D0840352

*Cambridge Studies in Social and Cultural Anthropology*

Editors: Jack Goody, Stephen Gudeman,
Michael Herzfeld, Jonathan Parry

73

# PROPERTY, PRODUCTION, AND FAMILY IN NECKARHAUSEN, 1700–1870

*For other titles in the Cambridge Studies in Social and Cultural Anthropology series, turn to page 512.*

# Property, production, and family in Neckarhausen, 1700–1870

DAVID WARREN SABEAN
*Cornell University*

PUBLISHED BY THE PRESS SYNDICATE OF THE UNIVERSITY OF CAMBRIDGE
The Pitt Building, Trumpington Street, Cambridge CB2 1RP, United Kingdom

CAMBRIDGE UNIVERSITY PRESS
The Edinburgh Building, Cambridge CB2 2RU, United Kingdom
40 West 20th Street, New York, NY 10011-4211, USA
10 Stamford Road, Oakleigh, Melbourne 3166, Australia



First published 1990
Reprinted 1997

Printed in the United States of America

Typeset in Ehrhardt

*A catalogue record for this book is available from the British Library*

*Library of Congess Cataloguing-in-Publication Data is available*

ISBN 0-521-38538-5 hardback
ISBN 0-521-38692-6 paperback

*This book is dedicated to*
Mark, Emma, *and* Lucas

# Contents

# Tables

*Tables*

# Abbreviations

| | |
|---|---|
| D | Döte/Dote |
| G | Gevatter(in) |
| GRTZ | Grötzingen |
| fl. | Gulden |
| kr. | Kreutzer |
| M. | Morgen |
| NH | Neckarhausen |
| NTLF | Neckartailfingen |
| NRTG | Nürtingen |
| OBENSG | Oberensingen |
| RDWG | Raidwangen |
| x | Kreutzer |

*Dates* are given in the form: day, month, year: 12.1.1832: 12 January 1832.

# Abbreviations of sources

|  |  |
| --- | --- |
| Communordnung | Ordnung für die Communen, auch deren Vorstehere und Bediente in dem Herzogthum Württemberg (1758), in Reyscher, vol. 14, pp. 537–777 |
| Gericht | Gerichts- und Gemeinderatsprotocolle, Neckarhausen |
| STAL | Staatsarchiv Ludwigsburg |
| HSAS | Hauptstaatsarchiv Stuttgart |
| Kirchenkonvent | Kirchenkonventsprotocolle, Neckarhausen |
| LKA | Landeskirchliches Archiv Stuttgart |
| Nürtingen Stadtgericht | Stadtgerichtsprotocolle, Nürtingen |
| Oberamtsgericht | Nürtingen Oberamtsgerichts protocolle, STAL |
| Reyscher | August Ludwig Reyscher, ed., *Vollständige, historisch und kritisch bearbeitete Sammlung der württembergischen Geseze*, 19 vols. (Stuttgart and Tübingen, 1828–51) |
| Schultheißenamt | Schultheißamtsprotocolle, Neckarhausen |
| Vogtruggericht | Vogtruggerichtsprotocolle, Neckarhausen |
| Beschreibung Nürtingen | Königliche statistisch-topographischer Bureau, *Beschreibung des Oberamts Nürtingen* (Stuttgart and Tübingen, 1848) |

# Weights, measures, and coinage

**Land**
1 Morgen = 0.78 acre = 0.32 hectare
1 Jauchert, 1 Mannsmahd, 1 Tagwerk = 1.5 Morgen = 0.47 hectare
1 Viertel = 0.25 Morgen

**Cubic measure**
Grain: 1 Scheffel = 8 Simri = 1.77 hectoliters
Wine: 1 Imi = 16.7 liters
Hay: Wannen
Straw, willow wands: Buschel

**Weights**
1 Pfund = 467.59 grams = 0.97 pounds

**Coinage**
1 Gulden (fl.) = 60 Kreutzer (kr., x)
1 Pfennig = 2 heller (h.)
1 Pfund pfennig = 43 Kreutzer

# On reading kinship diagrams

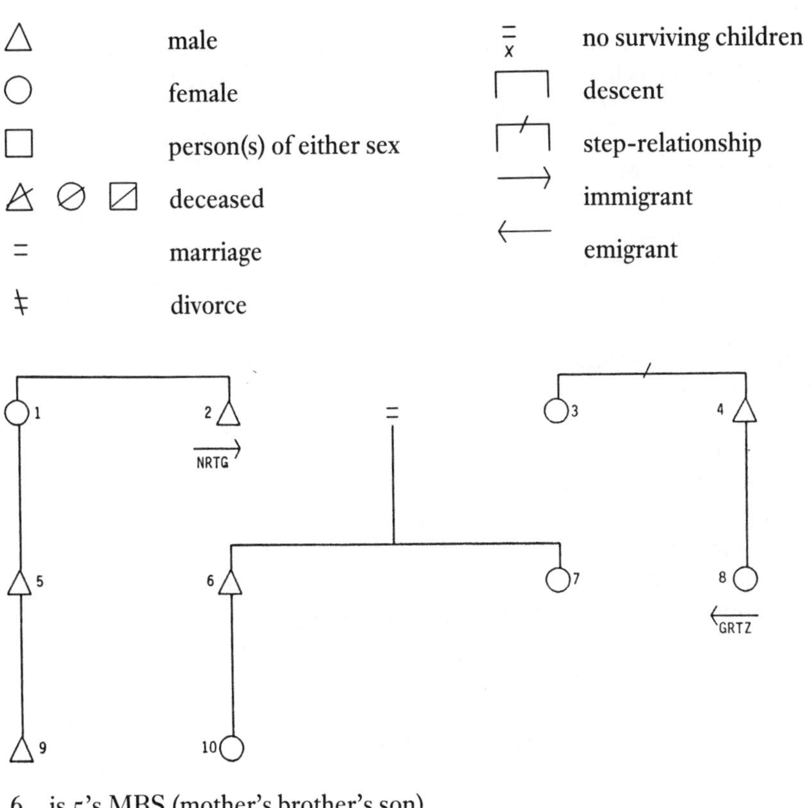


6 is 5's MBS (mother's brother's son)
7 is 6's Z (sister)
8 is 7's MxBD (mother's step-brother's daughter)
3 is 2's W (wife)
5 and 6 are first cousins (*Vettern*)
6 and 9 are first cousins once removed
9 and 10 are second cousins
2 immigrated to Neckarhausen from Nürtingen
8 emigrated to Grötzingen

# Glossary

German words are italicized when they occur for the first time in the volume and italicized in block quotations (or put into roman type in italicized passages) when attention is focused on their use.

**Abrede** agreement, arrangement
**Acker** arable
**Actuar** accountant, clerk
**allatum** endowment, personal possessions
**Allmendeteil** commonland portion
**Amt** bureau
**Amtmann** officer, official, administrator
**Amtschreiber** district clerk
**Amtstadt** district capital
**Arbeitslohn** wage, fee for services
**Ausding** retirement annuity
**Auslöser** one who redeems property
**Bauer** agricultural producer, peasant, local inhabitant with sufficient land and equipment to be obligated to certain types of corvée labor
**Bauerlohn** fee or wage for plowing or harrowing
**Bauernbefreiung** peasant enfranchisement, emancipation
**Bauerngeschirr** agricultural apparatus, gear
**Baumwiese** orchard-meadow
**Befehlbuch** copybook of mandates, edicts, and orders
**Beibringen** marriage portion, endowment
**Beisitzer** legal inhabitant of a locality without citizenship rights; can enjoy only "water and air" free
**Bürger** enfranchised member of a locality, citizen
**Bürgerausschuß** committee representing inhabitants of a locality
**Bürgermeister** chief financial officer of a locality
**Bürgerrecht** citizenship, full rights in a locality
**Bürgerschaft** citizens of a locality
**Bürgschaft** pledge, bond, surety
**conferieren** to return a marriage endowment to an estate

**Dekan** deacon, ecclesiastical district administrator, superintendent
**Dorfschütz** bailiff, peace officer of a village
**Dote** godmother (relation to child)
**Döte** godfather (relation to child)
**Dötle** godchild
**Ehegericht** marriage court
**Ehepact** marriage contract
**Ehepredecessor** marital predecessor (spouse's previous spouse)
**Ehesuccessor** marital successor (spouse's subsequent spouse)
**Ehevogt** marital guardian, overseer, governor (office held by husband)
**Eigentum** personal or owned property, possessions
**Einbringen** marriage portion, endowment
**Einbuß** loss
**Errungenschaft** acquisitions
**Errungenschaftsgesellschaft** community of acquisitions
**Fahrnis** movables
**Feld** furlong, partition in a field (Zelg)
**Flachsland** strip devoted to cultivation of flax
**Freieigenes** freehold
**Fuhrgeschirr** wagon apparatus, gear
**Fuhrlohn** freight charge, fee or wage for carrying services
**Gemeindepfleger** village financial officer
**Gemeinderat** local council
**Gericht** court
**Gerichtsbuch** volume of court minutes
**Gerichtsverwandte** justices of the court
**Geschlechtsvormundschaft** gender tutelage
**Gevatter(in)** godfather (mother) (relation to parents)
**Gleichstellung** equalization; establishing heirs on an equal footing
**Gült** rent paid in kind
**Gültlosung** redemption of land sold outside a rental unit
**Güterübergabe** property devolution
**Güterbuch** cadaster, register of real property
**Hanfland** strip devoted to cultivation of hemp
**Hauptrecht** death duty, laudemium
**Haus** house
**Hausbuch** household ledger
**hausen** live together, be married, get along, do well, be diligent
**Hausgenossen** members of a household
**Haushalter** householder
**Haushaltung** household, economy
**Hausherr** head of a household
**hausieren** colporting
**Hausleute** tenants

**Heiratsgut** marriage portion, endowment
**Herrschaft** lordship, authority, domination, dominion, rule, power; domain, seigniory
**Inventarier** member of an inventory commission
**Inventuren** marriage inventories
**Kaufbuch** register of real estate sales
**Kirchenkonvent** church consistory
**Knechtdienst** farmhand service
**Konventsrichter** church consistory elder
**Kriegsfrau** court ward (woman); correlative to Kriegsvogt
**Kriegsvogt** curator ad litem; court guardian, overseer, protector
**Land** strip outside of arable rotation
**Landrecht** law code
**Landschaft** estates general, parliament
**legitima** Pflichtteil, obligatory portion
**Leibgeding** retirement annuity
**Leibrente** life annuity
**Liegenschaft** immovable property
**Losung** redemption
**Losungsrecht** right to or law of redemption
**Loszettel** lists of goods to be drawn by lot
**Ludimagister** village schoolmaster; literally, singing master
**Marklosung** redemption of land sold outside of village
**Markung** village territory
**Mundtod** incompetent, in state of civil death
**mütterliches** maternal inheritance
**Nachlaß** inheritance, estate
**Nachthut** night watchman
**Oberamt** district
**Oberamtmann** district administrator
**Oberamtsbeschreibung** district gazetteer
**Oberamtsgericht** district court
**Oberamtsstadt** district capital
**Pactum** contract
**Parzellenbauer** peasant farmer with a few small plots
**Pfleger** curator, guardian, overseer, protector
**Pflichtteil** legitima, obligatory portion
**Pfand** pledge, mortgage, security
**Pfandgesetz** law of pledging, mortgage, security
**Pförch** sheepfold
**Pförchgeld** receipts from sheepfolding
**Pförchmeister** sheepfold administrator
**Presser** marshal, debt collector
**Rat** council; member of council

**Rechnungen** accounts
**retrait lignager** redemption of property sold outside the family line or kin group
**Richter** justice, member of the court (Gericht)
**Ruggericht** periodic assembly; court of accusation
**Schreiber** clerk
**Schreiberei** clerk's office
**Schreiberamt** district clerk's office
**Schultheiß** chief administrator of a village
**Schultheißamt** bureau of the Schultheiss
**Schultheißenamtsprotocolle** protocol volume of the office of the Schultheiss
**Skortationsprotocolle** protocol volume of fornication cases
**Spinnstube** spinning bee
**Stammtisch** table reserved for regulars
**Steuerbuch** tax register
**Stube** sitting room
**Substitut** underclerk
**Superintendent** ecclesiastical district administrator, deacon, superintendent
**Teilung** estate division or partition
**traditio bonorum** property devolution
**Unteramt** local bureau
**Untergang** boundaries commission
**Unterpfand** mortgage, pledge
**Unterpfandsbuch** register of mortgages and pledges
**väterliches** paternal inheritance
**Vergleich** settlement, compromise
**Vermögen** property, wealth
**Vermögenstradition** property devolution
**Vogt** representative, guardian; chief regional official
**Vogtruggericht** periodic court of visitation by district administrator
**Voraus** preferential portion
**Waisengericht** justice of the orphans' court
**Waldmeister** forest administrator
**Wasen** grassland
**Weide** pasture
**Weingarten** vineyard
**Wiese** meadow
**Wohnstube** sitting room, parlor
**Zelg** field (of a three-field system)
**Zins** money rent
**Zinslosung** redemption of land sold outside a rental unit
**Zubringen** marriage portion, endowment

# Preface

This book has taken shape in discussion with many people. In 1968, as I was searching for ways to extend the questions about family dynamics and social change first raised in my dissertation on the Peasant War of 1525, I had the benefit of many talks with several anthropology colleagues at the University of East Anglia. Christopher Turner, Robert Groves, and George Bond encouraged me to think in terms of a village study. I spent many hours discussing my plans with Morley Cooper and began a debate with him about the usefulness of anthropology for historical study. At that time, I also met Jack and Esther Goody, who made it possible several years later for me to spend a year in Cambridge reading the literature on kinship. Jack read the final manuscript and made many helpful suggestions.

During the early 1970s, I had the good fortune to be at the University of Pittsburgh, which was one of the great centers of methodological innovation in social history. Sam Hays set the standards for conceptual work, and Larry Glasco encouraged me to computerize the records from Neckarhausen. Discussions with members of the peasant studies group at Pittsburgh, and with Jonathan Levine, the editor of *Historical Methods*, were important for formulating the project. Sandy Dumin and Ella Jacobs keypunched and verified all of the parish register forms in record time and with professional care. Eva Savol and Raymond Monahan prepared some of the tax records and inventories for keypunching by Lena Crnovic.

In 1976, I went to the Max-Planck-Institut für Geschichte in Göttingen on sabbatical and stayed for seven years. The director, Professor Rudolf Vierhaus, provided superb working conditions and presided over one of the most creative centers for innovative historical work in Germany. I benefited considerably from Peter Kriedte's extensive knowledge of agrarian history. Alf Lüdtke directed my attention to the issues of *Herrschaft*. Jürgen Schlumbohn discussed theoretical and methodological issues with me and commented incisively on everything I wrote over the many years. He also introduced me to the bewildering varieties of bread available in Göttingen. My study of Neckarhausen owes most to daily – almost hourly – conversations with Hans Medick, whose patience knew no bounds. We discussed at high intensity our respective Swabian villages, anthropological history, the perspective of "everyday life," issues of practice, and just as important, the culinary ins-and-outs of Göttingen, Stuttgart, Laichingen, Paris, and London. Loli Diehl and Gerlinde Müller prepared the difficult and complex inventories for computerization, and Kornelia Menne entered the protocols and inventories on the terminal. The computerization of the Neckarhausen material was made possible by the historical data base system "Kleio" developed by Manfred Thaller, without which the study would have been impossible. Manfred is one of the pioneers in developing relational data bases for complex, nonstandardized historical sources.

The Max-Planck-Institut was host to a number of people who were important for my thinking at various stages of research: David Gaunt, David Levine, Jonathan Knudsen, Vanessa Maher, Gerald Sider, and Robert Berdahl. David Levine read and commented on the first draft and made me think through all of my assumptions once again. Several members of the continuing seminar on family history and the Round Table in Anthropology and History discussed various aspects of family and kinship with me: Barbara Duden, Michael Mitterauer, Heidi Rosenbaum, Karin Hausen, and Regina Schulte. Especially useful for aspects of Württemberg history have been talks with Carola Lipp and Wolfgang Kaschuba. William Reddy, who was a welcome guest at the institute, read every word of the manuscript and an early draft of the next one and offered a thoughtful and encouraging critique. During my last stay in 1989, I received useful comments from Gadi Algazi, Michaela Hohkamp, and Peter Becker.

Over the years, I have been graciously received at the Württembergisches Hauptstaatsarchiv in Stuttgart and in the Staatsarchiv in Ludwigsburg. They both continue to provide excellent working conditions for the practical historian. Dr. Dietrich Schäfer at the Landeskirchlichesarchiv made it possible for me to have the parish archival material microfilmed. Several people in Neckarhausen have offered me a great deal of assistance. When I started, Bürgermeister Schwarz gave me permission to use the sources in the Rathaus, and Gemeindepfleger Hagenlocher arranged to let me have them microfilmed. The present Gemeindevorsteher, Willi Knapp, has continued to provide access and microfilming privileges and has kindly helped me gain access to the material. A number of villagers consented to let me interview them, and their comments provided valuable insights into the historical life of the community.

During my years at the University of California, Los Angeles, several colleagues read the manuscript and offered comments. Scott Waugh, a kindred spirit, encouraged me to keep the details. Bill Clark fought for lucidity. Stanley Engerman from the University of Rochester read a draft of several chapters and sent me his detailed comments.

Carola Lipp and Isabel Hull kindly spent a day in Neckarhausen taking photographs for me, and Gilbert Shapiro furnished the picture looking toward the Alb from the arable fields. The maps were drawn by Henry Gayley.

Over the years, Frank Smith has been a very encouraging and patient editor.

Vicky Macintyre thought her way into the manuscript and rescued me from many inconsistencies and a plodding style.

My three children have lived with this book most of their lives. It is responsible in one way or another for their sense of humor, and their mother has only too willingly encouraged their wisecracks. They each wanted their own personal book for dedication but, given my track record, I think it best to collect them here. Ruth deserves another, but she, too, will have to be patient.

Philology is that venerable art which demands one thing above all from its worshipper, to go aside, to take one's time, to become silent, to become slow –, as a goldsmith's art and connoisseurship of the word, which has to execute nothing but fine delicate work and which achieves nothing if it does not achieve it lento. Just that it is what makes it more necessary today than ever, just by this it attracts and charms us most in the midst of an age of "work," i.e. of haste, of indecent and sweating hurry which wants "to have done" with everything in a moment, with any old and new book too: – while itself it is not so easily at an end; it teaches to read well; that means to read slowly, deeply, with consideration and carefully, with reservations, with open doors, and with delicate fingers and eyes.

Friedrich Nietzsche, *Morgenröte*

When beginning an investigation, one needs to construct methodological guidelines, not definitions. It is essential above all to get the feel of the actual subject matter – the object under investigation; it is essential to separate it from the reality surrounding it and to make a preliminary delimitation of it. At the outset of an investigation, it is not so much the intellectual faculty for making formulas and definitions that leads the way, but rather it is the eyes and hands attempting to get the feel of the actual presence of the subject matter.

Vološinov/Bakhtin, *Marxism and the Philosophy of Language*

# Introduction

> For what I really wish to work out is a *science of singularity*; that is to say, a science of the relationship that links everyday pursuits to particular circumstances. And only in the *local* network of labor and recreation can one grasp how, within a grid of socio-economic constraints, these pursuits unfailingly establish relational tactics (a struggle for life), artistic creations (an aesthetic), and autonomous initiatives (an ethic). The characteristically subtle logic of these "ordinary" activities comes to light only in the details.[1]
>
> – de Certeau

This book deals with the ordinary experiences of people living in one South German village. It focuses on the internal relations of the family and is part of a larger exploration of the dynamics of kinship, which will be developed further in a subsequent volume.[2] The study begins in 1700, by which time the village had largely recovered from the Thirty Years War and established the landholding patterns and occupational structure which would characterize it until the late nineteenth century, and ends in 1870, after the population had tripled in size, carried through a green revolution, and become enmeshed in regional and international markets.

Neckarhausen was not distinguished from many other villages belonging to the Duchy – from 1806, the Kingdom – of Württemberg in any special way, except for the fact that in the course of the nineteenth century it came to be well known for the quality of its flax. Despite major adjustments, its agriculture throughout the entire period was concentrated on raising spelt, a form of winter wheat widely grown in Swabia and particularly adapted to the weather conditions of the region. Spelt was cultivated in a progressively modified three-field system of crop rotation. Like most villages in the low country between the Black Forest and the Swabian Alb, Neckarhausen had adopted the practice of partible inheritance, which redistributed family property in each generation by according equal amounts of land and other assets to all the children. The region became a classic land of small peasant agriculture, characterized by ever more

[1] Michel de Certeau, *The Practice of Everyday Life*, trans. Steven Rendall (Berkeley, 1984), p. ix.

[2] Throughout this book, reference is made to another book in preparation on kinship in Neckarhausen. It is sometimes referred to as "Volume 2" or the "volume on kinship." It deals with the systems of marriage alliance and ritual kinship and examines the practices of child naming, guardianship, and underwriting debts. It examines the interactions of kin with each other, the language of kinship, and the strategic use of people related to each other by blood or connected through marriage. The volume has no title yet, but Cambridge University Press expects to publish it.

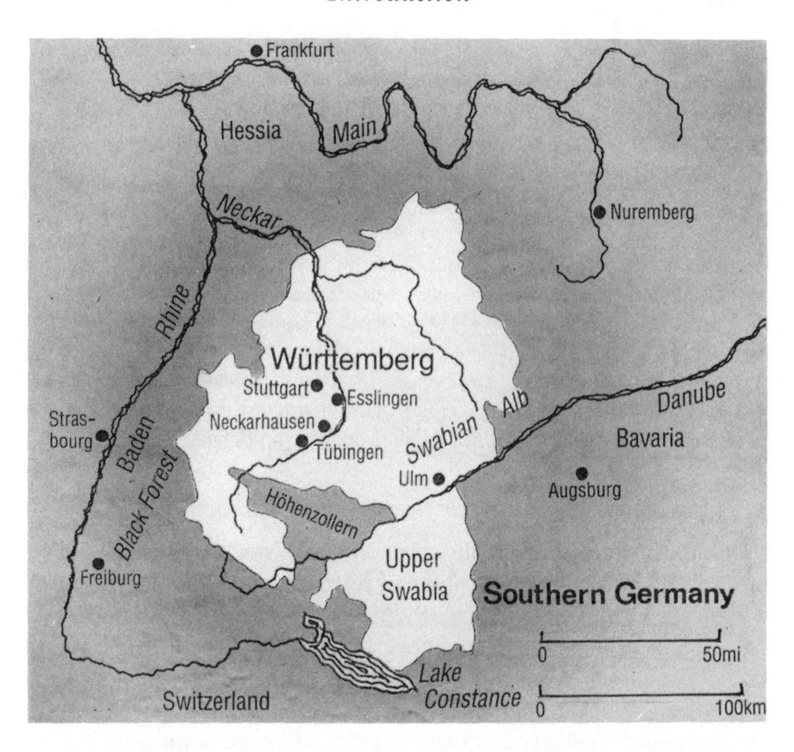
Frankfurt
Hessia
Main
Nuremberg
Neckar
Rhine
Württemberg
Stuttgart
Esslingen
Neckarhausen
Tübingen
Stras-
bourg
Baden
Black Forest
Swabian
Alb
Danube
Bavaria
Ulm
Augsburg
Höhenzollern
Upper
Swabia
Freiburg
Southern Germany
0
50mi
Lake
Constance
Switzerland
0
100km

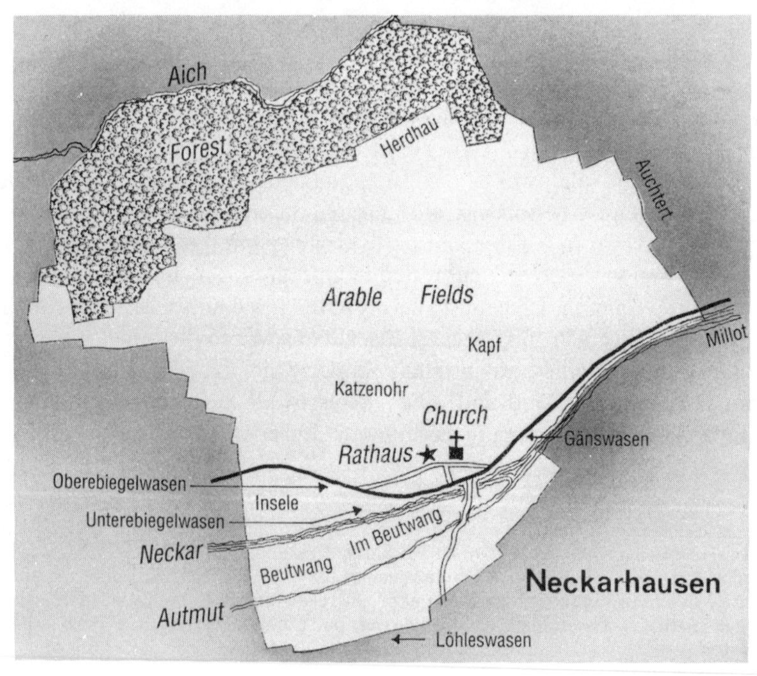
Aich
Forest
Herdhau
Auchtert
Arable Fields
Kapf
Millot
Katzenohr
Church
Gänswasen
Rathaus
Oberebiegelwasen
Insele
Unterebiegelwasen
Im Beutwang
Neckar
Beutwang
Neckarhausen
Autmut
Löhleswasen

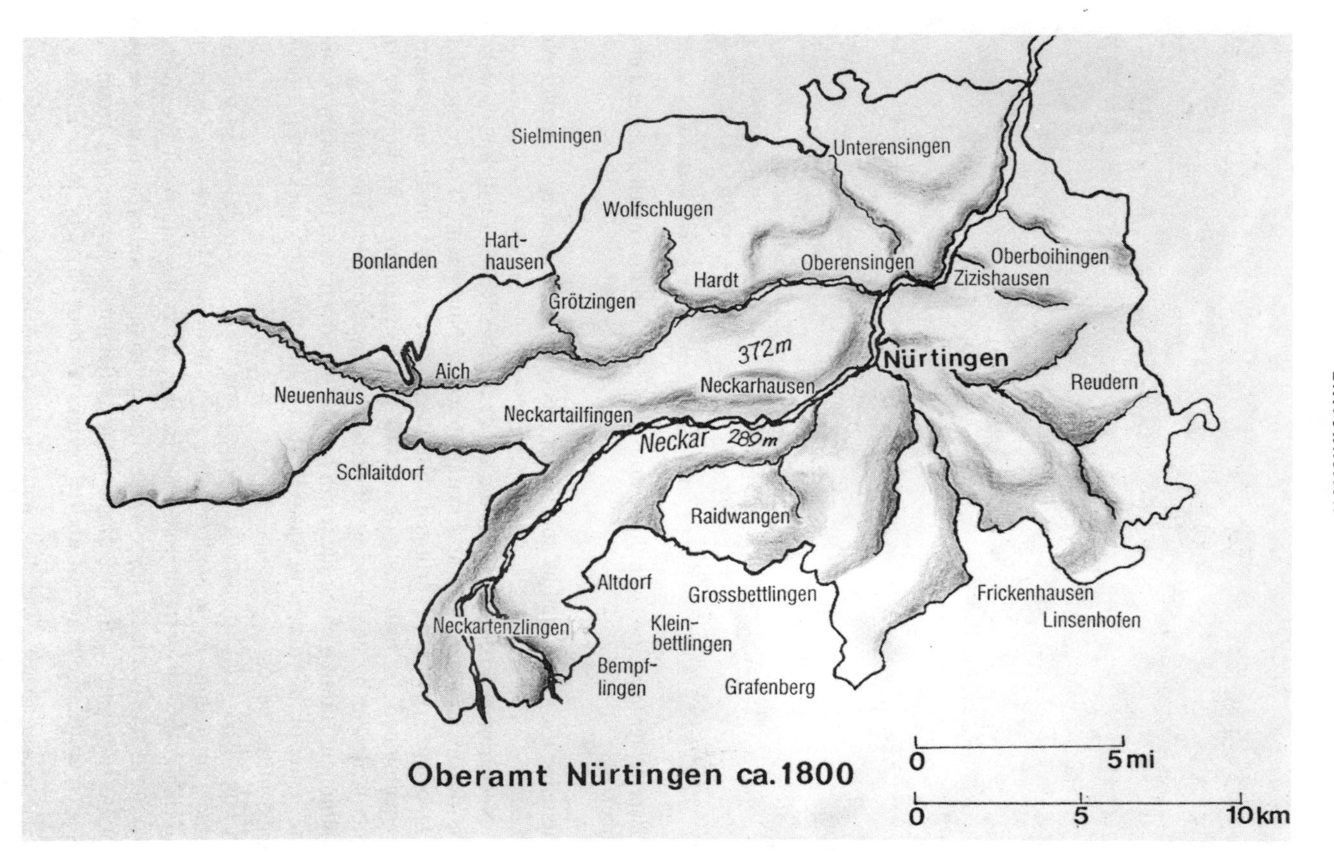

Sielmingen
Unterensingen
Wolfschlugen
Bonlanden
Hart-
hausen
Hardt
Oberensingen
Oberboihingen
Zizishausen
Grötzingen
372m
Nürtingen
Aich
Neckarhausen
Reudern
Neuenhaus
Neckartailfingen
Neckar
289m
Schlaitdorf
Raidwangen
Altdorf
Grossbettlingen
Frickenhausen
Linsenhofen
Neckartenzlingen
Klein-
bettlingen
Bempf-
lingen
Grafenberg
Oberamt Nürtingen ca.1800
0 5mi
0 5 10km

Village center facing east with the Rathaus on the left and the church at the end of the street.

intensive use of the soil as succeeding generations worked ever smaller plots of land.

Neckarhausen is situated on the upper Neckar River, a half hour's walk to the nearby administrative and market town of Nürtingen.[3] Today the village has become part of Nürtingen, but during the period under investigation it maintained its own institutions and jealously guarded its borders from encroachment by neighboring villagers and townspeople. The highway from Tübingen, running along the north bank of the river, used to go right through the center of the village but was relocated even before the Neckar was straightened in the 1830s.

The village is laid out on an east-west axis along the north bank of the river, which interrupts its general northeasterly flow just before Neckarhausen, turning eastward for several kilometers. Parallel to the course of the river on the north side is a long ridge, which rises up from the valley floor. In the early eighteenth century, the buildings of the settlement were grouped around the church and Rathaus a few hundred meters north of the river, in the manner of

[3] For an introduction to the village and surrounding communities, see Königlicher statisch-topographischer Bureau, *Beschreibung des Oberamts Nürtingen* (Stuttgart and Tübingen, 1848); and Hans Schwenkel, ed., *Heimatbuch des Kreises Nürtingen*, 2 vols. (Würzburg: Konrad Triltsch for the Kreisverband Nürtingen, 1950, 1953). See also *Pfarrbericht* (1828), LKA, A39, Bü 3060.

Arable fields with the village forest in the background.

a typical nucleated village. As the population grew, the inhabited area slowly expanded up the hill and eventually pushed along the slope of the ridge, especially eastward toward Nürtingen. Atop the ridge 100 meters above the valley floor is a broad flat plateau where the narrow strips worked by the villagers were distributed into furlongs (*Felder*), which in turn were grouped into three large fields (*Zelgen*). On the other side of the arable fields, a considerable forest of 447 Morgen (141 hectare, 348 acres) belonging to the village invited predatory incursions by villagers from Grötzingen and Oberensingen. From the Rathaus at the center of the village to the edge of the arable fields at the top of the slope, the distance is about 1 kilometer, and to the woods at the far side of the tableland, another 2.5 kilometers. Looking back from the fields in the direction of the village and river, one sees in the distance the long escarpment of the Swabian Alb, running in a northeast-southwest direction, with the rolling lowlands in between dotted with villages similar to Neckarhausen.

Proceeding back down the hill on either side of the inhabited area, we encounter the mixed orchard meadows which were developed at the turn of the nineteenth century and are so frequently found in the region today. They were the foundation for both stock raising and a considerable fruit harvest.[4] Some of

[4] The apple tithe itself frequently amounted to over 2,000 simri (44,300 liters, total harvest 443,000 liters) by the mid-nineteenth century; *Beschreibung Nürtingen*, pp. 65–7.

Arable fields facing toward the Swabian Alb.

the steeper slopes were devoted to viniculture until 1817, when everyone finally agreed that the wine was too sour to drink with any pleasure. At the bottom of the incline, all along the river, the village had its communal pastures and wet meadows, cultivated intensively from the beginning of the nineteenth century. Until the river course was "corrected," this area was subject to flooding in most years, and even today every other decade or so a destructive flood can disrupt the economy of various communities situated along the valley floor.

Scattered about the village territory (*Markung*) were areas set aside for vegetable gardens or for flax and hemp cultivation. Neckarhausen sold considerable amounts of raw flax, kept many people busy spinning, and had 30 weaving frames in use as late as the mid-nineteenth century.[5] In some of the meadows along the river and in some of the small communal parcels up the hill, villagers laid their linen cloths out to bleach, and pools by the river provided places to soak raw flax in preparation for extracting fibers. The geese were herded in one of the low-lying wet meadows until the 1830s. The district (*Oberamt*) of Nürtingen was one of the most important sheep-raising areas in Württemberg, and Neckarhausen had a considerable herd, which in the eighteenth century grazed on the fallow and in the nineteenth increasingly on intensive pastures set aside for its use.[6] Over toward Nürtingen in the Millot, there was a stone

[5] Ibid., pp. 177ff.
[6] Ibid., p.76.

quarry which produced building and paving stone, and whetstones were obtained from the valley of the contributory Aich. The Neckar River bank itself was a source of gravel and sand. Up on the hill there was a hut for producing saltpeter which the village leased out on an annual contract. Rights to fish in the river belonged to fishermen in Nürtingen, and the river was used by raftsmen for transporting timber from further upstream. Once the river was straightened, the village planted willows all along the bank and used the wands for basket production. Altogether, the agricultural and forest lands of the village included 1796 Morgen (measured in 1846: 566.2 hectares, 1368.5 acres), distributed among 77 families around 1700 (on average 23.2 M. or 17.7 acres) and 218 families by 1870 (on average 8.2 M. or 6.2 acres).[7]

Neckarhausen is situated in an undulating lowland under the Swabian Alb (*Albvorland*), where limestone plateaus alternate with valleys composed of clay and marl.[8] In contrast to the region north of Stuttgart, which is characterized by geological folding and relatively extended areas of consistent stratification, this southern territory shows signs of faulting and abrupt alterations, with a variegated pattern of micro regions. In general, the soils of the region consist of rich, heavy clays derived from the limestone substratum. In Neckarhausen, the soils on the plateau, which contains the arable fields, are mostly loess; those of the south slope with orchards and meadows consist of marl; and the valley floor with its wet meadows and pastures is made up of heavy clay with a limestone substratum.[9] The climate is influenced both by the oceanic and the continental systems, which can bring cold or mild winters and varying amounts of rain.[10]

Some readers might ask whether a study of this kind can produce results of general interest or comparative significance. These two questions are seldom distinguished from each other. Yet they can lead in quite different directions. In many instances, the comparative method is used precisely to establish the uniqueness of some institutional arrangement, pattern of behavior, or element of culture. In fact, comparative historians, anthropologists, or sociologists who are careful about their methodological procedures use comparison for the most part to establish the peculiar traits of a particular cultural area, familial structure, economic formation, or the like. Particularity, specificity, and context

[7] Ibid., Anhang. If we subtract the forest from the total, then the average household in 1700 had 13.3 acres (5.5 hectares) agricultural land; in 1870, 4.7 acres (2.0 hectares).

[8] I have based my description of the geography of the region on Friedrich Huttenlocher, *Baden-Württemberg, kleine geographische Landeskunde*, 3d. ed., Schriftenreihe der Kommission für geschichtliche Landeskunde Baden–Württemberg, vol. 2 (Karlsruhe, 1968), pp. 12–27, 41–50. See also *Heimatbuch Nürtingen*, vol. 2, pp. 590–2.

[9] *Heimatbuch Nürtingen*, vol. 2, pp. 591–2.

[10] The average annual temperature is 8°–9°C. (46°–48°F), ranging from 18°–19°C. (64°–66°F.) in July to just under 0°C. (32°F.) in January. The average annual rainfall ranges from 70 to 90 centimeters (27.6–35.4 inches); Huttenlocher, *Landeskunde*, pp. 40–6.

are usually the point of even the most general application of the comparative method.[11]

Generalization is itself not without ambiguity and can be thought of in at least three ways. First, there is the desideratum of typicality or statistical representativeness. In what way does Neckarhausen represent practices and behaviors which can be found elsewhere, either over a larger geographical area such as the district of Nürtingen, the Duchy of Württemberg, South Germany, Central Europe, or across cultures to embrace certain kinds of social formations – peasant, agricultural, partible inheritance, rural, Protestant pietist, and so forth? The answer has in part to do with scale. I could have studied one family or a region or a state, or I could have focused on a particular topic such as small peasant society in periods of intensification and capitalization, selecting as a case study one farm, one village, one epoch, or a series of different examples. It is not the scale of the exercise which determines the importance of its questions, since any unit of analysis is open to the same demand to go beyond its limits. In some ways, whether a territory is of satisfactory size is a matter of perspective. From the point of view of someone, say, in southern California, there is not a great deal of difference between Neckarhausen and Württemberg, and most people have heard of the latter only because their Porsche came from somewhere in the middle of it.

The relevance of scale has largely to do with the nature of the questions. For example, a philological investigation of a word such as "hausen" in the context of its daily use could not be carried out over a much wider area than I have done in Chapter 3. Moreover, it would be irrelevant to a general study of peasant societies as such. Hans Medick tells me that in Laichingen, a village about 30 kilometers from Neckarhausen, "hausen" was used in circumstances similar to those found in this study, but 50 years earlier. Such a comparative perspective shows how irritating the demand for generalization can be when complex issues of social interaction are raised. In the first place, it devalues the "merely local," and in the second, forces the researcher along the wrong path by implying that frequency of use and areal distribution are relevant criteria for judging significance. The fact that the terms of discourse in Laichingen are out of phase with those pertaining to Neckarhausen forces us to pose strong analytical questions about ideology, social differentiation, and the chronology of economic and social change rather than weak ones about statistical spread.

Another problem with areal significance is that it draws our attention away from social discourse. De Certeau makes a useful distinction between the "circulation of a representation" (e.g., by teachers and preachers) and its use, or between the production of an image and the "secondary production hidden in the process of utilization."[12] This kind of linguistic model, which distin-

[11] A good example is Jack Goody, *Production and Reproduction: A Comparative Study of the Domestic Domain*, Cambridge Studies in Social Anthropology, vol. 17 (Cambridge, 1976). But see George Peter Murdock, *Social Structure* (New York, 1949).

[12] De Certeau, *Practice*, p. xiii.

guishes between performance and competence, where speaking is not reducible to a knowledge of language, fixes our attention on particular acts of communication, on the appropriation and reappropriation of language by speakers. According to Bakhtin, "the task of understanding does not basically amount to recognizing the form used, but rather to understanding it in a particular, concrete context, to understanding its meaning in a particular utterance, i.e. it amounts to understanding its novelty and not to recognizing its identity."[13]

The second way in which generalization might be understood is in terms of a particular narrative of development; that is, Neckarhausen might be seen as an instance of a stage in the process of modernization, as a representative of a particular form of domestic group formation, as a typical instance of an economy of household production, or as a case of pre- or protocapitalist agricultural development. In this approach, the varieties of human society are considered a "sequence of specialized adaptations to different economic circumstances."[14] As a consequence, attention is turned away from the dynamics of social relations in a particular society to a grand narrative of human progress. Each new study recodes its findings to fit an objectified story already known to the observer. It is only the residue, when all the local color is washed away, which counts for essential knowledge of the subject. This approach does two things: It substitutes "our" story for "their" story, and it isolates us from interaction with "them." Every aspect of dialogue is erased, whether it is the historian's reciprocal fashioning of him- or herself in introspection – recognizing in "their peculiarities," as Edmund Leach says, a mirror of our own[15] – or whether it is the "cooperative" or "collaborative" construction of a narrative when the author no longer occupies the position of a transcendental observer.[16] More important, the nature of the inquiry shifts from intersubjective communication processes underpinning the objectivized account to "essential" and "substantial" being. But "once dialogism and polyphony are recognized as modes of textual production, [such] monophonic authority is questioned."[17]

A third form of generalization asks how a particular formation is to be measured against some criterion such as rationality: To what degree does it fulfill needs, master nature, or conform to an abstract concept of lawful behavior? Ultimately such questions come down to a notion of humanity which arose during the Enlightenment – namely, that each person represents its essence. The analytical problem is to go beyond the particulars to his or her essential

[13] V. N. Vološinov, *Marxism and the Philosophy of Language*, trans. Ladislav Matejka and I. R. Titunik (Cambridge, Mass., 1986), p. 65. For the argument that Bakhtin wrote the work, see Katerina Clark and Michael Holquist, *Mikhail Bakhtin* (Cambridge, Mass., 1984), pp. 146–7.

[14] Edmund Leach, *Social Anthropology* (New York, 1982), p. 121.

[15] Ibid., p. 127. James Clifford, "Introduction: Partial Truths," in *Writing Culture: The Poetics and Politics of Ethnography*, ed. James Clifford and George E. Marcus (Berkeley, 1986), pp. 1–26, here 23: "Every version of an 'other,' wherever found, is also the construction of a 'self.'"

[16] Stephen A. Tyler, "Post-Modern Ethnography: From Document of the Occult to Occult Document," in *Writing Culture*, ed. Clifford and Marcus, pp. 122–40, here 126.

[17] James Clifford, "Introduction," p. 14.

rational or sensual core. This approach may be criticized for adopting artificial standards and norms, and even a follower of the tradition such as Habermas tries to rescue rationality without a fixed concept of human nature.[18] According to the Enlightenment notions, individuals at their core are without relations, and as a result the individual is objectified and reified. This approach has been objected to in part because of the static nature of the categories. They are meant to catch common properties or, as Dumont puts it, the mere general as opposed to the universal.[19] And with the latter term, Dumont brings us back again to the problem of introspection. In contrast to the search for the general, which leads inevitably to objectification, the search for the universal enables one to find truth for oneself. For Dumont as for a large number of other writers, the "disintegration of 'Man'" appears to be rooted in a recognition of the arbitrariness of the criteria of rationality and the problematic boundary between nature and culture.[20]

If approaches to the "general" seem problematic, does that throw us back to a new historicism? Is the interest in the concrete, the local, and the particular based on an assumption of individualism? Meinecke, for example, was out to replace a "generalizing" with an "individualizing" science. Historicism was supposed to liberate us from an unhistorical and naturalistic conception of man.[21] It posited the existence of integrated, unique individualities, whether persons or nations, and in a similar fashion argued for an infinite variety of different historical forms. The facts of history are particular, individual, concrete, unrepeatable entities.[22] Historical narrative offers a form of knowledge which reconstructs events in their unique individuality.

What distinguishes this study from historicism is that it does not make individualism a starting point. The *local* is interesting precisely because it offers a *locus* for observing relations. And we must be careful not to confuse the particular and singular with the individual, a point made by both de Certeau (cited at the beginning of the introduction) and Norbert Elias:

> The traditional idea of the individuality of the single human being that underlies the historiography concerned with individualities presents a being standing completely alone, an isolated rather than just a single human being, a closed rather than an open system. What are actually observed are people who develop in and through relations to other people. By contrast, the individualistic historical tradition postulates individuals who are ultimately without relation.[23]

[18] Georg C. Iggers, "Historicism," in *Dictionary of the History of Ideas: Studies of Selected Pivotal Ideas*, ed. Philip P. Wiener (4 vols.: New York, 1973), vol. 2, pp. 456–64, here 463.

[19] Louis Dumont, *Homo Hierarchicus. The Caste System and Its Implications*, trans. Mark Sainsbury (Chicago,1970), p. 3.

[20] For example, see Leach, *Social Anthropology*, pp. 84–121. The phrase is from James Clifford, "Introduction," p. 14.

[21] Georg Iggers, "Historicism," p. 457.

[22] Hans Meyerhoff, "Introduction," in *The Philosophy of History in Our Time* (New York, 1959), p. 19.

[23] Norbert Elias, *Court Society* (New York, 1983), p. 24.

Once we center our attention on relationships, we are forced into research strategies which favor the local and the particular. That is why anthropology is concerned with small, particular localities.[24] And that is why the close reading of texts has come to dominate literary studies. When interest is centered on how consciousness is formed in social intercourse, on dialogical processes of value, and ideological construction, then "particular, concrete contexts" become the locus of serious work.[25] This brings us to the study of the quotidien, the everyday, which, as de Certeau has argued, does not at all imply a return to individuality: "Analysis shows that a relation (always social) determines its terms and not the reverse and each individual is a locus in which an incoherent (and often contradictory) plurality of such relational determinations interact."[26]

This work, then, is radically comparative. Throughout, it deals with matters from the perspective of different genders, age groups, and occupations. It is concerned with both the terms of *Herrschaft* and the many different opportunities for resistance. It sharpens the view of social processes in Neckarhausen by placing them against social scientific constructs of "peasant society," against regions characterized by other forms of inheritance, and against a variety of ideological notions of property. In only a few instances have I sought to make

[24] Edmund Leach, *Social Anthropology*, p. 127: "All the best work done by social anthropologists... has at its core the very detailed study of the network of relationships operating within a single very small-scale community. Such studies do not, or should not, claim to be 'typical' of anything in particular. They are not intended to serve as illustrations of something more general. They are interesting in themselves." Louis Dumont, *Homo Hierarchicus*, p. 5: "The true function of sociology is...precisely to make good the lacuna introduced by the individualistic mentality when it confuses the ideal with the actual....It has its roots...in the apperception of the social nature of man...;" p. 7: "One must underline the merits of anthropology as a *sociological* discipline."

[25] V. N. Vološinov (Mikhael Bakhtin), *Marxism*, p. 68; also p. 20: "Social psychology exists primarily in a wide variety of forms of the 'utterance,' of little *speech genres* of internal and external kinds – things left completely unstudied to the present day. All these speech performances, are, of course, joined with other types of semiotic manifestation and interchange – with miming, gesturing, acting out, and the like. All these forms of speech interchange operate in extremely close connection with the conditions of the social situation in which they occur and exhibit an extraordinary sensitivity to all fluctuations in the social atmosphere." Cf. Louis Dumont, *Homo Hierarchicus*, p. 3: "The adherents of a less radical sociology then accuse us of falling into 'culturology'...and of losing sight of comparison, which, in their eyes, is sufficiently guaranteed by concepts like 'social stratification' and by the mere consideration of the *similarities* which allow phenomena taken from different types of society to be grouped together under a common label. But such an approach can only ever achieve the general, as opposed to the universal, and with respect to our goal of comparison it represents another short circuit. In sociological studies the universal can only be attained through the particular characteristics, different in each case, of each type of society....In the last analysis, it is by humbly inspecting the most minute particulars that the route to the universal is kept open." See also Norbert Elias, *Court Society*, p. 26: "It is the task of sociology to bring the unstructured background of much previous historical research into the foreground and to make it accessible to systematic research as a structured weft of individuals and their actions. This change of perspective does not, as is sometimes asserted, rob individual people of their character and value as individuals. But they no longer appear as isolated people, each totally independent of the others." And finally, Edmund Leach, *Social Anthropology*, p. 148: "In fieldwork it is the details that matter and details cannot be discussed in general terms."

[26] Michel de Certeau, *Practice*, p. xi.

direct, explicit comparisons, but the driving force behind the narration is continually a comparative perspective. The tactics are also reversible. A local study can also be a point of departure for discounting the contextualization of other narratives. A consideration of the dynamics of property in Neckarhausen, for example, casts doubt on the coherence of the property/individualism account of social formation in England. The peculiarities of the English and the Württembergers lie somewhere else.

To argue for comparability is to underline the heuristic nature of those "studies that focus on meaning systems, disputed traditions, or cultural artifacts."[27] If I understand what is going on in present-day cultural studies, a reified notion of culture is giving way to socially specific, exacting accounts of power, resistance, and constraints *in loci*, where many voices contend each for its own view of reality. Rather than mapping and recoding the results onto new situations, the new perspectives offer a loose set of procedures and examples of possibilities for finding coherence or contradictions in any social context. In the study of Neckarhausen, the search for singularity, for particular coherence, for the contextual logics of performance suggests that significance does not lie in generalization or the extension of a particular paradigm or a plea for typicality. Nor does it lie in a presumption of individuality, whether it argues that each epoch or culture or polity is unique (historicism) or whether it presumes that continuous unity can be broken into "innumerable separated discontinuities" (sociology) which can then be matched for their common properties.[28] To say that Neckarhausen is not generalizable is not to presume some special kind of unity to the community, on the one hand, or the lack of similarity elsewhere, on the other. The many voices, the conflicting and overlapping sets of relations, the continuing arguments about this and that sometimes exercised couples; sometimes concerned households; sometimes brought family members, kin, or neighbors together; sometimes engaged the whole village; sometimes joined the capital city and village or spilled over communal territorial boundaries; sometimes threw beggars, wanderers, merchants, soldiers, police, officials, and bureaucrats together with villagers, who in turn were sometimes located in the locality and sometimes on the road. The many dialogues were structured by a variety of media – the "wanted" poster read at the church door, the inventory redacted by the town clerk, the *Presser* writ to attach a carpenter's tool kit, the protocol of a young woman's indiscretion, the bill for plowing presented by a father to his son, the epithet hurled at a husband by his wife. The task we have set for ourselves is to examine the regularities of context and the logic of action at the many different levels of discourse in this polyphony.

This book is about the ways in which property and production in a particular locality shaped and were shaped by the family. It deals with family dynamics

[27] James Cifford, "Introduction," p. 3.
[28] Edmund Leach, *Social Anthropology*, p. 87.

in a region where partible inheritance was practiced, that is, where all of the children, male and female, inherited not only equal amounts of property but also equal *kinds* of property from their parents. Partible inheritance systems in Europe frequently provided only for male children to share land, but in Württemberg society villagers were obsessive about according equal portions to all of the children, including daughters. They even carried such concerns with them to America, where they were shocked to find an English legal system which denied women full rights and limited their legal personalities.[29]

Most detailed studies of family dynamics in Europe have concentrated on regions where impartible inheritance is practiced, although there are the important exceptions of Martine Segalen's work on France and Michael Mitterauer's comparative investigation of the various regional practices of Austria.[30] Too little attention has been given to family relations in partible inheritance regions, considering the distribution of the practice. In Central Europe, it dominated a large part of the Rhineland, Württemberg, Baden, Lower Franconia, Hesse, southwest Westphalia, and parts of central Germany (Thüringen, southwest Saxony, and southern Hannover).[31] Most of the regions devoted to viniculture and many, but certainly not all, of the areas which developed protoindustry tended to partition real property among the children instead of arranging for one of them to continue the farming enterprise.[32] In France, people in the Paris basin and a large part of the northern region also followed the practice.[33] In

[29] A. G. Roeber, "The Origins and Transfer of German-American Concepts of Property and Inheritance," *Perspectives in American History*, n.s., 3 (1987): 115–71, here 162–3; see also, idem, "Erbberechtliche Probleme deutscher Auswanderer in Nordamerika während des 18. Jahrhunderts," *Zeitschrift für neuere Rechtsgeschichte* 2 (1986): 143–56.

[30] Martine Segalen, "'Avoir sa part,'" pp. 129–44; idem, *Quinze générations de Bas-Bretons: parenté et société dans le pays bigouden sud, 1720–1980* (Paris, 1985). Michael Mitterauer, "Familienformen und Illegitimität in ländlichen Gebieten Österreichs," *Archiv für Sozialgeschichte* 19 (1979): 123–88; idem, "Zur Familienstruktur in ländlichen Gebieten Österreichs im 17. Jahrhundert," in Heimo Helczmanovszki, ed., *Beiträge zur Bevölkerungs- und Sozialgeschichte Österreichs* (Vienna, 1973), pp. 167–222; idem, "Vorindustrielle Familienformen," *Wiener Beiträge zur Geschichte der Neuzeit* 2 (1975): 123–85; idem, "Familiengroße – Familientypen – Familienzyklus," in *Geschichte und Gesellschaft* 1 (1975): 235–55; idem, "Vorindustrielle Familienformen. Zur Funktionsentlastung des 'ganzen Hauses' im 17. und 18. Jahrhundert," in Friedrich Engel-Janosi, Grete Klingenstein and Heinrich Lutz, eds., *Fürst, Bürger, Mensch. Untersuchungen zu politischen und sozio-kulturellen Wandlungsprozessen im vorrevolutionären Europa* (Vienna, 1975), pp. 123–85.

[31] Barthel Huppertz, *Räume und Schichten bäuerlicher Kulturformen in Deutschland. Ein Beitrag zur deutschen Bauerngeschichte* (Bonn, 1939), pp. 25–7.

[32] For an exception, see the important forthcoming work of Jürgen Schlumbohm on the parish of Belm in the territory of Osnabrück. An early article: "Agrarische Besitzklassen und gewerbliche Produktionsverhältnisse: Großbauern, Kleinbesitzer und Landlose als Leinenproduzenten im Umland von Osnabrück und Bielefeld während des frühen 19. Jahrhunderts," in Mitarbeitern und Schülern, eds., *Mentalitäten und Lebensverhältnisse. Beispiele aus der Sozialgeschichte der Neuzeit. Rudolf Vierhaus zum 60. Geburtstag* (Göttingen, 1982), pp. 315–34; idem, "Bauern – Kötter – Heuerlinge. Bevölkerungsentwicklung und soziale Schichtung in einem Gebiet ländlichen Gewerbes: das Kirchspiel Belm bei Osnabrück 1650–1860," *Niedersächsisches Jahrbuch für Landesgeschichte* 58 (1986): 77–88.

[33] Jean Yver, *Egalité entre héritiers et exclusion des enfants dotés. Essai de geographie coutumière* (Paris, 1966), pp. 12–23, 91ff., and map.

England, Kent and much of the eastern part of the country were dominated for long periods by partible inheritance.[34]

One reason why partible inheritance regions have been studied less often is that the empirical work is difficult to carry out and the analytical assumptions are conceptually sterile. Such regions tended to have simpler household forms than those characterized by single-son inheritance, largely because, ceteris paribus, the farm holdings were smaller, and partitioning made impossible such complex forms as the stem family, with its continuity over generations between fathers and sons on the same farm. Partible inheritance, it is often thought, fosters individualism by the fact that a coherent patrimony is missing and residence for the most part is neolocal.[35] Since the object – the farm family – continually changes shape and appears to become subject to the individualized dynamics of expanded choices, it is less easy to make generalizations about and is less interesting, especially for those who want the premodern family to look premodern. In addition, there is the practical problem of keeping track of families in order to study them at all. Notarial records relating to continuous farm units are fairly accessible, in contrast to the documentation for a society which rearranges the holdings every generation and allows constant selling of land and subleasing of individual plots, whose houses are split into separate apartments, and whose barns are used by several tenants at a time.[36] In order to make the most of such material, the researcher must link together many pieces of information. It has only been with the development of family reconstitution techniques in the 1950s and 1960s that such research has become possible.[37] The framework of this book is a reconstitution of the village utilizing all the baptism, marriage, and burial records from the 1560s to 1870.[38] On that scaffolding, we have been able to organize thousands of records of land sales, mortgages, taxes, marriage and estate inventories, and criminal and civil court actions.

Interwoven throughout the book are several themes which touch on theoretical and comparative issues of considerable importance. We will continually circle around inheritance, property, capital, agricultural innovation, stratification, gender, and state. Before introducing the argument of the book, I should

[34] M. M. Postan, *The Medieval Economy and Society: An Economic History of Britain 1100–1500* (Berkeley and Los Angeles, 1972), pp. 145–7.

[35] This was the thesis of Wilhelm Riehl, *Die Naturgeschichte des Volks als Grundlage einer deutschen Social-Politik*, 3d ed. (Stuttgart and Augsburg, 1855), vol. 2, *Die bürgerliche Gesellschaft*, pp. 70–85; vol. 3, *Die Familie*, pp. 206ff.

[36] The individualism thesis, based on a land market and lack of a continuous patrimony linking generations, has been resurrected by Alan Macfarlane, *The Origins of English Individualism: The Family, Property and Social Transition* (Cambridge,1978), chaps. 4, 5, 6.

[37] A careful methodological study is offered by Andrejs Plakans, *Kinship in the Past: An Anthropology of European Family Life 1500–1900* (Oxford and New York, 1984).

[38] For a programmatic statement, see David Sabean, "Verwandtschaft und Familie in einem württembergischen Dorf 1500 bis 1870: einige methodische Überlegungen," in Werner Conze, ed., *Sozialgeschichte der Familie in der Neuzeit Europas: Neue Forschungen* (Stuttgart, 1976), pp. 231–46.

sketch in some of the considerations which underlie the analysis and give a short account of the conceptual apparatus which informs the narrative.

## Partible inheritance

The specific institutions of inheritance have to be carefully distinguished from the relative tendency to parcelization. As Cole and Wolf have demonstrated, adjacent regions with similar ecologies but with different inheritance systems could in fact emerge with farms of similar size.[39] Considerable ingenuity has been brought to bear on the question of the distribution of inheritance regimes in Central Europe, and scholars have considered such variables as cropping pattern, settlement type, ethnicity, customary law, and peasant enfranchisement.[40] But the general patterns appear to have been fixed, during the period of renewed population rise and market expansion of the "long" sixteenth century. In Upper Swabia, for example, where the ecology was suited to pasture, grain production, and forestry, the rules allowing families to distribute the patrimony to all the children created panic among the landlords threatened with problems of collecting dues on minifundia and among tenant farmers facing demands from an increasing number of small holders for a share in communal rights.[41] In the territory belonging to the monastery of Weingarten, for example, the abbot and tenants colluded in the preparation of an elaborate document, fixed with numerous seals, attesting to the "fact" that daughters had never had any rights to inherit land. And in all of the seigneuries of the region, lords took steps to establish single-son inheritance, either by reassembling farms through systematic repurchase or by revising the terms of contract.

In most of nearby Württemberg, the situation was quite different, although the forces at play were similar. There, too, a reciprocal interaction between state fiscal interests and peasant productive relations probably best accounts for the establishment of the particular inheritance regime in the law codes of 1555, 1567, and 1610 – the period of highest population density between the Black Death and the mid-eighteenth century. Viniculture, which was widespread in Württemberg, called for intensification, considerable risk, and orientation toward market relationships. Furthermore, vintners needed additional strips of land for other intensive crops to carry them over periods of bad harvest. All of this encouraged the development of densely populated villages of small producers whose pattern of farming underlay the long-term fiscal interests of the ducal state. Considerable work needs to be done on the

[39] John W. Cole and Eric R. Wolf, *The Hidden Frontier. Ecology and Ethnicity in an Alpine Valley* (New York, 1974), pp. 175–205, esp. 181–2.

[40] Theodor Mayer-Edenhauser, *Untersuchungen über Anerbenrecht und Güterschluss in Kurhessen* (Prague, 1942).

[41] See David Warren Sabean, *Landbesitz und Gesellschaft am Vorabend des Bauernkriegs*, Quellen und Forschungen zur Agrargeschichte, 26 (Stuttgart, 1972), pp. 36–48.

origins of inheritance practices, but there seems to have been a relation between partible inheritance and the production of wine, vegetable, and various industrial crops in many areas of the Rhineland and southwest and central Germany. Although state fiscal policies and seigneurial patterns of appropriation were developed with consideration for regional ecologies and marketing patterns, they were the main issue behind the practical activities of officials concerned with property and its devolution.

The specific regime of inheritance, of course, is only one attribute of a larger pattern of economic and social life. Even though the tendency in Württemberg may well have been toward small holdings, the process of fractionalization really set in during the eighteenth century as the population increased and land came to be used more intensively.[42] We want to fix our attention in this book not so much on economic issues as on familial strategies in a situation where land, capital, and labor were all undergoing considerable change, but of a kind rarely considered by historians to have been crucial in the transition from feudalism to capitalism. We want to show exactly how intergenerational transmission gave a precise form to relations between generations. The transfer of authority from parents to children was a gradual, long-drawn-out process. Resources were dribbled out in such a way as to ensure a labor supply, to build obligation, to form a specific dynamic of exchange between parents and children and within the wider system of alliance. To fix on the inheritance of land is to miss the point that the management of tool devolution was often more important and subject to finer calculation and more flexible practice. The usual marital portion of a young couple could not be exploited without the active assistance of their parents.

Inheritance, it turns out, was an inadequate means of managing property allocation during a period of extreme fragmentation. The system of kinship alliance became the main instrument for channeling land, credit, and labor in a way which ensured the reproduction of viable farms and the social distribution of power. A greatly expanded market integrated a wider set of kin at a time when endogamy and new patterns of ritual kinship were restructuring the patterns of alliance.

Both partible inheritance and the sale of land were central aspects of social reproduction. The rules governing them grew out of the exigencies of state fiscality, on the one hand, and an everchanging strategical intervention of officials to ensure order and productivity, on the other. Villagers developed their own strategies within the legal institutions which were provided for them. Parents wove a web of obligation through a calculated management of property devolution, and allied families took advantage of commercial institutions

[42] Paradoxically, the trend may first have developed during and after the population disasters of the Thirty Years War. In that situation, with the cattle and horse herds decimated, crushing back taxes, abandoned fields, and ruined buildings, many people seem to have sloughed off marginal or encumbered land. When the population began to increase again, the process of fissioning took place without any check.

designed to disencumber landed property to set up a flexible but regular system of exchange. To understand the history of the family one must track a peculiar dialectic between actions taken at different levels of abstraction and growing out of different logics of intention.

## Property

Property as an analytical category is a powerful but frequently neglected tool for social analysis. It is sometimes brought in to explain premodern social systems, but is used only in general terms to analyze the social dynamics of modern societies. Although studies rooted in the Marxist tradition are based on assumptions about ownership, the issues they raise concerning class and class consciousness have less to do with social reproduction than with the interplay of broad groups positioned against each other according to their access to the means of production.[43] There is not a great deal of interest in how, for example, the middle classes manage the distribution of property holdings, regulate succession to class membership, or develop strategies of inheritance.[44] In any case, property seems irrelevant to the internal relations of the working class and is interesting in the case of other classes primarily because of what it tells about the conditions for exploitation, on the one hand, and political coherence, on the other. Property remains a residual category for all classes except peasants, whose emotional lives appear peculiarly dominated by the dynamics of material interest.[45]

Although this book deals for the most part with peasants – or at least with rural dwellers, most of whom owned some land and carried out some agriculture – the argument about property will suggest the usefulness of the category for class situations well beyond this range. All social transactions take place within a field of rights, duties, claims, and obligations, which taken together comprise the system of property holding. Rousseau conveyed the essence of property when he described its origins as the act of one man drawing a boundary around some land and getting others foolish enough to respect it.[46] In Rousseau's analysis, property is fundamentally implicated with the social – society and property are constituted in the same act.[47] In the first place,

[43] For an exceptional example of property used analytically to examine class relations, see E. P. Thompson, "The Grid of Inheritance: A Comment," in Jack Goody, et al., eds., *Family and Inheritance: Rural Society in Western Europe 1200–1800* (Cambridge, 1976), pp. 328–60.

[44] Challenging departures are offered by Pierre Bourdieu and Jean-Claude Passeron, *Reproduction in Education, Society and Culture*, trans. Richard Nice (London, 1977); and Gilles Deleuze and Félix Guattari, *Anti-Oedipus: Capitalism and Schizophrenia* (Minneapolis, 1983).

[45] Hans Medick and David Warren Sabean, "Interest and Emotion in Family and Kinship Studies: A Critique of Social History and Anthropology," in *Interest and Emotion: Essays on the Study of Family and Kinship* (Cambridge, 1984), pp. 9–27.

[46] Jean-Jacques Rousseau, *Discourse on the Origin and Foundation of Inequality among Mankind*, ed. Lester G. Crocker (New York, 1967), second part, p. 211.

[47] Marx, of course, thought not about abolishing property but about changing its nature, for as a good Rousseauian he also understood that a "man without relationships is a man without

property is not a relationship between people and things but one between people about things. Davis puts it this way: "When we describe rights of ownership, or of use, or of tenancy, we are talking about relationships between people. Rights imply duties and liabilities, and these must attach to people. A hectare cannot be sued at law, nor is a boundary dispute a quarrel with a boundary."[48]

In other words, boundaries mediate between people. Land, houses, and tools are things which are held, managed, and argued about and are the stuff around which people in a village like Neckarhausen shaped their lives in concert with each other. In order to understand the trajectories of individual lives, the dynamics of particular families, the strategies of alliance and reciprocity, and the effects of state intervention and economic differentiation on village social practices, we have to examine the details of property rules, structures, and codes. We will look hard at contracts, agreements, testaments, gifts, sales, inventories, rental agreements, and crop-sharing arrangements. Land and other goods were part of a wider set of exchanges and reciprocities through which people were disciplined. And land and its exploitation provided a focus for socialization, character formation, emotional commitment, and the long apprenticeship which instilled obligation.

Our story about Neckarhausen peasants cuts across many of our expectations about what peasants do with property and how they organize themselves around it and express peculiar values about it. In Neckarhausen, property was owned by individuals, not by families. Children were not co-owners, and there was no joint enterprise to which they were all attached. The father was a proprietor, not a manager who could be replaced by another family member if he displayed incompetence. There was no special emotional attachment to particular pieces of land or particular houses, and partible inheritance and the property markets continually broke up what had been collected in one hand. There was little attempt to reassemble family or lineage property. Among family members outside of parents and minor children, there was no undifferentiated product. There was no continuing family enterprise over generations. Older parents and younger proprietors did not eat or cook together. Rights between adults of all kinds, married and unmarried, were carefully delineated and each person had different access to resources and rights to different things. Labor and equipment had to be paid for, and even adult married sons had to hire their fathers to plow and harrow their bits of inherited land. All the special encumbrances on property we associate with peasant societies – retirement annuities, conditional sales, *retrait lignager* – were residual at best and were designed to support the independence of households and generations from each other or were expressions of state fears that too much fractionalization of land might endanger the tax base. A lively market in land and buildings did not provide an unchanging mechanism for "individualism" or social transformation, nor was

property." The phrase comes from Jack Goody, *Death, Property and the Ancestors: A Study of Mortuary Customs of the Lodagaa of West Africa* (Stanford, 1962), p. 287.

[48] John Davis, *Land and Family in Pisticci* (New York, 1973), p. 73.

it inimical to a coordinated and highly structured system of family alliances. While on the one hand, many generalizations about traditional forms of property holding do not fit these peasants, on the other, precisely where the rules of property appear most "modern," the accompanying institutions of kinship and community run counter to expectations.

## Capital

The period we are studying in this book coincides, of course, with the great expansion of capitalism. This book does not deal in detail with the economic reordering of the village, but certain issues do continually intertwine with the story we have to tell. One aspect of capital which has been stressed in recent historical work is the great reorganization of labor which took place under its logic.[49] Even a village of small agricultural and handicraft producers underwent a restructuring of labor and became subject to new forms of discipline. As we shall see, after 1800 many village males became active in the building trades and construction outside the village. Until well into the nineteenth century, many such jobs were paid by piece rates or were subcontracted out. The key thing is that such jobs were often taken on with performance bonds, which the men offered by pledging their bits of property or by getting their wives, kin, or friends to underwrite their work. In this way, an intimate connection between village wealth and capital and infrastructural development in Württemberg as a whole developed. Mobile producers remained rooted in villages by the fact that they continued to own land and land offered guarantees for their labor. In both cases, labor was subject to the discipline of capital, which worked not through a new set of rules and management oversight, as in the factory system, or through specialization, payment schedules, and debt bondage, as in the putting-out system, but through the use of village wealth to underwrite the quality and tempo of labor. Because their wealth was at risk, kin, neighbors, and spouses became charged with monitoring the diligence of the mobile work force.

But it was not just the workers who exported their labor from the village who were subject to modern financial instruments. Innovation in agriculture and pressure on the price of land led to a considerable rise in the indebtedness of the average landholder. By and large, this debt was held by ducal or royal institutions or by officials and their widows. From the mid-eighteenth century onward, the long-term policy of the state was to disencumber land from all impediments to its marketability and to develop administrative and judicial practices to secure the debt. Above all, steps were taken to make the property

[49] See William M. Reddy, *The Rise of Market Culture: The Textile Trade and French Society, 1750–1900* (Cambridge, 1984); Jürgen Schlumbohm, "Relations of Production – Productive Forces – Crises in Proto-industrialization," in Peter Kriedte, Hans Medick, and Jürgen Schlumbohm, *Industrialization before Industrialization: Rural Industry in the Genesis of Capitalism*, trans. Beate Schemp (Cambridge, 1981), pp. 94–125.

of each spouse attachable for the debts of the other. In this way, agricultural production also became subject to the discipline of capital investment and debt. Village officials inventoried anyone who was suspected of bad management; they allied with the most effective commodity producer in a family to ride herd on the other partner; husbands and wives made new demands for diligence on each other; and villagers exercised new controls on each other through gossip and public discussion. Furthermore, most debtors needed to find other villagers who would place their own wealth at risk as third-party underwriters, offering again an effective external control on labor and husbandry.

Villagers were subject to radical changes in labor and capital markets, both of which shifted the terms of trade and the flow of resources between the village and the outside. Inside, the land market was driven by an increasing willingness for self-exploitation. As we shall see, the price of land rose at a rate which far outstripped the price of labor or that of any commodity. This was made possible by the enormous new inputs of labor and was conditioned by the reciprocal action of the capital market, which on one hand offered the financial power for competitors to drive up the bidding and on the other increased the percentage of land subject to servicing debt.

The commodity markets also underwent considerable changes during the period. Any discussion of small peasant agriculture during intensification must take into consideration the fact that villages and villagers developed new specializations. Studies of productivity have often concentrated on comparing yield data for a single crop such as wheat, but small peasant producers were extremely sensitive to market possibilities and usually put their energies into some other crop such as flax, hemp, vegetables, hops, fruit, or industrial dyes. Peasant specialization involved the development of unique marketing networks and specific connections with external markets. Neckarhausen sold its flax in Baden (and indeed developed the reputation for producing the best raw flax in southern Germany), a nearby village shipped snails to Bavaria, and another one saw the convergence of international buyers at its annual seed fair.

One of the most powerful influences on modern peasant studies has been Chayanov's notion that the peasant farm household was a viable economic form even in an environment dominated by capitalism. As a result, interest has become focused on the productive estate and on developing a management decision model of peasant production. In general, the Chayanov argument suggests a balance between the labor effort of a household and its consumer demands. This book suggests that the history of production in Neckarhausen in the context of capital investment and intensification involved a reorganization of the sexual division of labor, labor migration, interhousehold exchanges of labor and equipment, and specialization for new market opportunities. None of these essential changes is handled well from the Chayanov perspective. We will also find that the "household" was permeable and that the interconnections between households continually fractionalized, multiplied, and were redrawn, that they involved a multiplicity of dependencies and were organized hierarchically, and that the use of resources was continually reshuffled. The peasant household model flattens out history and disguises essential changes in the utilization of land, labor, and capital.

## Agricultural innovation

Württemberg may well have been characterized by small holdings, but the process of fractionalization that set in during the eighteenth century was accompanied by the systematic adoption of intensified agricultural techniques. Agronomists have left us a picture of innovation and experimentation developed first on large English estates and then propagandized by state agencies throughout the rest of Europe. Despite a nod or two in the general direction of the Low Countries, this picture ignores the fact that intensified rotation practices had long been in use in Holland and the Rhineland, and often on small holdings. To fully understand the dynamics of the agricultural revolution, one must take into account the mobilization of the ever-increasing labor force of the eighteenth century. The new agricultural technology was above all labor-intensive, and innovation in the agrarian sector has to be seen in the context of labor utilization in the economy as a whole – the "makeshift economy" of Olwen Huften – and in the context of the development of protoindustrialized production. In fact, the original insight of Franklin Mendels was that agricultural innovation was rooted in the smallholding regions of poor soil in Flanders, where protoindustrialized production was an aspect of intensified labor as a whole, and not in the nearby areas of large farms with rich soil.[50]

Our argument suggests that a certain population pressure was necessary for carrying out the kinds of innovation associated with the agricultural revolution.[51] And villages did not wait to be told what to do by agricultural experts. They recovered waste areas on their own, petitioned tithe holders to allow innovations in cropping, negotiated with shepherds to restrict grazing on newly planted fallows, substituted oxen for horses with consequent innovations in fodder crops and the introduction of stall feeding, introduced new crops into the rotation through trial and error, shifted many resources into the intensive cultivation of flax and hemp, and completely revolutionized the sexual division of labor.

Three-field rotation turned out to be very adaptable, and producers in Neckarhausen as well as all over southern Germany were able to develop complex rotation patterns. The interspersing of strips as such did not impede productivity, and the practice was not substantially modified. In fact, the highly

[50] Franklin F. Mendels, "Industrialization and Population Pressure in Eighteenth-Century Flanders" (Ph.D. dissertation, University of Wisconsin-Madison, 1970); idem, "Agriculture and Peasant Industry in Eighteenth-Century Flanders," in Peter Kriedte, Hans Medick, and Jürgen Schlumbohm, *Industrialization before Industrialization*, pp. 161–77.

[51] See the anti-Malthusian argument of Ester Boserup, *The Conditions of Agricultural Growth: Economics of Agrarian Change under Population Pressure* (Chicago, 1965).

mechanized, intensive agriculture found in Germany today is still carried on in "open fields" with interspersed strips. The rationality of small peasant production should not be measured directly against that of large estates. Nor does it make sense to use one crop such as wheat as a standard of the success of large versus small enterprises. One has to pay close attention to the whole economy of small peasants, who frequently concentrated their energies on crops for which they had a competitive edge. For example, large estate holders could not breed stock as cheaply as peasants nor could they afford the skilled labor to train ox teams. The efficiency of estate production was predicated on the fact that crucial costs were borne by self-exploiting small producers.

It is also not at all clear that breaking up communal lands and putting them under individual ownership was economically progressive. Certainly the move to parcel them out often came only on the heels of considerable communal investment. In Neckarhausen, the village continuously recovered wasteland and managed it flexibly and innovatively. Various plots were shifted from pasture to fodder crops to fruit or to commercial crops in tandem with the changing production schedules of individual villagers. Such investment required the financial strength of the village as a whole and the collective organization of its labor force. And the success of individual production was predicated on the considerable new inputs of the village community into protection agents, agricultural specialists, and agricultural services.

## Stratification

The particular history of stratification in Neckarhausen was the result of a combination of factors: institutionalized partibility; fractionalization caused by population pressure; the expansion of employment in building, construction, and navvying outside the village; the production of cattle, flax, hemp, and cloth for the market; and an alliance between state officials and the village oligarchy. Similar conditions existed in much of southwest Germany and the Rhineland, although the nature of village and regional specialization in each territory gave it a particular cast, and the timing of state policies and the peculiarity of state institutions and fiscal structures clearly affected the rhythms of change and the chances for accumulating wealth and power. In Neckarhausen, the more differentiated the economy became and the more that wage labor spread in agriculture and industry, the more tightly the proportionally ever smaller group of agricultural producers monopolized village magistrate offices and dominated the social and political life of the community.

"Even when a group was ostensibly defending class interests, it often happened that the latter were in fact merely a mask for family interests."[52] There was a language of class in Neckarhausen, but it was largely overshadowed

[52] Jean-Louis Flandrin, *Families in Former Times: Kinship, Household and Sexuality*, trans. Richard Southern (Cambridge, 1979), p. 2.

A smallholder's "Einhaus," with living quarters, barn, stall, and shed under one roof.

by the language of family. Occasionally people out of power referred to the "patricians" (*Ehrbarkeit*), or the lower villagers (larger houses, peasants) spoke about the "upper villagers" (smaller houses, artisans), or the pastor described the pauperized and proletarianized villagers. But, overwhelmingly, the language of class was expressed through family and kinship terms – "good householder," "trashy lot," "the Hillers," and so forth.

The concept of "stratification" is, in fact, quite inadequate to grasp the social processes in a village like Neckarhausen. The geological image it connotes is too static, and it masks crucial interconnections with kinship. After all, the flow of property was regulated and channeled through family and kin. Although there were times in the village when the distribution of resources was inheritance driven and times when it was regulated largely by the market, cutting across these shifts were compensating shifts in the alliance system. A large market in land was counterbalanced by tight familial endogamy. In general, it seems safe to say that endogamy among kin, first practiced around 1750 by the political elite of the village, which by no means coincided with the economic or occupationally leading groups at that time, led to endogamy within economic strata. But the relationship remains complex, and much of this volume is devoted to exploring the way family alliance formed the mechanism through which class relations were managed and reproduced.

Up to now, kinship has not been a central category in the social analysis of

European populations. It has often been seen as something ascriptive, and so the map of social history has looked something like "from kin to contract." A great deal is determined by where the observer stands. From a distance, differences become less sharp and people appear groupable in large, loose categories, which themselves become the characters in the particular story one wants to tell. The closer one looks, the more kinship and family appear to be the operative structures in which values are formed and meaningful action takes place. But we do not yet have the tools to generate theories about this kind of thing. Practice remains at the level of family and theory at the level of class. What we need are accounts of exchange, alliance, and reciprocity at the local level, at the level of practice, before we can begin to give an account of how practices connect up. Foucault puts the problem this way:

> One must suppose rather that the manifold relationships of force that take shape and come into play in the machinery of production, in families, limited groups, and institutions, are the basis for wide-ranging effects of cleavage that run through the social body as a whole. These then form a general line of force that traverses the local oppositions and links them together; to be sure, they also bring about redistributions, realignments, homogenizations, serial arrangements, and convergences of the force relations. Major dominations are the hegemonic effects that are sustained by all these confrontations.[53]

## Gender

St. Paul distorted matters when he overstressed the unity of the marital pair. Once such a conceptual move is made, then the family has to be seen as some kind of a small state with husband and wife ordered on hierarchical principles or the one spouse absorbed into the sphere and meaning of the other. St. Paul's borrowed model has always been useful for representing the family according to dominant norms of some kind, but it is a useless sociological tool. It has been part of Western culture and is therefore always part of every familial equation if for no other reason than as a rough map of an ideal terrain. But social historians find a better tool in the concept of alliance, which recognizes that both the husband and wife remain right-bearing persons and that they are inevitably connected differentially to kin, neighbors, and church and state officials. Both power and resistance are always part of marital relations, but there is no straightforward history to tell about improvements for women or men, greater independence, or more prestige.[54] One of the reigning myths about modernization is that when women withdrew from production they destroyed a good deal of their autonomy and status. Neckarhausen offers an instance in which women were brought into production of the main marketable agricultural products. And it did affect the balance of trade between husbands and wives, and all of

[53] Michel Foucault, *The History of Sexuality*, vol. 1: *Introduction*, trans. Robert Hurley (Harmondsworth, 1981), p. 94.

[54] On power and resistance, see Foucault, *History of Sexuality*, pp. 92–6.

their relationships were reordered during the period of transition to intensified agricultural production. Not only was the alliance between marriage partners redrawn in terms of the composition of their estate, the rules for governing marital property, their work schedules, and productive routines, but the nature of the kinship alliance and its reciprocities were also thoroughly restructured. Women developed new strategies for collaborating with the pastor and secular authorities and asserted their right to protection from attacks on their property and in a derivative fashion from attacks on their bodies.

Is it possible, then, to draw up a balance sheet to talk about greater autonomy for women? Such a question moves the inquiry away from alliance, which was its starting point. Globally speaking, there is not much meaning to the construct "autonomy," and history maintains a deeply ironic set of account books. Indeed, some have argued that freedom lies in interruptions of exchange or that alliance inevitably compromises self-direction, salvation, or whatever connects the individual to some sort of transcendence.[55] The point for us is to be as precise as possible about the living conditions, resources, strategies, and restraints of those who lived in Neckarhausen. We will want to know exactly what men and women did: how they held and managed property; how they formulated arguments; what precise values they had recourse to; what institutions, laws, and administrative controls they were subject to; and where they sought succor, support, and assistance. Santayana observed that it is impossible to be religious in general. And he might have added that it is impossible to be anything in general. Lives are always lived locally, and if the material does not overwhelm them, then the concrete does. The inhabitants of Neckarhausen do not exemplify some kind of generic peasantry, nor are the wives sisters to all other women who might concern themselves with their lives.

In this analysis, I have tried to look at several issues having to do with gender relations – work, production, marketing and the use and enjoyment of products and proceeds. Issues of autonomy and self-determination were affected differently for each of these aspects. For example, in the eighteenth century, women were not involved very substantially in field crop production, they did not have much say about marketing such crops, and their work routines went by without much comment from men. When they became substantially involved in agricultural and handicraft production, they had a great deal to say about the sale of the joint product and the schedules of consumption from the cash receipts, and men became observers of their work. Thus, just at the time when they began to take a greater share in the management of the agricultural enterprise, the autonomy of their labor routines disappeared. A similarly ambiguous shift took place with regard to property ownership and management. Until the third decade of the nineteenth century, women were always under gender

[55] For scattered examples, see Peter Brown's discussion of patristic ideas of sexual alliance, *The Body and Society: Men, Women and Sexual Renunciation in Early Christianity* (New York, 1988); Rousseau, *Discourse*; Sheila Jeffreys, *The Spinster and Her Enemies: Feminism and Sexuality 1880–1930* (London, 1985).

tutelage. They could never sell or alter the conditions of real property without the permission of their fathers, husbands, or guardians. However, institutional safeguards offered them substantial protection against their husbands, who could not carry out any transaction affecting a wife's property without going before a court and obtaining her consent, as advised by her court-appointed legal guardian (*Kriegsvogt*), who was almost always a close relative. In the 1820s gender tutelage was abolished, and a wife was free to sign her own property away or encumber it as she wished. This "autonomy" was in effect designed to make her property available to underwrite her husband's business activities and his debts.

## The state

The family is not an institution that can be opposed to the state, at least in any simply way. It would be hard to specify any aspect of familial relations in Germany in the early modern period which was not shaped in the crucible of state power. Yet the entry point for officials changed once the state learned to mobilize its resources and had gained several centuries of administrative experience.

I suggest that the state's interest in the family from the sixteenth to the eighteenth centuries was dominated by fiscal concerns and thereafter by productivity issues.[56] This shift was made possible by the long experience with measuring and listing land and tax liabilities. A large part of law giving from the mid-sixteenth century onwards was concerned with property law. Overall, there was a concentration of state effort in the processes of social reproduction. In Württemberg, the inheritance customs of each village were surveyed and a single law code promulgated in 1555. And a continual stream of emendations, corrections, and clarifications issued from Stuttgart over the next two hundred years. Detailed prescriptions were also laid down about the conditions of marriage and the degrees of incest prohibition. Accompanying the legal codes were a whole series of bureaucratic implements to ensure compliance. Beginning in the 1550s and 1560s, every baptism and marriage was registered. Around that time, officials revised or established cadastral surveys, and by the turn of the century, land tax volumes were set up in each village. The law codes insisted that each marriage begin and end with a complete and detailed inventory of all assets and debits held by a couple, and they set forth the conditions for maintaining vast public archives for such documents. Accompanying the detailed inventories of family holdings were volumes tracking all dispositions of real estate, whether by sale, trade, or gift. The state provided a marriage court to adjudicate between parents and children over the timing of marriage and the selection of mates and between husbands and wives over the consummation and dissolution of marriage and to regulate age discrepencies and permissible

[56] A parallel argument is offered by Foucault, *History of Sexuality*, pp. 135–59.

A wine cellar from the late eighteenth century.

degrees. At the local level, village elders fought to put control of the marriage market into the hands of family heads by keeping a watchful eye on such institutions as spinning bees.

The ideological collection point for all of the state activities in the second half of the sixteenth century was the notion of the well-ordered *Haus* under the administration of a *Hausvater*. Such a social formation cannot be understood outside of the dynamics of state fiscality – the drive to measure land, ascribe clear tax liabilities to it, and to track each piece as it moved from hand to hand. Considerable institutional complexity developed to ensure the adequate reproduction of the Haus and to protect the state against any default. The strategies of individuals were worked out within these institutions. Children negotiated with parents over property settlements, which were recorded, audited, and revised by inventory officials. A son-in-law who did not demonstrate sufficient diligence for his father-in-law might find his entire holdings subject to a humiliating village audit. Husbands and wives played out their squabbles in the law courts over issues of property management, inheritance, and the like.

In this early period, the logic of the state's intervention may well have proceeded from fiscal concerns, but from the point of view of villagers, many arrangements and procedures became internalized and were regarded as essential services to be expected from the state. A particular inheritance regulation may have violated the old custom of a particular village, but once in place for a generation or so would become part of the observed rule structure. In the two hundred years following the great law codes, state officials refined their ability to measure and track land, to limit mortgages and secured debt, and to audit individuals in danger of tax default or bankruptcy. Individual villagers used state-supplied institutions to assert their rights, develop strategies of aggrandizement, or maintain defensive alliances. By the early eighteenth century, officials had had sufficient experience to be able to develop a sophisticated land classification scheme to assess differential productivity. On that basis a thorough tax revision could be undertaken and a more rational, efficient, and precise fiscal policy developed.

During the course of the eighteenth century – after several centuries of measuring, tracking, and bureaucratic mobilization – state ideology began to put less emphasis on particular rights and obligations and more on productivity. By the time villagers clamored for the right to innovate in the field rotation system, officials were ready to see that increased productivity over the long run took precedence over the short-run protection of tithe rights. They were also quite willing to ally with wives, in contradiction to prevailing notions of gender hierarchy, in the interest of more efficient family production. In any event, the logic of state intervention shifted from property surveillance, measurement, listing, and appropriation to disencumbering, mobilizing, innovating, and development. We will be concerned with how this shift affected the strategies of husbands and wives and parents and children, and how the reciprocities of kinship were redrawn. Here we must be aware that root paradigm shifts such as that from rights to growth (fiscality to productivity) refashion not only the way officials and agencies interact with families, but also the way family members interact with each other.

The argument in this book is organized around four main topics: social and economic change, sources, and concepts (Chapters 1–3); the relationships between husbands and wives (Chapters 4–9); the relationships between generations (Chapters 10–13); and kinship and the transfer of property (Chapters 14–16).

Chapter 1 deals with the social and economic context of Neckarhausen village life and with Württemberg as a whole. Almost everyone was tied in one way or another to the logic of agricultural production throughout the period 1700 to 1870. Social dynamics took place within a situation which broke up or endangered property accumulations in each generation. Until the 1850s, strategical alliances between the state and village patriciate were determined by the fact that a large percentage of what was appropriated in rents, dues, and taxes was taken in the form of produce. And the interlocking interests of regional officials and the village oligarchy were also closely tied up with regulating village indebtedness. Over the period, social differentiation followed on the heels of population expansion, new labor conditions, and more effective forms of class exploitation. Artisans played an important role in eighteenth-century village life, followed in the nineteenth century by building and construction workers and farm laborers. By the 1760s, villagers were pressing for the reform of agricultural practices and began substituting new crops and developing the basis for intensive stock raising.

One of the important concerns of this study is the mobilization of women's labor, which had its own specific meaning in the context of small peasant production but which was part of a more encompassing change accompanying the agricultural revolution in Central Europe. The intensive hoeing which characterized the new fodder crops fell primarily to women. For intensive sugar beet cultivation in the estate regions of north-central Germany, this affected migration patterns and the utilization of mass labor. In the small peasant regions of the southwest, family work schedules, the terms of exchange between marriage partners, patterns of consumption and the use of time, and authority relations were all affected by the sexual division of labor.

We know about most of these matters because of the abundant records from village tribunals concerned with adjudicating disputes and arresting deviant behavior. Chapter 2 presents an account of the village constitution and the articulation of local officials and institutions with ducal and royal bureaus. It explains why Württemberg had such an unusually rich set of records, minutes, and protocols and how they can be read. This leads into a consideration of the strategies of negotiation between the parties to a dispute, the judges, and the recording officers. The exigencies of narrative style determined the form of such documents, which conceal just as much as they reveal.

Throughout this study, a comparative perspective is provided to help the reader understand the particular workings of the social system under consideration. One of the themes herein is that detailed examination of specifics sheds considerable light on important theoretical and conceptual issues. Before the records can be analyzed, however, certain terminological difficulties need to be cleared up. Thus Chapter 3 presents several different social scientific and historiographic traditions concerned with developing an analytically useful concept of the "house." It then becomes possible to examine closely the notions contemporaries used to grasp family processes and to use them to critique modern scientific preoccuptions.

Social scientists whose starting point is the individual use certain concepts to sort out and label the constituents of collectivities, of groups of individual people, attitudes, and values. By and large their theoretical practice is limited by this irreducible taxonomic core.[57] A good case in point is the quixotic cam-

[57] A consideration of these issues in a discussion of Jürgen Kocka's theory of social history is to be found in David Sabean, "Zur Bedeutung von Kontext, sozialer Logik und Erfahrung," in F. J. Brüggemeier and J. Kocka, eds, "*Geschichte von unten – Geschichte von innen*": *Kontroverse um die Alltagsgeschichte*, Publication of the Fernuniversität Hagen (Hagen, 1985), pp. 52–60. For Kocka's inadequate answer: "Antwort an David Sabean," in ibid., pp. 61–9. See also Norbert Elias, *The Court Society* (New York, 1983), pp. 1–34; and Edmund R. Leach, "Rethinking Anthropology," in *Rethinking Anthropology* (London, 1961), pp. 1–27; Louis Dumont, *Homo Hierarchicus: The Caste System and Its Implications* (Chicago, 1970), pp. 1–11, 39–42; and idem, *From Mandeville to Marx: The Genesis and Triumph of Economic Ideology* (Chicago, 1977), pp. 3–24.

paign to sort out all the world's households into a single onomatological set.[58] The point of such an exercise has never been fully apparent, but what has not been sufficiently remarked upon is that it shares the inadequacy of its starting point with a large number of other sociological programs. This does not mean that concepts are not fundamental for good historical or social analysis, but they do have to be adequate for maintaining contextual discipline by starting not with individuals but with relationships. It would be quite inappropriate, for example, to talk about fathers or husbands as such.[59] Both terms are radically correlative – father and son, father and daughter, father and fetus, husband and wife – just as the household is a locus of relationships and not an enclosed entity, however defined. One objective of this discussion is to convey a sense of the complex transactions which took place in households and to give a systematic account of the logic of relations and of the different forces, words, objects, and exchanges which mediated them. The concepts sought are ones that will ferret out the relations which dominated and provided structure and thereby help the reader to grasp process and historical change and to understand the mediations between practice and constraint. Two sets of crucial household relations are considered in this volume. At the outset, we concentrate on husbands and wives, in order to recover the changing logic of the internal relations of the house while giving a preliminary account of a couple's alliance as part of a wider system. Next, we examine relations between parents and adult children, moving in turn to the interrelationships between houses, then to hierarchies, dependencies, and the allocation of resources.

Chapters 4 to 9 deal with relations between husbands and wives. Many of the available sources exist precisely because particular couples were in such conflict with each other that they took matters to a court where the proceedings became part of the public record. They aired their disputes before the pastor and church elders (consistory) or before the secular officials (*Schultheiß* (chief administrative officer) and *Richter* (members of the village court, or *Gericht*)). In many cases, their purpose was simply to have the problem recorded, or, in their parlance, to *protocollieren*. This was often theatrical enough by itself to reestablish the household's "private" face. But a protocol could be just one of a string of episodes causing officials to become more and more involved in internal family affairs. We will simply offer an overview of the configuration of disputes, from which we tease an account of the claims, obligations, and expectations couples negotiated before the courts. The instances of marital conflict also provide an opportunity to examine the language of abuse for changes in the symbolic content of the most direct and compressed expression of value. At this preliminary stage, we provide considerable evidence of

[58] Peter Laslett, "Introduction: The History of the Family," in Peter Laslett, ed., with the assistance of Richard Wall, *Household and Family in Past Time* (Cambridge, 1972), pp. 1–89, esp. 28–51.

[59] This point has been made nicely by Jochen Martin, "Zur Stellung des Vaters in antiken Gesellschaften," in H. Süssmuth, ed., *Historische Anthropologie* (Göttingen, 1984), pp. 84–109.

a striking change in discourse about marital relations after 1800, which adds up to a veritable crisis in the household.

Chapters 5 and 6 examine issues connected with production and expand upon several of the patterns of conflict discussed in Chapter 4. A question of particular interest is how spouses constantly renegotiated their rights and responsibilities and reformulated their exchange relationships as the sexual division of labor underwent significant changes prompted by agricultural intensification and as the nature of work itself became restructured with the introduction of new crops and the integration of the village into a regional labor market. Population growth, increased social differentiation, and the pauperization of large parts of the community all significantly altered the terms of marital alliances. In fact, between 1800 and 1840, separation and divorce became common and were accompanied by new forms of violence and more types of abuse.[60] Associated with these changes was a novel discourse within families about household financial management, drinking, and housewifery. Therefore an attempt is made to delineate forms of exchange within the house; gender rhythms of activity; ideological and cultural models of order; alliances with neighbors, kin, and officials; and particularly critical points of contact between spouses.

Chapters 7, 8, and 9 turn to the dynamics of property holding. Although property is not the only thing which mediates relationships, no relationship escapes its formative power entirely. It is something which is continually talked about in peasant society, and its terms change as the context of that discussion changes. In Neckarhausen, strategic discourse depended on a particular family's position in the village hierarchy, the nature of its alliances, and the size and nature of the resources it controlled. Sometimes property claims were spelled out in written documents, which could be public or purely private in character. Sometimes negotiations were staged with important kin and relatives present, at other times with local officials. Family memories were embedded in different institutional and ad hoc arrangements, all of which afforded a couple and their kin endless possibilities for tactical and strategical moves.

The main concern in Chapter 7 is to lay out the details of formal negotiation about property. In Neckarhausen, the act of marriage was a fundamental part – but only a part – of a progressively formed alliance between spouses. In prenuptial negotiations, kinfolk gathered together to set the terms of exchange. At the final dissolution of a marriage, when a complete account was fixed in a concluding inventory, it was not unusual for 20 or so kin to gather together to dispute the reckoning. Between these two points there could be pacts, inventories, testaments, gifts, sales, and retirement contracts, each with representatives of the wider family present or not, depending on the rules of the particular transaction or the desires of the parties. Through the details of the system

[60] How unusual this was can be seen in Roderick Phillips's new history of divorce, *Putting Asunder: A History of Divorce in Western Society* (Cambridge, 1988).

Day-laborer/petty craftsman cottages.

of rights and obligations, property can become a flexible instrument for social analysis.[61] It enables us to explore marital reciprocity, for example, as a fundamental point within a larger context of reciprocities between groups of allied kin. We must not forget, however, that property as such was owned by individuals and couples and that they determined how it would be held, managed, and transferred. It is not that the kin group devolved property onto them so much as that they used kin as powerful instruments in defense of their rights. The chief interest of collateral relatives in the property situation of a particular couple was to see that rules were followed and values respected so as to secure themselves in their own expectations and management of property. Kinship provided an arena of concentrated involvement, which was derived less from residual claims to property than from a clear sense of obligation based on reciprocal exchange.

In Chapter 8, the focus shifts from ownership of familial property to its management. Every region in Europe had its own set of rules for the aggressive defense of resources and for sorting out gender-specific claims and duties. In much of the recent literature on property, loose connections have been made

[61] The classic statement is by Jack Goody, *Death, Property and the Ancestors*, pp. 273–327. See also the argument by Hans Medick and David Warren Sabean, "Interest and Emotion," pp. 9–27; and David Sabean, "Aspects of Kinship Behaviour and Property in Rural Western Europe before 1800," in Jack Goody, et al., eds., *Family and Inheritance*, pp. 96–111.

between individualism and private property, even though the content of individuality has been left largely unexplored. And it is not at all clear what bearing such discussion has on gender. Were women whose ownership disappeared with marriage less individualistic than their husbands? Or were their personal characteristics derived from their men, who provided a model for them to copy? Such questions are complex and cannot be discussed without some knowledge of how the system works. It is particularly important to understand the difference between ownership and management, the formal and informal institutions for controlling behavior, and the forms of recourse spouses had with respect to each other.

Rules and institutions are one thing, but it makes a great deal of difference whether a couple shares 1 acre or 20, tills land or makes shoes, owns a horse (plows for others) or a cow (cooperates with others in plowing), possesses a wagon and harrow or only a rake and hoe – in short, the nature of the mediation is fundamental for establishing a set of relations. And it makes a difference, too, whether property links families of different wealth and social standing or whether it serves to reinforce lines of stratification. Chapter 9 examines the composition of what we might call the "marital fund." The pertinent questions here are whether husbands and wives were equal to each other in the amount of wealth they brought to a marriage, whether marriage was a point of mobility, how a larger discourse about wealth and social standing related to marital strategies, what role marriage played in the social distribution of resources, and how family and class dynamics were interconnected.

Chapters 10 to 13 are about the relations between parents and adult children. Property not only provides a central focus of negotiation between spouses, but it also marks periods of transition between generations, demarcates areas of competence, and creates bonds of dependence. We must not think of property simply as a set of rules or hard structures, an account of which exhausts analysis. Property can focus attention and create expectations, provide opportunities to exhibit skill and character, and establish connections and cooperation or points of resentment and disruption. The fact that many small dramas repeat stereotypical performances attests to the power of the syntax established by property dynamics. But, like any language, its structure provides endless opportunity for innovation and creativity. Take the story of a younger daughter on a Saxon farmstead, who was repeatedly told by her parents that she was the child specially adapted to farm work, and that she had a unique touch with animals and a deep understanding of the rhythms of nature. That litany meant for her that she would inherit the farm instead of her older sister. Every pat on the head was a message about future expectations, the kind of husband she would find, the allocation of resources. She delayed her departure from the house and worked to maintain the substance of the farm during years of maximum productivity. She boiled over with indignation when her parents passed the farm on to her elder sibling. Every part of Western Europe has dealt with these matters in different ways, and while culture was built up through everyday considerations of real things, its direction was never predetermined, and any acquaintance with the variety of rural social forms demonstrates the endless creativity of the active appropriation of circumstance.

In Neckarhausen, two values seem to have marked the relations between generations: a preoccupation with treating all children equally and a shrewd sense that they should be set up in the world hungry. Adult, married children were independent and dependent in a curious mix, and the turnover in generations was never abrupt, but took place as a long-drawn-out process. Current accounts of peasant societies pay too much attention to the formal and most general aspects of ownership and inheritance and not enough to the details of production, labor utilization, and the interrelationships between separate farm enterprises. Neckarhausen offers a chance to examine peasant social dynamics in a situation where parents did not see themselves as trustees of lineal property, where rights in ownership were always specific and allocable, where parents and children established separate economies, where households assembled bits and pieces of real property which had no organic links with each other, where living space was divorced from property devolution, where the labor of children or parents was exchanged for cash, where the elderly did everything they could to maintain separate economies, where adult authority was not derived from property management, and where honor was dependent more on individual actions than on membership in a "house." Methodologically, we will handle these matters in two ways: first by a detailed examination of family histories (Chapter 10), and second by a systematic consideration of key issues such as access to capital equipment, the allocation of labor, and the life cycle of land ownership and craft production (Chapter 11).

Besides the continual negotiation over land and labor within families, there was also a set of general cultural values and state ideologies which played a central role in individual strategies. This theme forces us to consider the discipline exercised on the younger generation and how that discipline was justified during an early period marked by an ideology of patriarchal authority, in contrast to the following one in which competing state institutions intervened directly into internal family affairs (Chapters 12 and 13). The discourse of property also changed as the system of social stratification altered, accompanied by class endogamy, a more aggressive defense of family wealth, and a harsher interplay between groups of villagers.

The last three chapters of the book are concerned with the general problems of encumbrances on property and the alternative mechanisms for distributing resources in the society. There are two competing views about peasant family dynamics which fit similar phenomena into different schema. In one view, the family is a peculiarly moral unit, which takes care of its sick, mentally deficient, and elderly, but in the other the family is characterized by abandoned parents, rejected kin, and moral squalor.[62] Exactly how the available evidence can be

[62] The issues are summed up in Macfarlane, *Origins*, pp. 66–79, 83, 141–4.

used to arrive at a general set of values is a difficult problem, but we can talk more easily about how people justified the care they gave, how they ensured their own continued subsistence, and how they modeled relationships between generations at different points in the life cycle. I hope to show that the central mode of justification of the Fifth Commandment was exchange. Respect was due to parents because they were the source of wealth, and in terms of expressed value at least, the amount of effort – labor, services, produce – to be expended was directly proportional to the amount of property passed on. To understand the nature of negotiations between generations, one must look at retirement contracts, annuities, the allocation of land and buildings, conditions on sale, and the rights of lineal redemption (Chapter 14).

The second issue has to do with the mechanisms for distributing resources. It takes us to an analysis of the real estate market (Chapter 15). There has been considerable discussion about the degree to which market forces constitute familial relations, and attention has been focused on the problems of encumbrances on property, the degree of formality of transactions, the number of transactions, and the volume of trade. As might be expected, all of these matters changed significantly with the increase in population, innovations in agriculture, and the general monetization of relationships. Nonetheless, the startling finding is that the market did not transform the system of exchange in a linear fashion. Furthermore, the formal aspects of the land market are only half the story. Parents and children bought land and other real estate from each

An orchard meadow.

A cider press.

other in varying proportions over the study period, and their transactions were part of the larger market that was more or less dominated by kin (Chapter 16).

One of the reasons for undertaking this study was to document a particular rural social system as closely as possible. When I began, there was a general consensus that before "modernization" people lived in a world of kinship and that industrialization, mobility, and altered institutional arrangements brought the isolated nuclear family into being and reorganized society so that it moved away from solidarity toward competition and away from corporate groups to individuals sorted out into classes. Neckarhausen is a challenge to that sort of a linear story. As mobility came to dominate part of its work force, as agriculture was intensified and capitalized, as social strata in the village became more pronounced, as a land market came to be important in distributing resources, as most forms of feudal and familial encumbrances on property were done away with, as land was fractionalized, as producers became progressively tied into labor and product markets, and as a large part of the village became dependent on wages, kinship became more rather than less important. Close kin developed a flexible set of exchanges, passing marriage partners, godparents, guardians, political favors, work contacts, and financial guarantees back and forth.

What we find in this study are activities, structures, processes, and logics that simply are not visible outside of the local context. This, of course, does not mean that similar formations were not to be found elsewhere. If we want to know about the content of this "premodern" kinship system, we can only get at it by patiently tracing out genealogies from small geographical regions and piling up examples of kin actually interacting. If we want to recover the tenor of marital relations inside a particular context of production, we have to examine all the anecdotes we can find for the logic of confrontation, the strategies of subsistence and survival, the fabric of rights and obligations, and the coherence of life trajectories. If we want to understand the moral and social relationships which bound together and divided houses and families, we have to examine in detail the tactical language, spatial interaction, and practical everyday exchanges. This is no Montaillou, whose inherent interest lies in the uniqueness of its documentation and the strangeness of its social discourse. This is Neckarhausen, one of several villages with more or less the same name, whose stories can only reveal a strange world if we can penetrate the banality of repetitive written texts and fix our gaze on the everyday representations of social reality from the inside.

I

# Productive forces and social differentiation

The Schultheiss and Bürgermeister stick together because they are cousins, and the other magistrates support them, since they are all related to each other.
– The emigrant Jacob Hampf from Eglosheim, 1817[1]

The socioeconomic structures which developed in the half century after the Thirty Years War continued to characterize Württemberg until past the middle of the nineteenth century. Already in the eighteenth century, as Helga Schulz has ably shown, the density of handicrafts and trades in rural Württemberg was greater than in any East Elbian city.[2] But occupational statistics have always been difficult to put together for Württemberg – and bedeviled investigators until as late as the 1880s – because artisans almost always combined their trade with land and agricultural production. From a census of 1857, Wolfgang von Hippel has established that 92 percent of the families of Württemberg held property of some kind.[3] The transition between village and city was relatively fluid, and no great urban agglomerations developed by the end of our period. The capital city of the region (Oberamt) to which Neckarhausen belonged, for example, had a population only four times greater than the village as late as the mid-nineteenth century. It had well over three times as much arable and meadowland, and a considerable proportion of its inhabitants were occupied with agricultural production.[4] Around 1700, agriculture was probably the primary source of income for more than 70 percent of the Württemberg population. By 1820, the proportion had only fallen to 60 percent, and by 1860 a full 51 percent of all families still derived most of their support from tilling the soil.[5]

1 Günter Moltmann, ed., *Aufbruch nach Amerika. Friedrich List und die Auswanderung aus Baden und Württemberg 1816/17. Dokumentation einer sozialen Bewegung* (Tübingen, 1979), p. 131.
2 Helga Schulz, "Landhandwerk und ländliche Sozialstruktur um 1800," in *Jahrbuch für Wirtschaftsgeschichte*, part 2 (1980): 11–50.
3 Wolfgang von Hippel, "Bevölkerungsentwicklung und Wirtschaftsstruktur im Königreich Württemberg 1815/65: Überlegungen zum Pauperismusproblem in Südwestdeutschland," in Ulrich Engelhardt, Volker Sellin, and Horst Stuke, eds., *Soziale Bewegungen und politische Verfassung. Beiträge zur Geschichte der modernen Welt* (Stuttgart, 1976), pp. 353–4.
4 *Beschreibung Nürtingen*, Anhang.
5 Hippel, "Bevölkerungsentwicklung," pp. 306–10, 353–60.

Partible inheritance together with the freedom to alienate parcels of land created a smallholding peasantry, which in the course of time came to be dominated by what commentators have come to call "midget" *Bauern*. For example, by 1873 219 of the 220 households in Neckarhausen held at least some land.[6] Well over half (56.6 percent) of them had less than 1.5 hectares (3.7 acres), which together accounted for 20.1 percent of the usable land. The rest (43.4 percent) held 79.9 percent of the land. A substantial middle group (83, or 37.9 percent of the householders) held between 1.5 and 5 hectares (3.7 to 12.4 acres). Above that group, there were 10 landholders with 5 to 10 hectares (12.35 to 24.7 acres) and only 2 with more than 10 hectares. According to the careful calculations of Wolfgang von Hippel, 2.5 to 3 hectares was enough to keep a family fully occupied in agriculture by the mid-nineteeth century, although a contemporary put the figure at 0.72 to 2.6 hectares.[7] Much depended on how intensively the fallow field was used. In all likelihood, the considerable group of landholders in Neckharhausen with 1.5 to 5 hectares were either independent agricultural producers or combined a sedentary handicraft or trade with farming, which kept them fully occupied. Thus, out of 220 households in Neckarhausen, 125 had clearly less than adequate land to live from agriculture alone; another 83 could manage under normal conditions; and 12 were independent under most conceivable circumstances. By European standards of the time, these were smallholders, indeed.[8]

Most villagers in the Duchy of Württemberg either owned land outright or held it in tenure from the duke, the state church, or one of the ducal institutions such as the university or some other foundation. Those who held land in tenure owed various kinds of dues, but all land was subject to tithes, and everyone was liable for taxes. Although there was some *Freieigenes* (freehold) in Neckarhausen, much of the land was held in tenure from the duke and to a lesser degree from two regional foundations. During the Napoleonic period and at the Viennese negotiations, the new kingdom acquired various territories which practiced single-son inheritance, had insecure tenures, noble landlords, and considerable social inequalities.[9] By contrast, the older Württemberg territories had long been characterized by secure, heritable tenures, and villagers

[6] STAL, E10, Bevölkerungstabelle.

[7] Hippel, "Bevölkerungsentwicklung," pp. 306–7.

[8] On the basis of the 1857 census, Wolfgang von Hippel ("Bevölkerungsentwicklung," pp. 353–4) estimates that independent agricultural producers and handicraftsmen and tradesmen who were closely tied to agriculture, such as millers, weavers, and village artisans, and who held at least 5 M., made up 45.5 percent of the population of Württemberg and held 85 percent of the land. In our 1873 figures for Neckarhausen, the same occupations and level of land holding appear to have accounted for 43.4 percent of the population holding 79.9 percent of the land. In general, Neckarhausen seems typical of the smallholder/craftsmen structure of Württemberg as a whole.

[9] Wolfgang von Hippel offers a detailed account of rural institutions, rents, and taxes in *Die Bauernbefreiung im Königreich Württemberg*, 2 vols., Forschungen zur deutschen Sozialgeschichte, vol. 1, pts. 1 and 2 (Boppard am Rhein, 1977).

practiced the right to alienate holdings freely, parcel by parcel.[10] This gave a much larger population access to land, and no institutional limit was set on the ability of artisans and small tradesmen to purchase or inherit it. Furthermore, in most villages, and certainly in Neckarhausen, all Bürger had rights to commonland, which gave them garden plots and strips of land for flax and hemp, firewood, and pasture, and allowed them to have animals in the common herds (horses, cows, sheep, and geese). Consequently, almost everyone was tied in one way or another to the logic of agricultural production. Not only were people rooted in the village, but they also were able to put together enough resources to marry and produce children. The core territory of Württemberg, with a lower marriage age than elsewhere and higher fertility rates, developed the densest population in all of Germany.[11]

Throughout the period under consideration, the population of Württemberg was shaped by an unusually high fertility rate and an extraordinary infant mortality rate. Even in the nineteenth century in the Danube and Swabian Alb region of Württemberg, infant mortality was about 40 percent.[12] In the *Unterland* where Neckarhausen was situated, the mortality rate was much lower, which is why the whole Neckar Valley region had such a dense population. During the second half of the eighteenth century, the population increased at an annual rate of 0.63 percent. After a pause during the second decade of the nineteenth century, the annual growth rates fluctuated between 0.7 and 0.9 percent. From 1846 to 1855, there was a sharp decline to between −0.4 and −0.8 percent in the rates for the Neckar and Black Forest regions, but thereafter growth resumed at its earlier rate. Wolfgang von Hippel argues that Württemberg population fluctuations were driven largely by changes in fertility, and that the relatively moderate growth rates were due to the fact that between 1813 and 1871 some 60 percent of the population produced by the excess of births over deaths emigrated.[13] After 1830, the emigration rate increased rapidly, reaching a high point between 1846 and 1855. During this period and the following decades, far more young men than women emigrated, and this pattern had a severe effect on the balance of the sexes. Between 1813 and 1871, the population of Württemberg as a whole increased from 1,392,971 to 1,818,539.

The population levels attained in Neckarhausen before the Thirty Years War were not reached again until after the mid-eighteenth century (see Table 1.1). The population grew steadily throughout the eighteenth century except for a sharp fall during the 1760s. Between about 1700 and 1800, it increased by 70 percent and from 1700 to 1870 by almost another 70 percent.[14]

[10] Hippel, *Bauernbefreiung*, vol. 1, pp.76ff., 94–105, 120–4.
[11] Hippel, "Bevölkerungsentwicklung," pp. 278–91.
[12] The population statistics for Württemberg have been carefully analyzed by Wolfgang von Hippel, "Bevölkerungsentwicklung," pp. 277–301.
[13] Ibid., p. 283.
[14] The statistics up to the 1820s are based on church visitation records, after that on triennial Zollverein censuses. There are two series of visitations: in HSAS, A 261, and LKA,

Table 1.1 *Population in Neckarhausen, 1620–1869*

| | | | |
|---|---|---|---|
| 1620–29 | (516.3) | 1750–59 | (465.5) |
| ........................ | | 1760–69 | 419.5 |
| 1640–49 | (79.4) | 1770–79 | 444.0 |
| 1650–59 | 146.6 | 1780–89 | 515.6 |
| 1660–69 | 195.4 | 1790–99 | 549.8 |
| 1670–79 | 262.7 | 1800–09 | 621.6 |
| 1680–89 | (265.9) | 1810–19 | (743.3) |
| 1690–99 | (321.2) | 1820–29 | 738.0 |
| 1700–09 | 340.0 | 1830–39 | 858.0 |
| 1710–19 | 389.5 | 1840–49 | 953.3 |
| 1720–29 | 423.3 | 1850–59 | 910.7 |
| 1730–39 | 432.3 | 1860–69 | 924.3 |
| 1740–49 | 455.0 | | |

*Note*: Figures in parentheses reckoned from total parish data.

One of the principal concerns of modern students of the transition from feudalism to capitalism has been the problem of accumulation, which is closely tied up with social differentiation. Württemberg's path to modernization, if set against an external norm, was quite peculiar, but as Hans Medick has perceptively pointed out, the small peasant solution to accumulation is closely linked to the present-day economic strength of one of the most advanced industrial regions of the world.[15] The recent part of the story does not concern us here, but it does suggest that the complex social, economic, and institutional development of Württemberg needs to be examined in detail for its own inner logic and development. One of the consequences of secure tenures and partible inheritance was that accumulated landholdings were broken up in each succeeding generation and dispersed among the various heirs. As we shall see, there were considerable opportunities for the wealthier members of the village to profit from the poorer, but the earnings of one generation were constantly redistributed according to the demographic fortunes of the family.

*Synodus Protocolle*. For decades in which the statistics were given only for the parish, a ratio based on the prior and subsequent decades was used to sort out Neckarhausen proper from the hamlet of Raidwangen, which was also part of the parish. These data appear in parentheses in Table 1.1. The Zollverein statistics are found in STAL, E 10. For each decade, I have used averages based on all annual counts available. There are problems with the sources, which will be discussed in a later publication. For example, the 1848 gazeteer gives the village population as 1,034; Königlicher statistisch-topographischer Bureau, *Beschreibung des Oberamts Nürtingen* (Stuttgart and Tübingen, 1848), *Anhang*. Whatever the problems, Table 1.1 gives an adequate picture of the population changes over time and a fairly accurate one of the effective number of inhabitants over each decade.

15 Hans Medick, "Priviligiertes Handelskapital und 'kleine Industrie.' Produktion und Produktionsverhältnisse im Leinengewerbe des alt-württembergischen Oberamts Urach im 18. Jahrhundert," *Archiv für Sozialgeschichte* 23 (1983): 267–310, here pp. 309–10.

No account of the history of socioeconomic development in Württemberg can avoid the important impact of state fiscal policy.[16] Many of the specific structures and much of the society's peculiar development can be traced to the fact that the peasant's surplus was largely taken off as a *share* of the crop. From land which was held in tenure, the tenant paid most of his or her obligations in kind, and around 1800 those dues which went to the landlord made up a substantial 36 percent of the total taken from the producer.[17] Tithes were exacted on the gross production of all agricultural land, sheaves being collected as they stood on the field. Tithes on garden produce and hay were frequently abolished through forced purchase during the course of the nineteenth century, but not until 1848 did the state establish a program to have landholders redeem the "great," or grain, tithe.[18] In the state program, those obligated to render tithes were expected to pay off the capital value with interest over a set period.

As for taxes, in Württemberg they were usually paid in money and were already comparatively high in the sixteenth century. They were divided between those paid to the ducal or *Landschaft* (Parliament) treasuries and those paid to the village and regional (*Amt*) treasuries. State officials often found it expedient to transfer fiscal responsibilities to the localities, so that villagers were less likely to complain about ducal or royal than about local and regional exactions. For example, during the Napoleonic wars, villages were faced with quartering, forced requisitions of grain, additional taxes, carting services, and the like.[19] Each locality was given a quota which it had to provide and pay for out of its own income. As a result, most villages were forced into debt, and their inhabitants had to pay high amortization costs and carry substantial interest payments. Adam Rühle from Beutelspach testified in 1817 just before he emigrated to America that "the king's taxes account for very little, but those of the county [Amt] and village are unmanageable."[20] For Neckarhausen, when it came time to straighten the river or when the long stretch of highway had to be rebuilt or maintained, the village was responsible for a significant part of the costs.[21]

According to Wolfgang von Hippel, about 30 percent of the peasant surplus in old Württemberg around 1800 was taken off in rents, tithes, and taxes.[22]

[16] See the important argument of Hans Medick, "Teuerung, Hunger und 'moralische Ökonomie von Oben': Die Hungerkrise der Jahre 1816–17 in Württemberg," *Beiträge zur historischen Sozialkunde* 2 (1985): 39–44.

[17] Hippel, *Bauernbefreiung*, vol. 1, p. 291.

[18] During the period 1817 to 1821, various miscellaneous dues of small value and hay tithes under 10 fl. were amortized; Hippel, *Bauernbefreiung*, vol. 1, pp. 355ff., 437ff., 498ff.

[19] The details for Neckarhausen can be found in the annual *Gemeindepflegerechnungen*.

[20] Günter Moltmann, ed., *Aufbruch nach America. Friedrich List und die Auswanderung aus Baden und Württemberg 1816–17. Dokumentation einer sozialen Bewegung* (Tübingen,1979), p. 136: "Die KönigsSteuer beträgt fast nichts, aber der Amts- und FlekenSchaden ist unerschwinglich." And Christoph Schaar from Weinsperg complained in a similar fashion (p. 144): "Royal taxes are the least important, but the county taxes and the costs from the war have been unmanageable" (Die KönigsSteuer wäre das wenigste, aber der Amtschaden und die Kriegskosten sind unerschwinglich gewesen).

[21] For example, *Gemeindepflegerechnungen*, 1832–6.

[22] Hippel, *Bauernbefreiung*, vol. 1, pp. 278–304.

The fact that so much of the surplus was paid in kind had enormous consequences for the set of relationships established between the duke/king and villages and among inhabitants of the villages themselves. Fiscal officials created elaborate procedures for maintaining and systematically reviewing village financial records.[23] Besides the powerful Schultheiss, there was also a *Bürgermeister* in every village, who as chief financial officer kept volumes of detailed accounts, tax assessments and payments, bound receipts, and a running diary of all transactions.[24] The accounts were supposed to be read to the assembled villagers – although by 1800 this procedure appears to have been controlled by a small oligarchy – and were subject to a double audit by officials in the Oberamt.[25] In countless daily ways, the middle-range bureaucrats of the Oberamt were able to look into the affairs of each village. But most of their business was with the officials and patricians of the villages, whose hands they strengthened in their dealings with other inhabitants.[26]

The duchy's fiscal interests had important implications for many different levels of social, economic, and political development. For example, a substantial part of state income was built on the tithes and excise taxes on wine. Viniculture was supported by the fact that ducal officials forbade changing the cultivation of land devoted to grape production, which covered a much wider territory in the eighteenth century than later.[27] Neckarhausen, for example, had extensive vineyards which it only was allowed to abandon in 1817. State officials forced villagers to continue to produce wine and fought against changes in cultivation for many decades.[28] Since viniculture was always an intensive

[23] For the details, see David Warren Sabean, *Power in the Blood: Popular Culture and Village Discourse in Early Modern Germany* (Cambridge, 1984), pp. 12–20.

[24] See the "Communordnung" (1.7.1758) in Reyscher, vol. 14, pp. 537–777, here 729–45.

[25] Ferdinand Dieter from Neuenstadt testified in 1817 that "one cannot examine the village finances" (Man kann in unsere Gemeindehaushaltung nicht hineinsehen), Moltmann, ed., *Aufbruch*, p. 160. Christian Horrmann said that "no one looks at the village accounts. Only 10–12 Bürger come to their publication because one is allowed only to sign them, and if anyone objects, then it is held against him, and he is cursed as a rebel" (p. 163). (Es sieht Niemand in die GemeindeRechnung hinein; es kommen nur 10–12 Bürger zur Publikation, weil man nichts thun darf als unterschreiben, und wenn einer Einwendung macht, so wird es einem nachgetragen und man wird ein Rebelle gescholten). Gall Falter accused the Neckarhausen magistrates of not reading the Bürgermeister accounts according to law; *Gericht*, vol. 3, f. 25 (30.9.1780).

[26] The degree of control and censure varied over time, but even when there were serious charges, higher officials seldom exactly sprang into action. In some periods, they were expressly supportive of hierarchical relations in the village. The Bürgerausschuss, which represented the village, had brought charges against the temporary Schultheiss and Bürgermeister. The Oberamtmann announced that he would accept no further complaints from either the Bürgerausschuss or the whole village (*Bürgerschaft*); *Vogtruggericht*, vol. 2, f. 76 (26.11.1818).

[27] See the ducal ordinances, "Verbot, der Herrschaftszehendbare Weinbergen ohne höhere Erlaubniß mit Obst-Bäumen zu bepflanzen oder gar auszustocken" (20.9.1726) and "Erneuerung und Einschärfung des Verbots, in zehendbaren Weinbergen Bäume und andere Gewächse anzupflanzen" (1.10.1744), in Reyscher, vol. 16, pp. 572–3, 591.

[28] There is a constant refrain in the Gerichts- and Vogtruggerichtsprotocolle: *Vogtruggericht* vol. 1, f. 5 (1.12.1747); f. 56 (20.4.1763); f. 88 (18.3.1767); f. 100 (20.3.1770); f. 103 (11.3.1772); f. 109 (26.1.1773); f. 125 (12.12.1781); f. 127 (19.11.1783); vol. 2, f. 524 (11.3.1806); *Gericht*, vol.

form of production, was always tied up with the market, and could best be carried out on small holdings, it tended to support parcelization, especially since most viniculturalists had to balance their wine production with other agricultural products in order to bail themselves out in periods of bad harvest.[29] The close coupling of peasant production with state fiscal interests encouraged state officials to continue to allow breaking up landholdings throughout the early modern period despite their own ordinances and public warnings about arbitrary partitioning. They found a growing basis for income in intensified land use. By the second half of the eighteenth century, Württemberg cameralists argued that small peasant properties and a dense and growing population were a significant sign of economic health and well-being.[30]

Many Württemberg officials put their energies into mobilizing all of the productive resources at hand, although their perspectives and programs in each epoch depended on how their predecessors had created access to the village and to the individual peasant enterprise. In the sixteenth and early seventeenth centuries, they were concerned with measuring and recording land in cadasters and tax volumes.[31] And the postmortem and marriage inventories were also a way of defining tenure responsibilities and fiscal obligations.[32] By the mid-seventeenth century, control and measurement were further tightened by the establishment of *Kaufbücher* (registers of real estate sales) to record every change of ownership by sale (the inventories did the same for the premortem and postmortem inheritance and endowment of children), *Güterbücher* (registers of ownership) to maintain a current record, and *Unterpfandsbücher* (mortgage registers) to allow an overview of liens and mortgages.[33] Once this kind of work was accomplished, state officials could begin to reevaluate the quality of land in order to fine-tune the process of appropriation and develop strategies for encouraging increased production. During the third and fourth decades of the eighteenth century, a new cadaster was established which remeasured land, divided the arable into six classes, and surveyed the trades and handicrafts in order to extend taxation from real estate to occupation.[34] During this period, the central concern of state discourse shifted from rights and

1, f. 56 (28.12.1752); f. 60 (28.12.1753); vol. 2, f. 172 (29.12.1777); vol. 4, f. 128 (28.12.1789); vol. 6, f. 172 (7.10.1806); vol. 7, f. 9 (6.10.1807). Villagers continually tried to neglect their vines and plant beans or zwetschgen trees.

29 See Hippel, *Bauernbefreiung*, vol. 1, p. 64.

30 Discussed in ibid., pp. 49–56, 66–7, 77.

31 For a discussion of the Württemberg cadasters (*Lagerbücher*), see Gregor Richter, *Lagerbücher- oder Urbarlehre: hilfswissenschaftliche Grundzüge nach württembergischen Quellen*, Veröffentlichungen der staatlichen Archivverwaltung Baden-Württemberg, vol. 36 (Stuttgart, 1979).

32 On keeping inventories, see "2. Landrecht" (1567) in Reyscher, vol. 4, p. 376 and "3. Landrecht" (1610), vol. 5, p. 52. Also "General Reskript . . . Inventuren . . . betr." (24.7.1620), p. 371.

33 "3. Landrecht" (1610) in Reyscher, vol. 5, p.50; "General-Reskript . . . Inventuren . . . betr." (24.7.1620), pp. 369–70; "General-Reskript verschwiegene Beschwerden und Auslosung verkauften Güter betr." (15/30.1.1651), P. 448.

34 The results are in HSAS, A261, Bü 1344.

ownership to productivity and hard work. A typical village institution such as the *Spinnstube* (spinning bee) was talked about in terms of controlling sexuality and the marriage market (and thus the access to resources) in the sixteenth and seventeenth centuries and in terms of competition and production in the eighteenth.[35]

By the end of the eighteenth and beginning of the nineteenth century, state officials were concerned with clearing real estate of all encumbrances which affected its transferability and free mobility. To the late cameralists and early liberals, the complete marketability of land offered a means of increasing efficiency and therefore productivity.[36] At the same time, the state was willing to bear down harder and squeeze out all those whose "inefficiency" or "incapacity" had driven them into debt and made it difficult for them to pay their various dues.[37] During the first several decades of the nineteenth century, local officials were ordered to list every villager whose assets and debits were out of balance. This move precipitated local riots and considerable violence.[38] The Presser was sent to attach the property of anyone in tax arrears, and state officials directed local officials to force every villager to erase all tax obligations and public debts (which had piled up with the considerable capital costs of agricultural intensification and the expenses of the Napoleonic war period) each year or face bankruptcy proceedings – thousands of which took place in the decade or so after 1815.[39]

[35] Hans Medick, "Village Spinning Bees: Sexual Culture and Free Time among Rural Youth in Early Modern Germany," in Hans Medick and David Warren Sabean, eds., *Interest and emotion: Essays on the Study of Family and Kinship* (Cambridge, 1984), pp. 317–39.

[36] Hippel, *Bauernbefreiung*, vol. 1, pp. 323–9.

[37] Medick, "Teuerung," p. 41.

[38] In 1806, the Vogt wrote that Neckarhausen residents were not paying outstanding taxes and were falling into debt. The village magistrates were to report anyone who was not diligent; *Vogtruggericht*, vol. 2, f. 20 (11.3.1806). A list of people with too many debts was made for further investigation; f. 23. The concern for regular payment of tax arrears was mentioned again in 1808; *Gericht*, vol. 7, f. 27 (19.1.1808). By 1809, the Presser was a regular visitor to Neckarhausen. He forcibly seized property to be sold for taxes; f. 97 (19.1.1809). He came so often in 1812 that the Bürgermeister had trouble paying the pub bills for the soldiers (*Landdragoner*); vol. 8, f. 46 (3.9.1812). The Presser was attacked by a group of villagers in 1814; *Oberamtsgericht*, STAL, F190, vol. 11, f. 171 (14.11.1814). Again 1823; ibid., F190II, vol. 259, f. 445 (6.12.1823).

[39] Complaints along these lines were frequently heard from those who emigrated in 1815. Christoph Steinbach from Scheppach testified: "They repress the people beyond endurance. I had to sell my grain last fall in order to pay my debts for wood because the Presser stood right before the door" (Man drükt die Leute, daß es nicht mehr auszuhalten ist. Ich habe im vorigen Spätjahr meine Frucht verkaufen müßen um meine HolzSchuldigkeit zu bezalen, weil der Preßer gleich vor der Thüre steht): Moltmann, ed., *Aufbruch*, p. 151. Peter Kurz from Unterhambach said: "The Presser took away from them their axes, pans, and other things because they could not pay the interest on their debts to the poor relief foundation" (Der Preßer habe, weil sie ihre Zinnse zum Heiligen nicht haben bezalen können, ihnen Beile, Pfannen pp. weggenommen), p. 156. Johann Georg Nothurft from Weinsperg: "In order to make improvements, I sold a meadow and wanted to buy another from the proceeds. The magistrates garnished the proceeds, however, to pay my outstanding taxes. I cannot buy another meadow and therefore cannot keep any cattle, and if I cannot keep cattle, then I cannot cultivate any fields. In the present conditions of reduced fortune brought on by the difficult times, if I have to

As Hans Medick has pointed out, the fact that 20 percent of the total grain harvest was delivered to state departments meant that state and church officials became the greatest competitors and powers in the grain market.[40] They had close ties with grain traders and were interested parties in the politics of export to foreign territories. Even when the consequences of the disastrous harvest of August 1816 became clear, for example, state commerce in grain sent to foreign territories reached a new peak. The officials also supported the oligarchical developments in villages during the second half of the eighteenth and first three or four decades of the nineteenth centuries in many concrete ways. A case in point was the policy of developing a grain store in each village.[41] Everyone, including the poor – and often even those who did not actually produce grain – was obligated to deliver a certain portion to the central barn at harvest time, when the prices were at their lowest. Later, when the need arose, the poor could purchase grain or seed but at inflated market prices, often on credit at an interest rate of one-eighth of the value of the grain.[42] The earnings of the village storehouse went to pay off the tax bill of the village, which therefore meant a redistribution of resources in favor of those liable for the highest taxes. There were other ways in which the state method of appropriation was tied in with the local oligarchy. In the eighteenth and early nineteenth centuries, tithes were auctioned off for collection each year or for a period of years and were taken over by wealthy members of the village who could afford the capital outlay and the risk.[43] They profited by being able to keep the straw, which had been of little value at the beginning of the eighteenth century but by 1800 was worth 15 to 20 percent of the value of the whole plant.[44]

wait until the costs and debts from the war, which are outstanding for two years, are completely apportioned, then I will be a begger, since everything altogether is loaded onto farmland" (Ich habe meine Sache zu verbessern, eine Wiese verkauft und wollte eine andere für den Erlös kaufen. Die Obrigkeit aber hat mir wegen meinem SteuerRest auf den Erlös Arrest gelegt. Ich kann nun keine andere Wiese kaufen, und also kein Vieh erhalten, und wenn ich kein Vieh halte, so kann ich kein Feld bauen. Wenn ich bei meinen durch die schwere Zeit zerrütteten Vermögens Umständen noch zuwartte, bis die KriegsKosten und Schulden vollends umgelegt werden, was sich 2 Jahren rükständig ist, so bin ich ein Bettler, weil Alles und Alles auf die Güter gelegt wirt), p. 146.

[40] Medick, "Teuerung," p. 20.

[41] Ibid., pp. 40–1.

[42] Johann Jakob Strähle from Egolsheim testified: "When I told the Schultheiss and Bürgermeister in the presence of the whole community that I myself had no flour in the house since St. James Day and was myself in need, the Schultheiss said: It is the law and if you don't deliver grain, I will send the Presser to you." (Als ich dem Schultheiß und Bürgermeister in Anwesenheit der ganzen Gemeinde vorstellte, ich selbst habe seit Jakobi kein Mehl im Haus, und seye selbst in Noth, sagte der Schultheiß: so ist der Befehl, und wenn ihr nicht liefert, schike ich euch den Preßer): Moltmann, ed., *Aufbruch*, p. 132.

[43] Already in 1751, there was conflict in Neckarhausen about how the auction was rigged. Adam Falter and Hans Jerg Speidel were told not to call the villagers who had won the bid "scoundrels" (*Schelmen*). They should keep their well-known all-too-wide open traps shut (ihre wohlbekannte immerzuweit aufsperrende Mäuler besser zäumen), *Vogtruggericht*, vol. 1, f. 29 (14.12.1751). Here it was a case of the Nürtingen Vogt supporting the village oligarchy against criticism.

[44] Since it had become so crucial for stall feeding; see Appendix D, Table A.3.

State officials, in their excitement to create a free market in land, were not about to lose any income in the process. The so-called *Bauernbefreiung* (peasant emancipation) was paid for by the peasants themselves. It would be more precise to say that the *land* was freed step by step than to say that the Bauern were liberated. Only with great caution did state bureaus give up their income in grain and wine in favor of a revised taxation system, since they profited so heavily from the inflated values driven up by the population increase.[45] The process was drawn out over a long period, and villagers paid a considerable price for the privilege of exchanging their feudal obligations for modern state taxes. In each case, the value of the particular exaction was capitalized, and the subjects were obligated to amortize the capital and pay interest until the debt was extinguished. Between 1817 and 1821, miscellaneous small dues were abolished in this fashion, and in 1836 it was the turn of *Leibeigenschaft* (serfdom) and corvée labor to be capitalized for peasant liberation.[46] Only in 1848–9 were tithes finally set up for redemption in the following decade.[47]

The state continued to rely on payments in kind right through to the 1850s. Hans Medick has spoken of the "long eighteenth century," from 1648 to 1848, and there is much evidence to support that view.[48] Only in the ensuing decades did factory industrialization begin to compete with the decentralized cottage industry and the building trades for the labor pool. Throughout that long century, one important thread, which has never been systematically examined for its political effects, can be discerned. Part of the history of peasant production is a tale of ever-increasing debt, which in the nineteenth century swelled because of the enormous increase in land values. These values far outstripped other economic indicators such as wages or the price of grain.[49] By then, much of the mortgage money was supplied by officials, pastors, professors, doctors, notaries, innkeepers, and wholesale traders and their widows. In other words, the class which provided the state with its servants and officials became increasingly associated with *rentes* derived from peasant indebtedness. Some of the ferocity behind state controls and some of the effort put into increasing the marketability of peasant land appear to have been rooted in the interests of this class. Certainly the alterations in the *Pfandgesetz* (law of pledging) in 1825 and 1828 point in this direction. These law codes were aimed at mobilizing the properties belonging to women for the purpose of settling the debts of husbands.[50] This policy was designed to secure the risks of both the state and its

45 Hippel, *Bauernbefreiung*, vol. 1, pp. 54, 535–43.

46 Ibid., pp. 355ff., 437ff. In Neckarhausen, all that remained from the medieval form of villeinage was a death duty for males of 1.4 percent of the value of their estates.

47 Ibid., pp. 480ff.

48 Hans Medick, "Privilegiertes Handelskapital," pp. 269–70.

49 On the price of land, see Table 15.4. The argument about debt is based on a reading of the *Unterpfandsbücher* in Neckarhausen.

50 In 1781, lawgivers noted that a wife's property was not available for a husband's debts; "General-Reskript, Schuld- und Gantsachen betr." (14.4.1781), in Reyscher, vol. 7, p. 633. In 1828, just after gender tutelage was abrogated, the law code discussed the new freedom women

higher servants in the village. In the nineteenth century, village officials such as the Bürgermeister and Schultheiss had to post their property as bond for their performance.[51] Indeed, once the Pfandgesetz was revised, the property of their wives was put at risk as well. At the same time, the performance of village craftsmen who accepted extravillage projects had to be bonded by property pledged by parents, spouses, and other close kin.[52] The debts owed to the rentier class came to be underwritten not only by the specific pieces of mortgage land which were pledged but also by the rest of the holdings of the mortgagee and his spouse and by sureties offered by third parties.

As we examine the dynamics of the state–village interplay during the long eighteenth century, we cannot avoid looking at the specific effects of the specific form of appropriation. For the most part, the Württemberg duchy had no rivals for the peasant surplus, since there was no noble class between the peasantry and itself, and the small urban centers did not directly encroach on peasant land by purchase and sublease. Whenever villagers overextended themselves, their land was auctioned off to other villagers to satisfy the urban creditors, a process which also encouraged the breaking up of larger landholdings. The continuing tendency toward "minifundia" by itself does not explain the growing pauperization which characterized the long transition period from the third quarter of the eighteenth century to the middle of the nineteenth. The ever harsher and more systematic methods of state appropriation must be coupled with the continual official support of a growing village oligarchy which redistributed wealth and property upward. By 1800, one of the common political idioms which captured these relationships was the term "Vetterle" (literally cousin), which referred to the tight kinship network of the village patricians.[53]

had to pledge their property for their husbands' debts; see the discussion in Chapter 6. The problem of urban creditors for peasant mortgages was still part of the justification for central recordkeeping in 1806; "Circular-Rescript der königl. Ober-Landes-Regierung an die Ober- und Stabs-Aemter, die Aufmerksamkeit der Beamten auf Führung der Unterpfandsbücher betr." (29.5.1806), ibid., pp. 26–7.

51 See Chapter 6.

52 For example, five Neckarhausen builders were backed by a pledge (*Burgschaft*) for a job for a tavernkeeper in Hardt; *Gericht*, vol. 2, f. 135 (25.1.1847). The mother of Friedrich Krumm pledged 4,000 fl. so that he could take over a street repair and river bank construction contract: ibid., vol. 18, f. 72 (10.3.1866). When David Bauknecht agreed to build a house for Ulrich Sailer, he was underwritten by Salomon Köpple; ibid., vol. 10, f. 9 (6.6.1821). Anna Maria Deuschle pledged her property for her husband's performance as treasurer (*Pfleger*) of the poor relief foundation (*Stiftung*); ibid., vol. 14, f. 83 (18.7.1845).

53 Hans Medick handles the theme in "Teuerung," p. 41. See also the comments of Carola Lipp, Wolfgang Kaschuba, and Eckart Frahm, eds., F. A. Köhler, *Nehren. Eine Dorfchronik der Spätaufklärung*, Untersuchungen des Ludwig-Uhland-Instituts der Universität Tübingen, vol. 52 (Tübingen, 1981), pp. 164–6. Jacob Hampp from Egolsheim: "The Schultheiss and Bürgermeister stick together, since they are cousins, and the other magistrates also stick with them, because they are all related together" (Der Schultheiß und Bürgermeister halten zusammen, denn sie sind Vetter, und die andern MagistratsPersonen halten auch mit, weil sie alle zusammen verwandt sind): Moltmann, ed., *Aufbruch*, p. 131. Johann Jacob Strähle from Egolsheim: "The magistracy is one family. With street and other contracts, bread is taken out of the mouths of the Bürger" (Der Magistrat ist eine Familie . . . bei Strassen- und anderen Akkorden ist den Bürgern das Brod vor dem Munde weg), p. 132. Ulrich Walch from

Even then the duke/king was wily enough to tax his supporters for endogamy, maintaining a considerable fee throughout the period for the right to marry a cousin.[54]

Throughout the study period, one of the central developments in the story is the systematic creation of a "subpeasantry." By 1720 or so, when the population was well on its way to recovering from the Thirty Years' War, about 25 to 30 percent of Württemberg village populations were already involved in trades and handicrafts. In the 1740s, the fluid transition between Bauern and weavers is demonstrated by the frequent combination or alternate designation of the two occupations for the same persons in the various village records. In Neckarhausen, apart from the set of innkeepers, masons, carpenters, bakers, and smiths who catered to village needs, weavers were the most common handicraftsmen.[55] Exactly how they were tied into the market is not clear, but they appear to have worked with locally produced flax and sold their output to middlemen, who in turn were connected to an export market. As land continued to be divided, more and more people were added to the class of weavers, and the crafts represented in Neckarhausen multiplied – even a ropemaker was able to make a living, for example. Thus by the late decades of the century, there were many signs of more intensive use of all available resources. In the nineteenth century, house industrial production became extended to other crafts, such as shoemaking. During the 1830s and 1840s, competition from foreign cloth producers and the addition of new capital caused cloth production in Württemberg to begin servicing an internal market and forced many weavers to turn to the putting-out system.[56] Weavers made up about 20 percent of all those subject to the trade and handicraft tax around 1830. For the next

Schorndorf: "The poor Bürger demanded to have the commonland divided, which the lords at the Rathaus hindered because of the sheep pasture and because they are themselves sheep owners" (Die armen Bürgern haben verlangt, man solle die Allmand austheilen, was aber die Herrn auf dem Rathaus wegen der Schaafweide, weil sie selbst Schaafhalter sind, hintertrieben haben), p. 137. Christoph Ernst and Adam Schweikert from Wilspach: "The conflict between the Bürgerschaft and the Bürgermeister and Gericht, which has gone on for several years, is completely destructive of the locality" (Der Streit der Burgerschaft (*sic*) mit dem Burgermeister (*sic*) und Gericht, der schon ein paar Jahre währe, sey eben gar verderblich für den Ort), p. 153. Various people from Dahenfeld: "Our Schultheiss is guilty of stealing tithes and village grain stores, but he is still our chief administrator" (Unser Schultheiß hat sich eines Zehend Diebstahls und eines Diebstahls von GemeindsFrüchten schuldig gemacht, und er ist immer noch unser OrtsVorsteher), p. 165.

54 "Dekret des Geheimen-Raths an die herzogliche Regierung" (24.3.1798), in Reyscher, vol. 6, pp. 763–8. According to the rates set in 1808, it cost 20 fl. to marry a first cousin and 10 fl. to marry a second cousin; ibid., p. 745. But as usual, such fees struck the poor with greater force. Furthermore, those who were unwise enough (which meant most of the poor) to bear illegitimate children or get pregnant before marriage were slapped with the stiff fine of 20 fl., a considerable part of their start capital – which around 1800 was about equal in value to a cow.

55 According to the occupational census of 1735, the following trades were represented: butcher (2), baker (1), smith (3), cobbler (1), wheelwright (1), carpenter (1), tailor (3), weaver (18); HSAS, A261, Bü 1344.

56 See Wolfgang Kaschuba and Carola Lipp, *1848 – Provinz und Revolution* (Tübingen, 1979), pp. 36–7.

three decades the total number of cloth producers declined somewhat.[57] By contrast, the nineteenth century witnessed a sharp rise in the number of construction workers, which was particularly crucial for Neckarhausen.[58] Statistics for trades and crafts in Württemberg from 1820 to 1836 show that the number of construction workers rose from 107,000 to 148,000, or 38.3 percent. Figures for 1819–52 suggest that the number of construction workers doubled before midcentury.[59]

According to Wolfgang Kaschuba, most of the developments that we have chronicled are the result of the opening up of an internal market.[60] Colportage (*Hausieren*) may also have been a significant factor after 1815. However, we should not underestimate the important restructuring of village production into new forms of specialization for external markets. For example, Neckarhausen produced some of the best-quality flax in the entire kingdom, and much of it was exported to Baden. A nearby village specialized in raising snails for the Bavarian market. Another one specialized in the export of Kirchwasser, cherry juice for darkening red wine, and dried fruit sent to Bavaria.[61] This kind of specialization warrants careful study in itself. As Hans Medick has pointed out using the example of the trade in fine-quality handloom linens, Württemberg economic development in the nineteenth century was sparked by the village-based production of specialized, quality wares which were marketed through networks patiently developed by local traders.[62] The emphasis on quality, reliable markets, and limited production characterize Swabian production to this day – Porsche and Mercedes being two of the best-known examples.

Throughout the study period, land remained an essential component of the perspective not only of peasants but also of tradesmen and handicraftsmen. People were tied to village life through the land, citizenship rights to communal property and resources, and the rights to public assistance.[63] Within a system largely built on agricultural production, a significant sector of the population gradually became dependent on wage labor. Still, the ever-more intensive exploitation of land disciplined the small producer and continued to determine the dynamics of family life to a considerable extent.[64] Social and political life in nineteenth-century villages was frequently structured around the interplay

[57] Hippel, "Bevölkerungsentwicklung," pp. 319ff.

[58] See Appendix F.

[59] Between 1835 and 1852, the number of masons went up 30.4 percent from about 9,200 to about 12,000. On occupational statistics for Württemberg, see Kaschuba and Lipp, *1848*, pp. 36–8. A good comparative perspective is offered for the village of Kiebingen; Kaschuba and Lipp, *Dörfliches Überleben*, pp. 25ff., 43–53, 63. Wolfgang von Hippel is far more cautious about occupational statistics because of the close tie between agriculture and trades; "Bevölkerungsentwicklung," pp. 324, 331, 336, 353.

[60] Kaschuba and Lipp, *1848*, p. 36.

[61] *Beschreibung Nürtingen*, pp. 78ff., 146ff., 149ff., 173ff.

[62] Medick, "Priviligiertes Handelskapital," pp. 306–10.

[63] Kaschuba and Lipp, *1848*, pp. 20–1.

[64] Ibid., pp. 24–5.

between independent agricultural producers and the set of farm laborers, unskilled workers, and skilled construction craftsmen who left their wives and children in the villages to exploit the communal garden and manage the few strips of land while they sold their labor in the construction and agricultural markets.[65] Wolfgang Kaschuba reckons that from 1830 to 1870, on the average two people were gone for most of the year from the poorer families in Kiebingen, which appears to have been similar to the pattern in Neckarhausen.[66] In any event, the wages available to the best-paid building workers would have just covered the barest essentials for a four-member family, while those of a typical shoemaker or farm laborer would have fallen far short.[67] The possession of land and access to communal resources were fundamental to the continued existence of all families. The process of "proletarianization" was slow and took place without any radical restructuring of the economy or any abrupt break in the "traditional modes of life." It appears that the progress of pauperization was driven less by industrialization than by expropriation, redistribution of accumulated wealth, and the steady pressure of the state on the productive capacities of the population.[68]

Agriculture more than kept pace with the expanding population. By no means were Württemberg peasants "virulently conservative."[69] They began to put pressure on the state to change the systems of rotation as early as the 1760s and 1770s and found new products for the market into which they poured their resources. Even Kaschuba, whose knowledge of the economic history of Württemberg is so detailed, sees the history of agricultural change reflected in the ideology of the agronomists. Agricultural intensification in Württemberg was less the result of "biochemical" progress than it was the patient mobilization of labor and the communal reallocation of rights and privileges.[70] It has to be emphasized that the agricultural revolution was only possible because of massive new inputs of labor, the organization and mobilization of which ought to stand at the center of any story about agricultural progress.[71] By 1850, agricultural output in Württemberg was at least 20 percent in excess of the needs of the population in normal times.[72] The great crises of 1816–17 and 1846–7 were due not so much to the inadequacies of agricultural practices (the harvest failure in 1816 only brought a shortfall of 16 percent) as to state trade policies and the specific structure of village inequality.[73]

65 Ibid., p. 36.
66 Kaschuba and Lipp, *Dörfliches Überleben*, p. 53.
67 Hippel, "Bevölkerungsentwicklung," pp. 345–52.
68 Kaschuba and Lipp, *1848*, pp. 26–7.
69 Kaschuba's term, ibid., p. 27.
70 Ibid., p. 27.
71 This point was made forcefully by J. D. Chambers, "Enclosure and Labor Supply in the Industrial Revolution," *Economic History Review*, 2d ser., 5 (1953): pp. 319–43.
72 Hippel, "Bevölkerungsentwicklung," pp. 316–7.
73 Medick, "Teuerung," pp. 39–43.

## Agricultural intensification

The course of economic and agrarian change in Neckarhausen is an important part of the story which we will tell, and the subject can be approached in several ways, for example, by looking at changes in the use and productivity of commonland, or at cropping patterns, sheepherding, stall feeding, and animal traction. Some of these details can be found in Appendix A–D. In this section and the next, we focus on the trend of intensified land use and the way village communal resources were used. In both cases, we are looking for indicators of the rhythm of innovation and the direction of change. In Chapter 5, this information is used to assess innovations in the sexual division of labor.

Land in villages belonging to the Oberamt Nürtingen – as in Württemberg and South Germany in general – was categorized according to its use and the rights the individual owner had to farm it in certain ways. The arable (*Äcker*) in Neckarhausen was divided into three large fields (*Zelgen*), which in turn were divided into field segments or furlongs (*Felder*). These segments contained the numerous interspersed strips belonging to individual villagers. Originally, the arable was only planted with field crops, such as spelt, oats, and barley, and perhaps field beans and peas, all of which were subject to the large tithe. Most villagers also had meadowland (*Wiese*), which before the agricultural revolution produced primarily hay, harvested in a first and second cutting (*Heu* and *Öhmd*); hay was subject to a special tithe. Pasture (*Weide*) also existed, but in Neckarhausen most of it had been part of communal land, given out on short-term leases to individuals in the course of the nineteenth century. Another kind of agricultural land, called *Kraut-*, *Flachs-*, *und Hanfland* (small parcels which were available for intensive cultivation of flax and hemp and certain garden products such as cabbage), was cultivated outside the three-field rotation. There were also gardens, some close to the farm buildings, and some in other parts of the village territory, which were subject to the small tithe. Finally, some of the land was devoted to viniculture (*Weingärten*), which was also subject to a tithe. At the end of the eighteenth century, as villagers began to alter their cultivation practices, some institutions and jurisdictions that had rights to the various tithes were reluctant to allow land to be turned over to other crops, for fear of reducing their incomes, or were interested in capitalizing on increased production. They therefore usually allowed changes only after more or less protracted negotiations.

The evidence presented in Appendix C and D makes it possible to describe the contours of agricultural change fairly well. In general, the agricultural revolution in Neckarhausen began with the introduction of clover, alfalfa, and various grasses; leguminous plants such as beans, peas, and vetch; leafy members of the brassica family; and to a much more limited extent, root crops, such as potatoes. But the three-field framework was maintained, with a monocultural winter field of spelt. Already by the 1740s, peas, beans, and vetch were frequently found in the summer field, along with some cabbages and leafy brassica – kale or mangolds. By the 1760s, potatoes, maize, and lentils began to appear in estate inventories, although they were proabably introduced in the gardens and flaxlands. Within a decade, peas, vetch, clover, and other fodder grasses had found their way into part of the fallow and summer fields, and soon the size of the sheep herd had to be drastically reduced because it was being banned progressively from its traditional pastures. There is evidence that by the 1790s potatoes were being cultivated on the arable in the crop rotation, although the real growth spurt came after the crisis of 1816–17. At the turn of the century, stall feeding of stock became possible because of the widespread production of fodder plants, and the move away from permanent pasture was completed by 1830. Thereafter, root crops and other fodder produce requiring hoeing were steadily extended into the rotation. Greater production in the arable made it possible to shift about 10 percent of it to intensive meadowland by the 1840s. Over the course of the changes, the villagers themselves experimented with different crops and production routines and pioneered new forms of crop rotation. It would be a mistake to take the agronomists' self-congratulatory account of agricultural innovation too much at face value. More than anything else, cultivating root crops and nitrogen-fixing plants such as peas, beans, and vetch required new labor inputs, especially hoeing. That kind of hand work cleaned fields more thoroughly than plowing.

The central problem for villagers in the second half of the eighteenth century was the shortage of fodder, and innovations were sought to solve that problem. As we shall see, land reclamation projects were important, along the Neckar and in the areas of poorly drained, soggy soil, and productivity was increased by putting long-term pasture to the plow and planting clover, alfalfa, and sainfoin. The extensive vineyards, which did not produce a particularly good wine, were continually neglected or planted with zwetschgen trees. Along with a great deal of other land, they became mixed meadow and orchard, which still make up much of the landscape in the region today. Apple production replaced viniculture, and the cider, or "Most," made from the apples became the everyday peasant drink. At the same time that the meadow and pastureland were being developed – and after some debate – villagers switched to stall feeding. There is evidence of the careful saving of straw from the mid-eighteenth century, and by the nineteenth even the inventories of people with few food stores had some straw. Each type – spelt, barley, oat, and pea – was carefully listed and a differential value recorded. Straw was fundamental for manure production, and the whole system was oriented toward that and the development of hoe crops.

It was well known that simply introducing clover or other grasses into the rotation would soon lead to a field choked with weeds.[74] In fact, the old fallow was there precisely to be worked with frequent plowing in order to present as

[74] See, for example, J. G. Koppe, *Unterricht im Ackerbau und in der Viehzucht*, 5th ed., 3 vols. (Berlin, 1841–2), vol. 2, pp. 305–6.

clean a field as possible for the winter crop. Even then the field had to be sown thickly with seed in order to choke the weeds.[75] Better seed-yield ratios could only be achieved when weed-free fields could be presented, which was precisely the purpose of hoed crops. After a fallow of potatoes, for example, a field was far "cleaner" than it would have been after the four or five plowings it would have had without any crops.[76] Many of the other new crops – such as maize, beans, lentils, vetch, mangolds, beetroots, cabbage, and rape – required arduous, continual hoeing over the summer, which, as we shall see in Chapter 5, had a substantial effect on the sexual division of labor.[77]

While developing better pasture, new green fodder crops, more efficient meadowland, and stall feeding, the village progressively abandoned horses and increased the cattle herd. (Between 1710 and 1873, the horse population dropped from 72 to 8, whereas cattle increased from 147 to 566, and pigs from 12 to 127.) By the mid-nineteenth century, there were many ox teams in the village, but a considerable number of cows were also used for traction.[78] The village had never been a producer of young horses, but it became centrally involved in the production of young cattle for the market and in fattening cattle purchased in the many busy markets in the area. It does not appear that dairying was very important – at least there are few milk products such as cheese in the inventories, and the last mention of butter was in 1712.[79] The village was too far from an urban center to trade in fresh products such as milk. Cows probably produced milk for family consumption, but they were there primarily to produce young and manure and to provide traction. By the fourth decade of the nineteenth century, a good portion of the arable was turned over to intensive grass and green fodder production. The innovations were introduced step by step after careful experimentation. Changing the mixture of the stock herd had enormous implications for cropping patterns and labor schedules. It needs to be repeated that such changes were immanent to the peasant economy and were driven by their own responses to market forces, subsistence needs, and labor supply.

The village specialized in the production of flax and hemp. Neckarhausen became famous for its raw flax, and when state industrial trials were attempted, flax from the village was used.[80] The rise in the production of flax and hemp

[75] Koppe, *Unterricht*, vol. 1, p. 237.

[76] Ibid., pp. 204ff.

[77] Hoe crops are labor-intensive and require a great deal of manure. Summer stall feeding also requires a significant increase in labor inputs: Koppe, *Unterricht*, vol. 2, p. 306; vol. 3, p. 151.

[78] A note in the inventory taken after the death of Johann Georg Zeug's wife, Anna Catharina, reckoned the cow to his *Voraus* (inalienable portion) "because he presently plowed with a cow instead of with an ox as previously" (da er wirklich mit Küh statt vorhin mit Stier fährt), *Inventuren und Teilungen*, nr. 1403 (2.10.1815).

[79] Occasionally, there are references in the inventories to "Milchschmaltz," probably a sour milk product like *Quark*, which was eaten daily by Neckarhausen families. Butter may have been sold by women in the local market.

[80] *Erster Rechenschaftsbericht für das Jahr vom 1. October 1845 bis 1846 an die Gesellschaft für Hebung*

necessitated heavy inputs of manure and careful cultivation of the soil.[81] At first, such crops were grown on special *Länder*, but in the 1780s, there is already evidence that at times they were planted in the field rotation.[82] The important thing to note is that these crops required heavy inputs of labor. Storing, drying, soaking, breaking, combing, and spinning were additional chores that went into their production. And there was, of course, a good deal of weaving in the village. At certain times of the year, villagers would jockey for a position along the Neckar at the places where flax was laid into the water to soak. Consequently, the village put aside more and more areas for spreading out cloth to bleach. There was so much disorder that a leasing system was developed in 1823 and the places auctioned off each year. Apparently the lessees used their portions of the bleachery both to spread out their own cloth and to sublet space to others.

## Intensification of commonland

Communal land in Neckarhausen consisted of several types. The forest was exploited for kindling, building wood, beechnuts, acorns, grass, and oakbark for tanning. Garden plots and flax and cabbage lands were given out to villagers for individual use. The fallow field and stubble fields were managed collectively for sheep grazing, although proprietors had to pay for the right to have the herd folded on their individual strips overnight. The village also had a series of pastures for the communal livestock herds and for the village bulls. The most substantial lands belonging to the village were certain grasslands, or *Wasen*, which were used at various times as pasture, meadow, orchard, or garden and flaxland allotments. Most of them were in the floodplain of the Neckar south of the dwelling area, although there were also several on the plateau close to the woods. Appendix A follows the fortunes of several of the larger parcels from 1710 to 1870 as reflected in the village financial records.

The history of one of the Wasen, Insele, shows that it was small and subject to continual flooding at the beginning, produced little grass, and was largely covered in gravel. By the end of the eighteenth century, the village began to clear gravel from the parcel, plow it up, and develop a much-needed pasture. In subsequent years, it was partitioned into individual plots for intensive hay production and pasture, and the value of its production rose steadily. By 1870, it was again farmed in one block by the village, and its substantial output was sold to a large number of the villagers. What had been a small gravelly pasture

*der Linnengewerbe in Württemberg* (Erstattet von dem engeren Ausschuße derselben, Nürtingen, n.d.). Copy in HSAS, E70, Bü 1077.

81 See details in J. N. Schwerz, *Beschreibung der Landwirtschaft im Nieder-Elsaß* (Berlin, 1816), pp. 377ff.

82 Besides the evidence in Appendix D: In 1832, Friedrich Baur and many other villagers had recently turned meadowland into hemp cultivation without leaving a right of way for hay harvesting; *Vogtruggericht*, vol. 2, f. 156 (29.5.1832). In 1841, reference was made to flax being cultivated on arable land; *Schultheissenamt*, vol. 1, f. 46 (12.8.1846).

became a fairly substantial intensified meadow of just over 17 acres, or about 7 hectares. Much land was reclaimed from the Neckar when it was straightened during the 1830s, and the flooding controlled. This made it possible to clear the surface of gravel permanently. But the village had begun the clean up and the more intensive land use much earlier. Many of the other parcels such as the Obere- and Unterebiegelwasen, Beutwang, Im Beutwang, Löhleswasen, Millot, and the Untere- or Gänswasen had similar histories. The Auchtert to the east of the village and north of the highway and the Herdhau between the arable fields and the forest provided garden plots and intensive pasture for individual villagers.

This study shows that over time an attempt was made to account for each piece of commonland, but whether a particular parcel came into the financial records or not depended on its status as a source of income or expenditure. Despite the expansion of the common grassland through reclamation, the portion available for common use was constantly whittled away. In Insele, Biegel, Millot, Auchtert, and Herdhau, some commonland was divided up for *Allmendeteile* (communal portions), small strips of up to an are which were used for garden crops such as cabbage, commercial crops like flax and hemp, or for growing clover in rotation with root crops. As the population increased and agriculture became more intensive, the demand for such plots grew. Access was strictly accorded by Bürger or widow status and usually remained in lifelong tenancy, although some strips were reapportioned by lot every three years or so. As the number of landless or landpoor members in the community increased, such plots took on new significance. No annual fee or rent was charged, and the entry fee was minimal. Once land was dedicated to such use, it disappeared entirely from the account books and therefore from our view.

Most of the commonland remained dedicated to providing fodder for animals. At the end of the eighteenth century, good meadows were set aside in various parts of the village for the communal bull. At the same time, land reclamation projects were under way – these consisted of clearing up gravel, plowing up the land, grazing sheep and cattle, and planting clover and alfalfa. The long-term goal of the commonland policy was to step up the production of hay or green fodder, and by the third decade of the nineteenth century, considerable returns could be had by leasing such land in small plots as meadow.

But there were other ways to intensify the use of grassland. In the 1790s, some of these plots were systematically planted with fruit trees and willows. Already in the 1790 accounts, a tree specialist (*Bäumler*) had been hired by the village.[83] Thereafter each volume indicates an increase in the size and value of the fruit crop, part of which was divided among the villagers, usually for the cost of picking and bringing it in. The rest was sold at auction. During these years, the village landscape became characterized by meadows planted with fruit trees

[83] *Gericht*, vol. 4, f. 252 (23.4.1794). A *Bäumler* – tree surgeon – was hired, and reference was made to many trees – 2, 3, and 4 years old – planted on the *Allmende* (commons).

(*Baumwiese*). According to the Nürtingen gazetteer (*Oberamtsbeschreibung*) of 1848, the sale of fruit in the region was a primary source of income, and Neckarhausen was especially well known as an apple producer.[84] A measure of the effects of commonland intensification policies can be found in Table A.1 of Appendix B. The returns on fruit grown on the Allmende went from 55 fl. in 1810 to close to 1500 fl. in 1870.

Already in the eighteenth century, willows were grown in various parts of the village, especially along the river.[85] After the course of the river was corrected (1832–6), the bank was carefully maintained, and willow plantings played an important role in preventing erosion. In 1710, there was a rubric in the financial records for willow swathes (*Band*), but none were sold that year. That was the case throughout the eighteenth century. In 1810, 13 villagers bought willow grown on the commonland in Insele for 9.9 fl. Twenty years later, willow swathes were sold to 10 people (half from outside the village) for 67.2 fl. By 1850 the willow harvest had increased considerably. In that year, 65,150 willow swathes were sold in lots of 100 to 167 villagers at .1 fl. per hundred for a total of 67.2 fl. Another 2.9 fl. worth were purchased by 46 people. In 1870 every one of the 237 Bürger and widows received a *Buschel* of willow swathes for the cost of cutting and hauling them (.1 fl.). The remainder of the harvest was sold to 48 people for 33.9 fl. A second harvest was taken from the willows along the river bank, and again every Bürger received an equal portion of 14 swathes, this time at a cost of .5 fl. From the Beutwang, an additional crop was taken and sold to 46 buyers for 22.9 fl.

This kind of intensification, through dual-purpose pasture or meadow with trees, was only part of the story. Millot had a stone quarry and the Gänswasen a sand pit, and various grasslands were used for bleaching locally produced cloth. Once the Beutwang and Insele were cleared of gravel, they produced the richest hay crops in the village. Much of the pastureland was put to the plow in order to produce richer crops of clover and alfalfa. Sometimes plots were leased for a period of one, two, or three years, and the individual leaseholder was left to cultivate his own hay or clover. Alternatively, the village might hire out the job of plowing and harvesting to a small group of individuals, selling the product at auction. In either case, village land came to be used more intensively, and this pattern was part of the trend toward greater production.

A study of commonland use indicates that intensification was a long, slow process. First, the waste areas had to be recorded, measured, and brought into the regular village accounts. In the second half of the eighteenth century, villagers cleared areas of gravel or bushes and made their first attempts at putting meadow, pasture, and orchard to multiple use. By the last decades of the century, clover and alfalfa were sometimes planted on newly plowed land,

[84] *Beschreibung Nürtingen*, pp. 177ff.

[85] *Gericht*, vol. 1, f. 182 (3.4.1766), deals with a conflict between Bauern and day-laborers over the obligation to plant willows (*Felben*) by corvée labor. This planting involved 300 trees.

and the intensive meadow culture became integrated with the practice of stall feeding. Portions of the land were often carved up for individual cultivation of flax and hemp, garden produce, hay, and clover. Two bottlenecks developed in the shift to more intensive agriculture owing to the need for manure and meadowland. With stall feeding, straw became useful for composting, and allowed villagers to increase the production of manure, which could be used more rationally in the production of field crops or grass. During the late eighteenth century, villagers complained continually about the shortage of meadowland not just because of the pressure of population, but because of the need to produce fodder for the animals that were being kept in stalls for longer periods of time, especially over the summer.[86] By 1830, stall feeding had conquered, and much of the commonland was leased out or farmed for hay, which was sold to villagers. About the same time, viniculture was given up and cider produced from trees on the *Baumwiesen* replaced wine for domestic consumption.

An overview of the process of intensification can be obtained by looking at the number and rate of pay of agricultural specialists and protection agents for the village (see Tables A.2 and A.3 in the appendix). In 1710, for example, village protection agents amounted to baillif (*Dorfschütz*) and a night watchman. By 1810, these were joined by a second night watchman, a field guard, a vineyard guard, two forest guards, and a harvest watchman (*Nachthut*). The entire bill increased from 18 fl. in 1710 to 212 fl. in 1810, to 534 fl. in 1870. In the 1790s a permanent tree surgeon was appointed for the first time. Although the various herders disappeared with stall feeding, the bullkeeper eventually became a highly paid specialist, and a stock inspector was appointed in the 1830s. Another specialist, the mole catcher, was earning almost as much as the full-time bailiff by 1870.

The decline in stock herding and the establishment of stock inspecting can be interpreted as an individualizing process – each producer had his own stock in his own barns (and much of the considerably increased cost of protection went toward helping the individual villager against encroachments from his fellow villagers). There was a shifting balance between the individual and the collectivity, which, however, did not run in a direct path toward "individualism." At the same time that particular villagers were taking over grass plots to cultivate hay, the crop from the apple trees standing on the land was recorded as belonging to the village as a whole. The position of the shepherd illustrates the complexity of the balance between individual and communal production best. In the beginning, he was more or less a hired agent, under the control of the

[86] In 1769, reference was made to scarcity of fodder, and clover was to be planted in the Auchtert; *Vogtruggericht*, vol. 1, f. 96 (11.2.1769). In 1773, it was noted in the *Gerichtsprotocolle* that in "human memory" there had never been so many livestock on the pasture; vol. 2, f. 53 (23.10.1773). In 1778, there was a report about a lack of fodder, which brought a policy of planting clover in the Auchtert; ibid., vol. 1, f. 120 (11.12.1778). By 1820, the problem was to complete going over to stall feeding and turn some arable into intensive meadow and pasture; *Vogtruggericht*, vol. 2, f. 92 (16.2.1820). By 1823, many arable strips above Hofacker were changed to meadow; ibid., vol. 2, f. 106 (7.11.1823).

Schultheiss, Bürgermeister, and a *Pförchmeister* (sheepfold administrator, often the Schultheiss), who was responsible for apportioning sheep-folding equitably, collecting the fees, and paying the shepherd a salary. By 1810, the shepherd leased the privilege of running the village herd, collected the *Pförchgeld* himself, but rendered accounts to the village and paid the income to the Bürgermeister as he took it in. By 1870 he was simply an entrepreneur, leasing the rights to the herd from the village and collecting the Pförchgeld for his own income. Still the land which he used was village land and the stubble on which he folded the sheep was subject to the collective decision making of modified three-field agriculture. The village had undertaken a considerable long-term investment in the improvement of commonland and had continued to manage it flexibly and efficiently right through the period of agricultural innovation.

Another indicator of the rate of intensification in the use of village resources is the returns from the village forest (Table A.4). The ledgers for 1730 show that each Bürger received a *Teil*, or a portion of kindling, each year, although no details were given as to the amount and no one had to pay anything. Apportioning wood for burning went back to earlier centuries and remained a Bürger privilege well past 1870. Extra wood for burning, for building repairs, tools, and the like could be purchased from time to time – or stolen. Neckarhausen had a substantial forest of 447 M., which offered its Bürger considerable benefits. On that account, the bordering villages of Grötzingen and Oberensingen were out of luck, and their inhabitants were continually caught raiding the Neckarhausen woods. Besides the portions of kindling given out each year, substantial amounts of wood were sold. The rise in yield is an indication of a more careful rotation sponsored in part by state officials. In 1710, a few oaks were sold for 24 fl. By 1810, the sale of oak, white willow, beech, hornbeam, and linden, together with stumps, bark, and waste, amounted to 1,178 fl. At the end of our period, the return had jumped more than threefold to 3,777 fl. The forest guard's salary, equal in 1850 to that of the bailiff, increased almost four times by 1870. It may be that the drop in return from the woods in 1830 and 1850 was the result of the heavy demands on the forest for building purposes prior to and continuing after 1810. It was not just that the population increase made it necessary to build dwellings – the village was notoriously short of living space, and a building boom to solve the problem did not really get started until the 1830s – but, more important, the new agriculture increased the demand for barns, sheds, stalls, mangers, and cribs, and thus for material from the forest.[87]

It would be helpful to know precisely when the village went over to stall feeding. In 1818, some magistrates suggested that the answer to the economic difficulties of the village was to adopt stall feeding and to lease the Gross and Klein Beutwangwasen.[88] By 1820, an official from Nürtingen expressed the

[87] By the end of our period (1863), a 30-year plan of rotation was put together; *Gemeindepflegerechnungen*, 1870.
[88] *Vogtruggericht*, vol. 2, f. 54 (30.9.1818).

Table 1.2 *Requests at the annual assembly for wood for building stalls and cribs*

| 1780s | 1790s | 1800s | 1810s |
|---|---|---|---|
| 1 | 33 | 78 | 138 |

opinion that everyone should gradually go over to stall feeding in order to provide more manure for improving the arable land, to allow the planting of fodder grasses, and to increase production on the meadows.[89] A few years later, in 1823, the officials of the village debated whether to allow the cattle onto the late summer pasture.[90] Some of the villagers complained that without that pasture, the fertility of their cows would be reduced. Several members of the *Gemeinderat* countered that total stall feeding did not create such problems and that the common grasslands were now too poor to be used as daily pasture.

The discussion in 1823 took place against a background of partial stall feeding. Certainly most of the cattle were already being brought in during the winter, and some producers were keeping cows in the stall longer than usual. Even earlier, during the 1790s, a demand for wood for building stalls and cribs and the like had developed, which became quite substantial during the first two decades of the next century. Customarily, villagers requested building wood at the annual assembly (*Rüggericht*) held a few days after Christmas. By 1821, the demand for wood for cribs was so great that the Schultheiss forbade villagers to build them with oak. He feared that the forest would be depleted (see Table 1.2).

Table 1.2 reflects the trend of capital investment for intensive cattle production and manuring of crops. The first tentative steps were taken in the 1790s. In the first decade of the nineteenth century, most requests for wood were expressly for building feed cribs. By the second decade, it was only a question of time when the common herd would disappear. In 1814, the horse and cattle herds were combined, and in 1821 it was noted before the court that men no longer took herding seriously, leaving it in the hands of a few boys.[91] In 1830, the last herder was appointed for a year, 11 years before the disappearance of the last gooseherd.[92]

[89] Ibid., f. 92 (16.2.1820).
[90] Ibid., f. 117 (7.11.1823).
[91] *Gericht*, vol. 8, f. 109 (25.4.1814); vol. 10, f. 5 (24.4.1821).
[92] There is a discrepency between the village financial records and the court and council records about when herding was terminated. At the annual assembly where village jobs were given out, the last horse and cattle herder was appointed in 1830, *Gericht*, vol. 11, f. 194(27.2.1830); the last gooseherd, 1841, vol. 13, f. 130 (20.4.1841).

## Village social stratification

Social stratification in a village such as Neckarhausen is difficult to describe owing to a number of imponderables. For example, there were no sharp breaks in the scale of landholding at any period in its history. Almost every married, adult male held at least some property. Indeed, in the eighteenth century only 2 to 5 percent of the taxpayers were without any taxable land or buildings whatsoever. Even by the end of the 1860s this pattern had not changed very much, for if we exclude nonresidents and retired people on the tax list, only 5 percent of those remaining were without property.[93] (See Appendix F for a detailed review of the documentary evidence for the distribution of resources.)

A series of graphs detailing the distribution of wealth in the village at different points from the early eighteenth century through to 1870 would show no essential change over this period. For any year there is a fairly even curve of property ownership from the wealthiest to the poorest, with no sharp discontinuities. There was always some skewing in favor of the wealthy, and throughout the course of the eighteenth century the richest 10 percent held 28 percent of the taxable resources. During the nineteenth century, a few members at the top of the village hierarchy who had invested in taverns or the mill were able to accumulate fairly large fortunes, so that by 1870 the top 10 percent had increased their share to about 33 percent. By contrast, the lower 50 percent of the taxpayers held between 16 and 18 percent of the wealth in the eighteenth century, and this figure fell to about 14 percent by 1870. Although any lines we might draw to distinguish the different strata would be arbitrary, each particular decile or quartile clearly accommodated three times as many households in 1870 as in 1710, in keeping with the population growth. The overlapping Lorenz curves could, therefore, hide significant alterations in the system of stratification.

The principal "political" categories in Neckarhausen, as in all of Württemberg, were "Bürger," "widows," and "Beisitzer." Anyone born in Neckarhausen to a fully fledged resident – all but a few people could be described as such – had citizenship rights (*Bürgerschaft*). Although the term "Bürger" referred to all "citizens" of the village, it was most often used for men who had married and founded a household. They were all fully enfranchised and were required to pay a 1 fl. Bürger tax each year. When one of them died, his widow became the head of the household and a responsible political agent, paying a widow's tax equal to half a gulden. Now and then, a person could apply for the right to live and work in Neckarhausen (as a *Beisitzer*) without having full rights of Bürgerschaft, but there were never more than one or two such people in Neckarhausen at a time. Thus most of the inhabitants of the village were Bürger by birth or marriage and took part in all of the communal rights.

[93] The figures here are slightly different from those given earlier (n. 6), which were taken from a census based on households. By contrast, the annual tax lists contained everyone subject to any kind of tax – real estate, citizenship, or occupation.

At the beginning of the eighteenth century, the village consisted of a large group of Bürger who carried on agriculture and a smaller group of them who spent enough time at a trade to leave evidence of the fact in the records. There is no way of telling exactly to what extent an artisan was fully employed in his craft. We do know that in 1870 close to 40 percent of all the villagers listed in the tax list with a trade or handicraft were not taxed for it and presumably did not carry it on at the time. Most likely, those artisans in the top quartile of taxpayers who had accumulated enough land to keep themselves completely busy farming had given up their trade, but there were also men who worked at unskilled labor and seldom, if ever, carried on the craft they had learned. In any event, in 1710, about 1 in 3 married, adult males were artisans or tradesmen for at least part of the time or for part of their lives. This increased to 2 in 5 by 1790 and to about half in 1870.

Early in the eighteenth century, there was an easy dualism between subsistence agricultural producers and handicraftsmen. The English word "peasant" does not quite describe or differentiate the agricultural producers, since, on one hand, many of the craftsmen were not distinguished from them in any essential way, and, on the other, they formed part of a legal category, obligating those so designated to certain kinds of communal work, for example. We will stay with the contemporary term "Bauer" to describe someone who had sufficient land to be independent and who did not practice a trade or belong to a guild. In 1710, slightly more than half of the population were Bauern. By 1790, they had fallen to a third, and by 1870 to a quarter of the taxpaying Bürger. By the end of the eighteenth century, a group of farm laborers had emerged, but its size fluctuated, since many artisans and Bauern worked for daily agricultural wages for significant periods, and many laborers accumulated enough land over time to move into at least the lower ranks of subsistence farmers. At the turn of the century, there was also an increase in the number of people employed by the village as bailiffs, guards, street cleaners, and herders. This group remained relatively poor, and while their numbers grew throughout the century, few of them made a permanent career out of their posts, usually holding them for several years at a time. In the 1840s, a small group of relatively poor factory workers began to show up among the taxpayers; by 1870, they accounted for about 5 percent of the married population.[94] Those involved in the food industry – coopers, bakers, and butchers often founded taverns – had ample opportunity to accumulate wealth after the turn of the century, so that by 1870 several tavernkeepers were among the wealthiest members of the village.

The changes that took place can be assessed in part by comparing the

[94] A much larger number of unmarried men and women worked in factories, but there are no village statistics on the subject. The *Pfarrbericht* of 1862 reported that there were many factory workers in Neckarhausen, and that many families lived almost completely from factory wages; LKA, A39, Bü 3060.

Table 1.3 *Index of average tax bill by occupation*

| Occupation | 1710 | 1790 | 1870 |
|---|---|---|---|
| Bauern | 100 | 100 | 100 |
| Food services | — | 97 | 286 |
| Artisans | 74 | 39 | 40 |
| Day-laborers | — | 20 | — |
| Workers | — | — | 23 |
| Officeholders | 150 | 122 | 130 |

— None, or too few to count.

average amount of wealth held by various occupational groups.[95] Table 1.3 gives the mean taxable wealth held by each member of the various occupations in terms of an index based on Bauern. One can see the accumulation of wealth possible for the small group of tavernkeepers and the considerable decline in the eighteenth century for the ever-increasing group of handicraft producers.

We can compare the artisans and Bauern in a slightly different way by looking at the average share of village wealth each individual had (Table 1.4).

Table 1.4 *Average individual share of wealth by occupation*

| Occupation | 1710 | 1790 | 1870 |
|---|---|---|---|
| Number of Bauern | 36 | 41 | 49 |
| Percentage of total wealth held by Bauern | 54.5 | 48.3 | 32.3 |
| Mean percentage of total village wealth per Bauer | 1.51 | 1.18 | 0.66 |
| Number of Artisans | 22 | 32 | 71 |
| Percentage of total wealth held by artisans | 29.0 | 14.8 | 18.8 |
| Mean percentage of total village wealth per artisan | 1.32 | 0.46 | 0.26 |
| Mean artisan/mean Bauer | 0.87 | 0.39 | 0.39 |

[95] Tables 1.3 and 1.4 are based on tax registers from the relevant volumes in the *Gemeindepflegerechnungen.* For more detailed calculations, see Appendix F. For 1710, I have combined data for Bauern and people never given an occupation in any records as Bauern, on the assumption that Bauer was the default occupation. Artisans are those who were only given artisanal occupations in the tax and church registers and who were not also Bauern or village servants, for example.

Tables 1.3 and 1.4 both show a remarkable decline for artisans in relation to Bauern during the eighteenth century. At the beginning, although artisans were less numerous, on average each one was only marginally worse off than an independent agricultural producer. By 1790, a typical Bauer still had a significant share of the total village wealth, in sharp contrast to the ordinary artisan, who held about half as much as his great grandfather. During the course of the nineteenth century, the share of both groups eroded, leaving individuals by 1870 in the same *relative* position, although the relative size of each group changed substantially. The number of Bauern grew only slowly, altogether by about a fifth, while the artisan population more than doubled.

Such comparisons would be more telling if we could take into account the total amount of communal wealth measured in terms of output and standard of living. The available information does, however, clearly indicate the stages at which poor artisans and unskilled wage-dependent laborers emerged as a class.[96] The intensive competition among these people for bits of land slowly eroded the holdings of independent agricultural producers, reducing the amount of land available for their exploitation, but leaving them with enough resources to develop and maintain political hegemony and precipitating more intensive land use and family strategies for the defense of accumulated wealth.

The polarization between artisans on the one hand, and Bauern and the few propertied artisans and tavernkeepers who maintained parity with them, on the other, was increased by an important shift in artisanal activity itself. In the eighteenth century, a large percentage of handicraftsmen outside the necessary carpenter, smith, baker, and wheelwright were weavers. All of these crafts necessitated local residency. Increasingly, weaving became a part-time activity for some of the Bauern, and other sedentary crafts emerged, such as shoemaking, which kept many individuals rooted in the village. But after 1800, growth was concentrated in the building trades – among masons, stonecutters, pavers, plasterers, carpenters, and joiners – and most of these people worked outside the village for long periods of time.[97] There was also a significant increase in unskilled work in road, railroad, and canal construction, and in the burgeoning building industry.

The changes in the relative wealth of village groups and the new regional mobility of the growing wage-earning population had political consequences for the village itself. At the beginning of the eighteenth century, artisans were fully integrated into the power structure. They provided 2 of the 4 *Bürgermeister* (chief financial officer of the village), although none of them were ever *Schultheiß* (chief executive official). Altogether they held about half of the

[96] Compare the similar social development of the village of Kiebingen; Wolfgang Kaschuba and Carola Lipp, *Dörfliches Uberleben. Zur Geschichte materieller und sozialer Reproduktion ländlicher Gesellschaft im 19. und 20. Jahrhundert*, Untersuchungen des Ludwig-Uhland-Instituts der Universität Tübingen, vol. 56 (Tübingen, 1982), pp. 63–103.

[97] This was a typical development for the period as the history of Kiebingen shows; Kaschuba and Lipp, *Dörfliches Uberleben*, pp. 42–62.

offices in the *Gericht* (court) and *Rat* (council). By 1790, however, they held only 2 out of 23 offices, most of which were firmly in the hands of Bauern. By then, practically no one not in the top 25 percent of taxpayers was able to become a magistrate. Seven decades later, although fully fledged Bauern made up only 25 percent of the population, they still held 50 percent of the offices.

In summary, in the early eighteenth century, Neckerhausen was a village of about 80 households and was dominated by land but had plenty of political scope for artisans. At that time, the average share per household of the entire village land was about 17 acres. By the end of the century, the population had grown by about 70 percent, and the village was stratified in more complex ways. While the number of independent agricultural producers had expanded modestly, most of the population increase was taken up by wage-dependent, pauperized laborers and semiemployed craftsmen. The dualism of agriculture and petty commodity production gave way to a tripartite structure composed of relatively wealthy landowners, locally resident craftsmen (whose collective and individual wealth had for the most part been eroded), and a mobile group of workers available for seasonal opportunities in agriculture and construction. This last group grew throughout the nineteenth century, absorbing most of the 70 percent increase in population to 1870. By then, there were 220 households, and the average amount of land available for each of them had fallen by two-thirds, to around 6 acres. Fully subsistent Bauern now made up only 25 percent of the population. By the end of the eighteenth century, local village power was firmly in the hands of the landed agricultural producers. They maintained their political ascendency in the following period, sharing power with those artisans and tavernkeepers who were able to capitalize on the economic expansion and who themselves owned just as much land as the richest Bauern.

2

# Magistrates and records

Things are done according to how they are reported.
– Conrad Ischinger, 1844[1]

Various officials from the village and the region appear throughout this book. Villages in Württemberg developed a great deal of self-administration and, as we shall see, generated mountains of paper.[2] At the head of the local magistrates was the Schultheiß, who joined the pastor in deliberating many questions or in holding proceedings which had to do with religion or morals to compose the *gemeinsamen Unteramt* (joint lower bureau). The Schultheiss was responsible for directing all of the official business and for convening the deliberating and judicial bodies of the village. In Neckarhausen, he usually also held the office of *Schreiber* (clerk) and was responsible for keeping minutes – or protocols – of court sessions and the like. Various passages in the legal code and administrative revisions in the decade or so after the founding of the kingdom (1803) make it clear that many villages had no competent Schreiber and had to call on someone from the clerk's office in the district administrative center.[3] But in Neckarhausen, there is evidence that at least by the mid-eighteenth century, the top officials could keep some of their own records, although the local excise officer had to make do with tokens.[4] But there was still a sharp division between those records which the village officers could maintain and those which had to be written by the *Amtschreiber* (county clerk) or his *Substitut* (under clerk).

[1] See fn. 51.

[2] The information for this section is based on a reading of the protocols in the village archives; the "Communordnung" of 1858, in Reyscher, vol. 14, pp. 537–777; "Edikt über die Rechts-Pflege in den unteren Instanzen" (31.12.1818), ibid., vol. 7, pp. 667–780; "Edikt über die Gemeinde-Verfassung," in *Regierungsblatt* (1819), *Beilage* 1; "Edikt über die Oberamts-Verfassung," ibid., *Beilage* 2. For an excellent introduction to the local institutions, see Landkreistag Baden-Württemberg, ed., *Vogteien, Ämter, Landkreise in Baden-Württemberg*, 2 vols. (Stuttgart, 1975), vol. 1, Walter Grube, *Geschichtliche Grundlage.*

[3] See the earlier ordinance, "General-Reskript, die Beschränkung des Geschafts-Kreises der Dorf-Gerichts-Schreibereien betr." (16.10.1706), in Reyscher, vol.7, pp. 228–9; "Königliche Verordnung, die nähere Bestimmung des Geschäfts-Kreises der Gerichtsschreibereien betr." (20/28.7.1809), ibid., pp. 211ff.

[4] *Oberamtsgericht*, STAL, F190, Band 10, f. 1607 (2.6.1814).

The other chief official of the village was the Bürgermeister, who was responsible for the financial administration. In addition, there was frequently a second Bürgermeister, whose job was to care for village inventory, buildings, and land. The financial officer ran a complex household. He had to take in all the local and state taxes, Pförchgeld (sheepfold fees), pasture fees, fines, and other kinds of income, such as that from the sale of timber and firewood and bake oven and bleaching ground rentals. Besides the annual tax register, he kept a several-hundred-page account book, a diary, and a thick bundle of receipts.[5] The accounts were read (in principle) to the assembled villagers and were subjected to a complicated double audit, with the auditors carefully comparing the current accounts with the previous ones. All discrepancies were reported to the village for comment and then considered together by the regional administrators and village officials at a session held in the town. The results of each audit were sent to ducal/royal officials in Stuttgart.[6]

In the eighteenth century, the village had two deliberative/judicial bodies, the Gericht (court) and Rat (council). The officials on both bodies, like the Schultheiss and Bürgermeister, were appointed for life. The Gericht was the larger and more important institution and could be joined by the Rat when special issues had to be considered. Usually men first joined the Rat and then were promoted when a vacancy occurred on the senior body. The Bürgermeister and all the other important officials of the village such as the *Waldmeister* (forest administrator) and Pförchmeister were members of the Gericht, and a smaller group of *Richter*, or *Gerichtsverwandten* (members of the Gericht), made up the *Waisengericht* (orphan's court) and the *Untergang* (court dealing with boundary disputes). Altogether this small group of magistrates held all the administrative and judicial offices. In the administrative reorganization during the early years of the kingdom, a *Gemeinderat* was established, whose members were elected in the first instance for four years. A reelection gave a *Rat* a seat on the court for life. At the same time, an advisory body called the *Bürgerausschuß* was created, whose members held terms for two years. Every Bürger voted for as many seats as were available from among the Bürger as a whole, and those with the top number of votes were required to accept office unless they had just served a two-year term. This body, representing the village at large, was to be consulted by the Gemeinderat from time to time on issues affecting communal rights.[7]

Parallel to the civil hierarchy was a church hierarchy composed of the pastor, schoolmaster, and *Kirchenkonvent* (church consistory). The pastor was always an outsider to the village, normally someone born into a pastoral family, sent to one of the Latin schools, and trained in theology at the University of Tübingen.[8]

[5] A complete set of annual records is about a foot to a foot-and-a-half thick.

[6] See the more detailed description in David Warren Sabean, *Power in the Blood: Popular Culture and Village Discourse in Early Modern Germany* (Cambridge, 1984), pp. 19–20.

[7] "Allgemeine Verordnungen, die Organisation der Gemeinde-Deputirten betr." (7.6.1817), in Reyscher, vol. 15, section 1, pp. 916ff.

[8] On the social background of pastors, see Martin Hasselhorn, *Der altwürttembergische Pfarrstand*

Among other duties, he was responsible for keeping the church records, maintaining moral discipline in the village, administering the sacraments, and carrying out the various life cycle rituals, such as baptism, confirmation, marriage, and burial. The schoolmaster, who was under his supervision, was also usually from another village, although at the turn of the nineteenth century a father (who became Schultheiss) and son held long tenures in Neckarhausen. Until the nineteenth century, the term *Ludimagister*, or singing master, best captures the task of the village teacher. His job evolved from parallel church and civil functions, which consisted of preparing villagers for participation in church and local assemblies. State ordinances, wanted posters, and the like were read either from the pulpit or after church to a congregation well acquainted with oral texts.

A crucial institution in Neckarhausen was the Kirchenkonvent (church consistory), which met under the double chairmanship of the pastor and Schultheiss, who were joined by several members of the village magistrates as church elders. The institution was founded in 1644, although the protocols for Neckarhausen are only extant from 1727.[9] The Kirchenkonvent provides a good example of the close interdependence of the spiritual and civil instances of Herrschaft (lordship, authority, state domination). The pastor was supposed to chair the sessions in the consistory – he was literally the spokesperson, the one who controlled the word (*Wortführer*) – while the Schultheiss subjected people to the oath, counted votes, threatened, served notice, levied fines, and carried out civil punishments. The consistory was charged with overseeing the morals, religion, and schooling of the villagers. It acted as arbitrator of marital disputes, called young people to task for immoral behavior, saw to it that order and quiet were maintained on Sundays and holy days, looked into incidents involving blasphemy and superstition, and regulated school attendance and poor relief.

In an earlier book, I have described how the "sacral" and "fiscal" elements of the state were closely intermeshed.[10] Throughout the period of our study, officials in charge of delivering a fifth of the village produce to central storehouses and barns were the same officials in charge of family order, sober living, and practical piety. By the end of the eighteenth century, more and more administrative and judicial matters at the lowest level were being put exclusively into the hands of civil authorities, which concentrated power in the hands of the Schultheiss or town officials. By 1806, for example, illegitimacy and fornication, which had been the subject of a large part of the consistory protocols, came under the competence of the village Gericht, which soon set up a separate protocol book (*Skortationsprotocolle*, 1822ff.) and concerned itself less and less with moral questions and more and more with fines, paternity, and

*im 18. Jahrhundert*, Veröffentlichungen der Kommission für geschichtliche Landeskunde in Baden-Württemberg, Series B: Forschungen, vol. 6 (Stuttgart, 1958).

[9] On the founding, see "Synodal-Schluß, betr. die Einrichtung der Kirchen-Convente," in Reyscher, vol. 8, pp. 316–25.

[10] Sabean, *Power*, pp. 200–206.

support.[11] Although shortly after, marital disputes, according to the civil statutes, were also supposed to become a purely civil matter, they remained a concern for the consistory until 1839.[12] In that same year, the Schultheiss began his own protocols (*Schultheißenamtsprotocolle*) dealing with many matters of libel, petty theft, disturbance of the peace, and marital conflict, all of which had earlier occupied the village magistrates as a whole. The general administrative tasks of village officials multiplied to include animal inspection, inspection of weights and measures, observance of curfews, and a greatly expanded financial administration.

The village was closely integrated into the regional capital (*Oberamtsstadt*) of Nürtingen. In the Oberamt, a *Vogt* (later *Oberamtmann*) was the chief ducal/royal administrative official. The *Schreiberamt* (office of the clerk) was concerned with maintaining a vast series of inheritance, landholding, and administrative records both in the town and in all of the surrounding villages. A court of higher instance (*Oberamtsgericht*) received reports from the village court and officials and in the early nineteenth century became primarily a court of investigation, presenting evidence to higher courts in important civil actions and felonies.[13] One of the tasks of the Vogt was to carry out a triennial *Vogtruggericht* in Neckarhausen, where he looked into the state of village record keeping and inquired of every Bürger if he knew of any action against the interest of the state/duke/king (*herrschaftliches Interesse*).[14] The religious/school establishment was subject to a similar review when the *Superintendent* (later *Dekan*) made his annual visitation to hear the pastor preach, visit the school, and inquire into the conduct of villagers, officials, schoolmaster, and minister.[15]

At the beginning of the eighteenth century, the magistracy of Neckarhausen contained representatives of both landed proprietors and handicraftsmen. But positions in the village hierarchy came to be subject to oligarchical control. The judgment of the emigrant Jacob Hampf from Eglosheim in 1817 would have fit the Neckarhausen case perfectly: "The Schultheiss and Bürgermeister hold together, since they are cousins, and the other magistrates go along with them because they are all related together."[16] There were good political reasons why this came to be so. Over the course of the eighteenth century, the local officials were subjected to close observation and control, but at the same time their field of competence was extended. The population increase and expanding production created significant opportunities for capitalizing on administrative and judicial power. Ironically, the closer supervision created a tighter bond

[11] "Reskript der königl. Kreischauptleute, betr. die Untersuchung fleischlicher Vergehen durch die weltl. Aemter" (21.10.1806), in Reyscher, vol. 7, p. 65.

[12] "Edikt über die Rechtspflege" (1818), Reyscher, vol. 7, pp. 670–9.

[13] Most of the records of the *Oberamtsgericht* have been destroyed. A few volumes with detailed protocols exist for the period from 1801–1824.

[14] The results of his visit are in the *Vogtruggerichtsprotocolle* in the village Rathaus.

[15] The long series of church visitation reports (*Synodus Protocolle*) are in the LKA in Stuttgart.

[16] Günter Moltmann, ed., *Aufbruch nach Amerika. Friedrich List und die Auswanderung aus Baden und Württemberg 1816/17. Dokumentation einer sozialen Bewegung* (Tübingen, 1979), p. 131.

between those who mediated between the village and state and those who were supposed to watch over them. Local magistrates spoke in the idiom of the "house" and the ideology of the "good householder" to represent their perception of social reality to the Vogt and Oberamt officials. Increasing hierarchalization gave village oligarchs a significant opening for strategical maneuver.[17]

At the highest level, state officials were well aware of what they had created and described the forms of corruption in various ordinances in great details.[18] As long as they were dependent on the movement of grain to central storehouses, they were caught in a contradictory position. Consider the complex development of institutions for collecting tithes. By the mid-eighteenth century, the great tithe was auctioned off to a village collector just before the harvest. Working together with a series of Schultheissen, a close-knit group of people conspired to set the price. In some villages, a small group won the bid year after year by threatening an independent bidder. In others, those who could afford the considerable financial outlay formed separate syndicates which set the price by rigged bidding, rotating the business among themselves. They had considerable powers of patronage, since the job entailed security officers, carters, and threshers. But the whole corruption necessitated close interdependence between the wealthiest members of the village and the local magistrates.

## Sources

One of the most striking things about Württemberg villages is the enormous amount of written material in their archives. The parish houses, especially for Protestant communities, contain series of baptisms, marriages, and burials beginning in the sixteenth century.[19] In the nineteenth century, the pastor assembled all the records of vital events into a family register, adding supplemental information from sources outside the village.[20] Each parish also kept minutes and transcripts from the local church consistory. The Rathäuser have long series of inventories, village accounts, court records, cadasters, land sales, mortgage registers, tax lists, records of tithes, fines, and many other miscellaneous volumes, including the *Befehlbuch*, which contains a carefully written copy of mandates, ordinances, instructions, and wanted posters sent out by the central government. Altogether, for the period up to 1870, Neckar-

17 This process is discussed in Sabean, *Power*, chap. 5.

18 "Zweite Zehendordnung" (27.6.1618), in Reyscher, vol. 16, p. 301; "Anordnung gegen die heimlichen Uebereinkünfte bei Zehendverleihungen" (24.4.1660), p. 410; "Allgemeine Vorschriften, die Wahrung des herrschaftlichen Interesse bei Zehend- und Gülten-Verpachtungen betr." (17.7.1736); "General-Rescript, das diesjährige Ernd-Generale betr.", vol. 16, section 2, p. 47; "Ernd-General-Rescript für das Jahr 1808 . . . " (17.6.1808), p. 93.

19 The registers for baptisms in Neckarhausen begin in 1558, marriages in 1562, and burials in 1574. See, "Kirchenordnung" (1559), Reyscher, vol. 8, p. 256.

20 In Neckarhausen, complete from 1808. "General-Rescript, die Einführung neuer Kirchen- und Familien-Register betr." (15.11.1807), Reyscher, vol. 9, pp. 106ff.

hausen has over 300,000 pages of documentation available in the village itself.

This book is based on information from many village sources. One of the most useful series has been the marriage and postmortem inventories, which include the names of individuals faced with backruptcy proceedings or of people who had decided to retire and pass their property on to their children. Edicts and ordinances which mandated record keeping frequently justified their demands in some way or other, and some of these official concerns indicate the source of the problems of interpreting written local documents. According to the sixteenth-century *Landrecht*, there was good reason to list all the property belonging to a married couple:

> And therefore...so that people can sort out an inheritance with each other, and so that no one will be cheated or disadvantaged with respect to properties which are held in usufruct and which will fall to them, as soon after one marriage partner dies and is buried, or according to the situation and consideration of persons, not longer than one month, all possessions and property, immovable and movable, which the two married people held, whether having belonged to the survivor or deceased, without any difference, excluding nothing, shall be listed in an orderly fashion and inventoried by two competent members of the court [*Gericht*], or by other men delegated for the purpose by the chief official of the region [*Amtmann*], and the sworn clerk, in the presence of those who have a share and interest in the matter.[21]

In the great law code redactions of 1555 and 1567, ducal officials not only defined the law dealing with property but also established procedures for recording all rights and alterations of any kind. In typical fashion, just before a hundred pages of discussion of all possible inheritance procedures, the code provided for the keeping of detailed inventories.[22] As far as the government was concerned, the record and the rights were closely connected. Behind the formal practice of reducing all the scattered utensils of a household to formal categories and established values lies an event which gathered together a large number of claimants with all of their supporters and a set of officials charged with the task of watching out for the interests of the state and ensuring a fair and legal disposal of an estate. Here, as in the many other situations where complex, formal documents were to be composed, a key figure was the Schreiber. In the case of Neckarhausen, those many hundreds of thousands of pages of documents were the occasion for a visit from or to someone from the clerk's office in Nürtingen, either the Schreiber himself or one of his trained underclerks, a Substitut.

[21] "2. Landrecht" (1567), in Reyscher, vol. 4. p. 376: "Und damit...da man mit einander abtheilen, auch die Güter zum Widerfall nießlich besitzen soll, niemandt veruntrewt oder vernachtheilt werde, so soll als bald nach des einen Ehegemachts absterben und Erden bestetigung, oder nach gestalt der Sachen und ansehen der Personen, auffs lengst in Monats frist, alle Haab und Güter, ligende und farende, so die beide Eheleut besessen, die weren dem uberlebenden oder verstorbnen zugehörig gewesen, one underschid, nichts außgenommen, durch zwen verstendige Gerichts, oder andere vom Amptman darzuverordnete Männer, und der geschwornen Schreiber, in beisein deren, so Theil und Interesse daran haben."

[22] "2. Landrecht" (1567), in Reyscher, vol. 4, pp. 358–60.

Inventories were typical of record-keeping practices in Württemberg, but they were by no means exceptional. According to the law code (*Landrecht*) of 1567, a Schreiber or his Substitut was obligated to attend each meeting of a court or council and make a summary record of the proceedings called a *Protocoll.* He was supposed to record both the plaintiff's charges and the defendant's answers *substantialia* and briefly (*auffs kürzest*).[23] He was also responsible for keeping a separate volume (*Rugbuch*) of the annual or biennial *Ruggericht*, an assembly of all household heads, which sorted out various trespass complaints, boundary disputes, and petty delicts and required each person under oath to testify if he knew of any violation of the herrschaftlichen Interessen.[24] The clerk was also to attend the orphan's court and read and proof all the financial records of each guardian once a year.[25] The separate volumes for each purpose were supposed to be furnished with registers and indexes. All contracts and sales of real estate had to be carried out before a court and were also to be entered into the *Gerichtsbuch.*[26] Liens on property, mortgages, and pledges followed the same form.

The proliferation of separate records and volumes can be seen in Neckarhausen. The following series are still extant in the village archives: *Inventuren* (marriage inventories) and *Teilungen* (pre- and postmortem inventories) beginning in 1627 (ca. 3000 to 1870), *Kaufbücher* (real estate sales) beginning in 1653, tax registers from 1604 and 1726, *Unterpfandsbücher* (mortgages) beginning in 1747, *Gerichts-* and *Gemeinderatsprotocolle* beginning in 1746 (contains entries from the Gericht, later Gemeinderat, and Rat, later, transformed and enlarged, Bürgerausschuß, and Ruggericht), *Vogtruggerichtsprotocolle* (triennial visitation of the Vogt, later Oberamtmann) beginning in 1747, *Kirchenkonventsprotocolle* from 1727, *Gemeindepflegerechnungen* (financial records of the village), selected complete records from 1710, 1720, 1730, summary volumes every five years thereafter to 1794, and complete annual records from 1795 onward, the baptismal register beginning in 1558, the burial register beginning in 1574, the marriage register beginning in 1562, and the family register beginning in 1808. Many of the earlier documents from before the Thirty Years War appear to have been destroyed during the period of disarray.

By no means were the volumes kept just because ducal officials ordered that it be done. The various mandates and ordinances make it clear that record keeping was often done carelessly or in protest. A short review will show the great struggle that surrounded the practice and some of the official ideology. In 1620, the duke sent out an order concerning marriage inventories: "In our duchy a great many conflicts which cause long, drawn-out, difficult legal proceedings arise from the fact that marriage partners fail to have an inventory

23 Ibid., p. 199.
24 Ibid., pp. 203–4.
25 Ibid., pp. 203–4.
26 Ibid., pp. 204–5.

made [*inventieren*]."[27] The same order noted that mortgages were not being properly registered, with the result that properties were being loaded with more debt than they could carry. It was time then to see that a special register of mortgages and liens (Unterpfandsbuch) was kept. In 1645, the duke complained that many people were not getting inventories, and that this was causing difficulties for creditors, widows, and orphans.[28] Just after the Thirty Years War, a problem arose over the sale of deserted land where buyers were unaware of their rent obligations.[29] In 1717, owing to the lack of order in the Unterpfandsbücher, officials failed to learn in time about people who fell into debt, and therefore rents and outstanding taxes were left unpaid.[30] In 1730, the reason for keeping good books was clearly to spot those who were in danger of requiring public support.[31] An ordinance of 1736 made it clear that improper records were a threat to creditors.[32] It was repeated in 1743, when attention was also drawn to the problem of unpaid taxes.[33] At the turn of the century, the concern for overextended debtors was related to *Staatscredit* and private circulating credit.[34] The solution was proper registration. Throughout the seventeenth and eighteenth centuries, the constant concern of the ducal officials was to see that separate registers and protocol volumes were kept and entries made in good order. The purpose in each instance was to provide for the orderly processing of disputes (or to avoid them altogether), to protect the rights of widows and orphans so as to keep the number of propertyless poor in check, to shore up the tax and rent base of the ducal administration, and to protect creditors, who were by and large officials of the ducal government and their widows, or foundations belonging to the state or local authorities.

Various experiments were made using village personnel to keep records. In many villages, the schoolmaster acted as clerk, but by 1706 it was clear that he did not have the *Capacität*.[35] In most cases the Amtsschreiber was to take care of the protocols of the Gericht and of sales and mortgages. He was also to keep

[27] "General-Reskript . . . Inventuren . . . betr." (24.7.1620), in Reyscher, vol. 5, p. 371: "in Unserm Hertzogthumb, sehr vil stritt, und darauß erfolgte langwürige schwere Rechtfertigungen, daher verursacht werden, daß die Eheleut das Inventiren underlassen"

[28] "General-Reskript, das Inventieren betr. (5/31.4.1645), in Reyscher, vol. 5, pp. 437–8.

[29] "General-Reskript, verschwiegene Beschwerden und Auslosung verkaufter Güter betr." (15/30.1.1651), in Reyscher, vol. 5, p. 448.

[30] "General-Reskript, die Behandlung der Schulden und Unterpfänder bei Veräusserung der letztern und bei Theilungen betr." (27.2.1717), in Reyscher, vol. 6, pp. 278–9.

[31] "General-Reskript, die mögliche Verhutung und die Bestrafung selbstverschuldeter Vermögens-Zerrütung betr." (12.6.1730), in Reyscher, vol. 6, p. 358.

[32] "General-Reskript, das Vorzugsrecht der gleichsam öffentlichen und der gesetzlichen Unterpfänder betr." (19.3.1736), in Reyscher, vol. 6, p. 413.

[33] "General-Reskript, das gerichtliche Erkenntniß über Unterpfands-Bestellungen betr." (9.5.1743), in Reyscher, vol. 6, p. 471.

[34] "Circular-Reskript der königl. Ober-Landes-Regierung an die Ober- und Stabs-Aemter, die Aufmerksamkeit der Beamten auf Führung der Unterpfandsbücher . . . " (29.5.1806), in Reyscher, vol. 7, p. 26.

[35] "General-Reskript, die Beschränkung des Geschafts-Kreisen der Dorf-Gerichts-Schreibereien betr." (16.10.1706), in Reyscher, vol. 6, p. 228.

the financial records of the village. In Neckarhausen, evidence from 1774 and 1781 indicates that a Substitut maintained village financial records and evidence from 1781 indicates that he kept the poor relief records.[36] In the late eighteenth century, the Schultheiss Salomon Hentzler wrote the Gerichtsprotocolle, and his successors appear also to have done so.[37] After 1739, the Schultheiss kept the protocols of his own office. (He referred to himself as the "signing authority," *unterzeichnete Stelle.*) Inventories were always composed by someone from the Nürtingen clerk's office, and by 1828 there was an *Actuar* living part-time in the village, who was concerned with revising the mortgage volumes and keeping the increasingly complex financial records of the village. The Actuar was a trained accountant who took over much of the work earlier done by the Amtsschreiber. In asking for a raise, in 1828, he maintained that "in general in the countryside when a Bauer rose to become Schultheiss or Bürgermeister, he did not have the necessary exactness and knowledge of the law which a trained finance expert had to have."[38] In 1829, the Schultheiss announced that he was too busy to keep the mortgage volumes, so the court voted to give the work to an Actuar.[39] From that point on, an accountant from outside became a central figure in village life. In 1865, an Actuar from Nürtingen was actually elected Schultheiss. He combined the jobs of clerk of the Gemeinderat, village financial accountant, and mortgage volume keeper.[40] The trend in the nineteenth century was toward specialization and professionalization of the chief village administrative and financial positions.

From the middle of the sixteenth century onward, we find that the village was ever more closely bound together with officials in the *Amtstadt* and in Stuttgart through chains of paper. Every year the financial records of the village had to be audited in Nürtingen. The records of the poor relief institute and the books of each guardian were also audited annually. There may, of course, have been periods of neglect, but renewed ordinances and new generations of officials constantly brought the villagers to book. The volumes of mortgages, the cadaster, and the tax registers were completely revised every second or third generation, an action which could provide work for a commission for many months. Every year the superintendent visited the village and inspected the consistory protocols and commented on the state of the parish records. His report was sent to the highest church and state councils, who carefully noted their comments in the margins and sent instructions for correction and im-

[36] *Vogtruggericht*, vol. 1, f. 136 (22.11.1786); *Gericht*, vol. 2, f. 65 (21.1.1774); ibid., vol. 3, f. 66 (7.6.1781).

[37] Hentzler was Schultheiss from 1766–88; *Vogtruggericht*, vol. 1 (10.12.1788).

[38] *Gericht*, vol.11, f. 104 (29.6.1828): "Vor allen Dingen er nun bittet, den Umstand nicht aus dem Gesichtspunkt zu verlieren, daß überhaupt auf dem Lande von dem Bauersmann, wann solches sich auch zum Schultheissen oder Bürgermeister erhoben hat, doch bei weitem noch nicht die Pünktlichkeit und Kenntnis mit dem Gesetzen zu erwarten ist, die eine gelernte Rechnungsverständiger haben muß und die man von ihm als Rechnungssteller auch verlangt."

[39] *Gericht*, vol. 11, f. 131 (20.2.1829).

[40] *Gericht*, vol. 18, f. 12 (10.6.1865).

provement. Every three years, the Vogt, or Oberamtmann, visited the village and inspected all of the various Gerichtsprotocolle. In the visitation of 1820, for example, he noted that several court sessions lacked a date, that the name of a woman's court representative (Kriegsvogt) was missing, that court sessions frequently lacked the signatures of members of the Gemeinderat, that the obligations of guardians were not spelled out, that the Bürgerausschuss improperly sat in on meetings of the Gemeinderat, that there was no index of the protocols, and that village officials often levied fines which belonged to higher instances.[41] He went on to discuss various points of administrative form and activities that local officials were to watch over in particular. In 1823, he noted points which the village magistrates had ignored and stressed that they should leave no blank spaces in the records which could allow "evil people" (*bösen Menschen*) to insert something at a later date.[42]

The paper trail which we have been following was initiated by the duke and his officials. It is an unusual trail, and there are few territories in Germany with comparable amounts of material dealing with everyday life at the village level and probably none where the sources have been so well preserved. One reason why Württemberg generated so many documents is that there were no mediating instances between the duke and his subjects with rights over his subjects. The nobility had attained an independent status early in the sixteenth century, and thereafter their small territories were treated as foreign soil. After the Reformation, church properties and institutions became part of the state, and where they retained rights and property, they fell under the administrative oversight of the *Landeskirche* (state church). Therefore, except for a few exceptions here and there, there were no intermediate competencies, no lords with patrimonial courts, no seigneurial jurisdictions. As a result, the problem for the duke was to organize a hierarchical judicial system from the locality to his highest court. Just as the lordship held sway over justice, the duke was the only major landlord in the territory, and the various hospitals, schools, universities, and corporations which also held land were part of the state. In Württemberg, there was no possibility of an urban population buying out impoverished peasants and emerging as a class living from quitrents. Parallel to what we have found for judicial institutions, the problem was to organize a flow from the locality to the center and to develop a series of bureaucratic instruments to oversee it. A centerpiece of ducal policy was the *Schreiberei*, set up in every administrative town.[43] Much of the income of the chief clerk and his junior clerks was derived from fees levied according to the number of pages any document contained and assessed to the individuals and villages which used their services. It was very much in the interest of the Schreiber to see that ducal orders to keep minutes and registers of all kinds

[41] *Gericht*, vol. 9, f. 157 (11.11.1820).
[42] *Gericht*, vol. 10, f. 105 (22.9.1823).
[43] "2. Landrecht" (1567), in Reyscher, vol. 4, pp. 194ff.

were carried out. Any time it occurred to a high official that a problem could be solved by beginning a new series of records, there were ready and willing servants to carry out the task. It may also have been the case that the peculiar Reformation settlement and the intact school system encouraged an administrative practice based on widespread literacy, but we should not overestimate the familiarity of villagers with reading and writing. They did become used to *handling* written documents and signing their names to bills of credit and the like. During disputes, they presented their private records or official abstracts of public records for judicial officials to read and interpret. Since, for the most part, the village settlement in Württemberg presented large, compact, nucleated villages, there was always a critical mass of people for carrying on considerable administrative and judicial business at the local level.

At the center of state writing practice was the "protocol." Very seldom were there verbatim transcripts of complaints or trials. Instead, the protocol was meant to record the substance, reporting all the chief arguments, charges, answers, and transactions of a particular situation.[44] The verb form *protocollieren* runs like a bright thread through the laws and ordinances from the Landrechte in the sixteenth century to the end of the period under consideration. The obsession with protocols came to a head in 1730: "Every official of our duchy according to his office and obligations must each time in every case brought before him or investigated by him, no matter how trivial it may appear, make an orderly protocol."[45]

There is a great deal to be said about protocols, official memory – in fact, the duke spoke of his fear that continuous official memory might be lost[46] –, the various levels of reality (between an incident, its restaging before the court, and its redaction to a standard "case" by an official), and problems of interpretation. Although many strategies can be adopted for reading these texts, we will never encounter the "authentic" voices of the various villagers. Whatever took place in court was carried on in the Swabian dialect, but protocols were in what officials considered to be high German, liberally sprinkled with Latin expressions. We must think in terms of the strategies of different people, some mentioned in a protocol, some inferred, and some hidden. In a particular conflict before the court, the *Contrahenten* are all listed and are each given a voice: a complaint, a tale, an answer, an oath. But there may have been others present who supported one or more of the parties but who had nothing to say, at least at that point, which was noted. It is clear, for example, that a wife who had suffered her husband's abuse for several years did not do so in silence. Her own

[44] Ibid., p. 199.

[45] "General-Reskript, die Führung von Amtsprotocollen betr." (19.6.1730), in Reyscher, vol. 14, pp. 87–8: "ein jeder Beambter Unsers Hertzogthums, vermög seines Ambts und Pflichten sohin gehalten ist, in allen angebracht und von Ihm untersuchten Fällen, wann Sie gleich auch noch so gering anscheinen, jedesmahlen Ein ordentliches *Protocoll* zu führen."

[46] "General-Reskript, die Verwahrung fürstlicher Befehle bei den Amts- und Gemeinde-Registraturen betr." (2.7.1603), in Reyscher, vol. 12, pp. 591ff.

relatives and in-laws and maybe some of the neighbors listened, kibitzed, and sought to mediate long before she took the step of going to the authorities. Some of them might have been in the chorus in the Rathaus *Stüble*. The Schultheiss and the Konventsrichter were implied attendants at each theatrical event and are known to have been there not because they were part of the official story but because their signatures were affixed and because a punishment or judgment had been rendered. Unseen, of course, is the *Protocollant*, the one responsible for the protocol in the first place, and there is no direct evidence in most instances about who wrote the document.

The guidelines for keeping a record enjoined on the writer of a protocol certain practices which he might carry out with more or less skill and more or less verbosity. He was supposed to list the participants of the particular event, to summarize their statements, and to do so in such a way that the punishment described at the end formed a correct punch line to the narrative. Sometimes the Schreiber botched the job and was forced to add a description of the one most severely punished as a debauched enemy of all that was holy. The clerk also had to be careful, since he had to read his summary to the participants, who would accede or not to the description of their position, although he probably first read aloud from his notes and only after reading them back to the parties and the judges did he compose his protocol.[47] Since the Schreiber was either a member of the town elite or the pastor or Schultheiss himself, his strong hand in the shaping of each report represented the values of the closely allied magistrates of the *Amt*. Many protocols were copied and sent to the Vogt or Oberamtmann for further consideration, and they were all examined in the periodic visitations.[48] Each one, therefore, must also be considered as having been directed toward a higher audience, and even the form was affected by the relation. A Protocollant who reported in too much or too little detail would be brought up short by a higher authority.[49] Sometimes a villager was willing to

[47] An example of a protocol being read: to Jacob Gimmel in a breach of promise suit; *Kirchenkonvent*, vol. 2, p. 24 (7.2.1749). Another case in which one was explicitly read, this time to a mother after her son had been brought to court for mistreating his wife; ibid., p. 28 (4.4.1749). Michael Deuschle was not able to listen to the protocol because he was tipsy (*benebelt*); *Gericht*, vol. 12, f. 60 (26.9.1832).

[48] In 1867, for example, the Oberamtmann after examining the protocols criticized the Schultheiss for handling a case of injury to honor (*Ehrenkränkung*) which was beyond his jurisdiction; *Vogtruggericht* vol. 2, f. 242 (24.5.1867). One example of many protocols sent along to the Oberamt: *Gericht*, vol. 10, f. 31 (8.1.1822). Certain cases such as illegitimacy or fornication were always protocolled locally and sent on to higher authority for disposition. Sending on a protocol could be a threat. Two women were told to behave or the protocol would be forwarded to the Oberamt; *Kirchenkonvent*, vol. 2 (20.2.1774). Just because Conrad Reichle had scolded the magistrates, they made a record to be sent to the Oberamt; *Gericht*, vol. 14, f. 279 (4.8.1848). Sometimes the parties themselves wanted their dispute settled elsewhere and demanded either to have a copy or to have the protocol forwarded; *Gericht*, vol. 8, f. 131 (17.10.1714); vol. 7, f. 21 (2.4.1812). And someone could be very unhappy with the local magistrates and demand that a protocol be sent to higher authorities; *Schultheißenamt*, vol. 2, f. 97 (9.2.1846). Georg Wilhelm Hentzler was so outraged by the story retailed by Maria Magdalena Hentzler that he refused to make a protocol at all – which was recorded in a protocol; *Gericht*, vol. 10, f. 193 (18.8.1825).

[49] *Gericht*, vol. 9, f. 157 (11.11.1820).

accept a decision or punishment by the local magistrates in order to avoid dealing with officials in Nürtingen.[50] In any event, the power of shaping an account in a protocol was clearly recognized by villagers. In 1844, Conrad Ischinger complained that the local officials repressed the poor people in the village and that everything went according to how they reported matters.[51] Earlier the Oberamt itself had said it would take no more complaints about the Schultheiss and Bürgermeister but would consider matters only as they reported them.[52] Sometimes, in fact, officials used the protocol process as a public event. The pastor, who had been battling village drunkenness without much success, made an elaborate protocol (with the magistrates, who were the chief drinkers, present) about a man who had accidentally killed himself while intoxicated.[53] After one young Bürger had been disobedient and rude, the protocol was read to the assembled Bürger as a warning.[54] But a villager could make a public issue out of the action of the magistrates. Friedrich Geiger called the members of the Gericht who signed a particular protocol "a bunch of old whores" (*lauter alte Huren*).[55]

Being protocolled itself could be a matter for considerable disquiet or for careful strategies of planning. Wilhelm Hentzler boasted on the street that he had never yet been in conflict with anyone and therefore had never been in a protocol.[56] More specifically, after a young woman had been investigated and cleared of a suspicion of fornication, her mother was upset that any record remained at all and that her offspring was in the *Hurenprotocoll*.[57] Mathes Weiler in 1806 was angry over the fact that he had been listed as being indebted and wanted the whole Gericht to clear his name by making a formal record, which they did.[58] Other people sought to have an entry made so that they could use it as a basis for further action. One woman wanted her husband's behavior protocolled so that she could begin proceedings if he did not behave.[59] Jacob Häfner withdrew a complaint against his old and good friend Mathias Sterr, but wanted a protocol made in case there were further attacks on his family.[60] But it

[50] *Kirchenkonvent*, vol. 1, p. 38 (25.3.1736).
[51] *Schultheißenamt*, vol. 2, f. 68 (14.2.1844): "Wie man berichtet, so geschehe." Earlier Johann Georg Riempp expressed his disgust with the bias of a record by saying, "you are able to protocol what you want" (man könne protocollieren was man wolle); *Gericht*, vol. 4, f. 72 (2.7.1787).
[52] *Vogtruggericht*, vol. 2, f. 76 (26.11.1818).
[53] *Kirchenkonvent*, vol. 1, p. 168 (4.11.1746).
[54] *Gericht*, vol. 6, f. 114 (8.11.1805). The protocol about a son was read to his mother; *Kirchenkonvent*, vol. 2, p. 28 (4.4.1749).
[55] *Gericht*, vol. 4, f. 102 (7.4.1789).
[56] *Gericht*, vol. 9, f. 142 (18.7.1820). Johann Georg Hentzler was willing to take an oath that he had not stolen something he was accused of. He was 47, he said, and never come into a protocol; *Gericht*, vol. 12, f. 163 (26.9.1834). The officials themselves might attest to the fact that someone had never been protocolled; *Schultheißenamt*, vol. 1, f. 15 (3.2.1841).
[57] *Gericht*, vol. 3, f. 182 (23.9.1784).
[58] *Gericht*, vol. 6, f. 157 (29.5.1806).
[59] *Kirchenkonvent*, vol. 4 (6.11.1632).
[60] *Gericht*, vol. 11, f. 74 (6.8.1827).

could often be dangerous to bring someone before the court, since he or she could take the opportunity to counterattack with secrets not yet made public and punished.[61] Quite frequently, the plaintiff ended up with his own fine to pay. There was also the possibility of ending all talk by bringing someone before the court who had been spreading rumors. The chain of gossip would be followed back to the source, who would then provide evidence that the plaintiff had indeed committed the crime. Once the person was protocolled, fined, or jailed, that was an end to the matter. Anyone rash enough to continue to gossip about it could be sued for *Satisfaction.*[62]

We must be wary of taking the protocols at face value. Once a couple was before the court, for example, each would chose to describe an action to his or her own best advantage and to speak in an idiom that the magistrates would most clearly understand and be receptive to. In rewriting the drama, the Schreiber would also select and reshape, building a case for one party and undermining the case for the other or balancing unequal acts in order to create a situation where both parties needed correction. We will be looking closely at how words were used and how values were phrased in the protocols, but we must be aware that each term was part of a complex negotiation, perhaps actually spoken by a participant but just as likely chosen from a dictionary of official values and prejudices when the protocol was composed. That does not vitiate our argument. All the parties were part of the same complex negotiations and were trying to give form to unusual events as well as everyday incidents. Much of our account will be directed toward sifting out the view of this or that participant by piling similar incidents together, considering the positions of the actors, or by reading a dense text as closely as possible.

Before we begin to analyze our texts closely in the following chapters, it would be useful to take a critical look at several protocols, both to evaluate the forms that they could take and to consider the different voices and strategies which are overt and hidden in such texts. I have chosen to examine three protocols from the church consistory records. The first one concerns a magical attack by one neighbor on another, the route to the court through public opinion, and a redefinition of the incident by the consistory with the pastor at its head.

[61] For example, during a dispute about mowing hay, Johann Georg Riempp brought up the charge that Christoph Hentzler had moved a marker five years previously; *Gericht*, vol. 4, f. 72 (7.7.1787). In 1820, Johann Häfner told Georg Friedrich Baur to watch out or he would tell what had happened long ago; *Gericht*, vol. 9, f. 142 (18.7.1820). Friedrich Baur was angry because he was voted out as chairman (*Obmann*) of the Bürgerausschuss, so he accused two others of libeling him 18 months previously; *Gericht*, vol. 10, f. 31 (8.1.1822). Mathias Rieth in a dispute over garbage disposal accused Christian Sterr of stealing a pipe two years previously; *Schultheißenamt*, vol. 2, f. 109 (4.6.1848).

[62] *Kirchenkonvent*, vol. 4 (20.10.1832). The existence of earlier protocols could play into strategy, and they could be consulted. In various boundary disputes or trespass complaints, reference was made to an earlier record; *Vogtruggericht*, vol. 2, f. 211 (13.15.1845); *Gericht*, vol. 10, f. 25 (28.12.1821); ibid., vol. 5, f. 51 (9.7.1796). A protocol could be used to create a permanent memory. Two neighbors, e.g., agreed to let a boundary stone be covered but wanted a record so that rights would not be forgotten; *Gericht*, vol. 2, f. 124 (28.4.1776).

12 August 1770

Anna Barbara, the wife of Salomo Bauknecht, complains that Michel Häfner spreads the report (*ausschreie*) that she is the person who with a brazen attack wickedly assaulted his calf on July 27, so that he had to kill it on August 5. She asks to have her reputation restored.

Michel Häfner admits that he had not interpreted positively the fact that while his calf was fresh and healthy, Barbara Bauknechtin forced her way into the stall and, according to his wife's testimony, touched the calf, lifted its tail, and spoke various foolish words. He does not consider her to be a witch, although where she grasped the steer, there were broad red burn marks. He cannot prove anything further against Bauknechtin and wants to suffer his loss patiently in God's name and give Bauknechtin an acknowledgment that he will not now or in the future consider her to be a [illegible word].

Decision. You Michel Häfner must declare to Bauknechtin that you do not believe anything so wickedly dishonorable and will not abuse her, otherwise each instance will be punished. On the other hand, because of her inept invasion into a stranger's stall, Bauknechtin has to bear with patience all previous talk and both parties shall reconcile themselves with each other as Christians by shaking hands [*data dextra*], which they did.

Witnessed. Pastor M. Gentner
Salomo Hentzler[63]

It is not clear why certain cases came before the court. From internal evidence, we know that many incidents of a similar kind were never dealt with in a formal judicial forum. In this instance, there appears to be two possibilities. Whenever a rumor circulated through the village, it was incumbent on its target to purge him or herself by going before a court and having an official judgment entered. In fact, it was not unusual for a known thief to complain about an accusation even though he knew he would be found guilty. The court offered

[63] *Kirchenkonvent*, vol. 2 (12.8.1770)

Actum 12 Aug 1770

Anna Barbara, Salomo Bauknechts Weib klagt über Michel Häfner, daß er sie für diejenige Person ausschreye, die ihm sein Kalb durch einen kühnen Angriff d. 27te. July böser weiß angegriffen, daß er solches habe d. 5te. Aug. stechen müßen. Sie bitte um ihres Namens beschützung.

Michel Häfner gesteht, daß er der Barbara Bauknechtin nicht gut ausgedeutet hatten, daß sie ihm, da sein kalb frisch und gesund gewesen, in Stall eingedrungen seye u. nach Aussage seines Weibs das Kalb betastet, den Schwanz auffgehoben u. allerley närrische Worte geredt hatte. Er halte sie aber nicht für eine Hex, an denen Stieren seyen zwar wie die finger greiffen, rothe brandigte dicke Striche gewesen. Er könne aber nichts weiters wider die Bauknechtin beweisen, u. wolle seinen Schaden in Gottes Namen gedultig leyden, u. der Bauknechtin die Declaration thun, daß er sie weder jezo noch ins künfftige für eine... [illegible word] halten wolle.

Beschaid. Ihr Michel Häfner müßt der Bauknechtin wegen der angegebenen Klage bezeugen, daß ihr solches böse ehrenrührige nicht glaub noch sie schimpf wollt, oder es würde solches jedes mal mit Strafe angesehen. Hingegen soll die Bauknechtin wegen ihres ungeschikte Eindringens in fremden Stall solche bisherige Reden in Gedult ertragen u. sie beederseits data dextra sich als Christ versöhnen. So geschehen.

T. Pfarrer M. Gentner
Salomo Henzler

the possibility of paying for a crime by spending time in jail or forfeiting money or property. After that, no one could bring the matter up again or use it in village argument without being required in turn to render Satisfaction. In a sense, making a written record operated as a way of erasing memory in the everyday domain of oral discourse. Anna Barbara Bauknechtin may well have been following this kind of strategy, but the opening paragraph clearly offers details and expressions which she would hardly have put into a formal complaint.

It may have been the case, however, that she first went to the pastor either to reveal that her "benevolent" magical ritual had gone awry (although she probably would have known that he would have had no sympathy with her) or to complain that everyone was treating her as a witch. The pastor does not appear to have had much interest in dealing with the substance of a conflict between neighbors – he might well have dealt with that elsewhere – but was concerned with confronting superstition in an "open," public forum. He would have asked Anna Barbara to bring her complaint to the consistory or cited her to appear, entering her informal complaint to him as a formal plea.

In its narrative structure, this protocol is like many others. It describes a complaint, records the answer of the defendant, and renders a judgment. The complaint appears to contain more than the plaintiff would have brought forward herself. The "brazen attack" and "wicked assault" were clearly the phrases being bandied about in the round of village gossip. While ostensibly the case is one of Häfner against Bauknechtin, its hidden contest pits public opinion against the pastor, who in writing the protocol expanded Bauknechtin's story to include elements of the wider circulating narrative.

In the second paragraph, the pastor recorded Häfner's defense more or less as if it had been spoken out freely. Yet it moves back and forth between contradictions, which suggests that he was operating on two fronts. He knew this witch had killed his calf, but he also knew that the pastor would not allow him to say it. He inserted his empirical evidence – the healthy calf, the aggressive attack, the magic formula, and the burn marks – but he reinterpreted each element into a Christian framework. What looks like a summary of a testimony is actually the result of a series of questions which the pastor posed: (1) Did you accuse Anna Barbara Bauknechtin of killing the calf? (2) Do you believe she is a witch? (3) Can you prove (*beweisen*) anything against her other than the use of foolish words? (4) What is the proper way for a Christian to suffer a loss? (5) Will you acknowledge that she could not bewitch a calf? Formally, the consistory's procedures combined elements of interrogation and catechism recitation, which juxtaposed planes of experience and doctrine which did not jibe with each other very well.

The parties to the conflict appear to have shifted several times throughout the case. Apparently the issue was first joined by the two women, Anna Barbara and Häfner's wife. As long as the dispute remained at that level, it would have circulated in the village as "Weibergeschwätz" (female gossip), a form of public gossip that neither men nor the pastor would have had to pay formal attention to. While an issue remained in that field, even though public knowledge, no one would have had to go to court to be purged.[64] Once Michel Häfner himself made the accusation, then Bauknechtin could no longer afford to ignore the matter. Nor could the pastor. In formal terms, although the words are not used here, it went from mere *Geschwätz* (gossip) to *Sage* (knowledge) – she was now *ausgeschrieen*. Thus the deeply rooted conflict between two neighbor women entered the court as a contest between one of the women and the other's husband.

The pastor did not take up the general set of issues between the neighbors. Nor did he look at the specific instance of attack and examine the empirical evidence offered by Häfner. He turned the matter into one of ideology and doctrine and used his authority to repress any interpretation of events in a way which escaped God's control and his hermeneutic. The relief which Bauknechtin sought was denied her – the restoration of her reputation – since she had clearly spoken the "foolish" words. Häfner had to publicly disown a belief in witchcraft – that, and not his rumormongering, was what was "wickedly dishonorable" – and nothing was said about his wife's witnessing of the acts, only about their interpretation. The reconciliation was arrived at by treating the issue as one of belief, patience, and acceptance of God's justice and not by investigating the complex issues of real conflict that lay beneath the particular event taken up by the court. Doctrinal conformity and ideological controls rather than mediation were used to impose silence on the two parties.

A second instance which occasioned an appearance before the consistory also involved neighborly conflict.

Because dispute and discord over a suspicion of immorality have arisen between Andreas Feldmeyer and his wife Agnes on the one side and Anna Maria Stärrin and Elisabetha Geigerin on the other, the latter women reported to the parish office that the Feldmeyer house is a house of blasphemy [*Fluchhaus*] in which every day there is much swearing but throughout the year no praying.

Thus it was brought to their hearts and they could not deny that public prayer was not. . . established, but maintained that they prayed nevertheless as much as other people, and as for swearing, with many children it easily happens that one gets irritated and is brought to cursing. As an example, Agnes Feldmeyer was convincingly shown that just in the previous week she had called the pastor's maid, "you thunder gossiping cunt."

To begin with, besides a sharp rebuke because of this indecent, unchristian discourse, she was given a fine to the poor box of 10 Schillinge (22 Kreutzer), and Andreas Feldmeyer was earnestly enjoined to bring his house into better repute, and if in the future it is reported that people do not pray in his house according to Christian order, but swear instead, then each time a stern warning will be undertaken.

[64] See the discussion in Sabean, *Power*, pp. 148–50.

Agnes Feldmeyer took this scandalous departure, which will be punished at another time: she would charge it to the soul of the pastor's maid at the Last Judgment.

Witnessed. M. Gentner, pastor
Schultheiss Johann Georg Rieth
Alt Hans Georg Brodbeck
Johannes Bosch[65]

In this case there seem to have been three separate sets of parties. The elderly Anna Maria Stärrin and Elisabetha Geigerin were disturbed by the noise and strong language issuing forth from the Feldmeyer house and apparently had had bad relations with Andreas and his wife for some time (*Spän* suggests a long-term quarrel or feud). As for the pastor, here was a household which did not come to public prayer services and whose members were content with their own form of private worship. The very fact that they swore a great deal suggests that they were comfortable mediating between themselves and the higher dangerous powers they frequently called upon. And Agnes was sure she was going to get to talk at great length at the Last Judgment without the silencing power of the pastor. Then there was the arena of action on the street, the set of women controlling gossip, setting rumor in motion, commenting on behavior, and contributing powerfully to the construction of reputation and the hierarchy of honor and shame. In this situation, Agnes Feldmeyer and the pastor's maid were two chief contestants, and Agnes's turn of phrase made the issue of gossip the central point. The phrase "thunder gossiping cunt" suggests several possibilities of interpretation. Agnes Feldmeyer's use of "thunder" was unusual for women during the eighteenth century. All of the phrases having to do with the heavens and storms were almost always reserved for men. She was therefore crossing a line and asserting

[65] *Kirchenkonvent*, vol. 2 (18.6.1758)

Nachdem zwischen Andreas Feldmeyer, seinem Weib Agnes und anderntheils Anna Maria Stärrin und Elisabetha Geigerin Spänn u. Hadder wegen liederliche Argwohns entstanden, daß letztere Weiber dem PfarrAmt sollen angezeigt haben, es seye das Feldmeyerische Haus ein Fluch-Haus, darum tägl. viel geflucht, aber das Jahr nie gebettet werde.

So wurde es beeden Zugemüth geführt und könnte nicht läugnen, daß das öffentl. Gebett nicht... [illegible] angesetzt würde, wollten zwar behaupten, sie bäte dannoch so viel als andere Leute, und das Fluche anbelange, so seye es bey vielen Kindern leichtl. geschehen, daß man erzürnt u. zum fluchen gebracht würde. Z. E. wurde die Agnes Feldmeyerin uberzeugt, daß sie erst in voriger Woche zu deß Pfarrers Magd gesagt, du donners schwätzige Foz.

Wegen dieser unzieml. unchristl. Reden wurde das erstenmahl nebst ernstl. Verweiß ihro eine Straf in den armen Kasten von 10 Schilling (22 x) angesetzt, und dem Andreas Feldmeyer ernstl. beditten, daß er sein Haus in bessern Credit setzen solle, u. woferne künfftig eines anzeige würde, daß man in seinem Haus nicht nach christl. Ordnung bette, dargegen aber fluche, so solle allemahl ernstl. Ahndung vorgenommen werden.

Die Agnes Feldmeyerin nahm diesen ärgerlichen Abschied, sie wolle es der Pfarr Magd am jüngsten Gericht auf ihre Seel geben, welches ein anders mahl solle geahndet werden.

T. M. Gentner Pfr.
Schultheiß Johann Georg Rieth
Alt Hannß Georg Brodbeck
Johannes Bosch

power in a sphere women did not usually belong in. We also find words like "asshole," "cunt," "snotnose," and "blabbermouth" frequently used by women against each other in contexts of disputed power and contested social position. As we will argue later, social boundaries appear to have been modeled by bodily ones. The phrase which jumps out so clearly from the text appears to be the pivot around which the narrative turns. Although the story line shifts between three poles – the two neighbor women against the Feldmeyers, the pastor against the Feldmeyers, and his maid against Agnes Feldmeyer – the insult clearly governs the account.

What appears as the occasion of the court citation was hardly the issue. The two old ladies and the Feldmeyers had been on the outs for ages. Neither the swearing nor the church attendance was anything new. What was new was the attack on the pastor's maid and therefore on the honor of his house. He must have taken the occasion of their old complaint to cite the Feldmeyers before the consistory. In his protocol, he adopted a neutral narrative form, suggesting a feud and going on to what the two neighbor women did (went to the parsonage) and said (the Feldmeyers swear and fail to pray). The story holds back the pastor's knowledge and interest until the defendants' answer throws down a challenge to him, at which point he allowed his own issue to emerge from the narrative. The punishment appears to follow from the original complaint, and his honor was restored without himself having entered into the matter as plaintiff. Once the two women carried their gossip to him, he used it to open up the issue and then subtly entered his own complaint and fined the Feldmeyers for that, covering the whole matter in a field of neighborly conflict, which in turn remained unresolved except for instructions to Feldmeyer to get his house in order.

A key term in the protocol is "house." It is never clear who used it at any point in the hearing. Formally, the pastor bracketed the whole protocol with the term. At the beginning was the *Fluchhaus* and at the end an injunction to orderly householding. The conflict itself was between houses – the pastor's maid had been insulted by the Feldmeyers, who with their own house religion were already an affront to the cleric. It is inconceivable that Feldmeyer had not used the common term "house" in his self-confident and elaborate answer to the pastor's charges. But the pastor never ascribed the word to him. "House," as we shall see, was a central term of pastoral sociology and carried with it a significant capacity for ideological assertion and social discrimination. In concealing the real issues of the honor of his house and the uncontrolled independence of the Feldmeyers' house, he did not allow Feldmeyer to speak the word and claim its power.

In the final example, we encounter a family squabble.

On the 20th Sunday after Trinity, the church consistory met.

Johann Georg Zeug is living for quite some time in disunity with his wife, Margaretha, and hits her often, partly because he is incited by the children of his first marriage, and partly because he accuses her of wanting to become lord and master. Accordingly, before the midday church service today, he choked her over the trivial cause of a collar and while his daughter restrained herself, saying she would turn her eyes, pulled her [his wife] around the room by the braids. When she grabbed for his hair, he threw her violently to the ground, so that she received punctures on her head. He then tore her dress from her body and in the presence of the children beat her so badly on the bottom with a switch that she is swollen and has open wounds.

During the hearing, Zeug in no way recognizes his offence nor admits any injustice, despite the fact that he cannot say that his wife attacked him first with words or fist. Therefore he was enjoined under threat of higher punishment not to demonstrate his harshness against his wife but peacefully to show love in a Christian manner. At the same time, his wife is enjoined to carry out her duties in the house for him and is not permitted to run away so long as he does not chase her out and unless he treats her with blows or violent threats without her having given occasion by quarreling and strife. We will report this apparently "desperat" marriage with its circumstances to the Oberamt.

Because of unchristian treatment and scandalous behavior in front of the children, especially since it took place on Sunday, Johann Georg Zeug was fined 1 Pfund heller (43 x) to the poor box.

Although Zeug has earned jail several times over, this time he is let go in the hope of improvement, failing which the punishment is reserved.

Because during the hearing it was shown that the daughter Catharina Zeug tore the dress away from her sister who wanted to give it to the mother to put on and Catharina is already at the wine harvest, it is decided to punish the wickedness of the daughter at the next opportunity.

[A note added at the conclusion:] Catharina Zeugin denied the accusation and is backed by her father and thus let go with a stern lecture and warning for the future from God's Word.

Witnessed. M. Gentner, Pastor
Schultheiss Johann Georg Rieth
Alt Hans Georg Brodbeck
Johannes Bosch[66]

[66] *Kirchenkonvent*, vol. 2 (12.10.1755).

Dom. xx p. Trin würde Kirchen-Convent gehalten.

Joh. Georg Zeug lebt mit seinem Weib Margaretha schon geraumer Zeit uneinig u. schlägt sie öffters theils wegen seiner Kinder erster Ehe auffhezen, theils weil er sie bezüchtigt sie wolle seinen Meister und Herr werden. Gleichwie er sie denn heute vor der Mittags Kirch wegen geringer Ursache eines Göltleins gewürgt, u. da seine Tochter ihre selbst gewehrt, sagend sie verkehre die Auge, sie in die Stube an denen Zöpfe zuschleifft, u. weil sie ihm nach denen Haare gegriffen, sie heftig zu Boden geworffen, daß sie Löcher in den Kopff bekommen, hernach den Rock vom Leib gerissen, u. mit einer Weyden auff den untere Leib in Beyseyn der Kinder so geschlagen, daß sie Schwülen u. offene Wunden am untern Leib bekommen.

Dieweil aber bey dem Verhör der Zeug auff keinerley Weise sein Unfug erkennen, noch unrecht haben wollte, ohnerachtet er nicht sagen kan, daß sein Weib ihn mit Worte oder Faust zu erst angegriffen hätte, so wurde ihm bey höhere Straff aufferlegt, seine Härtigkeit gegen sein Weib nicht mit mehrern Proben zu beweisen, sondern christl. u. friedl. zu leben, gleichwie sein Weib gehalten seye, ihm in dem Haus ihrer Geschäffte zu versehen u. auch nicht darvon lauffen dürffte, wofern er also sie von sich jagen oder ohne daß sie ihm Gelegenheit zum Zank u. Hader gebe, mit Schläge oder heftige Drohworte tractiren werde, so wollen wir diese desperat scheinende Ehe mit Umstände an H. löbl. Oberamt berichten.

This protocol begins with a general statement about continuing conflict between a husband and wife but sets up the conclusion by making the husband's violence the central issue. Without giving voice to any particular person, it balances the points of view of both partners (the problem with her stepchildren – her complaint – and with her attempt to upset proper order in the house – his complaint). The particular offence becomes a metonymy, which suggests the whole course of their familial life: the step-daughter's connivance, the excessive brutality, the vain attempt to assert patriarchal authority. The setting, sketched in with a few words about the impending service and collar, deftly paints a picture of pious preparation for attending church, violently disrupted by Zeug's contrasting and unfitting action. At the consistory hearing, his defense was set aside and whatever justification he offered was dismissed out of hand.

The mediation offered by the court did not quite follow from the narrative: Johann Georg was threatened and Margaretha was warned about such matters as running away, which had not been brought up in the story. There was apparently much more said at the hearing than summarized by the pastor, and there are hints about Margaretha's inattention to her household duties. But the pastor was shaping his account to arrive at two points: sabbath-day desecration and patriarchal authority. The members of the Kirchenkonvent had a clear sense of proper hierarchy, and spanking the wife was well within the prerogatives of the head of the house. The offense lay in reducing the wife, who also had a position of authority, although derivative, to the rank of a child.

A further step was also taken by transcribing the protocol and sending it to the Oberamt. Since it was going to be read there, a justification of leniency was then tacked on to the argument. The whole narrative style represents a typical case of family conflict, from the introductory statement, to the measuring of punishment to fit the story. Relatives and neighbors who may have been involved for some time with the family dynamics do not appear. How the court knew there had been disunity for so long is not told. Why this particular

Wegen dieses unchristl. Tractaments u. gegebenen Ärgernißes denen Kindern zumahl es auch am Sonntag geschehen wurde der Joh. Georg Zeug um 1 lib. heller in armen Kasten gestrafft – 43 x.

Weilen nun der Zeug wohl mehrerer Straffe mit dem Carcere belegt zu werden verdient hätte, so würde er dißmal in Hoffnung der Besserung entlassen, widrigenfalls soll ihm die Straffe vorbehalten seyn.

Weil sich aber ohngefehr unter ihren Certirn ergeben, daß die Tochter Catharina Zeug ihrer Schwester, welche der Mutter den Rock anzuziehen geben wollte, hinweggerissen, u. dieser Catharina bereits im Herbst sich befindet, so wurde auf die nächste Gelegenheit diese bosheit der Tochter zu bestrafen beschlossen.

[added:] Die Catharina Zeugin hat solches abgeläugnet, ist von ihrem Vatter gestärckt mithin mit ernstl Bestraffung u. Vorwarnung wegen des künfftigen auß Gotteswort entlassen worden.

T. M. Gentner, Pfarrer
Schultheiß Johann Georg Rieth
Alt Johann Georg Brodbeck
Johannes Bosch

incident precipitated a court appearance is also not made clear. Perhaps the racket disturbed the neighborhood and produced a sabbath-day scandal, which had to be dealt with for that reason. The form of the story itself did not allow the daughter's action to be incorporated, so it was tacked on at the end.

These three protocols, although typical, do not represent the whole range of such documents. Nonetheless, they do offer examples of the kind of storytelling that we will encounter over and over in this book. The document itself seldom says directly who composed it, although we know from the context of these three cases that they were written by the pastor, whose job was to maintain such records. He even exercised his Latin from time to time as he wrote a clear copy. His presence as an active participant can sometimes be teased out of the structure of the text by the implied catalogue of questions, the arrogance with which evidence was disqualified, the silences imposed upon witnesses, the insertion of his own private interest, and the nature of rebuke and threat. The other members of the consistory remain more shadowy figures but were necessary participants in order for a fine to be levied.

The actual words and phrases used by the participants were seldom recorded, at least there are few grounds for us to assume that they were. However, terms of abuse such as those used by Agnes Feldmeyer in the second case are without any doubt authentic. Whenever a narrative relates what people said or did, we usually find a summary or a particular example, which is meant to reveal a pattern of discourse or behavior. What was put down in a protocol and how it was recorded were the result of complex strategical negotiations. The pastor suppressed information and terminologies which did not fit his representational intentions. Participants offered vivid descriptions or value-laden terms in the hope of having them fixed in the text. Alliances between the pastor and various villagers and tensions between the secular and religious authorities structured the staging of an event before the consistory. Public opinion, gossip, and rumor prepared the situation and made the participants known long before they appeared before the officials. Such considerations will guide our textual readings throughout the book and will be a central part of our first steps in critically examining the ideology of the house and its importance as an idiom of familial and official discourse.

# 3

# The ideology of the house

> The concept of "the household" implies a domestic unit with decision-making autonomy about production and consumption.
>
> – Jane Guyer[1]

This chapter deals with the way people in Neckarhausen conceptualized relations between husbands and wives. The analysis revolves around the word "Haus," which appears in the village records by itself only twice, but occurs in many compounds or other word forms, most frequently as the verb *hausen*. It is the equivalent of the English term "house," and is used in many contexts where we would today employ the word "family." And yet its field of meaning goes well beyond the latter term. Therefore, we need to examine closely the many ways in which it was used. *Familie* itself occurs far less frequently as it did not really become established until well after 1800, mostly in contexts where the need was felt to name an entity rather than describe an action or a role. We will assume that when "natives" used these concepts, they were asserting a view about reality, establishing relations among each other, and making claims about the partition of resources and the distribution of rights. Therefore, in each situation we will want to ask who used particular terms: a wife, a husband, the pastor, the village Schultheiss, or a state official. The sources for most of this investigation are court protocols, which provide a great deal of information about the wider field of action, related assertions of value, and relationships. This material allows us to move from a philological analysis of the words "hausen" and "Familie" in this chapter to an investigation of patterns of conflict between husbands and wives in Chapter 4, where we turn from purely linguistic concerns to the staging of confrontations, what spouses demanded of each other, and how officials expressed the interests of the state and constructed alliances with one or the other marriage partner.

First, we have to distinguish between the villagers' conceptions of "house" and "family" and those of social scientists, many of whom believe that the

[1] Jane I. Guyer, "Household and Community in African Studies," *African Studies Review* 24 (1981): 87–137, here 89.

study of familial matters is best approached through the house or household. They argue that in most European languages, the word "family" developed its present meaning rather late and that many of the world's cultures have no equivalent term. This suggests that comparative studies ought to take the household as their starting point rather than something so filled with assumptions as family. But the reasons for concentrating on the house are varied, so it might be well to review three of the main theoretical traditions which have dealt with it.[2]

The first tradition of note originated in European ethnology or *Volkskunde*. Its earliest formulations are to be found in the work of the nineteenth-century ethnographers, Frédéric Le Play and Wilhelm Riehl.[3] They saw the structure of the family as a continuous, functional whole with a head and dependent members – wife, children, servants, boarders, relatives, and retired people. The salient features of their model were developed from research on noble and large peasant households in which they focused on the dynamics of inheritance, the patriarchal power of the father/manager, and the moral capacities of the collectivity.[4] Some of their other concerns were class endogamy, reproduction of the line, and marriage alliances turning on female endowment. Both Le Play and Riehl stressed that authority and discipline were the key to understanding how the complex unity of the house could be welded together.[5] Above all, the logic of the functioning of what Le Play called the "stem family" (*famille-souche*) and Riehl "das ganze Haus" grew out of the need to maintain the integrity of the patrimony, and that fact also ordered the power relations in the family.[6] Some members had to be sacrificed to the goal of lineal succession and disciplined to collective "responsibility."[7]

2 For an earlier formulation of these issues, see my article, "The History of the Family in Africa and Europe: Some Comparative Perspectives," *Journal of African History* 24 (1983): 163–71.

3 M. Frédéric Le Play, *L'organisation de la famille selon le vrai modèle signalé par l'histoire de toutes les races et de tous les temps* (Paris, 1871); Wilhelm H. Riehl, *Die Naturgeschichte des Volkes als Grundlage einer deutschen Socialpolitik*, 2d ed. (Stuttgart and Augsburg, 1855), vol. 3, *Die Familie*.

4 Riehl, *Familie*, p. 208: "Und zwar wird 'das Haus' hier nicht bloß gedacht als die gegenwärtige Generation, sondern die große historische Kette unserer Familie in Vergangenheit und Zukunft ist es, vor deren Glanz und Macht das Interesse des Einzelnen verschwinden soll"; p. 116: "Die Familie steht unter der natürlichen Obervormundschaft der Eltern und speciell des Familienvaters"; p. 207: "Nun möge aber das Gegenbild folgen, ein Bild der deutschen Art, nach welcher der Mann nicht für sich allein fessellos zu seyn begehrt, sondern seine Freiheit sucht in der Macht und Ehre seines Hauses." Le Play, *Organisation de la famille*, p. 28: "Comme je l'ai indiqué . . . la famille-souche se recommande par le système d'etablissement de ses rejetons. Elle l'emporte sur les deux autres types par le mode adopté pour la transmission du foyer où la famille se réunit, de l'atelier où elle travaille et des biens mobiliers qu'elle creé par l'épargne. Sous ce rapport, la famille-souche offre un excellent terme moyen entre la famille instable qui etablit hors du foyer tous les enfants et la famille patriarcale qui retient dans ce foyer tous les fils, même après leur mariage. Les parents associent à leur autorité celui de leurs enfants adultes qu'ils jugent le plus apte à pratiquer de concert avex eux, puis à continuer après leur mort l'oeuvre de la famille."

5 Riehl, *Die Familie*, p. 118: "Autorität und Pietät sind die bewegenden sittlichen Motive in der Familie." Le Play, *Organisation de la famille*, pp. 6–7: "La principale source du bien se trouve dans certaines familles, soumises par leur tradition à la sévère discipline du respect et du travail."

6 Riehl's description of "Das ganze Haus," although not worked out in the same detail as Le Play's stem family, is clearly structured in the same way – one son follows the father on the same

In the recent ethnographic literature on the dynamics of the house, the contributions of Pierre Bourdieu, reformulating Le Play, and Otto Brunner, updating Riehl, have been widely discussed. Bourdieu studied social reproduction in stem families in Béarn, a region in the Pyrenees, and was particularly interested in practical schemes employed in structuring decisions (*habitus*). Like Le Play, he finds that the logic of the system follows from the need to maintain the integrity of the patrimony:[8]

> To assert that power over the land is indivisible and to place it in the hands of the eldest son amounts to asserting the indivisibility of the land and to making the eldest son responsible for its perpetuation. In short, as soon as we postulate the basic equation that the land belongs to the eldest son and that the son belongs to the land, in other words, that the land inherits its heir, we have established a structure that generates such practices as conform to the basic imperative of the group, namely, the integral perpetuation of the patrimony.[9]

At the heart of the system of practices, patriarchal rule ensured that the goals of property transmission and class endogamy would be carried out. The head of the house defined the claims of each member, controlled information, manipulated "rules," and indoctrinated the children, who emerged with strongly interiorized principles of the tradition and schemes of perception which fitted them for the tasks at hand.[10] The oldest son subordinated his interests to those of the line, and younger sons were socially primed to "embrace the traditional values" and "customary distribution of tasks and powers among brothers."[11] As Bourdieu puts it, "the sociology of the family, which is so

farm, with the household containing several generations living together; *Die Familie*, p. 156: "Das Haus erst ganz ist und auch der ganze Segen des Hauses erst in ihm wohnt, wenn Urahne, Großmutter, Kind und Enkel einträchtig bei einander wohnen und das Gesinde im Hause heimisch wird"; on the same page he discusses the issue of keeping the patrimony together. On pp. 206ff. he discusses the consequences of "individualism," the chief problem for the peasantry being the breaking up of family property. Le Play, speaking of the stem family (*Organisation de la famille*, p. 29), says: "Le testament du père est la loi suprême de la famille pendant le cours de chaque génération."

7 Riehl contrasts French individualism with German personality, rooting the latter in the social relations of the *ganzen Haus; Die Familie*, p. 208: "Ohne Vergleich sittlich tiefer als die modern französische scheint mir freilich die deutsche Auffassung, wonach das Individuum seinen Eigennutz und seine Fessellosigkeit zum Opfer geben soll an das Haus." Le Play, *Organisation de la famille*, p. 113: "En instituant à chaque génération un héritier, la famille-souche agricole ne sacrifie pas l'intérêt des cadets à celui de l'ainé. Loin de là, elle condamne ce dernier á renoncer toute sa vie, en faveur de ses frères, puis de ses propres enfants, au produit net de son travail. Elle obtient le sacrifice de l'intérêt matérial par une compensation tirée de l'ordre moral: par la considération attachée à la possession du foyer paternel."

8 "Marriage Strategies as Strategies of Social Reproduction," trans. Elborg Forster, in *Family and Society: Selections from the Annales*, ed. Robert Forster and Orest Ranum (Baltimore, 1976), pp. 117–44, originally published as "Les stratégies matrimoniales dans le système de reproduction," in *Annales ESC*, 27 (1972): 1105–25; p. 29 n. 18: "The 'right of the eldest' is but the transfiguration of the rights of the patrimony over the eldest."

9 Bourdieu, "Strategies," p. 129.

10 Ibid., pp. 127–9, 131–2, 139.

11 Ibid., pp. 129, 139.

often depicted as based on sentiment, might be nothing but a specific aspect of political sociology."[12]

Otto Brunner borrowed the concept of "das ganze Haus" from Riehl and like him put greater stress on the living unity of the formation and on the nature of its "economic" processes than on the transmission and defense of property as such.[13] In the peasant or noble house, ethical and social life, work, socialization, welfare, and emergency care were all combined in a complex whole. Such a formation, Brunner argued, characterized the basic peasant social grouping from neolithic times to the nineteenth century, although the literature he cited which articulates the ideology comes primarily from the sixteenth and seventeenth centuries.[14] The *Hausvaterliteratur* of that period mixed technical information for the household head with discussions of his relations with parents, spouse, children, and servants and with issues of piety. Apart from the domination (Herrschaft) of the Hausvater, such a set of complex functions could not be held together. Without question, power is the key to Brunner's interpretation of the house:[15]

> All relations of dependence in the house were based on the lord of the house [*Hausherr*], who as the directing head created a whole out of them in the first place. Only the man, who alone according to Aristotle had all of the necessary virtues, is fitted for this. The house [*Oikos*] is a whole which rests on the heterogeneity of its members, who are molded into a unity by the directing spirit of the lord [*Herr*]. Here is revealed the true meaning of the word *Hausvater*. . . . Father [*Vater*] was originally a concept of the legal order, which neither biological nor sentimental aspects sufficed to define. . . .The word in indogermanic languages designated the character of father as lord and master.[16]

Despite all the differences of emphasis and particular problems of focus in the ethnographic tradition represented here, the central element which fashions the collectivity of the house is discipline. However, the argument has been taken in two different directions, represented respectively by Brunner and Bourdieu. Brunner, because he thought of the house as a single, substantial entity, left the concept powerless to deal with questions about historical development or struggle either within households or between them. As far as he was concerned, the Hausvaterliteratur described a reality rather than a program, and he did not understand the representational character of "Haus" for state and church officials bent on hegemonic control through the con-

[12] Ibid., p. 135.

[13] "Das 'ganze Haus' und alteuropäische 'Ökonomik'," in Otto Brunner, *Neue Wege der Verfassungsund Sozialgeschichte*, 2d ed. (Göttingen, 1968), pp. 103–27.

[14] Brunner, "Ganzes Haus," p. 107.

[15] Speaking of the peasant "ganzen Haus" and its economy (*Wirtschaft*), Brunner says ("Ganzes Haus," p. 122): "Ihre innere Struktur und ihr eigentümliches Verhältnis zur Verkehrswirtschaft konnte nur mit Hilfe der Begriffe der modernen Wirtschaftswissenschaft erschlossen werden. Gerade die Anwendung dieser Begriffe hat aber auch gezeigt, daß in ihm notwendigerweise ein im modernen Sinn außerwirtschaftliches, herrschaftliches Moment erhalten ist, ohne dessen Wirksamkeit ein Funktionieren des ganzen Gebildes nicht möglich war."

[16] Ibid., p. 112.

struction of moral hierarchies. Bourdieu provides a more supple tool by concentrating less on aspects of unity than on elements of mediation such as the patrimony. In this way, he is able to sidestep artificial constructs and concentrate on relationships such as father and son or husband and wife and on practices which can be in tension with ideological formations.

Claude Karnoouh points out that the word "family" came to replace "house" in the eighteenth century in reference to the bourgeois domestic group, in contrast to the larger, more complex group formed by the aristocrat.[17] The latter notion served to designate those who lived in "society," the product of matrimonial alliances between aristocratic lineages. Family pointed to particularity, the mere union of two bourgeois holdings. Only in the nineteenth century did it come to be used universally to describe groups of domestic residence. Even today, the villagers he studied in eastern France make a distinction between family (*famille*) and house (*chez* = *in casa*), reserving the former term, in a reversal of meanings, for the wider kinship groupings.

If house tended to die out in the nineteenth century, it was not in fact widely used before the sixteenth. As the most recent survey of the literature makes clear, there was no "prescientific" word in the Middle Ages to designate the particular family at all.[18] The terms "Haus" and "domus" were originally confined to the spatial area covered by buildings. Before philosophers and theologians reconceptualized relationships, these terms never encompassed the domestic group as a unit, although various compound words were developed to designate roles of family members as marriage partners, parents, or brothers. The word *familia* itself included the household slaves or dependent serfs on an estate but, significantly, not the manorial head, his spouse, children, or relatives. For the late Middle Ages, it is still easier to demonstrate the existence of terms which designated wider kin who functioned together – *parentes, parentela, Sippe, Magschaft, Freund, Freundschaft* – than it is to find ones to cover the smaller living community.[19]

Clearly, the development of concepts designating the simple family living together in one dwelling came from the scholarly world, both from philosophy, which developed a theory of the house as a part of a doctrine of the state, and from theology, which was searching for a locus of practical morality. In each case, the starting point was a translation of the *pater familias*, an attempt to grasp a new unity bound together by Herrschaft relationships.[20] Moralists and churchmen described the various elements of marriage, parenthood, con-

[17] "Penser 'maison', penser 'famille': résidence domestique et parenté dans les societés rurales de l'est de la France," *Études rurales*, 75 (1979), pp. 35–75. Karnoouh is leaning on Norbert Elias's discussion of the noble household here. The former's series of articles are important reading for an understanding of peasant family relationships and local power.

[18] Dieter Schwab, "Familie," in *Geschichtliche Grundbegriffe. Historisches Lexikon zur politisch-sozialen Sprache in Deutschland*, ed. Otto Brunner, Werner Conze, and Reinhart Kosellek, vol. 2 (Stuttgart, 1975), pp. 253–301: 255–8.

[19] Ibid., pp. 256–9.

[20] Ibid., pp. 258–9.

sumption, and economy as welded into a unity under the domination of the lord of the house (*Hausherr*). Such a concept developed first in state and church discourse but not until the sixteenth century was it disseminated, especially in religious literature and sermons, to wider groups within the population.[21]

In general, in Central Europe the notion of the "Haus" was rooted in the fiscal needs of the state and the Reformation understanding of practical moral action.[22] In a recent local study devoted to the Hohenlohe region in southwest Germany, Thomas Robisheaux has brought together all the elements of the discourse in the second half of the sixteenth century, showing that the ideological formation underlying the Haus had three converging areas of support.[23] First, the Hohenlohe state was concerned with viable tax units, and during the second half of the sixteenth century officials revised and codified inheritance law and composed cadasters, and by the late sixteenth century succeeded in making the devolution of property a "publicly scrutinized process."[24] Robisheaux concluded that the sixteenth century state was engaged in a long struggle to regulate the property relationships at the center of the peasant family. But the state actually found among the peasants themselves allies willing to express their concerns through the idiom of the "house". The sixteenth-century population increase had brought considerable social differentiation and a consequent struggle on the part of the wealthy to maintain their position through the marriages of their children.[25] They wanted the state to support an extension of patriarchal control over their *Hausgenossen* and heirs. An only too willing and recently regenerated clergy, who were the key link at the local level between the state and the population, offered to strike an alliance with them. During the turmoil of the 1520s, reformers such as Luther had descried a crisis in the family and proposed a paternalist solution to its ills, stressing such values as order and stability. After midcentury they helped found marriage courts to support patriarchal authority over wives and children. Pastors had powerful support for the reform of marriage practices from peasant elders, especially wealthy tenant farmers. Protestantism became linked with making a peasant aristocracy.[26] In the end, the emergence of the patriarchal family conjoined peasant elders, church, and state in a program to preserve peasant property and to maintain the boundaries between the wealthy peasant elite and village poor.

The ideology of the house was formulated in the sixteenth century, with heavy borrowings from the literature of the ancient world, and was elaborated

21 Ibid., p. 259.
22 See my discussion in *Power in the Blood: Popular Culture and Village Discourse in Early Modern Germany* (Cambridge, 1984), pp. 199–209.
23 *Rural Society and the Search for Order in Early Modern Germany* (Cambridge, 1989).
24 Ibid., p. 124.
25 Ibid., pp. 68–91. In the Langenburg district, the wealthiest 20 percent of the population held 44 percent of the wealth in 1528. By 1581, they held 62 percent.
26 Ibid., pp. 95–120. The two sentences should be in quotation marks and are found in the original manuscript on p. 130. I cannot locate the exact wording in the printed version.

by "scientific" discourse long before strong chords were struck in a rural society undergoing sharp social differentiation and a struggle over resources. Brunner's assumptions about Herrschaft are based on the literature of that period, which was the time when the Haus became a crucial idiom of social contention and was continually used by wealthy rural elites as part of their ideological domination of the poor. The "good householder" was practically synonymous with the large, aggressive peasant proprietor, ever ready to throw his weight around and find support among the magistrates for his domination.[27] Das ganze Haus must be seen as part of a representational formation encompassing state and church rule; the struggle between families over prestige, honor, and property; and the establishment of patriarchal authority within the family over wives and children. The ethnographic tradition is right to focus on power as a constituent aspect of the house, but the latter concept itself has proved a weak instrument for the historical analysis of power itself. Most recently, Hermann Rebel in his study of sixteenth and early seventeenth-century Austria, has called into question the notion of the all-encompassing power and decision-making authority of the male household head.[28]

In the second theoretical tradition based on the house, the household is an autarchic unit of production and consumption. This concept has been associated with the economist Karl Bücher and his *Die Entstehung der Volkswirtschaft*, published in 1893.[29] He also formulated a stage theory of history which no longer finds much resonance, but modern historians and anthropologists have found useful his attempt to delineate an "economic" form not based on exchange. For him, the central economic problem was the relation between the production and consumption of goods.[30] He described the precapitalist historical epoch as a period dominated by a "domestic economy," wherein the house was autonomous and produced only for its own needs; the family was not involved in exchange relations and therefore also not in commodity production. In essence, the domestic group restricted its production and consumption activities to the exclusive circle of the household, the character and extent of its production being prescribed by the wants of the members as consumers. In this model, production and consumption are inseparably interdependent and form a single uninterrupted and indistinguishable process. In this case, the basic analytical concepts are "wants," "labor," "production," "means of production," "stores for use," "value in use," and "consumption." There is no division of labor, no capital, no sale of goods, no price, no circulation of commodities, no

[27] See, for example, Sabean, *Power*, pp. 144–73.

[28] Hermann Rebel, *Peasant Classes. The Bureaucratization of Property and Family Relations under Early Habsburg Absolutism 1511–1636* (Princeton, 1983), p. 50.

[29] I have used the 13th edition (Tübingen, 1919) and the English translation of the 3d edition, *Industrial Evolution*, trans. S. Morley Wickett (New York, 1912). Page references will be from the English edition. Later interest in his work can be gauged from Moses Finley, *The Ancient Economy* (Berkeley, 1973) and Karl Polanyi, et al., eds., *Trade and Markets in Early Empires*; see n. 32.

[30] Bücher, *Industrial Evolution*, pp. 88–9.

distribution of income, and no labor wages. Leaning on Rodbertus, Bücher revived the notion of *oikos* (house) husbandry as the unit of such an economic system encompassing both the dwelling place and people carrying on farming in common, each member laboring not for himself but for the pater familias.[31]

Some crities complain that Bücher did not understand the concept of exchange and put too much emphasis on the self-sufficiency of the *oikos* as the central unit of society. Historians such as Brunner, while building on Bücher's idea that the house economy cannot be analyzed in modern economic terms, also fault him for constructing his model of the closed household economy as a simple negation of modern exchange relations.[32] He had erroneously abstracted the house from its relations and activities as part of a wider system.

Like Bücher, the agronomist Chayanov denied the analytical value of neoclassical concepts such as wage labor for the peasant household.[33] He, too, attempted to develop a theory that would explain the relationship of family labor to consumer demands. His model of peasant farm organization, which sees production and consumption flowing together in a single uninterrupted process, is similar to Bücher's autarchic house. However, Chayanov extended peasant farm concepts to households of artisans and cottage industrialists, since their labor expenditure is a function of their demographic dynamics. In his analysis, the global economy did not have the same defining effects attributed to it by Bücher. As Shanin puts it, Chayanov "captured attention by the depiction of peasant farms as an economic form even in an environment dominated by capitalism."[34] Working with the two variables of production and consumption, Chayanov concluded that "self-exploitation" best described the fact that the burden on the worker is a function of the consumer demands of his household.[35]

The two sides of Chayanov's equation, consumption and production (to which he devoted Chapters 2 and 3, respectively, of *Peasant Farm Organization*), work rather differently when one is defining the household, on the one hand, and attempting to assess its dynamics, on the other. On the consumption side, the demand of the household is determined largely by its demographic cycle; on the production side,[36] labor is determined by aggregate output rather than

[31] Ibid., pp. 150–76.

[32] Brunner, "Ganzes Haus," pp. 124–5; see also Pearson's discussion in Karl Polanyi, Conrad M. Arensberg, and Harry W. Pearson, *Trade and Market in Early Empires: Economies in History and Theory* (New York, 1957), pp. 7–8.

[33] A. V. Chayanov, *The Theory of Peasant Economy*, ed. Daniel Thorner, Basile Kerblay, and R. E. F. Smith, foreword by Theodor Shanin (Madison, Wisc., 1986).

[34] Chayanov, *Theory*, p. 3.

[35] Ibid., p. 73.

[36] It was this problem that has been taken up by Hans Medick in his examination of the protoindustrial family and extended by David Levine. Hans Medick, "The Proto-industrial Family Economy: the Structural Function of Household and Family During the Transition from Peasant Society to Industrial Capitalism," *Social History* 1 (1976): 291–315, esp. p. 297; David Levine, *Family Formation in an Age of Nascent Capitalism* (New York, 1977). Both of them argue for the functional dependence between production and demographic reproduction in peasant, artisan, and cottage-industrial families.

by factor costs. This distinction between consumption and production has created a great deal of ambiguity concerning the appropriate criterion for isolating household units in the first place.

To give one example of recent attempts to define the household, the Laslett school has picked on the consumption side for the crucial variables. Laslett himself has been largely concerned with where a person is, not what he or she does – everything but residence (physical, spatial) is put in the category, "attitudinal."[37] The domestic group consists of those who share the same space to eat, sleep, rest, play, grow up, procreate, and bring up children.[38] Above all, he rejects production as a crucial variable, which suggests that he is applying the modern distinction between "public" and "private" to periods and places where it is less than useful. Richard Wall, following Laslett's lead, argues that the "basic building block of society" is the household as a consumption unit based on the provisioning of a fund on which all members of the household may draw. He expressly rejects reformulation of family in terms of elements of social reproduction such as property and transmission. The coresident domestic group marks out the living space that is private to a group of people.[39] Richard Smith, pushing the idea still further, tries to break the organic link between production and consumption altogether.[40] In a rather different manner, Hermann Rebel denies that the "peasant model" with the family making up a "unit of ownership, production, and consumption" is applicable to sixteenth- and seventeenth-century Austria.[41]

By contrast, a number of other observers find production to be the more interesting variable.[42] Jack Goody, for example, argues that the household looks different depending on which criterion is taken and that it is ambiguous because it includes processes and relations of quite different orders.[43] Examining African materials, he points out that consumption groups frequently center on women whereas production groups center on men.[44] In certain situations (matrilineal) in Ghana, the reproductive units, productive units, and units of

[37] Peter Laslett, "Introduction: The History of the Family," in *Household and Family in Past Time*, ed. Peter Laslett with the assistance of Richard Wall (Cambridge, 1972), pp. 1–73; see esp. p. 23.

[38] Laslett, "Introduction," pp. 24ff.

[39] Richard Wall, "Introduction," in *Family Forms in Historic Europe*, ed. Richard Wall in collaboration with Jean Robin and Peter Laslett (Cambridge, 1983), pp. 1–63, here pp. 1–7.

[40] Richard M. Smith, "Some Issues Concerning Families and Their Property in Rural England 1250–1800," in *Land, Kinship and Life-Cycle*, ed. Richard M. Smith (Cambridge, 1984), pp. 1–86, esp. p. 23.

[41] Rebel, *Peasant Classes*, p. 123. "We need to develop a new conceptualization of the collective status of the peasantry that can take into account the high degree of individual economic and social differentiation that existed within the house community, the peasant family, and the surviving forms of community corporations."

[42] Shanin finds Chayanov's analysis of the particular peasant economy of family labor and relative autonomy of its usage to be the center of interest in Chayanov.

[43] Jack Goody, "The Evolution of the Family," in *Household and Family in Past Time*, ed. Peter Laslett (Cambridge, 1972), pp. 103–24, here p. 106.

[44] Goody, "Evolution," p. 111.

consumption are distributed in different dwellings. Ultimately for agricultural societies, economic factors have mainly to do with rights in the means of production, especially in land. Consequently, Goody suggests, the household should be considered a "productive estate."[45] In the hands of most observers, the Chayanov synthesis of production and consumption, which he himself linked together rather uneasily, seems to break apart in favor of one aspect or the other, and it seems clear that the concept of the household fails to capture both sides of the relationship it was designed to grasp.

The question of the analytical usefulness of the concept of the peasant household raises a number of other important issues.[46] The integrity and self-sufficiency of most households in traditional Europe could not have extended to a majority of families in any case. Eighteenth-century figures for Central Europe, for example, show that at least 60 percent of families did not have enough land to feed themselves, which means that their labor was tied to the needs, work schedules, and productive capacities of other families.[47] Depending on the regional situation and the time of year, males or females, adults or children could be absent from home for more or less long stretches of time colporting, begging, laboring, building, repairing, and so on.[48] The food and drinking tabs of building workers at the local tavern were paid for by employers; agricultural laborers received meals; and seamstresses obtained room and board for the few days they worked for a family. Seasonality of employment, insecurity of the labor market, and forced idleness all sent members of a family in different directions and caused them to create temporary and permanent alliances with outsiders. Such a situation makes it difficult to analyze the household as a labor unit. And the consumption schedules of households were complicated by fostering, boarding, outwork, temporary migration, and remuneration in kind. In sum, the concept of the household obscures both the permeability of household economies and the hierarchical dependencies of families on each other.

The analytical power of the household is especially weak for dealing with historical change. Concentrating on questions of structure obscures real shifts within the family itself, such as alterations in the sexual division of labor. In Germany, for example, the agricultural revolution brought massive inputs of female labor into the arable fields. Such a fundamental global change demands proper tools of analysis. Otherwise it will be difficult not only to assess its meaning, but also to be sensitive to its occurrence in the first place. The critical remarks of Jane Guyer can be generalized far beyond her particular frame of reference:

45 Goody, "Evolution," p. 118.
46 See my earlier discussion of the issues in "The History of the Family in Africa and Europe."
47 Friedrich Wilhelm Henning, "Die Betriebsgrößenstruktur der mitteleuropäischen Landwirtschaft im 18. Jahrhundert und ihr Einfluß auf die ländlichen Einkommensverhältnisse," in *Zeitschrift für Agrargeschichte und Agrarsoziologie*, 17 (1969): 171–93.
48 See also Rebel, *Peasant Classes*, p. 50.

With a methodology based on household as a major analytical concept, one cannot look at three critical factors, all of which seem to be changing in Africa today, with very important consequences: the relationship between older and younger men; the relationship between men and women; and the relationships amongst domestic groups in situations where wealth or control of resources vary widely.[49]

The notion of the household is a substantialist concept that sees the farm family as a total unity rather than a locus of complex alliances and reciprocities. In fact, the household represents an alliance between a husband and wife, and if the notion is to be useful for historical purposes, it must capture the changing terms of that alliance from class to class and over time. Furthermore, the domestic group is also part of a larger set of reciprocities involving rich and poor, the wider kin group, and neighbors. Richard Smith, in summing up the evidence for late medieval England, describes "the extent to which at various points along a spectrum of land holding sizes the household economy was rarely the unit of production and consumption and was structurally linked with other economies through commodity and non-commodity relations."[50] If we pursue the implications of this idea, then the important factors are the relationships of family members to kin, neighbors, pastors, state agencies, schools, doctors, and the like.

Finally, the Bücher/Chayanov approach to the house obscures the facts of exploitation both inside the family and between households. Chayanov stressed the self-exploitation of the house as a whole, but that suggestion remains historically flat if the surrounding economic structures, particular demographic regimes, and the facts of domination are not taken into account. Historians such as Hans Medick have sought to understand how reciprocities between husbands and wives alter under changing structures of production.[51] His work on consumption and expenditure among protoindustrial producers raises important questions about differential male and female views of the household.[52] He called attention, for example, to patterns of conspicuous expenditure and lack of saving and analyzed changes in drinking practices

[49] Jane Guyer, "Household," p. 91.

[50] Smith, "Some Issues," pp. 30–1. Smith draws the wrong conclusions from his own theoretical point and ends up with a picture of each household being a node for individuals characterized by raw strategy. Jane Guyer suggests that a heavy emphasis on negotiability does not provide any point for comparative study. She argues that it is important to analyze constraints and sanctions in terms of the rights and duties embedded in complex groupings beyond the household, particulary in kin groups, even though from place to place, class to class and over time the connections will vary and have different purposes and consequences. See Guyer, "Household and Community," p. 93. Furthermore, Smith's theoretical position here underlies the analysis of Miranda Chaytor ("Household and Kinship") despite his and Houston's contrary analysis; Rab Houston and Richard Smith, "A New Approach to the Family?," *History Workshop Journal* 14 (1982): 120–31. See n. 50.

[51] Medick, "The Proto-industrial Family Economy."

[52] Medick's discussion of plebeian culture can be found in Peter Kriedte, Hans Medick, and Jürgen Schlumbohm, *Industrialisierung vor der Industrialisierung, Gewerbliche Warenproduction auf dem Lande in der Formationsperiode des Kapitalismus*. Veröffentlichungen des Max-Planck-Institut für Geschichte (Göttingen, 1977), pp. 138–54. An expanded discussion, "Plebejische

within "plebeian" culture in the eighteenth and nineteenth centuries. He asks in what way men and women viewed the production process and the use of earnings differently. If we subscribe to the theory that protoindustrial production involved increasing degrees of self-exploitation, it does not tell us whether the burden fell equally on the husband and wife. In any event, this kind of analysis suggests issues for social history about the differing perceptions of men and women toward the exchanges which take place inside the family – whether women produced and reproduced for a household economy or for some other end, or whether their own strategies were more complex than we are used to thinking. Perhaps the simple questions posed by Meillassoux should be our point of departure: Who works with and for whom, where does the laborer's product go, and who controls the product?[53]

The third theory of the "house" or "household" comes from historical demography, which has links with the other two traditions. One of its proponents is Peter Laslett, who was bothered by Le Play's assumption that the stem family is a widespread phenomenon and by the sociological myth that the history of the family reflects a progressive narrowing down of household size and structure.[54] Laslett was a member of the Cambridge Group for the History of Family and Social Structure, which rightly argued that the purely demographic research on families being carried on in France at the time had to be coupled with meaningful sociological questions before an appropriate concept of the household could be developed. Yet the "household," as it emerged from Laslett's analysis, was a unit largely abstracted from social processes. In the first place, he failed to recognize that the household lists he concentrated on were generated within the system of domination and were themselves strategic instruments of the exercise of power. They were tax lists or documents to be used for poor-law settlement, whose meaning cannot be dissociated from the fact that they served the interests of the tax collector, the rate payer, the state, or the church. Above all, they were generated in particular contexts of surplus extraction. Any lists created by the authorities ought to be considered first as strategic representations of social reality.

A second problem with demographic analysis is its statistical/structural approach, which, as Miranda Chaytor has pointed out, leaves the "content of social relations, both within households and between them, largely unexplored."[55] She argues that a close analysis of particular household lists,

Kultur, plebejische Öffentlichkeit, plebejische Ökonomie. Über Erfahrungen und Verhaltensweisen Besitzarmer und Besitzloser in der Übergangsphase zum Kapitalismus" is in Robert Berdahl, et al., eds., *Klassen und Kultur. Sozialanthropologische Perspektiven in der Geschichtsschreibung* (Frankfurt, 1982), pp. 157–204.

53 Claude Meillassoux, "From Reproduction to Production. A Marxist Approach to Economic Anthropology," *Economy and Society* 1 (1972): 93–105, here p. 98.

54 The first major publication was Laslett, ed., *Household*. This has been supplemented by Richard Wall, ed., *Family Forms*.

55 Miranda Chaytor, "Household and Kinship: Ryton in the Late 16th and Early 17th Centuries," *History Workshop Journal* 10 (1980): 25–60, here p. 26.

supplemented with other available data, shows that the boundaries between households were permeable and continually breaking down as people and property were constantly being redistributed between them. The particular kind of dependence being considered – producing, consuming, socializing – draws different boundaries and provides different kinds of links.[56]

Attempts to isolate the household statistically and structurally are based on assumptions about strategies of decision making. Laslett sets out to find a single isolable unit for which decisions apply to one and all.[57] He excludes children who have left home, nearby kin and affines even if they collaborate in productive work, and retired members who live separately even when supported by the family estate. The concept of the "household," as Jane Guyer succinctly puts it, "implies a domestic unit with decision-making autonomy."[58] The lack of fit between this conceptual move and reality has led most recent observers to the more flexible view that households should be considered from several aspects: production, distribution, transmission, reproduction, and coresidence.[59] Such a procedure leaves open both the question of where decision making is located and with respect to what. Even coresidence loses its power of definition where "the moral imperative of kinship and reciprocal obligation that flourish in the household context" allow a "household to operate effectively with some members who are not coresident for extended periods of time."[60]

The approaches discussed in the preceding paragraphs imply that the household is an individual thing which can be classified into types, and that each type has a specific quantifiable and comparative dimension. We cannot hope to understand much about societies by creating taxonomies of household types, since the relationships at the heart of social processes are thereby washed out of the picture. A valid concept of the "house" must (1) allow for a historical analysis of power, (2) account for hierarchical dependencies of families on each

[56] This is a point made by Jack Goody in his article in the original Laslett volume; "Evolution of the Family", pp. 119ff. It is also cogently argued in an important article by Claude Karnoouh: "Penser 'maison', penser 'famille'," pp. 41–2. Jane Guyer quotes Hoyt Alverson as saying: "The fabric of a rural life composed of systematic alliances *among* households, lineages and other institutions will be masked by a research methodology that defines *a priori* the household as an independent sampling unit," "Household and Community," p. 101; Hoyt Alverson, "Arable Agriculture in Botswana: Some Considerations of the Traditional Social Formation," *Rural Africana* 4–5 (1979): 33–47, here p. 41.

[57] Laslett, "Introduction," p. 27. Richard Wall, "Introduction," p. 12, makes this point explicit: "To include nonresidents in the household will give rise to problems with the concept of the household, which implies at least a certain measure of co-residence as well as dependence on a common budget." The ultimate conclusion has been drawn by Alan Macfarlane who finds in particularized decision making the roots of English individualism; *The Origins of English Individualism: The Family, Property and Social Transition* (New York, 1979), pp. 64, 77, 83, 85.

[58] Jane Guyer, "Household," p. 89.

[59] Richard R. Wilk and Robert McC. Netting, "Households: Changing Forms and Functions," in *Households. Comparative and Historical Studies of the Domestic Group*, ed. Robert McC. Netting, Richard R. Wilk, and Eric J. Arnould (Berkeley, 1984), pp. 1–28, here pp. 6ff. This volume is important reading for anyone interested in the concept of the "household."

[60] Wilk and Netting, "Households," p. 19.

other, (3) lead to an understanding of the social context of alliances and reciprocities, (4) take into account varying strategies of different family members and the location of different strands of support to "outsiders", (5) recognize the changing terms of alliance between husbands and wives, (6) deal with the representational and strategic character of lists, and (7) treat the issue of decision making as a problem.

"House" was an important concept to the villagers we want to study. They, of course, used it only in practical, everyday situations. As we have suggested, their adoption of the term has a specific history, which we are only beginning to understand, but which cannot be considered outside the system of state domination. There was a significant dialectic involved between pastoral propaganda and official policy, on the one hand, and local representations, intravillage struggle, and resistance to authority, on the other. Social stratification and gender are important aspects to consider in the analysis of discourse about the house. We have looked at current scientific notions critically, but we can also turn to our villagers for another critical focus. In the rest of this chapter, we will examine as closely as possible the language of house and family as we find it protocolled in the village court records before returning to a renewed reflection on our own theoretical practice.

## Hausen

Our purpose in this book is not to present a definitive study of the notion of the house. The economic and demographic structures will have to be treated in a separate volume. Our analysis of the house as a social formation begins with the way villagers and some of the local and state authorities used the term and its compounds. Therefore, our primary concern is linguistic elements and representations, and for the moment, ways of framing discourse abstracted from the context of action, which itself will be taken up in due course. We have already suggested that the house was a central idiom for expressing values, making claims, allocating blame, and struggling over resources. We will see that its use was always strategic and continually touched on issues of hierarchy, exchange, reciprocity, right, and obligation. It seems to me that the importance of the issues warrants extended treatment, which means taking up every occurrence of the different forms of the words "house" and "family" in the 8,000 or so village court protocols. The parts of the following text which are italicized can be read as a kind of lamentation, the pointillist style of which is designed to offer one form of impression of family life, which will be paralleled and supplemented by other techniques and styles throughout the book.

Note that the choice of terms varied from court to court. During the eighteenth and part of the nineteenth century, there were two main village courts, the church consistory (Kirchenkonvent) and the Gericht (court), which sometimes sat as a semiannual Ruggericht (court of complaint) and sometimes in ad hoc sessions to handle matters as they arose.[61] There was a court of higher instance in the town of Nürtingen, the Oberamtsgericht, but its records are only available for 1801 onward and are in various miscellaneous volumes. None of them contain details of actions after 1824.[62] Beginning in 1830, the office of the Schultheiss (Schultheißamt) acted as an administrative court in the village, protocolling complaints, levying fines, and reporting to the Oberamt.[63] Throughout the period, the Vogt, or Oberamtmann, held a triennial court (Vogtruggericht) in the village.[64] We will give more details about what each court dealt with. Suffice it to say here that the church consistory was the main forum for family disputes until about 1840, when the Office of the Schultheiss took over such cases. All along, some family quarrels ended up in the secular village court, especially those dealing with husbands not working. Certain difficult cases from all of the village courts (such as repeated drunkenness and failure to work, divorce, and the like) were protocolled at the village level first, but reported to the district court (Oberamtsgericht). The protocols of the church consistory were kept by the pastor, while those of the village Gericht were kept by a secular official, probably a town clerk in the early eighteenth century, but later on by the Schultheiss, who, of course, kept the records of the Schultheißamt. After each case mentioned in the following discussion, a letter with a date appears in parentheses, which will serve to mark the cases from the various courts and keep the temporal order straight: K = church consistory (Kirchenkonvent), G = village court (Gericht), S = Schultheißenamt, V = Vogtruggericht, O = Oberamtsgericht, and SK = Skortationsbuch (a separate register of illegitimate pregnancies, begun in 1822).[65]

As already mentioned, the word Haus appears only twice in all of the court records. We have already encountered the reference to the Feldmeyers' *Fluchhaus* (house of blasphemy) and the injunction to Andreas to bring his Haus in

[61] The minutes of the *Kirchenkonvent* are preserved in the *Pfarramt* in Neckarhausen and are bound in four volumes. Only volume 1 is consistently paginated. The date of the first entry is 11 May 1727 and the last, 31 October 1849. Altogether the volumes contain approximately 1,300 cases. The protocols of the village court are contained in 16 volumes from the first, dated 9 June 1746, through 1869, amounting to more than 4,400 "cases." (In some instances, several couples appeared before the court on the same day for separate but similar business reasons – e.g., to file a mortgage. I have counted such appearances as one case.) The complete series is housed in the village *Rathaus*. Not all of the volumes are consistently paginated.

[62] These volumes are found in the Württembergisches Hauptstaatsarchiv in Ludwigsburg (STAL) under the *Bestand* numbers F190 and F190II, numbered by *Band*: 9–11, 257–74. The first entry from volumes 9–11 for Neckarhausen residents was 3 January 1801 and the last, 19 August 1816. The first entry for volume 257 is 14 March 1817, and the last from volume 274, 4 June 1852. After 1823, lengthy protocols are seldom to be found, which means that these records only supplement those from the village in any detailed way for the period 1801 to 1823.

[63] These records are contained in three foliated volumes for the period beginning on 4 November 1839 through 1869 (last entry 23 November). They are housed in the village *Rathaus*.

[64] There are two volumes of the protocols of the *Vogtruggericht* in the village *Rathaus*. The first entry is 1 December 1747 and the last, 24 May 1867. Both volumes are foliated.

[65] The one-volume *Skortationsbuch* has 149 entries from the period 13 December 1822 to 2 March 1869. It is housed in the *Rathaus*.

order (K-1755).[66] In a case of a broken engagement, Caspar Fischer from Neckartailfingen testified that when the prospective bride was proposed to him, he said, "Wenn da so sey dass sie sich getreu sein Haus vorzustehen, wie es einer Frau zukomme, so sey es ihm recht" (If she would faithfully manage his house, as is fitting for a wife, then he was willing) (K-1747).[67] This verbal contract was made in the presence of her relatives and simply refers rather generally to her housewifely duties.

The most frequently used word form in which house appears in the records is the verb, hausen. It was the main term used to denote both the economic and physical side of marriage. Its basic meaning is to carry on a household or live together in a household (*Mit den Toten kann man net hausen* – You can't live with the dead). By extension, the word can be used to mean "manage" or get along together (*Mit dem kann man net hausen* – You can't get along with him). Living together as neighbors can prompt the word "hausen" (*Mit den Nachbarn muss man hausen* – You have to get along with the neighbors). One of the most direct meanings of the word is to live together in marriage (*Hausest du schon?* — Are you already married?). Finally, hausen means to carry on the economy of a household well, to save. Let us look at the uses of the term in chronological order.

*Conflict between husband and wife or between families often arose over the economic capabilities or attention to work of the husband. In an early example, David Falter's mother-in-law said he did not* hausen *(work) as he should (K-1743).*[68] *Mathew Falter's wife complained he beat her daily. She could not hausen (live) with him anymore (G-1799).*[69] *Johann Georg Riempp got into a fight with Johann Georg Falter, which the village cop (Fleckenschütz) broke up, hitting them both on the hands with his stick. Riempp then let loose and called him a "Traubendieb, Spitzbub, Hurenjäger, was machst du noch hausen" (grape thief, scoundrel, whore chaser, and whatever else you do) (G-1783).*[70] *Salomon Bauknecht reported that his bride of seven months had not come to live with him (K-1806).*[71] *She did not want to* hausen *with him. Margaretha Grauer's husband called her a* Hur *because he resented being told that he did not* hausen *(pay attention to his work). He refused to* hausen *(live) any longer with her (K-1808).*[72] *Johannes Bosch, caught up in divorce proceedings, maintained that he paid attention to his* Haushaltung *(work) and* Güterbau *(farming) (O-1809).*[73] *Since his wife was the one who left, she had to seek a divorce because he could not* hausen *(manage) alone. In a curious case, Anna Maria Renzler, wife of Johann Wilhelm, said she could no longer* hausen *with him, although she never had lived with him and claimed her parents promised she could live at home during the*

66 See Chapter 2; *Kirchenkonvent*, vol. 2 (12.10.1755).
67 *Kirchenkonvent*, vol. 2, p. 6 (30.8.1747).
68 *Kirchenkonvent*, vol. 1, p. 124 (6.10.1743).
69 *Gericht*, vol. 5, f. 133 (14.1.1799).
70 *Gericht*, vol. 3, f. 137 (1.9.1783).
71 *Kirchenkonvent*, vol. 3 (6.11.1806).
72 *Kirchenkonvent*, vol. 3 (20.11.1808).
73 *Oberamtsgericht*, HSAL, F190, Band 9, f. 460 (22.3.1809).

*first two years of marriage (O-1809).*[74] *Even though she was unwilling to go to her husband, she would not seek a divorce before the two years were up. In the higher court dealing with the divorce case of Salomon and Maria Agatha Bauknecht, she said she would not* hausen *with him (O-1809).*[75] *Again before the court she refused to continue to* hausen *(O-1810).*[76] *Johann Georg Lötterle could not* hausen *with his wife because she constantly brought up the subject of his wealth and did not allow him authority over her children (K-1812).*[77] *Mathes Häfner was caught breaking into his brother Georg's house. He said that Georg's wife* haust übel *(got along badly) with her husband (G-1817).*[78] *Maria Magdalena Zeug left her husband because he was driving them all into penury* (an den Bettelstab) *(K-1818).*[79] *She could not* hausen *with him, and he complained about her* Haushaltung. *Rebecca Häfnerin was separated from Michael. She did not want to* hausen *with him (K-1819).*[80] *Rebecca Feldmeier complained that her husband had been drinking for fifty-six days and no longer* hausten *(worked) (G-1821).*[81] *Katharina Falter said she could no longer* hausen *with her husband (G-1821).*[82] *She had always shown him love as long as she* hause *with him. Bernard Dieterle's wife reported she was willing to* hausen *(go back to live) with her husband (K-1821).*[83] *Maria Catherina Hentzler asked the court to ascertain why her husband no longer wanted to* hausen *in a way that befitted married people (G-1822).*[84] *She said she carried out all her duties and suppressed all comments on his shortcomings, but he alleged that she had started scolding* (schelten) *a year after the marriage and he had taken everything quietly so far. Barbara Bauknecht said it would be in vain to* hausen *with her husband (K-1823).*[85] *Michael Hentzler said he no longer wanted to* hausen *with his wife since she started talking about divorce (O-1823).*[86] *Johann George Waldner was asked why he so* übel hauset *(got along so badly) with his wife (K-1825).*[87] *He said she was hostile* (feindselig) *and scolded. Johann Georg Zeug's wife said she could no longer* hausen *with her husband because she was mistreated by her stepchildren (G-1826).*[88] *Margaretha Deuschle complained that her husband did not work, ran around, scolded, and swore, and tried to kill her (K-1833).*[89] *He called her a* Hur *and left home. He said "Sie sollen wie es recht sei mit ihm hausen, dann werde er wieder zu ihr gehen" (she should get along with him properly, then he would return). Mathias Ebinger complained that after a while his wife* gar nimmer gehaust *(never*

[74] *Oberamtsgericht*, HSAL, F190, Band 9, f. 481 (17.7.1809).
[75] *Oberamtsgericht*, HSAL, F190, Band 9, f. 366 (23.10.1809).
[76] *Oberamtsgericht*, HSAL, F190, Band 9, f. 389 (4.2.1810).
[77] *Kirchenkonvent*, vol. 3 (19.2.1812).
[78] *Gericht*, vol. 9, f. 14. (18.7.1817).
[79] *Kirchenkonvent*, vol. 3 (8.1.1818).
[80] *Kirchenkonvent*, vol. 3 (26.9.1819).
[81] *Gericht*, vol. 10, f. 10 (20.6.1821).
[82] *Gericht*, vol. 10, f. 15 (6.8.1821).
[83] *Kirchenkonvent*, vol. 4 (13.3.1821).
[84] *Gericht*, vol. 10, f. 48 (16.4.1822).
[85] *Kirchenkonvent*, vol. 4 (8.3.1823).
[86] *Oberamtsgericht*, HSAL, F190, Band 259, f. 325 (28.7.1823).
[87] *Kirchenkonvent*, vol. 4 (27.6.1825).
[88] *Gericht*, vol. 11, f. 29 (6.10.1826).
[89] *Kirchenkonvent*, vol. 4 (22.4.1833).

*worked at all) (K-1833).*[90] *Johannes Hentzler said he could not* hausen *with such a bad person as his wife, Christina Margaretha (K-1839).*[91] *She did not pay attention to the* Hauswesen *(household obligations). Christina Margaretha Hentzler complained that her husband* übel hause *from the beginning because her wealth was too small (K-1842).*[92]

Apparently the verb hausen was readily used by the villagers mainly in the period 1806 to 1842. That is to say, the protocolled use of the term was largely confined to that period. There was one use of hausen (in the sense of "to live together") in 1743, but then not again for 65 years. We will see a few other occurrences in the eighteenth century, when it was used by the pastor or the magistrates, which suggests that the term in its varied range of meanings already had common currency. But the sudden burst of use in the first four decades of the nineteenth century carried with it a distinctly normative accent. It was used to criticize a spouse or to suggest that cohabitation or continuation of a marriage was in doubt. In the entire set of records, the word occurred 33 times; in 25 of these instances it was used by villagers and in 8 by magistrates. Six of the times associated with magistrates occurred in the eighteenth century. In all but one of the instances where villagers used the term, a marital conflict was at issue, whereas the official use was not at all rooted in such a context. In other words, hausen came to be the popular term precisely when a house was put into question, either when one of the spouses was destroying the substance of the family or the couple was breaking up. Many marital squabbles and cases of severe conflict occurred in the eighteenth century without it becoming central in verbal exchange between marriage partners, nor had one or the other spouse described the situation to the magistrates with its use. After hausen was introduced as a significant part of discourse during what we will show was a period of crisis, it practically disappeared again by 1840. Indeed, only the church consistory records its use after 1831. At the end of the decade, when marital conflicts came under the jurisdiction of the Schultheiss's office, the word vanished completely from the records, except for one last recorded use, in 1842, still in the church consistory protocols. It may be that the pastor, keeping the consistory minutes, chose to substitute an already archaic expression for some other phrasing actually used by the villagers – for example, he noted the term *fortleben* (to continue to live with) in the 1820s (K-1828).[93] Or perhaps his ear picked it out, while the secular officials no longer heard it. In any event, the strongly critical use of the term in reference to managing or carrying on one's affairs comingled with its sense of living together during a period when divorce or separation frequently occurred. As we shall see in the next several chapters, this period of crisis in marriage seems to have ended in the late 1830s. The recorded expression was used by women

[90] *Kirchenkonvent*, vol. 4 (31.7.1833).
[91] *Kirchenkonvent*, vol. 4 (27.6.1839).
[92] *Kirchenkonvent*, vol. 4 (20.9.1842).
[93] *Kirchenkonvent*, vol. 4 (24.2.1828).

twice as often as by men, and even when men did use it, they often introduced it in reaction to the arguments already brought forward by their wives. This suggests that women or the writers of the protocols selected as a critical tool an expression, which, we shall see, was endowed with patriarchal and state authority.

In the eighteenth century, most of the times when the magistrates used the term hausen by itself, it was to emphasize the marital couple as a working and productive unit. The village was worried about the problem of a newly married couple founding a viable economic enterprise. Their concern had to do with sharing scarce resources, whether in reference to the use of the village commonland or community support of the poor.

*When Carl Ferdinand Fausel, a journeyman carpenter* (Zimmergesell) *from Nürtingen, became engaged to Dorothea Schach and wanted to become a Bürger of Neckarhausen, the council noted that he would have difficulty making a living (G-1779).*[94] *If they could not* hausen *(manage successfully), they would end up as a burden to the village. Another man petitioned in 1780 for Bürgerrecht, pointing out that the woman he wanted to marry was pregnant (G-1780).*[95] *His petition was denied because there were already many poor Bürger in the village who could not* hausen *(manage). Jacob Klein petitioned for his son-in-law to get Bürgerrecht in Neckarhausen (G-1798).*[96] *The whole council was against it because the village was full of Bürger and the couple could* hausen *better in Raidwangen, where they then lived. Michael Friess used to* hausen *(live) in Neckarhausen but after the death of his wife, he left (G-1808).*[97] *Now he was too old to care for himself and had returned. A council ordinance was established that each Bürger was to plant two trees when he began to* hausen *(set up an independent household) (G-1826).*[98]

The verb hausen was also occasionally used to mean behave in a general sense, beyond its more limited connotation of managing affairs or maintaining diligence.

*Johann Georg Falter said he was struck during an altercation with old Johann Waldner in the tavern. Waldner refused to admit it and was dismissed with a warning to* hausen *(behave) better (K-1748).*[99] *Ulrich Häfner and his wife Barbara and Andreas Köpple and his wife were referred to as "beide beisammenhausende Ehepaare" (married couples living with each other) (K-1751).*[100] *Barbara complained that Andreas Köpple's wife accused her of adultery. Köpple had come home drunk 10 days previously and met Barbara sitting outside on the stairs breaking flax. He put his hand under her apron and his finger into her vagina, whereupon she yelled to let her go. Köpple's wife came to the window just as he removed his hand. Although Andreas*

[94] *Gericht*, vol. 3, f. 201 (4.2.1779).
[95] *Gericht*, vol. 3, f. 15 (26.7.1780).
[96] *Gericht*, vol. 5, f. 89 (27.2.1798).
[97] *Gericht*, vol. 7, f. 33 (25.2.1808).
[98] *Gericht*, vol. 11, f. 19 (28.8.1826).
[99] *Kirchenkonvent*, vol. 2, p. 22, (21.12.1748).
[100] *Kirchenkonvent*, vol. 2, p. 69 (15.10.1751).

*Köpple had not done right and Barbara Häfner could have defended herself better, the consistory did not consider the case one of adultery. Köpple was put in jail to warn him to* hausen *(behave) more sensibly* (vernünftiger). *So closely tied up with his house, a man who frequented the taverns excessively and wasted his substance was an* Aushauser. *Johannes Rieth, "wegen vertunischen Leben und Aushausens willen" (because of a wastrel life and running around), was given four weeks in jail (G-1769).*[101]

Hausen was a multivalent word which sometimes expressed general behavior and could be used by the local magistrates to restore order and call a delinquent to book. But just because it was a lexical item with generally agreed upon signification did not mean that it was on everyone's lips. The very fact that it became so useful during a short period suggests alterations in the terms of reciprocity between husbands and wives. The house posed a new set of problems, and while a superficial view based on adding up the number of people physically present in a dwelling or around a hearth or in the sitting room or at the evening table might show no change, those who lived together reflected on their new relationships in agitated tones. Their recorded language circled around issues of producing for each other, balancing relative contributions to a complex enterprise, wielding authority, and exercising self-discipline. Their view of house involved a constant negotiation about the terms of alliance, which a mere concentration on terminology covers over, but which we will attempt to tease from all the sources available.

The most frequent form of Haus besides hausen found in the records is *Haushaltung*. It was often used in the sense of "household," or the people who live together as a group in a house. But a Haushaltung was also something that a person could possess or carry on, either in the general sense of household economy or management or in the more restricted one of housekeeping. Used as an activity or attribute, it usually did not refer to a common element of a collectivity but designated the area of competence of an individual. Occasionally reference might be made to the Haushaltung of a couple, but usually what was at issue was the management or diligence of a particular spouse.

*Barbara Petermann agreed to a mortgage taken out by her husband as the best for her* Haushaltung *(economy) (G-1751).*[102] *Reference was made to the* liederliche und verschwenderische Haushaltung *(disorderly and wasteful management) of Salomon Häussler (V-1755).*[103] *The schoolmaster wanted to quit and concentrate more on his* Haushaltung *(K-1756).*[104] *When Agnes Hess accused the pastor's widow of being a witch, Margaretha Bosch said that the old woman had a better* Haushaltung *and took special care of her animals (K-1756).*[105] *Andreas Köpple's wife accused him of drinking excessively and not caring for his* Haushaltung *(K-1757).*[106] *Johann Holpp said*

101 *Gericht*, vol. 1, p. 204 (22.11.1769).
102 *Gericht*, vol. 1, f. 40 (30.7.1751).
103 *Vogtruggericht*, vol. 1, f. 93 (22.2.1755).
104 *Kirchenkonvent*, vol. 2 (23.4.1756).
105 *Kirchenkonvent*, vol. 2 (27.12.1756).
106 *Kirchenkonvent*, vol. 2 (6.11.1757).

*he was talked into an engagement with Margaretha Hentzler, widow of Johann Georg, because of her need to have the* Haushaltung *taken over (K-1762).*[107] *Johannes Thumm was summoned to the parsonage "wegen seines übelen auf führens, zechens, und Sauffens halben, Verachtung des Gottesdiensts, und schlimmen Haushaltung daheim" (G-1763).*[108] *Ten* Haushaltungen *(households) of women* (Weiber) *applied for a church bench (K-1769).*[109] *In a dispute over thievery, it was noted that the two* Haushaltungen *in question baked with each other (G-1772).*[110] *Heinrich Pfaudler complained that the upper village* Haushaltungen *went through his field (G-1774).*[111] *The Köpple* Haushaltung *was forbidden to trespass on Johann Georg Speidel's land when leaving their kitchen (G-1775).*[112] *The brothers Johann Georg and Michael Häussler petitioned to be allowed to build a new sitting room* (Stube) *and chamber* (Kammer) *in the stall because of conflicts arising in their* Haushaltungen *(G-1780).*[113] *Wood was scarce, so two* Haushaltungen *which shared one sitting room* (Stube) *were to get only one and a half times the normal share of kindling from the village forest (G-1781).*[114] *Several men, living in houses with three* Haushaltungen, *petitioned for permission to build extensions (G-1793).*[115] *Johannes Bosch maintained against his wife's testimony that he did pay attention to his* Haushaltung *and* Güterbau *(farming) (O-1809).*[116] *The court stated that if Johannes Rieth continued to carry on his* Haushaltung *in the manner he now did, he would go through his property in three years (G-1798).*[117] *And reference was made to the* unordentliche Haushaltung *(disorganized management) of the village in a case leading to the resignation of the Bürgermeister and the suspension of three councillors (V-1813).*[118] *Johann Georg Zeug complained his wife did not do the* Haushaltung *(housekeeping) (K-1818).*[119] *She had her clothes sewn in other houses and could not prepare a meal on time. Maria Agnes Falter reported herself pregnant. She was without parents and had her own* Haushaltung *(SK-1830).*[120] *Mathias Häfner answered his wife's complaints by saying he had always taken care of his business and kept his* Haushaltung *in order. He scolded and beat her only when her* Haushaltung *did not please him (K-1831).*[121] *Margaretha Deuschle complained her husband had stopped his* Haushaltung *(K-1836).*[122] *Christina Rieth was told by the Schultheiss to end her scolding and decide "ihr Haushaltung mit Nutzen vorzustehen" (to manage her household profitably)*

107 *Kirchenkonvent*, vol. 2 (18.11.1762).
108 *Gericht*, vol. 1, f. 145 (29.3.1763).
109 *Kirchenkonvent*, vol. 2 (4.5.1769).
110 *Gericht*, vol. 2, f. 23 (29.7.1772).
111 *Gericht*, vol. 2, f. 85 (28.12.1774).
112 *Gericht*, vol. 2, f. 113 (28.12.1775).
113 *Gericht*, vol. 3, f. 6 (20.3.1780).
114 *Gericht*, vol. 3, f. 52 (28.2.1781).
115 *Gericht*, vol. 4, f. 222 (5.2.1793).
116 *Oberamtsgericht*, HSAL, F190, Band 9, f. 460 (22.3.1809).
117 *Gericht*, vol. 5, f. 84 (2.1.1798).
118 *Vogtruggericht*, vol. 2, f. 54 (30.9.1813).
119 *Kirchenkonvent*, vol. 3 (8.1.1818).
120 *Skortation*, f. 7 (12.7.1830).
121 *Kirchenkonvent*, vol. 4 (10.4.1831).
122 *Kirchenkonvent*, vol. 4 (13.11.1836).

*(S-1841).*[123] *Michael Murr kept all of the clothes of his* Haushaltung *in the attic (S-1841).*[124] *Catharina Brodbeck said she used the money sent from Switzerland by her daughter for the common* Haushaltung *(S-1843).*[125] *Salomon Hentzler explained he and his wife lived in* Gemeinschaft *(together) in a house with Johannes Feldmeyer and his wife, although they dwelt separately* (abgesondert) *(S-1843).*[126] *They had treated each other for years as expected from two* zusammenlebenden Haushaltungen *(households living together). Now the other party suspected them of stealing. Christina Rieth complained that Catharina Rieth said she was a* Hur *and ran her* Haushaltung *with* Hurengeld *(whore's wages) (S-1843).*[127] *A related term was used by Michael Hentzler, who arranged for his daughter to inherit before his death, her* Hausstand zu fordern *(to benefit her household) (S-1844).*[128] *Johannes Klein's wife refused to return to her husband (S-1845).*[129] *Leaving him with the* Haushaltung *was enough punishment, she said. Johann Georg Federschmid complained of his wife's* unreine Haushaltung *(filthy housekeeping) (S-1846).*[130] *Johann Georg Rieth said there was no more disorganized, dirty* Haushaltung *in the village than that of his wife (S-1847).*[131] *Conrad Reichle demanded back some pillows his divorced wife took from the common* Haushaltung *(S-1848).*[132] *Johann Georg Falter had been repeatedly warned by the consistory and Schultheiss about his "schlechte Aufführung und liederliche Haushaltung" (bad behavior and disorderly management) (G-1777).*[133] *The court refused Jacob Bauknecht's petition to have his fiancée made a Bürger. One of his daughters had returned four weeks previously to keep him from marriage and to take over his* Haushaltung, *but he threw her out (G-1850).*[134] *Three siblings had a* gemeine Haushaltung *(common household), each having a separate account (G-1854).*[135] *Johann Georg Sterr requested from the court a statement of his wealth to take with him to the village of Frickenhausen where he proposed to live. His wealth was divided into buildings and immovable property, on one hand, and* Haushaltung *in movables, such as livestock and grain, on the other (G-1858).*[136].

"Haushaltung," like "hausen" very often had a critical function. One can imagine that in everyday village discourse, the term was used in both a positive and negative sense, as a means of judging the quality of a good worker or manager. In courtroom dramas, of course, the concept emerged largely as a negative critical tool. As such, it was in use throughout the period of the records we

[123] *Schultheißenamt*, vol. 1, f. 43 (3.7.1841).
[124] *Schultheißenamt*, vol. 1, f. 64 (22.11.1841).
[125] *Schultheißenamt*, vol. 2, f. 18 (6.2.1843).
[126] *Schultheißenamt*, vol. 2, f. 25 (22.4.1843).
[127] *Schultheißenamt*, vol. 2, f. 26 (13.5.1843).
[128] *Schultheißenamt*, vol. 2, f. 60 (12.10.1844).
[129] *Schultheißenamt*, vol. 2, f. 77 (29.5.1845).
[130] *Schultheißenamt*, vol. 2, f. 126 (23.11.1846).
[131] *Schultheißenamt*, vol. 2, f. 140 (26.2.1847).
[132] *Schultheißenamt*, vol. 2, f. 158 (21.2.1848).
[133] *Gericht*, vol. 2, f. 146 (27.3.1777).
[134] *Gericht*, vol. 15, f. 29 (4.4.1850).
[135] *Gericht*, vol. 15, f. 293 (8.3.1854).
[136] *Gericht*, vol. 16, f. 204 (19.11.1858).

have to study. In the eighteenth century, it occurred most often in contexts of judging male behavior, but there are enough examples to show that both husbands and wives had Haushaltungen. There is also no hint of the term being used to denote a special territory for one or the other sex. Each had an area of competence to manage. Still there seems to have been a sense of hierarchy, with the man as the overall manager, as in the case of Johann Holpp, who agreed in 1762 to marry a widow who had to have her Haushaltung taken over. Or in a terminologically related instance: Michael Schober accused his wife of running a *treulose Haushalt* (disloyal household) (K-1753).[137] She had taken bread and flour to her father's house.

In the nineteenth century, there seems to have been a shift in meaning. If anyone took over (or abandoned) "the" Haushaltung, it was a woman. In fact, Johannes Klein's wife in 1845 saw the humor in her husband having to take over the Haushaltung, and in 1850 Jacob Bauknecht's daughter returned to the village to take over her father's Haushaltung. In this context, the term most readily means housekeeping. That was the issue for Johann Georg Zeug in 1818, Mathias Häfner in 1831, Johann Georg Federschmid in 1846, and Johann Georg Rieth in 1847. (Johannes Hentzler used a related word when he alleged his wife did not pay attention to the Hauswesen (domestic concerns) (K-1839).[138] Behind the continuity of terminology, there seems to have been an alteration in meaning accompanied by a new set of demands. Orderliness and cleanliness emerged as specific values related to a woman's Haushaltung. In fact, in one instance they were positively expressed by the court: Michael Hentzler's daughters and first wife were noted for their *Fleiss*, *Häuslichkeit*, and *Ordnungsliebe* (diligence, domesticity, and orderliness) (G-1843).[139] Such values became the nexus for discussion, contention, and conflict between husband and wife and were part of a shift away from an all-inclusive term for family, household, and economy with a patriarchal connotation. For women, Haushaltung came to mean the care of the house, more sharply defined in terms of domesticity. Housekeeping came to be singled out for consideration, perhaps for the first time, in everyday village discourse as the special area of competence of the wife. Enormous tension was generated in this conceptual move because at the same time that house cleaning, house tidying, cooking, and the like moved up front, women were being drawn into agriculture, as we shall see, on a large scale.

The person who had a Haushaltung was either a *Haushalter* or a *Haushalterin*, although most of the instances we find in the records are in the male gender. The one use of Haushalterin is rather ambiguous. It could have referred to a woman who took over the female half of the farm economy or to a housekeeper in a more restricted sense. In any event, a Haushalter was some-

[137] *Kirchenkonvent*, vol. 2 (2.9.1753).
[138] *Kirchenkonvent*, vol. 4 (27.6.1839).
[139] *Gericht*, vol. 13, f. 240 (16.1.1843).

one who had an *Oeconomie*, an area of competence over house, family, and farm, as a whole, which he managed.

*The density of language possible over the house is illustrated by a case from the 1740s. Dorothea Thumm complained about her son-in-law, David Falter (K-1743).*[140] *She accused him of hiring people to do his work and for loafing around several days at a time. "Er hauset nicht wie as sage solle" (He is not as diligent as he should be), and he neglected his* Haushaltung. *The conflict blew up with bitter recriminations. Dorothea said that she only required for* Satisfaction *that he be a better* Haushalter. *He claimed he only hit his mother-in-law when she scolded him as a "schlechter Hauser, Raissler, and Säufer" (bad manager, gambler, and drunkard). He denied that he neglected his* Oeconomie *(*Oikos = *house). Johann Falter stole some grain (V-1751).*[141] *He was such a bad* Haushalter *and* Prodigus *that he could not pay for it. Anna Fischer worked as a* Haushalterin *for Hans Jerg Sterr for six weeks (G-1769).*[142] *The tavern-keeper, Gottlieb Federschmid, was fined for allowing* liederliche Haushältern *(disorderly householders) and* Säufern *(drinkers) to stay so long in his place (G-1777).*[143] *Johann Falter was drunk all the time and beat his children and wife (K-1781).*[144] *He was put into jail for a day. The next time he was reported as a bad* Haushalter *and* Hausvater, *he would be reported to the Oberamt. Friedrich Bosch appeared before the court to bring complaint on behalf of his* Kriegsfrau *(court "ward") against her husband, Salomon Brodbeck, who had carried on his* Haushaltung *badly for a long time (G-1791).*[145] *His wife testified that he was a bad* Haushalter. *If he continued with his drinking and drunkenness her wealth would be destroyed, and she wanted him declared* Mundtod *(incompetent). An order from the Vogt about late tax payments in Neckarhausen: Officials were to keep a sharp eye on all* leichtsinnige Haushälter *(heedless householders) (V-1806).*[146] *Gottlieb Hentzler was warned by the Oberamt as a* leichtsinniger Haushalter *(O-1812).*[147] *If he continued to make the rounds of the taverns, his wife and father-in-law could bring suit to have him declared* Mundtod. *Mathias Häfner maintained he always kept his* Haushaltung *in order (K-1831).*[148] *But his wife complained that he drank, was not a* Haushalter, *and she did not feel safe with him.*

Haushalter was used mostly in contexts having to do with acting as the moral and economic incumbent of a household. A Haushalter was expected to be diligent, industrious, and sober, qualities which would go a long way toward making him an effective manager. We have already seen the word coupled with Hausvater, which perhaps emphasized a little more strongly the moral aspects of running a household in contrast to the more economic ones. An examination

140 *Kirchenkonvent*, vol. 1, p. 124 (6.10.1743).
141 *Vogtruggericht*, vol. 1, f. 26 (15.2.1751).
142 *Gericht*, vol. 1, f. 206 (27.12.1769).
143 *Gericht*, vol. 2, f. 146 (7.3.1777).
144 *Kirchenkonvent*, vol. 3 (16.12.1781).
145 *Gericht*, vol. 4, f. 175 (30.9.1791).
146 *Vogtruggericht*, vol. 2, f. 20 (11.3.1806).
147 *Oberamtsgericht*, HSAL, F190, Band 10, f. 1517 (1.12.1812).
148 *Kirchenkonvent*, vol. 4 (10.4.1831).

of terminological usage shows that officials gave a hierarchical slant to the term, while wives did not so much imply heading a house as managing that part of a complex enterprise under a husband's jurisdiction. The related terms *Hausvater* and *Hausmutter* help focus on this issue more clearly.

*Various* Hausväter *were called in for neglecting to send their children to school (K-1738).*[149] *Any* Hausvater *who interfered with the Kunkelstuben (spinning bee) ordinance was to be punished (K-1739).*[150] *No* Hausvater *was to hold a* Lichtkartz *(spinning bee) without permission (K-1748).*[151] *Several* Personen *and* Hausväter *were cited for contravening an ordinance (K-1745).*[152] *Each* Hausvater *was to see that the chimney sweep did careful work (V-1754).*[153] *Johannes Rieth was fined for letting a troup of young men hang around with a Catholic female* (Weibsperson) *(K-1773).*[154] *As tavernkeeper and* Hausvater, *he did not fulfill his obligations. Some Bürger sent their children to gather twigs, which led to pilfering and destruction to the hedges (G-1774).*[155] *Each* Hausvater *was to be warned not to let his children do damage.* Hausväter *were responsible for seeing that servants hired from outside registered with the Schultheiss and pastor (K-1778).*[156] *Johann Falter was drunk all the time and beat his children and wife (K-1781).*[157] *He was put into jail for a day. The next time he was reported as a bad* Haushalter *and* Hausvater, *he would be reported to the Oberamt. Michael Deuschle and his wife were in conflict over his drinking and bad* Haushaltung *(K-1836).*[158] *He complained that a* rechter Weib *stays at home. The consistory responded that a* Hausvater *also cares for his family and asked why he did not produce more from his craft as cooper? Anna Catharina Rieth accused her husband, Johann Georg, of drinking, loafing, and mistreatment (K-1839).*[159] *The court asked him about fulfilling his obligations as* Hausvater.

*The term* Hausmutter *does not occur in the sources with the same degree of frequency. It appears very early in relation to the* Kunkelstuben (Spinnstuben, *spinning bees) (K-1739).*[160] *The unmarried daughters or maids were allowed to go only if the* Hausmutter *went along. Two servants got into a shouting match (K-1741).*[161] *The* Hausmutter *of one of them ordered her servant to silence and to go to bed. Daughters were to go with their mothers, and maids with* Hausmütter *to* Lichtkärtze *(K-1747).*[162] *Several maids got drunk together with some boys (K-1784).*[163] *The widow in whose*

[149] *Kirchenkonvent*, vol. 1, p. 54 (3.4.1738).
[150] *Kirchenkonvent*, vol. 1, p. 60 (15.11.1739).
[151] *Kirchenkonvent*, vol. 2, p. 21 (28.10.1748).
[152] *Kirchenkonvent*, vol. 1, p. 155 (28.10.1745).
[153] *Vogtruggericht*, vol. 1, f. 36 (26.2.1754).
[154] *Kirchenkonvent*, vol. 2 (11.3.1773).
[155] *Gericht*, vol. 2, f. 88 (28.12.1774).
[156] *Kirchenkonvent*, vol. 3 (25.10.1778).
[157] *Kirchenkonvent*, vol. 3 (16.12.1781).
[158] *Kirchenkonvent*, vol. 4 (13.11.1836).
[159] *Kirchenkonvent*, vol. 4 (26.3.1839).
[160] *Kirchenkonvent*, vol. 1, p. 60 (15.11.1739)
[161] *Kirchenkonvent*, vol. 1, p. 95 (3.9.1741).
[162] *Kirchenkonvent*, vol. 2, p. 13 (10.11.1747).
[163] *Kirchenkonvent*, vol. 3 (28.4.1784).

*house this took place was referred to as the* Hausmutter *of the disorderly conduct* (Unordnung). *Finally there is an ambiguous reference to a widow with several unmarried sons living at home as a* Hausmutter *(G-1832).*[164]

From these instances, it is clear that Hausvater had an official connotation. It encompassed a view held by the magistrates and referred in most cases to the responsible head of the household. There are no examples of ordinary villagers using the term in everyday discourse. In this sense, Hausmutter was derivative, referring either to a household head in the absence of a man or to the specific relation of a wife to the (female) servants. No villager in any court case said, "My husband is not a proper Hausvater" or "My wife is not a proper Hausmutter." To the contrary, the terms were the lenses through which the village, state, and church officials viewed the family. They had a hierarchical connotation and authorized the male head of the house as the address of various communications. The state's guarantee of general order, proper behavior, and diligence was the Hausvater. Under him, or in his place when he was absent, stood the Hausmutter, also a figure concerned with order. The term Haushalter is almost exclusively used for males, the sole exception being an employee relationship where a woman took on the position of Haushalterin for a widower. It referred to a man's economy, his way of dealing with his livelihood, and carried with it the various layers of meaning of the word Haushaltung. Unlike Hausvater, however, it did not have a sense of patriarchal authority, even though assumptions of hierarchy might have underlain it. Women chose this latter word and avoided the expressly patriarchal vocabulary. In fact, they always chose terms which represented reciprocity and mutual obligation. Their discourse emphasized Haushalter as a person with duties and obligations before rights and power. When they used Haushaltung or hausen as critical tools, they were emphasizing the exchange elements of marriage. This can be seen most clearly in the context of scolding – *schlechter Hauser*, *übel hausen* (bad householder, manage badly), and the like. And precisely the reciprocal element was at issue when Anna Maria Häussler chose to call her husband *Lumpenhauser* (trashy householder) after he drank the profits from the sale of some lambs (K-1750).[165]

The notion of the "house" in its various configurations was one of those concepts through which people perceived a significant part of everyday reality and gave it form. Talking about the house was an activity: an argument, an expression of value, a claim, an acceptance of obligation. In the historical development of the word, two kinds of interchange gave it its characteristic effect: that between Herrschaft and subjects, and that between men and women. From the point of view of state agencies, the house was the smallest taxable unit and also the guarantee of order. It was understood as a functioning whole, a productive unity, with clear, hierarchical lines of authority. There

[164] *Gericht*, vol. 12, f. 53 (24.4.1832).
[165] *Kirchenkonvent*, vol. 2, p. 49 (24.8.1750).

developed a large secular and religious literature concerned with its properties, definition, and reform. In another context, I have explained how "good" and "bad householder" emerged in the eighteenth century as critical concepts used by both ducal officials and villagers to sort out the players in class conflict. Earlier, in the sixteenth and seventeenth centuries, the state had been primarily concerned with property rights, inheritance, and claims to sufficient resources to support widows, orphans, and the like. By the eighteenth century, it was increasingly concerned with production itself. At the macro level of the economy, it regulated manufacture and marketing, introduced new forms of production, and began to consider infrastructural problems. But it also started to view the house in terms of work, consumption schedules, and good management. More and more often, state directives instructed village officials to make lists of householders who were in danger of going too far into debt or whose expenditures seemed excessive. This was to serve as a warning, but also gave the opportunity for official observation. A Hausvater might soon find his belongings subject to inventory and, more drastically, forced sale. The eighteenth century, as we shall show, was the period when wives and officials often "contracted" together to take away a husband's right to manage the affairs of the house, declaring him *Mundtod.* And by the beginning of the nineteenth century, state agencies were willing to entertain arguments about a man's work and spending habits as grounds for divorce.

It is, of course, part of the dynamic of state intervention which prompted the construction of lists of all kinds: households attending communion, the number of people at a wedding, the householders in arrears with taxes, the resources available to orphans, the names and ages of inhabitants of households, the size and kinds of agricultural holdings belonging to a householder, the unmarried women allowed to attend a spinning bee, land sales, mortgages, tax assessments, and inventories.

It would be a futile exercise to try to sort out which part of house was composed of state ideology and which part was rooted in exigencies of peasant culture. There was constant reinforcement from both sides. Village ordinances such as those which attempted to regulate Lichtkärtze (Spinnstuben, spinning bees) eventually became state mandates, but then were continually contravened by villagers themselves.[166] Note, however, that village argument over household values took place under a reigning ideology of the house. There were good reasons for state officials to choose terms and forms of address which emphasized hierarchy and vertical relationships. From the beginning, women, as they appeared in court protocols, challenged official discourse by inserting words of horizontal relationships, exchange, and reciprocity into the argument. In part, they were relying on publicly expressed values but gave them an effec-

[166] See Hans Medick, "Village Spinning Bees: Sexual Culture and Free Time among Rural Youth in Early Modern Germany," in *Interest and Emotion: Essays in the Study of Family and Kinship*, ed., Hans Medick and David Warren Sabean (Cambridge, 1984), pp. 317–40.

tive twist in order to assert their own interests. In state ideology, the house was a whole, and recent historical scholarship has resurrected the term "das ganze Haus" (the whole house) from the university literature devoted to state policy. However, in Neckarhausen, villagers chose to give the terms "Haushaltung," "Hauswesen," "Haushalter," and "hausen" an individual slant. Women distinguished between their Haushaltung and that of their husbands. If they managed their own affairs well, then it was up to the authorities to get their husbands to hausen properly, declare them incompetent, or grant divorces. As we shall see, women were also tenacious about defending their own property rights inside a legal system which gave their husbands administrative rights over the family holdings considered as a unity.

We have also seen that the official use of the terminology of the house mediated an entire system of values. Once such values were part of public argument, administrative practice, and legal enforcement, there was room for villagers, both men and women, to use them with a critical edge. Yet there seems to have been, at least as documented in the court protocols, far more instrumental use of the ideology by women. They put the house with male authority at its pinnacle radically in question, although in time there was more room for maneuvering. At the same time that some women began to refuse to hausen, others were having illegitimate children with no marriage prospects in sight and no attempt to discuss them with the fathers of their children, and still others did not enter into a second marriage even when holding substantial amounts of property. Although the state viewed the house as a locus of an Oeconomie, that did not fit very well the situation of many families who did not have enough land or a substantial enough handicraft to be self-sufficient. The stress on the "good" household could play a role in social differentiation and conflict in a village. It was an idealization, rather than a reality for the majority of the population. Notions such as "Haushalter," "Hausvater," and "Hausmutter" could be and were used by authorities to control behavior, to transmit a value structure by which to define violators, and to set up alliances with village inhabitants.

How does our philological exercise suggest limitations on the three traditions interested in the house? We have seen that the stress on the functional whole characteristic of European ethnology must be balanced by an understanding of the values of reciprocity and the mechanisms of exchange which characterized the discourse between spouses. Furthermore, as I shall show in another context, while there is some support for the idea that a household was viewed from the outside as a moral unit, there is other evidence of household members divorcing their actions and reputations from their fellows.[167] Quite rightly, the notion of the ganzes Haus has captured a fundamental aspect of Herrschaft

[167] For example, a brother refused to back the testimony of his sister in a paternity case. He considered the issue of his truthfulness to be separate from that of the reputation of his sister; *Kirchenkonvent*, vol. 2 (20.2.1775).

relations, but, as we have seen, patriarchy was a program rather than an entity, or perhaps better, an idiom through which significant critical discussion always took place. The tradition of social analysis concerned with the peasant economy stresses the interrelationship of production and social and demographic reproduction. The results of this study suggest that the notion of the house producing and consuming together might be a male idealization. It is important to sift the data for contrasting male and female points of view and to consider the terms of exploitation. We have only hinted here at the possibility of different reproductive strategies and suggested that for many women in the period 1780 to 1840 and after family formation was not the central issue. They were often reluctant to found households even at the cost of bearing illegitimate children; they sued for divorce or failed to remarry when widowed even when they had sufficient resources to do so. Furthermore, the "fit" between reproduction of the house and the production and reproduction of more encompassing social relationships is not at all unproblematical. Beyond the dynamics of husband and wife are those of larger kinship structures and social class. Households were linked with each other in complex ways, and each one must be seen as the locus of many-stranded alliances and as a point of production of stratified relationships. As far as the third tradition of research on the house, that of historical demography, is concerned, we have seen that the primary data have usually been set up according to the needs of the state. Lists of households serve the tax collector and overseers of the poor and identify individuals who are not in properly administered groups. But that does not help us understand to what degree meaningful social interaction was focused on the house in actual fact. We will have to look in detail at the inner workings of families and households and examine the links between individuals and groups beyond the boundaries of it in order to put the house in its proper place.

## Familie

We have focused considerable attention on the concept of the "house," since it was such a critical notion for European political and social discourse in the early modern period and has become such a useful term in present-day social and historical analysis. "Family" has its own problems of definition, which are amply discussed in the literature, along with its suitability for comparative analysis. For our purposes, it is not necessary to dwell at length on current sociological concerns, but we must give some attention to its possible meanings in the rural society we are examining in order to set it against its companion term.

The term *Familie* occurs in the Neckarhausen court records 75 times. Only 6 of these occurrences appear before 1800, and the word first came into frequent use only during the decade of the 1820s. It does not supplant Haus as such, since, as we have seen, that term was used only once by itself. There were certain contexts in which it became useful to refer to collectivities or entities in some way, some of them living together and some not. In general, Familie was not subject to the same kind of complex word formation as Haus – such terms as *Familiendiebstahl* (family theft) and *Familienvater* appear only occasionally – nor was there a verb form parallel to hausen. In order to understand the context out of which the term arose in normal discourse, it is best to review all of its occurrences.

*On the earliest occasion where the word* Familie *is to be found in the Neckarhausen court records, Barbara Bauknecht said that her husband, Johannes, and his* Familie *were scoundrels* (Schelmen) *and thieves (K-1752).*[168] *Hans Jerg Falter and his* Familie *ate tainted meat from a slaughtered cow bitten by a mad dog (1758).*[169] *There was a street brawl between the Geiger and Bauknecht* Familien, *the parents of the two groups of boys being brother and sister (G-1784).*[170] *Friedrich Henzler was cited and asked why he had verbally abused the Häfner* Familie *(G-1784).*[171] *Because his brother was against his marrying into the Schober* Familie, *Andreas Falter wanted to break off his engagement (K-1786).*[172] *A mousetrap maker came through Neckarhausen with his numerous* Familie, *staying in Johann George Federschmid's barn (K-1795).*[173] *Matheus Falter petitioned for wood to build a house for himself and his* Familie *(G-1804).*[174] *After an altercation, Jacob Zeug and Christoph Hentzler, respective fathers-in-law* (Gegenschweher) *of a married couple, promised peace between the* Familien *(G-1807).*[175] *Ulrich Bauer received a building plot for himself and his* Familie *(G-1811).*[176] *Young Salomon Hentzler was accused by his brother-in-law, Matheus Sterr, of taking a great deal from his* Familie *and cutting down trees out of spite (G-1812).*[177] *Young Salomon Hentzler and Salomon Bauer reported that they were unable to support their* Familien *(G-1816).*[178] *Georg Falter complained about the filthiness of his tenants* (Hausleute), *the Häfners, and the father was told to clean up his* Familie *(G-1818).*[179] *Ulrich Bauer said that he wanted to support his* Familie *without public assistance (V-1820).*[180] *Wilhelm Hentzler and Ludwig Hiller complained about verbal abuse from Mathes Häfner against them and the whole* Familie *(G-1820).*[181] *Ludwig Bauknecht complained that as Mathes Falter went by the house drunk the night before, he yelled that the entire Bauknecht* Familie *was a bunch of witches* (Hexenkor) *(G-1820).*[182] *Barbara Bauknecht denied being the originator of*

168 *Kirchenkonvent*, vol. 2, p. 71 (4.2.1752).
169 Nürtingen *Stadtgericht*, Rathaus Nürtingen, vol. 19, f. 110 (4.1.1758).
170 *Gericht*, vol. 3, f. 173 (10.7.1784).
171 *Gericht*, vol. 3, f. 180 (22.7.1784).
172 *Kirchenkonvent*, vol. 3 (1.2.1786).
173 *Kirchenkonvent*, vol. 3 (1.11.1795).
174 *Gericht*, vol. 6, f. 55 (28.12.1804).
175 *Gericht*, vol. 6, f. 216 (11.6.1807).
176 *Gericht*, vol. 7, f. 210 (1.11.1811).
177 *Gericht*, vol. 8, f. 21 (2.4.1812).
178 *Gericht*, vol. 8, f. 215 (13.12.1816).
179 *Gericht*, vol. 9, f. 61 (28.12.1818).
180 *Vogtruggericht*, vol. 2, f. 90 (16.2.1820).
181 *Gericht*, vol. 9, f. 142 (18.7.1820).
182 *Gericht*, vol. 9, f. 144 (25.7.1820).

*the rumor against Jacob Häfner for stealing. She had suffered much from his* Familie, *and he would know directly if she had something against him (G-1824).*[183] *Johannes Zirn from Wolfschlugen was sent to Hamburg by the Schach* Familie *to fetch an inheritance (G-1825).*[184] *After punching the Bürgermeister, old Wilhelm Deuschle, in the mouth, Ludwig Federschmid called his wife's* Familie *a trashy lot* (Lumpenkor) *(G-1825).*[185] *Ulrich Bauer, who had emigrated, was turned back by the Bavarian authorities (O-1827).*[186] *He wanted to see if he could support his* Familie *in Neckarhausen. Christoph Sterr and Mathias Sterr called on Wilhelm Köpple to say what Jacob Häfner's wife said about them and their whole* Familie *(G-1827).*[187] *Young Mathias Häfner called his wife, her mother, and the whole* Familie *witches (G-1829).*[188] *Gottfried Hentzler's daughter had taken his schnaps to sell and was therefore accused of* Familiendiebstahl *(family thievery) (O-1831).*[189] *Margaretha Häfner complained that all the Weilers came to her house with stones and called her entire* Familie *a stealing trashy lot* (verstohlenes Lumpenkor) *(G-1833).*[190] *Salomon Bauer, the court pointed out, had to live as a poor man with his* Familie *(G-3534).*[191] *By selling beer yeast, Magdalena Stauch had supported her* Familie *for four years (G-1835).*[192] *Salomon Hentzler said to Ludwig Hiller that the whole Hiller* Familie *were pure trash* (lauter Lumpen) *(G-1836).*[193] *Michael Deuschle was told by the consistory that a* Hausvater *cares for his* Familie *(K-1836).*[194] *Later he received five days' arrest for libel against the Hiller* Familie *(O-1836).*[195] *Reporting on measures against the cholera epidemic, the consistory noted that the* Familien *in Neckarhausen did not live packed in together (K-1836).*[196] *When two different villagers applied for permits to open inns, the court reported that there were 959 souls (Seelen) and 213* Familien *in Neckarhausen (G-1838).*[197] *Barbara Hentzler, wife of Wilhelm, reported that Jacob Hentzler's* Familie *was eating in the room where she was making her bed (S-1840).*[198] *Jacob's wife, Maria Magdalena, hit her on the head for raising dust. Johannes Rieth's wife referred to "beide Familien, die in einem Haus zusammenleben" (both families which live together in one house) (S-1841).*[199] *As usual, the* Familien *had gotten into a squabble because of the children. She had called Johann Georg Falter's* Familie *a bunch of gypsies* (Zigeunerkor). *Two married brothers and their*

183 *Gericht*, vol. 10, f. 122 (2.1.1824).
184 *Gericht*, vol. 10, f. 166 (10.2.1825).
185 *Gericht*. vol. 10, f. 216 (26.12.1825).
186 *Oberamtsgericht*, HSAL, F190II, Band 257, f. 37 (14.4.1827).
187 *Gericht*, vol. 11, f. 74 (6.8.1827).
188 *Gericht*, vol. 11, f. 155 (6.11.1829).
189 *Oberamtsgericht*, HSAL, F190II, Band 265, f. 42 (31.3.1831).
190 *Gericht*, vol. 12, f. 107 (11.7.1833).
191 *Gericht*, vol. 12, f. 168 (11.11.1834).
192 *Gericht*, vol. 12, f. 184 (11.4.1835).
193 *Gericht*, vol. 12, f. 228 (10.4.1836).
194 *Kirchenkonvent*, vol. 4 (12.11.1836).
195 *Oberamtsgericht*, HSAL, F190II, Band 270, f. 75 (18.5.1836).
196 *Kirchenkonvent*, vol. 4 (20.11.1836).
197 *Gericht*, vol. 12, f. 2 (19.1.1838); f. 26 (10.9.1838).
198 *Schultheißenamt*, vol. 1, f. 11 (5.12.1840).
199 *Schultheißenamt*, vol. 1, f. 35 (19.5.1841).

*two sisters were in conflict over manuring a field (S-1841).*[200] *The Schultheiss said they were always quarreling and the magistrates had more to do with them than any other* Familie. *Johannes Hentzler excused his rudeness to his wife by saying that it was impossible to feed* (ernähren) *his* Familie *(S-1842).*[201] *He was told by the consistory that his property was not less than was owned by many others with larger* Familien *who support them well with thrift and hard work (K-1842).*[202] *Jacob Falter had had a stroke and could not work. If his rent was not paid by the community, he would end up with his whole* Familie *in an attic (G-1842).*[203] *In 1844, Michael Bosch's petition to marry a woman from another village was turned down on the grounds that he did not have the capacity to provide for a* Familie *(G-1844).*[204] *The term* Familie *occurs in eight more similar petitions through the 1860s.*[205] *Wilhelm Köpple applied for a communal garden in order to support his* Familie *(V-1845).*[206] *Michael Hentzler accepted apologies from Johann Georg Falter out of consideration for the latter's* Familie *for falsely accusing him of stealing potatoes from a cellar where they both stored sacks (S-1845).*[207] *This issue involved in a dispute about a common house entrance went back to a* Familie *which had owned a quarter of the house (G-1846).*[208] *Innkeeper Hihn came to Johann Georg Kühfuss's house while he was at the parsonage and asked the* Familie *sarcastically if the lord was at home (S-1846).*[209] *Christoph Deuschle complained that in his absence his Catholic neighbor August Baur used abusive language against his wife, children, and* Familie *(S-1846).*[210] *Johannes Klein did not pay attention to the needs of his* Familie *and continued to drink (S-1847).*[211] *Catharina Rieth complained that Margaretha Hentzler accused her of stealing potatoes from their common cellar and slandered her in the kitchen they shared. Apparently Margaretha said Catharina would find the culprit among her own* Familie *(S-1847).*[212] *An ordinance for the period of dearth forbade begging and threatened any* Familienvater *who allowed it with a day in jail (S-1847).*[213] *Christoph Deuschle complained about a Belgian flax specialist who had robbed him and his* Familie *of their good name (S-1848).*[214] *Michael Falter had been caring for his sick brother-in-law for a month and needed help because he had to support his own* Familie *from his earnings*

200 *Schultheißenamt*, vol. 1, f. 46 (12.8.1841).
201 *Schultheißenamt*, vol. 2, f. 7 (17.9.1842).
202 *Kirchenkonvent*, vol. 4 (20.9.1842).
203 *Gericht*, vol. 13, f. 185 (7.1.1842).
204 *Gericht*, vol. 14, f. 17 (15.8.1844).
205 *Gericht*, vol. 14, f. 27 (17.10.1844) (Johann Georg Bauknecht); f. 308 (7.4.1849) (Friedrich Walker); vol. 15, f. 124 (26.10.1851) (Anna Maria Scholl); vol. 16, f. 214, (9.2.1859) (Friedrich Sterr); vol. 17, f. 37 (30.7.1860) (Christian Falter); f. 136 (7.3.1862) (Johann Friedrich Müller); f. 228 (17.5.1864); f. 231 (6.6.1864) (Christian Schach).
206 *Vogtruggericht*, vol. 2, f. 210 (13.5.1845).
207 *Schultheißenamt*, vol. 2, f. 73 (28.3.1845).
208 *Gericht*, vol. 14, f. 108 (10.1.1846).
209 *Schultheißenamt*, vol. 2, f. 99 (9.2.1846).
210 *Schultheißenamt*, vol. 2, f. 120 (15.8.1846).
211 *Schultheißenamt*, vol. 2, f. 137 (9.2.1847).
212 *Schultheißenamt*, vol. 2, f. 141 (16.4.1847).
213 *Schultheißenamt*, vol. 2, f. 140 (15.3.1747).
214 *Schultheißenamt*. vol. 2, f. 172 (17.6.1848).

*(S-1850).*[215] *Ten Bürger appeared before the court and said that the necessities for their* Familien *were exhausted (G-1851).*[216] *Gottlieb Federschmid wanted to go to America where he would be better able to support his* Familie *(G-1853).*[217] *Friedrich Rieth, who was old and sick, was to be boarded in a proper* Familie *(G-1853).*[218] *Gottlieb Federschmid had a large* (bedeutende) Familie *of seven children, which he could not feed from his land (G-1853).*[219] *Ludwig Baur came back from Bavaria to support his* Familie *(G-1855).*[220] *Johannes Bauknecht was cited for drunkenness and reminded about his obligations to his* Familie *(S-1854).*[221] *Catharina Renzler and Daniel Hentzler both had* Familien *in the poorhouse. They complained about abuse against themselves and their* Familien *by Johann Georg Federschmid (S-1857).*[222] *Wilhelm Deuschle and his mother reported his father to the Schultheiss in order to prevent a further disturbance to the peace of the* Familie *(S-1857).*[223] *Friedrich Zeug shared a living room* (Wohnstube) *with his brother-in-law, Daniel Bauknecht. The latter had acted up and threatened him with a knife. Zeug's mother said that Bauknecht did not act as a* Familienvater *should (S-1858),*[224] *Ludwig Federschmid complained about Jacob Heinser disturbing him and his* Familie *(S-1858).*[225] *Christian Sterr requested documents so that he could move to another village with his* Familie *(G-1858).*[226] *Old Friedrich Baur wanted his son and* Familie *to move out of his house (S-1860).*[227] *The police reported that Ludwig Baur was disturbing the peace of his* Familie *(S-1862).*[228] *Catharina Baur complained that her husband's brother had been spreading the rumor that in the absence of her husband she had been living the high life* (Wohlleben) *with her* Familie *(S-1864).*[229] *Plasterer Schober accused Jacob Friedrich Post's* Familie *of drinking up his cider (S-1865).*[230] *Finally, there were four cases of men in the 1860s who petitioned to return to the village with their* Familien.[231]

Many uses of the term "Familie" emphasize the contractual aspect of a marriage. In the earliest example, a wife put her husband into the context of his whole family, all of them scoundrels. Such usage is ambiguous, because it could designate his closest relatives, his "nuclear family of origin," his

215 *Schultheißenamt*, vol. 2, f. 223 (29.5.1850).
216 *Gericht*, vol. 15, f. 138 (23.12.1851).
217 *Gericht*, vol. 15, f. 270 (19.10.1853).
218 *Gericht*, vol. 15, f. 219 (24.1.1853).
219 *Gericht*, vol. 15, f. 258 (29.7.1853).
220 *Gericht*, vol. 16, f. 15 (19.3.1855).
221 *Schultheißenamt*, vol. 2, f. 263 (6.11.1854).
222 *Schultheißenamt*, vol. 2, f. 271 (9.2.1857).
223 *Schultheißenamt*, vol. 2, f. 274 (19.11.1857).
224 *Schultheißenamt*, vol. 2, f. 277 (5.4.1858).
225 *Schultheißenamt*, vol. 3, f. 14 (18.10.1858).
226 *Gericht*, vol. 16, f. 204 (19.11.1858).
227 *Schultheißenamt*, vol. 3, f. 38 (14.8.1860).
228 *Schultheißenamt*, vol. 3, f. 63 (27.3.1862).
229 *Schultheißenamt*, vol. 3, f. 78 (8.2.1864).
230 *Schultheißenamt*, vol. 3, f. 104 (28.10.1865).
231 *Gericht*, vol. 18, f. 146 (5.8.1867) (Jacob Bauknecht); f. 154 (16.9.1867) (Christian Falter); f. 157 (13.11.1867) (Johannes Simmendinger); f. 249 (12.7.1869) (Friedrich Distel).

parents and siblings, or his whole set of relatives, his line of descent, the larger surname group. The latter meaning of family was especially emphasized in instances of witchcraft accusations where the line of descent was often made explicit. In 1829, for example, Mathias Häfner called his wife, then her mother, then their whole family witches. This larger use of family is frequently met with in the many instances of verbal abuse – where the suffix *-kor* was sometimes used (as in Hexenkor, Zigeunerkor, Lumpenkor – bunch of witches, bunch of gypsies, trashy lot). Sometimes a whole surname group was singled out (the Hillers), and sometimes related people complained of collective verbal abuse. In this general use of the term "family," an ill-defined larger collectivity of kin was involved, whose specific boundaries were left ambiguous.

Family could also be used to suggest differentiation, to define the line between two related groups or between people sharing a house or rooms or storage space. When a brother and sister and their children engaged in a street brawl, the protocol of the incident was rather unusually introduced by a title, emphasizing two Familien. Respective fathers-in-law promised peace between the families, or brothers-in-law showed aggression against each other's family. A father asked his son to take his family and leave. Inside a house, the term suggests differentiated groups – owners and tenants, economic collectivities, cells defined by marriage, commensal units. When two such groups were in conflict over the use of space or over the violation of property rights, the term "family" was especially useful. As we shall see in later chapters the term "family" came to be used frequently in such contexts precisely during a period when close relatives increasingly shared space and equipment, sold property to, became godparents for, and married each other. In a more general sense, the family was a group which lived together, had some of its own resources, and was supposed to live in peace. Still the boundaries could be expanded when two such groups lived in the same house, and a man acting up could be disturbing "the" family, meaning his wife, children, parents, and siblings or in-laws and wife's siblings. The fluidity of boundaries suggests that the term has to be understood in context. A larger group expecting an inheritance could be a family – differentiated from everyone not sharing in it – and two conflicting groups sharing such an inheritance could be designated separate families, differentiated by particular interests. A larger group of siblings, married and unmarried, could be a quarreling family, or their differences could be underlined by calling them separate families, especially when the interests of their offspring were at issue.

By far the most frequent use of the word family occurs in reference to a dependent economic group, in almost all cases the people for whom a *man* worked and earned. Men petitioned for building wood or plots for themselves and their families; they had trouble feeding their families or neglected them in favor of carousing and drinking; they wanted to emigrate or return in order to support them better; they were advised against marrying or refused permission to settle their "foreign" wives in the village on the grounds of not having the property, skills, or moral capacities to provide for their families. Of course, a woman could also support a family, but the court discourse is overwhelmingly concerned with men and their dependents. Just who the latter were is left ambiguous, but would certainly include wives and children and by extension servants, dependent relatives, and foster children. This coupling of a man with his family entered the records around 1800 and for a while paralleled the use of the word hausen, especially when the issue had to do with setting up a new economic unit through a marriage. By the 1840s, the court had shifted to the exclusive use of the term "Familie." It was clearly a concept used by village males and by magistrates in an official discourse about managing affairs, providing for dependents, and displaying diligence. In no instance did women use the term in a critical way to refer to their husbands's work habits, thrift, sobriety, or ability to provide a living, perhaps because they did not see the economy of their men set off in any special way from their own. At the time that the term was gaining currency, women were thoroughly involved in agricultural production and were quite prepared to support themselves and their children alone, if necessary. When they used the term "family," it was to stress the contractual aspect of family life, in the general labeling of the husband's relatives as a worthless lot. Still, taken altogether, women only used the term six times (8 percent of the cases) as far as the court records are concerned. For the rest, we have a discussion going on between village men and village magistrates. For a critical concept, especially during the period of the first four decades of the nineteenth century, women used the word hausen, suggesting a dynamic unity based on mutual dependence, reciprocity, and their willingness to stay in place, rather than a hierarchical structure with women dependent on men.

In this chapter, we have concentrated on a few key terms abstracted from the larger lexical field and the staged occurrences revealed in our sources. We have come to think of the household as a place where various exchanges took place, where one and the same act might have different meanings for a particular couple, their respective kin, and for the administrative agents of the wider polity. Conflicting linguistic strategies were embedded in conflicting needs, perceptions, and programs, and we can expect that a more encompassing consideration of language and action will deepen our understanding of the terms of discourse and of the particular concrete objects and forces which mediated them. Husbands and wives obviously thought about their respective performances on a day-to-day basis and with regard to fundamental issues that had to do with satisfying needs and fulfilling their goals and values. We cannot understand their reciprocities and exchanges without a clear idea of the material basis of their existence, but we must also be able to say how that was perceived, coded, represented, and shaped. We are well on the way to understanding just how rich and varied peasant culture across the face of Europe was, but we are only beginning to understand the great variety and complexity among the objects of everyday existence, about which peasants carried on a continual discussion with many strategical perspectives. If the house was a locus of exchange, then we can only understand it by looking in detail at the set of claims and obligations, demands and prestations, rights and performances which were expressed or carried out there. Production and property will offer us crucial analytical entry points to the patterns of relations between members of the house. As a next step in building up an understanding of the terms of discourse between husbands and wives, we will look at the recurring patterns of conflict, the dramatic forms of confrontation, the lexical context of familial relations, and the symbolic content of abuse.

4

# Patterns of marital conflict

> On Monday she scolded him rudely and then she looked him in the face, in response to which he of course defended himself.
>
> – Johann Georg Rieth, explaining why he beat his wife (1839)[1]

In discussing the idiomatic rendering of house and family so far, we have considered the villagers' use of the terms outside of the context of the dramatic situations in which they occurred. What we have at our disposal are re-creations before the pastor, Schultheiss, or village court of the original staging of some kind of conflict between husbands and wives. However, the action cannot be fully understood without on overview of the public airing of marital disputes, the frequency and kinds of complaint, changes in the nature of violence, and the symbolism behind the verbal abuse.

Family squabbles came before three different courts in the village, and, if serious, they would go on up to the various levels of higher instance, the next one beyond the locality being in the administrative town of Nürtingen, the level of the Oberamt. No records remain from any of the higher courts, except for a few cases heard in the ducal marriage court (*Ehegericht*). But none of these involve Neckarhausen residents. There are also several volumes "in causis fori mixti" and "in causis civilibus" from the Nürtingen Oberamtsgericht, covering the period 1806 to 1823. Most family quarrels were brought before the church consistory (Kirchenkonvent) from its inception in 1644 until 1840, when they were moved to the purely secular jurisdiction of the Schultheißenamt.[2] The consistory was a kind of morals court composed of the pastor, the Schultheiss, and two elders (*Konventsrichter*), who were usually members of the Gericht. For Neckarhausen, its records have been preserved only for the period after 1727. Occasionally, during the whole period, but especially in the 1820s (eight cases), conflicts were taken before the village Gericht, especially if they involved

[1] See n. 13.

[2] The two courts seem to have run parallel for a short time, with most cases going to the *Schultheißamt* from 1840 on, but with at least one case still being handled in the consistory as late as 1842. According to the *Regierungsblatt für das Königreich Württemberg*, nr. 62 (29.10.1824), marital cases were no longer supposed to be handled by the local church consistory. As late as 1840, many still did so; ibid. (1840), p. 131.

Table 4.1 *Frequency of marital conflict cases before local courts*

| Court | Inclusive dates | Number |
|---|---|---|
| Church consistory | 1727–1842 | 71 |
| Village court | 1754–1832 | 14 |
| Office of the Schultheiss | 1840–61 | 28 |
| District court | 1806–23 | 8 |

husbands accused of idleness. Altogether there are 121 cases in the records between 1727 and 1861, distributed as shown in Table 4.1.

The 121 cases are distributed over 134 years, which means that on average there was less than one per year. That does not seem like very much for a village as large as Neckarhausen. As already mentioned, behind each court appearance could lie a long history of marital problems and disunity. In many instances, perhaps, a husband and wife might squabble over quite serious matters without either of them ever appearing before the court. The cases we do have are not, therefore, "representative" of marital conflict in general. Sometimes less serious cases were brought before the consistory or Gericht and the couple was never "heard" from again. It is equally certain that some deeply disturbed marriages did not make it into the official records. Although our purpose here is not to measure the conjuncture of marital conflict, we must test a few simple counting procedures in order to find ways to handle the data.

The first steps in the analysis should be to document who brought the complaint, how old the complainants were, how long they had been married, and whether they were willing to continue in marriage. Many couples came before the court more than once, and altogether there are 70 of them to study. In Tables 4.2 to 4.4, however, we treat each court case separately, dividing the

Table 4.2 *Initiator of complaint in cases of marital conflict*

| Period | N | H | W | Hrel | Wrel | Other | NG |
|---|---|---|---|---|---|---|---|
| 1730–59 | 16 | 0 | 6 | 1 | 6 | 0 | 3 |
| 1760–89 | 15 | 4 | 4 | 0 | 0 | 0 | 7 |
| 1790–1819 | 16 | 1 | 6 | 0 | 1 | 0 | 8 |
| 1820–49 | 66 | 8 | 36 | 1 | 2 | 2 | 17 |
| Total | 113 | 13 | 52 | 2 | 9 | 2 | 35 |
| | | | | 78 | | | |

N = number of cases; H = husband; Hrel = husband's relatives; W = wife; Wrel = wife's relatives; NG = not given.

Table 4.3 *Age of spouses and duration of marriage, first time before the courts*

| Period | Number | Range | Percentage under 30 | Mean | Median | Mode |
|---|---|---|---|---|---|---|
| *Age of wife* | | | | | | |
| 1730–59 | 10 | 21–60 | 50 | 33.6 | 28.5 | |
| 1760–89 | 10[a] | 24–50 | 40 | 34.1 | 31.5 | |
| 1790–1819 | 14[a] | 18–43 | 30 | 28.9 | 31.5 | |
| 1820–49 | 28 | 20–56 | 57 | 31.8 | 27.5 | |
| *Age of husband* | | | | | | |
| 1730–59 | 9[a] | 22–61 | 44 | 38.3 | 36 | |
| 1760–89 | 11 | 25–47 | 27 | 34.0 | 32 | |
| 1790–1819 | 15 | 25–45 | 53 | 30.6 | 27 | |
| 1820–49 | 28 | 25–54 | 46 | 34.5 | 31 | |
| *Duration of marriage* (in years)[b] | | | | | | |
| 1730–59 | 10 | 0.5–17.0 | 50 | 5.8 | 3.0 | 0.5,2.5 |
| 1760–89 | 11 | 0.5–21.0 | 27 | 7.7 | 5.5 | 5.5 |
| 1790–1819 | 15 | 0.5–16.5 | 47 | 5.2 | 3.5 | 2.5 |
| 1820–49 | 28 | 0.5–31.5 | 46 | 7.3 | 3.5 | 1.5 |

[a] One age not given.
[b] Intervals of 0.5.

Table 4.4 *Frequency of divorce requests in local courts*

| Period | N[a] | Wife | Husband | Both |
|---|---|---|---|---|
| 1730–59 | 16 | 0 | 0 | 0 |
| 1760–89 | 15 | 2 | 0 | 0 |
| 1790–1819 | 16 | 7 | 2 | 1 |
| 1820–49[b] | 66 | 24 | 5 | 2 |
| Total | 113 | 33 | 7 | 3 |

[a] Number of cases of marital conflict before courts.
[b] Between 1822 and 1839 in 21 of 36 cases, women requested divorce. Between 1840 and 1848 in only 3 of 25 cases did they request divorce.

material for statistical purposes into periods of 30 years, ignoring the four cases before 1730 and the four after 1850.

Until about 1820, the number of marital conflicts that came before the courts appears to have been fairly constant, but the actual incidence of severe problems between husbands and wives is unclear. In one instance, the pastor wrote in the consistory protocols that a particular husband had been noted down in his diary on several occasions and that it was now time to bring his behavior to public notice.[3] At times there may have been more embarrassment associated with such a court appearance than at others. Or the reprisals by one spouse against another could have been more effective. Readiness to go to court is subject to a number of variables which are difficult to assess. If we were to take the number of cases as generally indicative of marital problems, then given the population increase up to 1820, we would be chronicling a decline in relative terms. In the third period (1790–1819), we would have to record a significant drop in problem marriages altogether because our figures are increased by the extravillage court records during that time. But I can see no reason for a decline in conflict, and there are other indications that the court records do not chronicle all the marital strains in the community. For example, several eighteenth-century inventories record that wives had their husbands declared incompetent, but there are no supporting records in the village Gericht protocols. Perhaps at that time many people went directly to the Oberamt, so that we only find an unknown percentage of instances in the village records. Nonetheless, given the sharp jump from the third period to the last, we might suspect that marital conflict was on the increase then, not perhaps, as the figures suggest, at a rate four times greater than before.

Perhaps a better measure of the seriousness of conflict is the demand for divorce. During the first 60 years of the records, few people mentioned divorce or permanent separation. Although the first recorded instance occurred in 1769, only after 1805 did the request for separation become frequent. By 1840, despite the fact that many conflicts still came to the village courts, the interest in breaking up a marriage fell off sharply. It seems possible to speak of a crisis in marriage between roughly 1800 and 1840, a period when many marriages seemed close to ending. That in itself does not mean that the problems between husbands and wives were any more acute or that violence and arguments were more frequent. But the phenomenon does suggest a changing structure in the relationships between men and women. In the overwhelming number of cases, wives sought divorce, not husbands. Out of 36 court appearances between 1822 and 1839, the wives explicitly refused to go back 21 times. And almost always their husbands either demanded or requested or hoped for their return. Just as women took the initiative when it came to demands for separation or divorce, they also instigated most of the proceedings altogether – and almost all cases came before the courts because of an explicit complaint. Table 4.2 shows that the plaintiffs in a majority of cases were wives. Of the 78 times when the person who brought the complaint was expressly mentioned, 75 percent were wives or their relatives. And when the initiator was not mentioned, the fact that the wife was usually questioned first and the husband appeared in a defensive position makes it fairly certain that the pattern of complaint throughout was the same.

[3] *Kirchenkonvent*, vol. 1, p. 113 (25.1.1743).

Women sought recourse frequently in the courts and were far more ready than their men to break up a marriage.

It was also common practice to report matters to the pastor. This could be done formally, and many women appear to have run along to the parsonage when violence or acute disagreement broke out. This did not mean that the pastor would agree to or suggest the need for a formal consistory session to consider the matter. He was just as likely to try to mediate between the spouses directly or to exercise his considerable authority to bring the offending party up short. Perhaps he was most likely to encourage a court confrontation when his authority or honor was put into question. He also had a great deal of leverage through communion, as villagers had to register at the parsonage before participating in it. This gave him a chance to discuss matters with an offender. According to one interpretation of the Pauline text about the disastrous consequences of sharing communion while in an "unworthy" condition, the pastor could suggest abstaining or could even withdraw the privilege altogether.[4]

Since women initiated most of the court cases, it was more likely that the sins of their husbands would get a full hearing. The latter were usually on the defensive and frequently refused to say very much or were defiant. Perhaps the ideology of the Haushalter or Hausvater helps explain some of the exchange in the courts. After all, the husband was supposed to be the manager of the smallest cell of the state, and whatever the details of the particular relationship between husband and wife, his understanding of its hierarchical character was being put in question. According to public ideology, he had the right to question the details of other people's actions inside the house without being answerable himself, but in the court scene the situation was reversed. His male prerogatives were put into question in an alliance between other men and his wife. In such an awkward situation, not knowing how to act, many men either kept silence, mumbled a few crude comments, or walked out. As we shall see later, women had a far richer vocabulary of abuse and complaint than men did. They forged powerful weapons in everyday exchange which served them well in court. Their articulateness was built on frequent street encounters and internal family discourse, and it was part of the techniques of power in the public forum of the village courts.

Table 4.3 gives the first appearance before the court by age and duration of marriage. Although the number of cases in the first three periods is rather limited, certain structures seem to emerge. Both the ages of the spouses and the duration of marriage are in most instance skewed sharply downward; that is, the median is a good deal less than the mean, which tells us that the extreme, high values of the range are not typical. In general, marital conflict which ended up in the courts could begin within a few years of marriage, during a woman's 20s, or could break out up to her early 40s. This roughly describes the period of

[4] David Warren Sabean, *Power in the Blood: Popular Culture and Village Discourse in Early Modern Germany* (Cambridge, 1984), pp. 37–60, 161–2.

fertility. After the child-bearing years were over, it was unlikely that the patterns of accommodation would break down. Most frequently, couples came before the court for the first time during the second or third year of marriage, and by the end of the third year almost half of the first cracks in the marriages had appeared. If we assume that people delayed a public appearance for some time, then the period of first conflict can be set back somewhat. If the strains were not apparent during these years, they usually became evident in the next three or four. In few of these cases were the husbands or wives particularly young; most were in their mid-20s to mid-30s. The evidence suggests that problems developed between husbands and wives soon after the first child was born or while there were two or three children under the age of six. It was not a problem of overly young people getting married, and both spouses had been well socialized to hard work routines by this time. It would seem that the conjunction of demands associated with domestic production and the reproductive cycle brought severe pressures at particular moments in a marriage. In the last period, the profile of the first marital conflict is more coherent than in the others. There, the median age for women was 27, and well over 50 percent of the cases occurred before the women were 30. Most frequently, conflict arose during the second year of marriage, with about half the cases coming to the courts before another two years were up. A recurring pattern of marital dispute during that period involved women in their late 20s in the early stages of childbearing, when they were at the height of their physical strength and productive vigor. This was the pattern during the period of marital crisis, when women frequently sought to walk away from their marriages and break up their households.

## Nature of complaints

It is possible to construct an overview of what husbands and wives complained about, although the protocols do not always provide details about specific charges. It may be that the local record keeper did not see the need for making explicit what everyone knew anyway, and sometimes village officials might not want to have prejudiced some villagers before courts of higher instance and the controlling eye of the Vogt. Taking all of the material together, however, we find enough evidence of the recurring patterns of dispute. Tables 4.5 to 4.10 only indicate what the spouses are explicitly recorded as saying. For example, for the period 1730–59, there are 16 protocols dealing with marital conflict, which contain 15 specific complaints voiced by husbands and 30 by wives (Table 4.5). Since scolding and swearing, violence, and drunkenness make up a considerable number of complaints, it may be useful to examine the general pattern before focusing on specifics.

There are certain differences in the way husbands and wives acted (see Table 4.5). To begin with, women articulated well over two times as many specific complaints as did men. And about 70 percent of them had to do with

Table 4.5 *Overall nature of complaints in cases of marital conflict*

| Period | Number of cases | Scolding and swearing | Violence | Other | Total individual complaints |
|---|---|---|---|---|---|
| *Husbands' complaints* (%) | | | | | |
| 1730–59 | 16 | 5 (33) | 1 (7) | 9 (60) | 15 |
| 1760–89 | 15 | 2 (18) | 0 (0) | 9 (82) | 11 |
| 1790–1819 | 16 | 0 (0) | 0 (0) | 7 (100) | 7 |
| 1820–50 | 66 | 17 (33) | 0 (0) | 34 (67) | 51 |
| Total | 113 | 24 (29) | 1 (1) | 59 (70) | 84 |

*Wives' complaints* (%)

| Period | Number of cases | Scolding and swearing | Violence | Drinking | Other | Total individual complaints |
|---|---|---|---|---|---|---|
| 1730–59 | 16 | 6 (20) | 11 (37) | 4 (13) | 9 (30) | 30 |
| 1760–89 | 15 | 3 (20) | 6 (40) | 3 (20) | 3 (20) | 15 |
| 1790–1819 | 16 | 7 (25) | 8 (29) | 6 (21) | 7 (25) | 28 |
| 1820–50 | 66 | 22 (18) | 36 (29) | 27 (22) | 40 (32) | 125 |
| Total | 113 | 38 (19) | 61 (31) | 40 (20) | 59 (30) | 198 |

abusive language, violence, and drinking – all three remained constant throughout the period, with an early shift in favor of drinking. The absolute level of violence and scolding certainly seems to have risen, while their relative incidence declined somewhat. Excessive tippling was never mentioned by a husband, and physical violence on the part of women seems to have been rare. Scolding and abusive language were commented on frequently by husbands, but there may have been some change in their incidence after 1820. Recall that women brought most of the cases before the court, and it may have been that men simply had to defend themselves as best they could. Still, they did not mention this one very often in the preceding 60 years. All the evidence points to a considerable rise in verbal quarreling after 1820. After verbal and physical abuse and drunkenness are subtracted, both men and women had about the same number of other things to complain about regarding each other in absolute terms.

As already mentioned, violence and drinking are practically missing from the complaints of men. It does not seem probable that no women ever imbibed too much. There is certainly gossip today about secret addiction to the bottle at home. Men, however, never made a point about the matter. As we shall see, complaints by women about men drinking always had to do with the fact that it was done in public with other men. (This issue is explored in some depth in chapter 6.) As for women and nonviolence, it is rather difficult to accept that

Table 4.6 *Specific complaints by husbands in cases of marital conflict*

| Complaint | 1730–59 | 1760–89 | 1790–1819 | 1820–49 |
|---|---|---|---|---|
| Money/independence | 4 | 1 | | 4 |
| Meister- /Herrschaft | 2 | | | 2 |
| Hausen | | | 1 | 5 |
| Work | 1 | 1 | 1 | 1 |
| Meals | | | 1 | 5 |
| Loyalty (*Treue*) | 1 | | 2 | 1 |
| Consumption | | 1 | 1 | |
| In-laws | 1 | 1 | 1 | 3 |
| Witchcraft accusation | 4[a] | | | |
| Sexual conduct | | | | 1 |
| Marital duty[b] | | | | 3 |
| Enmity[c] | | | | 2 |
| Stubbornness | | | | 2 |
| Ejection | | | | 2 |
| Leaving home | | 1 | | 3 |
| Scolding/swearing | | 5 | 2 | 17 |
| Violence | 1 | | | |

[a] Four court cases dealing with a continuing accusation by a woman that her husband was bewitching the family. The complaint was brought by the husband.
[b] *Eheliche Pflicht.*
[c] *Feindschaft.*

they never threw things, took up weapons to defend themselves, or, given the health and physical situation of people at the time, were never in a position to dominate physically.

There was a scattering of miscellaneous complaints by wives in the first period: troubles with in-laws and stepchildren, the fact that the husband did not fulfill his duties as a Haushalter well and that he used abusive terms like "witch" (*Hexe*). In the next period, there were a few more cases of sexual misconduct and in the third complaints that the husband ridiculed his wife, would not perform his marital duty (intercourse), was cold, unfeeling, stingy, lazy, or deceitful. Structurally, there is not a great deal to go on here, except to emphasize that increased complaints about the husband's ability to manage his affairs (hausen) went along with whatever hints there are about a new discourse of feeling. In the period after 1820, however, there was a considerable shift. Women complained that their husbands had driven them out, and let loose a flood of complaints about bad household management, inattention to work, intemperate language, anger, promiscuity, excessive drinking, and violent behavior. In general there seems to have been greater tension in sexual matters, with the introduction of the abusive term "whore" (*Hur*), complaints about sexual delicts, and lack of activity in the marital bed (this latter by both husbands and wives).

There was an important structural shift in male complaints as well. At the beginning, the central issues were about Herrschaft relations in the house, especially about the independent use of money. It was not until after 1790 that the woman's economy was mentioned – her Haushalt – her ability to work, the quality of her meals, and her ability to prepare them on time. By the 1820s, hausen, Haushalt, work, and meal preparation were all central matters. This development went together with conflicts over money and female independence, stubbornness, disobedience, and hostility, and above all a scolding and abusive tongue. There are even a few cases where the wife threw the husband out, but usually she was prepared to leave far more frequently than ever before.

In order to understand what was at issue in family confrontation, we investigate in detail five general themes suggested by this material: violence, verbal abuse, drinking, Herrschaft/obedience, and management/work. (The last three are discussed in Chapter 6.)

In the discussion which follows, we alternate structural accounts with statistical tables or logical reconstructions from instances of social interaction and extensive narratives of specific cases or excursive vignettes linked together in a kind of litany. Although these narratives are set off from the rest of the text

Table 4.7 *Specific complaints by wives in cases of marital conflict*

| Complaint | 1730–59 | 1760–89 | 1790–1819 | 1820–49 |
|---|---|---|---|---|
| Ridicule | | | 1 | |
| Business | | | 1 | 8 |
| Hausen | 4 | | 3 | 5 |
| Work | | | 1 | 7 |
| Failure to inform | 1 | | | 1 |
| In-laws | 1 | | | 1 |
| Stepchildren | 1 | | | 2 |
| Sexual delicts | | 2 | | 3 |
| Marital duty[a] | | | 1 | 1 |
| Lack of love (*Liebe*) | | | 1 | 1 |
| Anger | | | | 2 |
| Stinginess | | | 1 | |
| Deceit (*Betrug*) | | | 1 | |
| Scolding/swearing | 6 | 3 | 7 | 22 |
| Drinking | 4 | 3 | 6 | 27 |
| Ejection | | | | 11 |
| Violence | 11 | 6 | 8 | 36 |

[a] *Eheliche Pflicht.*

or confined to the Appendix, they do fulfill Flaubert's suggestion about God existing in the details.

## Nature of violence

Several factors must be taken into account when dealing with family violence. Current discussions are dominated by the widely held assumption that relations between men and women have always been characterized in some way or other by male aggression in the form of physical force. Too often, however, such an approach radically dehistoricizes violence and reduces it to what Eric Hobsbawm has called "the eternal struggle of the sexes." In this fashion, the problem is moved not just out of history but outside culture as well. If it can be handled at all, it becomes what we can best describe as part of the natural history of the species, which ironically reverses the standard image in Western civilization of the relationship of the sexes: Female is to male as nature is to culture. By seeing male violence as eternal, we put the male half of the gender relationship on the side of nature – which may be an emotionally satisfying thing to do, but one not likely to be analytically useful.

Yet in the cases from Neckarhausen, violence was almost totally on the male side. Only one husband ever reported that his wife had pushed him around. In typical fashion, she had grabbed him by the hair, which was the normal practice when women got into physical squabbles with women or with men other than their husbands. Male violence was almost always of another type: a slap with the open hand, a punch with the fist, a blow with a stick or club or with some nearby object, or occasionally a thrust with a knife. There are several cases of beating with a rope or whip. Almost never did a man kick his wife, although several times wives were thrown to the ground or down a flight of stairs. It is, of course, quite inconceivable that in the 140-year period covered by our records only one husband was attacked physically by his wife. Perhaps the embarrassment was too great to report it. What we are dealing with here is the public discourse of family relations, and for that, one central theme was male violence. And even the three men who had been kicked out by their wives did not say how it was done. Still, it is not our intent to question the real significance of violence or the suffering that went with it, but to try to understand the context in which it took place and to make our analysis historically specific.

In general, violence in Neckarhausen was of two kinds: either systematic chastisement or reactive striking out. Both types raised questions of legitimate force and the right of the husband to correct his wife physically. Chastisement, while it can take various forms, implies a hierarchical structure to family relationships in which the husband is jurally superior to the wife. His right to correct behavior physically is tied to implicit or explicit assumptions about the foundations of household unity. Power had to be located at one point in the house, and it was necessary to its existence; that is, it was understood as constitutive. Violence was integral to state ideology, and whether or not it was *douce*, it was still *violence*. But local officials had to be concerned with satisfying allied groups represented by a particular marriage and had to provide for the smooth running of households so that no threats to the security of property could get out of hand. Therefore, complaints about cruelty or about the inappropriate use of force got full hearing. Patriarchal values, however central for the eighteenth century, were negotiable. When we examine the details of the use of force, it appears that there was a general shift around the turn of the century in the direction of reactive violence. Rather than using the rod to enforce compliance or staging a carefully prepared beating, husbands boiled over in anger and wreaked immediate vengeance. There are several ways to demonstrate and describe this phenomenon. The least satisfactory is to tabulate the incidents available to us from the protocols.

Sometimes the actual part of the body which the husband struck is mentioned (Table 4.8). In the first period, blows above the shoulders were about evenly balanced with those below, although the numbers involved do not allow a definitive picture to be drawn. What does seem significant is the fact that in the last period 15 out of 18 cases involved blows above the shoulder. I would suggest that in the earlier period a strong sense of chastisement, of systematic punishment within the value system of patriarchy, was reflected. Men used a paddle or a rope or a sword or their open hand to punish or enforce compliance

Table 4.8 *Male violence – parts of the body struck (all cases)*

| Period | Face, mouth, side of head | Head, hair | Neck | Arm, shoulders | Body[a] |
|---|---|---|---|---|---|
| 1730–59 | 2 | 1 | 1 | 1 | 3 |
| 1760–89 | | | | 1 | |
| 1790–1819 | 2 | 1 | | | 1 |
| 1820–50 | 4 | 10 | 1 | 2 | 1 |

[a] Including being thrown down.

Table 4.9 *Male violence – weapons (all cases)*

| Period | Whip | Rope | Stick | Sword | Knife | Hand/ fist | Hard object[a] |
|---|---|---|---|---|---|---|---|
| 1730–59 | | 2 | 2 | 1 | 1 | 4 | 2 |
| 1760–89 | | | 3 | | 1 | | |
| 1790–1819 | | | 1 | | | 1 | 1 |
| 1820–50 | 1 | 1 | | | 2 | 4 | 5 |

[a] Chair, boot, hinge, flail, board, mug, stones, potatoes.

(Table 4.9). In the later period, fewer systematic attacks were in evidence – a blow to the head, a slap on the face, choking. The knife came out, the fist clenched, one threw what was to hand. Let us take a look at some instances of each kind of violence from each period.

*A good early example of violence to enforce compliance comes from the hamlet of Raidwangen, part of the larger parish of Neckarhausen (K-1742).*[5] *Anna Hentzler reported a quarrel with her husband, Jacob, a Bauer, who had tried to force her to lead the horse while he was plowing. She refused because she was sick, so he beat her on the shoulders with a stick. When she left to report the treatment to the pastor, Jacob followed and threatened to beat her with a rope. There were other issues aired at the deposition such as help she gave to her sister in another village, and Jacob was generally upset about her independence. In this instance, the consistory sided with the husband, judged that Anna had provoked him, and even considered putting her in jail overnight. In 1747 Agnes Speidel, wife of Hans Jerg, was brought before the consistory because of a fight with her husband (K-1747).*[6] *Her stepson had discovered a sack of money which she claimed had been saved from before her marriage. Her husband beat her with the flat of a sword while she was being held by the stepson. Her stepdaughter made it clear that the two men had carefully prepared the beating in order to punish her. Hans Jerg pointed out that several of the coins had been minted since the marriage. He complained that she had held the* Herrschaft *for nine years and that now he wanted to be his own master of the purse* (Säckelmeister). *The consistory concluded that the wife had given the most cause but punished the husband as well for using a sword, sentencing him to four hours in the local jailhouse and her to two. Barbara Bauknecht, wife of Johannes, a carpenter, had helped out a neighbor with a loaf of bread and with the returned money bought a loaf from a baker (K-1752).*[7] *Her husband was angry that she had done this behind his back and beat her with a rope. Both were warned by the consistory. Johann Georg Zeug often beat his wife because she wanted to become lord and master* (Herr *and* Meister) *(K-1755).*[8] *On the particular day in question because of a small amount of money she took, he choked her, threw her to the floor, tore off her dress, and beat her with a stick. He was fined largely because he did it on Sunday. He was also warned to live in a Christian manner. Jacob Falter, cooper, hit his wife hard because she had gotten the schoolmaster to write a letter to her sister in a nearby town, sending some money (K-1775).*[9] *Johann Georg Müller beat his wife because of her laziness and greed (K-1789).*[10] *Although she denied it, she was not able to convince the consistory. She was warned to greater diligence and he to more forbearance, and they shook hands. Eva Margaretha Bauknecht complained to the Schultheiss that her husband had treated her crudely* (gröblich behandelt) *(S-1840).*[11] *She said he hit her with a*

5 *Kirchenkonvent*, vol. 1, p. 111 (11.11.1742).
6 *Kirchenkonvent*, vol. 1, p. 178 (5.3.1747).
7 *Kirchenkonvent*, vol. 2, p. 71 (4.2.1752).
8 *Kirchenkonvent*, vol. 2 (12.10.1755); see Chapter 2.
9 *Kirchenkonvent*, vol. 2 (7.10.1775).
10 *Kirchenkonvent*, vol. 3 (13.2.1789).
11 *Schultheißenamt*, vol. 1, f. 3 (11.9.1840).

*rope, chased her to the attic, threw her on a bed, and choked her. That was because she wasted and stole all his things. She withdrew the complaint. Anna Maria Deuschle complained she was mishandled* (beleidigt) *by her husband, Friedrich (S-1841).*[12] *He had hit her with his fist and threw her out bodily when she failed to obey his order to leave. While she alleged she was green and blue over her whole body, he said he only gave her a couple of slaps. Since she complained to the Schultheiss, he had decided never to let her come back. The official said that she would not have reported her husband for a few slaps on the face, whereupon Deuschle said that if the Schultheiss did not believe him, he could "visit" his wife's ass* (seines Weibs Arsch visitieren).

The second form of violence was usually staged quite differently. The husband found himself in the position of having his weaknesses rehearsed in a torrent of abuse, to which he could answer in kind or with a blow from his hand or an object taken up for the occasion. In such situations, there was less

Table 4.10 *Scolding and violence in cases of marital conflict*

| | Wife's behavior | | | |
|---|---|---|---|---|
| Period | Number of cases | Scolds | Scolds/ husband scolds or swears | Scolds/ husband violent |
| 1730–59 | 16 | 8 | 3 | 8 |
| 1760–89 | 15 | 4 | 0 | 2 |
| 1790–1819 | 16 | 0 | 0 | 0 |
| 1820–49 | 66 | 20 | 9 | 14 |
| Total | 113 | 32 | 12 | 24 |

| | Husband's behavior | | | | | | |
|---|---|---|---|---|---|---|---|
| | Number of cases | Wife thrown out | Violent | Violent/ drunk | Scolds | Swears | Scolds/ swears/ violent |
| 1730–59 | 16 | 2 | 12 | 2 | 3 | 5 | 3 |
| 1760–89 | 15 | 1 | 9 | 4 | 1 | 1 | 2 |
| 1790–19 | 16 | 2 | 8 | 2 | 7 | 3 | 4 |
| 1820–49 | 66 | 13[a] | 35 + 4[b] | 7 | 21 | 3 | 10 + 2[c] |
| Total | 113 | 18 | 64 + 4 | 15 | 32 | 12 | 19 + 2 |
| | | | | | 44 | | |

[a] Between 1839 and 1848, 11 out of 26 cases

[b] Plus 1 *Drohung* (threat) and 3 *gröblich beleidigt* (maltreatment).

[c] Plus 2 *gröblich beleidigt*.

[12] *Schultheißenamt*, vol. 1. f. 48 (17.8.1841).

a symbolic demonstration of patriarchy as an exchange of firepower in a struggle over interpretations of reciprocal obligations. The weapons were of a different order, perhaps, but always a direct response to each other (Table 4.10).

We might take for our text an incident which occurred in the village in 1839 (K-1839), when Johann Georg Rieth answered the charges of his wife that he had struck her.[13] He said that she had scolded and looked into his face and he had only *defended* himself. If we set aside the truth of his account, this short text suggests a number of lines of investigation. First, Rieth put his physical act on a plane with his wife's verbal and visual actions. It was the proper response to what she had initiated. Furthermore, he implied by the word "defend" that her words and her glance were capable of doing him considerable injury. We should not dismiss this but consider the real power of the word and the look in that society. Then, too, his line of defense implies that any analysis of aggressive behavior which considers only the physical components is misleading. Finally, in Rieth's account there is a hint of weakness in the action of hitting his wife. He considered that he had no means of defense other than striking out. The use of physical violence does not always proceed from strength but frequently from the lack of an alternative. Not only is it extremely difficult to document that physical violence is a sign of weakness, but there is also the problem of how to define the terms of Herrschaft. It is not obvious from the many cases of male violence that domination was all on one side. Its central object was to slug the other partner into *silence.* The constantly repeated pattern to such dramas was the exchange of words and blows. At times the man started pounding and the woman answered with scolding. At other times the scolding started off the whole dispute. Both sides had weapons which were considered to be extremely damaging. Preoccupation with the look or angry glance went along with the increasing effectiveness of the male use of "witch" as an epithet in the nineteenth century, which often boiled down to fearful notions of the evil eye. Scolding and swearing were powerful acts, which brought about hundreds of court actions, precipitated brawls, and split up neighborhoods and families. As we shall see throughout this study, the complexity and effectiveness of female scolding stands out in contrast to the far simpler and repetitious vocabulary of men.

*A good example of the ambiguities present in many of the court cases comes from 1821 (G-1821).*[14] *Katharina Falter complained she could no longer* hausen *with her husband Anton. He beat her whenever he wanted to and she was no longer allowed to speak. She testified that he had hit her to the floor, stepped all over her, and threw her behind the table. She feared that he would beat her to a cripple. At least if she left now she could earn her bread with sound limbs. Anton said she swore continually for half a day, and after a warning, he had given her a few slaps* (Ohrfeigen). *That was all. It*

[13] *Kirchenkonvent*, vol. 4 (28.3.1839).
[14] *Gericht*, vol. 10, f. 14 (26.7.1821).

*was not necessary to protocol all that. His wife should just return, and he would not hit her again. Maria Catharina Hentzler was brought into the consistory because of continual marital disputes (K-1823).*[15] *She said that she tried her best to fulfill her duties, but her husband drank, and she was physically afraid of him. She had often run away. Michael, her husband, a Bauer, argued that she scolded all the time, and that is why he treated her so harshly* (hart tractieren). *The longer things went on, the more disorderly* (liederlich) *she got, and the less hope there was for improvement. Michael Bauknecht was cited for mishandling his wife Barbara (O-1823).*[16] *He had come from the mill, asked his wife for a coin which she no longer had, and punched her in the head. He also threatened her brother when he tried to interfere. Michael said that he had only hit his wife when she called him a "gypsy"* (Zigeuner). *Mathias Häfner had been punished several times for drunkenness and various "excesses" (O-1823).*[17] *On the latest occasion, he had come home drunk. He said his wife and sister-in-law had started a fight. His wife scolded, so he hit her. He pointed out that he had no property of his own and had to live in his wife's house where his sister-in-law could continually meddle in his* Haushaltung. *Friederika Beck complained her husband hit her so hard he practically knocked an eye out of her head (K-1833).*[18] *She would rather become a servant than be mistreated all the time because of her cooking. He said she gave cause by her wicked speech and scolding* (böse Rede und Schimpfworten). *Catharina Margaretha Hentzler wanted to leave her husband, Johann Georg (K-1833).*[19] *Her marriage had been one of continual disagreement for 10 or 20 years. This time he gave her a hole in her head and almost tore off her arm. He said she gave cause through her horrible blasphemy* (abscheuliche Lästerreden) *and scolding. If she stopped her wicked speech* (böse Reden), *he would not say things in anger.*

The evidence about violence shows that at the turn of the century disputes over practical everyday matters were no longer primarily hierarchical dramas, but exchanges in which women asserted themselves and made strong claims for the right to call their husbands to book. In their general deportment, they were quick to express their opinions about the ordering of marital reciprocities. From every indication available in the sources, such screaming matches entertained the neighbors for quite some distance, and it was not unusual for a passerby to come to the aid of a woman who made known her distress in loud tones. The labels a wife hurled at her husband were so telling because they were so public. His anxiety and distress were rooted in the fact that reputation counted in the hundreds of negotiations he was called upon to carry out. That reputation was built up in a round of public gossip in which women held the strings of power. A strong, supportive wife was an important point of power in a network of continual discussion. The words issuing from the "privacy" of a kitchen or sitting room were chosen for their effect.

[15] *Kirchenkonvent*, vol. 4 (8.3.1823).
[16] *Oberamtsgericht*, HSAL, F190II, Band 259, f. 196 (13.3.1823).
[17] *Oberamtsgericht*, HSAL, F190II, Band 259, f. 285 (3.6.1823).
[18] *Kirchenkonvent*, vol. 4 (27.3.1833).
[19] *Kirchenkonvent*, vol. 4 (5.6.1833).

## The symbolism of abusive language

Words hurled at someone in the pressure of the moment are chosen from a wider vocabulary of abuse. Some, of course, are stereotyped, and their form is just as or perhaps more important than the content. Many terms come to be used so regularly that few people reflect on their origins. Take, for example, the English epithet "bloody." In England, it is still a powerful, highly restricted term, whereas in America it carries little force and is used far less often. In neither country are people conscious of calling on Christ's blood when they use the term, even if they could trace its derivation. A complete catalogue of abusive language only tells half the story, since the more powerful words are perhaps the ones not used at all. Ivan Illich has suggested in another context a categorization useful for our purposes here.[20] Speaking of food habits, he notes that people divide things that can be eaten into the eatable, the tabooed, and things that are not food, such as, for most North Americans, geraniums, which Mexican peasants consume with relish. There are, I would suggest, many words, even powerful abusive terms, which simply are not thought of for particular occasions. Tabooed words, however, involve crossing boundaries and can be used to mark the seriousness of a situation. Their effectiveness depends on context, frequency of use, and the characters of the people involved. Establishing a hierarchy of the strength of terms is beside the point because that hierarchy is strongly tied to situation, the complexity of which is only accessible to the participants.

The following paragraph contains a complete catalogue of all abusive terms exchanged by married couples in Neckarhausen. The list is expanded in Chapter 13. Unfortunately, court protocols often referred to swearing or scolding without recording the terms, or, what is more frustrating, recorded some and noted that there were worse things said, better left unwritten. Although what remains is a partial list of abusive terms, when considered as a whole it should offer some insight into the relations under consideration.

*Hans Melchior Thumm called his wife a* Hund *(dog) (K-1727).*[21] *He called his mother-in-law an* unreiffte Baplerin *(unripe babbler). Conrad Meyer yelled to his wife, "du Hund komm herunter" (hey dog, come down here) (K-1728).*[22] *Then he hit and tormented her. Michael Häussler hit his wife on the head and said, "du Hund du muss sterben" (you dog, you must die) (K-1743).*[23] *Later at home he said, "der Hund muss sterben" (the dog must die). The next day he was throwing things around in the presence of the children who began to cry. He said, "wart du Hund" (wait you dog), and I will knife you when I get you alone. In the consistory, he said she screamed,* Lumpen *(trash) and* Schelmen *(scoundrel) at him. Hans Jerg Müller said his wife*

[20] Ivan Illich, *Gender* (New York, 1982), pp. 142ff.
[21] *Kirchenkonvent*, vol. 1 (11.5.1727).
[22] *Kirchenkonvent*, vol. 1. p. 7 (7.11.1728).
[23] *Kirchenkonvent*, vol. 1, p. 113, (–.1.1743).

*called him* Vogel *(bird, fool)*, Schelm, Dieb *(thief) and* Hund *(K-1744).*[24] *He said she inherited all that; she did not buy it* (erkauft). *He called his wife (and daughter)* Hexen *(witches). Anna Maria Häussler called her husband* Lumpenhauser *(trashy householder) and accused him of sleeping with the maid (K-1750).*[25] *Barbara Bauknecht's husband said she called him and his family* Schelmen *and* Diebe *(K-1752).*[26] *A wife called her husband* Saumägen *(pig belly) (K-1754).*[27] *Johannes Thumm said if a storm came up he hoped a* Blitz *(bolt of lightning) would drive his wife into the ground (K-1761).*[28] *Johann Falter's wife called her husband and his* Freundschaft *(relatives)* Hexenwahr *(pack of witches) and* Lumpenpack *(trashy lot) (K-1762).*[29] *Leonhard Weiler's wife said he worked magic on her, her livestock, and her children (K-1769).*[30] *(This case, together with subsequent court appearances, is not just one of name-calling or abuse but an actual accusation of witchcraft.) She would not allow him to eat with her. Her son had a swollen head. The sick boy wrote that the loom was bewitched. They all went to the Catholic town of Elchingen (where there was an exorcist) (K-1770).*[31] *There was no rest from Satan in their house. She said he was a* Hexenmeister *(sorcerer). When she ate alone she could digest the food, but when she ate from the bowl, she got sick. Weiler complained his wife kept calling him* Hexenmeister *and saying he killed her children and bewitched the livestock (K-1770).*[32] *Every time she ate with him she was bewitched and became sick. She would not allow her son from the first marriage to take a piece of bread from him. He went into other houses and ate more there, which proved that he was an adulterer. Leonhard Weiler complained that his wife continued to accuse him of witchcraft (K-1771).*[33] *He bewitched the children so that their bodies swelled up and turned them into* Hexen, *etc. Margaretha Agnes Bauknecht complained her husband Johann Georg Müller treated her like a* Hund *and almost killed her (K-1796).*[34] *George Friedrich Hörtz swore and fumed and called his wife* verekter Hund *(dead dog) (K-1803).*[35] *Johann Georg Beck called his wife a* Hur *(whore) and hit her on the mouth (K-1804).*[36] *The wife of Salomon Bauknecht complained he called her a* Hur *(K-1806).*[37] *This case went to the Oberamt, where the charge was repeated (O-1806).*[38] *Margaretha Grauer complained her husband scolded and swore (K-1808).*[39] *He called her a* Hur, *and alleged she was pregnant by someone else. Johann Wilhelm Renzler called his wife Anna Maria*

[24] *Kirchenkonvent*, vol. 1, p. 138 (24.8.1744).
[25] *Kirchenkonvent*, vol. 2, p. 49 (24.8.1750).
[26] *Kirchenkonvent*, vol. 2, p. 71 (4.2.1752).
[27] *Kirchenkonvent*, vol. 2 (12.4.1754).
[28] *Kirchenkonvent*, vol. 2 (16.2.1761).
[29] *Kirchenkonvent*, vol. 2 (12.9.1762).
[30] *Kirchenkonvent*, vol. 2 (22.1.1769).
[31] *Kirchenkonvent*, vol. 2 (13.7.1770).
[32] *Kirchenkonvent*, vol. 2 (13.7.1770).
[33] *Kirchenkonvent*, vol. 2 (11.1.1771).
[34] *Kirchenkonvent*, vol. 3 (4.6.1796).
[35] *Kinchenkonvent*, vol. 3 (21.8.1803).
[36] *Kirchenkonvent*, vol. 3 (26.9.1804).
[37] *Kirchenkonvent*, vol. 3 (6.11.1806).
[38] *Oberamtsgericht*, STAL, F190II, Band 9, f. 295 (2.12.1806).
[39] *Kirchenkonvent*, vol. 3 (20.11.1808).

liederlich *(dissolute) and a cripple (she would not live with him) (O-1809).*[40] *One court case provides an example of a wife swearing "all day" (G-1821).*[41] *Maria Catharina Hentzler called Michael* liederlicher Geselle *(dissolute fellow) (G-1822).*[42] *Barbara Bauknecht called her Michael* Zigeuner *(gypsy) (O-1823),*[43] *and Catharina Hentzler called her Michael* krummer Spitzbuben *(dishonest rogue) (O-1823).*[44] *Johann Friedrich Bross complained of his wife's scolding, blaspheming, and swearing. She had called on the devil. She called him* Spitzbuben *and* Gwerhengst *(randy stud) (K-1826/7).*[45] *The husband of Rebecca Häfnerin called her, her mother, and her whole family* Hexen *(G-1829).*[46] *She was no longer permitted to go to the pregnant women (she was the midwife). She said his family is* schlecht *(bad). Johann Georg Häfner called his wife a* schlechte *person and* Hur *(K-1832).*[47] *The husband of Catharina Margaretha Hentzler called her a* Reisen *(noisy woman – from* Rassel*) (K-1833).*[48] *He complained of her* abscheuliche Lästerreden *(horrible blasphemy) and* Schimpfworte *(insulting words). Mathias Ebinger called his wife a* Hexe *and her mother an old* Hexe *(K-1833).*[49] *Margaretha Deuschle complained Michael called her* Hexe *and* Hur *(K-1834).*[50] *He scolded and swore. Margaretha Häfner accused her husband Johann Georg of making Barbara Feldmaier pregnant (G-1834).*[51] *He ran around with other* Huren. *Fire should fall from heaven and burn him. Johannes Brodbeck said his father was as* liederlich *as his wife (S-1841).*[52] *Johann Georg Rieth said Catharina was the cause of the sickness of her children – or that she was a* Hexe *(S-1843).*[53] *He tore his three-year-old son from her bed so that she would not contaminate him. Christoph Deuschle called his wife, father-in-law, and her siblings a* Hexenkor *(bunch of witches) (S-1844).*[54] *He accused his father-in-law of killing his cow and doves and bringing him poison to drink. Johann Georg Rieth's wife called him* Lumpen *(S-1847).*[55] *Conrad Reichle complained his divorced wife called him* Lumpentier *(trashy animal) (S-1848).*[56] *He now had his* Lumpenbett. *She called him* Hurenbub *(whore chaser) on the street. Johann Georg Rieth's wife called him* Saukopf *(pig's head) (S-1848).*[57]

It is apparent from this list that there were significant differences in the terms

[40] *Oberamtsgericht*, STAL, F190II, Band 9, f. 481 (17.7.1809).
[41] *Gericht*, vol. 10, p. 14 (26.7.1821).
[42] *Gericht*, vol. 10, f. 48 (16.4.1822).
[43] *Oberamtsgericht*, STAL, F190II, Band 259, f. 196 (13.3.1823).
[44] *Oberamtsgericht*, STAL, F190II, Band 259, f. 325 (28.7.1823).
[45] *Kirchenkonvent*, vol. 4 (between 18.6.1826 and 11.2.1827).
[46] *Gericht*, vol. 11, f. 155 (6.11.1829).
[47] *Kirchenkonvent*, vol. 4 (20.10.1832).
[48] *Kirchenkonvent*, vol. 4 (5.6.1833).
[49] *Kirchenkonvent*, vol. 4 (24.11.1833).
[50] *Kirchenkonvent*, vol. 4 (24.3.1834).
[51] *Gericht*, vol. 12, f. 174 (12.12.1834).
[52] *Schultheißenamt*, vol. 1, f. 62 (25.10.1841).
[53] *Schultheißenamt*, vol. 2, f. 15 (9.1.1843).
[54] *Schultheißenamt*, vol. 2, f. 50 (1.6.1844).
[55] *Schultheißenamt*, vol. 2, f. 140 (26.2.1847).
[56] *Schultheißenamt*, vol. 2, f. 158 (21.2.1848).
[57] *Schultheißenamt*, vol. 2, f. 185 (10.10.1848).

Table 4.11 *Terms of abuse used by spouses in the eighteenth century*

| Husband to wife | Wife to husband |
|---|---|
| *Hexe* (witch) | *Hexenmeister* (sorcerer)<br>*Hexenwahr* (pack of witches) |
| | *Lumpen* (trash)<br>*Lumpenhauser* (trashy householder)<br>*Lumpenpack* (trashy lot) |
| | *Dieb* (thief)<br>*Schelm* (scoundral) |
| *Hund* (dog) | *Hund* (dog)<br>*Saumagen* (pig's belly)<br>*Vogel* (bird, fool) |

used by the two sexes and that there were changes over time. We can begin our analysis by examining the words that occur in the texts from the eighteenth century (Table 4.11).

The range of terms for women to choose from was much greater than that for men, which is true not only here but in the other contexts of abusive language. Women seem to have developed a rather flexible arsenal with which to arm themselves in scenes of domestic quarrel. Men, on the other hand, were either less quick witted or did not go so readily armed to the fray. It is also possible that the pastor, the town clerk, and the Schultheiss were more ready to record evidence for stereotypical female behavior and did not notice or need to note similar activity on the part of men. In any event, neither husbands nor wives utilized the rich German vocabulary of scatalogical phrases, which were used with such telling effect in other Neckarhausen squabbles.[58] Above all, given the evidence from other contexts, there were no *Loch* compounds – "asshole" and the like.

Both husbands and wives used words that emphasized the contractual aspect of marriage. They seem to have been conscious of the two sets of relatives who were brought together through their marriage. Women used several terms which linked their husbands to their origins: Lumpenpack, Lumpen, Hexenwahr. The sense here was that the husband was part of a scurrilous or trashy family or came from a line of witches. And the term Hexenmeister could be understood in the same spirit. From the male side, one of the two frequently used epithets was "witch." One husband said that his wife had inherited and not bought her disposition and added that she and her daughter were both witches. There is a good deal of evidence to show that

[58] Cf. Alan Dundes, *Life Is Like a Chicken Coop Ladder: A Portrait of German Culture through Folklore* (New York, 1984).

witchcraft was understood to run in families, either from mother to daughter or sometimes to son. Leonhard Weiler's wife thought that he was turning his son into a witch. And Johann Georg Rieth later on tore his son from his wife's bed so that she would not contaminate him with witchcraft. It therefore seems that an accusation of witchcraft or insult of witch went beyond the individual concerned and implied a wider culpability. Thus, whatever else the house was, it was always the product of continued negotiations between two larger parties. Inside the house each spouse viewed the other in terms of contending interests and conflicting loyalties and set him or her inside a configuration of character traits, blood lines, and moral force.

Not all the epithets used by women implied collective responsibility. There were also those terms which emphasized individual behavior: Dieb, Schelm, Hund, Vogel, Saumagen. Four of these were used by one woman in one breath, so it is difficult to weigh their typicality. Thief, scoundrel, and dog – probably here having a sense of being mean – suggest active characteristics, words which follow from specific incidents. Vogel is a word that is often coupled with Schelm. They are the few terms of abuse in this catalogue that can be tied to a man's Haushaltung. We are left with only pig's belly as an individual state of being.

In the eighteenth century, the use of the word *Hund* was frequent when a husband scolded his wife. It was used by Hans Melchior Thumm, Conrad Meyer, Michael Häussler, Johann Georg Müller, and Georg Friedrich Hörtz, and was recorded for the last time in 1803. Several times death and dog were brought together in the same context. Häussler coupled the term with the threat to kill his wife, while Hörtz referred to his wife as a dead dog. Margaretha Müller complained that her husband treated her like a dog and had witnesses to prove that he had tried to kill her. While we cannot unpack the total field of meaning associated with Hund, there are several suggestions in the ethnographic literature which seem to be helpful. We have seen that the use of the term in Neckarhausen was often coupled with particularly brutal behavior, several times with severe beating. The term may simply have been used as it is today, in the sense of treating someone shabbily – like a dog. But in folklore, dogs were often closely associated with death.[59] Their barking foretold its coming, but there is also another way in which the two things were conjoined. For example, it was possible to transfer sickness, especially fever, to a dog, perhaps by putting nail parings in its food. This obviously describes a situation of competition – the sickness either consumes the person or it consumes the dog. What seems to be implied in the image of Hund coupled with considerable physical aggression is precisely a situation of severe competition, a breakdown of exchange, the continued existence of the husband being possible only with the denial of existence of the wife. In any event, the use of the term "dog" arose in situations where the husband displayed extreme physical aggression.

[59] *Handwörterbuch des deutschen Aberglaubens*, art. "Hund."

Table 4.12 *Terms of abuse used by spouses in the nineteenth century*

| Husband to wife | Wife to husband |
|---|---|
| *Hexe* (witch) | |
| *Hexenkor* (pack of witches) | *Zigeuner* (gypsy) |
| *Hur* (whore) | *Gwerhengst* (randy stud) |
| | *Hurenbub* (whore chaser) |
| *Krippel* (cripple) | *Lumpen* (trash) |
| *Schlechte Person* (bad person) | *Lumpentier* (trashy animal) |
| *Reisen* (noisy woman) | *Spitzbuben* (rogue) |
| *Liederlich* (dissolute) | *liederlicher Geselle* (dissolute fellow) |
| | *Saukopf* (pig's head) |
| | Swearing: |
| | Calls on *Teufel* (devil) |
| | Calls on *Blitz* (lightning) |

In the nineteenth century the imagery changed somewhat (Table 4.12). The dominant words used by the husband are *Hexe* and *Hur*. Hur was new in the nineteenth century, and was often coupled with bad management. Either the wife complained of the bad Haushaltung of her husband, and he called her a Hur in return, or he complained of her slovenly housekeeping and called her a Hur to boot. While both terms express central dangers to the husband, Hexe ties the wife to her family, while Hur is more individualizing and stresses her own power and character. In fact, the two terms capture the essential parts of any marital alliance, the larger context of family and the system of exchange between the spouses. Calling the wife a whore, however, implies a fundamental threat to the husband's line, and it, too, cannot be analyzed outside the wider system of alliance. The marriage is supposed to ensure legitimate offspring, children who belong to both "lines," to both sides of the alliance. A whore and a bad cook are threats, on the one hand, to the house as a point in the larger network of exchange and, on the other, to the house as a productive unit based on reciprocity.

Some of the terms the wives used in the nineteenth century continued the tradition of the eighteenth: Spitzbuben, Lumpen, Lumpentier, Zigeuner. There were sexual terms to balance the new male use of "whore": Gewerhengst and Hurenbub. Liederlich is a term used by both wives and husbands, not only for each other but for all kinds of other people in the village. It came to be the expression that most frequently led to court action in the nineteenth century. There is no exact English equivalent. When coupled with *Geselle*, it means something like the archaic expression "lewd fellow," that is, dissolute, slovenly, disorderly. But by no means does it always carry with it sexual overtones. For example, a servant girl might be pregnant but not at all liederlich.[60] Perhaps the central meaning has to do with the manner in which one carried on one's affairs. It is the opposite of sober, honest, industrious, and diligent. If we have chronicled a crisis of the house in the early nineteenth century, its watchword was liederlich.

Until the nineteenth century, there are no examples of women swearing at, or in the presence of, their husbands. As we have seen, in both centuries men cursed and swore. If we look at the way relationships were modeled in the eighteenth century, hierarchically, with men in a position mediating between the state and all jural minors – women and children – then the Hausvater also stood in an intermediate position between God and the inner household. It was his privilege to enter into the dangerous sphere of the holy and call on thunder and lightning, invoke extraterrestrial power against his enemies, and to play with the dangers attendant on blasphemy. When we find women calling on the devil, blaspheming so heavily that their husbands intervened, or calling on lightning to act in their service, we encounter a break in a taboo. It was a fundamental challenge to hierarchically modeled relations and suggests a strong claim on the part of women for an altered understanding of reciprocities. The social shift underlying this new perception is discussed in Chapters 5 and 6.

Looking at the structure of abuse as a whole, we have suggested that the most fundamental terms used by husbands and wives emphasized the contractual aspects of the household as a node in a wider network of kinship alliances and as a production community continually engaged in negotiating its terms of reciprocity. Men shifted from the word Hund to Hur in the nineteenth century and thus exhibited an altered perception from passive to active competition. At the same time, both husbands and wives came to use more terms that had to do with the household and work. Part of the new tension seems to have been built around a changing sexual division of labor, which gradually reordered the map of mystical danger and noumenal power by reordering the spheres of production and breaking up the substantial supports for a hierarchical modeling of relationships.

Chapters 3 and 4 have demonstrated that conflict between husbands and wives changed its shape around 1800 and intensified for several decades after political peace was established. Although active disagreement and open dispute are what make our analysis possible, because so many documents were generated in the process, conflict itself is not what we are trying to study. Marriage and family life can be significantly altered without stress or without public notice, and we are only trying to use sources recording unusual events to get at the ordinary and mundane. Although there may have been an increase in

[60] On this point, see Regina Schulte, "Infanticide in Rural Bavaria in the Nineteenth Century," in *Interest and Emotion. Essays on the Study of Family and Kinship*, ed. Hans Medick and David Warren Sabean (Cambridge, 1984), pp. 77–102, here 84–5.

verbal abuse, just as important for us have been changes in its nature, the choice of epithets, and their symbolic load. In Chapter 1 we chronicled alterations in agriculture and craft production. The overall course of intensification coincides fairly closely with the new discourse on the house, and with the crisis over household management, diligence, and sobriety, as well as housewifery, obedience, and efficiency. Rage, tantrums, threats of separation, and actions for divorce became characteristic just about the time stall feeding became common. In Chapters 5 and 6 we shall see how the sexual division of labor changed with the alterations in agriculture, and how they in turn helped shape some of the issues that exercised marriage partners from the turn of the century onward.

# 5

# The changing context of production

> The task of understanding does not basically amount to recognizing the form used, but rather to understanding it in a particular concrete context.
>
> – Bakhtin/Vološinov[1]

Reading historical documents, particularly the kind we are dealing with here, is a little like catching snatches of conversation while moving along a crowded street. We know pretty much what the words signify, but their specific effect eludes us just because words only have meaning in the context of particular relations. We are, of course, interested in the details of individual lives to the degree that they illustrate the logic of social relationships or shed light on the alternative resources and strategies for action in the society under examination. Different forces underlie the patterns we find, but one area crucial for giving structure is the relationships of production, just because much of what people talk about, reflect upon, disagree about, embody, internalize, or escape has to do with labor, the problems and satisfactions of working with various people, and the things that are produced. Although most language is embedded in concrete, material practices and is directed toward appropriating everyday reality, how that appropriation takes place is open to the range of human talent, from ingenuity and creativity, to stupidity and callousness. To say that culture is about concrete existence is not to say that material existence produces particular cultural items or social relationships. It does mean that to parse a particular utterance, we do have to build up a complex understanding of the context in which it was projected.

In order to understand just how shifting relationships of production shaped the discourse between husbands and wives in Neckarhausen, one must focus on the details of agricultural practice, alterations in craft production, and the marketability of skills in construction and building trades. The problem has two sides: We need to study specific experience in village social life as well as subtle clues in the passing conversations that might reveal what villagers thought about these experiences. Rooted in the practices of everyday life, many fundamental

[1] V. N. Vološinov [Mikhail Bakhtin], *Marxism and the Philosophy of Language*, trans. Ladislav Matejka and I. R. Titunik (Cambridge, Mass., 1986), p. 68.

issues were never reflected upon in the kinds of sources we have at our disposal, and still others were hidden from the villagers themselves. For example, a generation which grew up with only cows and oxen for traction might not have been conscious of the way relationships between families were different from those dominated by horse traction. Certain forms of interaction might have been entirely restructured without anyone in the next generation being conscious of the shift. The few old people who remembered the change would have had nothing relevant to say about it for the active adults of the village. Even if some were conscious of the implications of the change, they would not have prefaced remarks in a court squabble with reflections on connections between new forms of productive relations and, say, verbal abuse, lousy cooking, or a slap on the face.

## Sexual division of labor

I have tried in Chapter 1 and Appendixes A, B, and D to be as specific as possible about alterations in land use and cropping patterns, for these details are crucial in examining changes in the sexual division of labor. Since the family's structure was based at least in part on its organization of work, we will not be able to understand its patterns of exchange and cooperation, strains, and conflicts without looking into the details of its labor processes. Although many of the trends in economic innovation and agricultural intensification in the village were part of a more global shift in the German economy as a whole, the particularities of timing and the context of small peasant production in the specific situation of Neckarhausen are also significant.

One of the important agricultural changes under way by the 1760s was the cultivation of various leguminous plants and leafy brassicae in the fallow field. These plants provided a basis for stall feeding. The period from 1800 to 1830 witnessed the development of intensive meadow cultivation, an end to horse traction, a concentration on livestock, intensified flax and hemp production, the disappearance of viniculture, and the restructuring of pasture for sheep as a result of the new systems of crop rotation. The exclusion of immigrants in the 1730s and 1740s, petitions to grow green fodder in the fallow during the 1770s and 1780s, crib and stall construction during the first two decades of the nineteenth century, a leap in potato planting in 1816–17, battles over bleaching places at the beginning of the 1820s – all were signs of the revolution in production. These changes were accompanied by the development of regional employment in the building trades, migratory farm labor, navvying, colportage, and a makeshift economy.

A particularly important agricultural innovation was the stall feeding of cows and oxen. How much of the new, heavy work, such as pitching manure and spreading straw, was sex-specific during this period, I do not know. It does appear from all reports that the care of small animals was largely in the hands of women, and milking certainly was. For the gathering of fodder, however, we have good evidence that this became largely women's work. Once regular pasturage was given up, fodder had to be carried to the village from the fields, which were on average more than 2 kilometers away. It would have been absurd to hitch the hungry cow to a cart, drive up the steep hill to the strip of clover, cut the clover and load it on the cart, only to bring it all back to the stall to feed the cow. It was much more practical to send the wife, for a man could not do such work without violating well-established cultural routines. Clover, alfalfa, sainfoin, and the like were carried in large kerchiefs on the head, a custom that seems to have been entirely female. Men, when they carried anything, did so in knapsacks, which were quite unsuitable for fetching such bulky products. There is a great deal of iconographic evidence from the period to show how normal it was for women to be seen with large loads of fodder on their heads.[2] In Neckarhausen, the resting benches constructed at the top of the hill for the use of these women consisted of four great stone slabs – one to sit on, two for the sides, and one at the top for setting down or picking up a load.

The fact that once stall feeding was in place women took care of fetching

Stone resting bench near the top of the hill on the way from the fields.

[2] See, for example, the frontispiece of various *Oberamtsbeschreibungen*. A good example in art is the painting by Gottlob Friedrich Steinkopf (1799–1860), "Schloss und Gestüt Weil bei Esslingen" (c. 1828) in the Staatsgalerie in Stuttgart. There are examples of women stealing hay kerchiefs from each other: e.g., *Gericht*, vol. 9, f. 43 (4.5.1818).

fodder is reflected in the list of forest delicts (*Waldrugungen*).[3] Every year, many villagers were fined for stealing from the woods. They took everything from logs, to kindling, to acorns and beechnuts, to grass. Those short of food for their animals continually raided the open, grassy plots. In the eighteenth century, grass filching, whenever it did take place, was done by men, but in the nineteenth, not only did the incidence of such crimes increase, but they were carried out almost entirely by women. In 1730, for example, 26 people were caught stealing grass, and all but two of them were men. In 1790, by contrast, most of the 24 people caught stealing grass "im jungen Hau" were women (20 women, 2 boys, and 1 man). Later on in that year, 10 more people were caught, 7 women and 3 boys. In 1820, 23 fines were levied on 20 women and 3 boys for stealing grass. During that same year, 22 people from the neighboring village of Oberensingen were also caught with grass, 20 women and 2 boys. With the introduction of green fodder crops, there were new labor inputs for women in stall feeding. From the 1770s onward, they were drawn more and more into such work, and there was a substantial leap in demand for their labor in the 1820s, when the cowherd was fired and the stragglers adopted year-round stall feeding.

Another new form of labor appeared when the village began growing root crops, the leafy brassicae, and légumes. As we have seen, potatoes were introduced in the 1760s and made slow headway during the next several decades, with the famines of the 1770s and 1816–17 spurring on production. Such crops have to be worked with the hoe. All the evidence for nineteenth-century Germany indicates that they were worked mainly by women.[4] Turnips or beets, for example, were frequently started in a garden bed and then planted in the rows of the field individually. Potatoes were planted by women in the furrows left by the plow. Individual seeds such as beans and peas would be planted with a dibble stick. Once planted, these crops demanded continual hoeing. It has been estimated that a hectare of turnips takes one individual about a week to hoe. This can be done four, five, or six times, depending on the care with which the crop is grown. If the fallow were totally given over to turnips, sugar beets, potatoes, and the like, the area under cultivation in a three-field system would increase by 50 percent. But unlike grain crops, root crops require an enormous amount of labor input between sowing and harvesting. The steady, arduous, individual effort that goes into weeding and aerating the soil can only take place if a large, cheap labor force is available. In the great estate areas of Germany, such as those around Magdeburg, which specialized

[3] The *Gemeindepflegerechnungen* for each year contain "extracts" from the *Feld- und Waldrugungs-protocolle*. References to dates in the text are to the relevant volumes of the *Rechnungen*.

[4] See the important work by Karl Kaerger, "Die Sachsengängerei," in *Landwirtschaftliche Jahrbücher*, 19 (1890), pp. 239–522. Friedrich Aeroboe, *Allgemeine landwirtschaftliche Betriebslehre*, 4th ed. (Berlin, 1919), pp. 128ff. Maria Bidlingmaier, *Die Bäuerin in zwei Gemeinden Württembergs*, Staatswissenschaftliche Dissertation Tübingen (Stuttgart, 1918), pp. 26–83.

in sugar beets, teams of women were imported from the east for the season.[5] But in Neckarhausen such labor was absorbed by the wives, daughters, maids, and young sons of the peasant families. The extension of hoe crops – legumes and vetch, followed by mangolds – beginning in the 1760s coincides with the increase in female labor on the fields. A substantial growth in such work took place in the period around and after 1815.

New forms of male labor were also available to village inhabitants. Intensification in agriculture went closely together with infrastructural development. Men were involved, of course, in building the stalls, barns, and sheds which housed the cattle and provided for storage. And they were also involved in communal and regional projects of improvement, such as the straightening of the Neckar River between 1832 and 1836.[6] The engineering for the construction and part of the cost were handled by the state, but the village provided much of the labor and paid for the rest of the expenses for its stretch of the river. Even before this project, which helped control some of the flooding, many fields were laboriously cleared of gravel, plowed up, and brought into cultivation, but afterward the banks of the river had to be constantly repaired, planted with willows to control erosion, and maintained. The main highway was rerouted south of the village next to the river and had to be continually repaired by village labor.[7]

For a long time, the village maintained a series of ditches to handle water runoff. The main fields were on a plateau up above the village, but many vineyards, meadowlands, orchards, garden plots, building sites, pastures, and some arable fields were on the steep grade rising from the river. To prevent erosion on the bank and to drain the soggy soil on the plateau or by the river bed, villagers built an intricate series of ditches, which placed a burden of overlapping and complex responsibilities on the individual owners who had to maintain them. In the nineteenth century, the village put in a system of drains to increase the efficiency of water control. But as soon as clover and alfalfa were introduced, individuals began constructing new drainage systems for their plots.[8]

Another issue, which increased as the fallow was planted with root crops, clover, alfalfa, and various other intensive field crops, such as fodder beans, peas and the like, had to do with access to plots. In the old system, everyone planted and harvested at the same time, which simplified access in the kaleidoscopic field pattern. Under the new system, the field map had to be simplified.

5 Kaerger, "Sachsengängerei."

6 The project as well as all of the receipts for construction costs are in the *Gemeindepflegerechnungen*. See also *Gericht*, vol. 12, f. 216 (11.1.1836).

7 Example of maintenance: *Gericht*, vol. 11, f. 14 (3.7.1826); vol. 15, f. 180 (1.7.1852); f. 244 (1.7.1853).

8 Details about drainage occur at every annual *Rugtag* in December and are found in the *Gerichtsprotocolle* for those dates.

One of the great construction projects had to do with the "Flurbereinigung," whereby the map was redrawn and a system of roads built, so that each plot, now of roughly similar length, was accessible at the bottom and top, from a series of branches off the main trunks.[9] This move prepared for the individualized management of plots which one finds in the open-field patchwork arable today. The management of the forest also offered the men of the village new labor opportunities, especially as it, too, had become subject to intensive exploitation by the end of the eighteenth century.[10]

Just as important for local labor as the straightening of the river and the rerouting of the highway was the construction of the railroad through the village territory at the end of the 1850s. A certain number of villagers were occupied outside during the period of railroad construction, but they were particularly busy when the tracks were laid through the village and the local station was built.[11]

Both men and women found considerable new employment outside the village. Although there is little to go on, some women seem to have been involved in migrant farm labor, and certainly many village girls worked for a time as servants in other places.[12] Some girls worked the military towns as prostitutes, occasionally being sent back to Neckarhausen under village arrest by the courts.[13] Still there seem to have been far more opportunities for men in outside employment than for women, especially in construction and the building trades. Masons, carpenters, joiners, stonecutters, and plasterers spent a good part of their time on building sites far from home.[14] Some men left the village permanently or semipermanently, so that they were no longer counted in the annual village census. But others were gone for long stretches of time, leaving their wives in the village to manage the farmland and inhabit the village communal rights to garden plots, kindling wood, and pastureland, which, according to the Neckarhausen magistrates, were considerable and highly prized by outsiders.[15] In the course of the nineteenth century, in fact, the sex ratio of the "permanent," adult population changed (see Table 5.1).[16]

Table 5.1 demonstrates that the percentage of women in the permanent population increased. There is some evidence that temporary immigration also

[9] The *Kaufbücher*, vol. 17ff., for the 1860s list properties taken for new paths and roads.
[10] Appendix B.
[11] *Schultheißenamt*, vol. 3, f. 9 (21.8.1858).
[12] Maria Margaretha Brodbeck sent money home from Switzerland; *Schultheißenamt*, vol. 1, f. 86 (20.4.1842). Also *Gericht*, vol. 11, f. 63 (20.3.1827); ibid., vol. 15, f. 29 (4.4.1850).
[13] For example, *Gericht*, vol. 14, f. 204 (14.7.1847); f. 214 (19.2.1848); f. 268 (4.8.1848); *Schultheißenamt*, vol. 2, f. 57 (14.9.1844).
[14] Compare the occupational census of 1735 (HSAS, A261, Bü 1344), where 30 artisanal occupations in the village were listed. Only one carpenter represented the building trades – there were 18 weavers –, with the 1870 occupations in Appendix F, where there were 67 nonfarming occupations, 27 of which were in the building trades (*Gemeindepflegerechnungen* 1870, *Steuerempfangs- und abrechnungsbuch*).
[15] *Gericht*, vol. 11, f. 113 (26.8.1828); vol. 14, f. 247 (14.4.1848).
[16] Based on periodic censuses, STAL, E10, *Bevölkerungstabellen*.

Table 5.1 *Ratio of men to women over 14 in Neckarhausen*

| Period | Ratio of men to women |
|---|---|
| 1830–9 | 1.01 |
| 1840–9 | 0.97 |
| 1850–9 | 0.85 |
| 1860–9 | 0.85 |

tipped the normal gender balance in their favor. Now and then, the triennial census gave figures on the percentage of the population that belonged to the village but was "absent" (*Ortsabwesend*). In 1846, for example, this group accounted for 9.8 percent of the total and in 1854, 12.2 percent. Unfortunately, there is no breakdown by sex for these figures, but given the job opportunities, we would expect a large percentage of them to be men. Furthermore, the census was counted at the end of the year, precisely when the least number of villagers would be absent, since the building, construction, and agricultural jobs available were at their lowest point. Even then, about 10 percent of the village was working elsewhere. Perhaps it is an exaggeration to speak of the "feminization" of the village in the second and third quarters of the nineteenth century, but the changing sexual division of labor appears to have rooted the women more in the village and agricultural labor, while dispersing some of the men into the surrounding countryside and cities, where they were constructing railroads, military roads, canals, public buildings, private homes, factories, and prisons.

The details of employment indicate that the work of men differed from that of women in two basic respects: It was usually carried out in the company of other men and involved "substitutability," whereas women's work was often carried out in isolation and could only be discharged by themselves. Take, for example, a typical male task such as carrying grain to the mill in the nearby town of Nürtingen. The wagon most often took several men together, either a father and his sons, a couple of brothers-in-law, or a few neighbors.[17] The job entailed moments of heavy labor, such as lifting sacks of grain, and a great deal of companionable standing or sitting around and talking. If a man was unable to go to the mill himself, he might add a few sacks to his brother's or a neighbor's cart. If he was absent, his wife would have to find someone to do the job, either as a favor or for hire, and she certainly would not go along for the ride. Many – judging from the evidence, most – male jobs were carried out in gangs, whether it was road work, lumbering, ditch digging, construction, or navvying.[18] Thus,

[17] E.g., *Schultheißenamt*, vol. 2, f. 8 (17.9.1842); f. 71 (6.3.1845); f. 200 (24.7.1849); vol. 3, f. 6 (27.7.1858).

[18] Alt Ludwig Federschmid and his son dumped manure together, *Gericht*, vol. 5, f. 207

when some incident brought men before the court, the story usually began with a group of men carrying on some activity together.[19] Even plowing involved more than one man, as someone had to lead the animals and someone else had to manage the plow. Here again a man could be "substituted" in either case through some mutual help arrangement or for cash. Given the distribution of horses in the eighteenth century, many people could not have plowed for themselves anyway and had to arrange for a richer farmer to do the job.[20] By contrast, women's work could not easily be done by someone else. It would have been impossible, for example, for a woman to ask a neighbor to fetch an extra load of clover while she was 2 or 3 kilometers away on a hill gathering her own. Although the women may have walked to the fields together, they soon divided to go to their own plots. Hoeing was another task carried out in isolation.[21] The fields may have been full of women hoeing at the same time, but each worked alone on her own plot. Although there must have been companionable moments in the village – around the pump, on the path to the fields, or on the road to market, each was carrying out her own task and did the job alone. Housework and stall work were other individualizing tasks.

Men also spent their "free time" differently, partly because of the nature of their work routines and partly as a result of the "political" aspect of their employment. In the first place, most male labor took place in fits and starts.

(28.12.1803); Johann Georg Häussler and several other men cut down a tree together, vol. 6, f. 48 (28.12.1804); two men cut down an oak, f. 75 (5.4.1805); Jacob Friedrich Bross and Friedrich Häussler cut down a tree together, f. 76 (5.4.1805); a similar case with Johannes Petermann and his son-in-law, f. 76 (5.4.1805); Young Salomon Hentzler was working in the woods with a group of other men, f. 93 (7.6.1805); two men worked in the woods together for half a day, f. 97 (18.6.1805); the Schultheiss and Bürgermeister cut a stump up together, f. 213 (6.6.1807); two men cut some of Friedrich Falter's wood together, f. 215 (10.6.1807); the Bürgermeister and Waldmeister cut wood from a tree together, f. 215 (10.6.1807); two men drove in a wagon over a sown field, vol. 8, f. 98, (29.12.1813); two men threshed together, vol. 9, f. 115 (4.2.1820); Salomon Baur and Salomon Hentzler travelled together to the Upper Alp to work in the harvest, vol. 10, f. 16 (27.8.1821); a group of men dug a hole for the foundation for a pump house, f. 113 (12.12.1823); Johann Georg Häfner and Alt Mathias Waldner threshed and stored grain together, vol. 12, f. 70 (5.12.1832); six men worked together on a building site, vol. 14, f. 61 (15.5.1845); two men rode to and from the Nürtingen mill together, *Schultheißenamt*, vol. 1, f. 17 (18.2.1849); three men worked together hauling stones from Millot, f. 33 (12.5.1841); two masons worked together on bridge repairs, f. 47 (16.8.1841); six men worked together on the Neckar correction, f. 85 (20.4.1842); two men worked together doing repair work for the village, f. 93 (7.7.1842); road repair work was carried out by seven men, vol. 2, f. 5 (14.9.1842); two masons worked on the pump together, f. 17 (30.1.1843); two men were cooperating together as masons, f. 62 (29.10.1844); a group of men worked on the Neckar bank together, f. 63 (4.11.1844); a carpenter and another man did some building work in Raidwangen together, f. 135 (25.1.1847); three men repaired the bridge in Neckartailfingen together, f. 151 (16.11.1847); two men brought in a wagon load of flax together, f. 200 (24.7.1849); three builders were working together on a tavern, vol. 3, f. 21 (8.3.1859); a carpenter and his mason brother were working on a house together, f. 37 (26.7.1860); a man and his son hired out together as day-laborers, f. 39 (25.8.1860).

[19] Certain places such as the smithy were natural gathering places for men, *Gericht*, vol. 8, f. 92 (5.6.1809).

[20] See Chapter 11 for discussion.

[21] In contrast to men, women were often found working in isolation, gathering grass or clover,

There were moments of extremely heavy labor alternating with moments of relaxation, which meant that the rhythm of their work was frequently punctuated with pauses, as in plowing or carrying. A man would begin by putting the complex harness on the horse or yoking and coupling the oxen to a wagon. After the slow trip to the field, man and animal would work steadily in the dust and the heat or the cold and the mud for as long as was fitting for the particular animal. Then it was back to the barn to unharness, rub down, and feed the animal, and after that to visit the tavern, where the rest of the plowmen would be gathering. Even business transactions were punctuated with a stop at the tavern, and every sale contract specified a certain amount for wine, which would be drunk by the two male parties and the Schultheiss, and perhaps a few Richter would gather at the tavern to conclude the business.[22] While male sociability may have been rooted in the rhythms of work, there were other important reasons for meeting one's fellows in the tavern. It was in such groups that the crucial networks of aid and information were set up. One can imagine the constant discussion about the upcoming cattle market and the merits of each calf villagers were thinking of selling. In such assemblies, a farmer learned to think about his chances on the market. Furthermore, the more villagers had to find employment outside of the village, the more the establishment of reliable networks among fellow villagers was necessary. News traveled constantly back and forth from worksite to village and was considered at great length at the *Stammtisch*. It is important to understand that work was always occasional – a few carpenters might be needed at a building site in Nürtingen, some gardeners in Ludwigsburg, a stonecutter in a nearby village – always for a task. To keep occupied, men needed reliable information about possible jobs, and they also wanted fellows to vouchsafe for their skills.

The rhythm of women's work appears to have been quite different. They hurried from task to task, and many of the jobs they did were ones that could be broken off and continued later. If men's work was heavy and sometimes dangerous, women's work was arduous, repetitive, detailed, and exact. Hoeing took long hours, yet could be broken off to hurry home to cook. The job called

hoeing, etc.: Jacob Falter's wife took clover from Young Andreas Feldmaier's field, *Gericht*, vol. 7 f. 133 (15.6.1810); Johannes Hentzler's wife fetched clover from their field, vol. 9, f. 9 (15.6.1817); Adam Falter's wife fetched fodder from her plot and saw Jacob Falter's mother doing the same, f. 43 (4.5.1818); Caspar Kuhn's wife was working alone on her field, f. 73 (2.3.1819); Maria Agnes Hentzler was cutting oats with a sickle, vol. 10, f. 196 (30.8.1825); Friedrich Köpple's wife hoed on her field, *Schultheißenamt*, vol. 2, f. 119 (14.8.1846); Catharina Rieth returned from hoeing, f. 178 (8.8.1848); a woman returned from harvesting potatoes alone, f. 267 (24.9.1855); Johann Georg Zeug's maid cut green fodder, vol. 3, f. 39 (25.8.1860); women also usually went to the pump alone to get water, clean potatoes, or to wash implements, *Gericht*, vol. 10, f. 74 (18.4.1825); vol. 12, f. 107 (11.7.1833); *Vogtruggericht*, vol. 2, f. 80 (26.11.1818).

[22] Most situations where men gathered to drink during the week involved the late afternoon at the conclusion of work. After dividing the firewood, men gathered for a drink, *Vogtruggericht*, vol. 2, f. 50 (28.9.1813); the wheelwright always got a few glasses of wine for communal work; building workers were paid partly in wine.

for precision and skill, so that the weeds would be destroyed without the plants being disturbed – just the right cut of the blade to aerate the soil and mound it around the plant while moving on rapidly to the next one.[23] Women did not gather to drink after the work was done, but hurried on to the next task. Whatever pauses occurred were more directly integrated into work – a rest on the bench (enough place for three or four women at most) before descending into the village, a pause to gossip at the pump while fetching water, leaning over the pitchfork in front of the barn to exchange words with the neighbor across the way, herself just finishing cleaning the stall. Even the pause at mealtimes was integrated into her work of preparation and cleaning up.

Long-term trends in the sexual division of labor are discussed again in Chapter 6, which focuses on the specific ways in which married couples adjusted to the ever-changing situation of productive effort, and the cryptic messages fired in the context of conflicting rhythms of work and widely divergent social conditions of labor. There is a more encompassing set of pressures as well, which have to do with the adjustments to a growing population and a more intense use of labor.

## The labor supply

We have suggested that the nature of work changed a great deal with the agricultural revolution. But what labor processes were like before is more difficult to establish, since the sources at our disposal more often give insight into novel arrangements which present problems of adjustment rather than into older ones people have learned to live with. I have suggested that the agricultural innovations were carried out over three or four generations, beginning in the 1760s. But there were changes in the village before which continued on into that period and made the new form of agrarian economy possible. Some of the changes are rooted in the population increase of the eighteenth century, which for Neckarhausen was on the order of 60 to 70 percent. With that came an increase in the absolute number of people who could not live from their own agricultural holdings. Weaving became important for the village, even during the first decades of the eighteenth century. By 1735, out of 80 adult male Bürger, 30 were engaged in some handicraft or other, 18 of them in weaving. The fact that people were listed as artisans did not mean, however, that they were exclusively devoted to that occupation. They often had land, sometimes more than many "Bauern." Thus, life for both groups was a mixture of handicraft, agriculture, and various by-employments. By the 1760s, the percentage of villagers with some handicraft or supplemental form of employment was rising. As the population expanded, rural inhabitants throughout the region began to piece a living together in more

[23] See the important work by Maria Bidlingmaier, *Die Bäuerin*, pp. 18–23, 33–7, 54–5.

complex ways. The rest of the century came to be characterized by what Olwen Huften has called an "economy of makeshift."[24]

By the 1770s in France, Hufton argues, the "family economy" was no longer viable for a larger proportion of the population.[25] The working poor were on the margin of existence, such that even a family with all members contributing to a single income had no cushion to fall back on should anything interrupt their fragile equilibrium. In contrast to the structural situation of widespread pandemics of the seventeenth century, the latter half of the eighteenth century was characterized by chronic undernourishment of large segments of the population exacerbated by their increasing numbers. In rural areas, the expanding population made it necessary to fractionalize holdings already by the 1740s and 1750s, and smallholders and farm laborers began a desperate search for new forms of ancillary incomes. It is important to understand that finding new sources of support involved a long process of learning over several generations. Holding multiple jobs, migrating with the seasons, or begging took place in a context of competition among large sectors of the population all in the same circumstances, and all establishing new networks and driven to find some niche or other for their activity. Heinz Reif has explored the phenomenon for Germany, chronicling the rise of such jobs as gathering manure from roads or horse hair from thorn bushes; colporting rosin – to grease wagon wheels –, mousetraps, or herbal remedies; ratcatching; dousing; pilfering; and providing magical protection for the horses and barns.[26] "The incomes of the poor are composed of too many component elements and imponderables to permit ready assessment."[27]

Although Hufton explores the "economy of makeshift" only for the end of the eighteenth century in France, it certainly characterized large sectors of the German population until well into the nineteenth century. Many of the same phenomena there have been described under the general rubric "pauperization." Abel shows, for example, that the situation developed during the second half of the eighteenth century as the price-wage scissors widened.[28] During that period a significant upswing in rural industry took place, as village inhabitants in many regions began spinning and weaving for a far-flung market.[29] For some regions, specialization in cloth production seemed to be the answer to the situation, but even where we cannot speak, perhaps, of protoindustry, many inhabitants of a village might find weaving or flax production profitable. In Württemberg, villages tended to find some specialization

[24] Olwen Hufton, *The Poor of Eighteenth-Century France, 1750–1789* (Oxford, 1974), pp. 69ff.
[25] Hufton, *Poor*, pp. 25–43, 108–9.
[26] Heinz Reif, "Vagierende Unterschichten, Vagabunden und Bandenkriminalität im Ancien Régime," in *Beiträge zur historischen Sozialkunde*, 1 (1981): 27–37.
[27] Hufton, *Poor*, p. 43.
[28] Wilhelm Abel, *Massenarmut und Hungerkrisen im vorindustriellen Europa* (Hamburg and Berlin, 1974), pp. 191ff.
[29] Peter Kriedte, Hans Medick, and Jürgen Schlumbohm, *Industrialization before Industrialization*, trans. Beate Schemp (Cambridge, 1981).

that would characterize them but perhaps leave the neighboring village untouched.[30] Neckarhausen was famous for the production of raw flax, the neighboring village of Necktailfingen for fine yarn, and the nearby village of Wolfschlugen for weaving.[31] Although all three of these villages carried on similar activities, each found a special niche. Local observers themselves made the connection between the new kinds of specialization and impoverishment.[32]

Hufton draws two important conclusions from her analysis. First, she argues that the ever-increasing poverty did not discourage people from marrying. Second, poverty worked like an "acid," corroding relationships inside the family. Men deserted their families in droves, leaving wives and children to fend for themselves. For Neckarhausen, both of these conclusions have to be modified. At least, the notion of a cultural learning experience can be usefully employed to determine how reactions to similar conditions could change with time. As we have seen, in the overwhelming majority of divorce and separation cases in the village, the woman provoked the split.[33] In case after case, the husband wanted to put the family back together because *he* could not make it on his own. Furthermore, after a generation or so of increasing illegitimacy, many women made it clear that marriage was not the intended aim of their pregnancy, and that they were not yet ready to consider setting up a permanent household with a husband because to do so would threaten their existence.[34] This issue will be explored in a later investigation, but it is important to understand here that the "economy of makeshift" was not necessarily a family economy, however much pathologically ordered.

How did the process of pauperization and the agricultural revolution interconnect? First, more than anything else, agricultural innovation was labor-intensive. In part, the agronomists of the time took labor for granted, and so they seldom discussed it, except in terms of discipline. Workers were so easy to come by and so cheap that the experts could concentrate their attention on anything else but those who were the major foundation for the change except as a factor cost. Whether it was shifting marl by the barrow full to new fields, or tiling a field for drainage, or carrying clover on long trips to the barn, or hoeing sugar beets for long hours, they were concerned, for the most part, only with the technology of doing it, or with bookkeeping exercises, not with who would carry it out. The new labor force was willing to work for very low wages and it could be utilized for the task at hand and then easily dismissed.[35] For the smallholder,

[30] See my discussion in "Intensivierung der Arbeit und Alltagserfahrung auf dem Lande – Ein Beispiel aus Württemberg," in *Sozialwissenschaftliche Informationen für Unterricht und Studium*, 6 (1977): 148–52; village specialization is fully documented in the *Oberamtsbeschreibungen* for Württemberg, published in the 1820s, 1830s, and 1840s.

[31] *Beschreibung Nürtingen*, articles on individual villages.

[32] See the *Pfarrbericht* (1828); LKA, A39, Bü 3060. Also *Pfarrbericht* (1796) for the district of Nurtingen; LKA, C2, 6/14.

[33] See Chapter 4.

[34] This is a consistent theme in the *Skortationsbuch*.

[35] Karl Göriz describes the rise of piecework in Württemberg from the late 1820s, *Die*

the situation was more complex. The family had to deploy its own labor on the farm but also find its way into the temporary labor market.

Not every village experienced pauperization, the development of makeshift jobbery, or the rise of labor-intensive agricultural production at the same time or at the same pace. We know that by the 1730s various handicraft trades, especially weaving, engaged the attention of close to 40 percent of the Neckarhausen Bürger at least part of the time.[36] The extension of labor-intensive production of hemp and flax was already obvious by midcentury.[37] In 1777, Johannes Thum complained of the mess made by his neighbors who broke their flax and hemp day and night out on the road around the Rathaus.[38] There were reports in the 1780s of stolen hemp that had been laid in the river to soak.[39] And in the 1790s, so many people were jockeying for position along the bank that fights broke out.[40] These kinds of problems were reported frequently during the first decades of the nineteenth century.[41] For years, officials tried to stop people from drying flax in the bake ovens.[42] In 1823, there was so much competition for bleaching places in the Gänswasen that a regular system of leasing was established.[43] In the parish report from 1828, the pastor said that the number of poor in the village was much greater than the number of well-off (*Bemittelten*). As a result, flax and hemp were grown in large quantities. The fact that parents needed their children to prepare the plants prevented the founding of an industry school. There are lists of people who rented the communal drying ovens in the 1840s and 1850s, usually 50 to 60 villagers each year.[44] Cases in which flax or hemp played a role indicate that most of the intensive labor that went into growing and preparing these crops was done by women – and their children.

Flax cultivation was, of course, only one response to the growing population pressure and slow splintering of land holding. In the 1770s and 1780s, various villagers applied to farm the river sand, the stone quarry, and the saltpeter shack. Others applied to keep the village fountain clean or to repair and maintain ditches and road surfaces.[45] The impression that one gets from the records is that the search for alternative sources of income increased sharply

*landwirtschaftliche Betriebslehre als Leitfaden für Vorlesungen und zum Selbststudium für Landwirte*, 3 Teile (Stuttgart, 1853–4), Teil 1, pp. 209ff.

[36] HSAS, A261, Bü 1344; see n. 35.

[37] In 1745, during the catechism lesson, many villagers were busy putting hemp to soak in the Neckar, *Kirchenkonvent*, vol. 1, p. 155 (28.10.1745); reference was made to breaking flax in front of houses, vol. 2, p. 69 (15.10.1751).

[38] *Gericht*, vol. 2, f. 170 (29.12.1777); see also *Vogtruggericht*, vol. 1, f. 118 (23.1.1777).

[39] *Gericht*, vol. 3, f. 17 (8.9.1780).

[40] *Gericht*, vol. 4, f. 237 (12.8.1793); see also f. 180 (28.12.1791); f. 208 (6.10.1792).

[41] *Gericht*, vol. 7, f. 67 (25.11.1808); vol. 6, f. 113 (8.11.1805); vol. 8, f. 173 (1.9.1815).

[42] *Gericht*, vol. 8, f. 129 (12.9.1814); f. 130 (29.9.1814); *Oberamtsgericht*, HSAL, F190, vol. 11, f. 78 (4.10.1814); f. 87 (10.10.1814).

[43] *Gericht*, vol. 10, f. 122 (29.12.1823).

[44] The lists are preserved in the *Gemeindepflegerechnungen* for each year.

[45] Auctioned off each spring at the annual assembly, protocolled in the *Gerichtsprotocolle*.

between 1815 and about 1835. There is evidence that village girls entered prostitution both at the local inns and in the court and garrison towns.[46] Throughout the period under study there were reports of villagers begging. In 1747, the church consistory said that the poor could not support themselves unless they could beg.[47] But there was also the problem of troops of beggars passing through the village. Everyone opposed the local enforcement of state ordinances against them because they were likely to set the village on fire.[48] There was some incidence of particular villagers begging from the 1780s onward, but the peak of this activity seems to have been the 1830s and 1840s. And there are examples of outsiders being arrested begging right through the 1860s.[49] Sometimes begging and colportage were combined. Various people, a majority of them women, either applied to the authorities for permission to sell goods from house to house or were apprehended for doing so illegally – they sold such goods as meat, grindstones, yeast, vinegar, linens, cottonwares, underwear, seed, paste jewels, eggs, butter, mousetraps, neckerchiefs, schnaps, sickles, breadrolls, soap, chickens, and geese.[50] Finally, the incidence of pilfering was very much on the rise in the three decades after 1810.[51]

From time to time, villagers or village officials commented on the conditions of village life. In 1756, permission for a man to marry into the village was resisted on the grounds that there were too many people already competing for farm

[46] E.g., *Oberamtsgericht*, STAL, F190II, Band 265, f. 77 (16.6.1831).

[47] *Kirchenkonvent*, vol. 2, p. 5 (29.6.1747).

[48] *Kirchenkonvent*, vol. 2 (17.4.1763).

[49] Many begging poor were coming through the village: *Gericht*, vol. 3, f. 47 (19.1.1781); there were wandering beggars: vol. 4, f. 90 (20.7.1788); people arrested; vol. 13, f. 89 (1.7.1840) and f. 144 (1.7.1841); a young man from Neckarhausen was warned about begging: vol. 15, f. 222 (18.2.1853); a villager was confined to Neckarhausen for begging from house to house: vol. 18, f. 121 (22.2.1867); the poor were not able to care for themselves if not allowed to beg: *Kirchenkonvent*, vol. 2, p. 5 (29.6.1747); the village was against the beggar ordinance because they were too busy to police the living area and were afraid of arson: vol. 2 (17.4.1763); men were posted around the village because of a stream of beggars: vol. 2 (7.4.1769); Johann Georg Bosch was arrested for begging: *Oberamtsgericht*, STAL, F190II, Band 262, f. 39 (11.2.1829); Salomo Schniring was arrested for begging: vol. 264, f. 126 (24.8.1830); Gottfrid Fausel was arrested for begging: vol. 265, f. 2 (3.1.1832); begging on the street was forbidden: *Vogtruggericht*, vol. 1, f. 127 (17.12.1782); no beggars were allowed to stay over night: vol. 1, f. 131 (13.12.1784); for many years Michael Friess was running around begging: vol. 2, f. 31 (17.2.1808); outsiders were arrested for begging: *Schultheißenamt*, vol. 2, f. 131 (29.12.1846); various parents were sending their children out begging: vol. 2, f. 145 (15.6.1847); a man and his two children were arrested for begging, vol. 2, f. 211 (14.5.1861); an outsider was arrested for begging: vol. 3, f. 49 (14.5.1871); see also vol. 3, f. 77 (20.12.1863); and f. 122 (8.5.1866).

[50] *Gericht*, vol. 10, f. 127 (14.2.1824) (meat); vol. 12, f. 29 (25.2.1832) (whetstones); f. 184 (11.4.1835) (yeast); vol. 13, f. 2 (19.1.1838) (vinegar); vol. 15, f. 321 (20.9.1854) (yeast); vol. 18, f. 103 (15.8.1866) (linen, cotton wares); f. 205 (paste jewelry); f. 235 (eggs and butter); *Kirchenkonvent*, vol. 3 (6.4.1794) (eggs); (1.11.1795) (mousetraps); *Oberamtsgericht*, STAL, F190II, Band 257, f. 166 (4.11.1817) (scarves, pins); Band 258, f. 376 (20.12.1821) (schnaps); Band 265, f. 42 (31.3.1831) (schnaps); Band 268, f. 39 (27.2.1834) (wine, cider, schnaps); Band 269, f. 41 (14.2.1835) (scythes, sickles); Band 271, f. 39 (27.4.1837) (not given); *Schultheissenamt*, vol. 1, f. 20 (5.3.1841) (not given); vol. 3, f. 93 (26.6.1865) (eggs, chickens, soap); f. 142 (9.12.1867) (geese).

[51] Appendix E.

labor positions.[52] Twenty years later, the village court agreed that the increased population in the village was driving the price of land too high.[53] At the end of the decade, Adam Fausel, a carpenter, was allowed to marry into the commune only reluctantly, since there were already two carpenters in the village and not enough work for them.[54] On the other hand, in the same year, Johannes Burkhart was welcomed, since two or three masons could be kept busy, and there was only one there already.[55] There were remarks during the 1780s and 1790s about the many poor Bürger who could not manage.[56] During the debates over the introduction of stall feeding in the first two decades of the nineteenth century, reference was made to the former excellent economic condition of the village. But by that time there were many poor in the village and large numbers of villagers were deeply in debt.[57] The pastor reported in 1828 that the number of poor (*Armen*) was greater than the number of well-off (*Bemittelten*).[58] And in 1848, the size of the *Proletariat* had increased.[59] By 1862, after the difficulties of the late 1840s and 1850s, the village had regrouped.[60] The Bauern (*Bauerstand*) were described as "wealthy, diligent, and thrifty" (*wohlhabend, fleissig, und sparsam*). There were many people working in factories, and they were beginning to spend more on clothes and pleasantries. The pastor in 1870 described the Neckarhausen villagers as leading a simple life; some were indeed needy (*dürftig*).[61]

In Chapter 6, we will be concerned with the implications of the nature of production and changes in production for the relationships between husbands and wives. The interconnection is not likely to be expressed directly in the sources. No woman angry over being beaten for getting the meal onto the table late was about to deliver an essay to the court on the effects of the agricultural revolution on the sexual division of labor, even if she was conscious of some aspects of the process. To understand many of the connections, we have to become masters in deciphering cryptic messages, unpacking tightly encoded metaphors, and analyzing symbolic language. We will be concerned with *relationships* between spouses, which suggests that we might best look for our evidence in moments of transaction. Marriage is, after all, an exchange relationship, composed of, if not reducible to, a property settlement, a labor contract, sexual privileges and duties, and reproductive claims and responsibilities. All of these elements are under constant renegotiation as conditions

[52] *Gericht*, vol. 1, f. 89 (6.5.1756).
[53] *Gericht*, vol. 2, f. 16 (22.4.1772).
[54] *Gericht*, vol. 2, f. 201 (4.2.1779).
[55] *Gericht*, vol. 2, f. 220 (8.11.1779).
[56] *Gericht*, vol. 3, f. 15 (26.7.1780); f. 56 (24.4.1781); f. 67 (26.6.1781); f. 189 (17.12.1784); vol. 5, f. 67 (19.1.1797); f. 89 (27.2.1798).
[57] *Vogtruggericht*, vol. 2, f. 54 (30.9.1813).
[58] *Pfarrbericht* (1828); LKA, A39, Bü3060.
[59] *Übersichtsbericht*, Dekanatamt Nürtingen, Akten I, nr. 3.
[60] *Pfarrbericht* (1862); LKA, A39, Bü 3060.
[61] *Pfarrbericht* (1870); LKA, A39, Bü 3060.

change, memories are built up, compliance is elicited, demands are resisted, and rights are installed, adjusted, and torn down. But there are certain structural moments when the exchange takes place or is symbolized, as in the preparation and consumption of food. In other words, to understand the way the *modes* of production affect family life, we have to look closely at the *nodes* of exchange. It is there that reciprocity and the values of reciprocity are most visible, and that expropriation can best be concealed or revealed. In Chapter 6, we discuss the periodization of divorce in Neckarhausen and three examples of conflict complexes that make the issues clear: "Meisterschaft," drunkenness, and cooking.

# 6

# Marital relations in the context of production

He works when he is not drunk, but then he wastes the earnings.

– Rebecca Häfnerin[1]

We now turn to certain key themes, words, concerns, and actions in the context in which husbands and wives observed each other's behavior. Our purpose is to explain why separation and divorce appeared and disappeared as a serious issue when it did, why the patriarchal concern for control of the family finances shifted to a problem of alienated labor, and why drunkenness became a theme for wives just when their husbands came to criticize their cooking. All these issues are related to the changes in the nature of production and the sexual division of labor described in Chapter 5. In our earlier discussion of divorce and separation, we simply looked at each case before the courts, without paying attention to whether certain couples appeared more frequently than others. And we were also interested in the demand for a divorce or separation, not whether a couple went through the legal system finally to effect one. In many testimonies, it was clear that the wife had left her husband already, sometimes for a considerable length of time. But it is usually impossible to find out whether a couple was separated, although the evidence suggests that some couples had broken up without attaining a formal divorce. When a husband was gone in search of employment for most of the year or when he left for America, as several did, a de facto separation took place. Table 6.1 shows only the instances which came before the court. By examining a later burial or marriage record, it is often possible to find out whether a divorce eventually took place. However, there were more divorces than recorded here, but we find them only by chance. For example, Eberhard Friedrich Denk, a surgeon and son of the pastor, married the daughter of the Schultheiss, Johann Georg Falter. After they were divorced in the 1830s, each remarried, she a teacher in Neckartailfingen and he the daughter of a cooper in Bernhausen. Since their marital conflict did not come before the Neckarhausen court, their case does not appear in Table 6.1.

[1] See n. 18.

Table 6.1 *Frequency of demand for divorce or separation in local court records*

| | Number | | |
|---|---|---|---|
| Period | Cases | Couples[a] | Divorces[a] |
| 1770s | 1 | 1 | 0 |
| 1780s | 0 | 0 | 0 |
| 1790s | 1 | 1 | 0 |
| 1800s | 9 | 4 | 3 |
| 1810s | 3 | 3 | 1 |
| 1820s | 12 | 8 | 3 |
| 1830s | 12 | 7 | 3 |
| 1840s | 3 | 2 | 0 |
| Total | 41 | 26 | 10 |

[a] By date of first demand.

The instances of requests for separation were sporadic from 1770 to 1800. Only after 1805 did the demand become frequent, but then it fell off sharply after 1840. As we have seen, between 1822 and 1839, out of 36 cases of marital conflict, 21, or close to 60 percent, involved a request for separation. By comparison, only 3 of the 25 cases between 1840 and 1848 did so (12 percent). If we take divorce, separation, or an attempt to separate as an indication of marital conflict, then there seems to have been a crisis in marriage between 1800 and 1840. In 1848, the pastor reported that the incidence of marital conflict (*Ehedissidien*) provided a good measure of moral depravity and that the village was no longer sunk so low in immorality as it once was.[2] In the 1862 parish report, the pastor reported that severe marital conflicts were infrequent.[3]

As already mentioned, the requests for divorce came overwhelmingly from women.[4] In more than half the cases,the first cracks in the marriages during this period of crisis came during the second year of marriage, during the early stages of childbearing, when the women were in their late 20s, at the height of their physical strength. We have shown that there was a rise in verbal quarreling after 1820 and suggested that many of the tensions developed around the changing sexual division of labor. Divorce and greater tensions in marriage correlated closely with the increasing intensification of agriculture, as women became heavily involved in stall feeding, hoe agriculture, and the preparation of flax and hemp. The shift speeded up at the turn of the century, got into full swing in the

[2] In the 1832 visitation, the Dekan wrote, "Processsucht, vernachlässigte Kinderzucht, und Ehedissidien gehören den weniger empfehlenden Eigenschaften"; Dekanatamt Nürtingen, Akten I, nr. 3; *Pfarrbericht* (1848); LKA, A39, Bü 3060.

[3] *Pfarrbericht* (1862), LKA, A39, Bü 3060.

[4] See Chapter 1.

1820s, and completed its structural break in the 1830s. The decline in divorce and leveling off of conflict in general during the 1840s and 1850s did not mean that women were less exploited or less self-exploited. If anything, the work only increased during the rest of the century. But the shift in role and structure meant that some accommodation between spouses had taken place. Culturally defined roles now made clear what women and men in their respective stations had to do under the new conditions.

It could be argued that pauperization rather than changes in work explain the crisis. Hufton's thesis that poverty works like an acid on family relations is perhaps more adequate for the situation: These were conflicts of the desperate and abandoned.[5] But that fails to explain why the conflicts slowly let up and divorce itself radically dropped during the crisis period of the later 1840s. If poverty explains the phenomena best, then we would expect that separation and divorce would be located overwhelmingly among the poorest of the village, among the farm laborers, village workers, the poorest artisans, especially those

Table 6.2 *Frequency distribution of couples involved in divorce: husband's occupation*

| Occupation | Frequency |
|---|---|
| Bauer | 10 |
| Farm laborer | 2 |
| Weaver/Bauer | 4 |
| Artisans | 8 |
| Food services | 2 |

Table 6.3 *Frequency distribution of couples involved in divorce: position in tax lists*

| Quartile[a] | Frequency |
|---|---|
| I | 3[b] |
| II | 3 |
| III | 9 |
| IV | 9 |
| NG[d] | 2[c] |

[a] In ascending order.
[b] Two absent from village.
[c] Both Bauer.
[d] Not given.

[5] Olwen Hufton, *The Poor of Eighteenth-Century France (1750–1789)* (Oxford, 1974), pp. 114ff.

who had to leave the village periodically to find work, and later among the factory workers who emerged in the 1840s, 1850s, and 1860s. Substantial Bauern and the better-off artisans would be the least touched. However, it is apparent from Tables 6.2 and 6.3 that conflict severe enough to break up a marriage was located most frequently among the more well-to-do villagers. And the artisans that did appear were most likely to be stable economically, and prosperous enough to have considerable amounts of agricultural land. Above all, peasant proprietors make up a significant proportion of the list. Even the farm laborers represented here were not impoverished and appeared in the third quartile of taxpayers, which means that they had more real property than half the inhabitants in the village.[6] It may well have been that as men spent more of their time outside the village, women became more assured of their role as director of the agricultural enterprise. In addition, the men were on the road and could not cause trouble at home.

## Master of the purse strings

The degree of autonomy attained in everyday household matters is not easy to determine. Although state ideologues might well have wished to view the house as a unit integrated by patriarchal authority, that hegemonic ideal may have been far from reality, and their notion masks fundamental processes of historical change by its static character. We have to pay close attention to the way that the family articulated with the state. When, for example, the household was considered from the point of view of tax revenue, the state was concerned with the regulation of inheritance, the apportionment of property rights, and the economic well-ordering of the house. Here, negotiations between the family and the state were most efficiently mediated through the symbolic figure of the Hausvater. But their concentration on patriarchal authority tells us little about family labor. Where male and female spheres were separated, a patriarch could not do much about the specifics of cleaning, cooking, child care, gardening, preserving, and the like. The pace and routines of women's labor were their own. The bedrock of custom determined when beds were to be made and with what degree of attention to detail and under what hierarchical circumstances among the women of the house.

Autonomy, then, is reflected in labor and the culture of gender. But it is also apparent in the use and enjoyment to which the product of labor is put. Andrew

[6] It might be objected that the poor were less likely to marry or would marry late, but the way the statistics are set up here allows for that problem. Table 6.3 divides all of the taxpayers – most of whom were married men, with only a sprinkling of widows, elderly widowers, and young single men and women. Even if we assume that half of the lowest quartile of taxpayers – a strong overestimation – were not married men and assume also that the rest of all taxpayers were, then we still get a strong correlation with wealth. Setting the population of taxpayers at 200, the ratio of divorce per household for the poorest two quartiles is 1:25 and for the richest two, 1:5.

Strathern has provided a useful example of how to approach the subject.[7] In traditional Highlands New Guinea, the separate spheres of men and women were quite marked. Women tended the gardens and raised the pigs, among other things. Men engaged in elaborate rituals of exchange in which pigs, provided by the women, were consumed in competitive rounds of feasting. In this situation, women did not seem to see the removal of the pigs which they had labored hard to care for as exploitative. But as the economic arrangements shifted and women began to produce products that could be exchanged for cash, they began to see that their labor was being appropriated for male politics. In this instance, we must distinguish between the autonomy of labor and autonomy of use inside the family. We can understand the social arrangements best by chronicling the history of the point at which the product passed between spheres of gender competence, which means that we should examine disputes over the control of family produce, resources, and income.

The social arrangements in Neckarhausen are reflected in the disputes over the control of money. In the eighteenth century, the key terms in the recorded discourse were "Meisterschaft" and "Herrschaft," used by the court and by men to assert a view of male and female prerogatives. In the nineteenth century, the terms of the disputes changed, and we no longer encounter men demanding to be master, partly because the alliance system between the state and the family had been renegotiated. We must look for fundamental changes in the relationships between husbands and wives with respect to the sexual division of labor against the backdrop of changes in the state's social objectives.

*We begin our analysis with four cases from the early eighteenth century. In the first, Hans Melchior Thumm complained that his wife Maria would not let him be master.*[8] *She had 20 Kreutzer which she wanted to use to pay the taxes and which she refused to give him. She had also kept a sack of grain in Tobias Häfner's house from which she sold a portion and kept the money. Maria said that the money was a confinement gift from her* Gevatter *(godparent to her children), which she used to purchase a badly needed pair of shoes. She had sold half of the grain to pay the family debts and needed the other half for food. Furthermore, she had borrowed 26 kr. from her mother to pay her husband's taxes with. She also complained that he had done some weaving for the wife of a tavernkeeper and took his wages in drink. He also drank excessively, especially when he was with his parents at the Amtpfleger's house in Nürtingen. The consistory decided to treat him leniently this time but threatened incarceration and a report to the Oberamt. Maria was told to let him have the* Meisterschaft *and not scold when he did something wrong.*

Meisterschaft here refers to holding the purse strings, and the officials certainly thought that the husband ought to have disposition over all cash reserves in the house. As the incident unfolded, the term "master" was used

[7] Paper submitted to the First Round Table on Anthropology and History, Göttingen, Max-Planck-Institut für Geschichte, 1978.

[8] *Kirchenkonvent*, vol. 1, p. 1 (11.5.1727).

primarily to refer to her independent access to resources, which she had gained by keeping the grain and the money she received from her *Gevatter* out of his hands and by contracting and paying debts. The husband demanded the right to use whatever money was available as he saw fit, and the consistory agreed. The village magistrates and state officials did not support the idea of a wife standing up to a wastrel husband by taking over the finances of the family or creating a fund for herself. At the same time, the court interfered directly with the husband's authority by making his Meistershaft dependent on good behavior, attention to work, and evidence that he was providing for the financial well-being of his family. There are several other issues here. Thumm's wife had borrowed money from her mother to pay his taxes, which indicates that her relationship to her own relatives played a role in the struggle for control over family finances. Maria also kept grain elsewhere, which argues for neighborly support of her independent action. And her Gevatter provided her with a substantial gift to be kept for her own needs. At least two other men, therefore, provided her with the means for challenging her husband's Meisterschaft, which appears to have received more support from the state than from the set of men in the village.

Maria Thumm also raised another issue with great effect. She complained about Hans Melchior's drinking, but the context in which he drank was important. He was with his father (the Schultheiss) and mother and was drinking in the Amtpfleger's house in Nürtingen. Essentially, she was attacking the way he spent the money of the family enterprise, but he defined his drinking by putting it in the context of family and "official" business. By throwing her husband and his parents into one boozing lot, she was denying both the claims of his kin on their substance and the articulation of her household with village politics. The consistory was chiefly concerned with Thumm's ability to work and brought in testimony over this matter: The upshot was that he both worked and drank. When the wife complained that Thumm had done some weaving and blew the wages, the accusation was not that the results of her direct labor were being appropriated, but that the exchange of the product of labor inside the family was at fault.

*Several years later, another dispute over* Meisterschaft *arose between David Falter and his wife Anna.*[9] *David accused his mother-in-law, Dorothea Thumm, of complaining to his mother that he hired others to do his work. He alleged that everything he said came before his parents-in-law for consideration and that they told their daughter to obey them first. There were charges of brutality about which Falter defended himself. He also denied he loafed around and neglected his* Oeconomie. *The consistory asked Anna if it was true that her husband was "not even master over a Kreutzer," to which she replied that all the money was under his direction except what she had obtained from selling her house. Falter complained that when he had ordered*

[9] *Kirchenkonvent*, vol. 1, p. 124 (6.10.1743); see further discussion of this case, Chapter 10.

*his mother-in-law from the house, she refused to go because it was her daughter's, and he demanded that his wife not visit her parents so often. After all the drama at the hearing, the pastor advised the old couple to leave Falter with the* Meisterschaft *in his own house. The consistory considered a report to the Oberamt and two days in jail for Falter, but gave him a verbal correction and a fine instead.*

The issues in this conflict were the general economic situation of the household and the relationship between the two families in the dispute over the control of the wife. She was the object of struggle between son-in-law and mother-in-law, and the essential point was expressly that of Meisterschaft. The issues turned around work, brutality, and control of the purse. In the end, the consistory wanted to arbitrate between the parties and ensure that matters would not get worse by treating the young husband too firmly. And they expressed the ideological viewpoint that a man should be master in his own family. Yet they suggested by their actions that the de facto right to be master in one's house involved reciprocity, and he was warned to deport himself with diligence. In this case, however, there is a hint that it was customary for women to retain control over large amounts of money they received from the sale of real property. Anna and her close kin maintained a separate account. The power situation in the family was also expressed by the idea that the house belonged to the wife, which gave her and her kin greater rights of autonomy vis-à-vis the husband. The consistory never spelled out exactly what rights the husband could have over his wife's property, but left the matter under the vague concept of Meisterschaft. While the law clearly specified that a husband had the right to administer his wife's property (see Chapter 8), it appears that de facto power relations were ordered rather differently.

*In 1735, a case came before the consistory which was a mirror opposite to the preceding one.*[10] *Maria Häussler complained that her mother-in-law had ordered her out of the latter's house and told her never to return. And she was angered by the fact that her husband always took his mother's side. Above all, he never told her when he would be busy with some matter, and when she asked, hit her. It turned out that Maria was opposed to her husband setting up a pub. She was supported by her father, who treated the consistory with disrespect and was crude and rough to Michael Häussler and his mother.*

In this case, the quarrel seems to have been about the proper use of family resources. Maria did not want her property committed to setting up a tavern, and her request for information was a demand to take part in economic decision making that affected the household. As in the previous case, the alliance between husband and wife was part of a wider alliance between two families. Judging from the relationship between son and mother, the pub was being set up in her house, which also implies that he was still integrated to some degree in the economy of his original family. On the other hand, the young couple

[10] *Kirchenkonvent*, vol. 1, p. 35 (19.5.1735); see further discussion of this case, Chapter 10.

had relatively little land, whereas the wife's father had enough to keep young Michael working for him. Perhaps Maria opposed the pub in order to tie her husband to her father's economy.

*Agnes Speidel, supported by her* Kriegsvogt, *came before the consistory in 1747.*[11] *She had been keeping money hidden away in a box, which she claimed had been saved during her years as a servant and was laid aside in the event of a future illness. Her husband, Hans Jerg, pointed out that the coins had not been entered into her inventory and that they bore dates subsequent to their marriage. Her stepson had discovered the box, and when she refused to open it, Hans Jerg forced it. He then beat Agnes with the flat edge of a sword, while his son held her. He complained that she had held the* Herrschaft *for nine years, and said that he now wanted to turn things around and become his own master of the purse* (Säckelmeister). *In the future, she could ask for any money she needed. The consistory sent them both to the local jail, he for four hours and she for two, but made it clear that Agnes had given the most cause and was chiefly to blame for what had happened. The only issue as far as local officials were concerned was that the husband had improperly used a sword to punish her.*

In this case, as in the others, the wife concerned was not without support for her actions from other members of the family, neighbors, or in this instance, her Kriegsvogt (legal spokesman), although just what position the latter took is not clear. He may not have supported her independence, while condemning the beating. According to the testimony, she had apparently run the finances of the family ever since the marriage. And there is the tantalizing point about saving for a future illness. Was she expected to have separate resources in such an eventuality? Or was she preparing for her widowhood? In any event, the consistory forthrightly supported the administrative rights of the husband over the money and goods of the household. It could well be that the local officials took the details of each family situation into account. Their lack of support may have been due to the fact that she had brought much less into the marriage than her husband (842.9 fl. to 387.6 fl.), whereas the implication in the three other cases was that the resources of the wives outweighed those of the husbands.[12] Or the issue could have been what was earned in the everyday life of the household, and no matter what was produced or by whom, the money was expected to go into the purse held by the husband. In the three other cases, the dispute centered on property the women had brought into their marriages, whereas in Speidel's case it was over coins that his wife had not entered into their inventory.

In all four cases, the rights of various individuals were in dispute. But the situations occur in contexts about which we know relatively little. In general, we are forced to work at the level of language, studying conflicting claims and interpretations of right. The official ideology of Meisterschaft overlay different arrangements in households, and women appear to have been far more in-

11 *Kirchenkonvent*, vol. 1, p. 178 (5.5.1747).
12 *Inventuren und Teilungen*, 494 (14.7.1729).

dependent than the legal codes suggested. Embroiled in the struggles were husbands and wives, steprelations, in-laws, neighbors, and friends. It appears that a simple patriarchal solution to running a household was not enforceable. Although the consistory – under leadership of the pastor, who strongly represented state ideology in the issues – may have thrown its weight behind the husband in the question of who should control family finances, it had to take into consideration the allied forces involved in the dispute and recognize in practice that the husband's right to autonomy in that realm was based on reciprocity. There is the additional tension between the ideology of patriarchy and the strong alliances established between the pastor and village women, and women often found a space for developing their own strategies within the field of conflict between the pastor and their husbands. In the end, men could assert a claim to mastership over the purse as part of their Haushaltungen. Many of the cases complaining about a husband's Haushaltung mentioned in Chapter 3 reflect the powerlessness of women in certain financial matters. The husband represented the family at the cattle market, the mill, and the tax collector's office. In the eighteenth century, he was generally concerned with producing the chief products of the family – grain, cattle, cloth, barrels – which were sold in exchange for cash. Later in the century, there is evidence that men kept a Hausbuch, containing their accounts, but there is no evidence that women kept any similar records.[13] This did not mean that women did not themselves sell some products of their own – chickens, butter, eggs, and vegetables at the local market – but that the income of the family was derived mainly from products in which women were only peripherally involved. Whatever negotiations took place between spouses and whatever the variations in practice, the husbands seem to have secured a firm place as the marketing and financial agents of the family.[14]

We suggested in Chapter 5 that toward the end of the century, women became more centrally concerned with the production of cash crops. They were drawn into agriculture by the new demand for hoe labor and were crucial agents in the shift to stall feeding. As the village became ever more a prime producer of flax, hemp, and yarn, women were brought into the intensive production of industrial raw materials. Two cases at the turn of the century illustrate the changing nature of exchange within the family.

*In 1796, Margaretha Agnes, the wife of the weaver Johann Georg Müller, came to the consistory to report that her husband had beaten her severely and that she had only been saved from death by the intervention of their journeyman weaver* (Weberknecht).[15] *Müller claimed that his wife had stolen thread from him. He had thrown a*

[13] See, for example, *Oberamtsgericht*, STAL, F190, vol. 9, f. 460 (22.3.1809).

[14] For example, all of the cases of sales of animals, grain, or hay were transactions involving only men; *Vogtruggericht*, vol. 2, f. 70 (5.4.1815); f. 26 (17.2.1808); *Kirchenkonvent*, vol. 4 (21.4.1837); *Schultheißenamt*, vol. 3, f. 23 (19.7.1861); f. 30 (8.2.1860); vol. 2, f. 212 (30.10.1849); f. 147 (27.8.1847); vol. 1, f. 80 (9.3.1842); f. 78 (22.2.1842); *Gericht*, vol. 11, f. 93 (3.3.1828); vol. 6, f. 53 (28.12.1804).

[15] *Kirchenkonvent*, vol. 3 (4.6.1796).

*rope around her neck and slugged her in the mouth a few times. She said he treated her like a dog and resented every little bit that she ate, but he replied that she took everything he did not lock up and sold it. The consistory counseled Müller to eat together with his wife and not resent everything she consumed. He got 24 hours in jail for using the rope, and she was told not to spend a Kreutzer without her husband's permission.*

The relationships in this household are a little difficult to figure out. Apparently, the Müllers did not eat together, and Johann Georg kept his wife on short rations. She was used to purchasing the food that she needed by selling some of the yarn that she produced and that her husband wove into cloth with his assistant. In this family, there was no ambiguity about who kept charge of the purse. The new issue was that the direct product of the woman's labor was being used by the husband, and the wife developed strategies to reappropriate it. In this rather bizarre situation, we find illustrated the altered conditions of family production. In the nineteenth century, women increasingly wanted to know about, or share directly in, what they produced for the market. In this case, the wife provided yarn for her husband, but many other families were selling yarn for cash. It was already a commodity. In many clashes between husbands and wives, an oft-heard refrain among the women was that their husbands did not consult them and among the men that their wives were meddling in their business. It appears that these complaints were two sides of the same thing. The wife now wanted to know how much the husband received at the market for the calf that she raised, while the husband did not think that marketing was part of her Haushaltung. The husband had little control over the pace of the wife's work or the quality of her care of the animals, but he demanded the right to appropriate her product and decide what she would get in return. Even a responsible Haushalter, who plowed back all of the proceeds into the family enterprise, might well have resented the interference of a concerned wife in his affairs.

*The second example from this period illustrating growing women's interest in produce marketing comes from 1808. Margaretha, the wife of Johannes Grauer, reported to the consistory that her husband had been swearing at her and using abusive language.*[16] *He called her a whore and said that if she had a clear conscience she would go to the pastor and report him. Apparently what started the whole thing was that he had sold a cow and resented her scolding him for going drinking afterward. She maintained he was throwing their money away, but he was not about to put up with an accusation that he did not* hausen *properly.*

*Some of the nuances of conflict can be seen in a number of cases from the 1820s, 1830s, and 1840s. Two brothers of Maria Agnes, the wife of Johann Georg Zeug, complained she was ill-treated by her husband and her stepchildren, especially Johann Georg, Jr.*[17] *She said that whenever she sold butter or eggs, every Kreuzer had to be accounted for, and when she had to buy anything, she was treated ill-manneredly.*

16 *Kirchenkonvent*, vol. 3 (20.11.1808).
17 *Gericht*, vol. 11, f. 29 (6.10.1826).

*Maria Agnes was, in fact, the sister of Johann Georg's first wife and aunt to the step-children who abused her. She was supported by her brothers, their uncles. In this instance, the quarrel was over the proceeds from the direct products of her labor. In 1831, Rebecca, the wife of Mathias Häfner, reported to the court, among many other things, that she could not weave any more with her husband, since he blew the earnings on drink.*[18] *A complicated case from 1832, eventually leading to divorce, involved accusations between the couple's parents and siblings.*[19] *Apparently the central issue was that the husband worked for his own father and not for his wife, in whose father's house they lived. Friedrich Bauknecht beat up his wife for continually stealing from him.*[20] *Johann Georg and Christina Rieth were at loggerheads because he drank and she did not spin enough thread.*[21]

At some point during the nineteenth century, the magisterial ideology caught up with the shift in labor conditions and the balance of power in the family. Especially when the family threatened to fall back on the dole or was already receiving help from the village, the local officials were apt to ally with the wife.

*The wife of the carpenter Johann Georg Federschmid complained to the Schultheiss that her husband did not come straight home after work.*[22] *Since they were so poor, he should be more careful with his earnings. In fact, the Schultheiss had been ordered by the Oberamt to collect his wages and give them directly to her. Johannes Bauknecht broke open the locked box which contained money the village had given the family.*[23] *His wife searched him out in a tavern. She asked the Schultheiss to call him in and count his money, which was duly done. After he received a sentence of 24 hours in the local jail, however, she withdrew her complaint. Twelve years later he was brought before the Schultheiss for a similar offense.*[24] *He had gotten his wages and gone straight to a tavern. When his wife found him, he swore at her and railed against the magistrates for helping her. His wages were supposed to be withheld, and his wife had waited a long time for them to pay off his debts. A running battle characterized the marriage of the cobbler, Johann Georg Rieth, and his wife Catharina.*[25] *She was concerned that her property was being wasted because he did not pay enough attention to work. She complained about his selling fodder. Furthermore, she had purchased leather for shoes for her and the children, which he either sold or made into shoes for sale. As far as he was concerned, he had been silent long enough about his wife, who ran the dirtiest household in the whole village. The Schultheiss put him in jail several times, scolded him for not working hard enough, and made a point about the family property being mostly the wife's marriage portion.*

All these examples indicate that the discourse over family expenditures no longer revolved around Meisterschaft, but around alienated labor. This

18 *Kirchenkonvent*, vol. 4 (10.4.1831).
19 *Kirchenkonvent*, vol. 4 (20.10.1832).
20 *Schultheißenamt*, vol. 1, f. 3 (11.9.1840).
21 *Schultheißenamt*, vol. 1, f. 43 (3.7.1841).
22 *Schultheißenamt*, vol. 1, f. 89 (16.5.1842).
23 *Schultheißenamt*, vol. 2, f. 29 (26.6.1843).
24 *Schultheißenamt*, vol. 2, f. 268 (5.12.1855).
25 *Schultheißenamt*, vol. 2, f. 54 (6.8.1844); f. 140 (26.2.1847).

correlated closely with changes in the sexual division of labor. As women became producers of products which were exchanged for cash, they began to demand considerable say in the disposal of both the products and the proceeds. The fact that husbands and wives met on more of an equal footing does not mean, however, that their labor became interchangeable. Throughout the study period, male and female spheres of work remained separate. When women were drawn into agriculture, they did not take over tasks traditionally belonging to men, nor did they and their husbands share the new tasks.[26] Hoeing was a woman's job and the only males that might have been present with them were half-grown sons. We do have the hint in the case of Rebecca Häfner that husband and wife worked together weaving, but such combined activity seems to have been rare. Usually while a man wove in the cellar, his wife was busy on the street breaking flax, or pulling hemp out of the river, cultivating the plot where such products grew, or spinning upstairs close to the baby. The activities of husbands and wives were embedded in separate gender spheres, which were given contour through the web of village gossip and formal institutions of arbitration and control. This ensured that most conflicts between spouses would be over exchange, over how they would share what they both produced or how the traditional division of rights and duties would intersect with the new distribution of productive labor.

Over the period, the courts shifted in the way they related to the family. In the beginning they sought to effect control by enhancing the authority of the Hausvater, while at the same time exercising a careful watch over his activities. With time, they came to act more flexibly, allying with whichever spouse seemed to be the most effective commodity producer. Throughout the period, the issue of reciprocity between husband and wife included a wider group of allied figures, whose concerns the courts had to take into consideration. Women were not just part of a gender set, with sanctions mediated through the powerful control of reputation-dispensing mechanisms, but they were surrounded by other male figures, who had forged an alliance with the husband through their daughter-sister-cousin-Kriegsfrau–neighbor.

## Patterns of drinking

One of the common complaints that wives voiced about their husbands had to do with drunkenness. As mentioned in Chapter 1, the number of cases in which drinking behavior played a role increased considerably after 1820. Earlier, however, we were concerned with the frequency of the complaint about drinking in relation to other complaints. It is possible to look at the evidence from a slightly different angle and ask in what percentage of cases drunkenness played a role in marital conflict (see Table 6.4).

[26] Here I disagree with Ivan Illich's interpretation of my data, *Gender* (New York, 1982), pp. 173–4.

Table 6.4 *Percentage of marital cases in which husband's drinking mentioned*

| Period | Number of cases | Drinking | Percent |
|---|---|---|---|
| 1730–59 | 16 | 4 | 25.0 |
| 1760–89 | 15 | 3 | 20.0 |
| 1790–1819 | 16 | 6 | 37.5 |
| 1820–49 | 66 | 27 | 40.9 |

Clearly, excessive drinking, and perhaps alcoholism, were grounds for dispute between husband and wife throughout the period. Whether the consumption of alcohol rose around the turn of the century or the tolerance level of village and state officials and wives dropped is not clear. Exactly how new forms of alcohol affected the situation is also difficult to sense from the documents. In the eighteenth century, most villagers produced their own wine, and there are a few inventories with schnaps. But the beverage kept in most cellars around the turn of the century was cider (*Apfelmost*). Apparently there was a good deal of steady drinking – even today a farmer with a bright red face is called *Mostkopf* – and it is safe to say that a good many men were under the influence of alcohol during most hours of the day. We also find increasing amounts of schnaps in the inventories. The fact that vines were replaced with zwetschgen trees in the vineyards is another indication of the trend. Indeed, by the 1820s there were three licensed stills in the village. In the tavern, wine was the chief beverage consumed. In many protocols reference is made to the "Schoppen Wein" and to no other beverage. Since some taverns were licensed to offer schnaps, some of it must have been consumed there, but male society usually preferred wine. In every case before the courts in which wives mentioned or complained about drinking, the men either came expressly from the tavern or came home from drinking, from which it can be inferred that they had been at the tavern. There are no recorded instances in which a man got drunk at home and then carried out some "excess."

The tavern seems to have been a male preserve. In the many incidents in which some brawl or similar activity took place, all the witnesses from inside the establishment were men. The occasional references to women being in the pub come from holidays or church festivals. On a day-to-day basis, the only women who seem to have been there were the wife or daughter of the owner or a serving maid. It may have been possible on Sundays or at certain times during the week for women to frequent the tavern or at special events such as a wedding, but the sources remain silent about their presence. By contrast, there is no reticence about the attendance of men.

There were, of course, many different forms of drinking, although they all fall into certain regular patterns. An occasional figure is the man who started early at the tavern and built up a drunk very slowly over the whole day, ending with a bout of loud abuse of the village officials, the pastor, or neighbors, delivered with considerable hollering and truculence. After leaving the tavern, he moved slowly down the street, rocked back on his heels from time to time, and let loose with a shout. This form, although repeated and stereotyped, was exceptional, and most drinking seems to have been done together in company with one's fellows. Alcoholism certainly existed, but that could not have been a problem only for males. Today in every village, there are certainly rumors about the woman silently tippling at home. And yet there is not one case of a woman accused by her husband or by the authorities of alcoholic abuse. It was simply not a theme for public discourse. Although it is clear from many cases that alcoholic men abused their wives and children and broke up many homes, the issue for us is whether this was a new phenomenon during the early years of the nineteenth century.

During the eighteenth century, the secular and clerical officials of the village were engaged in a running battle about drinking. In the case of Hans Melchior Thumm (1727) already cited several times, the protocols of the consistory clearly sided with the wife in her criticism of her husband's drinking.[27] But the protocols were written by the pastor, and Hans Melchior was drinking with his father the Schultheiss, his mother, and the Amtspfleger in the latter's house in Nürtingen. Every year the superintendent from Nürtingen visited the parish officially and took evidence from the secular officials about the pastor and from the pastor about the villagers and the secular officials. Year in, year out, the pastor complained about the bad example of the Schultheiss and the other magistrates, about their excessive consumption, and about the fact that heavy drinking was common in the village.[28] On one occasion, a villager tripped coming out of the tavern and killed himself, which gave the pastor the opportunity to set aside several pages in the consistory protocols to describe the tragedy in detail and draw the proper moral lessons.[29] This, of course, was done in the presence of the lay consistory members who themselves were part of the drinking culture. All the evidence suggests that men frequented the drinking establishments regularly, that they drank heavily, and that women did not make the same heavy weather about it that they would in the nineteenth century. By the 1830s, the pastor was reporting that the bad example set by the village magistrates had ended, and it seems that the Schultheiss had some time before begun to lend his ear more readily to complaints from wives about their husbands' drinking habits.[30] Yet I see no reason to believe that the magistrates

[27] See above, "Master of the purse stringes."

[28] See the reports on Neckarhausen in the *Synodus Protocolle* throughout the eighteenth century; LKA.

[29] *Kirchenkonvent*, vol. 1, f. 168 (4.11.1746). The pastor called everyone together to warn about drinking; vol. 3 (14.6.1781); (1.4.1782).

[30] In 1840, the Dekan wrote in the margin of the *Pfarrbericht*: "Allmählich Ärgernisse und zerstörende Einfluß auf die öffentliche Sittlichkeit beseitigt wegen Wechsels des Ortsvorstehers"; Dekanatamt Nürtingen, Akten I, nr. 4.

were in fact more temperate, and I suspect that they met the pastor's approval because they were more ready to control the behavior of others. Perhaps there was some differentiation of habits, and with the proliferation of taverns, different kinds of people could congregate with their fellows.

The chief problem about drinking, aside from the brutal behavior of drunken men, was that it went with idleness. At least that was the stereotype. Sloth and tippling were coupled over and over in the wives' testimonies, the one being alternately derived from the other. When a poor man came before the wealthy court members in the nineteenth century, he was treated as a wastrel and a drunk even if he did not drink more than they did. Because of the very nature of the documents we have to study, it is impossible to sort out the alcoholic idlers from the underemployed mates. For the woman who objected to her husband being at the tavern, there was a prima facie case that he was wasting his time. Yet the issue does not seem to have been so simple. For example, the parish report for Nürtingen at the end of the eighteenth century (the file for Neckarhausen is missing) stated that men drank a great deal but they also worked very hard.[31] This is a theme repeated continuously by the men themselves when accused of excessive drinking. They made it abundantly clear that they had to work hard and that they did work hard, and they insisted that they did not neglect their Oeconomie or Haushaltung. In some cases, the court or the wives made the point that although the husband worked attentively for a time, he would punctuate his diligence with a period of drinking and hanging around, which implies that the rhythms of the wives and husbands were out of synch.

There were regular cultural forms which dictated when men gathered in the tavern for a glass. We find them there after every business transaction. Every contract to sell real property specified an amount for a *Weinkauf*, which was shared by the Schultheiss and perhaps a few magistrates and the parties to the transaction. The tavern seems to have been the locality where a great deal of business was transacted. In fact, all sales of land and livestock could be rescinded within 24 hours, precisely to allow the parties to sober up and consider things in a fresh light. Men also came to the tavern after work – a man and his servant would go along after finishing the plowing, or the work teams would assemble there after a day of lumbering or ditching. Many workmen were paid in part by meals and drink in the pub.[32] Whenever men went to Nürtingen to take some sacks of grain or testify in court, they would stop in the Brückenwirt just on the other side of the river on the way home to the village. Frequently, quarrels began there and continued on the road home.[33]

Since many of these practices seem not to have changed over the period, we might do best to search for an explanation for the rise of complaint about

[31] *Pfarrbericht* (1796); LKA, C2, 614.

[32] Receipts in the *Gemeindepflegerechnungen* demonstrate the practice. Schultheiss Krumm was accused of writing off too many drinking bills for several village builders; HSAS, A214, Bü 714.

[33] For two examples, *Schultheißenamt*, vol. 2, f. 93, 3.2.1846; *Gericht*, vol. 6, f. 101 (25.8.1805).

drinking in the altered relationships between men and women. The increasing complaints about alcohol reflected a changing tolerance on the part of wives for their husbands' drinking in the tavern. Part of the issue was that since the women themselves were now producers, they saw the husband dropping off in the tavern with the proceeds from the sale as a direct expropriation of their labor. They were, perhaps, no longer willing to have the husband treat the local magistrates to a drink after selling their land. Men were not doing anything different when they expended family resources in male socialization – they did that in the eighteenth century and they continued to do it in the nineteenth. The difference was that what was produced was sold increasingly for cash, and the relationships of exploitation were unmasked.

Only part of the meaning of the structural shift in productive relations is understood, however, through recourse to the issue of exploitation. One of the effects of change was to differentiate men and women radically in the rhythms of their work. Women who rose early, jumped into the stall, fetched green fodder, tended the children, prepared the meal, ran to the field to hoe, dropped the hoe to prepare the next meal, and so on, were developing a new sense of time. At the beginning of the twentieth century, one observer characterized Württemberg peasant women in intensive agriculture as being dominated by *Eile* (hurry), and recently when I asked an old peasant woman what characteristic a woman had to have to be successful, I received the same answer.[34] Hurry was a characteristic of peasant women's lives brought about by the agricultural revolution. It would be incorrect, perhaps, to say that men were unaffected by new rhythms of time – the ringing of the clock at regular intervals seems to have become an issue. But they were still dominated by old routines. In agriculture, they still plowed and harrowed, which meant putting the gear on the animals, going to the field, working until the animals tired, and returning to the barn to unharness and care for them. Much male work – gang labor on the roads, lifting heavy sacks at the mill, or lumbering timber in the forest – was similar. It was characterized by heavy labor, with short bursts of energy punctuated by pauses. By contrast, the arduous routines of the women simply flowed from task to task, without significant break. During the day, women were unlikely to pause for very long in the company of other women. When the plowmen gathered in the late afternoon at the pub, their wives were hastening off to prepare a meal. Therefore, the objection to drinking appears symbolic for a much more inclusive clash between men and women over the organization of time.

Note that the tavern played a central role in male work. It was not just a place to relax after laboring. In the pub, a continual discourse took place about work and business. It was there that a man learned to assess his chances in the market and to estimate the bargaining position for his cow.[35] It was also there that the

[34] Maria Bidlingmaier, *Die Bäuerin in zwei Gemeinden Württembergs*, Tübinger staatswissenschaftliche Dissertation (Stuttgart, 1918), p. 105.

[35] A good example is provided by *Gericht*, vol. 6, f. 53 (28.12.1804).

chain of negotiations took place over a land sale – a neighbor might persuade another to sell him a strip of land if the latter could get another strip from the former's cousin. Village politics were, of course, the subject of continuous *raissonieren* over the Stammtisch. Increasingly in the nineteenth century, the tavern became important as a place where work could be discussed. There the villager learned about opportunities outside the village. If the principal craft in the eighteenth century had been weaving, in the nineteeth century its place had been taken over by the building trades – masonry, carpentry, stonecutting, plastering. The tradespeople depended on occasional jobs in other places, just as many nonspecialists in the village depended on farm labor, work on the roads, railroad construction, and the like. The tavern was part of a network of information, a place where jobs were to be found, where outside contractors sometimes hired people, where travelers dropped tips about employment, or where the locals shared information. It was also at the pub where friendships were negotiated and alliances forged, where a person could get called on when a friend found employment. We often find that where one villager was on a job, others were to be found there as well. Thus, drinking at the tavern was serious male work. But women failed to understand why it was necessary to hang around to find something to do. Seeking employment in this fashion was interpreted as sloth in itself. The impatience of these women or the control mechanisms of officials were reflections of a new structure, a large, cheap, and underutilized work force available for short-term employment. These men were supported by the intensive, hurried, and harried labor of peasant women.

## Häuslichkeit

From scraps of evidence, a case can be made that around the turn of the century pressure was put on women to raise themselves to new standards of cleanliness. Various measures were introduced to ensure that the areas around the house were kept cleaner. People were ordered to tidy up their manure piles, and schoolchildren were forbidden to pee around the school house – a new nineteenth-century ordinance, abrogating a century-old practice.[36] There seems to have been a new sense of smell among the villagers, which manifested itself in many ways – ranging from a woman rejecting her fiancé for his fetid breath to neighbors complaining about the smell of urine from small children.[37] Complaints about people leaving a mess around the village fountain or throwing water out the window brought the village council into action.[38] Inside the house, there was a new ideology of Häuslichkeit. In the 1840s, the Schultheiss

[36] *Kirchenkonvent*, vol. 2, p. 75 (7.4.1752); *Gericht*, vol. 7, f. 150 (22.11.1810).

[37] *Gericht*, vol. 4, f. 180 (28.12.1791); vol. 6, f. 126 (28.12.1801); vol. 9, f. 69 (15.1.1819); *Kirchenkonvent*, vol. 2, p. 25 (7.4.1752). One man complained that his tenants were dirty (*unsauber*), and they were told to get cleaned as quickly as possible; *Gericht*, vol. 9, f. 61 (28.12.1818).

[38] *Gericht*, vol. 6, f. 57 (28.12.1804); vol. 10, f. 174 (16.1.1843).

praised a woman and her daughter for their housewifely diligence.[39] Part of this new ideology was based on "order" in the house, but I think that there were two foundations for the new expectations. One was the greater interest in the care of clothes and the other interest in the care of children. Women needed sufficient firewood to keep the water boiling to wash the diapers every day.[40] Dirty laundry could reflect on a woman's reputation. It seems to be the case that with the shift from woolen clothes to the lighter cottons and homespun linen, laundry day became the important matter that we are so familiar with at the end of the nineteenth century. Household inventories included far more cloth and clothing, dirty laundry being stored up for long, arduous days of labor. Sewing more complicated clothes, and constant mending and repairing of the lighter materials made far more demands on women than earlier. This, of course, was part of the trend toward turning out children in better condition for school. The very demand for enough wood to boil the nappies every day bespeaks a new standard of cleanliness for children.

Men complained quite frequently in the nineteenth century, but not in the eighteenth, about the housekeeping, cleanliness, and orderliness of their wives. And the epithet Hur was so often coupled with such criticism that perhaps the word alone symbolized the issue of slovenliness.[41] It may be that the complaints of the husbands were part of a new ideology of cleanliness and good housekeeping. Words having to do with the specific chores of maintaining an orderly house appear for the first time in the nineteenth century, in contrast to the more inclusive term for the wife's entire Haushaltung in the eighteenth. That part of her labor which had to do with the physical house seems to have been singled out for comment.

Along with the issues of housekeeping came frequent complaints about how food was prepared. Sometimes, the problem seems to have been that the meal was not prepared on time or the wife had not gotten to it at all. In such a situation, the husband might leave for the tavern to take his meals there – which would then lead to accusations by the wife that he drank too much.

*The only example in the eighteenth-century cases of a complaint about food was from Michael Häussler.*[42] *He said that he had to work all day and found no meal when he arrived home. That was countered by his wife, who complained about his drinking in the tavern with his mates. By the nineteenth century, there was a flood of complaints about food and meal preparation. In 1818, Johann Georg Zeug, a Bauer, complained that his wife could not prepare meals on time and that she failed to do her own*

[39] *Gericht*, vol. 13, f. 240 (16.1.1843).

[40] See Karin Hausen, "Große Wäsche. Technischer Fortschritt und sozialer Wandel in Deutschland vom 18. bis ins 20. Jahrhundert," in *Geschichte und Gesellschaft*, 13 (1987): 273–303. A woman in a divorce case sued for wood, since she had to wash her child's things every day; *Gericht*, vol. 12, f. 77 (9.1.1832); similar case, f. 139 (17.1.1843). After 1800, the retirement contracts (*Leibgedinge*) begin to mention expressly that children had to furnish wood for washing; e.g., *Inventuren und Teilungen*, 1494 (25.3.1826); 1522 (23.6.1826).

[41] See Chapter 3.

[42] *Kirchenkonvent*, vol. 1, f. 113 (–.1.1743).

*sewing.*[43] *Michael Bauknecht left for the tavern when he could not eat with his wife.*[44] *Mathias Häfner, according to his wife, would go berserk when her houskeeping did not please him.*[45] *Friederika Beck was continually mistreated because of the way she prepared meals.*[46] *Mathias Ebinger said that his wife had never cooked a proper meal for him.*[47] *Johann Georg Federschmid alleged that most of what his wife cooked was so hastily done that it was raw dough.*[48] *Johannes Hinzler pointed out that his wife was sloppy in her household chores.*[49] *Johann Georg Federschmid had had it with the fact that his wife had not done the washing and the house was dirty. He dumped cold pease porridge on the meal she was preparing.*[50] *When Johann Georg Rieth's wife told him that she would not cook for him unless he had earned it, he threw the potatoes at her.*[51] *He complained that she had one of the dirtiest and most disorganized households in the village.*

While there may have been new standards of household cleanliness, they could only have exacerbated an already difficult situation. The terms that were tossed around about Häuslichkeit may perhaps better be explained not by new demands but by old chores in a situation of new agricultural labor demands. None of the jobs that women used to do were taken over by their husbands. Instead, they were carried out in addition to stall feeding, flax breaking, hoeing, and the like. The burden was on the wife to speed through her day and get all the parts organized. Perhaps the one place where husband and wife met was at the meal. In any event, it was the primary node of exchange, where the woman demonstrated her ability to get her work done and get a properly cooked meal on the table on time. Any breakdown on her part was answered by an immediate withdrawal of the husband to the tavern if he did not stay around to smash things up. Not every husband acted in a brutish manner, of course, but the frequency of meal preparation as a symbol of the sexual division of labor is apparent. A dirty house, ill-clad children, an unaccomplished chore could be pointed out specifically, but food preparation was a much better point to focus on because of the multiple strands of exchange mediated through it. But many times the husband said nothing at all. He just went drinking, leaving the wife and the courts to divine its implicit meaning. The more they focused on his behavior, the more uncommunicative, surly, and enraged he might become.

The nature of conflict between husbands and wives is complex. It is difficult to ferret out all of the forces which combine in each specific situation. The general impoverishment of Neckarhausen may have played an important role in structuring relationships within households, but we have found that even

[43] *Kirchenkonvent*, vol. 3 (8.1.1818).
[44] *Oberamtsgericht*, STAL, F190II, vol. 258, f. 94 (23.5.1820).
[45] *Kirchenkonvent*, vol. 4 (10.4.1831).
[46] *Kirchenkonvent*, vol. 4 (27.3.1833).
[47] *Kirchenkonvent*, vol. 4 (24.11.1833).
[48] *Kirchenkonvent*, vol. 4 (13.8.1837).
[49] *Kirchenkonvent*, vol. 4 (27.6.1839).
[50] *Schultheißenamt*, vol. 2, f. 126 (23.11.1846).
[51] *Schultheißenamt*, vol. 2, f. 140 (26.2.1847); f. 185 (10.10.1848).

where resources were the greatest there were significant new patterns of activity that caused spouses to have great difficulties adjusting to each other. Wherever land was a factor, women were drawn into new productive routines, but this characterized almost everyone in the village, since most of them had at least some land. Perhaps the strains were greater the more resources people had to manage. As the average size of the farmholding shrank, the input per unit of land rose considerably. Cutting across this trend were other cultural changes having to do with the kind of clothes people bought or made and the pressure to keep them clean and repaired, the kind of children people wanted to turn out – clothed, schooled, scrubbed – and the kind of order necessary to a house. We know, for example, that pietism made important inroads into Neckarhausen at the beginning of the nineteenth century.[52] The pietist group gathered weekly in different homes to read and discuss the Word, which opened a house to new kinds of inspection and put new demands on order and discipline. The conjunction of forces resorted the lines of responsibility and patterns of labor for men and women and brought strains as they viewed each other across unfamiliar temporal rhythms, through changed commodity relations, and from different social and political platforms. Until the adjustments were lived through for a generation or two, families were apt to break apart or find themselves adjusting with great difficulty.

[52] On the pietist group, see *Vogtruggericht*, vol. 2, f. 102 (16.2.1820); *Pfarrbericht* (1840), LKA, A29, Bü 3060; *Pfarrbericht* (1834), Dekanatamt Nürtingen, Akten I, nr. 4; *Pfarrvisitation* (1832), Dekanatamt Nürtingen, Akten I, nr. 3. The pietist group which met regularly had 60 members in 1820; "Privatversammlungen" (1821), Dekanatamt Nürtingen, Akten I, nr. 3.

# 7

# Marital estate

They both describe how their marital affection toward each other has lasted for a long time, and how they cannot avoid taking it to their hearts and have taken thought about how they can reward each other.

– Will of Michael Hauer and his wife (1731)[1]

A great deal of discussion between husbands and wives in Neckarhausen turned on issues having to do with property. We have already seen that one public justification for divorce was the threat a husband posed to the wife's portion. Perhaps this theme runs through so many cases before the courts in part because state officials were willing to entertain that argument. Any threat to life or to property became the business of the state, and much of the discourse about violence and idleness may have been shaped by what its agents were willing to listen to. There seems to have been a window for a few decades after the turn of the century in which officials were concerned with redefining property rights and destroying all kinds of encumbrances on property and the cracks in marital relations were allowed to develop into severe ruptures. Once officials saw what was happening, they began to subject women to a new discipline, putting them in prison for ever-increasing periods on short rations or bread and water to encourage them to think better about their demands for divorce.[2] This reading of the situation requires more research into the details of official family ideology and practical policy. But various matters do seem interconnected. At the same time that feudal dues and tithes were under attack (in an effort to redefine property in terms of what could be exchanged for cash) and that law codes were being revised with respect to surety, mortgage, and gender tutelage (in an effort to open all property to public and private claims in

[1] *Inventuren und Teilungen*, 539 (21.1.1731).

[2] *Oberamtsgericht*, STAL, F190, Band 9, f. 473 (12.6.1809). Friderika Regina Bosch was ordered to return to her husband. When she refused, she was given 14 days to reconsider, then 8 days in the tower. This was repeated three times and then she was given 4 days with bread and water, which also was repeated three times. In the end, she persevered and won her divorce. During the next decades, this kind of treatment was extended, and to attain a divorce required increasing determination.

debt action), women gained the right to negotiate with the state over the emancipation of their property from wastrel husbands.

Unfortunately, the literature on the social history of the family gives few details on property ownership and management. Although the shape of relationships between spouses is not determined by property in any predictable way, it certainly is the outcome of interaction with the system of property holding. In Chapters 7, 8, and 9, we explore the issues raised by family dynamics in Neckarhausen and argue that the way married couples got along with each other, their parents, siblings, and children, and the way they articulated with the wider set of kin can only be understood when property dynamics are examined in detail. The various court transcripts should provide some evidence of how husbands and wives asserted their claims against each other, sorted out their rights, and adjusted mutual and conflicting interests in and through a continuous discussion about property.

This approach should not be taken to imply that the relations between husbands and wives in peasant families were or can be reduced to "property." What we mean is that claims to ownership are rights of exclusion or inclusion which define positions between different people with regard to things.[3] They are not essentially statements about relationships between people and objects. Property is nothing apart from the set of relations of which it is composed. That is to say, it is the complex totality of rights, claims, duties, and obligations between people with regard to things. Although we loosely speak of things or objects as property, what makes them so is not the relationship between themselves and persons but that between persons.

This position has important implications for social analysis. There is a tendency in a good deal of recent sociology and anthropology to reject older structural and functional paradigms of social relations in favor of analyses of raw strategy. The problem is, there is nothing to be strategic about if there are no systematic structures which mediate social existence. Much of the old functional school of anthropology was founded on individualistic assumptions about needs, and social forms were read off from their fulfillment. What investigators found was assumed to be rational once an account could be given of individual needs. Of course, anything could be explained in this way, and dissension, conflict, repression, exploitation, and sheer stupidity were ignored. Models of strategy or power and resistance at every point, while recognizing that objective social forms are frequently hammered together through raw assertion, are robbed of sociological penetration by their own presuppositions about

[3] The classic statement of this position by an anthropologist is Jack Goody, *Death, Property and the Ancestors: A Study of the Mortuary Customs of the Lodagaa of West Africa* (London, 1962), chaps. 13–15; see also Georg Simmel, *Philosophy of Money*, trans. Tom Bottomore and David Frisby (Boston and London, 1978), pp. 128–9, 304, 306, 324, 342, 353–4. A recent attempt to suggest some of the issues is Hans Medick and David Warren Sabean, "Interest and Emotion in Family and Kinship Studies: A Critique of Social History and Anthropology," in *Interest and Emotion: Essays on the Study of Family and Kinship*, ed. Hans Medick and David Warren Sabean (Cambridge, 1984), pp. 9–27.

individualized interest. We can begin to give a systematic account of social structures by utilizing such concepts as property once we rid the notions of their individualistic assumptions. This particular concept enjoins us to give a systematic account of claims and obligations ranging from publicly backed principles embodied in codes to demands or requests on the most informal basis. Property can be a flexible instrument for analyzing what people are arguing about.

In this study, we are concerned with the way men and women combined resources to found houses and passed their wealth to the next generation. Württemberg had a peculiar set of rules about family property which distinguished it from its neighbors. In many areas of peasant Europe, farms descended to a single child – male, if possible – and were combined with movable wealth brought by an in-marrying spouse. The monetization of marriage arrangements proceeded at a different pace throughout Europe, but there is evidence to show that where a market economy developed, dowries brought by women could be more substantial and, above all, contained in a more negotiable form. The custom of providing endowments which in turn could be used to set up noninheriting children slowly developed into a legal practice which gave the in-marrying spouse greater ownership rights. In fifteenth-century Bavaria, a wife became an immediate coparcener and heir to the property of her husband, a development which is only understandable in terms of the considerable monetary endowments which developed at that time.[4] Market forces, of course, did not create any uniform practice, and the range of inheritance forms in mercantilist Europe were extremely varied.[5] Although many historians have considered the practices in dichotomous or disjunctive terms – namely, partible inheritance versus unigeniture – and have attempted to correlate particular social and economic developments with them, their accounts of the rules are somewhat simplistic and usually abstracted from other crucial matters which affect family economies. If we combine three points in the life cycle – the establishment of the marital estate, premortem devolution, and postmortem inheritance – with or without a will, then we find that no two areas in Europe are quite alike. Partible inheritance in Normandy, for example, was combined with rules about the marital estate which were so different from Württemberg that we must consider them totally dissimilar forms of property distribution.[6] Even abstracting "partible inheritance" is misleading, since these systems vary

[4] David Sabean, "Aspects of Kinship Behaviour and Property in Rural Western Europe before 1800," in *Family and Inheritance: Rural Society in Western Europe 1200–1800*, ed. Jack Goody, et al. (Cambridge, 1976), pp. 96–111, here 106–7. For a general discussion of dowry, see Jack Goody, "Bridewealth and Dowry in Africa and Eurasia," in *Bridewealth and Dowry*, ed. Jack Goody and S. J. Tambiah (Cambridge, 1973), pp. 1–58. Paul Hradil, *Untersuchungen zur spätmittelalterlichen Ehegüterrechtsbildung nach bayrisch-österreichischen Rechtsquellen* (Vienna, 1908), pp. 26ff., 57ff., 77ff.

[5] Sabean, "Aspects of Kinship Behaviour and Property," pp. 103–6.

[6] Jean Yver, *Egalité entre héritiers et exclusion des enfants dotés. Essai de géographie coutumière* (Paris, 1966), pp. 91ff.

as to whether only sons share in land, whether sons and daughters get equal portions, whether one child gets the house, whether particular children get equal value but not similar things, or whether intestate practices predominate. It also makes a great deal of difference whether children are sharing arable land, vineyards, or livestock. Modern research has not yet adapted models based on matrices, which can isolate specific regional characteristics when the variables – themselves considered continua – are combined. Postmortem inheritance, for example, offers a continuum: At one pole, all children, male and female, inherit equal things in equal proportions, and at the other pole, one child receives everything. This second pole most likely does not describe any actual situation, but some primogeniture situations such as those Sigrid Khera describes for Austria come close.[7] Inheritance rules are part of an interlocking structure of which another feature has to do with the rights of each marriage partner to their common estate. Questions of management, alienability, sustenance, and survivorship were solved in multiple ways all over Europe, and they in turn can be fit onto their own continuum, ranging from coparcenership in a community estate to holding separate properties from two lines whose temporary representatives were the two parties to a marriage.

In what follows, I outline in detail the way property was held, managed, and argued about by marriage partners in Neckarhausen. Intergenerational transmission is discussed in Chapter 8. The Württemberg case is interesting on both accounts because it stands at one end of one continuum and toward one end of another. All children, male and female, inherited equally, which meant that both husbands and wives brought the same kind of property – land and movables – to a marriage. In this situation, the concept of a dowry was peculiar, since there was no special word for what women brought to a marriage. The "dowry," or *Heiratsgut*, was something both the husband and the wife had, and various terms were used to describe it: *Zubringen*, *Beibringen*, *allatum*, *dos*, *dota*.[8] Each marriage inventory detailed first the Heiratsgut of the husband and then gave that of the wife under the same headings of "arable," "meadow," "flaxland," and so forth – all of the *Liegenschaft* or immovable property – followed by the movables (*Fahrnis*), under the rubrics of "cash," "linen and bedding," "furniture," "kitchen stores," and the like. There is a special term, *Voraus*, for sexlinked personal property of the survivor that often appeared in

[7] Sigrid Khera, "An Austrian Peasant Village under Rural Industrialization," *Behavior Science Notes* 7 (1972)): 29–36.

[8] There is a series of about 3,000 marriage and postmortem inventories (*Inventuren und Teilungen*) housed in the Neckarhausen Rathaus covering the period 1627 to 1870. They will be cited by number and date. Many of the details of the following discussion come from reading through the series. For an excellent summary of Württemberg inheritance law, see Rolf-Dieter Hess, *Familien- und Erbrecht im württembergischen Landrecht von 1555 unter besonderer Berücksichtigung der älteren württembergischen Landeskunde in Baden-Württemberg*, Veröffentlichungen der Kommission für geschichtliche Landeskunde in Baden-Württemberg, Series B: Forschungen, vol. 44 (Stuttgart, 1968). A recent discussion from the vantage point of social history is A. G. Roeber, "The Origins and Transfer of German-American Concepts of Property and Inheritance," *Perspectives in American History*, n.s., 3 (1987): 115–71.

the inventories prepared upon the death of one of the spouses. But that only involved a small proportion of the total wealth, usually the clothes the wife wore plus a few basic pieces of jewelry or a horse and some of the tools belonging to the husband. Land was never part of it. As soon as a couple were joined, each received rights in the other's goods. The survivor was one of the heirs of the deceased spouse whether there were children or not, as I shall explain, and had lifelong use-rights to the whole property if there were surviving children.[9]

In this chapter, we concentrate on the marital estate, which will take us a long way toward understanding the peculiarities of the Württembergers. We begin by examining how inventories were constructed and offer examples of how mutual rights and claims were sorted out. Then we will look at the practices of making marriage contracts and writing testaments. In Chapter 8, we examine how family property was administered, how the rights of women were protected, and how the state intervened when the estate was in danger. In Chapter 9, we will consider the issue of equality; although husbands and wives brought the same kinds of things to a marriage throughout the period under investigation, for a considerable part of the village history they did not bring the same amount.

## Marriage inventories

By the late sixteenth century, documents had become part of the strategy of all marital unions. Ducal officials insisted that complete accounts of family property be made at various points in the course of a marriage. This practice developed for several reasons, one of which had to do with the fiscal interests of the state. Officials first developed a detailed knowledge of land holdings. They went about this business from several directions. They made lists of all the property in each village, sorting out which land owed dues of various kinds to the duke or to some institution of his realm. By the end of the sixteenth century, tax lists could be composed on the basis of such records, and revenues could be raised from parcels which were not subject to ducal rent. At the same time that the system of land registration was becoming more sophisticated, the state began demanding that families prepare public inventories of their entire wealth. This, too, involved state financial matters. In Neckarhausen, for example, every man owed a death duty, or *Hauptrecht*. It was imperative to be able to sort out exactly which goods belonged to the husband and which to the wife and which were already passed along to the children in order to assess the heriot. As one would expect, the costs of making all these documents were born by the subjects of taxation themselves.

The series of Württemberg inventories contained in every village are divided

[9] "2. Landrecht" (1567), in Reyscher, vol. 4, pp. 367–93.

into "Inventuren" and "Teilungen."[10] The latter documents were inventories dividing up a property, whether prompted by the death of a spouse, the full or partial retirement of a parent, backruptcy, or divorce. The former – the *Inventuren* – listed the property of a newly married couple and was called *Zubringensinventarium* or *-inventur*, *Zusammenbringensinventarium*, *Beibringensinventur*, *Inventarium allatorum*, or sometimes, just simply *Inventarium*. The property of each spouse was specified in detail, and carefully classified, in the case of a first marriage, as *Heiratsgut* (endowment) and *Eigenes* (personal property of the individual). This distinction only applied to the claims each partner had with respect to their parents. If a servant girl had managed to save some money over the 10 or more years she had worked or if a young Bauer had bought himself a few shirts from earnings as a laborer, that was brought to the marriage as Eigenes. When the time came to reckon inheritance claims from their parents, only the Heiratsgut would be returned for a final settlement. The distinction, then, had to do with inheritance rights and not with claims each of them had against the other.

It was possible, according to Württemberg law, for a couple to make a marriage contract (*Pactum*) in which they specified which properties were not to be considered part of the marital community.[11] But no such agreements were ever composed in Neckarhausen as far as first marriages were concerned. In any event, neither spouse could conceal any holdings or charges against the estate, and if such were discovered later, it could have important consequences. When, for example, Hans Jerg Speidel beat his wife with a sword for concealing money, he pointed out that she had not entered the coins in their marriage inventory.[12] Concealed debts could eventually be deducted from a spouse's portion at the moment of an inheritance partition (*Teilung*). After Hans Jerg Falter died, the plea of his fourth wife for an increased inheritance portion was successful because he had failed to list some of his debts in the inventory.[13] In another instance, Johannes Sterr had led a "prodigal life" and run through (*durchgejagt*) his own property and part of his wife's, as reference to the marriage inventory showed.[14] After the debts were paid, the rest was to go to her.

Not all property rights were complete and not all were final. Whatever parents gave to a child as Heiratsgut would eventually be "returned" or "conferred" (*conferiert*) at the moment when an inheritance was to be divided. This was a matter of intestate law, which the overwhelming majority of adults in Neckarhausen followed by leaving their estates behind without testaments. Even with a testament, a parent could only dispose of part of the property,

[10] "2. Landrecht" (1567), in Reyscher, vol. 4, pp. 358–60, 376–8.

[11] "2. Landrecht" (1567), in Reyscher, vol. 4, pp. 330–3, 367; "Communordnung" (1758), in Reyscher, vol. 14, pp. 537–777. I used a separate edition called *Ordnung für die Communen auch deren Vorsteher und Bediente in dem Königreich Württemberg* (Stuttgart, n.d. [1758?]), pp. 54–60.

[12] *Kirchenkonvent*, vol. 1, p. 178 (5.3.1747).

[13] *Inventuren und Teilungen*, 493 (17.11.1728).

[14] *Inventuren und Teilungen*, 664 (17.9.1745).

which meant that some portion followed the rules of intestate inheritance in any event. At the division, a new reckoning took place and real estate was reapportioned by lot. Thus, even a strip of land given in full ownership to a son or daughter might well fall to a sibling in the final division. In almost all instances where there were more than two children to inherit, they all made a return. There are a few cases in which a child declared that he or she was satisfied with the portion, but it is not at all certain that he or she received more than the others. Perhaps it was usually advantageous to share in the final inheritance, since most parents seemed to have followed the Swabian proverb: "You don't put young bees into a full hive."[15] But I have found one instance in which a daughter actually received a smaller portion by returning her Heiratsgut.[16] Sometimes newly married people received their immovable property not in full ownership but only in usufruct, with ownership remaining in the hands of parents. In the period immediately after the Thirty Years War and again in the nineteenth century, this practice was common. Above all, it appeared in periods of heavy debt when parents could not clear the liens from a parcel so as to pass it on in clear title to a child, although some parents in the nineteenth century chose this looser form of devolution in order to control the behavior of sons- and daughters-in-law.[17] Even then the usufruct rights passed on to a child became part of the joint property of the spouses, and a parent could not arbitrarily divest either spouse of those rights. In addition to these formal agreements, written up in inventories, there were many informal arrangements whereby children worked their parents' land for part of the produce or for wages, or held the land in usufruct, rented it, or exchanged support, aid, or comfort in return for its full or partial use.

Exactly when a family estate was founded is not clear, since inventories were always made following a marriage. There are some indications in the sources about prenuptial negotiations, at which property settlements were presumably discussed and promised (see Chapter 11). Sometimes prenuptial agreements were quite specific, but other times they seem to have been vague. Only a few documents provide insight into the process, especially in the eighteenth century. By the nineteenth century, however, such negotiations were carried out in far more detail and with ever greater formality. An early case suggests that agreements were subject to continuing negotiation carried out over a long period of time.

*In 1696, as the shepherd Hans Zeug's estate went into bankruptcy* (Gant), *his stepson Heinrich Pfeiffer put in a signed "bill."*[18] *Zeug had promised him 15 fl. "wages" per year for seven years work. During the eighth year Pfeiffer got married, and Zeug promised him a further 10 fl. "und sein Sach noch darzue schaffen" (and to get*

[15] Hermann Fischer, *Schwäbisches Lexikon*, 6 vols. (Tübingen, 1904–1936), art. "Immen."
[16] *Inventuren und Teilungen*, 490 (2.8.1728).
[17] The particular case has to do with Schultheiss Hiller and his son-in-law Jacob Bosch; see Chapter 8, n. 44.
[18] *Inventuren und Teilungen*, 429 (–.–.1696/7).

*his things for him). In other words, Pfeiffer had begun working for his stepfather with a seven-year agreement, after which he was to receive 115 fl. plus whatever inheritance he had coming from his real father, or perhaps the necessary clothes and tools from his stepfather ("sein Sach"?). Four years prior to the incident, Pfeiffer had married and three years later was inventoried, bringing 63 fl. worth of immovable property (land and a quarter house) but no movables. It appears that the resources coming from Zeug had not been meant to be paid out all at once; at least, three years after Pfeiffer's marriage, he still did not have what had been promised. All he had had to negotiate with before marriage were claims arising from an informal but real agreement.*

Such documents as this one were inserted into estate inventories. Although they are not rare, they are not uniform. Each family had specific agreements, which come to light only upon an unexpected death. Usually, agreements were worked out orally with various kin present, and that seemed to suffice. The important point is that relations between generations were always under negotiation on the basis of both implicit and explicit agreements which were steadily revised. By dribbling out resources a bit at a time, parents built up obligation and trust and continued to maintain a hostage to compliance. An early example of a rare formal contract comes from 1679. Two years after Georg Klein, widower, married a widow, he drew up an agreement with his wife about property devolution.[19] He wrote that if his two stepchildren remained obedient and worked hard to maintain his property up to the time they married, they would each get a strip of arable and a piece of meadow. Even here a written document demonstrates the vagueness of promises and the importance of negotiations. It is not clear whether Klein formalized their relations at the moment of making an inventory, or whether he had made some promise to their mother at the marriage negotiations two years earlier. However, the period between engagement and drawing up an inventory allowed a good deal of discussion and give-and-take. In both of these cases, stepchildren who had no expectations to inheritance directly from their stepfathers were involved. Although many documents involving claims between family members can be found in the inventories, those with promises to stepchildren are exceptional. The logic of all other arrangements suggests that it was uncommon to shift devolution onto nonheirs and perhaps the unusual conditions were what prompted the drafting of formal documents in the first place.

The fact that vague promises and negotiations continued after the formal marriage ceremonies took place can be illustrated by yet another case. In this instance, the differentiation of households itself took some time, and each aspect – consumption, production, and housing arrangements – was subject to different timing.

*In 1729 the shoemaker Jacob Häfner died, leaving five unmarried children aged 7 to 19.*[20] *His married son, Hans Jerg, had predeceased him by eight days. The latter had*

[19] *Inventuren und Teilungen*, 220 (21.11.1679).
[20] *Inventuren und Teilungen*, 501 (8.4.1729).

*been married for less than half a year to Anna Maria Hentzler, daughter of the Schultheiss in Raidwangen. Hans Jerg had received at his marriage and up to the time of his death absolutely nothing from his father. His widow claimed he had been promised an arable field: "Er seye aber nicht zu seiner Richtigkeit gekommen" (He did not get what was coming to him). The son's widow had no children, was not pregnant, and even after four months of marriage, there had been no inventory. Sharp disagreements* (Unpässlichkeiten) *between the two families then broke out over her inheritance rights. According to intestate law, a surviving partner where there were no children inherited half of the deceased's property, the rest falling to collateral heirs.*[21] *In this case, however, Hans Jerg had not yet completely owned anything. However, testimony made it clear that the father, Jacob Häfner, had declared that each of his children would get part of their maternal grandfather's legacy* (Ehnigut). *On this basis, the village officials worked out an agreement according to which Hans Jerg's expectations from his mother's and grandfather's estates were reckoned and declared as his property. According to the inventory drawn up at the occasion of the mother's death, each child was to get 31 fl. 56 kr. The maternal grandfather's legacy gave them each a further 7 fl. 56 kr., bringing the total of Hans Jerg's* Heiratsgut *to 39 fl. 53 kr. The widow was to get her proper inheritance of half the estate left by her husband, with the rest falling back to his siblings. The marriage had lasted only four months, and the young couple had not established a separate* Haushaltung *until a few weeks before its dissolution. Since neither spouse had received a* Heiratsgut, *one could not speak of a win or loss. The widow's spokesman pointed out that the son had helped the father in his craft without receiving any wages, and while the children's guardian did not dispute that, he pointed out that the young couple had shared meals with the father and because the son was sick he could not have earned much. It was agreed that the widow would keep her husband's everyday clothes and would not have to pay costs of an inventory. Altogether, she got 19 fl. 56 kr. and gave up any further pretentions to the inheritance.*

It is unusual to find a case in which a child died so soon after being married. Such a rare event makes it all the more useful for us. Neither family had given out Heiratsgüter to the newly married couple, although each spouse entered the marriage with expectations based on discussions between the families. At the beginning of the marriage they had both been well, and property devolution had not been put off on account of illness. Jacob Häfner had promised to let some of the children's maternal inheritance go in due course but was not prepared to give up any of his own property yet. Meanwhile, Hans Jerg remained integrated into his father's household, both in production and consumption, with the understanding that as his labor was to be withdrawn, some of the property could go as well. But the differentiation of households was a process extended over a period of time. In this case, as can be shown for many others, marriage did not provide a sharp break between households and families but only established one step in a long, drawn-out transition. Of course, a newly married couple had to

[21] "2. Landrecht" (1567), in Reyscher, vol. 4, pp. 369–73.

have a material foundation for their existence, but that could be accumulated slowly.

The young couple left the Häfner household and established a separate consumption unit three months or so after the marriage. Hans Jerg continued working for his father, however, since he had no land yet, not from his own family or that of his wife. The whole history revealed in the discussions shows that emancipation took place in a series of steps carried out over time – one of which was to set up a separate marital estate, with contributions from two different families. In this particular instance, the future property settlement was still extremely vague at the time of the marriage ceremony and subject to negotiation between the parents and children. Jacob Häfner was a widower, and although he had three teenage daughters (14, 16, 19), the 23-year-old daughter-in-law, Anna Maria, might have been a welcome additional hand in the household. Perhaps the vagueness of the promised Heiratsgut was a useful instrument for eliciting cooperative work from her. Accordingly, the more "obedience" and trust she demonstrated, the higher the possible Heiratsgut of her husband. What was at issue was more than the material inheritance, since, for the Hentzler family, at least, the disputed 20 fl. was insignificant. It represented fair treatment and a proper conclusion to an alliance which had terminated with an unexpected death.

Although the state required inventories for every marriage by the late sixteenth century, it was not until the mid-seventeenth century that the duplicate set in the village was preserved with care. Many couples took their time about calling in the officials and only entertained meeting the expenses when the officials caught up with them. The poorest people in the village frequently pretended that they did not know anything about the rules. Throughout the study period, inventories were made only after a marriage took place, but the gap between the two events narrowed considerably and became more and more subject to bureaucratic routine.[22]

The point to note is that the legal description of what a couple had was always completed *after* they had committed themselves to a marriage. In some cases,

[22] To develop the following figures, I took 35 marriage inventories from the seventeenth century, 33 from the eighteenth, and 64 from the nineteenth. In the seventeenth century, inventories were often made several years after the date of the marriage ceremony. Over half took more than a year to complete – a few took four, five, or six years, and one took more than nine, the mean being two years and one month and the median precisely half of that, one year and one month. In the eighteenth century, bureaucratic procedures were regularized, so that while inventories still always postdated the marriage, in the normal case they were completed within a year – over half by the end of 5 months. There were still a few that took two or three years and one that took four years seven months, but they were clearly unusual. The mean was 11 months and the median 5. In this period we can clearly speak of a mode, the most frequent practice – 3 and 4 months, accounting for a third of the cases. In the nineteenth century, the lapse between the marriage date and the inventory was narrowed down even more. The mean dropped to less than half of that in the eighteenth century – 5 months – and the median was 3 months, which means that half of the inventories were completed within that time. The most usual instance – the mode – was now 1, 2, and 3 months.

either when a spouse died before the inventory or when it had simply been neglected, it is clear from the description that the young couple had long been in actual possession of what was now being inventoried. So we cannot see the making of the inventory, especially in the seventeenth century, with its long delays, as the moment of property settlement. On the other hand, the period of negotiation between parents and children, in which promises were to be fulfilled, could last up to that point. The timing of an inventory was frequently a matter of dispute between spouses or between parents and children, and the period provided an opportunity for considerable strategical maneuvering. In a complicated divorce case from the nineteenth century, while a wife accused the husband of mismanaging her property, he complained that his father was delaying a property settlement by putting off the inventory.[23] Where a second or third marriage for one or both of the spouses was in question, there might have been a necessary period of time in which one or the other child from a previous marriage came of age and received his or her marriage portion. In any event, the delay in making a legal description and the consequent period of negotiation suggest that an alliance between the various families was forged in steps. Not only did the two families of origin have to make a settlement, observing each other closely over several months, if not several years, but the neogami themselves had to work out the terms of reciprocity with their parents. As we shall see, the young couple usually had obligations to the parents, either by being at least partly integrated into their production routines or by paying them some form of retirement dues. Still, the period of negotiation – at least that associated with the legal description of the new family's property – was sharply narrowed down and regularized by the nineteenth century. Nonetheless, the progressive forging of an alliance remained an extended affair. For one thing, the age structure of landholding in the nineteenth century changed, and fewer and fewer resources were to be found in the hands of the newly married (see Chapter 5). Paradoxically, their hope for any significant independence at all depended on all kinds of informal agreements with their parents.

## The composition of the marital fund

Making an inventory was never a purely procedural matter. Even after the officials mediated for hours and literally papered over the fissures, relatives gathered to participate in the division of a deceased parent's estate might cap a final break with each other. At any marriage inventory, there was ample opportunity for accusations of bad faith. But in between marriage and death there was a special significance to having property listed again in a public document. One villager caused a riot by alleging that the Vogt had ordered the Schultheiss to inventory a large number of villagers suspected of being

[23] *Kirchenkonvent*, vol. 4 (27.6.1825).

hopelessly in debt.[24] If the main satisfaction of a peasant was *durchzukommen*, to arrive at death with an increase commensurate with the number of children to be established, the visible shame of a man *durchgefallen* (failed) was an inventory while he was still alive. Not even in death could one rest easy as the phrase "unter dem Boden vergantet" (bankrupted in the grave) testified – in the final inventory after death, one stood in negative balance.[25] What one *increased*, however, was a source not only of personal satisfaction but of public estimation. One man panicked at the suggestion of official action to prevent his economic slide with the thought that his *Runges* and *Gewonnes* (*Errungenes* = acquisitions and *Gewonnenes* = earnings) would end up in the hands of his hated sons-in-law.[26] Each marital union was considered in terms of its own economic history, and a spouse would be inventoried as many times as he or she married. Each marriage was subject to its own set of negotiations, depending on the size of the endowment, future expectations and the claims of existing children. All of the strategies open to people were played out within a set of rules, however different the cards each person held.

The property of a married couple was always made up of three parts: what the wife brought, what the husband brought – each one's allatum or Zubringen or Beibringen together with any inheritances – and what they acquired (*errungen*) or lost (*eingebüßt*) in community during their marital life. In Chapter 8 we discuss the husband's administration of the couple's holdings. Here we are concerned with the claims that each spouse could make on the estate. A marriage inventory detailed each spouse's share of the wealth, which the couple then lived from as an undifferentiated whole. Upon the decease of one or the other partner, the respective rights to the estate were listed all over again, mutual claims were regulated, and the lines of devolution were specified. Let us look at one concrete case to see how the system worked.

Rudolph Schober, son of Hans Jerg Heinrich Schober, married Elizabetha, daughter of Hans Jerg Beck, in 1705. They were both born in Neckarhausen and were being married for the first time. Three months after the wedding their property was inventoried.[27] Each strip of land – arable, meadow, vineyard, garden, flaxland – was listed, with its exact size and location, its rent and obligations, and value, as follows:

| | Husband | Wife |
|---|---|---|
| Land | 135 fl. | 242 fl. |
| Movables | 0 | 90 fl. 36 kr. |

[24] *Oberamtsgericht*, STAL, F190, Band 11, f. 171 (14.11.1814).

[25] Christoph Zeug mocked Salomon Bauer's dead parents in this way, which began a fight and ended up in a fine for Zeug; *Gericht*, vol. 11, f. 42 (28.12.1826).

[26] *Inventuren und Teilungen*, 1397 (17.4.1815). See the discussion of Fridrich Ludwig Zeug in David Warren Sabean, "Young Bees in an Empty Hive: Relations between Brothers-in-law in a South German Village around 1800," in *Interest and Emotion*, ed. Medick and Sabean, pp. 171–86, here 180–2.

[27] *Inventuren und Teilungen*, 308 (28.7.1705).

In 1731, Elizabetha died, leaving her husband, Rudolph, a Bauer, with a 14-year-old daughter, Elizabetha. Three months later the family property was inventoried.[28] The house and barn and each field were listed separately, with the location given, and the value specified. Each item of movable property was also listed and evaluated under standard headings, such as "iron cooking utensils," "field and agricultural implements," "kitchen stores," and "linen and bedding." The total family property amounted to

| | |
|---|---|
| Immovable property (Liegenschaft) | 1130fl. 59 kr. |
| House and barn, 300 fl. | |
| Land, 830 fl. 59 kr. | |
| Movables (Fahrnis) | 214 fl. 29 kr. |
| Credits | 4 fl. 58 kr. |
| Subtotal | 1350 fl. 26 kr. |
| Debits | −72 fl. 20 kr. |
| Total | 1278 fl. 6 kr. |

The next step was to sort out the share each partner had in this total property.

| | Husband | Wife |
|---|---|---|
| Marriage inventory | 161 fl.[a] | 272 fl. 11 kr.[a] |
| Inherited, from | | |
| Father | 79 fl. 20 kr. (1710) | 32 fl. 53 kr. (1726) |
| Father | 40 fl. (date?) | |
| Grandfather | | 16 fl. 30 kr. (1708) |
| Voraus[b] | 53 fl. 1 kr. | |
| Total | 333 fl. 21 kr. | 321 fl. 34 kr. |

[a] Adjusted to present value of land.
[b] Clothes and tools to carry on profession (Bauer).

Together their claims on the total property amounted to 654 fl. 55 kr. This amount, minus the burial costs of the deceased wife, was subtracted from the total current value of the estate, giving an increase (Errungenschaft) of 630 fl. 11 kr. That sum was divided in half (315 fl. 5 kr.), with each half being apportioned to a spouse. The deceased wife's estate then, was composed of her Einbringen, inheritances, and half Errungenschaft:

[28] *Inventuren und Teilungen*, 529 (31.1.1731).

| | |
|---|---|
| Zubringen | 272 fl. 11 kr. |
| Inheritances | 49 fl. 23 kr. |
| Half Errungenschaft | 315 fl. 5 kr. |
| Subtotal | 636 fl. 39 kr. |
| Burial costs | −7 fl. |
| Total | 629 fl. 39 kr. |

The wife's estate was then apportioned, one third to the husband and two-thirds to the surviving daughter. If there had been two children, each of the heirs would have gotten a third, and three children or more would simply have given each heir (including the father) an equal share.[29] Similar principles existed where no children remained, with the survivor inheriting half and the rest distributed to collateral heirs by stem. In this instance, the family property was divided in the following manner:

| | Husband | Daughter |
|---|---|---|
| Zubringen | 161 fl. | |
| Inheritances | 119 fl. 20 kr. | |
| Voraus | 53 fl. 1 kr. | |
| Errungenschaft | 315 fl. 5 kr. | |
| Portion of wife/ mother estate | 209 fl. 53 kr. | 419 fl. 46 kr. |
| Total | 858 fl. 19 kr. | 419 fl. 46 kr. |

This bookkeeping did not hand over any property to the daughter or her court-appointed guardian. All her property remained in her father's hands in usufruct for his lifetime or until he allowed it to be *tradiert* (passed on). No attempt was made to specify which pieces of land or which pots and pans belonged to the daughter. She only had a claim on the total estate, her *Mütterliches*, to the value specified. By contrast, in the nineteenth century, specific immovable properties would go into the Eigentum of the child, or a pledge would be established on the surviving parent's property as insurance. The daughter in this instance, of course, remained the heir of her father. Were he to remarry, in the normal course of events, she would be an equal claimant on her father's property along with his new wife and children. In her father's new marriage inventory, the total property would be listed, usually with her Mütterliches given as a lien on his property *Masse*. In any event, her rights to her mother's inheritance acted as a prior claim on his total allatum in the event of his decease.

In this instance in 1733, the 52-year-old Schober married a widow, Veronica Häfner (57), who brought only 26 fl. 15 kr. worth of movable property to the

[29] This practice no longer reflected the law of 1567; "2. Landrecht" (1567), in Reyscher, vol. 4, pp. 378 f. If there were four children, the survivor received half, and if more than four, a third.

marriage.[30] The couple appended a legally drawn up pact to the inventory about how the property would be treated when one died without issue from the marriage. In the inventory, all of Schober's goods, including his daughter's Mütterliches, were listed, with no differentiation, which was not necessary, since no new children were to be expected and the new wife was excluded from any inheritance. Such marital pacts were unusual, and we will have cause to review all of them, together with all of the testaments. The point to this one was to concentrate all of Schober's property on his young daughter.

We should note that at each inventory the Schultheiss was present together with two members of the village Gericht who sat in their function as *Waisenrichter* (jurors from the Waisengericht or orphan's court) or *Inventarier.*[31] A town clerk from Nürtingen was also present together with all other interested parties. If the daughter had been married, her husband would have been present. In this instance, a guardian (*Pfleger*), her maternal uncle, was appointed to care for her interests. In the majority of cases during this period – as we shall demonstrate in a later volume – the Pfleger was chosen from among the close relatives of the deceased spouse. If the wife had been the survivor, she would have been provided with a male spokesman, a Kriegsvogt (*curator ad litem*) (see Chapter 8). At such an inventory, with several married children, and several unmarried, especially when two or more marriages had produced heirs, there could be four officials, three or four Pfleger (usually relatives), a survivor, a Kriegsvogt (also usually a relative), and half a dozen heirs, together with their spouses present – upward of 20 people. They represented all the complexities of the alliance system centered on the neogami or newly separated couple, and the public arbitrators represented the interests of the state and mediated among family members present in strength.

In the normal course of events, the children from different marriages were treated separately. All the children from a marriage had a claim to the marital fund established at its inception. But their unique claim was only to the property of the parent who died first. That was apportioned "before" the surviving spouse could remarry. In the case of the children from two different marriages, their fortunes could be quite different where the Mütterliches or Väterliches were of different sizes. So they were set apart from each other and differentiated in this fashion.[32] Yet they all shared in the inheritance of the common parent, which gave them a recognition of unity (symbolized by having common godparents[33]).

Again, it is useful to examine a specific case.

*Michael Schober married Agatha Renzler in 1693 (both were previously single) and*

[30] *Inventuren und Teilungen*, 542 (9.1.1733).

[31] *Communordnung*, pp. 54–60.

[32] It was possible under certain circumstances to treat the children from more than one marriage as a unit (*Einkindschaft*); "2. Landrecht" (1567), in Reyscher, vol. 4, pp. 415–9. I have found no instance in Neckarhausen from 1627 onward where this was done.

[33] See the volume on kinship to appear with Cambridge University Press.

*was inventoried in 1695.*[34] *Their respective* allata *were husband, 142 fl. 36 kr.; wife, 174 fl. 30 kr.*

*The wife died in 1720 after they had accumulated an* Errungenschaft *of 465 fl. 59 kr., and about ten months later Schober married Agnesa Zeug the widow of Jacob Weiss.*[35] *He had seven children ranging in ages from 7 to 28, and she had two married daughters. Into this marriage, the husband brought 1057 fl. 2 kr. (including 473 fl. 20 kr.* Mütterliches *belonging to the seven children); the wife, 181 fl. 44 kr.*

*Schober died in 1741, and his estate was inventoried.*[36] *In this second marriage there was an* Errungenschaft *of 558 fl. 28 kr. One of the children had died, and five had received marriage portions, which were now conferred in order to take part in the inheritance. All the values of the properties were reassessed at the current rates. In the end the parties took away the following amounts:*

| | Widow | Each Schober child (6 children)[b] |
|---|---|---|
| Zubringen | 418 fl. 29 kr.[a] | |
| Half Errungenschaft | 279 fl. 14 kr. | |
| Portion from husband/father | 153 fl. 19 kr. | 153 fl. 19 kr. |
| Mütterliches | | 164 fl. 5 kr. |
| Total | 851 fl. 2 kr. | 317 fl. 24 kr. |

[a] Reassessed at current value.
[b] × 6 = 1,904 fl. 2 kr.

A few years later, in 1745, when the widow died, her property was assessed at 835 fl. 31 kr.[37] Her sole surviving child from her first marriage to Jacob Weiss, Anna Catharina, wife of the Bauer, Georg Waldner, was her universal heir. In this example, the second wife contributed a fifth of what the husband brought into the marriage, but ended up with almost three times as much as any of his children got, and passed that on to her own child. Looking at the situation from the point of view of the latter child, she watched her poor widowed mother marry a wealthy widower and herself ended up with considerably more than any of his children.

## Marriage contracts

When two people married, some kind of property settlement was always involved. If the newly married couple had both been single and their parents were alive, then both families would have to commit some of their resources. They were not only establishing and altering relationships with the young

[34] *Inventuren und Teilungen*, 275 (13.1.1695).
[35] *Inventuren und Teilungen*, 407 (10.12.1722).
[36] *Inventuren und Teilungen*, 621 (10.11.1741).
[37] *Inventuren und Teilungen*, 660 (20.4.1745).

couple but also establishing an alliance with each other through them. The permutations depended on the number of children in each family, their ages, the birth order, the ages of the parents, the size of the properties, the state of the economy, previous alliances, and so forth. A widow or widower was no longer subject to a settlement from parents. He or she brought a Heiratsgut which consisted of the settlement of a previous marriage, part of its acquired wealth, and an inheritance from the deceased spouse. More could well have been expected from the parents by way of inheritance, but not in the form of a Heiratsgut. In any event, each alliance brought together strands of devolution transmitted through the various *Lini* (lines) to form a particular estate.

The question that immediately arises is the degree to which marriage partners had a right to dispose of their own property. We learn a great deal about a society when we know whether a spouse is willing to alienate property that would fall to collateral heirs in favor of his or her partner, or, contrariwise, to redirect property that might fall to the partner or their children to other kin or people not related at all.[38] There are three times during any marriage when such an exercise of free will could take place: by contract at its inception, by testament during its course, or through gift or sale inter vivos. The issues associated with giving or selling property are discussed in Chapter 16. Here we examine the practice of making an *Ehepact* (marriage contract) and testamentary rights.

As already mentioned, it was possible for a couple to make a "contract" at the beginning of a marriage, although we must distinguish between a Pactum, a written covenant regulating rights and claims to each other's property, and an *Abrede*, an oral or written agreement concerning the size and nature of marriage portions. In those cases where the latter were written, they remained private documents, and only one of them has ended up inserted into an inventory file. But most of the evidence suggests that such agreements were oral, "mit lauttern Zusagungen und Worten, und mit bestimpten Gütern oder Summa" (with reliable promises and words and with specific properties or amounts).[39] The Landrecht of 1567 echoed what was probably the normal custom when it said that marriage preliminaries should take place in the presence of the closest blood relations (*gesippten Freund*).[40]

The only copy of a *Heiratsabrede* I have found comes from the 1630s and involved the 49-year-old, twice-married baker Michel Ruockher from Neckarhausen and Maria, the single daughter of Jerg Laubengeür, baker, from Oberensingen.[41] The date of the document is obliterated but must have been written shortly before the banns were posted on 7 January 1638 and was done in the presence of the pastor from Neckarhausen, who wrote it, the schoolmaster

[38] This is one of the central questions for Alan Macfarlane, *The Origins of English Individualism* (New York, 1978), pp. 80–92.
[39] "2. Landrecht" (1567), in Reyscher, vol. 4, p. 330.
[40] Ibid.
[41] *Inventuren und Teilungen*, 35 (13.3.1639).

from Nürtingen, and the widowed mother of Maria. "After long urging and persuasion both sides were convinced and in agreement: that Michel should take Maria in marriage, accompany her to church and on the street (according to old, laudable custom), and behave toward her as is fitting for an honorable husband, and in return she should love and honor him (as her head)." The bride's mother promised her daughter or future son-in-law 50 fl. cash as Heiratsgut. He in turn gave and bestowed the paternal and maternal inheritance, which he considered his. In this instance, the negotiations seem to have been about the size of the dowry from Maria's mother, since Michel had only a very young son and could not yet have been considering passing on some of his property to his heirs.

A pact was necessary only when a couple agreed from the beginning to exclude one of them from the rules of intestate inheritance, to set up a special endowment for the survivor, or to exclude the husband from the administration of part of the wife's property. It was a public instrument, and of course, would have to be included or abstracted in any marriage or postmortem inventory. In actual practice, they were very rare, and I have only found three of them in the roughly 700 extant inventories from 1627 (when the series begins) to 1750 (50 inventories from the 1820s are missing). In the next half-century, there were seven, but between 1800 and 1870, I have found only one (1849).[42] Apparently most couples were willing to follow intestate rules. As we shall see, it was frequently the practice in the early part of the century for widows and especially widowers to marry people with little or no property at all. Under such conditions, it was useful to restrict the poorer partner from a major share in the resources of the richer one, which intestate law would have specified. By the late eighteenth century, marriage portions were evenly balanced, and the inheritance belonging to children was guaranteed by the survivor's estate. In such a situation, spouses offering similar amounts of property "purchased" full rights to each other's wealth, which made special contracts unnecessary. The declining frequency of contracts seems to reflect the change in strategies for setting up an estate.

There are no examples of pacts for first marriages. Whenever such an instrument existed, it was there to protect the inheritance rights of children or to protect one of the contracting parties – usually the wife – from any loss. One can well imagine the pressure brought by adult children or collateral heirs when an elderly man with considerable property decided to marry an impoverished widow; yet agreements even in such conditions were very rare. In Appendix G, I have summarized all of these documents.

The only way to explain the rarity of such agreements is to suggest that they

[42] In an 1850 marriage inventory, a contract from 1881 has been inserted; *Inventuren und Teilungen*, 2030 (21.1.1850). In this instance, Johannes Schach (81) and his wife Rosina Barbara Hess, widow of Johann Georg Stükle (75), made a contract to give up inheritance rights from each other. Her property was to go to her grandchildren in Philadelphia and his to the children and grandchildren of his siblings. Their house was to remain the property of the survivor.

were not usually necessary. A wife past childbearing, as most of these women were, could not cause the established lines of inheritance to deviate. When a fairly elderly man married, in many instances Heiratsgüter were bestowed at that time on the adult children, if they were not already in possession of what they would receive. In any event, what the surviving parent held from the children's inheritance in usufruct had to fall to the children at his or her death. Furthermore, the law specified that parents were not allowed to delay the marriages of their children unduly after they came of age at 25.[43] Many of the contracts appear to have been composed in order to protect a wife with meager resources. If, for example, a man with 1000 fl. married a woman with 50 fl., a small decline in their total fortunes could wipe her out. In such a situation, the husband contracted to bear any loss. There is also little evidence from these documents of an inclination on the part of neogami to injure the rights of collateral heirs. With the Schultheiss and court members present at the composition of public documents such as marriage and postmortem inventories, any and all disputes received full airing, and the officials were obliged to keep everyone talking until an agreement was reached.[44] This was a powerful institution for ensuring that families followed the social and legal norms. Seldom did squabbles among kin make it to the higher courts outside of the village, even though inventories frequently attested to the furious disagreements among interested parties. An old parent trying to hold on too long would be pressured by the village magistrates to give over. As far as marriage contracts were concerned, they provided little possibility of getting around the laws of intestate – or customary – inheritance.

## Testaments

The issues of testamentary rights are complex, since everyone over the age of 16 was legally capable of expressing his or her will over property, and yet there were restrictions on what a person could do.[45] Property was individual in the sense that the bundle of rights always pertained to a particular person. Whatever ownership one had, even if that comprised only a usufructory right, could be sold, given, exchanged, pledged, or mortgaged.[46] Certain persons, such as married women, could not alter the substance of their property without the consent and knowledge of their husbands, but they maintained full ownership, and with that consent, could sell it at will. Property which belonged to legal minors, such as women or children, or property in usufruct, was not subject to the arbitrary power of someone else. For example, a husband could not mortgage his wife's meadow without her consent, nor could a father sell a barn from his daughter's maternal inheritance which he held only to "use and

[43] "3. Eheordnung" (1687), in Reyscher, vol. 6, p. 91.
[44] *Communordnung*, p. 57.
[45] "2. Landrecht" (1567), in Reyscher, vol. 4, pp. 333–4.
[46] Ibid., p. 299.

enjoy" unless it was for her benefit and with the consent of her guardian (Pfleger).[47]

Despite the full-blown rights to ownership which we encounter in Württemberg law and practice, when it came to a last will and testament a person appears to have been more hedged in.[48] We will look at the main legal descriptions of the testamentary right and then examine the practice of making testaments, particularly the values expressed or implied about the wider network of kin. Anyone above the requisite age of 16 could make a will as long as he or she was of sound mind, not being extravagant, and undertook the act with due consideration (*in Acht*).[49] One could not take away parents' usufruct rights, violate the terms of a marital contract, or specify over more than half the acquisitions of a marriage (since each spouse had rights to only half). In any event, while everyone had the right to express their will in a testament, that freedom was not to be used lightly.

The chief restrictions in making a testament had to do with the obligatory portion (*Pflichtteil*, *legitima*) which had to go to the spouse or to the children. Furthermore, a will had to be prepared with certain witnesses present and according to certain forms, which if violated voided the instrument.[50] Collectively, the children were entitled to a certain portion of the estate, a third if there were one to three surviving children, and a half if there were four to six, and a spouse had a legitima equal to that of any child. The lineal descendants of a deceased child counted for one portion. In making a testament, a person had to leave a Pflichtteil or disinherit with the exact, legal reason given. If either of these conditions were violated, the will was voided. Furthermore, a child could not be disadvantaged through excessive gifts or dowries while the parent was alive. When the estate was finally divided, the property values at that date were the valid ones, and an heir could demand a revocation of some of the conditions of a will with reference to insufficient funds. When a person was disinherited with cause, it was up to the other heirs to prove the validity and truth if it was not to be set aside. Among the valid reasons for disinheriting a child were striking the parent, acting dishonorably or disgracefully (*unehrliche Schmach*), charging the parent with crimes, using witchcraft or poisoning a parent, sleeping with the stepparent, betraying a parent, or failing to spring one from jail. If children did not care for parents according to their means, then they were to be disinherited with or without a will – a good idea but one apparently never used in Neckarhausen, at least. A spouse could be disinherited for any of these reasons or any act, such as adultery, which could lead to divorce. In the normal case, without any significant reason to disinherit a child or spouse, it seems that a person could, in legal principle, dispose of roughly a third to a half of his or her own estate.

[47] Ibid., pp. 318, 332.
[48] Ibid., pp. 333ff.
[49] Ibid., pp. 333–4.
[50] Ibid., pp. 330–44, 353–8.

Table 7.1 *Frequency of wills in Neckarhausen*

| Period | Inventories | Wills | Ratio |
|---|---|---|---|
| 1627–49 | 55 | 7 | 1:8 |
| 1650–99 | 244 | 9 | 1:27 |
| 1700–49 | 456 | 3 | 1:152 |
| 1750–99 | 480 | 10 | 1:43 |
| 1800–49 | 790 | 18 | 1:44 |
| 1850–69 | 1,251 | 23 | 1:54 |

Despite the fact that testamentary rights existed, we do not encounter frequent use of them in the Neckarhausen records. Out of 700 or so inventories from between 1627 and 1750, there were only 19 wills, and they occurred with distinctly declining frequency. After the mid-eighteenth century, the percentage of villagers dying intestate stabilized. It is quite impossible to give the exact number of people who made wills, since a testament was only included in an inventory if it was relevant. A survivor's will would not be included, for example, if its provisions had had to do with the predeceased spouse. In Table 7.1, the ratio of testaments to all inventories is given, but a better perspective would be gained if we only included postmortem inventories. However, such a count is difficult to make in view of the missing documents and the complexity of those that do exist. If a parent retired, no will would have been mentioned, for example. About half of the inventories were *à cause de mort*, which suggests that after 1750 roughly 96 percent of Neckarhausen villagers died intestate.

There has been a good deal of discussion, especially among English historians, about the practice and meaning of wills. It is argued that if kinship had any significance outside of the immediate family, then people would partition their estates according to some system of claim.[51] Wills and testaments would then offer the best possibility of finding out what kind of valence kinship had in any particular society. In the second volume of this study, we will show that this approach is based on a misunderstanding of kinship. In any society, the rights and obligations are territorialized in such a way that kin have different purposes for each other, depending on some sort of schema. The rules of property devolution are quite different from the rules of marriage alliance, faction formation, or religious ritual. A particular hunter may feel obligated to share the hind haunch of a wildebeest with his third cousin twice removed, but would be shocked by the idea that his spear would ever fall into that fellow's hands. Because the issues are so important and because there are no detailed studies of inheritance for German territories, I have decided to go through each of the

[51] E.g., Macfarlane, *Origins*, pp. 73–93.

wills available for Neckarhausen in Appendix H in chronological order, drawing attention here to important details after each 50-year period.

In the instances from 1627 to 1649, a strong attachment to collateral heirs is evident. A surviving spouse, where there were no children or lineal ascendants, might get control of the property or an extra portion for a lifetime, but the substance was to fall back to the collateral, intestate heirs. It was not usual to alienate lineal property permanently. Some people might be singled out from among the various kin for special bequests, but they were the particular ones who offered care in sickness or old age. We find the desire to reward loyalty especially strong in the disarray following the Thirty Years War, when relatives and children had died by the hundreds and villagers had fled with their belongings to the town, only to drift back slowly to derelict houses and weed-clogged fields. Except for the unspecified relation between Maria Laubengeyer and Georg Klein, all those people who helped each other appear to have been the closest or among the closest living relatives. In none of the cases did tensions or problems between spouses lead to attempts to deprive them of part of what would have fallen to them without a will, and in only one case did a woman, Friederich Clewer's wife, permanently remove property with cause from her siblings to her husband. Furthermore, in these wills there was no interest at all in using one's wealth to care for the poor or unfortunate in the society, with the one exception of Michel Hermann. The overriding concern was with rewarding kin and family members who had offered individual attention to the testator.

In most of the cases in the second half of the seventeenth century, the testaments were still concerned with rewarding various family members, children, spouses, or an occasional relative for care in sickness or old age. Usually, the intestate heirs, whether other children, siblings, nephews and nieces, or collateral heirs from the larger kin-group, were not cut out, even where that was possible. Given the fact that testaments were not frequent in the first place and that only in rare instances was property permanently alienated from the "line" in favor of a spouse, and even less frequently in favor of nonkin (if such they were), we can conclude that "lineal" values were strong. We will investigate the nature of the line in the next volume. Let us not forget here that people may have agreed to care for the testators only if the latter made a will giving them some kind of reward.

All the documents from the first half of the eighteenth century are concerned with issues of family and kin. In many cases, a spouse was providing for the care of a partner when they had not produced any heirs. They themselves were often old, or one of them, being sick, was in fear of death. In most instances, the collateral heirs were hovering in the background, often not specifically mentioned, sometimes nieces and nephews, but also first cousins or their children, or even more extended kin. Property was something which "belonged" inherently to the line, and few people considered permanently alienating it. If they could not act as a conduit for further devolution, it seldom occurred to any of them to let its substance go to the poor or end up in the hands of a spouse, only eventually to fall to his or her line. Such an act would have violated the fundamental nature of marriage as part of an alliance structure. The tension between kin groups mediated by property would have been broken. But it was certainly all right to pick out specific kin to favor, and all of the evidence points to a strong obligation on the part of kin to care for each other, which does not imply that all kin were equally interested in helping one another out. Claims and obligations existed as part of an idiom of kinship, which implies only that within it people displayed their characters, defined relationships, and perceived reality. Friederich Clewer's limping wife had been disappointed in her claims for emotional support from her relatives, and Agatha Rieth's investment in her son had not paid off. In any system of values, claims can be disappointed, which does not make the claim any less real or the values any more false. To deny a claim established on the basis of family ties no more calls the system of kinship into question than the failure to fulfill a contract announces the fall of capitalism.

In the second half of the eighteenth century, testaments performed much the same purposes as they had in the earlier periods. When an older couple had no children or grandchildren, they sometimes provided for each other by making over all of the property to the survivor, either totally or with lifelong use-rights. Sometimes specific collateral relatives were singled out for particular small bequests, but it was unusual to disinherit anyone specifically. On occasion, a close relative who had emigrated and had not been heard from again would be excluded, but the attachment to family could be so strong as to set up a fund specifically for someone who had disappeared. There was always a special gift for the person – most often a niece or nephew, a grandchild, or a cousin – who cared for the elderly person after retirement.

In the first half of the nineteenth century, we find frequent efforts to concentrate succession on some members of the kin group. Specific collateral heirs were singled out, sometimes with a remark about care or services – which suggests that these particular kin had developed closer links than others. Above all, wills were used to reward people for care in illness or for unspecified services or for the display of love or consideration. From the internal evidence of a few of the documents, it is possible to see that a testament was frequently made when an old person moved in with a particular relative. Apparently, the terms of the agreement between the parties involved an exchange of property by will. In all cases, the range of people under consideration were the closest living relatives, and the testaments simply picked and chose among them according to the relations they had developed over time. The will could be an instrument for punishing the ill behavior, neglect, rudeness, and prodigality of the closest possible kin. Frequently, when a legal heir was disinherited, the testator left a small sum to one of the welfare agencies in the state, probably in the hope of associating powerful interests with the particular disposition. Sometimes the succession of emigrants was regulated, but given the number of villagers who left for the Caucasus or America, sending money abroad does not seem to have been much of a problem. Perhaps some of those who emigrated did so under extreme tension with relatives and were excluded from inheritance as a result. However much testaments were an instrument for adjusting relations among close kin, they appear in only 4 or 5 percent of the instances of property devolution. In the overwhelming majority of instances, the rules of intestate inheritance were followed, and even in many wills they were only modified to take into consideration some particular arrangement. The ideology of equality among the children – which we will deal with in detail in Chapter 10 – and the rights of collateral heirs were principles seldom put into question.

In the 20 years after midcentury, many of the same concerns found in the earlier wills reappear. Close relatives were sometimes singled out from among others of similar kind because of services rendered or long mutual support – or to spite the disinherited or disadvantaged. Occasionally parents were concerned with equality when one child had earlier received an advantage in some way. In several instances, parents wanted to ensure that none of their property would fall into the hands of a particular son- or daughter-in-law, and built in institutional guarantees to see that only the grandchildren were advantaged. In like fashion, parents skipped over children in favor of grandchildren or siblings in favor of nieces and nephews. There were also a few cases where minor children, especially from a second marriage, were accorded an extra portion in order to provide for their support. In such instances, and in others, we often see that the issues had been discussed in the family, or at least that the testator had acquired formal acquiescence from the other heirs. Finally, more and more frequently in this period, married couples, whether they had direct descendants or not, made wills together giving each other complete ownership rights in survivorship, which involved the right to alienate any and all property in any manner whatsoever. Nonetheless, at the death of the survivor, the property would be treated as one mass, without any differentiation as to the origin of any particular piece or the balance of wealth provided by each partner to the marital estate, divided into equal portions, and given out to the collateral heirs on both sides. This practice suggests a number of issues that will be discussed further on: the rise of the average age of property holders and greater equality of wealth of marriage partners. In most of the cases we have examined here, couples made testaments together in this fashion seldom before they were well into their 50s. During this period just as at the beginning of the study period, the rights of collateral heirs were always taken into account, and property falling to them was at most delayed by the few years between the death of the spouses.

Property rights in Neckarhausen were sorted out around two focal points. On the one hand, there was an alliance between larger, interested groups, frequently referred to as "lines," and on the other there was the specific alliance of a married couple. By law, property was invested in individuals and they could alienate it as they saw fit. Yet the state always expected such rights to be exercised with sobriety and discipline. Every seller had a day to think over a sale just in case he had considered matters too hastily or, more realistically, just in case he was drunk. The state also created institutions to ensure that the equal input of children's labor into the capital formation of the farm enterprise was rewarded with rough equality. Any child could object if a parent gave too much away to another. From inside the village, the dominant values of equality were exercised as social control as well. Marriage was a carefully worked out contract which put together the economic basis for a productive household, but it also brought different families into contact with each other, who then continued to exchange goods and services such as godparents, guardians, Kriegsvögte, and pledges. They bought from and sold land to each other and worked out political alliances among themselves. Practically no one in the history of the village ever forgot the collateral heirs. No matter how long a couple lived together, no one ever considered giving to a spouse final ownership in what they had. The rights of the residual heirs, of the "lines," were continually respected. The substance of a marital estate itself was always considered something temporarily joined together, and the children did not inherit from their parents but received lineal property designated, respectively, as Väterliches and Mütterliches. There was considerable ambiguity about the lines, however, since they were always considered in pairs, the mother's line and the father's. Since each in turn inherited from two lines, and so on, any number of them ultimately intersected for a particular couple. Despite the constant bifurcation when considering the ancestral lines, people always modeled the situation in terms of two lines, the two sets of relatives allied together by a particular marriage. Yet people did not see themselves as guardians of property belonging to a kindred or of property held by them for a time. No particular piece of land or real estate was inherently family property, and parts of houses or arable strips constantly entered into the market. The value of a wife's estate had to be partitioned in part to her heirs, but a particular field might end up in the hands of her husband's nephew. Parents were expected to provide for their children and help establish their independence, but there was no sense of a continuing house whose substance would pass from one manager to another.

# 8

# State and estate

> So that one knows how to proceed against prodigals and wastrels, we do ordain and establish that against whoever squanders his property unprofitably . . . at the complaint and appeal of friends and relations of the wastrel, or of his wife, . . . as soon as enough evidence for such complaint is demonstrated . . . the administration of his goods and chattels shall be taken away from him.
>
> – 2. Landrecht, 1567[1]

Discussion between husbands and wives about common and conflicting goals, the nature and pace of work, or shares in what they produce takes place within concrete institutional arrangements. We have seen how rights to ownership in land and other forms of property in Neckarhausen were sorted out, but there were other kinds of rights which we also have to examine. Ownership by itself does not tell us about conditions of management, use, or alienability, nor does it tell us how relations between husbands and wives were structured by the actions of state officials in practice. The capacity to own property, for example, was not differentiated by sex, but the ability to manage or sell it was. Such a situation is not surprising, but it would be far too simplistic to classify it under a heading such as "patriarchy." Throughout the period under study, the husband under Württemberg law was the administrator of the family property "mass." But there were guarantees to protect wives, which hemmed husbands in and made them continually responsible to the public and to official observation and intervention. Since the institutions which protected women changed over the period, the different strategies which husbands and wives pursued cannot be fully understood without some knowledge of the general principles and main turning points.

## Administration, Vogtschaft

The husband was the administrator of the family property. This meant that before the law, decisions about farming or about the craft were ultimately his. In theory, at least, the purse strings were in his hands, although in Neckarhausen,

[1] Reyscher, vol. 5, pp. 222–3.

there were many disputes, as we have seen, over who was to hold Meisterschaft. The situation cannot be compared to an employer-manager/employee one – each spouse had his or her own area of activity or Haushaltung, which was subject to tradition and the watchful eyes of neighbors, relatives, and village officials. Nor is this a simple case of an exploitation relationship. In the village assembly, it was the husband who dealt with the issues of planting, harvesting, and pasturing. He did the plowing, sowing of grains, and harrowing, kept the buildings in repair, dug the drainage ditches, and so on. His job was to maintain the household inventory, both his own movable property and that of his wife. He bought and sold land and decided what to do with the proceeds. He sold the produce of the family and paid the taxes, borrowed money, and paid the mortgage. In fact one of the external signs of an adult male was the leather money pouch he carried – the other was his knife. None of this, of course, tells us about practice. We find women, for example, laying aside money for the tax bill and trying to protect such funds from raids by their husbands.[2] Nonetheless, when the bill was paid, in the tax register only the man's name was noted. If a woman determined to sell some of her land, in the court records, formality enjoined a description of male activity. When a father sold land to his daughter, the transaction was recorded as a sale to his son-in-law.

Until 1828, at law women were "Vogtbar." That meant that they were always subject to an "overseer" or "administrator." The term "Vogt" was used in the general sense of "administrator," but also had a special legal sense of "representative."[3] Before the court, the Vogt became the Kriegsvogt (*curator ad litem*), the one who spoke for and represented someone else. In any event, the husband was first and foremost the Vogt and legal Kriegsvogt of his wife – her *Ehevogt*. She could not sell, mortgage, or pledge property without his knowledge or consent, as the second Landrecht (1567) made explicit.[4] A woman could not contract over *her* immovable property or considerable amounts of her movable property without her Ehevogt. If unmarried, she would be provided with a Vogt by the court. However, as we have seen, it was possible for a couple to make a pact together, excluding certain properties from the husband's administration.[5] Even though the wife would then be able to contract over that property without her husband's consent, she would still have to be represented in the court by a Vogt.[6] It is not exactly clear how much this legal provision was ever used in Neckarhausen. In all of the inventories, I have only found one formal agreement exempting certain property from a husband's administration.[7] But

[2] An early example, *Kirchenkonvent*, vol. 1, p. 1 (11.5.1727).

[3] "2. Landrecht" (1567), in Reyscher, vol. 4, p. 325; "Gesetz, die vollständige Entwicklung des neuen Pfand-Systems betreffend," *Regierungsblatt für das Königreich Württemberg*, nr. 34 (24.5.1828), pp. 362–3.

[4] "2. Landrecht" (1567), in Reyscher, vol. 4, p. 325.

[5] Ibid., p. 231.

[6] "3. Landrecht," in Reyscher, vol. 5, p. 82.

[7] *Inventuren und Teilungen*, 509 (28.11.1729). Even that reference is ambiguous, since although the woman kept ownership of the property, she had put it into the usufruct of her children.

there was one court case where a wife mentioned by the way that the proceeds from her house sale were not in her husband's hands.[8] It is quite possible that out of view of the public record various practices were possible, but my sense of the situation is that the property of wives was seldom formally excluded from the direction of their husbands.

In almost all cases in Neckarhausen, husband and wife constituted what was called an *Errungenschaftsgesellschaft* – a community of acquisition. That meant that the marital estate was composed of his Eigentum (or property) and her Eigentum and a mutual, communal wealth (*Vermögen*) composed of what they had acquired (errungen) during the marriage. The husband could make debts and contracts, and sell or mortgage his own property. But as far as the wife's property was concerned, he had to have her consent to alter its substance in any way.[9] On the other hand, the wife could not alter any property or enter into contract nor bring suit in court without her husband's consent: "Wir wollen auch das kein Ehefraw klagen oder antworten möge . . . ohne ires Ehemanns wissen und willen, sonder soll das der Mann thun, der dann ihr rechter Vogt ist" (We ordain that no wife shall plead or defend herself without her husband's knowledge and consent; rather, such shall be done by the husband who is her legal representative).[10]

Significant protections for wives were built into the legal system. Even the laws denying them administrative competency were ambiguous in a way. The third Landrecht (1610) explicitly stated that wives could not bind their husbands to contracts.[11] But a clause provided an exception – that it be done for "common use" and that the business be carried out before a court. Furthermore, a creditor would have to prove that the contract was to the woman's and her children's advantage. The passage in the second Landrecht (1567) was even more revealing in the manner in which it pulled both ways at once. Part of the statement was a direct, unambiguous prohibition while the subclause pulled its teeth, so to speak:

> . . . kein Weibsbild, so . . . in der Ehe ist, sich für ihren Ehemann auß desselben Geheiß (es were dann, das sie es ausser selbst freiem ungezwungenem willen, unnd gemeiner Haußhaltung fürstendingen, billichen, bewegenden ursachen thete, sich auch ein solches vor Gericht gnugsamlich erscheinte) in kein weiß noch gestalt umb Schulden oder in andern Contracten unnd Handlungen, verpflichten oder verbinden . . . (No woman who is married may in any way or manner bind or obligate her husband for debts or in other contracts and transactions even at his bidding [except she do it from her free, unconstrained will, act with prudent, proper, and urgent cause for their common household, and appear fittingly before a court]).[12]

[8] *Kirchenkonvent*, vol. 1, p. 124 (6.10.1743).
[9] "3. Landrecht," in Reyscher, vol. 5, p. 221.
[10] "2. Landrecht," (1567), in Reyscher, vol. 4, p. 231; see also "3. Landrecht," in Reyscher, vol. 5, p. 96.
[11] "3. Landrecht," in Reyscher, vol. 5, p. 221.
[12] "2. Landrecht," (1567), in Reyscher, vol. 4, p. 324.

All of this assumes that a woman was vulnerable and had to be protected, not only from third parties, who had to prove that contracts were in her interest, but also from her husband. While a couple's relationship may have been asymmetrical, there were significant obligations he had to assume. To balance, for example, his administrative rights and duties, all of his property was tacitly pledged as a protection of her marriage portion, nothing of hers was pledged in return.[13] In fact, creditors could not proceed against her property for his debts. A husband, despite the fact that he was the administrator of the wife's property and her legal Vogt, could not pledge or mortgage or contract with respect to her property without her consent.[14] Since all selling, mortgaging, and pledging of property had to take place before a court and be duly entered in the various registers (Kaufbuch, Unterpfandsbuch, Grundbuch, Steuerbuch [registers of land sales, mortgages, land holdings, and tax valuations]), there were strong guarantees for proper procedures.[15]

Despite the fact that correct action before a court was necessary for a woman's property to be altered, a further guarantee was created. Already in the sixteenth century, if not earlier, the principle was established that if a wife was uncertain about a transaction of her husband, she could have a court-appointed Kriegsvogt, whose job was to read aloud all the documents, clarify all points, and see that her free will was exercised.[16] By the eighteenth century, the village court protocols registered hundreds of instances of Kriegsvögte being appointed, which suggests that such a figure had become obligatory. Most of them were close relatives of the wife, who in all likelihood took advantage of this legal provision in order to ensure that property which "they" had provided was not encumbered to the advantage of the husband's side of the alliance.[17] Kriegsvögte were usually appointed in the context of borrowing money or mortgaging a strip of land, either because the rest of the family property was supposed to be pledged at the same time or because a lien was being established on the wife's Eigentum. The wife had to appear before the court with her husband and Kriegsvogt and under oath release her *weibliche Freiheiten* (female privileges).

The Kriegsvogt was appointed by the court and had to take an oath. In most cases, he held his office over a long period of time and was not just appointed on an ad hoc basis for a particular occasion. Important for his function was the ability to read and write, since he had to read the contractual terms of a transaction explicitly to the woman (his *Kriegsfrau*). In one way, the Kriegsvogt can be seen as an instrument for informing a woman and attaining her will through a neutral or supportive third party in a period when few women were literate, and perhaps part of the reason for finally ending the institution was the

[13] Ibid., p. 285.
[14] "3. Landrecht," in Reyscher, vol. 5, p. 318.
[15] "2. Landrecht," (1567), in Reyscher, vol. 4, pp. 297, 316.
[16] Ibid, p. 325; "3. Landrecht," in Reyscher, vol. 5, p. 221.
[17] See volume 2.

fact that literacy had become the property of most women. While it lasted, however, legally the two acted together, and they could, further, appoint a solicitor (*Anwalt*) to represent them before the court.[18] In any event, the two of them could not act together for any substantial matter outside the court.[19] After 1828, when the institution of the Kriegsvogt was abolished, women were still allowed to bring along a supporter (*Beistand*), and one frequently finds in the records that a father or brother had been present in the court with the couple. Nonetheless, from that date onward, a woman's simple signature was legally binding and sufficient evidence of her will.

In 1825 and 1828 two major revisions of the *Pfandgesetz* (law of pledging) took place, which led in the later year to the abolition of *Geschlechtsvormundschaft* (gender tutelage).[20] From then on, adult women were *Verwaltungsfähig* (administratively competent), and their signatures sufficed to attest to their intentions. They were no longer under the Vogtschaft of their husbands nor was a Kriegsvogt required in action before the court. This meant that a woman could pledge her property (in *Bürgschaft* or *Intercession*) and validly contract with her husband without the intervention or presence of a third party. The husband kept the right of administration over their common and her particular property, and a woman could not contract over property over which that right extended without his permission. When it came to her intercession or Bürgschaft (pledge), such was still only valid when formally expressed before a court.[21] The law required court officials to explain all details and point out any dangers and to ask a wife if she were taking on an obligation in free will. But that was no longer essential for the validity of the transaction. "Jede einfache Unterschrift einer in der Errungenschaftsgesellschaft lebenden Ehefrau in dem auf ihren Ehemann lautenden Schuldscheine begründet die rechtliche Vermuthung, es habe dieselbe sich als Mitschuldnerin unterzeichnet" (Any simple signature in a husband's bill of debt of a wife living in a "community of acquisition" establishes the legal supposition that the said wife signed it as co-debtor).[22]

The general tendency of the law over the period we are considering was to make ever more explicit what was implicitly there in the first place. While calling upon the aid of a Kriegsvogt was legally permissable in the sixteenth century, by the eighteenth century one came to be formally required. By 1825, a court had to have at least three officials present for a woman to pledge her property.[23] This last formality was clarified shortly before women emerged from under the tutelage of their husbands. The new law in 1828 specified that all the immovable property a woman brought to or acquired during a marriage

[18] "3. Landrecht," in Reyscher, vol. 5, p. 80.
[19] "2. Landrecht," (1567), in Reyscher, vol. 4, p. 325; "3. Landrecht," in Reyscher vol. 5, p. 221; "Pfandgesetz," *Regierungsblatt*, nr. 17 (1.5.1825), p. 199.
[20] *Regierungsblatt* (1828), pp. 362–3.
[21] Ibid., pp. 363–4.
[22] Ibid., p. 366.
[23] "Pfandgesetz" (1825), p. 199.

was to be entered into the registers as her Eigentum.[24] Furthermore, a woman could require a general pledge of all the husband's immovable property to guarantee her movable property. At the making of the marriage inventory, she could request that particular pieces of land be pledged against her movables, although in Neckarhausen in almost every case women formally renounced this right and simply maintained the possibility of requiring it should the need arise. It was also possible if a husband did not have enough land to put a general note in the mortgage volumes to the effect that future acquisitions by him had to be formally pledged.

These were the legal institutions within which negotiations between marriage partners took place. The law quite clearly stressed the nature of marriage as an alliance, one in which property played an essential role. It distinguished the property of each spouse unambiguously and, while concerned with authority relations in the family as a productive unit and temporary property holding society, nonetheless created rules and procedures to maintain the relationship as an alliance. Behind and around the married couple were the "lines" which transmitted property to and through them. As far as property was concerned, spouses acted as the temporary incumbents of the many strands of devolution collected at that particular point. More narrowly, they were the incumbents of two families making up an alliance, and the law specified what was certainly the custom anyway that discussions before marriage were to take place within the circle of close relatives.[25] In any court appearance of a married couple, there would be two male representatives of that alliance, the husband and the wife's Kriegsvogt – which was usually a close relative of the wife. Brothers-in-law frequently appeared in court together to transact business concerning the wife/sister. Both of them were Vögte of the woman, yet she was a legal person in her own right who had to express her free will. Beyond and above the interests of family alliance was the court, which had to recognize that a transaction was in her interest and protective of her property and had to mediate publicly under strong pressure from private interests.

When the institution of Kriegsvogtschaft was abolished, there also seems to have been a shift in the focal point of alliance. What was at issue in the 1820s as far as the lawgivers were concerned was the practice of Bürgschaft, or pledging. There was the old issue of debt arising from a mortgage situation, when a particular strip of land or building securing a loan did not suffice in a default. In such a situation, the rest of the borrower's property was tacitly pledged and could be attached to satisfy the debt.[26] A problem arose, however, when the ability to proceed further did not include the wife's property because at the original mortgage transaction she had not agreed to place her wealth at risk. This became more and more of an issue in the eighteenth century, and many

[24] Ibid., p. 201.
[25] "2. Landrecht," (1567), in Reyscher, vol. 4, p. 330.
[26] Ibid., pp. 273–5.

lenders refused to extend money without the guarantee: therefore the frequent appearances of Kriegsvögte with their Kriegsfrauen in the court. Increasingly, land became subject to debt after the mid-eighteenth century, and the beginning decades of the nineteenth witnessed a rash of bankruptcies. In at least one case in Neckarhausen, after the bankruptcy of a farmer, his wife bought back all of the land sold at public auction.[27] Had she pledged her property, much of it would have gone to settle her husband's debts. Other women were called on after the fact to save the honor of the family by allowing creditors to attach their properties.[28] The revision of the law of pledging took place on the heels of the crisis in money lending, and the Kriegsvogt was banished from the court, leaving the wife alone to represent her interests and those of her family vis-à-vis her husband.

Early in the nineteenth century, pledging changed somewhat. Property was more and more put at risk to guarantee performance. A carpenter laboring outside the village might need to post a security for his work. And very important for the state was the development of a general system of "Caution" for officials who handled money.[29] When a Bürgermeister, for example, entered office, his wife had to appear before the court and pledge her property for his performance – of course his own was pledged at the same time.[30] By extending the system of guarantee to the whole marital estate, the relationships between husbands and wives were subtly changed. By standing as a guarantee for her husband's good faith, competence, and moral capacity, a wife was implicitly mandated to observe and comment on his activities. Wives had much more to lose from the improper behavior of their husbands and certainly took up the opportunity to comment more frequently and vociferously. It was in the context of extending the liability of the community estate that the law in 1828 was formulated. Its primary concern can be inferred from the fact that it took up Bürgschaft (pledging) in the next sentence after abolishing Geschlechtsvormundschaft (gender tutelage).[31]

## Mundtod and Pflegschaft

The law protected the husband's administrative rights over his wife's property and over his own only as long as he acted soberly and with good judgment. Bad (*Unnutzen*) householders, prodigals, and wastrels (*Geudern*) could lose their

[27] The records of land sales are kept in a series of registers called *Kaufbücher*. The example occurred during the first decade of the nineteenth century.

[28] *Kaufbuch*, vol. 3, f. 6 (7.8.1733); *Inventuren und Teilungen*, 3704 (12.3.1792).

[29] Formulae for transaction of such business are found in the *Regierungsblatt* (1863/4), pp. 65–84.

[30] E.g., *Unterpfandsbuch*, vol. 4, f. 57 (23.11.1813): "Johann Salomo Bauknecht, Friedr. Sohn, nebst Eheweib Johanna und ihr Kriegsvogt Kaspar Kuhn sezen für die dem Ehemann anvertraut Commun Rechnung als Bürgermeister der hiesigen Commun zu gerichtlichen Unterpfand der Eheleute ganzes jeziges und kunftiges Vermögen mit der rechtlichen Wirkung ein."

[31] "Pfandsystem," pp. 362–3.

freedom to act.[32] At the behest of a relative or his wife, a man could be declared *Mundtod*, that is, incapable of entering into any contracts – no debts at the tavern, no credit on the purchase of a calf, no sale of a strip of land. All of his property would be put under the administration of a Pfleger (guardian).[33] Even if matters did not go that far, at the first complaint of his wife and a warning, any transaction touching his wife's property could be revoked. Once under a Pfleger: "derselbig soll gentzlich kein Gewalt noch Macht haben, ichtzit zuverendern oder sich zuverbinden und zu obligieren, in keinerley weiß noch weg, ohn Vorwissen und Willen seiner Vogt und Pfleger" (He shall have absolutely no power or authority at any time to obligate, bind, or alter, in any manner or way, without the knowledge and consent of his administrator or guardian).[34]

Law enunciates clear principles and establishes boundaries to action. But, as in any situation, when a man was clever enough and determined enough to circumvent the rules, he very often could go further than anyone would have expected. Indeed, at the turn of the nineteenth century one man went through one of the largest fortunes in the village even though he was under a legal guardian and his wife's two Kriegsvögte, her brothers, kept a sharp eye out and continually visited the courts.[35] If a husband was just a bad manager or if times were rough, there was probably little a wife could do if they did not agree on common procedures. She had to point to character faults which made him incompetent, such as drinking or loafing. She could go before the court herself, although occasionally the court intervened when family squabbles became notorious. She could also come with the support of a male relative – her father, occasionally her brother – or with her Kriegsvogt. As a first step, she could request interference on the part of the court and expect her husband to get a scolding, a few days in jail, or a fine. The problem with a fine was that it affected the economy of the household, and once it was levied, the woman frequently withdrew her complaint. Often, it was enough just to effect a judgment in her favor or to gain a condemnation of her husband's behavior, which could be the basis of further complaints leading to more drastic action, such as a request for a *Vermögensseparation* (officially withdrawing her property from the administration of her husband) or a Mundtod declaration, putting him under a guardian. In no case did a woman then become an independent agent capable of contracting debts on her own, at least before 1828.

In general, actions leading to the withdrawal of a man's competency over his own affairs, at least insofar as they were brought by wives, were a distinctly eighteenth-century phenomenon. After 1828, women were capable of administering their own affairs, so that when matters came to a head, they demanded

32 "2. Landrecht" (1567), in Reyscher, vol. 4, pp. 325–6.

33 "3. Landrecht" (1610), in Reyscher, vol. 5, p. 221; "7. Landesordnung" (1621), vol. 12, pp. 782–5.

34 "2. Landrecht," (1567), in Reyscher, vol. 4, pp. 325–6.

35 Case of Johannes Rieth discussed below.

divorce rather than staying married to a man under a court-appointed administrator and asserted the right to a greater degree of self-determination. Even well before the change in the law, however, women increasingly sought divorce as a solution rather than simply having their husbands declared incompetent. Or sometimes a Mundtod declaration was just a preliminary step, freezing all the family assets, while proceedings leading to a legal separation or divorce ran their course. In the following paragraphs, we run through a number of cases in roughly chronological order, looking particularly at the way women sought help from local institutions to control the behavior of their husbands or to win a degree of independence.

*We have already encountered the case of Hans Melchior Thumm (1728).*[36] *The pastor, reacting to complaints of Thumm's wife, reported to the consistory that he had begun his disorderly life and boozing again. Thumm came home drunk and subsequently visited more taverns that day, continuing his drunkenness the whole week. Finally he came home from Nürtingen and chased his wife and children from the house. At that point the pastor sent for Thumm's father, the Schultheiss, to order him to keep the peace, and a complaint was formally brought by Thumm's wife before the consistory. It was noted that he had already been reported to the Oberamt, and now a second report was to be made.*

In this instance, the pastor had first attempted to control matters by his authority and had tried to mediate between Thumm, his wife, and his father. Many cases appear to have been handled in this way in a kind of half private, half public manner. The pastor noted in one case that a man had come into his diary several times, and it was now time to make the matter public and take official action.[37] The pastor could seek to bring in the power of the relatives or the secular authorities – in the case of Hans Melchior Thumm, the father/Schultheiss. Before the consistory or village court, fines could be levied, matters made public, and recalcitrant individuals threatened. A more drastic step was to report someone to the administrative and judicial officials of the Oberamt, where more severe fines could be levied, longer jail sentences given out, and civil rights taken away.

*In 1747, the abandoned wife of Michael Schill ("Michael Schillens deserta"), Anna Barbara, complained to the* Vogt *together with her* Kriegsvogt, *her brother Johann Adam, that her husband had returned to the village in 1738 and given a meadow that had been part of her marriage portion to Joseph Häfner and Hans Jerg Schill without her knowledge and consent.*[38] *The latter was Michael's brother and Pfleger. She pointed out that recently, with the lowering of the Neckar, the land had become usable again and she wanted to have it back. The official said that Michael Schill was a declared* Prodigus *and* liederlicher Geselle *(dissolute fellow), and*

[36] See Chapter 6; *Kirchenkonvent*, vol. 1, p. 6 (25.1.1728).
[37] *Kirchenkonvent*, vol. 1, p. 113 (–.1.1743).
[38] *Vogtruggericht*, vol. 1, f. 2 (1.12.1767).

*despite Hans Jerg Schill's claim to have a legal document, the wife should have the power to take possession of the plot again.*

*Andreas Köpple, mason, beat his wife badly enough to leave bruises (1757).*[39] *She accused him of drinking excessively every day and not caring for his* Haushaltung. *He promised the consistory to avoid the pub in the future and not to provoke his wife. As a warning, he was put in the village jailhouse for the night and threatened with a report to the Oberamt. In turn, his wife was lectured for her anger and scolding and was told she would only have herself to blame if she fell into distress. She promised peace and improvement.*

Both of these cases are typical of many others which came before the local courts. A woman seldom appeared before officials without bringing support of her family members, one of whom was usually singled out to act as her Kriegsvogt. In the Schill case, one family, brother (Kriegsvogt) and sister, disputed the property rights of two brothers. In the court's mediation, the character of the husband was a central consideration. Local officials had ways of disciplining behavior, from the lecture and warning given to Köpple's wife to the night in jail for Köpple himself. Such a punishment was not at all taken lightly, and people frequently ran away to avoid going to jail even for a few hours, and there are many expressions of shame associated with the threat.

*The case of Johannes Rieth (1749–1805), a butcher, is especially instructive.*[40] *He was the son of the Schultheiss, Johann Georg Rieth III, and married to the daughter of a butcher and Richter from the neighboring village of Neckartailfingen, Maria Rebecca Baur (in 1773). Four years before he married, he had his first entry into the court protocols for being drunk and rowdy on the streets. There is no mention of this kind of behavior again until 1781, when he was cited before the consistory for drinking late and running around, but above all for drinking heavily before and after going to confession and communion. His wife reported him for getting worse, yelling at her, and giving her a beating. Most nights he spent in the pub. She fetched her brothers from Neckartailfingen, who testified that Rieth was followed around by a carousing crowd. During the next few years, he was repeatedly cited for drinking, especially on holidays. In 1784, his wife was appointed a new* Kriegsvogt, *a cousin (or brother-in-law, Johann Caspar Häussler), from Neckartailfingen, and Rieth was put under a* Pfleger (curator), *Johannes Bosch, Rat. By 1785, Maria Rebecca had received a divorce, and her brother was appointed* Pfleger *of the children. Shortly before, Rieth had admitted getting the maid pregnant, which may in fact have been the formal cause of the divorce.*

[39] *Kirchenkonvent*, vol. 2 (6.11.1757).

[40] *Kirchenkonvent*, vol. 2 (13.8.1769); vol. 3 (14.1.1781); (1.7.1781); (12.8.1781); (1.4.1782); (7.4.1782); (25.1.1784); (20.1.1785); (19.5.1786); (16.7.1789); (7.1.1790); (25.4.1791); (23.10.1791); (7.3.1796); *Gericht*, vol. 3, f. 153, (2.1.1784); f. 156 (17.2.1784); f. 179 (30.7.1784); vol. 4, f. 18 (30.4.1785); f. 130 (7.1.1790); vol. 5, f. 84 (2.1.1798); f. 105 (13.7.1798); f. 105 (13.7.1798); f. 167 (11.11.1801); vol. 6, f. 521 (9.8.1805); Nürtingen, *Stadtgericht*, vol. 28, f. 93 (24.10.1785).

*The next year he was before the consistory for fornication with two different women, and three years later was cited again. During the 1790s, Rieth was repeatedly brought before the courts for drinking and carousing. He was reported in 1791 for making noise on the village streets when he was supposed to be in jail in Nürtingen. Apparently he had the jailhouse key and had let himself out for the evening. In 1796, some of his friends broke down the wall of the village jail to go off with him to the pubs. By 1798 everyone had had enough. The Schultheiss wrote that if he continued his* Haushaltung *in this manner, he would go through his entire property* (Vermögen). *His divorced wife's brother as* Pfleger *of the children requested that all of his properties be rented out, but the Oberamt officials went further and ordered them to be sold, that he be declared* Mundtod, *and that Friedrich Krumm be appointed his* Pfleger. *No transactions were to be completed without his guardian, and especially no pub debts were to be honored. The story then gets rather dense, with repeated interventions of his children's* Pfleger *and his wife's* Kriegsvogt. *Under Krumm's administration, Rieth managed to go through a very large fortune, a scandal which ended up with a special investigator visiting the village. In the end, Krumm, himself, was found liable for several thousand Gulden worth of debts, and Rieth was appointed a new* Pfleger, *Johann Falter, baker, and the rest of Rieth's land and house were auctioned off.*

This story illustrates how closely a woman could rely on her own near kin in official positions having to do with her family and marriage. Her brother became Pfleger of the children, and as such had the right to intervene with regard to Rieth's property, even after the divorce. He brought suit in order to protect the children's rights to sustenance and to their inheritance. Maria Rebecca's own Kriegsvogt was a close relative (either a cousin or a brother-in-law) named in fact after her own father – Johann Caspar. Both before and after the divorce, she intervened in her husband's administration through her male kin. Just exactly how Rieth was able to circumvent the restrictions put on him for so long is unclear. For one thing, he was the son of a former Schultheiss and very rich. Even well into his *asotisches Lebenswandel*, he continued to have large funds, and was able to drive up incredible bills at the various pubs. He was especially popular, it was said, because he never liked to drink alone, and he always paid for everyone. In a sense, a very large part of the village treated him as ripe for picking and profited from his profligacy. In the end, however, his Pfleger had to pick up the bill, which shows not only that the wife and children were protected through court action, but also that being a guardian or administrator entailed serious risks.

*Friedrich Bosch brought suit before the village court because of his Kriegsfrau, the wife of Salomon Brodbeck (1791).*[41] *The latter had led a bad* Haushaltung *for a considerable time, and Bosch would no longer put up with it, and wanted the magistrates to intervene. After the wife was called in, she testified that she "could not deny" her husband was a bad* Haushalter *and that she had come to the end of her tolerance of the situation. Her property was in danger of being dissipated. He drank*

[41] *Gericht*, vol. 4, f. 175, (30.9.1791).

*heavily and had not been home for two nights. She wanted him declared* Mundtod *so that no one could transact anything with him.*

In this instance, the Kriegsvogt acted independently of his Kriegsfrau, at least formally, and brought suit himself in court. She quickly moved from being a witness to acting as plaintiff, and the burden of her case had to do with the threat to her own property. There was no suggestion of not continuing the marriage, but the administration of the husband's Haushaltung was to be removed from his own direction.

Not every case led to demands of a property separation or a declaration of incompetency. To take the latter step was possible only if the husband could be convicted of drunkenness or dissoluteness. When a wife was no longer able to live with her husband, she could go to the court to see that he provided for her support. For example, the wife of Mathäus Falter came to the court because her husband hit her so often that she could no longer hausen (live with him).[42] Because she complained to the Schultheiss, Falter locked her out, and she demanded that he support her and her child with the necessary victuals.

By the turn of the century, women were less likely to seek a declaration of incompetency than to threaten divorce.

*Friederica Regina Hentzler complained that her husband Salomo was drunk and violent.[43] Her parents argued that a divorce was necessary, for otherwise her property would decline. "Sie wird vollends nach Leib und Seele zu Grund gehen" (She will be completely ruined, body and soul). He denied everything and said a lot of women have been beaten and it was not necessary on his account to bruise a quill ("Sein schon Viele Weiber geschlagen worden. Man dient seinethalben kein Feder eindruken").*

*Another case of some interest because of the way property was dealt with, involved Johannes Bosch and his wife Friederica Regina, daughter of the Schultheiss and former schoolmaster.[44] They had gotten into violent dispute soon after the marriage, partly because he had falsified information about his income and she had expected to be able to live better. For one thing, he had changed the figures on his military pension document to a much higher monthly sum. He also subsequently had to pay a considerable amount in a paternity suit. Friederica Regina charged he was wasteful, lazy, and quarrelsome and liable to convulsions when angry. The village officials (her father was the Schultheiss) had reported to the Oberamt that the wife wished to leave Bosch because of horrible mistreatment and an ever-increasing mountain of debt. She had left, taking all of the household inventory with her, leaving him only with a straw mattress to sleep on. Already a considerable part of her marriage portion had been wasted, and to rescue the rest, she was determined to separate, and she simply could not* hausen *with him any more. Bosch defended himself by saying that the falsification of his documents was discovered before the marriage, and his two illegitimate children were also known about. He had only gone through with the marriage when she cried. He did drink when she*

42 *Gericht*, vol. 5, f. 10, (25.1.1795).
43 *Kirchenkonvent*, vol. 3 (7.12.1799).
44 *Oberamtsgericht*, STAL, F190, vol. 9, f. 460 (22.3.1809).

*caused trouble, but he worked hard at his tasks. By no means was he a drunkard or lazy. At the moment he had nothing to do because since she took everything, the* Haushaltung *had been destroyed.*

It is clear that the Schultheiss himself opposed the marriage from the beginning and that he refused to let his daughter have any land in clear title as a marriage portion.[45] As problems arose, he encouraged her in her growing resolve to get out of the marriage. For him and for her, the discourse circled around the amount of Bosch's wealth, his ability to earn, and the danger to her property. It probably became clear to Friederica Regina that her father would never endow the marriage sufficiently and that as long as he lived she would always have a restricted income. In this instance, there was no strong sense on the part of the wife or her father about keeping the marriage going. It was not a question of restricting or taking away the administration of the household, but of dissolving it altogether.

*An example of a wife still determined to keep the marriage going while restricting her husband comes from 1812.*[46] *Gottlieb Hentzler had been reported the previous year as a* leichtsinniger Haushalter *by his wife and father. He improved for a while but now was going the rounds of the pubs again. After Hentzler was reported again by the wife and father, the Oberamt threatened to declare him* Mundtod *and put him under* Pflegschaft.

The steps that were necessary to declare a man incompetent are clearly laid out in this example. Such a drastic move did not take place without considerable negotiation among family members on both sides, village authorities (lay and spiritual), and the higher power of the ducal officials. Sometimes the strains in an alliance simply pitted wife against husband. But more often other constellations can be observed: The wife could be supported by her parents, her brothers, her sisters' husbands, or even more distant kin, or as in this instance by her husband's closest kin. They were seldom able to separate the issue of good treatment of the wife from the necessary resources for her support.

*In 1825 Christina Waldner had already been separated from her husband of one year for several weeks.*[47] *She complained that he was going through her wealth as fast as possible. Already 200 fl. had come into his hands, and when she questioned him, he beat her bloody. He claimed she was hostile and offensive and scolded all the time and denied taking her wealth and piling up debts.*

Occasionally women used their marriage portion to symbolize the whole issue of living together with their spouse. It appears that few of the problems or details were discussed in court, but rather the whole course of a marriage was represented by the request to live off the Heiratsgut and let the wife go. Georg Zeug's wife was told in October of 1826 by the court to exercise patience. In

[45] *Unterpfandbuch*, vol. 4, f. 48.
[46] *Oberamtsgericht*, STAL, F190, vol. 10, (29.10.1812).
[47] *Kirchenkonvent*, vol. 4 (27.6.1825).

May of the following year, she said she could not hausen with her husband anymore and just wanted her Beibringen paid out to her in money or kind.[48] Catharina Margaretha Hentzler was tired of her husband's persistent brutality.[49] She wanted to have her *zugebrachte Vermögen* (marriage portion) to support her. Once she had her things, she simply wanted to leave.

Not all of the property that a husband and wife fought over during a divorce had to do with their personal wealth. As a household was breaking up, the question of access to communal rights also became important. Mathias Ebinger and Johann Georg Häfner were going through severe marital conflicts.[50] Häfner and his wife both had requested that the annual wood supply be held up until their conflict was resolved. Ebinger wanted to know if the kindling wood should follow the male or female line (*Geschlecht*).

The village officials could intervene directly, especially when a family was on the dole. Johannes Bauknecht's wife complained he had returned to drinking.[51] He had forcibly taken from the money-box 5 fl., which had been given to them from public funds. She had trailed him to another village and confronted him in the pub, and he followed her back and threw stones at her. She requested that the court call him in and check his money. When it was found that he only had 1 fl. 1 kr., he was sentenced to 24 hours, whereupon she withdrew her complaint.

*Katharina Rieth came before the Schultheiss to complain about ill-treatment from her husband, which started when she reminded him to return a wagon (1844).*[52] *He threw several heavy objects at her and kicked her out of the house. When cited before an official, Rieth maintained he acted according to right. He was told that he was running his property down, and that while he worked diligently as a cobbler for a while, he would intersperse that with a month of idleness. Slowly he was wiping out the family estate, which was composed primarily of his wife's* Beibringen. *Rieth said that if his wife were supported by the officials, he would go into decline* (abgehen). *After leaving without permission and being sent for, he said he would not return to the Rathaus where they wanted to help his wife.*

*Catharina Bauknecht complained about her husband Johannes (1855).*[53] *He had earned money and then spent the day in various taverns. She finally went to drag him out of one of them, but was treated to abuse instead. She had waited a long time for his earnings to pay off his debts, and now all of her promises were brought to disgrace. She pointed out that all of his wages were supposed to be garnished* (in Arrest).

Over the several centuries after the establishment of the legal framework for family property and the recourses available for offended parties, villagers worked out a set of procedures. The pastor, an outsider, was concerned with a

[48] *Gericht*, vol. 11, f. 61, (19.4.1827).
[49] *Kirchenkonvent*, vol. 4 (5.6.1833).
[50] *Gericht*, vol. 12, f. 139, (17.1.1834).
[51] *Schultheißenamt*, vol. 2, f. 29 (26.6.1843).
[52] *Schultheißenamt*, vol. 2, f. 54 (6.8.1844).
[53] *Schultheißenamt*, vol. 2, f. 268 (5.12.1855).

particular moral program and had various disciplinary measures at his disposal. No one could avoid his summons without incurring sanctions, and he had the power to exclude offenders from communion, which could in itself be a powerful weapon. After all, a pastor in a nearby village was murdered for exercising that kind of discipline.[54] He had an important mediating function and could intervene in family squabbles before making them "public." But he and the courts had to mediate between wider groups concerned with a particular marriage as well. The staging of any confrontation in the courts brought male representatives from both sides of an alliance together to air the issues, and frequently the entire matter was framed in a discourse about property. The ultimate threat was to restrict or take away a man's independence and put him under tutelage. For many husbands, interference from village officials was in itself a threat to their subsistence. This became an obsession by the 1840s and 1850s especially when women were willing to run their own independent households. It would be interesting to examine the second half of the nineteenth century to see if the rising court discipline exercised on women was part of a new model of marriage which no longer represented it in terms of an alliance between property-holding groups.

[54] David Warren Sabean, *Power in the Blood. Popular Culture and Village Discourse in Early Modern Germany* (Cambridge, 1984), p. 156.

# 9

# Marital fund

Christina Margaretha Henzler, née Henzler, wife of Johannes Henzler . . . complains about her husband with whom she has gotten along badly from the beginning of her marriage because her property was never enough for him.
– Kirchenkonvent (1842)[1]

A social history of marital property is concerned in the first instance with the bundle of rights sorted out among spouses, children, families of origin, and a wider set of kin, as demonstrated in Chapters 7 and 8. But equally important are the terms of the "balance of trade" between spouses. They are the subject for this chapter.

We have noted that in Neckarhausen there was no general distinction between the kinds of property brought to a marriage by men and by women. The fact that women almost always included land in their dowries is a rather unusual feature of Württemberg family life considered in a European context. Does that mean that marriage portions balanced each other, one wealthy spouse attracting another? The way the discussion among historians and ethnologists has developed suggests a return to the problem of the "house," that is the continuity over generations of the household, which combined both social and demographic reproduction. To provide for children and to ensure continuity, the family farm had to remain a viable economic unit: Hence, all those strategies to favor one son at the expense of others or to prejudice the descent of land in favor of sons over daughters.[2] No matter what the formal rule, so the expectation goes, children had to be treated unequally if the system was to reproduce itself. This inequality among siblings, however, contrasts sharply

[1] *Kirchenkonvent*, vol. 4 (20.9.1842).

[2] See, for example, Pierre Bourdieu, "Marriage Strategies as Strategies of Social Reproduction," *Family and Society, Selections from the Annales*, ed. Robert Forster and Orest Ranum, trans. Elborg Forster (Baltimore, 1976), pp. 117–44; Bernard Vernier, "Putting Kin and Kinship to Good Use: The Circulation of Goods, Labour, and Names on Karpathos (Greece)," *Interest and Emotion: Essays on the Study of Family and Kinship*, ed. Hans Medick and David Warren Sabean (Cambridge, 1984), pp. 28–76; Alain Collomp, "Tensions, Dissensions, and Ruptures inside the Family in Seventeenth- and Eighteenth-Century Haute Provence," *Interest and Emotion*, pp. 145–170; Martine Segalen, "'Avoir sa Part': Sibling Relations in Partible Inheritance Brittany," *Interest and Emotion*, pp. 129–44.

with the equality – at least social equality – of spouses. A farmer inheriting a great deal of land expected to be able to attract a woman with a correspondingly large dowry as working capital or, in turn, to pay off the dowries of his siblings, or to pay the entry fine to the holding in situations where tenure was not inheritable.

How equality is perceived in a community is a more complex question than it seems. Some people may define it in terms of wealth and others in terms of social position. In the first case a woman with a large dowry would not necessarily have to be from a family of the same social position as the young farmer she hoped to marry. The demographics, simply the number of siblings sharing movable wealth, would determine how large a dowry could be, all other things being equal. A rich farmer with many daughters might give far smaller dowries than a considerably poorer farmer with only one. If the amount of a dowry was closely calculated in terms of the size of a farm, then each generation would see a general mixing of property-holding families, especially if the size of farms remained stable no matter how many heirs and if dowries varied in size according to the demographic properties of households.

In other cases, the size of a dowry might not be as important as the relative standing of the families. The honor of two wealthy farmers might still be served even when a daughter was sent off with a meager dowry shared with too many sisters. Such an alliance would make brothers-in-law of two men of similar resources. Too narrow a focus on the married couple instead of the larger system of alliance would miss the essential point. In any event, on the basis of either form of calculation, equality between spouses seems to have been the operative value – not sexual equality as such – but a balanced alliance of wealth or station. Assuming some validity to these various arguments, we would expect to find in peasant families strategies working for inequality among children and "equality" between spouses. Neckarhausen offers a fascinating case because for part of its history the situation was quite the reverse. In Chapter 8, we will detail the lengths to which people went to ensure equality among all children. Here we look at equality in the marital estate.

In order to calculate the balance in marriage portions between husbands and wives, I have taken two sets of inventories, one at the beginning of the eighteenth century and one at the beginning of the nineteenth.[3] The first and simplest question to ask of the sample is how the balance was struck between

[3] As the basis for the sample, I took the 10 sibling groups used for the study of godparents (vol. 2) for each of the "cohorts" 1700–1709 and 1820–9. (The sample began with 10 individuals married in a particular decade, selected to include the range of occupations and wealth groups. It was expanded to include all the siblings of the original 10 no matter when married.) In the first cohort sample, there were 10 sets of parents of the sibling groups, who, when remarriages are taken into consideration, contracted altogether 12 marriages in the period 1642 to 1679, evenly spread in each decade. The sibling sets had 58 members, including a few adult children for whom there are no marriage records. Taking all of their marriages and remarriages and those of their spouses and parents, the sample has a total of 108 marriages. There are inventories available for many of the marriages and a large number of postmortem inventories. The latter figures

what the wife brought to the marriage and what the husband brought. Was there a tendency for the male side to be wealthier, or did that side provide more productive resources, more immovables? Were first marriages different from subsequent ones? Did artisans differ from peasants in the way they put their property together?

## Phase 1: inequality

The startling fact is that in the early eighteenth century husbands and wives seldom brought similar amounts of property to a marriage. In the negotiations between prospective neogami, their parents or closest relatives, their guardians and wider kin, it does not seem that a close matching of fortunes was of great concern. The evidence suggests a tendency toward hypergamy (i.e., a tendency for women to marry upward), yet there were many unions in which the woman brought far more property than did the man. We will show that one of the partners' contributions to the marital estate far outweighed that of the other.

I was able to locate the marriage inventory or a summary in a postmortem inventory for 81 marriages contracted between the 1640s and 1750s (40 after 1700).[4] I measured the relative contributions of spouses in two ways: first, by looking at the total property, including movable and immovable wealth plus assets and minus debts, and second, by considering immovable wealth alone, since a person with a large property, property assessment, and relatively high

include a few similar documents of premortem devolution (*Übergabe*) or bankruptcy (*Gant, Schuldenverweisung*).

*Documents for the marriage sample from the first cohort (ca. 1650–1750)*

| | Marriage inventories | | Postmortem inventories | |
|---|---|---|---|---|
| | Number | Period | Number | Period |
| Parents | 11 | 1647–79 | 15 | 1659–1723 |
| Children | 63 | 1657–1746 | 81 | 1685–1761 |

[4] To measure the relative contribution to the marital fund, one might take into consideration all the property that eventually came into a spouse's hand either through inheritance or purchase from parents. Future expectations might have played a large role in marriage choice. If, for example, a single heir was given a few strips of land from a large farm, that heir might well expect in the course of time to get the rest of the farm. Thus, simply to measure the property at the moment of marriage could be regarded as misleading. One problem is that to restrict the study to families with complete sets of records reduces the size of the sample, and does not seem to affect the nature of the argument. After inspecting the data, I found that in most cases where there was sufficient information, the amount brought to a marriage was proportional to future expectations. Taking the whole history of a family into consideration, the difference between spouses was usually only exacerbated by the process of inheritance. In those families where there was a significant amount to expect from a future inheritance, in this period, the young couple was tied primarily to one set of parents.

debts had more productive capacity in his or her hands than someone with less land, although debt-free. Looking at land by itself also helps to clarify whether husbands or wives tended to contribute more productive resources to a marriage.

A quick measure of the relative disparity can be obtained by assuming that if a couple were negotiating on an equal basis, then in a large percentage of cases neither would contribute less than 40 percent or more than 60 percent of the marital property. To make calculations simple, I have figured the percentage contribution to the whole that wives made. Looking at the overall property figures, we find that only 14.7 percent of the women made a contribution falling between these two figures – a good deal less than if the figures had simply been distributed randomly (i.e., 20 percent).[5] When we examine land and buildings alone, the figure is reduced by half, to 7.8 percent.[6] The inescapable conclusion is that as far as property was concerned, husbands and wives were far from following a policy of balancing fortunes (see Tables 9.1 to 9.6).

In my calculations, I divided the share of wives in the marital fund into equal thirds. In each case the middle third represents the broad area of equality – where what the wife brought was not much different from what the husband brought. Each of the bracketing thirds represents inequality of the spouses: Either the wife brought much less or she brought much more than the husband. Taking property as a whole, women were more or less equal with their husbands in just about 30 percent of the cases (29.9), which means that in the

Table 9.1 *Wife's percentage of the marital fund by period, 1640–1759*

| Period | Not given | 0–33.3% | 33.4–66.6% | 66.7–100% |
|---|---|---|---|---|
| *All property* | | | | |
| 1640–69 | 2 | 6 (54.5) | 1 ( 9.1) | 4 (36.4) |
| 1670–99 | 8 | 6 (30.0) | 7 (35.0) | 7 (35.0) |
| 1700–29 | 3 | 13 (41.9) | 9 (31.0) | 7 (24.1) |
| 1730–59[a] | 1 | 3 (42.9) | 3 (42.9) | 1 (14.3) |
| Total | 14 | 28 (41.8) | 20 (29.9) | 19 (28.4) |
| *Land and buildings* | | | | |
| 1640–69 | 2 | 6 (54.5) | 1 ( 9.1) | 4 (36.4) |
| 1670–99 | 6 | 9 (40.9) | 5 (22.7) | 8 (36.4) |
| 1700–29 | 4 | 15 (53.6) | 3 (10.7) | 10 (35.7) |
| 1730–59[a] | 2 | 5 (83.3) | 0 (0.0) | 1 (14.3) |
| Total | 14 | 35 (52.2) | 9 (13.4) | 23 (34.3) |

[a] All the marriages after 1730 involved remarriages.

[5] Out of the 81 cases studied, 68 offered data for this calculation.
[6] Out of 64 cases with suitable data to study.

Table 9.2 *Wife's percentage of the marital fund by position of couple in tax list (by quartiles[a]), 1640–1759*

| | Not given | 0–33.3% | | 33.4–66.6% | | 66.7–100% | |
|---|---|---|---|---|---|---|---|
| *All property* | | | | | | | |
| Not given | 6 | 6 | (46.2) | 2 | (14.3) | 5 | (35.7) |
| I | 0 | 2} | | 2} | | 3} | |
| II | 1 | 4} | (40.0) | 2} | (26.7) | 2} | (33.3) |
| III | 3 | 4 | (26.7) | 6 | (40.0) | 5 | (33.3) |
| IV | 3 | 13 | (52.0) | 8 | (32.0) | 4 | (16.0) |
| Total | 13 | 29 | (42.6) | 20 | (29.4) | 19 | (27.9) |
| *Land and buildings* | | | | | | | |
| Not given | 6 | 7 | (53.8) | 1 | ( 7.7) | 5 | (38.5) |
| I | 0 | 3} | | 1} | | 3} | |
| II | 2 | 3} | (42.9) | 1} | (14.3) | 3} | (42.9) |
| III | 4 | 6 | (42.9) | 4 | (28.6) | 4 | (28.6) |
| IV | 2 | 16 | (61.5) | 2 | ( 7.7) | 8 | (30.8) |
| Total | 14 | 35 | (43.2) | 9 | (11.1) | 23 | (28.4) |
| Magistrates | 4 | 8 | (72.7) | 0 | (00.0) | 3 | (27.3) |

[a] In ascending order.

overwhelming majority of instances the spouses were distinctly unequal. If we consider only basic productive resources (land and buildings), the case is even stronger. Spouses were more or less equal in 13.4 percent of the cases. Breaking down the data into time series (Table 9.1) does not seem to offer any clear trend. If the overall property figures suggest a slow rise in the percentage of cases in the middle third, the numbers are too small and are contradicted by the data from immovable property. Neither of the bracketing thirds shows any statistical trend except in the period 1730–59, but the numbers are too small to support any firm conclusions. All of the marriages after 1730 involved widows or widowers, and their property relations were different from those of people marrying for the first time.

Did a man or woman with a large Heiratsgut attract a spouse with a similar amount? Actually, the relationship is directly inverse (Table 9.4). Men in the lowest quartile made no marriages where their wives contributed less than one-third of the marital fund. And in over three-fourths of their marriages, the wives contributed more than two-thirds. As we go up the wealth scale of men, we find that the wives contributed an ever smaller proportion. Close to 90 percent of the men who brought the largest Heiratsgüter married wives who contributed less than one-third to the marriage. This means that "poor" men found wives who were much richer than themselves, and "rich" men found

Table 9.3 *Wife's percentage of the marital fund by occupation of husband, 1640–1759*

| Husband's occupation | Not given | 0–33.3% | 33.4–66.6% | 66.7–100% |
|---|---|---|---|---|
| *All property* | | | | |
| Not given | 6 | 5 (26.3) | 4 (21.1) | 10 (52.6) |
| Bauer/ shepherd | 4 | 9 (39.1) | 9 (39.1) | 5 (21.7) |
| Artisan | 4 | 12 (54.5) | 7 (31.8) | 3 (13.6) |
| Day-laborer/ officer | 0 | 2 (66.7) | 0 (00.0) | 1 (33.3) |
| Total | 14 | 28 (41.8) | 20 (29.9) | 19 (28.4) |
| Gericht | 4 | 4 (36.4) | 5 (45.5) | 2 (18.2) |
| *Land and Buildings* | | | | |
| Not given | 5 | 7 (35.0) | 3 (15.0) | 10 (50.0) |
| Bauer/ shepherd | 2 | 15 (60.0) | 3 (12.0) | 7 (28.0) |
| Artisan | 7 | 11 (57.9) | 3 (15.8) | 5 (26.3) |
| Day-laborer/ officer | 0 | 2 (66.7) | 0 (0.0) | 1 (33.3) |
| Total | 14 | 35 (43.2) | 9 (11.1) | 23 (28.4) |
| Gericht | 4 | 8 (72.7) | 0 (0.0) | 3 (27.3) |

wives who were much poorer. The relationship is the same from the woman's point of view, although not so strong.

Although the data point to a disproportion between husbands and wives, they also suggest that over the whole period wives "married up"; that is, they brought less overall property and less land and fewer buildings than their husbands. In Table 9.1 we see that 57.1 percent of the women brought less than one-third of the marital property, whereas 28.4 percent brought more than two-thirds. The comparable figures for land and buildings are 52.2 percent and 34.3 percent. What accounts for the "marrying up" is the greater propensity of men to remarry and the accumulation in marriage of wealth. On average, men brought larger Heiratsgüter than women did, the mean portion for men being 404 fl. and median 202 fl. For women the comparable figures are 229 fl. and 171 fl. Note, however, that the average Heiratsgut for men marrying for the first time was much smaller than for widowers, the mean and median for first marriages for men being 157 fl. and 135 fl. The top 15 Heiratsgüter (from the 71 where known) were all brought by widowers, and the 5 cases in which nothing was brought were first marriages. In Table 9.6, there are 30 widowers

Table 9.4 *Wife's percentage of the marital fund by size of Heiratsgut, 1640–1759*

| Quartile[a] | Not given | 0–33.3% | 33.4–66.6% | 66.7–100% |
|---|---|---|---|---|
| *Husband's Heiratsgut: all property* | | | | |
| Not given | 10 | — | — | — |
| I | 1 | 0 (00.0) | 4 (23.5) | 13 (76.5) |
| II | 1 | 4 (23.5) | 8 (47.4) | 5 (29.4) |
| III | 0 | 11 (61.1) | 6 (33.3) | 1 ( 5.5) |
| IV | 1 | 14 (87.5) | 2 (12.5) | 0 (00.0) |
| Total | 13 | 29 (42.6) | 20 (29.4) | 19 (27.9) |
| *Husband's Heiratsgut: land and buildings* | | | | |
| Not given | 8 | 2 | — | — |
| I | 0 | 2 (11.1) | 1 ( 5.5) | 15 (83.3) |
| II | 1 | 7 (41.2) | 5 (29.4) | 5 (29.4) |
| III | 2 | 12 (75.0) | 1 ( 6.3) | 3 (18.8) |
| IV | 3 | 12 (85.7) | 2 (14.3) | 0 (00.0) |
| Total | 14 | 35 (52.2) | 9 (13.4) | 23 (34.3) |
| *Wife's Heiratsgut: all property* | | | | |
| Not given | 9 | — | — | — |
| I | 1 | 10 (58.8) | 3 (17.6) | 4 (23.5) |
| II | 3 | 8 (53.3) | 4 (26.7) | 3 (20.0) |
| III | 0 | 7 (38.9) | 8 (44.4) | 3 (16.7) |
| IV | 0 | 3 (16.7) | 5 (27.8) | 10 (55.6) |
| Total | 13 | 28 (41.2) | 20 (29.4) | 20 (29.4) |
| *Wife's Heiratsgut: land and buildings* | | | | |
| Not given | 8 | — | — | — |
| I | 0 | 12 (66.7) | 3 (16.7) | 3 (16.7) |
| II | 3 | 11 (68.8) | 1 (6.3) | 4 (25.0) |
| III | 2 | 7 (43.8) | 3 (18.8) | 6 (37.5) |
| IV | 1 | 5 (29.4) | 2 (11.8) | 10 (58.8) |
| Total | 14 | 35 (52.2) | 9 (13.4) | 23 (34.3) |

[a] In ascending order.

and 19 widows. Only one widow was married more than twice whereas 7 men married for the third or fourth time. The mean and median Heiratsgut for first marriages of women were 182 fl. and 161 fl., respectively. Both of these figures are higher than for men marrying for the first time, but lower than for widows. For both sexes, accumulation within marriage and inheritance from the deceased spouse frequently increased the amount available for the next marriage, even when the inheritance portions held in usufruct from the children were deducted.

Apparently differences in occupation (Table 9.3) did not play much of a role, although within occupations wealth was important. To begin with, the category

Table 9.5 *Wife's percentage of the marital fund by residence, 1640–1759*

| Residence | Not given | 0–33.3% | 33.4–66.6% | 66.7–100% |
|---|---|---|---|---|
| *All property* | | | | |
| Both NH[a] | 4 | 18 (47.4) | 10 (26.3) | 10 (26.3) |
| H NH | 7 | 11 (55.0) | 6 (30.0) | 3 (15.0) |
| W NH | 2 | 0 (00.0) | 4 (40.0) | 6 (60.0) |
| Total | 13 | 29 (42.6) | 20 (29.4) | 19 (27.9) |
| *Land and buildings* | | | | |
| Both NH | 7 | 19 (54.3) | 6 (17.1) | 10 (28.6) |
| H NH | 5 | 15 (68.2) | 3 (13.6) | 4 (18.2) |
| W NH | 2 | 1 (10.0) | 0 (00.0) | 9 (90.0) |
| Total | 14 | 35 (52.2) | 9 (13.4) | 23 (34.3) |

[a] NH = Neckarhausen, H = husband, W = wife.

Table 9.6 *Wife's percentage of the marital fund by marital order, 1640–1759*

| Marital order | Not given | 0–33.3% | 33.4–66.6% | 66.7–100% |
|---|---|---|---|---|
| *All property* | | | | |
| H1/W1[a] | 10 | 9 (28.1) | 11 (34.4) | 12 (37.5) |
| H2+/W1 | 2 | 15 (83.3) | 2 (11.1) | 1 (5.6) |
| H1/W2+ | 0 | 0 (00.0) | 3 (33.3) | 6 (66.7) |
| H2+/W2+ | 1 | 5 (55.6) | 4 (44.4) | 0 (00.0) |
| Total | 13 | 29 (42.6) | 20 (29.4) | 19 (27.9) |
| *Land and buildings* | | | | |
| H1/W1 | 10 | 14 (43.9) | 6 (18.8) | 12 (37.5) |
| H2+/W1 | 3 | 13 (76.5) | 3 (17.6) | 1 (5.9) |
| H1/W2+ | 0 | 0 (00.0) | 0 (00.0) | 9 (100.0) |
| H2+/W2+ | 1 | 8 (88.9) | 0 (00.0) | 1 (11.1) |
| Total | 14 | 35 (52.2) | 9 (13.4) | 23 (34.3) |

[a] H = husband; W = wife; 1 = first marriage; 2+ = second and subsequent marriages.

"NG" (not given) comprises a substantial number of villagers. Until 1730 or 1740 it was not usual to find occupations listed in many of the records. A strong association with a particular craft such as "smith" was often noted, so that where occupations were never mentioned, the individuals were probably agriculturalists for the most part. In this sample, those "without occupation" brought smaller Heiratsgüter than did Bauern: mean 258 fl. median 165 fl., compared with a mean of 503 fl. and median of 255 fl. The problem is that in profile, they appear to be the reverse of the Bauern. It would seem that among the agricultural producers, the more independent the husband was – the wealthier – the smaller the contribution from the wife. Those in the lower three tax brackets (Table 9.2) were as likely to be dominated by the wife's wealth or land as by the husband's. It is only in tax category IV, the wealthiest members of the village, that the husband's wealth predominated over the wife's. In that group the husband was two to three times more likely to have made the major contribution than the wife. This fits the profile of both artisan and peasant families, and no clear occupational difference can be ascertained.

Marrying into the village generally meant marrying up (Table 9.5). When a husband came from outside, his wife was most apt to contribute the lion's share of the property. At least we have no cases in which the husband in such a situation contributed more than two-thirds of the marital fund. When we look at immovable property, the balance is entirely on the wife's side. The overall situation was reversed when the wife married into the village, although occasionally she still contributed the better part of the family resources. When both neogami came from Neckarhausen, one spouse overwhelmingly contributed the lion's share of the resources, with the frequency skewed toward husbands because of their greater propensity to remarry.

Although serial marriages concentrated wealth in the hands of the surviving partner, we still have to look at the overall balance (Table 9.6). In the case of a woman remarrying and choosing an unmarried man as a spouse, the woman almost always contributed over two-thirds of the land and most of the wealth. This factor is independent of residence, since 7 of the 9 cases here involved couples who were both from the village. The reverse overwhelming precedence for male wealth existed whenever a husband remarried, whether he married a single woman or widow. Perhaps what is even more significant, where both spouses were marrying for the first time, they were just as likely to set up a household dominated by the wife's resources as by the husband's. How the process worked can be seen in the case of Anna Agatha Falter (1648–1706), daughter of Johannes Falter (1612–81), smith and member of the Gericht (Figure 9.1).

> Marriage 1. In 1669 Hans Alle from Oberensingen married into the village.[7] Both he and Anna Agatha Falter were single.

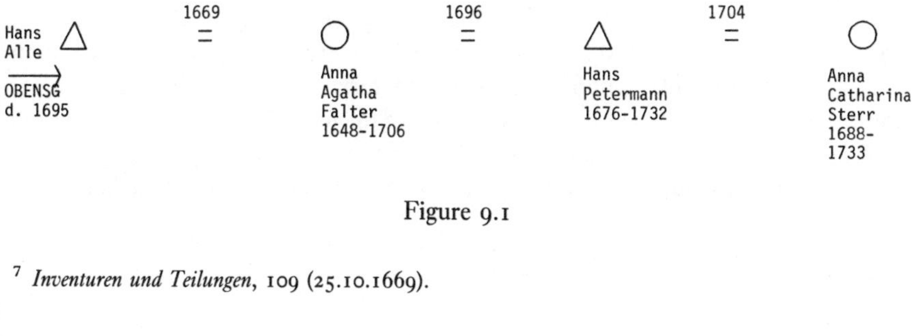

Hans Alle △ —→ OBENSG d. 1695
1669 =
○ Anna Agatha Falter 1648-1706
1696 =
△ Hans Petermann 1676-1732
1704 =
○ Anna Catharina Sterr 1688-1733

Figure 9.1

[7] *Inventuren und Teilungen*, 109 (25.10.1669).

Since his home village bordered on Neckarhausen, the property he brought to the marriage could have been worked by him or easily exchanged for parcels in Neckarhausen. In the marriage inventory, the land and buildings were not evaluated:

| Husband | Wife |
|---|---|
| | Hofstatt (building plot) |
| 4 Jauchert arable | 4.5 Jauchert arable |
| 5 Tagwerk meadow | 1 Mansmahd meadow |
| 1 Viertel vineyard | 2 Simri flaxland |
| Movables: 200 fl. 20 kr. | Movables: 41 fl. 11 kr. |

Marriage 2. In 1696, the widow Allin married Hans Petermann, single, from Neckarhausen:[8]

| Husband | | Wife | |
|---|---|---|---|
| Land | 32 fl. | Land/bldgs | 955 fl. |
| Movables | 33 fl. | Movables | 47 fl. 57 kr. |
| | | Debts | 324 fl. |
| Total | 65 fl. | Total | 678 fl. 57 kr. |

Marriage 3. In 1707, the widower Petermann married the single daughter of Johannes Sterr, Catharina, from Neckarhausen:[9]

| Husband | | Wife | |
|---|---|---|---|
| Land/bldg | 855 fl. | Land | 242 fl. |
| Movables | 141 fl. 52 kr. | Movables | 83 fl. 50 kr. |
| Debts | 183 fl. 39 kr. | | |
| Total | 813 fl. 13 kr. | Total | 325 fl. 50 kr. |

A number of conclusions can be drawn from this information. First, the *kind* of goods brought by men and women to a marriage did not differ, at least not in terms of the two grand categories "Liegenschaft" (immovables) and "Fahrnis" (movables). The basic productive resource, land, was not in any way particularly male, and women frequently provided the material base – or most of it – for a marriage. There are differences, however, particularly under "Fahrnis" which must be studied in detail in another context when production and material culture are considered. With first marriages, for example, the majority of women (63.0 percent) had a cow as part of their Heiratsgut, whereas few men did so (12.5 percent). Such differences, material and symbolic, might offer important clues about gender construction. Still it is important to understand that land and other immovable properties were not sex-linked. Men may have provided houses more frequently (33:18), but this seems to have been part

[8] *Inventuren und Teilungen*, 309 (29.7.1705).
[9] *Inventuren und Teilungen*, 326 (23.11.1707).

of the accumulation process associated with remarriage. With first marriages, the ratio is 9:8.[10]

The second conclusion is that in most cases the marriage partners, insofar as their contribution to the material resources of the marriage were concerned, were distinctly unequal. In first marriages, the balance could be tipped in either direction, with no tendency for property to be more in the hands of men or women. Note, however, that, overall, women had on average *more* property than did men when only first marriages are taken into consideration – they had between 15 and 20 percent more, depending on whether one measures the mean or the median. At the start, then, women were definitely not disadvantaged. It was remarriage which altered the situation. With successive marriages, the accumulation process was such that the (comparatively) really large fortunes in the village were mostly in the hands of widows or widowers. The main difference had to do with the frequency of remarriage for men and women, with men having a distinct edge and being capable of marrying three or four times. The difference in the mean size of portions for widowers and widows was reflected in the very large accumulations of some widowers. Overall, the latter had on the average about 75 percent more property than the former at remarriage, although the difference of the medians was far more modest – on the order of 20 percent. It could be that wealthy widows were less interested in marriage, given the rules of male administration of property, but it seems more likely that widows transferred property to children more readily than widowers.[11]

Several observations can now be made about the strategy of remarriage. Widowers overwhelmingly contributed more than two-thirds to the marital fund, whether they married single women or widows. Widows, on the other hand, contributed the lion's share only when they married single men. The balance of the system seems tipped toward hypergamy – women marrying upward – because widowers married more frequently and accumulated larger amounts of wealth. The phenomenon of hypergamy is, however, not an easy one to deal with. For one thing, we can only compare the size of marriage portions. A woman coming from a wealthy or politically powerful family, sharing the property of a large sibling group, might not be marrying "up" at all even if her Heiratsgut were small relative to that of her husband. Unfortunately, the tax records which might be used to study the families of origin do not exist for the very early period, but there are some clues. In those cases where Neckarhausen residents married people from outside the village, where presumably the status of their families was irrelevant inside Neckarhausen, the contributions of the in-marrying spouses were usually less than one-third of the

[10] Based on sample, Table 10.1.

[11] In Chapter 12, we show that few widows in the eighteenth century held substantial amounts of property, in contrast to the nineteenth century. Those who inherited a great deal and did not marry apparently retired.

marital estate. Marrying in, at least, seems to have meant marrying up. Perhaps we should look at the fortunes of one family to explore the meaning of differential Zubringen; although this will take us into numerous details, it is the only way to examine the issues.

*This exercise takes us through the marriages of Conrad Geiger (d. 1703) and his children. Geiger married into the village in 1661 from Grossbettlingen, and a year later he and his wife, Catharine Häfner (1640–1712), the daughter of Laux, had their property inventoried.*[12] *Catharine was the only child of Laux, who had died three years after her birth. Although the property which each brought to the marriage was not evaluated, we still can compare the size of the land each of them had. She brought more than twice as much arable and 51 fl. in movables, while he had no movables. To offset her assets, she had 20 fl. in debts. In the course of time, they gave each of their five children land worth between 57 fl. and 80 fl. and movables worth between 5 fl. and 13 fl.*[13] *Part of the difference in land valuation had to do with inflationary values over the period of their marriages, 1685–1700, and part had to do with small differences in size. In 1703, at Conrad's death, each child conferred his or her* Heiratsgut *and then shared in equal proportion – each one-fifth – from the entire estate valued at 535 fl. 42 kr.; that is, each ended up with 107 fl. 8 kr. Any more that each of the children brought to their marriages was apparently earned or saved.*

*The first child, Hans Conrad Geiger (1664–90) married Maria Catharina Rieth (1665–1721), the daughter of Michel.*[14] *She was one of six children, all of whom married, and five of whom remained in Neckarhausen. Her marriage portion, then, was proportionally comparable to her husband's, who was one of five children himself. However, she had twice as much arable. She also had credits and movables worth 61 fl. 2 kr., whereas he had none. To offset her property were 59 fl. 22 kr. in debts. Judging by the size of the marriage portions, the wife came from a family which was about twice as wealthy as the husband's.*

*The second son, Heinrich (1666–1710), was a Bauer and appeared in the 1710 tax list in the top quartile.*[15] *He first married Dorothea Sterr (1653–93), the widow of Hans Ulrich Häfner, member of the Gericht (1649–90), who brought four children into the marriage. Two of her married brothers lived in Neckarhausen and one sister had married out. In her first marriage, she had brought over twice as much as her husband (514 fl. 15 kr. to 232 fl. 48 kr.), who was one of seven children, all of whom married (five remaining in Neckarhausen).*[16] *Her husband became a Richter, and one of his brothers, Bürgermeister. Here one could argue that the families of origin were of similar wealth, with the larger sibling group having to be satisfied with smaller portions. In this instance, Dorothea, although with a larger portion, married into what became the politically more powerful family. When she married Heinrich Geiger 23 years later, her property was valued at 1,450 fl. 9 kr. compared to his 164 fl. 42 kr.*

12 *Inventuren und Teilungen*, 96 (14.12.1662).
13 *Inventuren und Teilungen*, 301 (19.10.1703).
14 *Inventuren und Teilungen*, 230 (–.–.1686).
15 *Inventuren und Teilungen*, 296 (25.4.1693).
16 *Inventuren und Teilungen*, 188 (28.11.1679).

*After debts were subtracted, the value came to 1,261 fl. 11 kr. to 151 fl. 59 kr. However, contained in her property were 432 fl. 13 kr., the paternal inheritance of her children, to be held in usufruct and thus under Heinrich's management only for her lifetime. When that is subtracted, she still had 829 fl. 58 kr. In this marriage, it is clear that Heinrich was moving up. His wife was the wealthy widow of a Richter and his new brother-in-law was about to become Bürgermeister. Three years later, after her death and his remarriage, he was able to take 433 fl. 3 kr. (minus 131 fl. 30 kr. maternal inheritance of his daughter = 302 fl. 33 kr.) as a portion, at least twice as much as he had had in his previous marriage.*[17] *He married a widow from Notzingen whose marriage portion was 48 fl. 33 kr., and who never inherited any more, and was thus clearly a woman of much less wealth and standing than himself.*

*The third sibling, Georg Geiger (1667–1740), was a cooper, and in the 1710 and 1720 tax lists appeared in the third quartile. He married Barbara Reich from Wolfschlugen, who brought a portion in movables to match his, and eventually inherited a substantial amount in addition.*[18] *His* Zubringen *was composed of 132 fl. 20 kr. land and 16 fl. 20 kr. movables, which together amounted to 148 fl. 40 kr. She brought 143 fl. 7 kr. Eventually he inherited another 60 fl., totaling 208 fl. 40 kr., while she inherited 250 fl., a total of 393 fl. 7 kr.*[19] *Georg thus married a woman of equal wealth, with good expectations, but whose family had no status in Neckarhausen.*

*The fourth child, Elisabetha Catharina Geiger (1672–1742), married (1698) Johann Sturtz from Schnier (d. 1724). He brought absolutely nothing to the marriage, while she provided 34 fl. in land and 35 fl. 47 kr. in movables.*[20] *Eventually she inherited, after conferring, 107 fl. 8 kr., whereas he inherited nothing. He became the village gravedigger and never rose above the second quartile on the tax lists.*

*The last child was Jacob Geiger, who eventually became a Richter and Bürgermeister. His first marriage (1700) was to Agnes Rentzler (1661–1729), the widow of Andreas Grauer.*[21] *She came from a family of eight siblings, four of whom married out of the village. All received equal marriage portions and inheritances. Her father, Michel, from another village, had married a daughter of the Schultheiss. She married Andreas Grauer (d. 1699) from Grossbettlingen, who had a marriage portion of 156 fl. 55 kr. to match her 99 fl. 22 kr.*[22] *He was marrying into a solid Neckarhausen family, whose numerous children had had to be content with relatively small portions. At his death, the couple had increased (*errungen*) their wealth by 673 fl. 28 kr. Thus in the new marriage, her property was worth 806 fl. 33 kr. to Jacob Geiger's 297 fl. 28 kr. Her property included 238 fl. 57 kr. paternal inheritance of her children and 277 fl. 14 kr. debts, reducing the value of her own property to 290 fl. 22 kr. However, Jacob was marrying into a situation which gave him considerable property*

17 *Inventuren und Teilungen*, 271 (12.1.1695); see also 341 (10.4.1710).
18 *Inventuren und Teilungen*, 243 (19.12.1687).
19 *Inventuren und Teilungen*, 452 (12.3.1726).
20 *Inventuren und Teilungen*, 285 (16.9.1698).
21 *Inventuren und Teilungen*, 254 (2.12.1700).
22 *Inventuren und Teilungen*, 246 (30.8.1699).

*to administer. At his second marriage (1729), he brought 1327 fl. 43 kr.*[23] *Since his two children had already received large* Heiratsgüter, *his wealth contained only 73 fl. 37 kr. of their maternal inheritance. His new wife, Anna Elisabetha (d. 1743), who had been married to a Schultheiss, had given out substantial portions to her children. She brought 579 fl. 42 kr. to the marriage.*

It appears that the children of one family receiving equal portions attracted a variety of spouses, some from families of equal standing but with different amounts of property to bring to a marriage, others of distinctly lower or higher standing. Overall, families of both similar and different status exchanged children regardless of the sizes of the marriage portions available. Marriage portions were not matched, field for field, gulden for gulden. There was considerable mobility involved with marriage negotiations, downward as well as upward, and the alliances contracted at marriage brought people of different status, political standing, and wealth together.

This brings us back to hypergamy. We have seen that especially single men frequently married up, which demonstrates that traffic was not in one particular direction. But because of the process of accumulation within marriage, the balance of the system meant that men more frequently had larger portions than their wives. By the time of the third or fourth wife, some men had accumulated relatively large fortunes. But precisely this fact makes the term "hypergamy" seem rather ironic. Some of the men seem to have been largely concerned with finding housekeepers or nannies for their children. And in a few cases, the large property contained significant proportions of maternal inheritance belonging to the children of an earlier marriage and still in usufruct to the husband.

*In 1746 Johann Martin Zeug,* Weberobmeister *(grand master of the weaver's guild) for the Amt Nürtingen and Richter and Bürgermeister in Neckarhausen took as his third wife Agnesa, widow of Jacob Speidel from Hardt.*[24] *He had a sizable property, which was listed but not evaluated. She brought only 81 fl. 21 kr. At the time of the marriage, she was 51 and childless. He had three children from his first marriage, who were already married by that time. The couple made a pact excluding her from any increase* (Errungenschaft) *or decrease* (Einbuß) *in the marriage. Instead she would take her* Beibringen *and 100 fl. should he predecease her. If she should die first, he would get 50 fl., with the rest going to her lineal heirs. In other words, Agnesa was prevented from sharing fully in an inheritance and at the same time protected from any disaster. Zeug got his housekeeper, a necessity for an active man of business and a substantial landowner. It was not a question of her marrying up, but rather of achieving a secure position. Everyone considered her past childbearing at 51, but just in case, Zeug specified that the pact would be invalid if she should produce an heir that survived him. We have already mentioned the case of Rudolph Schober, widower, who married Veronica, widow of Johann Häfner, in 1732.*[25] *He brought 1,322 fl. worth of property,*

[23] *Inventuren und Teilungen*, 509 (28.11.1729).
[24] *Inventuren und Teilungen*, 685 (13.12.1746).
[25] *Inventuren und Teilungen*, 542 (9.1.1733); see Chapter 7, "Composition of the marital fund."

*with a house and substantial amounts of land (worth 784 fl. 30 kr.). She brought 26 fl. 15 kr. worth of movables. He was 52 at the time of the marriage and had no surviving children from his first one. She was 56 and had two married daughters and a married son. In this instance the wife would share in an increase but no decrease. That is, if he should predecease her, she would get her* Zubringen, *half the* Errungenschaft, *and 50 fl. He was not to share in her property. All this, of course, assumed that they would have no children. In 1729 Jacob Geiger, 52, Richter, Bürgermeister and widower, married Anna Elisabetha, 39, the widow of David Böbel.*[26] *She had earlier been married to Michael Hess, Schultheiss. Geiger had two and she had three married children. Both neogami brought significant amounts of property to the marriage, he 1255 fl., she 580 fl. In their pact, she expressly gave some parcels of land to her children in usufruct. They were not to come into her husband's hands nor was he to have administration over them. The property which each brought was to remain* eigentumlich *and not to be common property* (gemeinschaftlich), *although each one was to have half of the increase or decrease. Whoever survived was to receive 100 fl. from the other's wealth* (Vermögenschaft), *which the heirs could pay off in land or cash, as they saw fit. One might also note that in 1722 she had called in the* Heiratsgüter *of her three children, ranging from 198 fl. to 233 fl. and then gave out their inheritances in equal shares of 565 fl. 40 kr.*[27] *She was left at that point with a similar amount herself. This is an instance in which the wife certainly was not marrying up, despite the inequality of fortunes. She was the widow of a Schultheiss and had given out three large portions to her children, keeping a substantial property for herself. The couple did not expect to produce children and limited the mutual claim on each other's wealth. Since both were substantial enough to take the risks of fortune, both got to share in the increase or decrease.*

A third conclusion we have come to is that larger fortunes were not used as counters to attract equal amounts of wealth. The larger the Zubringen of one partner, the less likely that of the other partner would be of similar proportions. This had the effect of distributing wealth more equally among villagers, rather than providing strategies of accumulation. Matching fortune with fortune would have driven a sharp wedge between classes. Instead, lines of different "strata" were constantly interwoven together. This does not mean that some wealthy families did not create alliances or that the very poor had equal chances with the rich and powerful. It did mean, however, that the play between families and groups was relatively open. Alliances were cast among families of differential fortune.

In addition, the power balance within the family was affected by the different amounts brought to a marriage. If the size of the Zubringen could symbolize a person's status and worth, it is possible to see why those in a powerful enough position would be interested in taking a spouse whose property did not signal too much independence. Many villagers, male and female, sought spouses

[26] See Appendix G.
[27] *Inventuren und Teilungen*, 394 (26.5.1721).

from outside the village with no status inside and little fortune. Whenever accumulation within marriage allowed it, both widows and widowers cast their lots with people who could not muster independent positions. One must also note that parents frequently gave their children Heiratsgüter in land or buildings which remained Eigentum of the parents, that is to say, usufruct of the children. In such a case, the spouse with the greater amount of property attracted a dependent spouse, who would be integrated into the parents' enterprise. The young couple would either live with the parents or be expected to work for them. It is important to understand this point, since married children remained tied for many years to their parents' farm (see Chapter 10). All the evidence suggests that differential portions were part of a strategy of marital power. If we ask why a spouse with a good deal of property could not attract someone worth more, the answer is that he or she probably did not want to. But still the tendency was stronger for men than for women, since once married women and their property were under the administration of their husbands. A man with no property at risk was a gamble: To dominate was one thing, but to put oneself under a weak character or a wastrel was another. If a husband had no property to lose, the effects of bad management would fall completely on the wife. Perhaps this explains why even women bringing among the most substantial portions still sought out equals or spouses richer than themselves more frequently than men in a similar position did. In any event, a consideration of marriage property and power suggsts that the picture so dear to ethnologists of the house ordered hierarchically according to clear social values was subject in practice to calculation and constant negotiation, and asymmetricality was based more on wealth than on gender.

## Phase 2: equality

By the end of the eighteenth century, the whole structure we have been examining had changed. Husbands and wives came to match their respective portions much more exactly, which can be seen by comparing our quick measure for the two periods. In the first, the percentage of women bringing between 40 and 60 percent of the combined property was 14.7 percent, while in the second, fully 52.0 percent fell into those rather restricted parameters – 32 percent more than a random distribution would suggest. Prospective spouses were eyeing each other rather exactly during the period of agricultural innovation and increased social differentiation.[28] We have, then, a sharp contrast between the

[28] This sample is based on the cohort of 1820–9 godparents from the volume on kinship to appear. As before, there were 10 sets of parents of the sibling sets chosen, this time comprising 13 marriages from the 1760s to 1790s, most of them (11) in the later two decades. The sibling sets had 60 members who survived to marriage age, a few never marrying. Their marriages and those of their spouses totaled 64 – considerably fewer than the 96 in the earlier sample, owing to the decline in the frequency of multiple marriages. As before, we do not have a complete set of inventories. Under the rubric "postmortem inventories" are included separations at divorce, premortem devolution (*Übergaben*), and bankruptcies (*Vermögensuntersuchung, Gant*):

first period from the close of the Thirty Years War until well into the eighteenth century and the second from the closing decades of the eighteenth century extending well past the mid-nineteenth century.

There came to be far more discussion in the records about the amount of property of prospective spouses and married couples. A spouse who failed to bring enough into a marriage might constantly be reminded of that fact. Toward the end of the eighteenth century, young people bringing their fiancé(e)s home would find their parents undertaking a businesslike investigation of the potential dowries.[29] No promise of a marriage portion from an unknown parent would do. The family sent emissaries to a Schultheiss or to the tavern to make inquiries. Women, especially, now coupled any complaints about a husband's Haushaltung with a specific worry about their own Einbringen.[30] In many cases, they expressly sued for divorce on the grounds that continuing the marriage would ruin them, as it was eating at the substance of their wealth. In the larger context of village affairs, the theme of wealth came to be expressed openly, especially in exchanges of verbal abuse.[31] Thus the move toward closer weighing of the future partner's material contribution to a marriage was accompanied by a remarkable increase in the overall discourse about marriage property.

In this sample, I have been able to locate either the marriage inventory or the summary contained in a postmortem inventory for 50 marriages. However, the data are constructed a little differently from those in the earlier sample. From the 1780s up to about 1830, immovable property was most frequently given to the children at the time of their marriage only in usufruct. In such cases, the size of the property was usually recorded without any evaluation, and so it is difficult to compare the respective spouses' contributions efficiently. Strips of land given in *Nutzniessung* would usually be returned at the death or retirement of the parents when all the siblings were "made equal" (*gleichgestellt*).[32]

*(n. 28 cont.) Documents for the marriage sample from the second cohort (ca. 1780–1860)*

| | Marriage inventories | | Postmortem inventories | |
|---|---|---|---|---|
| | Number | Range | Number | Range |
| Parents | 12 | 1763–99[a] | 25 | 1774–1850 |
| Children | 57 | 1790–1859 | 62 | 1807–70 |

[a] Eleven between 1782 and 1799.

In general, the parent's marriage inventories came from the 1780s and 1790s and those of the children from the 1790s to 1850s. Thus the data provides a good guide to the period 1780–1860.

29 For early cases, *Kirchenkonvent*, vol. 2, p. 82 (26.5.1752); (5.16.1753); vol. 3 (21.10.1793).

30 See Chap. 3.

31 *Oberamtsgericht*, STAL, F190II, vol. 258, f. 107 (16.6.1820); *Gericht*, vol. 11, f. 42 (28.12.1826).

32 Especially the frequency of bankruptcy in the period 1810–30 meant that many endowments fell back, not to be recovered.

Sometimes the parents could not give up a piece of land because it was mortgaged and the children were not in a position to assume the lien. Despite these problems with the sources, the Beibringen of each spouse can often be measured by reference to its summary in a postmortem inventory. At that point a definitive valuation of the property at the earlier marriage inventory might be given.

By sharp contrast with the earlier period, in this period inheritance often changed the contribution of a spouse radically. Therefore I have preferred to look at the *Nachlass* (estate) inventory, where one exists, adding together the Zubringen and inheritances throughout the life of a couple. This takes into consideration both the actual and expected wealth of each partner. On one occasion a young wife put no Liegenschaft into her marriage inventory but on the next day inherited a very large property. Clearly, it would distort the situation not to take such an expectation into account. Only a chance inheritance, from a deceased sibling or aunt, might not have been part of a couple's calculations, but in no case did these figures substantially reflect such a windfall. In this material, I have therefore preferred the data from the inventories *à cause de mort*, where they are available. Moreover, only six times did calculations of the two inventories lead to substantially different results, and only half of these put the wife's contribution into different thirds. Close inspection of the results from both samples indicates that they are directly comparable and that no distortion arises from the two modes of calculation. As in the previous section, I have used the percentage that a wife contributed to the whole marital fund as a way of summarizing the results.[33]

Upon inspecting the data, it seems superfluous to offer separate tables for both total wealth and immovable wealth. In this period, calculations comparing the latter category would often distort matters, because one partner might have brought equal amounts of cash to be invested in land. In many cases, the property falling to a minor was sold and invested at interest, with various outstanding obligations called in during the early years after marriage and reinvested in land. This was the case, for example, of the future Schultheiss Krumm who matched his wife's substantial landed wealth (the fifth highest marriage portion in any of the 100 studied) with twice as much in cash and loans (the second highest fortune brought to a marriage).[34]

Tables 9.7 to 9.13 show that a substantial majority of couples brought more or less equal amounts of property to their marriages. Whereas in the earlier period just about 30 percent of the cases fell into the middle third, in this period that figure doubled. The time-series data (Table 9.7) seem to suggest that the trend was even stronger after the third decade of the nineteenth century. Perhaps the lower figures for the first three decades reflect the economic troubles of the Napoleonic and post-Napoleonic wars period. Many villagers

[33] All 50 are used in the calculation.
[34] *Inventuren und Teilungen*, 1106 (7.7.1787).

went bankrupt, and children frequently had to return a marriage portion to the father's creditors. Above all, there is no indication of the hypergamy we found in the previous period in the overall figures – just as many women brought more than two-thirds of the family property as brought less than one-third. The issue of hypergamy, however, is more complicated. When we discuss marriage alliance in the context of kinship, we will suggest other ways of looking at the data. In the nineteenth century, daughters generally received larger endowments than sons did. That meant that where husbands and wives had equal marriage portions, women from less-well-off families were marrying men from better off ones. As a result, there was a systematic tendency for women to marry upward, but with no great leaps from relatively poor to relatively rich.

As in the earlier period, there were absolutely no differences among occupational groups (Table 9.9). Both peasant agriculturalists and artisans were overwhelmingly prone to match portion to portion. And as for the overall wealth of the families as measured by their position in tax lists (Table 9.8), all wealth categories display the same general propensity to bunch up in the middle third, although the wealthiest (IV) seem more likely than others to have put together family property dominated by the husband's wealth. Still we must stress that far more of the wealthiest families more or less evenly matched endowments. Just as in the previous period, in overall terms men brought larger Heiratsgüter than women – mean 693 fl., median 431 fl. to mean 574 fl. and median 371 fl. In comparison with first marriages, this meant: men – mean 624 fl., median 451 fl.;

Table 9.7 *Wife's percentage of the marital fund by period, 1760–1859*

| Period | Total | 0–33.3% | 33.4–66.6% | 66.7–100% |
|---|---|---|---|---|
| 1760–99 | 10 | 3 (30.0) | 6 (60.0) | 1 (10.0) |
| 1800–29 | 20 | 3 (15.0) | 10 (50.0) | 7 (35.0) |
| 1830–59 | 30 | 3 (15.0) | 15 (75.0) | 2 (10.00) |

Table 9.8 *Wife's percentage of the marital fund by position of couple in the tax lists, 1760–1859*

| Quartile | Total | 0–33.3% | 33.4–66.6% | 66.7–100% |
|---|---|---|---|---|
| I | 0 | — | — | — |
| II | 14 | 2 (14.3) | 9 (64.3) | 3 (21.4) |
| III | 16 | 2 (12.5) | 11 (68.8) | 3 (18.8) |
| IV | 17 | 5 (29.4) | 10 (58.8) | 2 (11.8) |
| Not given | 3 | — | 1 (33.3) | 2 (66.7) |
| Total | 50 | 9 (18.0) | 31 (62.0) | 10 (20.0) |

Table 9.9 *Wife's percentage of the marital fund by husband's occupation, 1760–1859*

| Husband's occupation | Total | 0–33.3% | 33.4–66.6% | 66.7–100% |
|---|---|---|---|---|
| Bauer/shepherd | 19 | 3 (15.8) | 12 (63.2) | 4 (21.1) |
| Artisan[a] | 26 | 5 (19.2) | 16 (61.5) | 5 (19.2) |
| Day-laborer/officer[b] | 5 | 1 (20.0) | 3 (60.0) | 1 (20.0) |
| Total | 40 | 9 (18.0) | 31 (62.0) | 10 (20.0) |

[a] Includes 3 weaver/Bauer.
[b] Officers = minor village officials such as bailiff, or cowherd.
Note that there are only three magistrates in the sample – two in the middle and one in the low category.

Table 9.10 *Wife's percentage of the marital fund by size of husband's Heiratsgut, 1760–1859*

| Quartile | Total | 0–33.3% | 33.4–66.6% | 66.7–100% |
|---|---|---|---|---|
| I | 12 | 0 (00.0) | 4 (33.3) | 8 (66.7) |
| II | 13 | 1 (7.7) | 11 (84.6) | 1 (7.7) |
| III | 13 | 5 (38.5) | 8 (61.5) | 0 (00.0) |
| IV | 12 | 3 (25.0) | 8 (66.7) | 1 (8.3) |
| Total | 50 | 9 (18.0) | 31 (62.0) | 10 (20.0) |

Table 9.11 *Wife's percentage of the marital fund by size of wife's Heiratsgut, 1760–1859*

| Quartile | Total | 0–33.3% | 33.4–66.6% | 66.7–100% |
|---|---|---|---|---|
| I | 12 | 2 (16.7) | 5 (41.7) | 5 (41.7) |
| II | 13 | 5 (38.5) | 7 (53.8) | 1 (7.7) |
| III | 13 | 2 (15.4) | 9 (69.2) | 2 (15.4) |
| IV | 12 | 0 (0) | 10 (83.3) | 2 (16.7) |
| Total | 50 | 9 (18.0) | 31 (62.0) | 10 (20.0) |

Table 9.12 *Wife's percentage of the marital fund by residence, 1760–1859*

| Residence | Total | 0–33.3% | 33.4–66.6% | 66.7–100% |
|---|---|---|---|---|
| Both NH | 36 | 7 (19.4) | 22 (61.1) | 7 (19.4) |
| H NH | 12 | 2 (16.7) | 8 (66.7) | 2 (16.7) |
| W NH | 2 | 0 (00.0) | 1 (50.0) | 1 (50.0) |
| Total | 50 | 9 (18.0) | 31 (62.0) | 10 (20.0) |

Table 9.13 *Wife's percentage of the marital fund by marital order, 1760–1859*

| Marital order | Total | 0–33.3% | 33.4–66.6% | 66.7–100% |
|---|---|---|---|---|
| H1/W1 | 33 | 4 (12.1) | 22 (66.7) | 7 (21.2) |
| H2+/W1 | 7 | 4 (57.1) | 2 (28.6) | 1 (14.3) |
| H1/W2+ | 7 | 1 (14.3) | 4 (57.1) | 2 (28.6) |
| H2+/W2+ | 3 | 0 (00.0) | 3 (100.0) | 0 (00.0) |
| Total | 50 | 9 (18.0) | 31 (62.0) | 10 (20.0) |

women – mean 551 fl., median 367 fl. Note that if daughters consistently received larger endowments than sons, this calculation suggests even more strongly that the general tendency for women was to marry from poorer into wealthier families. The discrepancy between the fact that families gave larger endowments to daughters at marriage and the fact that men on average had higher marriage portions arises from three factors: high celibacy rates for women, high out-migration rates for men, and higher wages and more opportunity for men to accumulate property as personal wealth outside of family endowment.

The radical difference between the first and subsequent marriages we found earlier no longer existed, even though remarriages appeared on average to have a little more wealth. In the first period, the top 15 Heiratsgüter all belonged to widowers. This time the breakdown was men, first marriage: 7; second marriage: 2; women, first marriage: 5; second marriage: 1.

The data on residence (Table 9.12) and marital order (Table 9.13) offer no surprises, except that we should note the decline in the frequency of both sexes marrying into the village but above all the relative lack of men doing so. If anything, the women marrying in were under greater pressure to match the wealth of their husbands, since their consistency in this regard is noticeable. There is no hint of the earlier practice of the local spouse providing the lion's share of the wealth. The table on marital order offers some interesting observations. First, we should note the decline in frequency of remarriage. In the earlier period, marriages where at least one party was widowed accounted for about half of all marriages (48.1 percent). Now they made up about one-third (34.0 percent). It is clear that where both were being married for the first time the policy was to match fortunes rather closely – in two-thirds of the cases, well above the mean overall figures. If anything, when close eyeing of each other's property failed, then it seems more likely that women contributed the lion's share. But the situation was reversed when a widower married a single woman. There we find hints of the accumulation process observed in the eighteenth century, but the tendency was not as strong – 83 percent compared with 57 percent where the wife contributed less than one-third. Although the numbers are too small to draw strong conclusions, that is part of the trend itself

Table 9.14 *Wife's percentage of the marital fund, all remarriages*

| Period | N* | 0–33.3% | 33.4–66.6% | 66.7–100% |
|---|---|---|---|---|
| Eighteenth C | 36 | 20 (55.6) | 9 (25.0) | 7 (19.4) |
| Nineteenth C | 17 | 5 (29.4) | 9 (52.9) | 3 (17.6) |
| *NGs disregarded | | | | |

– proportionally fewer widowers remarrying. When widows remarried, they tended to match fortunes with their single husbands. When both spouses were remarrying, they brought similar amounts, a departure from the earlier situation. The typical poor widow marrying the wealthy widower has disappeared.

The material from the nineteenth century suggests two conclusions. First, there was a strong, positive urge to match wealth at marriage, especially in first marriages. In the first period, in about two-thirds of such marriages one or the other spouse brought more than two-thirds of the property to the marriage. In the second, in about two-thirds of the cases, each spouse brought about the same amount. Second, we find the virtual disappearance of the kind of hypergamy characteristic of the eighteenth century, partly because of the decline in the frequency of remarriage and partly because in such marriages inequality itself declined. Table 9.14 presents the overall figures for all remarriages. Clearly, the great decline is in the percentage of women in such situations bringing less than one-third of the wealth.

We have also offered data about the proportion of wealth measured in terms of the size of the Heiratsgüter (Tables 9.10 and 9.11). In the earlier cohort, we discovered that the men with the smallest portions sought out wives with much more wealth than themselves – or perhaps the wives sought them out. The same tendency exists in the later period as well but is balanced by the fact that the men bringing the largest portions no longer contributed the lion's share. The smaller the marriage portion, the less likely the portions would match evenly, which suggests that for this period, inequality was embedded in poverty. A husband with a few clothes and some bedding, for example, married a woman with a quarter of a house and the eighth part of a vegetable garden. The proportional difference in their wealth was no longer a measure of a difference in circumstance. For such people, the choice was to marry locally and participate in some of the communal rights of the village or go on the road. By contrast, the more substantial the marriage portion, the more likely a couple would match each other rather closely. Sometimes the disproportion that did occur simply reflected the narrowness of choice. As we have already pointed out, when Friedrich Krumm, the future Schultheiss, married Christina Margaretha Bosch, the daughter of a member of the Gericht, she brought less than one-third of the property to the marriage. Yet she brought the fifth largest marriage portion in the entire sample – he was simply that much richer.

In the later period, wealth came to attract wealth (and poverty, poverty). As far as Neckarhausen is concerned that general notion about peasants having calculating marriage politics really only fits the period of rapid economic and social change associated with the agricultural revolution. And yet, in a way both periods we have studied involved calculation. In the first, people with wealth avoided each other, while in the second they sought each other out. Everything points to a a greater differentiation of class in the village by the late eighteenth century. In the heat of argument, villagers began to hurl insults at each other about their relative standings in the wealth hierarchy. This suggests the decline of a general intravillage connubium and the development of class endogamy.[35]

At least that is one way of looking at the situation, and class endogamy was certainly the effect of the new practices. But there was also meaning at the level of the couple itself. Bringing similar amounts of wealth to a marriage meant that neither spouse was dominant from the outset. We can imagine that when a widow brought all the land and a house while her husband contributed his clothes and a few personal effects that must have affected the power balance in the family. In any event we would have to argue either that wealth was not important in establishing hierarchies so that whatever was in play at a marriage, it had little power to adjust the situation – or that wealth was a crucial variable, and people sorted out their respective positions by taking advantage of whatever resources they had. Either way contrasts sharply with the situation in the nineteenth century. The balancing of wealth can only be interpreted in terms of a politics of calculation. It also suggests that the relative power of each spouse was more closely adjusted to the other. The labor situation of men and women underwent considerable change, as women were increasingly drawn into agriculture. Equality of fortune, balance of power, and cooperation in agricultural production seem to have developed together.

In our account of the marital estate, we have seen that houses in Neckarhausen may have looked the same to external viewers over the period – with the same number of residents, similar distributions in age, and a relative stability in terms of servants and relations attached to the nuclear core – but that they underwent considerable change in the material conditions of alliance. In the early eighteenth century, husbands and wives came from families which were quite different from each other in demographic makeup, wealth, and political standing. The power situation inside the house was derived from the fact that the spouses were distinctly unequal. Such a family was a connecting point of allied families ordered hierarchically or asymmetrically to each other. Struggles between husbands and wives were often about the terms of alliance. Sometimes the parents or siblings of one of the partners interfered too much in their house. In many instances, their relative power was an issue and it was very difficult for a husband with a comparatively small portion to fulfill the legal and ideological

[35] To be discussed in detail in the second volume.

tasks of administration. This was doubly so for the frequent situation where he was coupled with a widowed, propertied, older wife.

By the late eighteenth century, marital alliances connected people of equal wealth, and the divisions between landed agricultural producers and small artisans were constructed ever more clearly. People with power constructed alliances among themselves – in fact, members of the Gericht began an endogamous marriage system in the 1740s, several decades before the peasants began to close themselves off as a group.[36] There was greater stress on equal contribution to household production and more disputes over the dividing lines between gender spheres of authority. Expropriation of labor became an issue in the house, and the small differences between allied families came in for continual comment. The different families were continually weighed and balanced from the moment of a proposed marriage on through its duration. Much of the discourse about social stratification became narrowed to one about family and kinship, this at a time when classes began to break ties of marriage alliance and fictive kinship with each other, and Herrschaft and resistance became more visible.

[36] To be discussed in detail in volume 2.

# 10

# Generational transition

It was explained to Daniel Henzler, Schreiner . . . , [who thought] that the offence was not so great that his parents should have complained before the court, to his face, that the property originated from them.

– Schultheiss and Gemeinderat[1]

The transition between generations in peasant society is thought to be an abrupt one.[2] It is signaled by a set of public and private ceremonies, the most important of which is probably the marriage of the heir. Either the young couple has had to wait for the death of the parents, or the father or widowed mother has moved to the retirement cottage or west room of the farmhouse. Most discussions of European peasant social systems suggest that marriage is marked by patrilocality. It is, of course, possible for the young couple to set themselves up in a new location, leaving the old one with their house and reduced property. A great deal depends on the capital value of house and outbuildings, the legal, economic, and social interdependence of land and house, and the partibility of the holdings. Nonetheless, marriage appears to signal a change in authority relations between parents and children, in the distribution of resources in the family, and in the domestic division of labor.

In Neckarhausen, the transition between generations did not follow this model at all and was not characterized by a sharp break. In the first place, the marriage of one child did not have the same importance to the system that it might have had in an area of impartibility. And since land did not just pass to sons, daughters and sons-in-law had a structural significance which might have failed elsewhere. Partibility, however, did not mean that children were independent of their parents' resources, and the dynamics of intergenerational

[1] See n. 40.

[2] The literature on this subject is particularly fascinating. See Lutz K. Berkner, "The Stem Family and Developmental Cycle of the Household: An Eighteenth-Century Austrian Example," *American Historical Review* 76 (1972): 398–418; George C. Homans, *English Villagers of the Thirteenth Century* (Cambridge, Mass., 1941), pp. 144ff.; Martine Segalen, *Mari et femme dans la société paysanne* (Paris, 1980); Michael Mitterauer and Reinhard Sieder, *Vom Patriarchat zur Partnerschaft* (Munich, 1977), pp. 66–93, 169–85; David Gaunt, "Formen der Altersversorgung," in *Historische Familienforschung*, ed. Michael Mitterauer and Reinhard Sieder (Frankfurt, 1982), pp. 156–91.

transmission played a central function in giving form to their relationships. In Neckarhausen, the transition from generation to generation was much more gradual than it is thought to have been in European peasant societies, and it involved an integration between parents and married children that the notion of the "house" has failed to discern. In this chapter and Chapters 11 and 12, we want to examine the degree to which parents differentiated among children, how the turnover between generations took place, ways in which households of parents and children were tied together, how authority was understood and practiced, just how pivotal marriage was in signaling change, how stepparent-stepchildren relationships were ordered, and the manner in which abusive language highlighted the points of tension in many of these relationships. We begin this chapter by examining the ideology of equality among siblings and show how intestate practices and wills institutionalized equal treatment.

In Chapter 7, we noted that in most peasant societies in Western Europe some children were favored over others. In many instances, a single male heir received the lion's share, and the farm fell by custom usually to the oldest son or, in some areas, to the youngest. Family dynamics were organized in such a system around the father-(eldest) son dyad, and authority relations, character development, and class formation could not be understood outside it.[3] Apparently, wherever the father could choose among suitable heirs, patriarchal power was emphasized. In some areas, property was divided rather equally among all of the sons, although one of them might have been especially privileged, so that a core of family power and interest could be maintained.[4] There seem to be two implications in all of these practices. First, concentrating immovable wealth on one son or all the males appears to have been part of a strategy of reproduction. The house maintained its position, expanding according to the demographics of each generation for a time and then contracting and concentrating on a holder of lineal interest. Alternatively, the males collectively reproduced the position of the line, expanding or contracting as lines developed or died out.[5] In any event, social reproduction of viable farm units seems to

[3] Leonard Kasdan, "Family Structure, Migration and the Entrepreneur," *Comparative Studies in Society and History* 7 (1965): 345–57; Meyer Fortes, "Pietas in Ancestor Worship," in *Time and Social Structure and Other Essays*, LSE Monographs on Social Anthropology, vol. 40 (New York, 1970), pp. 164–200; Pierre Bourdieu, "Marriage Strategies as Strategies of Social Reproduction," trans. Elborg Forster, in *Family and Society. Selections from the Annales*, ed. Robert Forster and Orest Ranum (Baltimore, 1976), pp. 117–44, originally published as "Les stratégies matrimoniales dans le système de reproduction," in *Annales ESC*, 27 (1972): 1105–25; Bernard Vernier, "Putting Kin and Kinship to Good Use: The Circulation of Goods, Labour, and Names in Karpathos (Greece)," in *Interest and Emotion. Essays on the Study of Family and Kinship*, ed. Hans Medick and David Warren Sabean (Cambridge, 1984), pp. 28–76.

[4] Claude Karnoouh, "Le Pouvoir et la parenté," in *Paysans, femmes et citoyens*, ed. Hugues Lamarche, Susan Carol Rogers, and Claude Karnoouh (Le Paradou, 1980), pp. 143–210; "L'oncle et le cousin," *Etudes rurales* 42 (1971): 2–53.

[5] On the reproduction of the line, see Jean-Marie Gouesse, "Parenté, famille et mariage en Normandie aux xvii^e et xviii^e siècles," *Annales ESC* 27 (1972): 1139–54. On the house, see A. Collomp, "Famille nucléaire et famille élargie en Provence au xviii^e siècle," in ibid., pp. 969–75. See also Jack Goody, "Marriage Prestations, Inheritance and Descent in Pre-Industrial

have been a central issue, with the power and prestige of a family tied to the long-term fortunes of the male line or agnatic group. One can easily understand how such systems also imply the existence of male lineages, of which each house is only the visible representative. Indeed, sometimes the inhabitants of a house even took its name as their surname, emphasizing how lineage is derived from the patrimony, the dynamics of reproduction, and concern for succession.[6] The house and its integrity seem to have been central, and even where landed resources were partitioned more equitably among children, they were concentrated on sons, letting the more successful – economically, politically or demographically – piece the patrimony back together over time.[7] Patrimony and patriline, reproduction of the farming enterprise, and agnatic kinship principles appear to be closely interlocked, deeply rooted in the dynamics of peasant society and in aristocratic culture as well, at least since the High Middle Ages.

In Neckarhausen, as we have seen, immovable property was divided in each generation among all the children, male and female. But we will have to examine whether strategies were developed to privilege one child among others or sons against daughter.

In principle, the entire property belonging to the father and mother was inventoried at the death of either one, although sometimes the move was delayed while the survivor made up his or her mind to retire or die. As long as the survivor wished to maintain the integrity of the property, rights to the wealth of the deceased were spelled out and the children accorded a specific amount to be held in *Verfangenschaft* by the still-living parent. In the eighteenth century, only the total value was specified, but in the nineteenth a proportion of immovable property was reckoned and entered into the property registers as "Eigentum" of the children. In either period, what was held "Verfangen" was reckoned collectively for all the children and remained in the usufruct of the surviving parent. When one or the other child married, a parent could allow a part of the inheritance to be hived off for marriage portions – the child receiving his Mütterliches or Väterliches as Heiratsgut.

When the second parent died, the legacy was divided up definitively. At that point, whatever marriage portions had been given out were "thrown in" to (*eingeworfen*) or "brought together" (*conferriert*) with the property mass of the parent and reapportioned. In the early eighteenth century, the heirs to a particular inheritance had the right within a year to buy out any purchaser of

Societies," *Journal of Comparative Family Studies* 1 (1970): 37–54; Walter Goldschmidt and Evelyn Jacobsen Kunkel, "The Structure of the Peasant Family," *American Anthropologist* 73 (1971): 1058–76.

6 Pflaumer-Resenberger, *Die Anerbensitte in Altbayern. Eine rechts- und wirtschaftsgeschichtliche Untersuchung* (Munich, 1939), pp. 54ff.

7 A good example is offered by P. Bonnassie, "Une famille de la campagne barcelonaise et ses activités economiques aux alentours de l'an mil," *Annales de midi* 76 (1964): 261–303.

family property for the price set in the transaction, whether by private sale or public auction.[8] Later on in the century, the heirs had to specify at the time of the division that the right to redeem was a condition of the apportionment (*die Teilung war anbedungen*). By the mid-nineteenth century, there were frequent examples in which this condition was expressly abrogated. Over time, then, the de jure rights of collateral heirs were increasingly restricted, but de facto, close kin gained greater access to each other's land (see Chapter 16).

*Let us take one early example of a legacy division to see how the rules actually worked.*[9] *In 1689, Jerg Bauknecht's property was divided among his children, three from the first marriage and six from the second. His first wife had died in 1667 and the second in 1685, three years before himself. The two oldest daughters had each received marriage portions amounting to about the same value: Anna Barbara – 31 fl. immovables and 36 fl. 38 kr. movables; Catharina – 33 fl. immovables and 40 fl. 10 kr. movables. Their younger sister, Margaretha, 31, who married the year following the inventory, had received 12 fl. in movables already. The second set of siblings, three boys and three girls, ranged in age from 8 to 21, and were all unmarried. After the marriage portions were conferred, Bauknecht's property was divided into equal ninths, each child receiving roughly equal amounts of immovable property. Each half-sibling group, however, received their* Mütterliches *as well, the older group dividing theirs into thirds and the younger theirs into sixths. In the end, the three older daughters shared 321 fl. 26 kr., and the younger six children shared 374 fl. 46 kr.*

In this example, we see that full siblings were treated with total equality.[10] Women inherited exactly the same amount as men did. In all of the inventories I have studied, the same equality is to be found.[11] At times it seems obsessive. If, for example, there were three items of a particular good, say three mixing bowls, there would be three marks against the item indicating that each had fallen to a separate heir. The usual practice with movables was to provide as many lists (*Loszettel*) as there were heirs, each one containing the same total value as the other. The lists were then apportioned by lot. (Occasionally, the children agreed to reserve one or two pieces of movable property, with the rest being divided in the usual way.) Immovable property was often treated in a similar fashion. For example, in 1837, after Anna Maria Federschmid died, her husband Ludwig decided to retire. All of his property was listed on separate sheets of paper (Loszettel) and distributed among the five children by lot.[12]

A phrase which recurs continually in the postmortem inventories is "equalizing" (*Gleichstellung*). Whatever the children had received already was

[8] See the discussion in Chapter 24.

[9] *Inventuren und Teilungen*, 287 (19.1.1689).

[10] See the interesting discussion by A. G. Roeber, "The Origins and Transfer of German-American Concepts of Property and Inheritance," *Perspectives in American History*, n.s., 3 (1987): 115–71.

[11] I took all the inventories used for the study of *Heiratsgüter* in Chapter 2. In the first cohort, I examined the details of 57 and in the second of 43 postmortem inventories, while at the same time reading through all the others.

[12] *Inventuren und Teilungen*, 1740 (14.11.1837).

accounted for, and all the children, married and unmarried, were then gleichgestellt. This did not necessarily happen without considerable wrangling, and frequently an inventory concluded with the remark that there had been a good deal of conflict and emotional outburst during the property division, but everyone finally accepted the fairness of the arrangements and was at peace with the others. The considerable heat over small amounts of advantage attests to the enormous pressure exerted by each child to get an equal share. The village officials were always the middlemen at these formal occasions, and their job was to keep everyone talking until an agreement (*Vergleich*) had been reached. In the few cases where parents violated the sense of equality, the Schultheiss and Richter quickly set aside the advantage. For example, in 1683 Hans George Beck and his sister Elisabetha, the wife of Georg Fausel from Nürtingen, were in dispute.[13] Their parents had given Hans Georg an arable field to cultivate in usufruct during their lifetime and specified in a will which meadows were to go to each child. The use of the field and the inheritance of better-quality meadowland was meant as a reward for taking care of the elderly parents. Perhaps the son had even extorted the concessions in return for his help. In any event, Agnesa objected to the partition of the meadowland on the grounds that her brother had frequently been disobedient and that her parents had often complained to her about his behavior. The Schultheiss effected an agreement between the brother and sister, whereby Hans Georg gave Agnesa a meadow in order to reestablish equality.

Testaments were not composed by Neckarhausen residents very frequently.[14] Perhaps a parent who gave up property while still alive could have privileged one or two of the children. But whenever anything like that occurred, advantage was a minor adjustment upon a basic practice of equality. The widow Barbara Speidel retired in 1684.[15] To make her two unmarried children equal to the married daughter, she gave one of them, Barbara, a cow and some furniture, and the other, Georg, a horse and two wheels from a cart. Since the unmarried children had been taking care of her for some time, they were given 1 *Jauchert* of arable land off the top *im Voraus*. The rest of the property was to be divided according to the law of intestacy (*nach dem Landrecht*), in three equal portions.

Even when a testament existed, the siblings could simply set it aside. Johannes Kühfuss in 1841 gave a large portion of his considerable wealth to his eight children.[16] The immovable property was divided according to 8 *Loszettel* with values ranging from 671 to 706 fl. and apportioned by lot. However, one son, Johannes II, had lived a disorderly life and had been put under administration, which meant that his portion had to be handed directly to his court-appointed administrator. When the elder Johannes died in 1849, there

[13] *Inventuren und Teilungen*, 210 (10.4.1685).
[14] See Chapter 7.
[15] *Inventuren und Teilungen*, 218 (–.–.1684).
[16] *Inventuren und Teilungen*, 1820 (25.8.1841).

was still a very large estate to be divided.[17] His will disinherited Johannes II and specified that the youngest son, Jacob, was only to get an obligatory portion (Pflichtteil). In fact, by this time Johannes II and Jacob had emigrated to America, and the older of the two had died as a soldier. The five children (another had died in the meantime) still in Neckarhausen gathered to make the inventory and agreed that Jacob should get an equal share. The portion going to Johannes II was formally entered into the document on an equal footing with the others, although his Pfleger had given up any rights even to a Pflichtteil because he had already died. Johannes's portion was to be held for a possible heir, or it was in turn to be divided among his siblings. What this unusual case demonstrates is the length to which siblings among themselves could go to express their rights to an equal share, even, in this case, for two absent brothers, one of them already reported dead. Even the father had tried to establish equality, not disinheriting or disadvantaging his wastrel namesake in 1841, by which time he had already been declared incompetent. Apparently, old Johannes had only cut down Jacob's portion because he had received extra money for his passage to America.

One way to advantage a child was to give him or her an extra large marriage portion. Even if a return had to be made at the final division of property, the child could profit during the interim period. It is difficult to weigh the differences, because over a period of time the monetary equivalent of goods could change, and various children might have been getting similar things but with different value. Or children might marry at quite different moments of an economic cycle, and be slightly advantaged or disadvantaged accordingly. In the nineteenth century, the practice of giving land in usufruct meant that such property did not have to be "brought together" because it had never been alienated, and therefore it is difficult to know who actually had been farming a particular plot. Over the whole study period, daughters do seem to have been systematically advantaged in favor of sons. From our sample of inventories, there are 19 cases with unambiguous information. In 14 of these cases, daughters had an average value higher than sons (73.6%). In about half of the instances, they received more than twice as much as their brothers. Perhaps this was part of a strategy of obligating sons-in-law and attaching them more fully to the interests of the family. But also, given the fact that husbands and wives brought relatively equal portions during the nineteenth century, this is evidence of a systematic hypergamy, the analysis of which will take us into the alliance system.[18]

The one piece of property which stood out for special consideration was the house, which frequently was divided up among the heirs. There are many instances in the court protocols to indicate that more than one family was living in a dwelling, and it appears that barns and outbuildings could be permanently

[17] *Inventuren und Teilungen*, 2012 (23.3.1849).
[18] Vol. 2, devoted to kinship.

broken up into use areas just as fields were.[19] There were many instances in which the individual portions of a house were sold to one of the heirs – sometimes such transactions were recorded in the inventory after all the business of partition had taken place.

*In 1741, four Schober siblings sold their house to their brother Jacob on the condition that the house would be a place of refuge, especially for the sisters in case of illness – as long as they remained single.[20] Adam and Agatha Bauknecht sold their shares in the house to their younger brother Johann.[21] Their widowed mother received the right to live there until her death, and Agatha could remain as long as she remained unmarried. Three Zeug siblings sold their portions of a half house to Johannes, their brother.[22] The two Dalm brothers split the house.[23] The five Rieth siblings split the house in five equal parts.[24] The son-in-law of Johannes Sterr bought the quarter house before the division began and the money became part of the estate to be divided.[25] The nine children of Hans Jerg Heinrich Schober sold their portions of the house to Rudolph.[26] In 1728, one of the sons of Hans Jerg Schober wanted to purchase the house, but the other children did not think he could afford it.[27] The Oberamt ordered an auction, and it was sold outside the family to Salomon Häussler.[28] Michael Schober's children sold the house to one of the sons-in-law.[29] The three unmarried children of Johannes Petermann each kept their share in the house.[30] When Barbara Falter retired, her eldest son Adam bought the quarter house in which she retained life-long rights to live.[31] In 1686, Michael Rentzler's eight children divided the house.[32] Nine years later two of the siblings sold their eighths to Michael. Since three of the daughters were living in other villages, it appears that they must have rented their portions to those who stayed in the house, or perhaps had sold them.*

In the nineteenth century, the house, or whatever portion of a building was included in an estate, was not chopped up as frequently as before and was often treated separately from other immovable property. All the land would be divided equally among the heirs, but the house would fall to just one of them. That one, sometimes chosen by lot, took over the aged surviving parent. Since it

19 A typical example is the sale of a quarter barn (*Scheuer*); *Kaufbuch*, vol. 5, f. 237 (9.1.1782). The buyer was obligated to cut a new door. Different parts of the main floor and attic were specified for each owner. In another instance, a house was partitioned into quarters, which the village Gericht disallowed as being against regulations. The buyer appealed to the Oberamtsgericht, which gave him permission; *Kaufbuch*, vol. 3, f. 241 (10.12.1788).
20 *Inventuren und Teilungen*, 620 (2.11.1741).
21 *Inventuren und Teilungen*, 710 (21.3.1749).
22 *Inventuren und Teilungen*, 747 (22.11.1752).
23 *Inventuren und Teilungen*, 351 (15.3.1712).
24 *Inventuren und Teilungen*, 385 (11.7.1720).
25 *Inventuren und Teilungen*, 664 (17.9.1745).
26 *Inventuren und Teilungen*, 340 (8.5.1710).
27 *Inventuren und Teilungen*, 490 (2.8.1728).
28 *Inventuren und Teilungen*, 236 (19.12.1687).
29 *Inventuren und Teilungen*, 621 (10.11.1741).
30 *Inventuren und Teilungen*, 536 (19.4.1732).
31 *Inventuren und Teilungen*, 691 (13.5.1747).
32 *Inventuren und Teilungen*, 213 (4.11.1686); 299 (5.7.1694); 278 (14.1.1695).

was usual for most families to be considerably in debt, the child who took over a house simply assumed a corresponding amount of the debits to balance his or her excess assets.

*When Eva Barbara, widow of Jacob Friedrich Zeug, died, the value of the building was determined by an auction among the five siblings.*[33] *When Ludwig Federschmid retired, his son Johann Georg got the house and the father as well by lot.*[34] *In this instance, the children divided the land by Loszettel into lots ranging in value from 165 fl. to 192 fl. On top of his land worth 185 fl., Johann Georg got the house worth 260 fl. with the obligation to pay off the other children for their interest. In 1870, Ludwig's son Ludwig retired, dividing his property among four children.*[35] *The one who got the house received it in addition to an equal portion of land, paying off the others. Johann Georg Schach left his children only the house and movables.*[36] *The oldest son took the house and paid the rest of the children their share. Johannes Ebinger, who had begged in order to support his family, died in 1812.*[37] *He left only a small house worth 130 fl. His seven children, ranging in age from 10 to 29, were allowed by the Oberamt to take the house over in common* (gemeinschaftlich). *There was another case of unmarried children taking a house in common in 1836.*[38]

In all the other examples in the nineteenth century where a house was part of the property, it went to one child in some fashion or other, was either taken over with a corresponding portion of debt, sold to one of the siblings, or apportioned in lieu of cash. In that period, as well, the house almost always went to the eldest son, in sharp contrast to the practice in the eighteenth century (Table 10.1).

*The children of Salomon Hentzler, who were all adults, arranged matters among themselves.*[39] *The youngest son, Salomo, 22, was in America and was represented by his guardian. Catharina, married to Christian Eppler, lived in Neckartailfingen. Johann Jacob was married and Johannes still single. True to form, Jacob had received a* Heiratsgut *very much smaller than that of his sister: in movables, 35 fl. 15 kr., compared with 179 fl. Salomon had received 220 fl. for his trip to America.*

Table 10.1 *Inheritance of houses when assumed by one of a group of siblings of mixed sex*

| Period | Eldest son | Other son | Daughter (son-in-law) |
|---|---|---|---|
| Eighteenth century | 2 | 6 | 4 |
| Nineteenth century | 8 | 1 | 0 |

[33] *Inventuren und Teilungen*, 1733 (21.7.1837).
[34] *Inventuren und Teilungen*, 1740 (14.11.1837).
[35] *Inventuren und Teilungen*, 3331 (6.5.1870).
[36] *Inventuren und Teilungen*, 1673 (19.3.1835).
[37] *Inventuren und Teilungen*, 1372 (6.8.1812).
[38] *Inventuren und Teilungen*, 1701 (29.1.1836).
[39] *Inventuren und Teilungen*, 3029 (11.3.1854).

*All the "advances" were "thrown-in" in value, that is, reckoned as a claim against an equal share of 893 fl. 39 kr. of the assets:*

| | Jacob (m, 30) | Johann (s, 27) | Catharina (m, 24, NTLF[c]) | Salomon (s, 22, America) |
|---|---|---|---|---|
| Total portion (fl./kr.) | 893/39 | 893/39 | 893/39 | 893/39 |
| Received already | 35/15 | — | 179/— | 220/— |
| Claim | 858/24 | 893/39 | 714/39 | 673/39 |
| Immovables outside lot | 475/—[a] | 171/—[b] | — | — |
| Immovables by lot | 689/30 | 706/— | 736/— | 740/30 |
| Movables by lot | 32/32 | 32/32 | 32/32 | 32/32 |
| Liquid assets | 89/39 | 62/54 | 89/47 | 5/35 |
| Debt | 429/— | 78/37 | 113/20 | 104/38 |

[a] house
[b] arable field
[c] Neckartailfingen

In this instance, Johann, the unmarried son, appears to have been given an extra advantage in land to compensate for Catharina's marriage portion and Salomon's travel money. Jacob, the eldest, received the house, which he paid for by taking a corresponding portion of the debt – he also drew the smallest bundle of land. Salomon, who was not in a good position to manage extended credit, did not take over any loans, but only received a small amount to balance everything to the penny.

Family strategies are never simple, and parents dividing up their assets have to take many different factors into consideration, some of which are in tension or conflict with each other. An octogenarian going into retirement with all of his children long since married is carrying out a different exercise as far as property devolution is concerned from a widow threatened with the withdrawal of labor of several sons itching to get married. Different points in the life cycle and the characters of the various children call for different considerations. It would not do to be cheap setting up a daughter who had a shot at an advantageous marriage, since alliances were fundamental for access to important resources for both generations. Everything had to be balanced by the commitment to "equalizing" all the children, at least in the end. This always meant setting each of them up with meager resources at the beginning, which kept the younger generation dependent, as we shall see, in many ways. Daughters were offered a bit more to counter the pull of their households into the orbit of their husbands' families. Everyone understood that property was laden with obligation, and any child who forgot that would receive a stern lecture from the Schultheiss or pastor.[40] However, no one was so naive as to think that gratefulness would go a very long way by itself. The exercise of fairness was something continually staged publicly, and equality was subject to repeated

[40] E.g., *Gericht*, vol. 14, f. 73 (2.3.1840).

demonstration. On the one hand, such a practice shored up obligation, and siblings and officials joined in on the chorus. On the other hand, parents dribbled out resources over a very long period of time, keeping tight reins on their children. Those who did not show the right degree of filial piety and respect or looked too longingly at the parents' land would be brought up sharply. Care was always exercised on the part of the senior generation to maintain authority and independence as long as they could. This meant a considerable alteration in the material situation as the age structure of property holding underwent fundamental change.

## Age and the distribution of wealth

Because of the way village resources were distributed in the nineteenth century, there was a trend toward increased inequality. The fact that most households had some access to land meant that there was less to go around, given the considerable rise in population and decline in the average holding size. There were no great disjunctions as one would find in neighboring areas such as Upper Swabia, where large farmers confronted small cottagers or landless laborers. Nonetheless, there was increasing disparity in Neckarhausen as the upper 10 percent of the village increased their share of the taxable resources from 28 to 33 percent between 1790 and 1870, while the lower 50 percent declined from 18 to 14 percent. One of the significant changes was in the role

Table 10.2 *Percentage of total tax paid by various age groups of male Bürger*

| Year | 15–29 | 25–34 | 35–44 | 45–54 | 55–64 | 65+ |
|---|---|---|---|---|---|---|
| 1710 | 0.0 | 18.3 | 19.1 | 35.9 | 6.7 | 3.2 |
| 1790 | 4.0 | 13.4 | 19.5 | 36.5 | 7.9 | 5.4 |
| 1870 | 0.2 | 13.7[a] | 15.5 | 26.0 | 18.3[b] | 11.7 |

[a] Subtracting the new, immigrant miller from Switzerland = 10.9 percent.
[b] Subtracting the wealthiest villager, an innkeeper = 15.3 percent.

Table 10.3 *Distribution of mean tax per male Bürger by age group (in heller)*

| Year | 15–29 | 25–34 | 35–44 | 45–54 | 55–64 | 65+ |
|---|---|---|---|---|---|---|
| 1710 | 0 | 229 | 302 | 449 | 399 | 256 |
| 1790 | 325 | 287 | 310 | 514 | 432 | 205 |
| 1870 | 130 | 1,429[a] | 1,700 | 2,065 | 2,176[b] | 2,001 |

[a] Subtracting the new, immigrant miller = 1,162 h.
[b] Subtracting the wealthiest villager = 1,874 h.

age played in that phenomenon. In Appendix I, I have given data from three tax lists from 1710, 1790, and 1870, which detail the tax liability of the various age cohorts in the village (also see Tables 10.2 and 10.3).

In all three periods, the average amount of property held by individuals in each cohort rose steadily, to a peak at age 45–54. Young, married Bürger did not get their hands on significant amounts of property at marriage, but accumulated it until their early 50s. In the first two periods, there was a tendency to pass on some real estate as a man grew older. In sharp contrast, however, in the last period, there is no suggestion that parents gave up a great deal before they died or became totally enfeebled, and the average amount of property men over 65 held was about the same as for the two adjacent younger cohorts.

It is not a simple matter to compare the size of each age group with the average amount of wealth held by it. For the most part, the tax lists contain married Bürger, widows, and widowers. Since there are no population or household lists available for the village, there is no easy way to estimate the age distributions for different periods, and complex demographic calculations have not yet been undertaken. We would expect that the younger age groups would be the largest and that their property holdings would be inversely related to their size. In terms of the total wealth of the village, the younger members remained dependent upon the older ones. The dependence seems to have been real enough, but as older age groups not only expanded their holdings and held onto property longer, their numbers grew in absolute and relative terms. As the period of age dependency lengthened and as prospects for younger people dimmed, many of them emigrated, especially in the late 1840s and 1850s. The average amount of the total wealth for each individual married taxpayer did not change very much: For example, the ratio of mean tax of the age groups 25–34 compared with those 55–64 was 0.57, 0.66, and 0.65, respectively. But the expansion of numbers in the older age groups increased their overall share significantly. The total percentage of wealth held by men over 45 was 1710, 45.8; 1790, 49.8; 1870, 56.0. Over 55, it was 1710, 9.9; 1790, 13.3; 1870, 30.0. In all of this, there seem to have been three changes in the nineteenth century which increased the phase of dependence. Parents lived longer; they did not pass on as much property as they got older; and widows tended to hold on to what they had accumulated for significantly longer periods of time.

All the tax lists show that the ages 45–54 were dominant in terms of the share in the total wealth of the village. Once individuals had achieved their peak holdings, they hung on until death or enfeeblement in old age. By contrast, until age 30, little wealth fell to villagers. During the age period 30–44, individuals received marriage portions and inheritances or bought property, completing the process as a group with age 45 or so. Not all of the dynamics of wealth accumulation and property holding are captured in these figures, however. One might venture the following characterization. Young, strong, capable men remained largely excluded from property ownership until they reached their 30s. Thereafter property was accumulated gradually until age 45 or 50. Then a phase of maintenance set in with perhaps the beginnings of the process of devolution of wealth. In the eighteenth century few widows held onto land in their own right. They either married soon or devolved property onto the next generation. At least they appear very seldom as taxpayers in the upper brackets. In the nineteenth century, the accumulated wealth was more likely to remain in their hands. Unmarried women had little property and little possibility of getting any as long as they remained single. They, like their brothers, remained dependent until marriage. Thereafter, they shared in the fortunes of their husbands. These data tell us little about female "ownership" as a whole, for as long as the husband was alive he was always listed as "owner" of the family property. Underneath this formal category lies a great deal more complexity for both married women and unmarried sons and daughters, which we have explored to some degree already.

The slow trend toward inequality during the nineteenth century was partly due to the fact that accumulation took place over a relatively long period for each couple and that the increasing number of older people held onto their resources for a much longer time. The men over 55 tripled their holdings from the beginning of the eighteenth century to the end of the 1860s. If we add the widows, who by then also held on to their considerable fortunes, then the situation seems even more revolutionary. The traditional practice of devolving resources piecemeal had quite a different meaning in the new context. These practices in ever-changing circumstances shaped relations between generations in ever different ways. In Chapters 11 and 12, we explore the reciprocal relations between parents and married children and point up the complex ways in which households depended on each other.

11

# Reciprocities of labor and property

> Then the father slapped the son on the face and threw him to the ground. Then the mother grabbed old Weiler by the hair and tore him from the son. As soon as the son, Bauknecht, felt some air, he grabbed a stick and struck his father on the head so that blood immediately flowed.
>
> – Gerichtsprotocoll[1]

In many instances over the course of the period we are considering, parents and adult children cooperated in work or shared living areas, storage, and tools. Sometimes they advanced each other cash or covered each other's debts. The manner in which people interacted raises questions about the cultural meaning of property within the exigencies of production. These issues have been at the center of a recent attempt to distinguish fundamental historical differences between various regions of Europe.[2] Those areas which were dominated for centuries by a system of private property have been differentiated from others characterized as peasant. According to the theory, ownership in peasant societies is not individualized, but belongs to the whole family. Children work as part of a joint productive effort, and as co-owners of an estate are quite distinguishable from wage-laborers. The father, rather than being a proprietor, acts as a manager who can easily be replaced by another family member if he is incompetent. In any event, he has to give over when the son becomes capable of leading the enterprise. In a peasant system, land seldom comes onto the market, and when it does, it has such symbolic value that families put great effort into reassembling the pieces. Since land is not treated as a capital investment, they also avoid mortgages and other forms of contact with financial markets. And because the family is essentially a subsistence enterprise, there is little place for wage labor and servants. In general, the size of a farm determines the number of people who can live from it, the ideal being to include as many family members as possible. Frequently, households contain parents and married children and sometimes groups of married siblings, sharing the same

[1] See n. 41.

[2] Alan Macfarlane, *The Origins of English Individualism. The Family, Property and Social Transition* (Cambridge, 1979).

space, tools, and equipment and living from an undifferentiated product, caring for each other and taking meals together.

It would be out of place here to argue about models and the justification for keeping this or that element intact. Nor would we gain much insight by holding each local situation in Europe up against a particular ideal type in order to measure its relative distance from a notional peasant social formation. As soon as we examine the details of any region, we find that the issues have been badly posed and that social formations are too complex to allow such a method to capture essential social dynamics. Württemberg law, for example, defined the central characteristic of property as a matter of individual will and enforced this conception in its detailed prescriptions; nonetheless, it does not seem profitable to think of Württemberg villages as less than peasant.[3] However property was related to the family in practical terms, when the father was a wastrel, the village did not appoint another family member as manager. His affairs were put under a court-appointed guardian, just as they would be in most modern Western nations today.[4] Nor was a declaration of incompetency easy to come by. Property was not transmitted in Neckarhausen when the next generation was competent to manage. In most documents of *Tradition*, the parent or parents passing on property stated that he, she, or they could no longer do the work or manage affairs. Not the needs of the coming generation but the will, desire, and interests of the retiring generation defined the situation. It is possible to take any element of the "peasant" or "individualist" model and show that it partly fits the Neckarhausen situation. This is true not because the village lies somewhere in a transitional zone between autarchic peasants and capitalized farmers, but because land was a chief means of production. Like every other region in Europe, the village had to deal with its distribution, and with labor utilization, generational turnover, subsistence, markets, and socialization by linking production and reproduction in a never-ending cycle, and like them, it solved its problems in its own way.

The problem in this chapter is to discover an adequate way to represent the system parents and adult children used to sort out their various claims and obligations with respect to property. To uncover the logic of social experience and the nature of practice, we have to find a way to analyze a host of individual confrontations. We will have to read a number of texts and then string some together to recapture the continuous discourses that our evidence presents to us in discontinuous forms. At the core of kinship dynamics are assertions of rights, but it is analytically simple-minded to regard cases where expressed claims are rejected as evidence for the weakness of kinship. Kinship is a language in which rights are accorded to various people, obligations are adjusted,

[3] "2. Landrecht," (1567), in Reyscher, vol. 4, p. 299: "Whoever has a possession of (*Besitz*), use of (*Gebrauch*) or benefit from (*Niessung*) some goods may sell them to another for a time, and the owner (*Eigenthumbsherr*) is obligated to allow such use or benefit to the buyer so long as the seller has the right."

[4] See Chapter 4.

and duties are taken on and sloughed off. Its dynamics are a continual story of expectations fulfilled and denied. It is therefore in the details of narratives that we must search for the system of expressed values and the practices they entail. This long chapter is composed of a set of rather ramshackle stories about eight different families. Each one was chosen because of the interesting details of one court appearance, which, when examined for its context and linked to many other court protocols, reveals some of the complex workings of Neckarhausen society. I prefer to expose them to the reader without streamlining them too much, partly as an heuristic of discovery and partly as an efficient way of becoming familiar with the terms of social interaction in the village before we make some general remarks. These are not *illustrations* of the way people acted but are the ways *some* people actually did act. I will not justify them as typical stories, although they may be so, because we are concerned with the logic of social action not its typicality, which is a rather uninteresting problem, better left to the taxonomical sciences. We will center our attention on the conflicting claims people made against each other with regard to space, property, and productive resources, and we will gather any evidence we can find about living arrangements. However peasant this village was, people always had individual rights to things, a fact that has to be underlined in order to clear away the misunderstandings which characterize many of the discussions about precapitalist, "traditional" rural society.

## Example 1

The first story deals with how rights in shared space were carefully delineated, how the practical exigencies of farming threw separate family units together, how specific properties were uncoupled from inheritance claims, and how the ideology of authority was unconnected with any notion of a common family enterprise. The genealogy of these family units is presented in Figure 11.1.

*Christoph Rieth, 60, complained to the church consistory in 1743 about the behavior of his son-in-law, Michael Häussler, 30.*[5] *Michael had been drinking in Nürtingen with his brother and Johannes Häfner, arriving back in Neckarhausen after the curfew. All three of them had a few glasses of wine at Michael's house before his brother and Häfner set off for Jacob Geiger's pub – Geiger, 41, was Häussler's brother-in-law. Michael soon followed on the pretext that he had to fetch something in the stall but was quickly sought out by his suspicious wife, Anna Maria, 29. When they got home, Michael threw a jug at the wall, turned over two tables, and smashed the lamp. Then he went after his wife, yelling that "the dog now had to die." She hid behind her mother-in-law, Barbara, 56, and managed to crawl out to fetch her stepfather-in-law, Johannes Heinser, 40. A few days later, after coming back from the mill, although his meal was waiting on the table, he started to throw things and cried that he had to*

[5] *Kirchenkonvent*, vol. 1, p. 113 (–.1.1743).

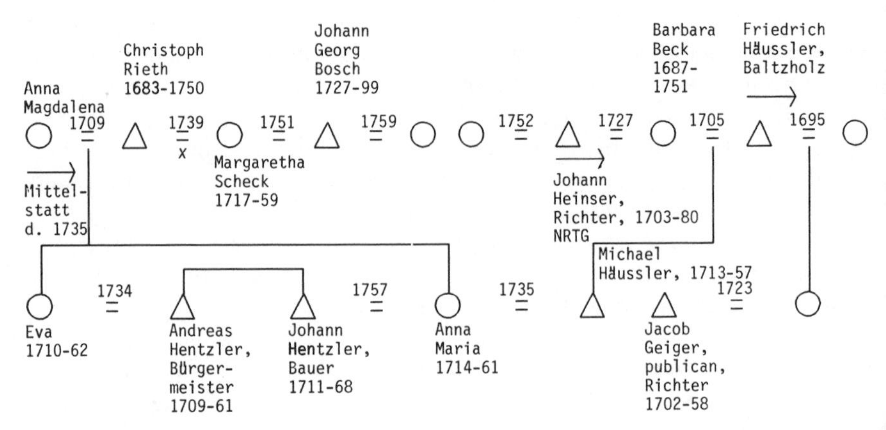


Figure 11.1

*work all day and found no slops (*Fresssen = *animal food) at home. As the children began to cry, he threatened to get his wife alone and stab her.*

*The next day, Anna Maria, after receiving no comfort from her mother-in-law, fetched her father, Christoph, and her stepmother, Margaretha, 26. When Michael told his father-in-law that he had little authority in the former's home, Rieth threw him to the floor. Häussler's mother in turn knocked Margaretha Rieth down, and Michael called her a "whore." At the hearing, the pastor warned Häussler's mother that she was responsible for exercising authority when her husband (Johannes Heinser, 40) was absent.*

*Eight years earlier, Anna Maria had complained that her mother-in-law had ordered her from the house and told her never to come back.*[6] *She alleged that Michael always took his mother's part. He always failed to inform her when he would be busy and hit her when she asked questions. At the hearing, it became clear that she objected to her husband opening a pub (over the next 15 years, he was frequently referred to as a pubkeeper* [Gassenwirt]*).*

*The physical location of the young couple involved here can be teased from the story and developed with aid of some of the inventories. To begin with the senior generation: According to Christoph Rieth's marriage inventory from 1740, he brought a "fine" house, with two sitting rooms* (Stuben), *and a barn under one roof in the Biegelgasse.*[7] *Since he owed each of his two daughters money for a house purchase, it appears that he had bought the shares they had each inherited at their mother's death in 1735. By the time of the inventory in 1740, his eldest daughter and son-in-law held half of the house in usufruct – presumably each family used one of the two sitting rooms. From the fact that Barbara Heinser had ordered her new daughter-in-law from the house in 1735, and that she was present in 1743 when Michael was threatening his wife,*

[6] *Kirchenkonvent*, vol. 1, p. 35 (19.5.1753).
[7] *Inventuren und Teilungen*, 604 (22.3.1740).

*we can conclude that the younger couple was living in his mother's house. It was in fact worth considerably more than Rieth's "fine" house, so must have been large enough for two families, and since Michael's father had been a "Wirt" before him, it probably had been a pub.*[8] *When Michael and Anna Maria got married, Barbara let her son have about 30 percent of her land as a marriage portion (7 strips), while Christoph Rieth provided 2 arable strips from his own 23 in usufruct.*[9] *Michael had enough land to support his own family at least in part, but since his widowed mother had married a much younger man, his labor was not necessary for his parents' economy. In order to support himself, he opened a pub, which was abandoned just as soon as he could accumulate enough resources to become a full-time farmer at the death later on of his father-in-law.*

*Michael Häussler's father had brought two-thirds of the house into his marriage and subsequently purchased the other third.*[10] *In her second marriage, his widow, Barbara, brought an estate of 2,379 fl. compared to that of her new husband, Johannes Heinser, who had only 222 fl.*[11] *In 1735, when Michael married, he received 509 fl. worth of land and movables. Later on, in 1751, when Barbara died, her husband inherited a third of the house, and her son, Michael, two-thirds. The son ended up with a considerable fortune of 1,737 fl., and the widower came away with a handy profit, altogether 1,105 fl. – five times more than he started with. Two years later, when Heinser remarried, he had already sold his portion of the house to his next-door neighbor, Johann Georg Rieth.*[12] *By 1757, when Michael Häussler died, he then owned the former house of his father-in-law, Christoph Rieth.*[13] *He and his wife had inherited 1.5 quarters of it and purchased the rest during their marriage. In fact, he owed his brother-in-law and his stepmother-in-law's new husband, Johann Georg Bosch, for their shares in the house. At his death, half of the house fell to his wife, Anna Maria, and half was secured for the children. When she married again in 1757, both neogami brought similar houses, but by the time she died four years later, they were reduced to her half-house.*[14] *In 1765, Johannes Hentzler, her widower, took the whole house into his third marriage, having purchased his stepson's portion.*[15] *In 1768, when Johannes died, his son and son-in-law from his first marriage bought up all the property from the widow.*[16] *They had already been carrying on much of the agriculture and were owed considerable wages for their labor by the estate.*

The fortunes of the house in the Biegelgasse are illustrated in Figure 11.2. Neither house had followed a straight line of descent in any way. The Häussler house had first come into the immigrant Friedrich Häussler's hands through his in-laws. Eventually it fell not to the children by his first wife, through whom

8 *Inventuren und Teilungen*, 472 (11.5.1727).
9 *Inventuren und Teilungen*, 604 (22.3.1740); 736 (27.4.1751).
10 *Inventuren und Teilungen*, 736 (27.4.1751).
11 *Inventuren und Teilungen*, 736 (27.4.1751).
12 *Inventuren und Teilungen*, 741 (15.3.1752).
13 *Inventuren und Teilungen*, 782 (30.1.1757).
14 *Inventuren und Teilungen*, 796 (25.11.1757); 1838 (17.4.1761).
15 *Inventuren und Teilungen*, 899 (19.1.1765).
16 *Inventuren und Teilungen*, 941 (28.4.1768).

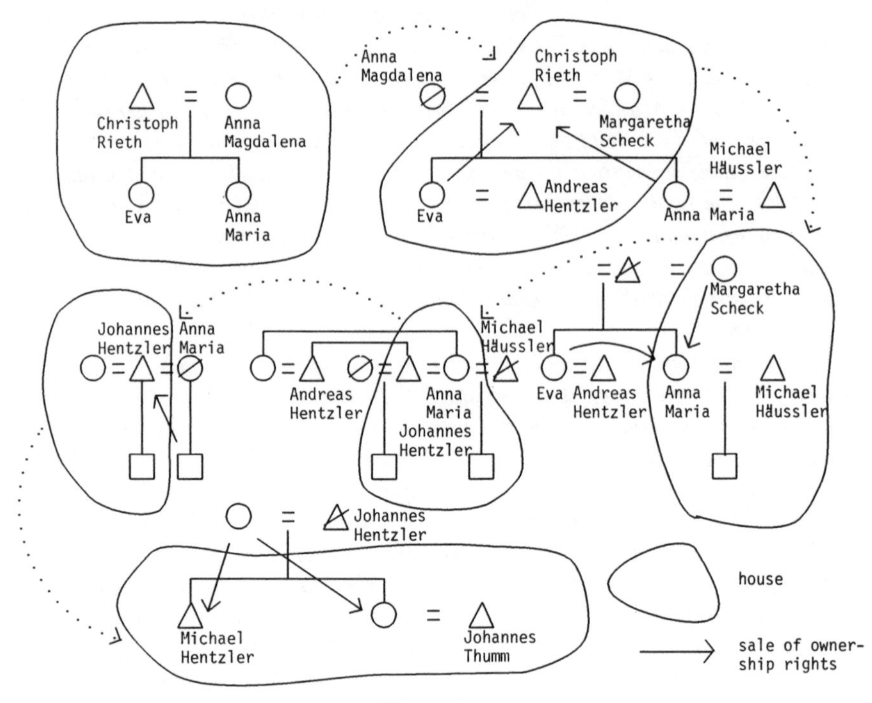


Figure 11.2

it came to the marriage, but to the child and second husband of his second wife, who in turn sold it to a nonrelated neighbor. The Rieth house first sheltered Christoph's oldest daughter and son-in-law, went later to his second daughter and son-in-law, then to her second husband, and finally to the latter's son and son-in-law from his second marriage. In this constant movement "sideways" as well as downward, there was no sense of a line of devolution. Children, especially the oldest, continually had to find new places to live inside the village. We also see that individuals in households were continually negotiating alliances with people in other households. Anna Maria sought for backing early on in her marriage from her father and stepmother, while her husband used his own mother in the struggle. Much of the problem appears to have been the direction of economic orientation for the young couple. Michael was not needed for his mother's farming, which would have made him dependent on his father-in-law's considerable resources. If Anna Maria could have prevented him from opening a pub, his only recourse was to act as a drudge for Rieth for many years to come.

Apparently any number of possible groups could use the space in the house in the Biegelgasse in complex ways – multiple generations, parents with children from other marriages, married siblings, and families with servants. Some sources give indications of boarders, relatives, wards, and foster children continually circulating in and out of households. It would have been a fundamental strategic mistake for anyone to identify too closely with any household without holding open as many options as possible.

If Anna Maria had had problems with her mother-in-law as a 21-year-old bride and suffered under the dependent position in the latter's house as her husband went about his publican activities there, she got really exercised over relations with her stepmother. Both she and her sister had married about the same time as their mother died. And since Christoph appeared content not to remarry, Eva, the elder daughter, and her husband had moved in with him. But in 1739, he did marry – at the age of 56 – the 22-year-old Margaretha Scheck, whose Beisitzer father occupied the *Römerhof* in Neckarhausen. Margaretha was pregnant at the time of the marriage with someone else's child – the father being apparently a noble military officer.

*The first conflict seems to have come with the older sister, Eva. In 1740, a little over four months after Christoph and Margaretha had been married, the latter reported a family quarrel to the pastor.*[17] *She said that Eva had secretly kept a pot of lard* (Schmalz) *which should have been shared with Margaretha as her new mother. Apparently Christoph had told Eva quietly that she still had some lard to share, and although Margaretha had overheard the conversation, she did nothing about it. Eva's sister, Anna Maria Häussler, complained about a lack of lard to her father as he visited her at home one Sunday evening. He told her to come to his house whenever she wanted because Eva had a jarful which she ought to have shared. The next morning Anna Maria came to her father's house, and Christoph told Eva to find the jar and share the lard, but she said there was no more there. When pressed, she called her sister* Glunte *(whore),* Bestie, *and* Schleife *(wanton) and ordered her out of the house. At that point her father, Christoph, demanded the key to the cupboard and threatened to break it open with an axe. Once Eva opened it, however, there was no lard to be found, so Christoph told Anna Maria to leave and return when his son-in-law Andreas was home. As she was going, Margaretha suggested she get her father to break the lock on the attic door, since the arrival of her brother-in-law would only bring more drama. Anna Maria and her father then made their way to the attic, Eva after them, followed by Margaretha. Eva turned on her stepmother, saying "tausend sakraments Bestie, what are you doing here?" In the ensuing altercation, Eva ended up on the floor with Margaretha pounding her and Christoph breaking it up by hitting his daughter with a rake handle. As Eva ran down the stairs, she called back* Schelmvater *(scoundrel father) and said to her stepmother, "You did not get my father honorably but by* Schelmerei.*" Margaretha was upset that Eva had called her a* Schlutte *(slut), suggesting in addition that she had killed her child. At the court, Christoph demanded that his daughter and son-in-law let his wife go by without rude comments and obey her in proper* (billig) *matters, and if not, to find another place to live.*

Among the various actors in these stories, there was a strong sense of ter-

[17] *Kirchenkonvent*, vol. 1, p. 67 (2.2.1740).

ritory. Michael Häussler in 1743 told his father-in-law that in his own house he had the greater right. Christoph Rieth visited his daughter's house in a formal manner – on a Sunday evening – and invited her to visit his house, which emphasized the sense of separateness. When Eva got angry, she ordered her sister out of her house. She and her husband lived with her father and stepmother in the same house, but with well defined territories. Eva kept a lock on the attic and on the cupboard, and her father and stepmother did not have access to either. The father, in fact, only violated the closed areas when his son-in-law was not home and his other daughter was present. Eva gave in under his authority but specifically attacked her stepmother for following them to the attic. She not only pointed out that Margaretha had illegitimately crossed a boundary but in her verbal abuse suggested a lack of boundaries ("beast", "slut") or a crossing of social boundaries ("scoundrel," dishonorably married). She used similar words for her sister – "whore," "beast," "wanton" – coupling them with the demand that she leave her house. The struggle was over the right to divide up lard for use in separate households, not access to a common store. In fact, throughout the entire family history, access to resources was characterized by specifying rights to different things. Michael Häussler had usufruct rights in some strips and Andreas Hentzler in others. Hentzler had rights to half the house with territory demarcated rather clearly. Indeed, the locks in the house served to keep other house members out. Furthermore, the younger couple drew strong boundaries around their territory by rude and violent behavior.

Houses in Neckarhausen frequently contained more than one married pair; in fact, throughout the eighteenth and nineteenth centuries they averaged almost always about 1.4 families. Sometimes a house was divided into separate and autonomous apartments. Perhaps more frequently, one or two rooms were shared because of the problems and expense of heating and cooking. If a house only had one heatable room – the *Stube*, sitting or living room – then whoever lived there likely shared in its use. In the case of the Rieth house, there were clearly two Stuben, which allowed the two families separate living space. By contrast, however, as in this case, the kitchen was an area that could be shared – it all depended on how many fireplaces a house contained. Each year, every Bürger was entitled to a full portion of kindling from the communal woods unless a fireplace was being shared.[18] Two families with one chimney combined one-and-a-half portions of firewood. Wherever more than one family shared an inheritance or strangers purchased separate sections of a house or someone rented space from someone else, families were likely to share cooking and living areas. Segregation of such spaces depended on the number of fireplaces and heating ovens in a house.

The issue of sharing space has to be kept separate from that of particular

[18] *Vogtruggericht*, vol. 2, f. 13 (11.3.1806).

economies. Two women cooking in the same kitchen, for example, could have separate supplies, storage areas, and separate schedules for use. The evidence suggests that for a period of time, sometimes perhaps up until the young couple made their inventory, parents and married children often formed one household. However, that period was usually short, and separate households were commonly established rather quickly. All it took was a complaint to the consistory, and the officials would advise the young people to move out or the older couple to see that separate households were established. If a daughter-in-law could not get along with her mother-in-law, the court would advise that the son be accorded Meisterschaft in his own household – that is, that he and his wife form a separate economy. Even then, there would normally be a long transition period until a family acquired its full set of resources. During that period, a son would ply a trade, open a pub, seek agricultural labor, work his own land, and work for his and his wife's parents. Because the younger couple had their own economy, parents did not have an unconditional call on their labor. Indeed, Johannes Hentzler had to pay for the agricultural labor of his son and son-in-law, and there is no reason to think that that was in any way extraordinary. Wherever a young couple shared a house with older relatives, the in-marrying spouse emphasized the break and called the other spouse to his or her primary allegiance. As in Anna Maria's case, a strategy was worked out allying various relatives and the court to insure that the son turned his attention to his own family.

We are suggesting that although marriage marked a turning point and began a process of redistributing resources, the period of transition was a long one. Independence marked the first stage, but even then there was no sharp generational turnover, and it was a very long time before a young couple got their hands on the old people's property. When Christoph's first daughter married, he was 51. Out of 38 strips of land, his 23-year-old son-in-law (Andreas Hentzler) received 6 in usufruct. From his own father, the Schultheiss in Raidwangen, the latter received a modest marriage portion and no final inheritance until 1760, 26 years after the couple married and 1 year before Andreas died. Christoph Rieth himself died 16 years after his oldest daughter's marriage. When Anna Maria married a year after her sister, she and her husband got 2 arable strips in usufruct and set up their household in his mother's house, getting 4 arable strips, 2 meadows, and a garden from her. Not until his mother died 16 years after his marriage would Michael Häussler inherit a substantially greater portion. Just after his father-in-law and just before his mother died (1750, 1751 respectively), Michael Häussler moved to the Rieth house and set himself up as a substantial farmer. When he died in 1757, he was called "Bauer," whereas in the 1740s, he had been a "Wirt" (innkeeper). The four young people were in their early to mid-20s when they first married: Andreas, 25; Eva, 24; Michael, 22; and Anna Maria, 21. At that time, they were modestly set up with land and provided with living space in their parents' houses. The children even sold their claims to the houses to the surviving parents, even when they subsequently got portions in usufruct. At the time that they married, their surviving parents were in their late 40s and early 50s. Not until the children reached their late 30s did they receive final settlements from the latter as they died or retired. In the case of Andreas Hentzler, his father did not retire until he was 50 and his father 73.

During the years between marriage and a final settlement from the senior generation, the children might lease land from their parents, purchase it, cultivate it for a wage, or cultivate it for part of the produce. As the parents aged, the younger generation might be brought increasingly into the economic orbit of their parents. Jacob Geiger, Michael Häussler's stepbrother-in-law, for example, retired in 1758 at the age of 56, one year after his wife died.[19] He was unable, he said, to cultivate his land without servants, which demonstrates that his children's labor was not available to him. Therefore he "tradiert" a substantial portion of his property with the condition that his son and two sons-in-law cultivate all the land he kept without any payment, including plowing, harrowing, sowing, harvesting, threshing, carting, and storing. All work was to be given out to the children on an equal basis. They promised life-long obedience, faithfulness, and aid. This settlement, which is typical of many retirement contracts in the village, lays out clearly the terms of reciprocity. The children's labor became available because they had received productive resources from the parents. At the end of the document, Jacob sold his house to his son, and the daughter living in Grötzingen sold all of her landed inheritance to her sister's husband.

In the case of the children we are dealing with, they were in competition with their stepparents for property and position in the family concern. Johannes Heinser, Michael Häussler's stepfather (who was supposed to exercise authority over him) was only 10 years his senior. He entered his marriage with Barbara with 222 fl. compared with her 2,370 fl. and left it with 1,105 fl., not much less than Michael (1,737 fl.). Margaretha Scheck was seven and four years younger, respectively, than her stepdaughters. She only brought 91 fl. worth of movables to her marriage, compared with her husband's estate of 2,192 fl.[20] When her husband died, she ended up with 761 fl., but she was also pregnant. The posthumous child received 515 fl. from his father's inheritance, equal to what each daughter got. When his portion, which was held in usufruct by the widow, is added to hers, Margaretha ended up with 1,276 fl., compared with the 868 fl. Väterliches and Mütterliches each daughter received.

The discipline that was to be exercised between "generations" was one of position and did not flow from hierarchical structures of large family enterprises. Johannes Heinser was supposed to exercise authority over Michael Häussler, his 10-year-younger stepson, despite the fact that they had separate

[19] *Inventuren und Teilungen*, 804 (18.4.1758).
[20] *Inventuren und Teilungen*, 604 (22.3.1740).

economies – Heinser's farm was too small to need Häussler's regular labor, and Häussler had his own land and a pub. In fact, Häussler's mother's authority, according to the consistory, was derived from that of her husband – she was expected to control her son's behavior in the absence of his (step-)father. Eva and Anna Maria were both supposed to treat their stepmother with the deference due to a mother, despite the fact that she was younger than they. In a later case, the pastor would see their behavior as a violation of the Fifth Commandment. The relationship did not grow out of Margaretha's taking part in a larger family enterprise. Eva and her husband had a separate apartment and separate resources, while Anna Maria and her husband did not live in the same house at all.

*Five months after Christoph Hentzler died, Anna Maria and Eva used abusive terms behind the back of Margaretha – no dog would ever take a piece of bread from her again.*[21] *As far as the pastor was concerned, such behavior was a violation of the Fifth Commandment and the daughters were forced to apologize. A month later, Anna Maria was at it again (the two daughters were now 36 and 33, respectively).*[22] *A week previously, Michael Häussler had come home from Nürtingen and gone into the barn to work. Anna Maria came and complained that he and the maid had not threshed enough and called him a* Lumpenhauser, *whereupon he chased her with the flail and told her to do the work herself if she was not satisfied. Anna Maria called the maid a* Bestie *and said she whored with her husband. Several days later, Margaretha advised Michael to punish his wife rather than run away all the time. Later that day Anna Maria and Margaretha got into a quarrel, and Michael from down below yelled that his wife was now quarreling with her "own mother" just as she had with his. He came up and said he would finally shut her mouth. During that altercation, Margaretha was interrupted when she ran to get a piece of bread for a beggar, and Anna Maria ordered her away from the door, whereupon the stepmother went off to take care of some animals. Anna Maria flung abuses at her, accusing her of taking a husband on the same day she buried one. Margaretha responded that it was none of her business and that she was not waiting for her husband's death like Anna Maria. The latter then called her stepmother* Canallie *(cunning, malicious person) and* Bestie *and accused Margaretha of stealing an egg. At one point in the hollering match, she said to her stepmother: "lick me"* (leck mich). *She raised her dress and said, "Du Scheckwahr" (a reference to her family name, Scheck, with the suffix* Ware, *which is the same as* Pack *– baggage, pack, bunch, often used with* Lumpen *as in* Lumpenware, Lumpenpack, *trash).*

*At the next hearing, Anna Maria complained Margaretha called her names.*[23] *She had said one man was not good enough for her – she needed two or three to bugger her* (die du den Hinterst verhuren). *She also accused the maid, Agnes Grauer, and another woman of sleeping with her husband. In 1751, Michael and Anna Maria Häussler were brought before the consistory together with Margaretha (34), now*

[21] *Kirchenkonvent*, vol. 2, p. 48 (25.7.1750).
[22] *Kirchenkonvent*, vol. 2, p. 49 (24.8.1750).
[23] *Kirchenkonvent*, vol. 2, p. 54 (28.8.1750).

*the wife of the 24-year-old Johann Georg Bosch.*[24] *Earlier, before the village court, Margaretha had complained that Anna Maria alleged she had gotten too large an inheritance portion.*[25] *Since then there had been a steady stream of abuse: "du Bestie, Cannallie, Glunt." The stepdaughter said she was called in return,* Faullentzerin *(lazy person) and* Laman *(lethargic person) – "your husband is not man enough for you." In the Vogt's court Michael Häussler and his wife were fined for the "shocking wickedness" of stealing food stores from Margaretha – rye, oats, barley, peas, salt, fruit, and flour.*[26] *Michael was also ordered to pay 8 fl. he still owed on the sale of the house by his stepmother. By the time things had gotten this far, they all lost perspective and started flinging charges of gross immorality at each other, and so the Vogt ordered an investigation before the village consistory.*

The choice of abusive terms does not seem to be totally arbitrary. At least they strongly parallel the issues at hand. The accusations against the maid of whoring arose in the context of inattention to work. The abusive terms Canallie and Bestie, accusations of adultery, and Anna Maria's invitation to her stepmother to lick her ass, all went together with disputes about property – the right to give bread to a beggar, the use of an egg. Margaretha herself was not without verbal resources – accusing her stepdaughter of insatiable sexual desires and buggery. Taken together, the two women traded insults that had to do with false sexual boundaries, while the issues at hand had to do with lines of inheritance, ownership of foodstores, and unpaid debts. Issues of property devolution and legitimacy were sharpened and focused in the rhetoric of abuse. Michael Häussler maintained that Margaretha had slept with Bosch before the first proclamation (Christoph Rieth died 5 March 1750, the first banns were posted on 15 November, and the couple were married 19 January 1751). He had said to Margaretha, "Scratch my back and I will scratch yours." Conflict arose when Michael told Johann Georg Bosch he could not order him around. Bosch admitted he had slept with his wife after the first proclamation, but apparently there was suspicion that he had slept with her before Christoph died (which would imply that the posthumous child who had taken such a large inheritance portion was not Christoph Rieth's at all). Margaretha wanted put into the protocol that her two stepdaughters had lain in a bed together with their prospective mates before they had been married. But Anna Maria denied that she had said more than four words to her husband before the wedding. While her father was alive she would not have been so fresh (*keck*) as to allow an unmarried man into the house.

What caused the two couples to bring all of the family secrets out into the open was a fundamental issue of authority. In principle, Margaretha's authority as "mother" was derived from the authority of the Hausvater – her husband, Christoph Rieth. The consistory and village court had relied on the ideology of the Haus and Fifth Commandment on several occasions. How then was the

[24] *Kirchenkonvent*, vol. 2, p. 62 (22.2.1751).
[25] *Gericht*, vol. 1, f. 31 (28.8.1750).
[26] *Vogtruggericht*, vol. 1, f. 26 (15.2.1751).

new situation to be understood? Upon Rieth's death and Margaretha's remarriage, the generationally "senior" couple was composed of Johann Georg Bosch and Margaretha, yet Bosch was 14 years and Margaretha 4 years *younger* than Häussler. It was not long before the crisis in authority separated the couples altogether. In Margaretha's marriage inventory, we find that she and Bosch had sold their portions of the house to Michael Häussler.[27]

This case history shows us that private property is not a straightforward matter that can be easily correlated with a particular kind of character formation or economic type. Rights were always carefully delineated and couples drew careful boundaries around their areas of competency. There was no notion of a family enterprise encompassing several generations, nor any sense of particular properties being under the temporary management of a patriarch who would have to pass them on to the junior partners. Beyond the husband and wife, there were no coparceners in an estate, and inheritance was regulated not unlike it is in most Western societies today. Authority, in any event, was not derived from the necessity to hammer together a continuing productive unit and was continually involved in the contradiction between Fifth Commandment ideology and the facts of remarriage. Related families were, in fact, frequently dependent upon each other for space, labor, and tools, but what they contracted about had to do with the distribution of productive resources and labor and not with "peasant" notions of property, ganzes Haus, or a particular peasant economy.

## Example 2

The second story deals with the gradual separation of households and practical strategies for demonstrating the volitional aspects of inheritance and for building obligation and dependence. The families involved are shown in Figure 11.3.

*In 1740, David Falter, 25, was quite exercised about the size of his marriage portion, so he removed some straw and hay from his father's barn against the wishes of his stepmother, Dorothea, 31.*[28] *He called her "dog" and "thunder" and pushed her around. His brother Salomon, who lived separately, blocked her brother's entry to the house, while David made disparaging remarks about her poor origins. David and his future wife, Anna, were about to receive modest but by no means insignificant marriage portions of over 300 fl. each, giving them considerable productive resources.*[29] *At the time of the marriage, nine months after the incident, he was 25 and she 22, while their parents were in their late 40s or early 50s except for David's stepmother, who was only six years older than himself. The young couple would wait 11 years (at the unexpected accidental death of Salomon Falter) and 17 years for further inheritance. Apparently David and his wife moved out of the parental home at marriage and*

[27] *Inventuren und Teilungen*, 735 (27.4.1751).
[28] *Kirchenkonvent*, vol. 1, p. 76 (24.2.1740).
[29] *Inventuren und Teilungen*, 614 (7.1.1741).

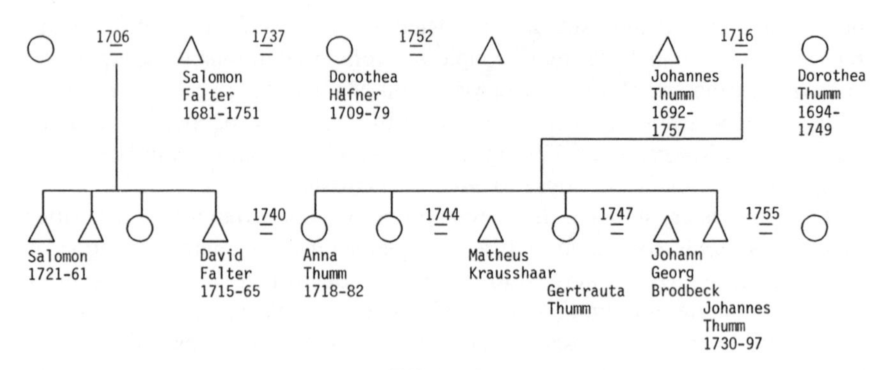


Figure 11.3

*rented living space and storage, since they had no buildings. In 1751 at the estate division of Salomon Falter, after many disputes, the house belonging to Salomon senior was sold to Salomon junior.*[30] *However, the 41-year-old stepmother got the house back* (wieder an sich erhandelt) *right away to remove "inequalities." In any event, both Salomon and David set themselves up in houses separately from their parents. Still Salomon felt strongly enough about territory to refuse his stepmother's brother entry over her wishes.*

David Falter and his wife married with the expectation that they would have to wait 15 to 20 years before they would come into their full inheritance. His marriage portion, which was modest but "adequate" was a negotiable matter between himself and his parents. They were expected to provide him with the necessary property, but the amount was subject to cultural expectations, the current economic situation, the honor of the two families, and their demographic structures. Negotiations began long before his marriage date and were not just a matter of words.

*Three years after the incident with his stepmother, David Falter had an altercation with his parents-in-law, Johannes and Dorothea Thumm.*[31] *David had hit Dorothea with a flail head when she brought soup to her daughter. He was angry because she had complained to his stepmother about his poor householding and loafing. He called her an "old cunt" and told her to "kiss his ass." Because she complained to the pastor, he then said he would not live in peace with his wife until her mother was pushing up daisies* (grüne Brusttuch trägt). *He was upset about his parents-in-law constantly interfering with his affairs, and his mother-in-law had even refused to leave the house upon his orders. David was fined for his behavior, but the older couple were told to leave him with the* Meisterschaft.

In this incident, it is clear that the young couple were living separately from both sets of parents. Mother and daughter wandered back and forth, but each

[30] *Inventuren und Teilungen*, 739 (16.11.1751).

[31] *Kirchenkonvent*, vol. 2, p. 124 (6.10.1743); see the discussion of this incident in Chapter 3, "Hausen."

household had its own economy. David was in the early years of asserting his authority, but his mother-in-law claimed the right to enter her daughter's house. In the end, the village authorities put pressure on the older couple to maintain a lower profile.

In the incident between Falter and his mother-in-law, we see that the women of the senior generation had carried on a running commentary about the young couple. But David and his wife lived separately, apparently in rented quarters. There was no indivisible unity between dwelling and barn and farmland. Just as strips belonging to a family were scattered across the village fields and could easily be detached in the process of passing them on to children, so storage space and stalling could be partitioned. The young Falters did not need to be set up in an apartment in the family homestead but could easily find rented space somewhere else in the village. Not only did a particular house and yard (*Haus und Hof*) not form an indissoluble unity with specific fields, but there was also no association of the house with a particular line or lineage. When the father died, there was so much jealousy among the three sons and daughter, that an opening developed to let the stepmother, who shortly remarried, get the house.

Seventeen years after their marriage, the Falters received a quarter house from the Thumm inheritance.[32] Falter's sister-in-law, the wife of Johann Georg Brodbeck, sold her share at the estate division to young Johann Thumm. Within a few years, a continuing quarrel developed between Thumm and Falter, who now shared the house.[33] In the meantime, Thumm had bought out another brother-in-law, Matheus Krausshaar, and now the court forced David to sell the remaining quarter to Johannes and seek a dwelling elsewhere. In this instance, the "family homestead" was eventually divided among a brother and sister – or between brother and brother-in-law. The only son had purchased shares from two sisters, which made the divisions unequal: three quarters to one quarter. Once the difficulties between the two families got fierce enough, the family with the smaller portion was forced to move again to rented quarters.

*Johann Georg Brodbeck and his wife Gertrauta Thumm had had their own problems with living space. In 1748, after a year of marriage, they were cited for marital problems.*[34] *Both sets of parents-in-law were involved. Hans Jerg's father was concerned with the dishonesty* (malhonnet) *with which his son was being treated by his bride* (Braut) *and her parents with whom the young couple lived. His son was resolved to have his own* Oeconomie, *either in his parents' house or elsewhere. The consistory advised them to find another place to live.*

In the case of young Brodbeck, he and his wife had not yet established a separate economy or account. The expectation does not seem to have been that they should get along with her parents for very long but that after a short

[32] *Inventuren und Teilungen*, 791 (2.6.1751).
[33] *Gericht*, vol. 1, f. 122 (9.6.1759).
[34] *Kirchenkonvent*, vol. 2, p. 18 (10.5.1748).

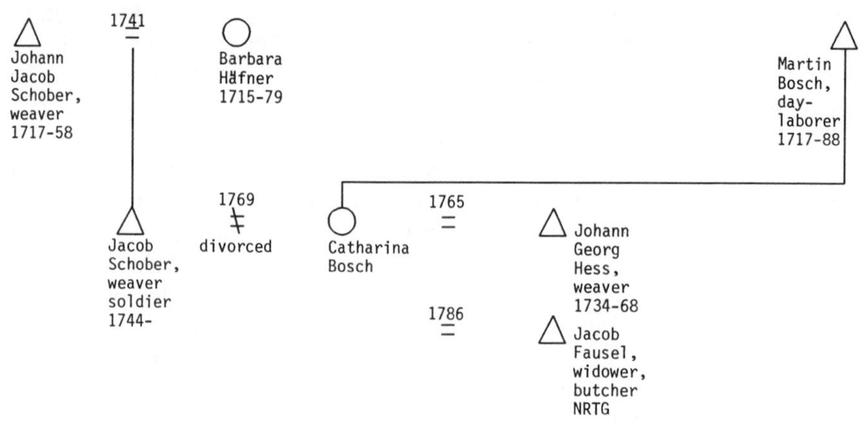


Figure 11.4

start they would establish their independence. The notion of being treated "dishonestly" suggests the impropriety of keeping the young around too long as a work force without their own resources and without pay. The general idea, however, seems to have been that the transition to independence would not be abrupt. First the young couple would work for the parents for several months, then make an inventory and set up their own accounts, establish their own living quarters, perhaps after the birth of the first child. Property expectations established one major link between the two generations, and negotiations around the settlement openly established obligation. By the very fact that the period of separation and the exact amount of property was left vague, the young people were shown that their separate existence was rooted in the will of their parents. The terms of their independence were meant to build obligation. Just because the young couple would get power over their own resources, a period of time was necessary so that negotiation leading to the establishment of bonds of reciprocity could take place. As in any social practice, one side or the other could be inept, impatient, selfish, or cruel.

## Example 3

*Jacob Schober's father, a weaver like himself, died in 1758, leaving a widow with three small children and a shack worth about 100 fl. Several pieces of land had had to be sold to pay debts, and even on the shack the widow had to pay off 90 fl. at 8 fl. per year. She was described as "one-eyed" but "strong", and she earned a living spinning, washing, and doing occasional agricultural labor.*[35] *In 1769, Jacob, 25, married Catharina, 26, widow of Johann Georg Hess and daughter of Martin Bosch, a day-*

[35] *Kirchenkonvent*, vol. 2, (14.1.1760); (6.1.1761); (12.4.1762); (25.4.1765).

*laborer and village servant (see Figure 11.4). From the beginning, she was treated with blows and abuse, and was thrown out of the house on at least one occasion.*[36] *She and her husband had moved into the shack with his mother, who apparently incited Jacob, who, according to the consistory, was lazy and wasteful* (leckerhaftig). *A few months after Catharina's first appearance before the consistory, Jacob complained that upon his return home from laboring in Nürtingen, he found she had moved to her father's house with bedding, household equipment* (Hausrat), *and cow.*[37] *Martin Bosch said that his coparent-in-law* (Gegenschwieger), *Barbara Schober, was full of enmity* (feindselig) *and regarded his daughter as a witch. He therefore wanted to take back the marriage portion he had provided. The consistory said the* Haushaltung *had to be continued in the Schober house but that Schober was to run a proper* (treulich) *household. Sometime later but before 1779, Schober had deserted his wife, and after a divorce, she married Jacob Fausel in Nürtingen (1786).*[38]

In this example, we encounter the other end of the economic ladder. Jacob had grown up in a poor household with his widowed mother. Eventually he brought his bride home, and mother and daughter-in-law must have shared a very small space together. The issue for Catharina and for her father was a separate household inside a house. When she left, she took the chief symbols of that household – her bedding, her cow, and some furnishings – and her father threatened to pull out its economic underpinnings altogether by withdrawing the marriage portion he had provided. For the consistory as well, the issue was a separate household for the young couple – Jacob was admonished to run a *treuliche Haushaltung.* In his marriage inventory, Jacob listed a newly built house, valued at zero until his mother's death.[39] He also had usufruct of 2 strips of land. Catharina brought 11 pieces of land, all in usufruct. His clothes made up most of his movables, while she brought bedding, furniture, utensils, many food and grain stores, a calf, and a sheep.

In this instance, we see a reversal of the usual notion of the in-marrying spouse. The wealthier partner by far went to live with the poorer. We normally think of such a situation the other way around, but where a young couple lived was a separate issue from the composition and origin of their resources. It was mostly a matter of available room. Apparently Martin Bosch did not have enough space for them, since after his daughter's divorce, he repeatedly applied for and was eventually granted permission for her to build a cottage (*Häuslein*).[40] Jacob Schober had helped build a new house for his mother sometime before he married and thus had some claim to use but no ownership rights – therefore the house was entered into his inventory but given no value. He and his mother tried to set the wealthier young bride straight on authority

[36] *Kirchenkonvent*, vol. 2, (13.8.1769).
[37] *Kirchenkonvent*, vol. 2, (2.10.1769).
[38] *Gericht*, vol. 2, f. 226 (28.12.1779). On Schober's later existence as a soldier and his disappearance, see *Inventuren und Teilungen*, 1103 (20.2.1787).
[39] *Inventuren und Teilungen*, 954 (7.5.1769).
[40] *Gericht*, vol. 2, f. 226 (28.12.1779).

in the house, but she expected independence. One of the ways she and her father kept a tight rein on her husband was to take only usufructory rights to land into the marriage.

### Example 4

*Leonhard Weiler, 60, reported in 1791 that his "son" Johann Georg Bauknecht, 31, had mistreated him (the family is shown in figure 11.5).*[41] *The latter had returned to the shed* (Werkstatt) *with the plow after sowing hemp and complained that a part of the instrument was missing. Just then Anna Maria, Leonhard's wife, came on the scene, and young Bauknecht told her his (step)father had the missing piece, whereupon Leonhard slapped him in the face, knocking him to the ground. After Anna Maria pulled her husband off by the hair, Bauknecht hit him on the head with a stick. According to his own testimony, Johann Georg had told his mother to look for the missing part, which she then found. His half-brother, Mathes Weiler, 25, called him a "scoundrel"* (Spitzbub), *which heated up the argument until he and his stepfather went at each other. Only the intervention of his mother and the two daughters-in-law* (Söhnerrinnen) *had separated them. According to Bauknecht, when Mathes attacked him with a pitchfork, he had swung wildly with a stick to protect himself and accidentally struck his father. Mathes testified he had been stacking hay and only joined the fray when he heard the noise. Bauknecht had already made accusations about stealing the part the night before. The local court sent the matter to the Oberamt, and the Vogt sentenced Leonhard and Johann Georg each to 24 hours in jail.*[42] *To prevent such occurrences in the future, young Bauknecht and Mathes Weiler were ordered to leave their parents' house and find other accommodations.*

*The stepbrothers had been raised in the house together and were five years apart in age. Their relationship seems at times to have been close and at others to have been full of conflict. In 1785, for example, Mathes, then 20, had been part of a group of young men in a tavern who had been cited for throwing clubs at another young villager.*[43] *Weiler denied having taken part, and Bauknecht, having interrupted the consistory to chew the officials out for being unjust, was severely reprimanded and reported to the Oberamt. The two stepbrothers further cemented their relations by marrying sisters.*

*The house the two young couples and their parents lived in had been inherited by Johannes Bauknecht, Anna Maria's first husband, and his siblings, whom he bought out.*[44] *When Johann Georg Bauknecht married in 1788, he received a quarter of the house and barn and garden as part of his marriage portion.*[45] *Mathes Weiler, who married two years later, did not get part of the house, although he and his wife lived there until the time of the incident.*[46] *From this information, we know only that all*

[41] *Gericht*, vol. 4, f. 166 (28.4.1791).
[42] *Vogtruggericht*, vol. 2, f. 7 (12.12.1791).
[43] *Kirchenkonvent*, vol. 3, (7.5.1785); (12.5.1785); (3.6.1785).
[44] *Inventuren und Teilungen*, 850 (14.11.1766).
[45] *Inventuren und Teilungen*, 1116 (26.6.1788).
[46] *Inventuren und Teilungen*, 1140 (25.10.1790).

## *Example 4*

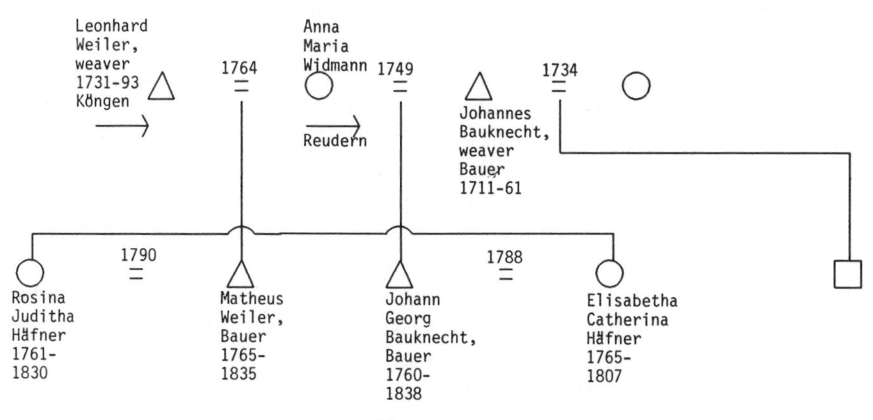


Figure 11.5

*three families were in the house together, but not what the living arrangements were. A little earlier, Bauknecht had complained to the village court that his father did not allow him a fair share of the wood.*[47] *This suggests that the Bauknecht family heated and perhaps cooked separately, although a single wood supply implies that there was only one fireplace or chimney and therefore only one kitchen. It was unlikely that all three families had separate sitting rooms and kitchens, so perhaps Mathes Weiler was still living in his parents' apartment.*

The conflict raises a number of issues. In this case, Leonhard and his wife were not young (60 and 64), yet the marriage of neither son represented a break in control of property or in family power. Young Bauknecht got 564 fl. and Mathes Weiler 387 fl. worth of immovable property, together just about half of what Leonhard and his wife kept for themselves.[48] Each son, adding the property of his wife, had a substantial landed holding to work, but they continued to live in and share the house and agricultural buildings. At the time of the incident, Mathes was stacking hay, Leonhard was working in the shed, and Johann Georg was returning with the plow team. Mother and daughters-in-law were quickly on the scene. Despite the fact of mutual residence, there was a strong sense of separate space and property. Neither Johann Georg nor Mathes had brought any agricultural tools into their marriages, which meant that they depended on their father for those necessary means of production. They apparently did not work land in common, and I presume that space was demarcated, yet they were implicated enough with each other to share tools. As Johann Georg set up his own household, he got a quarter of the house and a quarter of the barn, but he received no implements.

The issue between father and son had to do with a piece of the plow, which

[47] *Gericht*, vol. 4, f. 135 (26.2.1790).
[48] *Inventuren und Teilungen*, 1884 (17.2.1793).

had been discussed over a period of two days. Mathes and his father were on one side of the argument against Johann Georg and his mother. However insignificant the object, the dispute over use rights seemed crucial to the participants. Leonhard considered the piece to belong to him and, for whatever reason, was maintaining that right by hiding it. We know no more than what was related before the court, but clearly a larger set of reciprocities was also in dispute. The symbolic importance of the part was great even if its real importance was not – after all, Johann Georg was able to plow without it. Still he and his mother both felt strongly enough about the matter to label it "stealing." Leonhard, on the other hand, was being challenged on significant grounds. For a farmer, the property most clearly associated with his person was the set of agricultural implements, the *Bauerngeschirr*. In every postmortem inventory, a man's Voraus (inalienable portion) – consisting of his horse, its gear, and his tools – was set aside from the common reckoning of the property of a married couple. Johann Georg was trespassing on his father's independence – which, as we shall see, had been radically put into question by the mother many years before. Mathes, however, identified more closely with Leonhard, especially since he had no separate property rights in the house or barn as his brother did.

In the end, the court ordered a radical separation of the three households altogether, which apparently was not carried out at that time. That the village officials frequently took this tack, suggests that villagers eventually expected to set up separate households and that there was no overwhelming economic advantage for families to remain in one building, since each family had its own agricultural enterprise. That did not mean that Leonhard did not continue to use his sons as a labor force. When he died in 1793, his estate owed both of them wages for agricultural labor and service (*Güter-, Bauern-, und Lidlohn*), which argues again for separate enterprises and the lack of an unpaid labor pool, since the father had to hire them. What Leonhard required of his sons, he had to pay for in some manner or other. Perhaps, giving children land without tools was part of a system of exchange – labor for implements. In many families, the exchange may well not have been reckoned down to the penny but subject to informal balance or good will. Nonetheless, wages for parents working the land of children, or vice versa, are to be found frequently in the postmortem inventories.

Once again, despite close and overlapping relations, we find that the enterprises of different families were not part of one production and consumption unity. There may have been a transition lasting several months to a year or so, but the resources – land, barns, stalls, rooms – were specific to the individual families. That, of course, was not always necessary. If a family shared a heated sitting room for a year, there was no need to stop doing so for many more years. Most likely the presence of children was the crucial turning point in the fissioning process. And perhaps the makeshift arrangements worked best when the parties occupying common space scrupulously avoided sharing things.

## *Example 4*

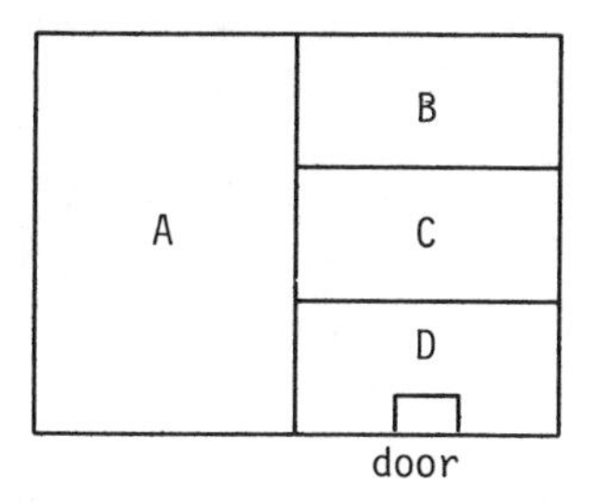


Figure 11.6

There were, of course, many possible ways to divide up space, informally, formally, with selfishness, or with good grace. One formal arrangement for sharing space is seen in Figure 11.6.[49]

Here a barn was divided up among four parties, one half going to one man, and the other half divided up in thirds. A conflict arose when B trespassed on A's side because C had placed a wagon all the way across his space. The only entrance was through the door on D's portion, and B only had the right to get to his part of the barn by entering the door and crossing across D's and C's portions.

When Leonhard Weiler died, his widow decided to retire. She sold the rest of the house to Johann Georg on the condition that she could continue to live there for the rest of her life.[50] From the sale, Mathes was to get enough money to build himself a house, and he was given two years to live in the homestead with use of the barn without charge. Each son had to pay the mother 4 fl., 2 Scheffel spelt, 3 Simri barley, and 6 Pfund lard each year, which suggests again the exchange of produce for productive resources. The fact that the mother was accorded food supplies implies that she would continue to maintain a separate household, and we can infer that the house continued to support three separate households for two years. If we assume that the house had two heated sitting rooms, then the Bauknechts formed one separate unit, and the Mathes Weilers and his mother the other. However, the fact that inside the Weiler half of the house the mother maintained her own food stores argues for a lack of commensality.

*The relationships within the Weiler family had a strange history, which is worth dwelling on for a moment, in order to examine some of the later situations. After Johannes Bauknecht died in 1761, Anna Maria became engaged to Johann Georg Häussler, but soon after broke it off because he stole some grain and called her "whore," "witch," and "Canallie."[51] Rather than marry him, she said, she would suffer death. Shortly thereafter she married Leonhard Weiler from Köngen, providing the*

[49] I have not been able to locate this particular case again, but it is typical of many examples found in the Gerichtsprotocolle.

[50] *Inventuren und Teilungen*, 1184 (17.2.1794).

[51] *Kirchenkonvent*, vol. 2, (10.10.1762).

*house and land – altogether including her child's property worth 1,001 fl. He brought 182 fl. in cash and movables.*[52] *In the inventory, it was noted that she still owed Häussler 25 fl. for breach of promise. He had to sue in court that year for a judgment against her.*[53] *Two years later, someone else was suing her for the unpaid bill Häussler had ceded.*[54] *By 1769, she was threatened with jail and still later with forced sale of property.*[55] *As late as 1777, the case was still in the courts.*[56] *In all of this, Anna Maria displayed a definite stubborn streak, and relations with the man she actually married were not any smoother.*

*In 1769, Leonhard complained his wife alleged he bewitched her and that she would not allow him to eat with her.*[57] *Her son (Johann Georg Bauknecht – then nine years old) was very ill and his head was badly swollen. She had sent him to Elchingen, a Catholic town famous for its exorcist, which action, according to the consistory, was opening the door to Satan. They suggested that her beliefs stemmed from enmity toward her husband and her own* liederlichen Hausen.[58] *One of the quarrels between the two marriage partners was over work and cultivation of the land she had brought into the marriage. For example, she had sent her husband to pick stones from a field, and all he did was push them under.*[59]

*The next year, he was back complaining about his wife again.*[60] *The family had left for five weeks to go to Elchingen to get advice. He was tired of being called a warlock* (Hexenmeister) *and having to eat alone. Whenever she ate out of the common dish, she was in pain. A few weeks later, she said he was killing the children and bewitching the animals.*[61] *Whenever they ate together, she got sick, and she would not allow Johann Georg to accept a piece of bread from him. He said he could not keep animals because she would not gather grass for "other people." She complained that he entered other houses and frequently ate there, which proved that he was an adulterer. The pastor wrote that his pen could not describe what crazy, foolish, wicked, unproven tripe* (Gewäsch) *she reported. People in the village were saying that she only wanted a divorce and that she was sorry she married Weiler. In 1771, Leonhard again came to the consistory with similar complaints.*[62] *The bodies of both children were swelling up because of his bewitchment. He said that he was unable to keep any animals or make fresh cheese* ([Milch]Schmalz) *because of her. Although this was the last appearance of the two before the courts over this issue, during the next several years, the whole family developed a reputation for being witches.*[63]

52 *Inventuren und Teilungen*, 3093 (11.1.1765).
53 Nürtingen *Stadtgericht*, vol. 22, f. 90 (3.6.1765).
54 *Vogtruggericht*, vol. 1, f. 87 (18.3.1767).
55 *Vogtruggericht*, vol. 1, f. 92 (11.2.1769); f. 98 (20.3.1770).
56 *Vogtruggericht*, vol. 1, f. 117 (25.1.1777).
57 *Kirchenkonvent*, vol. 2, (22.1.1769).
58 She had been before the court twice before for spreading rumors about people being witches; *Vogtruggericht*, vol. 1, f. 80 (4.10.1765); f. 86 (18.3.1767).
59 *Kirchenkonvent*, vol. 2, (22.1.1769).
60 *Kirchenkonvent*, vol. 2, (25.2.1770).
61 *Kirchenkonvent*, vol. 2, (21.11.1773).
62 *Kirchenkonvent*, vol. 2, (11.1.1771).
63 *Kirchenkonvent*, vol. 3, (21.12.1783); *Gericht*, vol. 3, f. 176 (15.7.1784).

Leonhard's contention that his wife would not gather grass for "other people," meaning him, was an extreme statement of the husband as stranger, a complete denial of reciprocity. She would not gather fodder – which only a woman could do – which made it impossible for him to raise animals. She also would not eat with him, yet underlined commensality as a symbolic part of a legitimate marriage – only an adulterer would eat in another house.

*The two boys experienced all of this when they were very small, and it probably played into their relationships. In 1790, they were in a court squabble about a debt.*[64] *In 1794, a year after the father died, Bauknecht went to court to complain that he had been short-changed in the partition* (Tradition) *of the estate of his mother.*[65] *The same year, Matheus Weiler's wife complained her brother-in-law had thrown a milk can, striking her in the head.*[66] *Johann Georg and his mother were in the chamber discussing the estate division and when she wanted to enter the argument, Bauknecht called her a* Schelm *(scoundrel) and suggested she had made improper advances to him. When she answered, he threw the pitcher. Bauknecht claimed he was discussing barley he owed his mother. He said he would not thresh any for her until she paid him what she owed him. When his sister-in-law butted in, he threw the pitcher. In this scene, we see demonstrated once again the various aspects of this family's life – the proximity of the households, tension over the partition of property, and work the son did for the mother.*

*In 1796, Mathes Weiler was sowing hempseed on a half strip of land he held next to that of his brother.*[67] *Johann Georg came along, discovered that Mathes had been taking earth from his side, called him a "thief," and threw a hoe at him. Bauknecht said in court that Mathes called him an* Elchinger *– an allusion to the childhood trip to the exorcist – to which Johann Georg responded he had not gone alone; Mathes's father had taken them both there. He abused his brother and called him a* Hexenmeister *just like his father.*

Here again, a piece of property was divided rather than farmed in common, and the two brothers were jealous of their rights. The split in their interests was paralleled by the social split suggested in the metaphors of abuse they hurled at each other. The family lore had Leonhard as the witch and Johann Georg as the bewitched. Mathes emphasized the split in their position by abusing his brother with the epithet *Elchinger*, meaning something like "superstitious Catholic dupe." Since the mother had forced the family to go there, the family dynamics of mother/Bauknecht were emphasized. Johann Georg countered by allying Mathes and his father together – if it was wrong to go, Mathes's father, after all, took him. And then came the clincher – witchcraft was inherited, father and son were both Hexenmeister. The split of the land and the illegitimate aggression – taking earth – paralleled the split in family interests.

[64] *Vogtruggericht*, vol. 2, f. 6 (15.12.1790).
[65] Nürtingen Stadtgericht, vol. 30, f. 329 (12.5.1794).
[66] *Gericht*, vol. 5, f. 2 (13.12.1794).
[67] *Gericht*, vol. 5, f. 17 (4.5.1796).

We know that Weiler had moved out of the family house within a few years of the estate division. Half of the new house he built, he sold to the unrelated Jacob Bauknecht, and the two of them were in constant conflict. In 1809, they were cited to court and told to measure the building and divide it into two by lots.[68] They were no longer to share the sitting room and each side was to have its own. Here we see two unrelated families sharing a sitting room. What brought them together was not the exploitation of a single family enterprise but the practical exigencies of finding an apartment and maintaining body heat in a house with a single fireplace and chimney.

*In 1810, Johann Georg Bauknecht went bankrupt, and his son Michael was put under the guardianship of the half-brother Mathes. Bauknecht had to sell most of his property, and Weiler as guardian was entrusted with selling what belonged to Michael.*[69] *During this transaction, Weiler purchased three-quarters of Bauknecht's house, leaving the rest at that time to Bauknecht. By 1823 at the latest, Weiler had bought the remaining quarter.*[70] *In 1820, Weiler applied to the court for increased money from Michael's estate for boarding him, which suggests that although Johann Georg was still alive, his son lived with the half-brother/uncle/guardian.*[71]

*A final part of the history of the family came with the deaths of the two brothers. When Mathes's wife died, he still had his unmarried daughter, Maria Catharina, 40, Margaretha, 25, divorced, and Michael, 18, at home. Another daughter, Rosine, 27, was at that time in service in Stuttgart, and a son, Matheus, was married. The unmarried children petitioned to allow no estate division to take place. They wanted to live "in common" with their father.*[72] *When Weiler died in 1836, the unmarried children kept the house together to live in common – each getting a quarter.*[73] *The land was apportioned by lot. In the division, Michael took over the half set of agricultural implements and traction gear still left in the father's estate, the other half of which Matheus had gotten sometime after he married. The oldest daughter received 50 fl. for having carried on the household* (Hausführung) *for their father. When Johann Georg Bauknecht died in 1838, his son Michael got 375 fl. worth of land, but there was no house to inherit.*[74]

*The descent of the Weiler house is depicted in Figure 11.7.*

Let us examine the strategy of the Weiler children. After their mother's death, they stayed together with their father for five years, except for one son who was already married and endowed. One daughter had been married, endowed, divorced, and was back home. The oldest child, Maria Catharina, already 40, never married, and died in 1859 at the age of 67. She was one of

[68] *Gericht*, vol. 7, f. 81 (10.3.1809).

[69] *Gericht*, vol. 7, f. 119 (10.2.1810); (26.2.1810). There is a series of volumes recording all sales of land and buildings (*Kaufbücher*) beginning in 1653, altogether 19 volumes through 1870. The sales from this transaction were recorded in vol. 9 (17.3.1810).

[70] *Vogtruggericht*, vol. 2, f. 109 (7.11.1823).

[71] *Gericht*, vol. 9, f. 161 (1.12.1820).

[72] *Inventuren und Teilungen*, 1587 (19.4.1830); 1592 (6.9.1830).

[73] *Inventuren und Teilungen*, 1701 (29.1.1836).

[74] *Inventuren und Teilungen*, 1750 (27.2.1838).

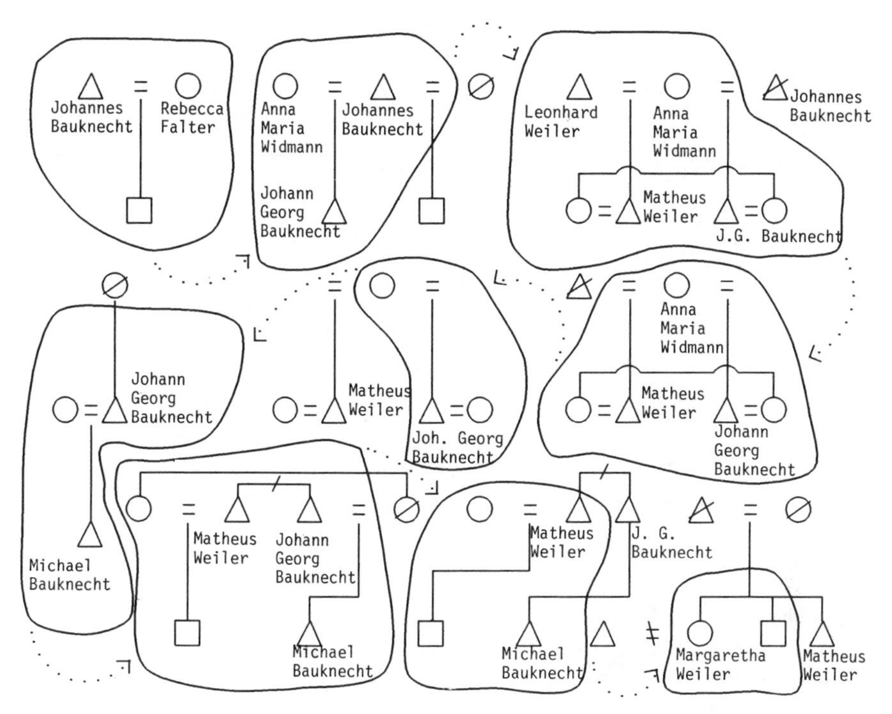


Figure 11.7

the growing number of women in Neckarhausen in the nineteenth century who either married very late or lived out their lives as single women. At the time of the petition to stay together with the father, the youngest son was 18 and too young to take over a farm. The children provided a work force for the father, but they expected remuneration. When he died five years later, there were outstanding wages due to Maria Catherina for leading the household. The children, with Rosina back from service, now intended to stay together, yet each received a separate share of land. The implements were divided between the two sons, one still at home and the other long married and living separately. About five years later, Rosina and Michael married and Margaretha married again. The five-year period after Mathes' death when they lived "in common" did not mean that they farmed a single family enterprise. Each had separate resources, and not even the tools were held in common.

The agricultural implements were, of course, absolutely necessary for the economy of each separate enterprise. Even before the mother died, half of them had gone to young Matheus. Presumably father and son had to pool the tools to work the land. After the father's death, the set was divided between the two brothers, and again pooling was necessary. In 1821, when young Matheus married, he did not have any agricultural implements. However, by 1830, when

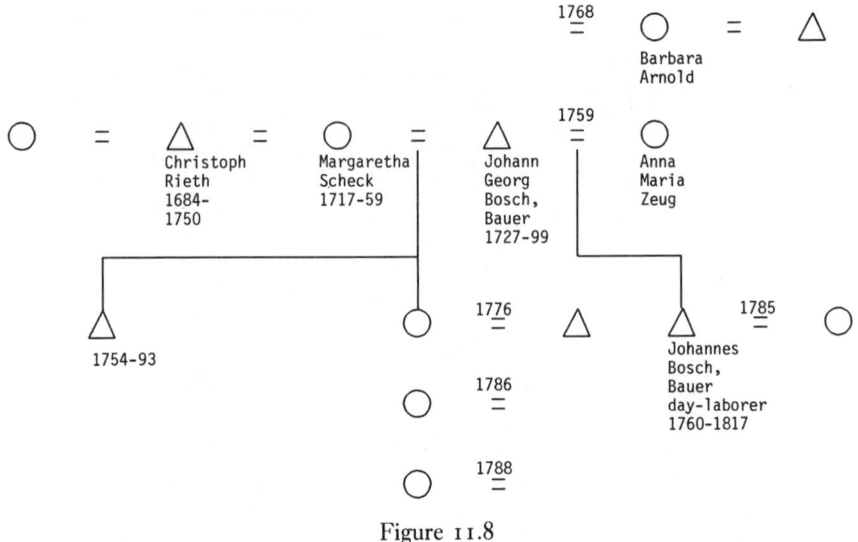


Figure 11.8

old Mathes's wife died, he had half a set, which argues for a partition in the intervening period. Mathes had a half wagon, half cart, half plow, half harrow, a yoke, a wooden sled, and a pair of oxen. The fact that the two families could not carry out their production without cooperation gives an insight into one of the chief ways that adult kin were tied to each other. They each needed the other half of the tool kit. In fact, during the early years of his marriage, young Mathes had no implements at all to work his land. They had neither production nor consumption in common: They each had separate rights to land, but they had to pool the capital equipment. It was furthermore unlikely that young Mathes had a pair of oxen like his father. He would have had to borrow them or hire them with cash or labor services. Later on, his father could not plow without a whole plow or with only half a harrow. From this evidence, however, it is unclear exactly how they cooperated. We do not know whether the plow, wagon, cart, and harrow were divided ideally or whether each of the parties had parts which had to be fitted together to make up a single piece. We will have to come back to the evidence on these practices in Chapter 12.

This family history reveals that rights were jealously guarded by separate households. Space and tools might have been used jointly, but that had to do with capital formation, wealth, and available labor. Sons and daughters expected to be rewarded for their labor through wages when their parents were young and through land when they were older. In fact, by providing children with a few strips of land, parents ensured their dependence because they would not have the necessary equipment to work it. In some instances, parents and children or siblings could own a set of tools together. In the case of the Weiler family, the two boys eventually shared the equipment and plowed their sisters' land in return for services, but the women sued their brothers in court for not doing a careful job.[75] The Schultheiss exclaimed no family fought with each other as much as the Weilers or caused him more trouble.

## Example 5

*In 1792, the Richter Christoph Hentzler complained that as young Johannes Bosch was carrying manure to his own father's meadow, he rode over Hentzler's meadow and caused some damage.[76] In this instance the younger man was laboring for his father. Young Johannes was 32 and married; his father was 65. (Family relatives are shown in Figure 11.8.) During that year, Johann Georg Bosch had let the maternal inheritance of his children pass on to them.[77] In the previous year, he had appeared before the village court to petition for building wood so that his son could build a house in the garden.[78] By the end of the same year, Johannes had completed the house, and it was entered into the tax rolls.[79]*

In this example, the son built a house six years after he was married. Neither he nor his wife had brought a house or a part of one into the marriage.[80] They had tried to purchase a suitable one in 1788, but it was redeemed by a relative of the seller.[81] Perhaps they lived in his parents' house until they were able to build on the latter's property. In any event, it is clear that there were two households with separate resources. In the 1792 incident, Johannes carried manure to his father's field, perhaps for a wage or in exchange for some service. Only three years later at the property transmission (*Güterübergabe*) of the old man did Johannes become obligated to work for his father. In return for getting land, the son and son-in-law agreed to cultivate the father's reserved portion for free.[82] As far as Johannes was concerned, even after the father transferred much of the property in 1795 to his son and son-in-law, their resources were considered separate.

*In 1798, when old Johann Georg was 71, Johannes, then 38, sold some wine to the Brückenwirt, whose establishment was just outside Nürtingen on the road to Neckarhausen.[83] The tavernkeeper deducted 4 fl. owed by Johann Georg from the price, but Johannes told him to approach his father for it. An altercation ensued in which Johannes was thrown out. Later, back in the village, his father struck him for being drunk.*

This short family history is once again about property rights. Father and son did not pool their property nor did they have a single account. Yet they lived

[75] *Schultheißenamt*, vol. 1, f. 46, (12.8.1841).
[76] *Gericht*, vol. 4, f. 188 (20.2.1792).
[77] *Inventuren und Teilungen*, 1193 (17.1.1795).
[78] *Gericht*, vol. 4, f. 158 (2.4.1791).
[79] *Gericht*, vol. 4, f. 169 (18.6.1791).
[80] *Inventuren und Teilungen*, 1096 (17.2.1786).
[81] Nürtingen *Stadtgericht*, vol. 29, f. 110 (8.12.1788).
[82] *Inventuren und Teilungen*, 1193 (17.1.1795).
[83] *Gericht*, vol. 5, f. 122 (17.12.1798).

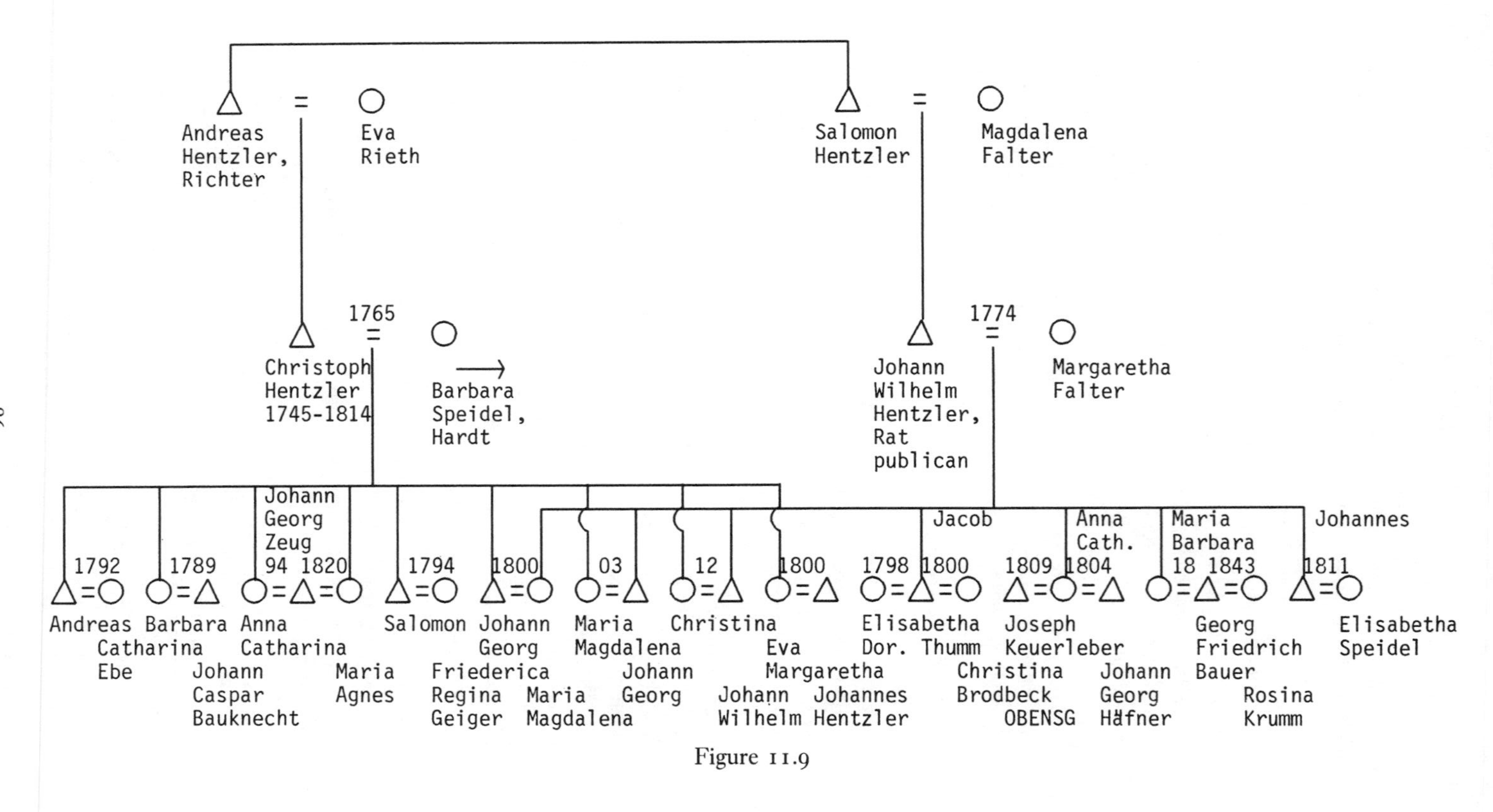

Andreas Hentzler, Richter
Eva Rieth
Salomon Hentzler
Magdalena Falter
1765
Christoph Hentzler 1745-1814
Barbara Speidel, Hardt
1774
Johann Wilhelm Hentzler, Rat publican
Margaretha Falter
Johann Georg Zeug
Jacob
Anna Cath.
Maria Barbara
Johannes
1792
1789
94 1820
1794
1800
03
12
1800
1798
1800
1809
1804
18 1843
1811
Andreas Catharina Ebe
Barbara Johann Caspar Bauknecht
Anna Catharina
Maria Agnes
Salomon Friederica Regina Geiger
Johann Georg Maria Magdalena
Maria Magdalena Johann Georg
Christina Johann Wilhelm
Eva Margaretha Johannes Hentzler
Elisabetha Dor. Thumm
Christina Brodbeck
Joseph Keuerleber OBENSG
Johann Georg Häfner
Georg Friedrich Bauer
Rosina Krumm
Elisabetha Speidel


Figure 11.9

cheek-by-jowl, with Johannes setting up house in the garden. He also was available to work for his father, and even into his old age, the latter exercised authority over the son, castigating the 38-year-old for drunkenness. Such a thing would have been unthinkable in an impartible inheritance region where the father would have relinquished all authority at retirement. From the outside, however, they were so closely identified that the one could be seen as responsible for the debts of the other – especially the small obligations such as pub bills and the like. There are frequent indications in the sources that fathers and sons settled debts for each other from time to time – sometimes brothers did the same. Since in incurring a debt there is an element of trust, those people most closely associated with each other, whose obligations were most intertwined, often covered for each other. In a parallel fashion, fathers could sign documents for absent sons, sons for fathers, and brothers for brothers.[84] Despite the rough-and-ready exchange system, there was no legal claim on a third party for a debt, and it was not necessary, as Johannes pointed out, for a son to meet an obligation of his father. They were not running a single account.

## Example 6

*Only a small part of a very complex family history (Figure 11.9) is of interest for our problem here. We will start with a dispute in 1812 between Christoph Hentzler, 67, and his married son Salomon, 36, when they came to the village court to settle their debts.[85] Salomon produced a list beginning in 1800. In Stuttgart, he had lent Christoph 8 fl. 16 kr. for wedding clothes for his sister, Eva Margaretha. Three years later, he again lent his father cash for another daughter's wedding (Maria Magdalena), this time 15 fl. He had paid a 5 fl. tax bill for his father. In 1803, he lent him 69 fl., from which nine years of interest amounting to 31 fl. 3 kr. had accrued. In 1805, he had lent him 22 fl. 11 kr. in Esslingen and the same year had paid a bill at the smithy for 2 fl. There were various other sums for smith work, leather goods from the saddler, wine during an illness (6 fl.), and wood. Including interest on some of the loans, the total was 181 fl. 20 kr. In turn, the father claimed 8 fl. for a debt he paid to a baker in Nürtingen. There was also 7 fl. for two sheep, 16 fl. for wine, and other sums for piglets and more wine. He had made rent payments and settled debts for his son. He also claimed wages for carting manure and plowing the son's fields – further evidence that the younger generation often did not have a set of tools. Altogether the son owed 145 fl. 50 kr.*

In this case, we find a father and son settling debts for each other in the various market towns and cities of the region. They were identified closely enough for people to claim a payment from either of them. Other evidence suggests that villagers did not have ready cash available at all times. People

[84] Based on a reading of the *Kaufbücher*, see n. 69.
[85] *Gericht*, vol. 8, f. 48 (9.10.1812).

frequently ran up bills at the pub or had outstanding bills at the apothecary, the grocer, or the agricultural supply merchant in Nürtingen. Practically the only people who had money in the bank were servant girls. It appears that whenever a farmer cashed in on a pig or sold a bag of grain, he settled an outstanding debt of his own or lent the money to someone else with cash-flow problems – the money moving from hand to hand settling a chain of debts. In this instance, we see that one member of a family who had money when the other needed it passed it along. Each kept separate books and did not regard the accounts as making up one pool. Not even work for one another was free. Family and neighbors might well have helped each other out continually, but they at least kept a rough balance in their heads. But perhaps Salomon was absent from the village for long stretches of time – or he did not have the necessary equipment to farm his own land. In any event, his father charged him for carting and plowing.

Salomon was one of nine children, many of whom were involved in one way or another with their father's agriculture. In 1801, Johann Georg, 24, married for one year, was walking along with his father to one of his father's plots when they discovered two women stealing grass.[86] The fact that Johann Georg chased them with a hoe suggests that the two men were going to carry on some agricultural work together on the father's land. Another example in the family history of an adult son working for his father comes from 1849. Georg Friedrich Bauer, who married the daughter of Wilhelm Hentzler and eventually succeeded him on the council, was absent for a period from the village. His son Ludwig Friedrich, a carpenter living in the neighboring village of Oberensingen brought a load of manure to his father's plot one day and was busy manuring another the next.[87] These examples of cooperation in work do not mean a lack of careful delineation of rights. In 1808, for example, Christoph and his children were in conflict over the boundaries of a plot of land, and since they could not agree took each other to court.[88] Even there they would not accept arbitration, so the court sent the officials concerned with such matters (*Untergang*) to make a judgment. Similar issues occurred frequently with houses and buildings.

*In 1805, Salomon Hentzler was in conflict with his father-in-law and brother-in-law, Alt Friedrich and Johannes Geiger, over space allocation in the house they all lived in.*[89] *Since the house was supposed to be apportioned by equal halves to the two brothers-in-law, the court measured it, divided it exactly in half, and had the disputants draw lots.*

*Christoph Hentzler had nine children who eventually married and lived in Neckarhausen. Young Salomon was actually raised and endowed by Christoph's childless*

[86] *Gericht*, vol. 5, f. 165 (9.6.1801).
[87] *Schultheißenamt*, vol. 2, f. 195 (13.6.1849).
[88] *Vogtruggericht*, vol. 2, f. 28 (17.2.1808).
[89] *Gericht*, vol. 6, f. 63 (21.1.1805).

*elder brother, Salomon, the Schultheiss.*[90] *Three of the children married children of Christoph's first cousin, Johann Wilhelm Hentzler, who himself had seven children. Altogether, counting remarriages, there were 16 couples in the generation following the two first cousins. In 11 instances, the neogami did not have a house or portion of one as part of a marriage settlement, which meant that they had to rent space from their parents or other villagers.*

*Before his death, Christoph sold half of his house (1814) to his son-in-law, Wilhelm.*[91] *The other half belonged to his daughter Maria Agnes, who married her dead sister's husband, Johann Georg Zeug, at 36 in 1820.*[92] *Since Zeug already had a house, she sold her half to Wilhelm, who held the whole house until his death in 1835.*[93] *A few years after that, the house was divided between Johann Georg Hentzler, Christoph's son, and Johann Georg Hentzler, Wilhelm's son.*[94]

Allocation of living space became a serious problem in the early decades of the nineteenth century. Despite the fact that the children of Christoph and Johann Wilhelm Hentzler intermarried so frequently and two sisters married the same husband, all counteracting in effect the fissioning of property which the large size of these two families had brought about, most of the children had no space of their own. Houses were constantly chopped up, reconfigured, traded, and sold, and the cramped quarters led to a good many squabbles.

*Johann Georg Hentzler – Wilhelm's son – soon after his marriage was living in a house with an unrelated family.*[95] *By 1825, living in the same house with him as his renter was his sister-in-law, Eva Margaretha, daughter of Christoph, and her husband, Johannes Hentzler, called Raidwanger.*[96] *Johannes and Johann Georg's wife got into a squabble about keeping animals secure in the stall. Nineteen years later, in 1844, when they were still coresidents, Johann Georg accused Johannes of stealing a rag from the common kitchen.*[97]

*Christoph Hentzler's son-in-law (who married two of his daughters), Johann Georg Zeug, during the early years of his first marriage rented space from the unrelated Heinrich Pfautler and was in constant dispute with him.*[98] *Sometime after 1800, he bought half a house; the other half belonged to Johann Falter, also unrelated.*[99] *The house had originally been split a century earlier (1711). In the current dispute, it was decided that Johannes Falter would hold the back stall and that Zeug would have the right to carry manure through it two times a week.*

*A daughter of Christoph Hentzler married Johann Caspar Bauknecht in 1789. Caspar brought a house in the Brückengasse into the marriage.*[100] *Three years after*

[90] *Inventuren und Teilungen*, 1191 (67.1.1795).
[91] *Inventuren und Teilungen*, 1388 (23.2.1814).
[92] *Inventuren und Teilungen*, 1470 (13.1.1822).
[93] *Inventuren und Teilungen*, 1672 (18.3.1835).
[94] *Inventuren und Teilungen*, 1818 (–.5.1841).
[95] *Gericht*, vol. 11, f. 132 (7.2.1829).
[96] *Gericht*, vol. 10, f. 196 (18.8.1825).
[97] *Schultheißenamt*, vol. 2, f. 46 (22.4.1844).
[98] *Gericht*, vol. 5, f. 102 (27.6.1798); f. 107 (17.7.1798); f. 146 (28.12.1799); f. 156 (29.12.1800).
[99] *Gericht*, vol. 5, f. 181 (4.7.1802).
[100] *Inventuren und Teilungen*, 1139 (22.1.1790).

*they were married, her brother-in-law Johannes accused her of stealing yarn from a trunk.*[101] *Apparently he lived with them in the same house. The same year Barbara complained about the renters. Ludwig Federschmid's wife had accused her of stealing firewood, kohlrabi, and a goose. Barbara in turn accused her of stealing from the kitchen and stall, offering her maid as a witness.*[102] *Thus in the house lived the Bauknechts, his unmarried brother, a maid, and the Federschmids. There was a great deal of access to common space – kitchen, stall, trunk – but all the objects were accorded to specific people.*

These three vignettes exhibit various villagers, some related to each other and some not, sharing living space but jealously guarding separate rights to various objects – a kitchen rag, some firewood, yarn, and vegetables. A stall space while shared could be subject to overlapping use and multiple rights. The space that Johannes Falter owned in his stall could be sold, given, rented, or lent like any other piece of immovable property. Furthermore, it was his to use for his animals and so forth as he saw fit. Nonetheless, Johann Georg Zeug's right of way was also a property right. He was just as free to alienate his stall and with it his right of way.

*When Johann Georg Hentzler, Christoph's son, died in 1841 leaving eight children, he left a problem for the family to clean up.*[103] *He had gone bankrupt in 1826 and because of his poor health would have been unable to support himself without his children's help. The oldest, Gottlob, went to work in one of the baths in Cannstatt and through "thrift and hard work" accumulated enough money to send to his father to buy half a house and a few strips of land. Johann Georg was supposed to have purchased the property in his son's name but failed to do so. When he died, Gottlob and the other two elder sons were faced with the loss of everything they had saved. However, under pressure from the local court, the creditors in the earlier bankruptcy gave up their claims, and the house and land fell to Gottlob. He and the other two older children agreed to support their widowed mother with a specified amount of grain, money, and lard each year. She also received lifelong rights to live in the house.*

The fact that Gottlob had sent money home to his father argues for close ties but not for parents and children as part of a single enterprise. The son had treated his earnings as an investment and had trusted the father to keep the ownership rights straight. By sending back the money to the village, he had attempted to fulfill two purposes, the honorable support of his parents and the investment in property in preparation for his return. In the final contract with their mother, the three sons provided the produce for her separate household in return for the village defense of their property.

The involved dealings of the Hentzler family exhibit typical behavior of Bauern at the turn of the century. While the two first cousins of the senior generation were substantial landholders and each had held office or were

[101] *Gericht*, vol. 4, f. 203 (3.7.1792).
[102] *Gericht*, vol. 4, f. 212 (26.11.1792).
[103] *Gericht*, vol. 4, f. 212 (26.11.1792).

siblings of those who did, the facts of partible inheritance and the economic difficulties of the post war period pushed the next generation into the artisan stratum. And they frequently had to find support for themselves outside the village however much they retained roots there. Each decade brought greater pressure on the available living space and considerable conflict over its use. None of these families – which were continually allied with each other through marriage, godparentage, pledging, and guardianship – ever pooled their resources to create larger economic units. On the one hand, exchanges of labor and land were paid for, but on the other closely related people had claims on each other for work opportunities and a kinship (*Freundschafts-*) price for real estate. The reason relatives fought with each other is that they lived with each other.

## Example 7

*Michael Hentzler, 69, tavernkeeper, pointed out to the Schultheiss that after the estate division of his late wife, Maria Catharina Kraussharr, what fell to his daughter Eva Barbara could have remained in his usufruct for his lifetime.*[104] *However, for her sake, he had divided the estate into two parts, letting 9/11 go to her in full ownership, keeping 2/11 for himself to use. However, the condition of this transaction was that his son-in-law, Georg Waldner, was to take care of his land and to cart wine twice in the fall. During the ensuing nine years, Waldner had often been contrary, especially since Hentzler's daughter died. He either failed to do the work or sent Hentzler away with abuse. Since the contract had been broken, Michael wanted his property returned. After Waldner promised to do better, Hentzler took back his complaint. Several years later, they were still squabbling.*[105] *Michael complained that Waldner was not doing the carting he was supposed to. When Hentzler (now 72) remonstrated, Waldner (48) threatened to throw a fork full of manure on him if he did not go indoors.*

*Michael Hentzler (1775–1864) was a substantial Bauer and, from 1834, tavern-keeper in the village. Shortly after his first marriage in 1789 (Figure 11.10), he joined the Rat and in 1813 became a member of the Gericht.*[106] *At the revised constitution forming an eight-member Gemeinderat as the higher organ, with lifelong membership for those elected to a second term, and a nine-member Bürgerausschuss with two-year terms of office, Hentzler resigned, declining a position on the new Gemeinderat. Thereafter in 1822, 1826, and 1830, he was elected to terms on the Bürgerausschuss.*[107]

*At the death of his first wife in 1834, the couple had a very considerable estate worth 5,135 fl., and Hentzler after letting much of his wife's estate go to his daughter ended up with 3,230 fl.*[108] *He also shifted the focus of his labor to his new tavern.*[109]

104 *Schultheißenamt*, vol. 2, f. 60 (12.10.1844).
105 *Schultheißenamt*, vol. 2, f. 138 (11.2.1847).
106 *Vogtruggericht*, vol. 2, f. 54 (30.9.1813).
107 *Gericht*, vol. 9, f. 88 (3.6.1819); vol 10, f. 61 (20.7.1822); vol. 11, f. 20 (9.8.1826); f. 188 (5.7.1830).
108 *Inventuren und Teilungen*, 1675 (19.3.1835).
109 *Oberamtsgericht*, STAL, F190II, 268, f. 39.

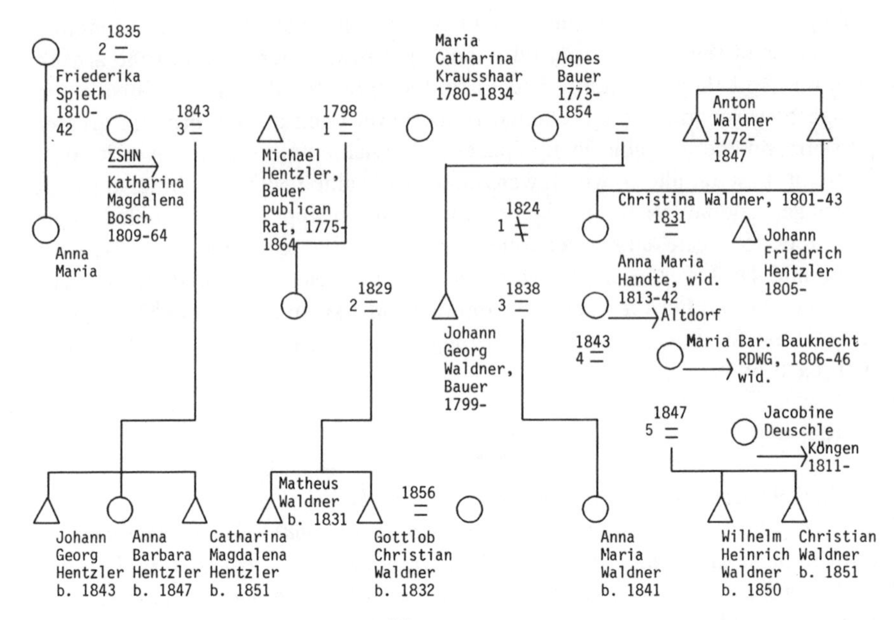


Figure 11.10

*Just before his second marriage in 1835, he gave his daughter and son-in-law another 400 fl.*[110] *He had begun his first marriage as a fairly well off but undistinguished farmer. By 1805, he and his wife were in the third quartile of tax payers.*[111] *Twenty years later, he was the fifth highest taxpayer out of 194 (top 3 percent), and in 1830 was the tenth from 253 (top 4 percent). With the settlement of most of his wife's estate on his daughter, he dropped to position 21 in 1835 (top 8 percent) and stayed there throughout his second marriage.*[112] *By 1849, when he was 74 and in his third marriage – he brought 3,022 fl., while his wife brought only 55 fl.*[113] *– he had improved his position to eighteenth from 298 (top 6 percent). Thereafter his holdings declined as he helped provide marriage portions and made gifts to his children and grandchildren. He ended up in the upper half of the third quartile of taxpayers (1859). The total value of his estate when he and his third wife died within a few days of each other in 1864 was 3,384 fl.*[114]

Hentzler clearly was a very capable manager. He and his first wife accumulated a substantial holding during the early decades of the century, when many other villagers were driven into bankruptcy. During his 60s, with the death of two wives, he maintained a considerable position in the village, turning

[110] *Inventuren und Teilungen*, 1694 (24.9.1835).
[111] The figures for position in the tax registers are taken from the *Steueraufnahm- und Abrechnungsbücher* in the *Gemeindepflegerechnungen*.
[112] *Inventuren und Teilungen*, 1675 (9.3.1835); 1694 (24.9.1835).
[113] *Inventuren und Teilungen*, 1864 (31.3.1843).
[114] *Inventuren und Teilungen*, 3193 (13.2.1864).

his attention to tavernkeeping. At the age of 68, he married for a third time – a 34-year-old woman – and fathered four more children, three of whom survived him. When he died at 89, he was still a substantial landholder.

*Hentzler's son-in-law, Johann Georg Waldner, Bauer, was first married to his first cousin, Christine Waldner, in 1824. At the time of their marriage, her parents were dead, and they lived with her uncle and aunt, his parents. Soon after they married, she complained to the consistory that Johann Georg was going through her property.*[115] *When she asked about what was going on, he would hit her. She had left because of his abuse, and his parents refused to take her back. He alleged that she was truculent* (widerwärtig) *and hostile* (feindselig) *and continually scolded, and he denied that he was failing to manage her property well and settling her debts.*[116] *Part of the situation, as we shall see, is explained in their marriage inventory, which Johann Georg's father, Anton, wanted to delay until such time as he could pass on land free of encumberance.*[117] *Christine requested security for her movable property and assets, but her husband did not yet have any land to secure anything with. By 1827, the couple had been divorced, and they divided up their small estate of 353 fl., encumbered by 160 fl. worth of debts.*[118] *He assumed all of the debts and an equal amount of property, while she took 191 fl. worth debt-free.*

*When Waldner married Michael Hentzler's daughter, Eva Barbara, in 1829, he brought property worth 289 fl., and she, worth 575 fl.*[119] *Between the marriage and the death of Eva Barbara's mother in 1835, Michael Hentzler sold the young couple half of his house for a substantial 1000 fl.*[120] *By the time she died in 1838, the Waldner estate was worth 2,626 fl., 94 percent of the land having been brought in by the wife.*[121] *Waldner married his third wife in 1838, the two of them putting together 3,004 fl.*[122] *At his fourth marriage in 1843, he and Maria Barbara Bauknecht combined 4,928 fl.*[123] *Finally, at his fifth marriage in 1847, the couple combined 3,408 fl.*[124] *We can chronicle his rise by looking at the amount he brought to each marriage:*

| *1* | *2* | *3* | *4* | *5* |
|---|---|---|---|---|
| *1824* | *1829* | *1838* | *1843* | *1847* |
| *Christine Waldner* | *Eva Barbara Hentzler* | *Anna Maria Handte* | *Maria Barbara Bauknecht* | *Jacobine Deuschle* |
| *0* | *289 fl.* | *1,301 fl.* | *3,514 fl.* | *2,734 fl.* |

Waldner's big break came with his marriage to Eva Barbara Hentzler. Not only did Michael let a substantial portion of his daughter's maternal inherit-

115 *Kirchenkonvent*, vol. 4, (27.6.1825).
116 See also *Gericht*, vol. 10, f. 192 (2.8.1825), where she secretly stole his bed.
117 *Inventuren und Teilungen*, 1505 (18.8.1825).
118 *Inventuren und Teilungen*, 1541 (27.11.1827).
119 *Inventuren und Teilungen*, 1570 (20.3.1829).
120 *Inventuren und Teilungen*, 1675 (19.3.1835); 1694 (24.9.1835).
121 *Inventuren und Teilungen*, 1756 (19.5.1838).
122 *Inventuren und Teilungen*, 1767 (26.2.1839).
123 *Inventuren und Teilungen*, 1843 (2.4.1842); 1855 (26.1.1843).
124 *Inventuren und Teilungen*, 1951 (22.10.1846); 1861 (25.5.1847).

ance fall to them, but he also forgave much of the purchase price of the half house and gave them a horse worth 200 fl. and all the instruments of cultivation.[125] When Eva Barbara died, Waldner not only inherited a considerable property but had even more in usufruct, the maternal inheritance of his children. In 1825, a year after his first marriage, Johann Georg was in the lowest quartile of taxpayers. By 1830, married to Eva Barbara Hentzler, he was already in the third quartile. From 1835 to 1859, he went from being the 24th highest taxpayer to the 15th, and in the 1865 and 1870 tax records was respectively in eighth and seventh place. Another way of putting it is to say that in his 20s he was among the lowest 15 percent of taxpayers. By his mid 30s, he was in the top 9 percent. From then through his 50s, he hovered around the top 6 percent. In his 60s, he rose to the top 3 percent and then 2 percent of taxpayers. During the 1830s and 40s, Waldner was elected consistently to serve on the Bürgerausschuss. We should note that his father, Anton, through the 1830s had consistently been in the top quartile of taxpayers, even though he did not contribute substantially to Johann Georg's property accumulation. The Waldners and the Hentzlers were in the same league of substantial property holders and peasant producers.

Let us now look at the relationships Johann Georg found himself in. In his first marriage, he and his wife lived in his parents' home. While the property settlement was delayed, he probably worked for them. The relations at home were intimate, and it is not clear whether the young couple had their own economy, although Johann Georg was managing his wife's property, which consisted largely of loans that had been set up after her parents died. She apparently suspected her uncle and husband of using her property to free their own of debt, and she quickly backed out of the marriage. Even then, young Johann Georg was trying to establish his own independence, insisting on an inventory despite his father's attempts at delay. Shortly after he married Eva Barbara Hentzler, he apparently moved into her father's house, half of which they purchased in 1834. In that year, when Michael was 59 and Johann Georg, 35, the older man set up the deal whereby the younger carried on the agriculture for both families while he turned to his tavern. Waldner got extra land, the horse, and all of the agricultural equipment.

In 1845, seven years after the death of Eva Barbara Hentzler, Waldner complained about the use of the house.[126] He said that he had been living with Michael Hentzler "in Gemeinschaft" for 10 years (at that point Johann Georg was married to his fourth wife and Michael to his third). Waldner had purchased the half house on the condition that apart from the front sitting room, the rest of the house and barn would be possessed in common, unpartitioned (*unverlost*). He noted that at the time of the sale, his father-in-law had had more land than he, but now the situation was reversed, and Waldner wanted

[125] *Inventuren und Teilungen*, 1694 (24.9.1835).
[126] *Schultheißenamt*, vol. 2, f. 83 (29.9.1845).

the entire house divided up, especially the cellar, so that his potatoes could be locked up. After consulting the sale records, the authorities discovered that except for the sitting room, the rest of the house was supposed to have been divided up. Either owner had the right to ask for a partition and division by lot. In this situation, we see that for ten years there had been no effective subdivision of the buildings. Waldner had worked his father-in-law's land, while Hentzler had set up a pub in the front room. Wives had come and gone, and each husband had produced children. Michael Hentzler himself had married a woman who had had four illegitimate children (Friderika Spieth) and adopted the two who were still living.[127] His last wife also brought an illegitimate child – the survivor of 5 – to the marriage in 1843. The tensions which existed between old Hentzler and Waldner were especially acute during the early 1840s after Eva Barbara died and Michael Hentzler married for the third time at 68 and began producing more children. Once the house was partitioned, tensions between them seem to have attenuated, and when Michael died in 1864, Waldner paid for his funeral costs.[128]

As far as the issue of using the house was concerned, we have an example here of two very substantial landholders, one of them very old, who probably lived 20 years longer than anyone expected. When Johann Georg took on the contract essentially to do all the agricultural labor for both families, there was no great necessity to divide up space, since he was the one who needed the agricultural storage and stall areas. Only when he accumulated enough land to become an independent producer did he force a partition. He was especially keen to keep his father-in-law and the latter's wife out of the produce storage areas.

A final few comments can be said about Michael Hentzler. During the 1820s, conflicts had broken out between him and his first wife.[129] She claimed that Michael would not eat or talk with her and that he had even beaten her with a whip. Apparently, he had accused her of having an affair with the temporary Schultheiss Brodbeck and then gave her the silent treatment for four years.[130] She complained of his drinking, and she had had to run away several times.[131] By 1828, the consistory minutes refer to him as "godless."[132] But during all this time, he was building up the property and serving on the Bürgerausschuss, which meant that he had considerable respect from his fellow villagers in order to get the necessary votes. When he applied for Bürgerrecht for his prospective bride in 1843, his petition was denied.[133] He was 68, and she had had five illegitimate children and was pregnant (with his child) again. The court referred to debts that had accumulated in his previous marriage and a term in the work-

127 *Inventuren und Teilungen*, 1843 (2.4.1842).
128 *Inventuren und Teilungen*, 3193 (13.2.1864).
129 *Oberamtsgericht*, STAL, F190II, 259, f. 325.
130 *Gericht*, vol. 10, f. 48 (16.4.1822).
131 *Kirchenkonvent*, vol. 4, (8.3.1823).
132 *Kirchenkonvent*, vol. 4, (31.10.1828).
133 *Gericht*, vol. 13, f. 240 (16.1.1843).

house. He had always been in conflict with his two previous wives and with his daughter and had gone to none of their funerals. He had therefore come under universal contempt among the villagers. Despite their opposition, Michael was soon married, and his wife became a Bürger. There was no way that a villager of his wealth could be denied the right to marry whomever he liked. In 1850, he composed a testament to restrict his adopted daughter, the illegitimate child of his second wife, because of her behavior.[134] Six years later he wrote a new will, this time wanting to restrict the children of Eva Barbara, who used insulting speech (*beleidigenden Reden*) despite the fact that their mother had received a considerable property from him. Apart from obligatory portions, all the rest was to go to the children of his third and final marriage. However, his wife was not to profit in any way, including gaining the usufruct of the property, since she had shown insufficient marital fidelity (*Treue*) by not being thrifty and hard-working enough.

Michael Hentzler's grandchildren's behavior was so galling to him because he had been the conduit of their wealth, and he had expected the rules of reciprocity to be tacitly understood. As so often, there was here no sense of the parent as trustee of family property but as the source of wealth. When he was in conflict earlier with Waldner, Michael pointed out that he had passed on property as an act of free will. In this later situation, he was making the same point. The reciprocity built into the transmission of property was also very much a part of the ideology of the magistrates.[135] On several occasions, young married men were enjoined to have respect for their parents because they had been the source of their property.

## Example 8

*This case deals with Christoph Deuschle, cooper, born in 1813 and married in 1838. His brother became one of the most substantial members of the village and served on the Gemeinderat, and their father had been a Richter. The year he was married, he received a license to brew beer and later on that year to serve it.[136] According to the court, he had an unblemished reputation, a solid property worth 1,600 fl., and a house and barn in common with his father-in-law, Johannes Kühfuss, one of the wealthiest men in the village. He and his wife lived separately, however, with their own rooms. Sixteen years later, Christoph's property had fallen in worth to 500 fl.[137] At the time, he received a license to deal in yeast, which he purchased in the Oberämter of Biberach, Riedlingen, Saulgau, and Tübingen and sold in Tübingen, Kirchheim, Esslingen, and Stuttgart. He noted that there was not enough work for him as a cooper in a village with no viniculture. By 1858, he had left Neckarhausen altogether for Ottendorf. Apparently some of the family went with him, since at least one daughter married there*

[134] *Inventuren und Teilungen*, 3193 (13.2.1864).
[135] *Gericht*, vol. 13, f. 73 (2.3.1840).
[136] *Gericht*, vol. 13, f. 26 (10.9.1838); *Oberamtsgericht*, HSAL, F190II, 272, (19.9.1838).
[137] *Gericht*, vol. 15, f. 321 (20.9.1854).

*and his wife bore him another child there in 1861.*[138] *On the other hand, his son Christoph, who was 10 in 1858, was still in the village in 1869 when he applied for papers to move to Gaildorf.*[139] *The court said that it could not give details about his wealth, since his father had left the village 11 years earlier.*

*Christoph Deuschle's economic decline seems to have been closely related to excessive drinking. Until he was 25 and married, he had had an "unblemished reputation." Three years later, his wife complained of beating and being thrown out of the house.*[140] *Christoph was rude and truculent to the Schultheiss and told him that if he wanted to see whether his wife was black and blue he could examine* (visitieren) *her ass. That incident set off a litany of complaints about him. His wife came back to the Schultheiss two years later, and there was a blowup between himself and his brother, Wilhelm, who refused to be a guarantor for him any longer.*[141] *The pastor summoned the consistory together to talk about the increasing drunkenness among the villagers, but since he only mentioned Deuschle and one of his brothers-in-law, they must have been very noticeable indeed. One of them publicly insulted the pastor and swore when he went by the parsonage.*[142] *Every so often the Schultheiss put Christoph in jail for a day or two.*[143] *His father- and a brother-in-law complained about his renewed drinking in 1844.*[144] *Apparently he had accused old Johannes Kühfuss of killing his cow, attacking his doves, and bringing him poison. Christoph had broken the lock on the wine cellar many times. He had also forced his way into the part of the house apportioned to his father-in-law – the latter's residence and sleeping rooms* (Aufenthalts- und Schlafzimmer) *– to confront him about some matter. In 1849, he drove his family out of the house in a drunken rage.*[145] *The same thing happened the next year.*[146]

*In 1857, the year before Deuschle left the village, the incident we want to dwell on occurred.*[147] *His son Wilhelm, 19, came home one evening from threshing for wages. His mother and siblings were sitting at the table eating supper, while his father sat behind the stove. The cat began acting up, so Wilhelm started to chase it out of the sitting room, whereupon his father came at him with a broomstick. The children held Christoph back but later he attacked his son again and threw him to the floor. Only help from a neighbor made it possible to get the father off. Wilhelm went to the Schultheiss to prevent further disturbance to the peace of the family. His mother came along with two of her daughters to complain that Christoph had been drunk the whole morning. He had begun the day driving out his own cows and those of the other people in the house, which she then had had to fetch back. He went out to his fields with his day-laborer but returned in an hour to sit behind the stove. He abused her and the*

138 Pfarramt Neckarhausen, *Familienregister*, vol. 2, f. 45.
139 *Gericht*, vol. 18, f. 257 (27.9.1869).
140 *Schultheißenamt*, vol. 1, f. 48 (17.8.1841).
141 *Schultheißenamt*, vol. 2, f. 24 (5.4.1843); f. 46 (9.4.1844).
142 *Schultheißenamt*, vol. 4, (20.4.1843).
143 E.g., *Schultheißenamt*, vol. 2, f. 48 (25.4.1844).
144 *Schultheißenamt*, vol. 2, f. 50 (1.6.1844).
145 *Schultheißenamt*, vol. 2, f. 187 (16.1.1849).
146 *Schultheißenamt*, vol. 2, f. 222 (18.4.1850).
147 *Schultheißenamt*, vol. 2, f. 274 (19.11.1857).

*children and criticized the midday meal in front of the laborer. After lunch, he drove her from the house and slammed the doors and scolded when she returned in the late afternoon to begin preparing the evening meal. He said she had whored with a Jew, a Belgian, and the Schultheiss, which got him 16 hours in the local jail. He excused his behavior with his drunkenness.*

Young Deuschle was working as a day-laborer at the same time as his father was hiring labor. In several other instances, we have seen that parents frequently hired their adult, married and unmarried sons for wages. In this instance, young Wilhelm, single, was involved with occasional labor outside the house. Since Christoph's hand was being hired by the day, it does not seem to have been difficult for him to have used his son. The fact that Wilhelm did not work for his father suggests that their accounts were to some degree already separate. Although still part of the consumption unit and probably paying for room and board, the son worked for himself just when his father needed extra labor. There was no sense of a single family enterprise with all family members contributing their labor to it. Although Christoph's drunkenness and bad management created special conditions, and there may not have been enough regular work to keep Wilhelm busy, nonetheless, the labor of unmarried, grown sons had for a long time not been available to their parents. The late teens and early twenties was a period for going into service, often outside the village. Many sons began to work for themselves well before they started to think about getting married. Sometimes marriage must have meant coming back home for the first time again after being away. For a while, children would then be integrated into their parents' households before receiving rights to particular strips of land and occasionally to parts of buildings. For a long period of transition after that, they were dependent on the older villagers for farm labor, occasional jobs, and handicraft employment, or they found sources of income outside the village itself. During the 1840s, 50s, and 60s, village men became increasingly involved in building and construction outside the village. Not until they reached their 40s or 50s would they attain the maximum extent of their resources.

Some of the issues which we have discovered in these stories are dealt with more systematically in Chapters 12 and 13. We have seen that, from well before marriage, parents and children often began protracted negotiations over property which continued until the parents died. Ownership, use rights, tools, and labor were the elements of complex reciprocities which structured the relationships between parents and their adult children. The senior generation maneuvered the situation through the control of property, and they had a strong sense of themselves not so much as the managers of a family estate as the source of wealth for their heirs. In all of the complex negotiations between generations, houses, barns, and fields were all detachable and subject to reassembly by each household. Land might well have descended through various lines, but there was no specific attachment of a patriline or extended family to any particular house or plot of land.

## *Example 8*

The group of people sharing a building or living in one of its apartments was constantly reformed, and individuals within them had alliances with other households, receiving goods, work, ritual aid, or political support. The permeability of groups, flexibility in the use of space, and the multiplicity of ties called for a careful delineation of rights and the maintenance of boundaries and the guarding of passageways. Family groups were nested in a kaleidoscopic field, constantly rearranged by second and third marriages, the consequent scrambling of age hierarchies, and the shifting of inheritance rights. Certain boundaries were established by commensality and common – but hierarchical – access to food stores. Others were set up by tool and equipment utilization and still others by cooking and heating facilities. The "family" circle in which an individual moved was continually reinscribed over the course of the day. The dynamics for each set of families were different from others, but all were tied to the logic of land holding. All the way through the period under study, subsistence was rooted in land even, and especially, for those with the smallest amounts of it. Children were never set up with enough resources to be independent, but the conditions for them changed considerably over time. At the beginning of the eighteenth century, the fact that even artisans had considerable amounts of land meant that the reproduction of farm and craft enterprises could follow a more or less smooth cycle. However, the increase in the population and social differentiation left many children facing continued poverty at the end of the century or continued dependence over a much longer period of time. The children of even the largest peasant holders were forced to spend a long period as handicraft producers and day-laborers. By the 1830s and 1840s, large numbers of young men were working outside the village during the agricultural and construction seasons. Their wives frequently minded the agricultural work at home. With older men accumulating more and more property, the village was populated by them and a large cohort of women for much of the year.

# 12

# Reciprocities in parent–child relations

I have cultivated a Morgen arable for my mother and sown one Morgen for her.

– Michael Hoyh[1]

The case histories in Chapter 4 indicate that tool distribution is as important for understanding social hierarchies and household interdependencies as land distribution. Other sources available to us suggest further complexities in family relationships. In this chapter, we examine marriage and postmortem inventories for clues about tool ownership and agricultural production, and about the exchange of labor for cash, which linked parents and children or senior and junior kin in two ways. The wealthy, established producers could offer work with a plow team and equipment, while the poorer, less well equipped could offer hand labor in return. We also discuss some of the ways handicraft production supplemented land for part of the life cycle before the junior generation emerged as full-time agricultural producers.

## Agricultural implements

We saw in Chapter 9 that young Johann Georg Bauknecht received no agricultural implements at his marriage and fought with his stepfather, Leonhard Weiler, over a piece of the plow. Mathes Weiler, sometime after his oldest son married, divided up the rights to the wagon, plow, harrow, and cart so that each of them owned "half." (Perhaps he had learned something from the earlier conflict between his father and half-brother.) When the old man died, his younger son, not yet married, took over the father's rights, each of the two brothers sharing the entire set of tools. When Michael Hentzler decided to pull out of cultivation altogether and devote himself to his pub, he gave the implements of cultivation and the horse to his son-in-law. All these incidents suggest that the land the younger generation received was unworkable without help from the older generation. More generally, cultivators with small amounts of land had to depend on larger landholders for plowing, harrowing, and

[1] See n. 37.

carting, either through the use of equipment – borrowed or rented – or through their actual work, paid for in money or in kind.

The various inventories provide some clues to the structuring of relationships around the ownership of tools. To gain further insight into these relationships, I selected five decades in the study period (1700–1709, 1740–9, 1780–9, 1820–9, 1860–9) and examined about 50 inventories in each.[2] These sources contain detailed lists of land and a complete inventory of household goods, including the *Fuhr- und Bauerngeschirr* (transportation and cultivation equipment). From this information, we can estimate the size of an enterprise which supported the capital equipment necessary to plow, harrow, and cart. Occasionally, we can see how the farming implements were passed on to the next generation. Not every farm had the animals necessary for traction. In a few inventories, there are outstanding wages to be found, further evidence about the interrelations of people with and without the proper equipment to work their land.

To simplify the reckoning of the relation between land and equipment, I have taken the strip as the unit of measure, adding up for each enterprise the total number of arable, meadow, flaxland, garden, and vineyard parcels. The size of strips of land are analyzed in Chapter 15.[3] In most cases involving marriage inventories, the first land to be given to young people was arable. Frequently, a child received one strip in each field plus a meadowland.

In the marriage inventories (see Table 12.1) only those couples who combined more than 30 strips of agricultural land consistently had a large equipment inventory, replete with wagons and carts, plows and harrows. Whereas such couples were frequently encountered in the first half of the eighteenth century, they were not found at all in the latter half of the century or in the next, which is to be expected considering the rise in the average age of land holding and the decline in the frequency of remarriage. By the mid-nineteenth century, almost all of the newly married couples had a small number of strips of land (none in the sample had more than 15). There was an increasing tendency for equipment to be held by smaller landholders. For example, there were 5 wagons in each of the samples III–V. In sample III, four wagons were held by people with 16–30 strips, but there were only 2 in sample IV. By the last sample, all of them were held by people with 15 or fewer strips. Plows exhibit a similar pattern of increasing concentration. The postmortem inventories demonstrate the same phenomenon. Until the mid-nineteenth century, none of the families holding 15 or fewer strips had a wagon, at which point well over half did so. What we are witnessing is a growing capitalization of agriculture

[2] The sample for each cohort either included all the relevant inventories, and covered roughly half marriage and half postmortem inventories, or went beyond the particular decade involved to get enough to make up at least 50, or was chosen randomly to get a roughly even distribution over the decade: cohort I (50 cases), 1694–1712; cohort II (53 cases), 1739–51; cohort III (53 cases), 1779–89; cohort IV (52 cases), 1818–29; cohort V (54 cases), 1859–69.

[3] An economic analysis based on the distribution of farm sizes will be offered in future publications.

which paralleled a decline in the size of farm holdings. The size of parcels of land also declined over the period, so that on average nineteenth-century farms with the same number of strips were smaller than eighteenth-century farms (see Chapter 15). What matters, of course, is output, and land was used far more intensively in the nineteenth century. Farms employed more labor and equipment per unit of land.

In the eighteenth century, the normal means of traction was the horse. With one exception, yokes do not show up until the 1780s (see Tables 12.1, 12.2). Thereafter, they slowly increased in frequency, and by the mid-nineteenth century at the latest they had become standard equipment. Teams of oxen were occasionally found in the eighteenth century but their incidence gradually increased in the nineteenth. By the mid-nineteenth century, the half-yoke was often listed in the inventories, an indication of the practice of hitching a single ox or cow to a cart. In Tables 12.1 and 12.2, I have listed all farms which had at least one fully grown cow, ox, or horse. Naturally, the larger enterprises were able to keep larger inventories of better-kept animals. For example, in the decade 1700–1709, only 30 percent of the newly married couples combining 15 strips or less had a horse. For couples in the next category, the rate rose to 50 percent, while all of the couples with more than 30 strips had at least one horse. A similar correlation is to be found in the postmortem inventories (see Table 12.2). This suggests that in general, since cows were not used for traction in the early period, the smaller enterprises depended on the larger to cultivate their land, carry manure to the fields, bring hay and grain stores to the barns, cart rocks from the fields, and take grain to the mill in Nürtingen. If, for example, we take the frequency of farms with horses from both tables in period I, we see that 22 families provided the traction power for 52 (themselves and 30 others). In the case of several of the smallest holders, however, the horse was noted as being old or decrepit. In addition, the smaller holders did not have the complex gear – collars, straps, saddles, harnesses, chains, and so forth – necessary to equip an animal. Only the largest farmers had horses, gear, carts, and plows to make up a fully equipped work unit. This means that the dependency ratio was far greater than 3:2 and may have been more on the order of 3:1 (plows, wagons) or 4:1 (harrows, carts).

The dependency seems to have been of two types: the poor on the rich, and the young on the old. Up to the 1820s, the families in the postmortem inventories having more than 15 strips averaged about 60 percent of the whole, while for the marriage inventories, they constituted about 36 percent. This reflects the fact that property was usually accumulated by a couple over time. But there is also an indication that, given the same amount of land, the older villagers had more equipment. Looking at all the families holding 16–30 strips in Table 12.1 and 12.2, we find that about 61 percent of the deceased or retiring farmers had at least one large piece of farming equipment, compared with 48 percent of the newlyweds. This latter figure would be less if remarriages were factored out. The fact that none of the smallerholders reflected in the postmortem inven-

Table 12.1 *Marriage inventories: frequency of farms with various items of agricultural equipment by number of parcels agricultural land*

| Equipment | I (1700–1709) | II (1740–9) | III (1780–9) | IV (1820–9) | V (1860–9) |
|---|---|---|---|---|---|
| *0–15 strips* | | | | | |
| Number of cases | 13 | 16 | 14 | 15 | 22 |
| Wagons | 1[a] | 1[b] | 1[c] | 3[d] | 5 |
| Carts | 0 | 1 | 2 | 2[d] | 0 |
| Plows | 1[a] | 1 | 1 | 2[d] | 5 |
| Harrows | 1[a] | 0 | 2 | 2[d] | 2 |
| Yokes | 0 | 0 | 0 | 0 | 5[e] |
| Horses | 4 | 0 | 1 | 2 | 0 |
| Oxen | 0 | 0 | 0 | 0 | 1 |
| Cows | 9 | 5 | 3 | 4 | 5 |
| *16–30 strips* | | | | | |
| Number of cases | 8 | 6 | 7 | 4 | 0 |
| Wagons | 3 | 1[f] | 4[g] | 2[a] | — |
| Carts | 3 | 0 | 5[h] | 2[a] | — |
| Plows | 2 | 2 | 3[h] | 2[a] | — |
| Harrows | 1 | 1 | 2[d] | 2[a] | — |
| Yokes | 0 | 0 | 0 | 0 | — |
| Horses | 4 | 3 | 4 | 1 | — |
| Oxen | 1 | 0 | 0 | 1 | — |
| Cows | 6 | 4 | 6 | 3 | — |
| *31+ strips* | | | | | |
| Number of cases | 5 | 3 | 0 | 0 | 0 |
| Wagons | 5 | 1 | — | — | — |
| Carts | 3 | 2 | — | — | — |
| Plows | 5 | 2 | — | — | — |
| Harrows | 4 | 1 | — | — | — |
| Yokes | 0 | 1 | — | — | — |
| Horses | 5 | 3 | — | — | — |
| Oxen | 1 | 0 | — | — | — |
| Cows | 5 | 3 | — | — | — |

[a] One had half the equipment.
[b] One had a front (*vordere*) wagon.
[c] Part of a wagon (*am Wagen*).
[d] Two had half of the equipment.
[e] Three half-yokes for use with a single animal.
[f] One had a front and a back (*hintere*) wagon.
[g] Two had half a front and a back wagon, one had half a wagon, and one had a rear wagon.
[h] Three had half the equipment.

Table 12.2 *Postmortem inventories: frequency of distribution of farms with various items of agricultural equipment by number of parcels*

| Equipment | I (1700–1709) | II (1740–9) | III (1780–9) | IV (1820–9) | V (1860–9) |
|---|---|---|---|---|---|
| *0–15 strips* | | | | | |
| Number of cases | 9 | 15 | 9 | 12 | 19 |
| Wagons | 0 | 0 | 0 | 0 | 11[a] |
| Carts | 0 | 0 | 0 | 0 | 5 |
| Plows | 0 | 0 | 0 | 0 | 6 |
| Harrows | 0 | 0 | 0 | 0 | 6 |
| Yokes | 0 | 0 | 0 | 0 | 4 |
| Horses | 0 | 0 | 0 | 0 | 0 |
| Oxen | 0 | 0 | 0 | 0 | 5 |
| Cows | 4 | 2 | 2 | 8 | 7 |
| *16–30 strips* | | | | | |
| Number of cases | 10 | 4 | 19 | 16 | 9 |
| Wagons | 2 | 2[b] | 3[c] | 8[d] | 8[d] |
| Carts | 4 | 3 | 11 | 7 | 4 |
| Plows | 3 | 4 | 12 | 10 | 7 |
| Harrows | 3 | 3 | 9[d] | 9 | 8 |
| Yokes | 0 | 0 | 2 | 4 | 7[e] |
| Horses | 5 | 3 | 8 | 3 | 0 |
| Oxen | 0 | 0 | 1 | 4 | 8 |
| Cows | 10 | 3 | 18 | 10 | 9 |
| *31+ strips* | | | | | |
| Number of cases | 5 | 7 | 6 | 4 | 0 |
| Wagons | 5[f] | 6[g] | 5 | 4 | — |
| Carts | 1 | 7 | 5 | 3 | — |
| Plows | 5 | 7 | 6[f] | 3 | — |
| Harrows | 2 | 6 | 6[f] | 3 | — |
| Yokes | 0 | 0 | 0 | 0 | — |
| Horses | 4 | 6 | 5 | 2 | — |
| Oxen | 0 | 1 | 0 | 0 | — |
| Cows | 4 | 6 | 4 | 2 | — |

*Note:* Includes premortem transfer (*Übergabe*) inventories.
[a] Three had front and rear wagons, one had half front and rear wagon.
[b] Two had front and rear wagons.
[c] One had front and rear wagon.
[d] One had half equipment.
[e] Three half-yokes for single animals.
[f] Two with half equipment.
[g] Four had front and rear wagons.

tories had any equipment up until well into the nineteenth century is perhaps to be explained by life cycle mechanisms. In the process of retiring, parents might give up more and more of their land over a period of years, and at some point the agricultural equipment as well. What we find at their deaths are the parcels of land they kept for themselves, probably worked by their children who now had the tools and horses. The evidence suggests that although newly married couples hived off bits of their parents' land, they remained dependent on them for the equipment and traction animals to work their land. As long as parents kept considerable amounts of land themselves, no matter how much the younger people acquired, they often retained ties to them through the instruments of labor. When parents retired, another major land transfer often took place, and apparently the tools were given up as well. At that point, the younger generation became responsible for cultivating their parents' remaining land and carrying out all of the accompanying carting services.

During the 1780s and 1820s, we find an increasing propensity to share equipment. Although a few postmortem inventories list shared equipment, the phenomenon appears to have been far more usual among newlyweds. We have seen at least one example in which a father and son each had half of the Bauerngeschirr, but such sharing was more common among brothers and brothers-in-law.[4] This is a crucial point, because it was unusual for any other kind of movable property to be shared – now and then a cow or a calf. Close relatives of the same generation developed a system of mutual interest in agricultural tools – there are no examples of such sharing in any of the trades (e.g., masonry, weaving, tailoring, or carpentry), except for one instance of a father and son sharing blacksmithing tools. Usually only one generation owned them at a time, while at a particular generational level, several people might share in them together.

Many postmortem inventories provide the details of inheritance of equipment, but this does not happen as frequently as one would wish, since tools were often disposed of before a parent died or retired. When one parent died, the other usually took all the tools. Here are the details from all the examples I have found in the 257 inventories in the sample, arranged chronologically by cohort.

*There are only a few examples of a woman bringing* Fuhr- und Bauerngeschirr *into a marriage, and almost all of these are second or third marriages.*[5] *In most cases where such tools were partitioned among the children, they went to sons, although the few examples from the early eighteenth century run counter to this generalization. When Heinrich Geiger died in 1710, he left four children ranging in age from 7 to 17.*[6] *All of the* Bauerngeschirr *went to the widow. When Anna, the widow of Mathes Zeug, died in 1711, she was survived by six daughters (four married) and one son.*[7]

[4] Mathes Weiler and his son, Chapter 11.
[5] *Inventuren und Teilungen*, 346 (17.3.1712); 639 (20.6.1743); 1092 (19.3.1784).
[6] *Inventuren und Teilungen*, 341 (10.4.1710).
[7] *Inventuren und Teilungen*, 345 (19.5.1711).

*The* Bauerngeschirr *was divided into sevenths, with, for example, one son-in-law getting one wheel of the wagon, another a second, still another a third, and a daughter the fourth. Various chains, hitches, and straps were parceled out. A plowshare went to one son-in-law, another to a second, the front cutting piece to a third, a plow ring to another, and the plow frame to the son. When Nicolas Spendler died in 1712, his unmarried 25-year-old son got the* Webergeschirr *(weaving implements), while his son-in-law and daughter got all of the* Fuhr- und Bauerngeschirr.[8]

These early examples indicate that agricultural equipment was either passed on integrally or broken up altogether. In most marriage inventories in this early period, a man with any equipment at all tended to have whole pieces and several items at a time. Therefore it does not seem to have been the practice to chop up the inventory. In those few instances where a wagon or a plow was divided into its constituent pieces, all the participants would have had to cooperate to use any element, since a wagon, for example, with one, two, or three wheels is not very serviceable.

*In 1740, Johann Georg Rieth, Schultheiss, died, leaving considerable property (59 strips) and farm inventory.[9] His married daughter received the rear wagon, one of two harrows, and half rights in the plow, while his son, also Schultheiss, got the front wagon, with its two wheels. A page is missing from the document, but he presumably got the other harrow and half rights in the plow, and a cart. The rest of the gear was parceled out. It is not clear whether the plow was divided up or each retained half rights in the whole – it was listed as a "halber Pflug," (a half plow) in contradistinction to the later phrasing usually found: "die Hälfte an. . . ." (half of a . . .). In any event, in this instance most of the property each child received consisted of whole, integral, usable things. Georg Geiger's widow passed on various gear to one married daughter, but the other got all the large equipment, the front and rear wagons and a complete plow.[10] The rest of the gear remained with the widow. When Hans Jerg Geiger, a wealthy villager and Bürgermeister, died in 1743, the inventory of his estate noted that his son owned two-thirds of all the agricultural equipment.[11] The latter and a nephew inherited rights to the remaining third, which meant that they owned five-sixths and one-sixth of it, respectively, including two plows, a cart, a front wagon, a rear wagon, and a harrow. At Michel Schober's death in 1746, he left a married daughter and minor son.[12] Although the son got an equal share of land, all the* Bauerngeschirr *and the horse were sold to the son-in-law. Christoph Rieth's inventory divided the* Bauerngeschirr *among the widow, the two married daughters, and posthumous child.[13] The widow got a complete rear wagon, while Eva got a complete plow and Anna Maria, a front wagon. The posthumous child received a cart. All the rest of the gear was parceled out. The mother and unborn children shared half rights in a*

[8] *Inventuren und Teilungen*, 350 (4.3.1712).
[9] *Inventuren und Teilungen*, 609 (10.8.1740).
[10] *Inventuren und Teilungen*, 612 (2.1.1741).
[11] *Inventuren und Teilungen*, 637 (25.4.1743).
[12] *Inventuren und Teilungen*, 679 (20.10.1746).
[13] *Inventuren und Teilungen*, 730 (15.5.1750).

*horse and steer, while the rest of the livestock was given out piecemeal. At the death of Barbara, wife of Johannes Heinser, member of the Rat, the widower took a complete rear wagon, a cart, plow, and harrow.*[14] *The son, Michael Häussler, received a front wagon and a cart. The rest of the gear was divided up.*

*In 1780, Dorothea, the wife of Johannes Häfner, Richter, was inventoried.*[15] *Two children from an earlier marriage inherited a front wagon, a chain, and a horse collar together. The widower got a rear wagon, the plow, a cart, and the rest of the considerable gear. Johann Georg Häfner's estate parceled out to the widow and three minor children a front wagon, an oxcart, and some gear.*[16] *One daughter got the rear wagon, a son some gear, another a cart, and the rest of the gear was parceled out. At the death of Barbara, widow of Johann Georg Hentzler, the two daughters received no* Bauerngeschirr, *while the son took it all, including a cart, plow, and harrow.*[17] *However, they each had third rights in a horse, a cow, and a calf. Johannes Kittelberger took the most important implements when his wife Anna died, including a front wagon, a rear wagon, and half rights in a plow and harrow.*[18] *One married daughter received some wheels and a cart. Gertrauta, wife of Michael Friess, left considerable property and equipment, including two carts and a plow.*[19] *Two married daughters each got quarter rights in all the* Bauerngeschirr, *and the children of the son collectively got half rights. Johann Georg Speidel's married daughter took half rights in the wagon and the whole plow and harrow, while the unmarried son got the other half rights in the wagon and a cart.*[20] *They partitioned all the other gear. Johann Georg Sterr, Bauer, transferred his rights to his land and implements, including half rights in a front wagon, a rear wagon, a cart, plow, and harrow, and a whole cart to three children by different marriages. One son took the whole cart. The other son took half rights in both wagons, cart, plow, and harrow. Together they partitioned the rest of the straps, saddles, collars, chains, and so forth, while the daughter took no implements at all. The two sons of Margaretha, widow of Johannes Heinser, each took half rights in the considerable* Bauerngeschirr, *including a wagon, plow, and harrow.*[21] *Salomon Hentzler, Bürgermeister, left a very large estate, including 56 strips of land.*[22] *The widow kept two horses and a cow but took no implements. Two sons, one living in Aich, and a daughter shared equally in land and each took one animal, but they did not take any* Bauerngeschirr. *Two other sons took half shares each in all the implements, including two wagons, two carts, a plow and harrow, and a complicated set of wheels, chains, bolts, ladders, connectors, straps, collars, saddles, reins, ropes, and harnesses. One of them, Friedrich, listed his half rights a week later in his marriage inventory.*[23]

[14] *Inventuren und Teilungen*, 736 (27.4.1751).
[15] *Inventuren und Teilungen*, 1039 (29.2.1780).
[16] *Inventuren und Teilungen*, 1063 (14.2.1782).
[17] *Inventuren und Teilungen*, 1064 (21.2.1782).
[18] *Inventuren und Teilungen*, 1067 (2.12.1782).
[19] *Inventuren und Teilungen*, 1072 (18.12.1782).
[20] *Inventuren und Teilungen*, 1079 (13.1.1783).
[21] *Inventuren und Teilungen*, 1082 (16.2.1785).
[22] *Inventuren und Teilungen*, 1095 (6.2.1786).
[23] *Inventuren und Teilungen*, 1105 (16.2.1786).

*Barbara Bauknecht's three sons split up the inventory, one taking a plow and cart, another a cart and some gear, and a third another cart.*[24]

The equipment inherited in the 1780s contrasts sharply with that from the 1740s. All three strategies were present in each period: It was possible to pass on shared rights in the implements, parcel them out piecemeal, or pass them on to one of a number of heirs without division. In both decades, the last strategy does not seem to have been utilized very often. A few cases demonstrate a mixture of strategies – some important pieces going to one person, or being shared, while the rest was divided up. Nonetheless, the dominant practice in the 1740s was to parcel out individual pieces of property to separate heirs, whereas in the 1780s shared rights were often passed on. There was a tendency to split rights between two children, and to show a slight bias toward sons, but there were also examples of three and four people sharing Bauerngeschirr, and many of these rights descended through daughters. Since these instruments – wagon, plow, cart, harrow, and all the harnessing and field gear – were closely associated with male work, this practice of transferring shared rights in implements created horizontal connections between brothers-in-law and maintained a link between brothers, each of whom farmed his own land at his own pace. The several decades before and after the turn of the nineteenth century were characterized in many ways by the development of many other close links between adults of the same generation. It seems possible that the slow move to more intensive agriculture, the increased use of cows and oxen for traction – which made it possible for small producers to put together a team – and the shortage of capital consonant with new investment in agricultural innovation all combined to encourage small producers to pool agricultural instruments. Such a move would have made the poor less dependent on the rich and created a more or less well-integrated generational cohort sharing tools among themselves, the dynamics of which were structured by kinship. When a child married and received land, he or she would be dependent on the parents' access to tools. In some cases, the parents would have a full tool kit, especially if they had a large enough estate to support it. In other instances, the parents would have shared rights with their siblings and in-laws. Of course, some parents would have had no implements or any share in a pool. When they passed on portions of an estate, they passed on dependence relations with other wealthier villagers.

*In the 1820s, most of the postmortem inventories which contain* Bauerngeschirr *involved a surviving spouse who kept them all. Nonetheless, there are data from the marriage inventories which show the results of partition. Salomo Hentzler, son of Andreas, took his half rights to all* Fuhr- *und* Bauerngeschirr *into his marriage.*[25] *Several months later, his brother David took the other half into his marriage.*[26] *When*

[24] *Inventuren und Teilungen*, 1126 (9.3.1789).
[25] *Inventuren und Teilungen*, 1512 (20.3.1826).
[26] *Inventuren und Teilungen*, 1521 (17.6.1826).

*Johann Georg Zeug died in 1827, each of his four children ranging in age from 14 to 32 received quarter rights in the* Bauerngeschirr, *including a wagon, a cart, plow and harrow, and a yoke.*[27] *Only the oldest son was married. The other two sons were 27 and 14, and the daughter was 17. A year later, when Johann Georg Zeug, the second oldest son, married, his claim was now up to half of all the implements, which probably means that the guardian of the two younger children transferred their rights to the older two.*[28] *When Johannes Bauknecht died in 1829, his right to half a wagon fell to his 30-year-old married son, making him a co-owner with an uncle or perhaps a cousin.*[29]

All of this evidence suggests that Bauerngeschirr was frequently shared during the first several decades of the nineteenth century. By the time older people were inventoried, however, the most usual situation was full ownership in whatever tools they had. From Table 12.2 we see that a substantial number of medium holders (16–30 strips) accumulated the more important tools of agriculture by the end of their working lives during the 1780s and 1820s.

One pronounced trend in the nineteenth century was for the average farm to grow ever smaller, which, for those who accumulated tools, meant an increasing capital/land ratio. Although many observers at the end of the century remarked that the small peasants were somewhat overcapitalized, the process set in long before it was subject to analysis.[30] By the 1860s, all of the farms with 16–30 strips had a full set of Bauerngeschirr, in contrast to half of them in the 1780s and 1820s and a third around 1700. This time a substantial proportion of the smallest holders (0–15 strips) had cultivation instruments (about a third, measured by plows, harrows, and carts; over 50 percent when measured by wagons), whereas those in this group in the earlier periods had not had any implements at all. Almost a quarter of the newlyweds, all of whom had less than 16 strips, had wagons, or plows, or yokes.

*When Catharina, the wife of Salomon Häfner died in 1859, all the agricultural implements (now called* Fuhr- und Reitgeschirr*) went by lot to Jacob, one of six children.*[31] *When Louise, wife of Johann Georg Schlecht, died, she left half rights to a wagon in her estate, which went to her husband.*[32] *At Salomo Hentzler's death, all the* Geschirr, *a wagon, cart, plow, harrow, and yoke, went to the oldest son of three children, all unmarried, aged 21–27.*[33] *When Anna Maria, the wife of Johann Hentzler, died, the estate contained half rights to a wagon, plow, harrow, and half-yoke.*[34] *At the death of Johann Georg Kühfuss, his three wagons, cart, plow, and harrow were all sold to strangers, rather than going to his son or married daughter.*[35]

[27] *Inventuren und Teilungen*, 1539 (19.11.1827).
[28] *Inventuren und Teilungen*, 1557 (16.10.1828).
[29] *Inventuren und Teilungen*, 1569 (20.3.1829).
[30] See, e.g., Friedrich Aeroboe, *Allgemeine landwirtschaftliche Betriebslehre* (Berlin, 1923).
[31] *Inventuren und Teilungen*, 3138 (13.12.1859).
[32] *Inventuren und Teilungen*, 3229 (9.9.1865).
[33] *Inventuren und Teilungen*, 3231 (9.9.1865).
[34] *Inventuren und Teilungen*, 3241 (28.3.1866).
[35] *Inventuren und Teilungen*, 3273 (17.7.1866).

*The next year, the* Bauerngeschirr *of Wilhelm Deuschle, Gemeinderat, was all sold.*[36] *A son-in-law purchased a plow and a son bought a cart, wagon, and half-yoke. Another wagon, a harrow, two yokes, and a cart were sold to unrelated individuals.*

The evidence for this last period is not very substantial. Perhaps the two examples of shared implements in the postmortem inventories of two individuals are the results of an earlier practice. At least, there are no examples of such property being transferred onto children who would have to retain mutual rights. For the rest, the Bauerngeschirr either was passed on integrally to one child among several or it was sold off piecemeal to the highest bidder. In this situation, individuals added to this or that piece of equipment, but may not have kept a full set. The trend back to individualized holding of specific objects took place in a completely different context from the early eighteenth century. Although agriculture was more intense, in some ways the technology was simpler. Complex gear for horses was no longer necessary. A cow hitched to a cart with a half-yoke might move slower, but was available to a wider group of the population. Some people could put together a plow team by themselves, but others would have had to contribute their ox or cow to make up a team with someone else. The fact that more people with small holdings had some equipment, together with hints that tools were circulating around the village as they came up for sale, suggest that cooperation was just as important as it had been earlier in the century, but that it did not take the form of mutual rights to a complete set of Bauerngeschirr. Instead, it involved reciprocal trading to make up the tool set necessary for a particular task.

Over the study period, young people who were in the first years of marriage seldom had any heavy agricultural equipment to go with the few strips of land they received from their parents. This was the case both for children of Bauer families as well as for those artisans who combined farming with their handicraft. When the parents aged, retired, or died, they frequently worked out strategies with their children to maintain the farm inventory intact. In the early years of the eighteenth century, one child might get the wagon and another the plow, which would ensure cooperation for a time. The goal, however, for each enterprise was to accumulate all the important tools, especially by the time the next generation was being set up with a few strips. From the 1780s until the mid-nineteenth century, the cooperation of brothers and brothers-in-law during a phase of their adult lives was enforced by joint ownership. Either the capital costs of intensive agriculture, coupled with the declining size of farm enterprises, made equipment so expensive that direct joint ownership was a useful strategy, or the competition was so great and kinship relations so full of tension that sharing became the only way to ensure access to fundamental tools. By the 1860s, although joint ownership was sometimes still in evidence, the dominant practice was single ownership of individual pieces. The splintering of land for the *Parzellenbauern* may well account for the large number of people with very

[36] *Inventuren und Teilungen*, 3276 (6.7.1867).

small amounts of land giving up the possibility of maintaining heavy farm equipment at all. By that time, an even clearer system of dependence of young/poor/women an old/propertied/men was established.

## Wages

The inventories also provide clues to the wage relations between villagers and between family members. Few inventories contain outstanding debts of this nature, since people would have had to die at precisely the right time for an outstanding wage to be listed, and in those situations where debts were owed to heirs they might not have been mentioned if they canceled each other out or would have been moot given the fact that heirs would come to own what they had recently labored on. Nonetheless, what we do find suggests a certain degree of congruence with the patterns of tool ownership. We would expect to find evidence of richer villagers plowing and carting for smaller holders in the early eighteenth century, which would give way to parents doing the same for children in the later part of the century. At the retirement of parents, children would take over the responsibilities of cultivation. Horizontal relations would be harder to find precisely because they might well be posited on non-monetary reciprocity.

*In the first decade studied (1700–1709), in 1709, the widow of Georg Klein died owing her son Michael Hoyh 24 fl. wages for seven years of cultivation* (Bauerlohn).[37] *The supporting documents include a running bill with an annual entry beginning in 1695: "I have cultivated* (gebaut) *a Morgen arable for my mother and sown one Morgen for her." It is not known how old each of them was, but she married Klein in 1678, bringing her son into the marriage, so he was at least 24 when he began to work for her. There is also a bill from 1692 from Balthas Hentzler for what he did for his mother-in-law. This consisted of 21 trips with horse or horse and cart or wagon and various chores. He had brought her portions of inheritance from her native village, gone on official business to Stuttgart or Tübingen, brought in the sheaves of grain, fetched wood (with an ox), and carried hay. At her death, Agnes Klein had seven strips of land and no* Bauerngeschirr. *This single example from the decade could not have involved a retirement contract, since the son and son-in-law charged for their services. The mother had too little land to support the heavy equipment, but in any event would not have used it herself. The son-in-law had a large enough farm to support both a horse and oxen.*

*The documents give a little more information for the next period. In 1739, Anna Maria, the wife of Adam Bauknecht died.*[38] *The couple had a small farm of six parcels, and, judging from his tools, he worked as a carpenter. They owed her brother, a Bauer, 2 fl. 40 kr. wages* (Ackerbauerlohn) *for cultivating the fields that year. When old Michael Schober, a substantial Bauer with 34 strips of land, died in 1741, his son-*

[37] *Inventuren und Teilungen*, 342 (6.7.1709).
[38] *Inventuren und Teilungen*, 601 (17.11.1739).

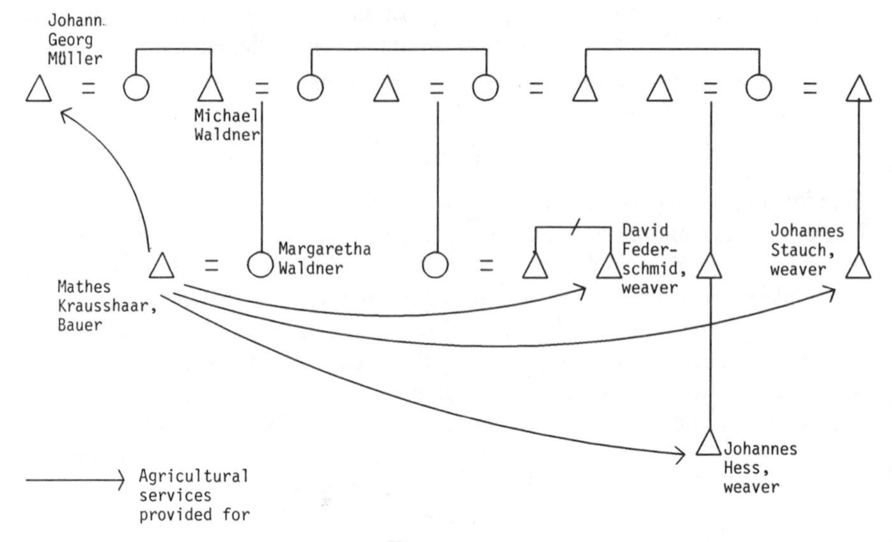


Figure 12.1

*in-law owed him 10 fl.* Bauer- und Fuhrlohn *(cultivation and carting wages).*[39] *In turn, he owed his son 10 fl. wages for having provided servant labor* (Knechtdienst) *since his youth. At the death of his wife Rosina, young Michael Schober (44), a Bauer with 28 strips, was owed wages* (Ackerbauerkosten) *for cultivating fields of Salomon Falter (29) and Johannes Feldmeyer (41).*[40] *These men were married to Michael's sisters. When Mathes Krausshaar (42), a substantial cultivator with 30 strips, died, there were various outstanding wages owed to him: Johannes Stauch (43), weaver, for cultivation* (Ackerbauerlohn)*; Johann Georg Müller (age and occupation unknown), for carting hay and manure* (Dung- und Heufuhrlohn)*; Johannes Hess (28), weaver, for cultivation; Johann Georg Schill (54), cooper, and David Federschmid (46), tailor, for cultivation* (Güterbauerlohn).[41] *Krausshaar owed Johann Georg Hentzler for a trip with a horse* (Rosslohn).

Krausshaar had moved into the village, with his wife bringing the immovable property. Most of the people he cultivated land for were in one way or another related to her: FZH (Müller), MZDHB (Federschmid), MZHZSS (Hess), MZHZS (Stauch) (see Figure 12.1).

It could well be that they all had inherited portions near his through the process of partible inheritance and inheritance of spouses. Johann Georg Müller was poor and had only a few strips. The others exercised handicrafts and at this point in their lives had not accumulated much land. Krausshaar may well have plowed their nearby land when he plowed his own. He also owed

[39] *Inventuren und Teilungen*, 621 (10.11.1741).
[40] *Inventuren und Teilungen*, 622 (17.11.1741).
[41] *Inventuren und Teilungen*, 628 (4.7.1742).

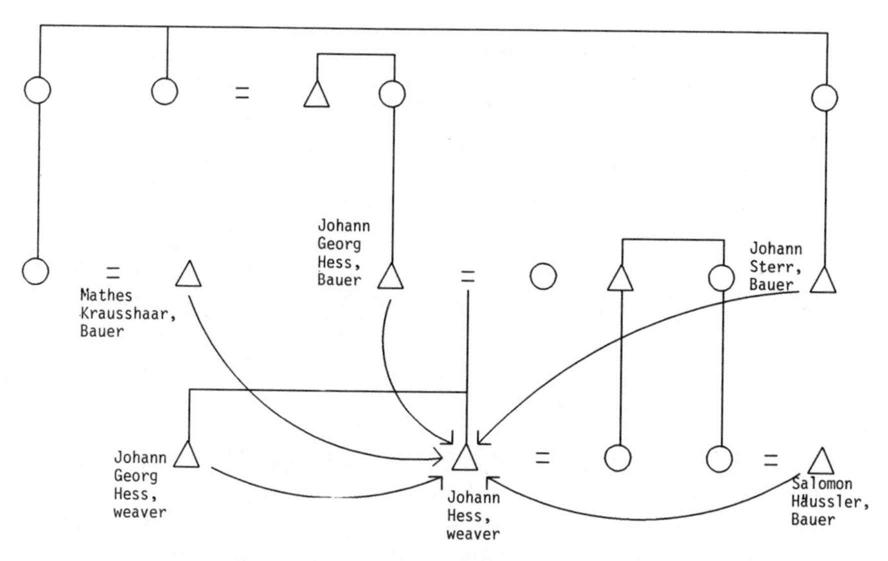


Figure 12.2

wages to Johann Georg Hentzler, a day-laborer, his wife's first husband's first cousin (WHMBS).

*When Rebecca, wife of Johann Hess (28), weaver, died, the estate owed wages for cultivation to five people: Johann Georg Hess (24), weaver, for mowing; and Johann Sterr (50), Bauer; Johann Georg Hess (51), Bauer; Salomon Häussler (43), Bauer; and Anna Maria Krausshaar (7) for* Ackerbauer- und Fuhrlohn. *The total amount owed was 14 fl. 27 kr.*[42] *Johann Hess had 15 strips of land and no* Bauerngeschirr *to carry on the cultivation and carting himself. The wages owed to Anna Maria Krausshaar were originally to her father, Matheus, Hess's FMBWZDH. Johann Georg Hess, Bauer, was his father, and Johann Georg Hess, weaver, his brother, Johann Sterr his FMBWZS, and Salomo Häussler his WFZDH. Hess had arable parcels adjacent to those of Sterr and Häussler, and a vineyard next to Häussler's.*

In this instance, we find a set of relations similar to those of Matheus Krausshaar in the previous case; there Krausshaar offered cultivation services, here Hess received them. The extended set of relations that Krausshaar had through his wife's mother, Johannes Hess also had through his father's mother (with Krausshaar himself and Johannes Sterr) (see Figure 12.2). He also bought services from his wife's cousin's husband, Salomo Häussler, and his own father. Cultivation had to come from men with implements, and most efficiently from those with properties near his. His younger brother, a weaver like himself, worked for him mowing hay (*Mäderlohn*), a job not requiring animal traction and large equipment. Johannes Hess died a year after his wife, still a weaver, but his younger brother ended life as a Bauer. In this instance, we see that an

[42] *Inventuren und Teilungen*, 632 (11.9.1742).

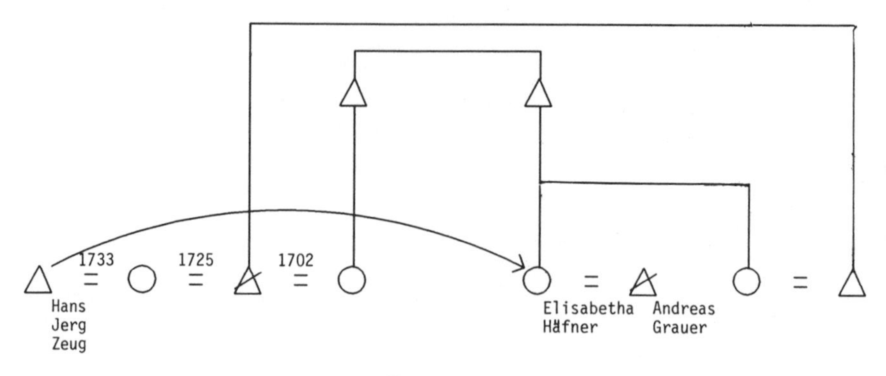


Figure 12.3

older generation provided services for a younger one, which would in turn offer them when it had accumulated enough land to support the equipment.

*In 1742, when Johann Jacob Neckh, who had eight parcels of land, died, he had two debts (4 fl. 54 kr., 2 fl. 37 kr.) to Georg Hentzler and Johannes Häfner for cultivation and carting.*[43] *Neckh was an immigrant to the village and had no relatives there. At Andreas Grauer's death (32 strips), he was owed 2 fl. for cultivation and carting from Johann Georg Zeug, weaver.*[44] *The two men had adjacent strips in the middle field* (Zelg Mittel). *In 1742, Johannes Hess died owing cultivation costs to Salomon Häussler, Bauer, his deceased wife's first cousin's husband (WFZDH) and Johannes Waldner, Bauer, his MZH (see Figures 12.1 and 12.2).*[45] *Hess had arable strips adjacent to ones of Häussler and Waldner in the Ensingen field* (Zelg Ensingen). *The Bauer Salomon Häussler also cultivated land and carried out carting services for Johann Stauch, Dorfschütz, with 12 strips, according to the description of his wife's estate.*[46] *They do not seem to have been closely related. When Catharina, the widow of Johannes Falter, weaver, married in 1743, she had a large debt for cultivation and carrying services (15 fl.) to her father-in-law, Salomon Falter.*[47] *Elisabetha, widow of Andreas Grauer, owed Hans Jerg Zeug for cultivation and carrying. They were related in two ways: She was his WHBWZ and WHWFBD.*[48] *They also had adjacent arable parcels in the middle field* (Zelg Mittel) *(see Figure 12.3).*

*In the next period (1780–9), at the death of Catharina, wife of Johann Georg Ebinger (39), weaver and later Bauer, who had 28 parcels of land but no* Fuhr- und Bauerngeschirr, *the estate owed* Güterbauerlohn *to his son-in-law, Hans Jerg Gneiting from Hardt (7 fl. 30 kr.), and* Bauer- und Fuhrlohn *(3 fl. 20 kr.) to Friedrich Häfner (53), Bauer, his wife's ZH.*[49] *When Ebinger remarried the next year, he*

[43] *Inventuren und Teilungen*, 636 (18.11.1742).
[44] *Inventuren und Teilungen*, 640 (6.7.1743).
[45] *Inventuren und Teilungen*, 641 (9.7.1743).
[46] *Inventuren und Teilungen*, 642 (12.7.1743).
[47] *Inventuren und Teilungen*, 645 (26.9.1743).
[48] *Inventuren und Teilungen*, 651 (25.7.1744).
[49] *Inventuren und Teilungen*, 1073 (3.1.1783).

*owed Johannes Häfner (59), Bauer, his MB, 5 fl.* Bauerlohn.[50] *Ebinger had 2 strips next to Johannes Häfner's in the Grötzingen field* (Zelg Grötzingen) *and 1 adjacent to Friedrich Häfner's in the same field, 2 in the Ensingen field, and 3 meadows. At Johannes Häfner's remarriage, the same outstanding wage was listed.*[51] *Häfner had 23 strips – less than Ebinger – but a complete set of* Fuhr- und Bauerngeschirr. *At Johann Georg Hess's death, his estate (12 strips) owed Leonhard Weiler 1 fl. for* Fuhr- und Bauerlohn.[52]

*In the next period (1820–9), Johannes Petermann, weaver, owed his son-in-law, Friedrich Brodbeck, Bauer, 4 fl. for carting* (Fuhrlohn). *Petermann had 19 strips and a plow and cart but no wagon.*[53] *Christoph Schmid, weaver with 14 strips and no agricultural equipment, owed Matheus Grauer, Bauer, 6 fl. 5 kr. for* Güterbaukosten.[54] *Grauer was Schmid's MBDH. In 1824, Friedrich Arnold, weaver with 10 parcels of land, died. He owed Friedrich Falter, Friedrich Haüssler, and Michael Hentzler altogether 16 fl. 12 kr. for* Fuhrlohn.[55] *Arnold came from Hardthausen and his wife from Neckartailfingen, and they had no relatives in Neckarhausen. At Jacob Friedrich Bross's (butcher) death, he owed Georg Friedrich Häussler, Bauer, his step-daughter's husband (WDH) 1 fl.* Fuhrlohn.[56]

*The final period to be dealt with is 1860–9. In 1863, Jacob Friedrich Falter, a carpenter, with two strips of land in his estate, although more land had been sold shortly before, owed Friedrich Hess 36 kr.* Bauerlohn *for plowing* (Sturtzen) *a field, Gottlieb Zeeb 2 fl. for sowing* (Saatlohn), *and Salomo Hentzler 2 fl.* Fuhrlohn.[57] *Hess was Falter's ZH, but the other two do not seem to have been related. Jacob Friedrich Häfner, day-laborer, with five strips, owed 1 fl. 13 kr.* Fuhrlohn *to Johannes Hentzler (unmarried) and 1 fl. 30 kr. to Gottlieb Hentzler, 18 kr.* Bauerlohn *to Friedrich Hentzler, and 15 fl.* Arbeitslohn *to his own son Ludwig.*[58] *Between Häfner and the various Hentzlers, I can find no relationship.*

This material demonstrates clearly that over the entire period it was usual to charge for services with a plow or wagon or for labor by hand. Parents charged children, children parents, in-laws in-laws, cousins cousins. All of the evidence shows that people with farm inventory relied on kin to offer them the opportunity to work their land. In many situations, reciprocal, nonmonetary arrangements could have been made, or people could have worked for each other to pay off their debts. The kinship part of the claim had to do with work opportunities and reliability, and kin did not work for free. In many instances, the situation was built in. A father could give a child a half or quarter strip. In fact, by the later eighteenth century most parcels sold or passed on were frac-

[50] *Inventuren und Teilungen*, 1091 (18.3.1784).
[51] *Inventuren und Teilungen*, 1094 (22.3.1784).
[52] *Inventuren und Teilungen*, 1077 (10.1.1783).
[53] *Inventuren und Teilungen*, 1448 (26.4.1822).
[54] *Inventuren und Teilungen*, 1471 (–.–.1821).
[55] *Inventuren und Teilungen*, 1493 (26.8.1824).
[56] *Inventuren und Teilungen*, 1560 (20.3.1829).
[57] *Inventuren und Teilungen*, 3171 (17.1.1863).
[58] *Inventuren und Teilungen*, 3174 (19.1.1863).

tionalized strips with no boundaries between them. This meant that the two, three, or four parcels had to be plowed together in order to make use of the headland and not to waste soil by introducing new boundary strips. Therefore, when a father passed on a half strip, he was also passing on the requirement that his son or son-in-law pay for plowing services. A generation or two down the line, cousins plowed for cousins or arranged together for a third party to do the work. This phenomenon can already be seen by mid-eighteenth century, but was structurally dominant by the 1820s. As more and more smallholders worked outside the village as laborers and construction workers and eventually in the factories, a portion of their earnings went to support the older men with significant accumulation of land and tools.

## Life cycle and the exercise of handicrafts

There have been indications in the preceding material that the dependence of the younger generation on the older also involved the exercise of a craft. While the older generation held onto the landed resources which it had accumulated, the children had to develop various strategies for supporting themselves. In many instances, they were trained in artisanal trades, which occupied much of their attention from the time of their marriage until they accumulated enough land to devote most of their energies to agriculture. Since every family had a complex and unique bundle of resources and labor available, there was no single, or perhaps even dominant, life cycle form. In order to explore the possibilities, I have taken the male descendants of Jerg Bauknecht (1624–88) from Raidwangen, who by the third generation were all living in Neckarhausen. The point is to examine the property accumulation of those who ever exercised a handicraft. Therefore, only the individuals who lived a substantial portion of their lives after the tax records become available – from 1790 – can be analyzed. Furthermore, by 1825 those who were actively carrying on a trade were subject to a handicraft tax (*Gewerbesteuer*), which allows us to follow their careers over time.[59] From the 53 descendants of Jerg Bauknecht, 17 who exercised a craft sometime during their lives offer sufficient evidence in the tax records to enable us to gain some insight into the role of artisanal professions in the life cycle. By the first half of the eighteenth century, there were just about as many Bauern in the family as there would be in each generation (Table 12.3). The rest of the family members had to spend some time in their lives as artisans – or after the mid-nineteenth century as factory workers.

*The best way to discuss our findings is in a rather detailed monographic treatment. Johann Jacob Bauknecht (1796–1869), Weaver and Bauer, first appeared in the tax rolls (taken every five years) in 1825 in quartile 3. In that year he paid a handicraft tax. After his father died, he moved up to quartile 4 (1835), remaining there and still paying a handicraft tax until 1845. From 1849, until the last record in 1865, he*

[59] I have computerized the tax lists beginning in 1790 at five year intervals.

Table 12.3 *Occupations of Jerg Bauknecht and descendants*

| Period Born | Number | Bauer | Handicraft |
|---|---|---|---|
| 1600–49 | 1 | 1 | |
| 1650–99 | 3 | 1 | 2 |
| 1700–49 | 8 | 5 | 3 |
| 1750–99 | 20 | 6 | 14[a] |
| 1800–49 | 22 | 7 | 15[b] |

[a]One day-laborer.
[b]Two factory workers.

*no longer paid the handicraft tax.*[60] *He appears, then, to have exercised his craft from the time of his marriage in 1821 until shortly after 1845, when he was in his mid-50s, after which he tended to his farming. His son, Johann Friedrich Bauknecht (1808–49), was also a weaver and Bauer. In 1840, he was in quartile 2 but paid no handicraft tax. By 1845, he had moved up to quartile 3 but was now exercising his craft. At the time of his death at 41, he had put together enough land to come just short of quartile 4 and had apparently given up weaving. Another son, Johann Georg Bauknecht (1813–), remained in quartile 1 from his marriage in 1844 until our records stop in 1870. His profession, butcher, was always listed in the tax records, but he never paid a handicraft tax, so he apparently never practiced it. Johannes Bauknecht (1767–1846), weaver and day-laborer, was in quartile 2 from his marriage (1796) until his father's death, when he moved up to quartile 3 (1820). In 1825, he paid a handicraft tax, but by 1830 until his death, he no longer carried on his trade as weaver and had fallen down to quartile 1. His son Johannes (1797–1867), also a weaver, began his married life in quartile 2 (1825) and paid the handicraft tax. During the period when his 60-year-old father fell back to quartile 1, he advanced to quartile 3 (1830), where he stayed until his father died (1846). In the next tax record, young Johannes had risen to quartile 4, and in the ensuing years sometimes practiced his craft and sometimes did not. His son Heinrich (1829–), mason, moved from quartile 2 (1865) to 3 (1870) after his father's death. In both years he paid the handicraft tax. Salomo Bauknecht (1802–), weaver, remained in quartile 3 from his marriage (1832) through the period under consideration (1870). Only in the last year when he was 68 did he fail to pay the handicraft tax. Salomo's brother Friedrich (1805–), day-laborer, weaver, Bauer, went from quartile 1 (1845) to 2 (1849) after his father's death, but never paid a handicraft tax. Their uncle, Salomon Bauknecht (1780–1834), weaver and Bauer, went from quartile 2 to 3 (1820) when his father died. In 1825 and 1830, he paid the handicraft tax. Michael Bauknecht (1795–), smith, began in quartile 2 in 1820. By 1825, he had moved up to quartile 3. Five years later he was in quartile 4 and for the only time through 1870 was taxed for his*

[60] The tax lists for 1850 and 1860 are missing, so I untilized those from 1849 and 1859.

*craft. By 1835, his father was 75 years old and Michael had abandoned his smith work. Three years later when he was 43, his father died. Johann Ludwig Bauknecht (1764–1849), brickmaker (Ziegler), was in tax quartile 1 from his marriage until 1825. From 1830 to 1840, he had advanced to quartile 2, but by 1845 was back in quartile 1 again. From 1825 until 1849, when he was 61–85, he never paid the craft tax, and we might note that during his late 60s and 70s he was rather wealthier than in his earlier life. Johann David Bauknecht (1762–1846), carpenter, moved from quartile 3 (1795) to 4 (1800) a few years after his father's death. He remained there until he was 68 (1830), when he fell back to class 3. He continued to pay the handicraft tax until he was at least 73 and presumably exercised his profession, although he had enough property to keep himself busy as a farmer. Perhaps he functioned as an entrepreneur and left the actual work to younger men. His brother, Johann Bauknecht (1764–1838), weaver, moved up from quartile 2 (1790) to 3 (1795) upon his father's death. By 1825 when he was 51 and his fortunes began to decline, he was not carrying on his trade. His son, Johann Friedrich (1790–1844), weaver and day-laborer, jumped from tax quartile 1 (1825) to 3 (1830); at the same time, his father began to descend. From 1825 until 1835, Friedrich paid his handicraft tax. By 1840, just after his father died and he was 50, he stopped weaving. Matheus Bauknecht, his son (1821–), carpenter, carried on his craft early on in his marriage (1844–9), but stopped by 1855 at 34, moving a few years later from quartile 2 to 3. His brother Johannes (1818–), mason, fluctuated between quartile 2 and 3 from his marriage in 1841 to 1870, always paying the handicraft tax. Their other brother, Johann Michael (1816–), cobbler, moved from quartile 1 (1845) to 3 (1849) when his father died, but continued to exercise his craft through to 1870 when our data stop.*

In this series of seventeen short biographies, we see that men frequently jumped a whole tax class at their fathers' death (eight cases) or went up as their fathers went down (two cases). This is only an indication of the phenomenon, since movement within a quartile is not registered, nor did I correlate the death of widows or parents-in-law with the tax movement of sons and sons-in-law. These data suggest once again that there were two crucial points at which property moved between generations – at marriage and at the death or the retirement of parents. In this group, men married in their mid- to late 20s (mean 27.8, median 25, mode 25). They frequently had to wait 10 or 20 years before their fathers were dead. The period between marriage and final property devolution would be even longer when widows are considered, and in the nineteenth century, as we have seen, they frequently held onto property until they were into their old age.

The issue of the exercise of a craft is more complex. Occasionally, even an older, propertied man carried on a trade, if the fact that he continued to pay the handicraft tax is any indication. But most men, as they acquired enough property to become full-time agriculturalists, abandoned their crafts. Some were able to do so soon after marriage. Our evidence suggests that men tended to give up a craft in their early 50s when they could get enough land (median 51, mean 51.6 from nine cases). None of these figures should be accepted lightly, given the size of the sample, but we might tentatively suggest the following. Even in propertied families, a strategy had to be found to maintain children for the potentially long period between marriage and entrance to the full set of family resources. Some Bauern sons simply remained close to their parents' enterprises and called themselves Bauern even though they did not have enough land for their own subsistence. Others considered themselves day-laborers, although this category could include a wide range of property holders – some day-laborers had more property than some Bauern. Many families invested in an apprenticeship in a trade for their children, or the son learned a craft with his father. Many were weavers, but the full range of building trades was also represented. In the nineteenth century, the builders, along with cobblers, slowly supplanted the weavers. Certainly, many of the artisans remained active in their trades throughout their lives, but some quite noticeably never exercised their crafts at all. Their profession remained simply a part of their name – Hans Bauknecht, *Metzger* (butcher). More interesting for our purposes is the fact that for many families the exercise of a craft was part of the life cycle. Men entered their marital estate with several parcels of land and a trade, which they exercised more or less intensely throughout their 30s and 40s. Attaining full landed status by their late 40s or early 50s, they abandoned their artisanal professions and tended their crops for the next decade or two. Official documents still designated them by their crafts in order to distinguish men with similar names. Depending on when a family is studied in its life cycle, it could be seen as primarily peasant or artisanal. Generations of carpenters, for example, transmitted both land and skills. During the phase of dependence, when the older generation held their resources, young married men carried on a multitude of handicrafts, some fixed in the village and some traveling in the surrounding territory. When they moved over to full-time agriculture, their sons were ready to supplant them in the skilled and semiskilled trades.

Conditions changed in the village over the period we are dealing with. In the eighteenth century, the few artisans in the village frequently combined significant amounts of land, and the logic of their lives was closely bound up with agriculture. Handicrafts were resources frequently passed on from father to son (sons-in-law practically never had the same craft as their fathers-in-law), to be exercised for a part of the life cycle. By the 1730s and 1740s, a significant group of weavers developed in the village, but they were often designated "Bauer" for a few years and "weaver" for a few others. Especially during periods of cyclical depression, landowners moved into that kind of craft production. When their parents died, they were often left with enough property to stick to farming. By the early nineteenth century, young couples as a group received fewer landed resources and had to wait for a significantly longer time to get more. During the decades of shiftover to intensive agriculture, their labor was available inside and outside the village but schooled and disciplined at home. Almost all of the younger generation got some land, and the logic of their productive lives remained closely aligned with its exploitation, the use of rights

# 13

# Authority, solidarity, and abuse

Because Johannes Bosch reproached young Hans Jerg Hess with his father . . . , so Johannes Bosch is fined for a grievous misdemeanor.

– Gerichtsprotocoll[1]

On many practical levels, households of married, adult children were intertwined with those of their parents. Generally speaking, the younger generation was provided with just enough land to keep them anchored in the village and tied to the interests of their parents and to the needs of their property-owning elders. The wisdom of the practice was embedded in the proverb already cited: "Don't put young bees in a full hive."[2] Although we can pinpoint two important structural moments in the devolution of property – the marriage of the young couple and the decease or retirement of the older ones – there were all kinds of makeshift arrangements which allowed real estate to be passed on in fits and starts, with tentative agreements and reversals. Even land and buildings passed on to married children as their legal property (Eigenthum) would be thrown back into the estate of their parents to be redistributed among all their heirs. However, frequently, and above all in the nineteenth century, land found in marriage contracts was given to children in usufruct only. In those instances where the parents went bankrupt, such land found its way to the auction block to satisfy the demands of creditors.[3] In any event, the relationship established between parents and children through the devolution of land was complicated during that period by the addition of third-party mortgage interest. Between marriage and the retirement of parents, more strips could be given to the children for their use, and every conceivable practice can be found: outright gift, sale, devolution in return for an annual rent, usufruct, sharecropping, and rent. The access to property by the younger generation was

[1] See n. 18.

[2] Hermann Fischer, *Schwäbisches Wörterbuch*, 6 vols. (Tübingen, 1904–36), art. "Immen."

[3] Sometimes adult children would negotiate a takeover of a bankrupt parent's property in order to avoid an auction; e.g., the case of Johann Georg Riempp discussed in my "Young Bees in an Empty Hive: Relations between Brothers-in-Law in a South German Village around 1800," in *Interest and Emotion: Essays on the Study of Family and Kinship*, ed. Hans Medick and David Warren Sabean (Cambridge, 1984), pp. 171–86, here 179; *Inventuren und Teilungen*, 1340 (9.2.1808).

subject to constant negotiation. It is not surprising, then, that despite the expectation that a young couple would shortly form their own household and establish an "independent" economy, parents retained a good deal of power over them.

There are interesting shifts in the way patriarchal authority was talked about in Neckarhausen over time. In the eighteenth century, village institutions relied on assumptions about paternal authority in the exercise of their own power and often called on fathers to discipline their adult sons. For example, when Hans Melchior Thumm started his disorderly life and boozing again (1728), throwing his wife and children out of the house, the pastor sent for Thumm's father, the Schultheiss, to quiet him down.[4] In this instance the roles of father and village official may have been confused, but the text makes it clear that Thumm's *father* was sent for. By the time of the incident, Hans Melchior was 30 years old and had been married for three years. The father and the church consistory relied on each other to enforce discipline on the son.

We have already investigated a slightly different case in some detail.[5] Michael Häussler, 30, married for eight years, got into a scuffle with his father-in-law after he had mistreated his wife. The pastor told Häussler's mother that she was supposed to exercise authority over her son and be a restraining influence, since her husband was absent working in the forest. This text is interesting because it suggests that the person with paternal authority was young Häussler's stepfather, only 10 years older than himself. The stepfather's position was not based on his being the head of a joint household because Häussler had a separate economy and apartment. His mother's authority was derivative and not the result of her own maternal-filial relation. There is even the suggestion that she was required to act with authority and restraint only in the absence of her husband. Be that as it may, parental authority continued well into adulthood and was firmly rooted in the father or stepfather.

*Georg Heinrich Dorfschmid knocked his wife to the ground and swore at his father-in-law, Mathäus Krausshaar, when the latter interfered.*[6] *Dorfschmid's father reprimanded his son but insulted Krausshaar in his turn. After hearing the case, the consistory told Georg Heinrich to offer his hand to his parents-in-law and to beg their pardon. He also had to promise not to attack his wife verbally or physically. His father agreed to protect his daughter-in-law against his son.*

During the eighteenth century, there was no attempt to justify paternal authority to grown children. The pastor or the Schultheiss might try to use it or express values through it, but it was taken for granted. And as far as small children were concerned, there was never any official, protocolled interference with parental authority in the village at all. Over the 140 years that village court records exist, there is not one direct complaint of a parent's maltreatment of

[4] *Kirchenkonvent*, vol. 1, p. 6 (25.1.1728). See the discussion in Chapter 6, "Master of the purse strings."

[5] *Kirchenkonvent*, vol. 1, p. 113 (–.1.1743). See Chapter 11, "Example 1."

[6] *Kirchenkonvent*, vol. 2 (26.8.1767).

a child. Occasionally, the treatment of children was mentioned in connection with other issues, but action was never taken ostensibly in that regard. Children were sometimes officially taken away from parents but only, or primarily because, they could not support them. For example, when Ludwig Hentzler's two children fell to the village because of his incompetence (*Leichtsinniger Mann*), they were auctioned off to the lowest bidder to be boarded and fed.[7]

In the nineteenth century, the nature of the discourse about parental authority shifted somewhat. In the first place, the courts found it necessary to justify parental power. For example, when Daniel Hentzler and his wife complained of mistreatment from their two sons and sought legal punishment from the court, the Schultheiss told the sons that they owed their parents respect *because their property came from them.*[8] Such a lecture would have been unnecessary in the eighteenth century, perhaps because the springs of power were hidden in the ideology of practice. But by the nineteenth century, parental authority was more difficult to assert.

If the court relied on parents to discipline adult children in the earlier period, the situation was reversed for the later. A typical case is provided by Gottlieb Hentzler who came before the courts because of his excessive drinking.[9] Gottlieb's father and his wife requested a declaration of incompetency. Johannes Brodbeck, Gemeinderat, complained to the Schultheiss about his son, Wilhelm.[10] The latter had treated his wife so badly that she had had to call on her father-in-law. Wilhelm said to his father that he was as silly (liederlich) as his wife, which prompted Johannes to ask the court to have his son prove his remarks. For rudeness to his father, he got 12 hours in the local jailhouse.

It is not a simple matter to account for the shift in the way parents and courts interacted. Perhaps with the structural changes in the economy, sons were increasingly exercising their independence. Many of them would be spending years looking for casual labor opportunities outside the village. It could be that the conflicts between fathers and sons were rooted in tensions over labor and property expectations. However, it also appears that the authority of the parents was slowly undermined by the village and state institutions themselves, as the school had begun to play a great role. The conflict over school attendance was a central one for the village. For the parents, the issue was not just the time spent in school – the hours were short and the vacations were long – but rather the challenge to parental authority. As parents understood it, the issue was whether the children belonged to them or to the state. For one thing, children could be summarily punished by the schoolmaster, and the consistory and court could sentence children to be whipped in the school. Above all, children could be punished when their parents kept them home.

*In 1738, various* Hausväter *were cited for neglecting to send their children to the*

[7] *Gericht*, vol. 7, f. 182 (23.4.1811).
[8] *Gericht*, vol. 13, f. 73 (2.3.1840).
[9] *Oberamtsgericht*, STAL, F190, vol. 10, f. 1493 (29.10.1812).
[10] *Schultheißenamt*, vol. 1, f. 62 (25.10.1841).

*winter school.*[11] *The parents said they kept their children home when necessary to give them food and clothing. Before the consistory, they said that they would go to the Oberamt to force the pastor to stop interfering with them and their children. Several months later, the issue was the required attendance three mornings a week at summer school.*[12] *The pastor had ordered the schoolmaster to keep a record of unexcused absences, and learned that many children of all ages had missed classes 10 to 20 times. He was now threatening to levy a fine of 1 kr. per day for failed attendance. Hans Jerg Hentzler, a member of the village court, led the parents in their protest against the school ordinance, which, he argued, was inhumane. The children belonged to them and the pastor should understand that there were many ordinances from the state that no one paid any attention to. When the pastor said he was concerned for the children, Hentzler said he was a better swineherd* (Sauhirt) *than a shepherd of souls* (Seelenhirt).

In their protest against school attendance, the parents saw the issue quite clearly to be their authority over the children. In part, that authority was rooted in control of the children's labor which seems to be the point to the argument about keeping them home to feed and clothe them. But more important was the discipline that the school had over the children independent of the parents. For example, Andreas Falter complained about a neighbor hitting his child for climbing in an apple tree and giving him an extra slap for a rude rejoinder.[13] Hentzler said he was quite capable of raising his own children. The neighbor got six hours in the local jail, but the son was to be punished in the school as an example to the other children. In this instance, just precisely when a father objected to interference with his parental right of correction, it was taken from him and meted out by the schoolmaster. In a later example, Friedrich Walker rousted the schoolmaster out of bed to berate him for beating his son too hard.[14] He called him a *Lausbub* (rogue) and said he would be better at taking care of cows than children. Walker got four hours in jail for his offense. Over time, I am suggesting, parents became used to the school disciplining their children, even when a good deal of tension continued to exist for many families. The shift to school as a disciplining agent was symptomatic of a general shift to extrafamilial institutions – the village court, the consistory, and the Schultheiss office. Parents brought adult children before them for ill behavior, drunkenness, rudeness, laziness, and marital discord.

## Alliance for the defense of property

Although devolution and the control of labor may have caused many tensions inside a family as one generation replaced another, outsiders often saw only

[11] *Kirchenkonvent*, vol. 1, p. 54 (3.4.1738).
[12] *Kirchenkonvent*, vol. 1, p. 56 (25.7.1738).
[13] *Gericht*, vol. 5, f. 108 (16.8.1789).
[14] *Kirchenkonvent*, vol. 4, (13.7.1834).

a tight network of coordinate interests. Sons and fathers sometimes settled debts for each other and were often closely identified with each other morally. Sometimes we find them in a defensive posture, protecting property and reputation, and sometimes we encounter them on the offense, in search of new resources or just flexing collective muscle. One of the best places to view family solidarity is the street brawl, for in the pressure of the moment clear sides were taken and actions had strong symbolic content.

*An excellent example of an intricate battle developed as Salomon Brodbeck, temporary holder of the office of Schultheiss, Wilhelm Deuschle, Bürgermeister, and Johann Georg Lötterle, wheelwright, were placing supports along the Neckar bank below the bridge.*[15] *Lötterle was standing in a garden belonging to a Bauknecht when Johannes Winkler came along and started an argument. Brodbeck ordered Lötterle to move from the garden to prevent a dispute. At that point Jacob Bauknecht, 57, Caspar Bauknecht, 54, and Johannes Bauknecht, 52, came out of their houses, together with two of their sons and Mathes Braun, 27. They all jumped on Lötterle and one of them chased his stepson, Salomon Vogler, along the bank. The Bauknechts and their son hurled abuse at Lötterle and Vogler, and Jacob Bauknecht reproached them both with their insignificant wealth. Bürgermeister Deuschle was angry because when he had announced the need for a donkey* (Esel), *Caspar Bauknecht had said one should only use those from Neckarhausen – meaning Deuschle and Brodbeck. Since then, the joke had been going around the village. During the altercation at the river bank, Caspar Bauknecht challenged the two magistrates to do something about the remark. Winkler yelled that they should throw the* Donnerwetter, *meaning Lötterle, in the river and said that he was a greater* liederlicher Himmelsakrament *(wretched heaven's sacrament) than all the* liederlichen Spitzbuben *(slovenly rascals) in the village. Jacob Bauknecht yelled that they should beat him to death. After Brodbeck left the scene, the three elder Bauknechts and Johannes Geiger accused him of being* liederlich *(lewd, disorderly, dissolute, slovenly) and suggested that he and the Bürgermeister were doing the Neckar work in their own interests. Hans Jerg Bauknecht, 25, one of the sons, said that even schoolchildren had more intelligence, and Mathes Braun said that the Bürgermeister was not needed at the job but just came along for the day's wages. Salomon Vogler testified that all five Bauknechts chased him and that young Hans Jerg threw him into a ditch. Caspar Bauknecht complained that the corvée work was being done poorly and that Brodbeck and Deuschle were only interested in the day wages. Mathes Braun was angry that Bürgermeister Deuschle in the heat of the exchange referred to his outstanding tax bill and that of his father (Deuschle was fined for that remark). In the conclusion of the case, the judge said that it was clear that the Bürgerausschuss – but especially the Bauknecht family – was concerned with the river eating away land from their gardens and was very unhappy with the way the repair work was being undertaken by the magistrates.*

There are a number of important points to consider here. First, there were the three Bauknecht brothers who lived close to each other near the river. They

[15] *Oberamtsgericht*, HSAL, F190II, vol. 258, f. 107 (14.6.1820).

were the organizational node for opposition to the magistrates. Caspar had started the joke about the two donkeys available for work in the village and openly challenged the two leading magistrates to do something about it. The central part of the action played around property and its defense. In fact, the issue itself was the threat to the Bauknechts' gardens. They accused the other side of working in their own interests, demeaning them in the process, since they were suggesting that the magistrates would threaten landed property for a mere day's wage. They belittled the villager that the magistrates brought along to help by saying that he was a man of little wealth. In return, the Bürgermeister attacked one of the chief supporters of the Bauknechts, Mathes Braun, for not being able to pay his tax bill, blaming his father for the same thing.

If one views the structure of the conflicts as being embedded in property relations – substantial Bauern against the magistrates – with one side using the Bürgerausschuss as their chief weapon, the form of the action reveals something about the identification of father and son in the defense of property. The Bauknechts only physically went after Lötterle and his stepson, confining their attack on the Bürgermeister and temporary Schultheiss, also substantial landowners, to words. Lötterle had been hired to do the job, and he had brought along his son to help. In the attack, two of the Bauknecht sons were present, and one was particularly active. Mathes Braun was identified with his father. (Another family connection in the dispute seems important. Johannes Winkler, an immigrant from Kleinbettlingen, was a stepbrother to Mathes Braun's wife. He was married to the daughter of Conrad Hiller, the previous Schultheiss, at that time under investigation for malfeasance and replaced by Brodbeck.) In this instance, the senior generation took the initiative, and the sons followed their lead. But there is also the larger issue of identification between individuals, people coupled together in verbal abuse, which suggests more about the lines of cohesion than a spur-of-the-moment street fight. For example, there are no instances in the records of anyone insulting a young man's mother or sister to get at him. Although there are occasional examples of a general insult cast at a person's relatives, such cases do not occur very often. In the Neckarhausen records, there is only one case in which a father was reproached for his son.[16] In contrast to these possibilities, young men were frequently attached to their fathers, socially and morally, by the insults and abuse directed at them. The fact that Bürgermeister Deuschle dared insult Mathes Braun for his father's tax bill drew an immediate and stiff fine. Among the many other instances of such behavior, there was Jacob Klein who called to Ludwig Friedrich Hentzler: "Du Spitzbub, du liederlicher Gesell, du Schindensknoch, dein Vater geht geistweise" (You rogue, you lewd fellow, you shabby bones, your father is crazy).[17] Johannes Bosch, after he was thrown out of the Brückenwirt, was followed by Johann Georg Hess, who

[16] *Gericht*, vol. 7, f. 61 (2.11.1808).
[17] *Kirchenkonvent*, vol. 3, (14.5.1790).

threw him to the ground.[18] Bosch yelled that he was a *Kerl* (fellow) and a *Spitzbube* (rogue) just like his father, which made Hess angry. He asked in court how Bosch could reproach him with his father, and Bosch received a fine for it. Wilhelm Brodbeck brought the Waldschütz to court for slandering his parents.[19] Christoph Zeug called Salomon Bauer's parents names: *schlechtes Lumpen* (trash), *verstohlenes Wahr* (thieving pack).[20] He said they were a *Lumpenbrut* (trashy brood) and that they were *unter dem Boden vergantet* (posthumously bankrupted). Such injuries to the reputation of the deceased brought him a stiff fine.

One of the ways that the parties squared off against each other had to do with their wealth. Jacob Bauknecht blamed Lötterle for being poor. In that year (1820), the latter's property was valued at 357 fl., while Bauknecht's was not quite twice as much: 633 fl. Lötterle was by no means among the poorest Bürger of the village but was just low enough to be subject to Bauknecht's taunt. The tax evaluations for the combatants were as follows:

| | |
|---|---|
| Johannes Bauknecht, Bauer, 52 | 733 fl. |
| Wilhelm Deuschle, cooper, Bürgermeister, 49 | 711 |
| Caspar Bauknecht, Bauer, 54 | 644 |
| Jacob Bauknecht, Bauer, 57 | 633 |
| Salomon Brodbeck, Bauer, Schultheiss, 47 | 615 |
| Johannes Winkler, Bauer, 33 | 401 |
| Johann Georg Lötterle, wheelwright, 40 | 357 |
| Johannes Geiger, Bauer, 52 | 218 |
| Mathes Braun, Bauer, 27 | 214 |
| Hans Jerg Bauknecht, Bauer, single, 25 | 139 |
| Jung Jacob Bauknecht, weaver, single, 24 | 5 |
| Salomon Vogler, wheelwright, single, 20 | — |

The chief combatants in the central dispute were the two magistrates and the three senior Bauknechts. They were all in the substantial Bürger class. They had larger properties and enough land to need the work of adult sons. In fact, there were only six men in the village assessed higher than Johannes Bauknecht, the highest being 1,008 fl. At its core, the dispute was between equals, men of the same generation, ranging in age from 47 to 57, and the same wealth. They were seconded by younger and poorer men, and the core of support was significantly drawn from sons tied to fathers through property. In the case of Lötterle, he and his stepson were both wheelwrights, working together in the same shop. With a middling amount of property and a handicraft, he was not among the poorest men of the village by any means, but he was dependent on wage labor and subject to the problems of loyalty to one of the village factions. On the other side, Mathes Braun, in tax arrears, was also

[18] *Gericht*, vol. 5, f. 122 (17.12.1798).
[19] *Gericht*, vol. 10, f. 225 (28.12.1825).
[20] *Gericht*, vol. 11, f. 42 (28.12.1826).

one of those men dependent on a network of patrons and kin for his livelihood.

*Another brawl offers examples of fathers and sons defending common interests.*[21] *Michael Deuschle reported to the court that he, his father Wilhelm, Bürgermeister, and his siblings were abused by Ludwig Federschmid and his sons, Jacob and Friedrich. On his way from Oberensingen with a barrel of Schnaps, he met the three of them coming from Nürtingen. Ludwig sent his two sons to stir up an incident and then pushed Deuschle to go another way. When Michael smashed him in the chest with a barrel, all three went at him. After he broke loose to go to his father, Ludwig managed to grab and choke him. Michael's brother, young Wilhelm, heard the commotion and joined the fray but was choked by Ludwig and beaten bloody by Jacob Federschmid. Old Wilhelm's wife sounded the alarm, and when he arrived was greeted by Ludwig Federschmid: "There you are you shitty Bürgermeister. You I have always wanted to get." He slugged Deuschle twice on the eye, shoved his hand into his mouth, and yanked out a tooth. He called Deuschle a perjurer and said if he was not Bürgermeister, he would go under* (krepieren). *He alleged that Deuschle provided dowries from his office and gobbled* (fressen) *pork all he liked because he took bribes.*

*At the hearing, old Wilhelm Deuschle explained that four years previously he had helped Johannes Bosch arrange some loans and had refused to be paid. In his absence, Bosch's wife had brought three pounds of pork and told his wife to give it to him when he returned. That was an honor and to one honor belongs another. Deuschle tried to repay Bosch a few days later, but the latter refused to accept payment, so he gave him a tax break. He complained that Jacob Federschmid often called him perjured and a* schlecht liederlicher Lumpenkor *(slovenly trash) and that Ludwig said the entire council was full of snots and ass lickers* (Lekker) *and should be run under the Rathaus. Federschmid had also called him an election thief. When Ludwig got so worked up that the Schultheiss had to send him home, he yelled that the Schultheiss was exactly like the Bürgermeister.*

In this instance, the identification of fathers and sons was again very close, yet the conflict essentially concerned the two fathers. Wilhelm Duschle was 54 and Ludwig Federschmid, 51, the former assessed in 1825 at 1,334 fl. and the latter at 509 fl. Deuschle was a wealthy landholder, a cooper, and a leading member of the village hierarchy, while Federschmid was a middling landholder and weaver. All of Federschmid's sons became artisans – Friedrich and Johann Georg, carpenters, and Jacob, a weaver, later a shopkeeper – and one of his daughters actually married Michael Deuschle in 1838 after his divorce. What exactly lay behind the dispute is not completely clear, but it does appear that the real target of the Federschmid wrath was the Bürgermeister. Ludwig Federschmid was traveling with his 25-year-old married son, Friedrich (tax assessment 434 fl.) and his unmarried 22-year-old son. Michael Deuschle, the son they attacked, was 27 and already married for four years (tax assessment, 421 fl.). Young Wilhelm Deuschle was 20 and single. What emerges clearly in the dispute is the strong association of sons – even independent,

[21] *Gericht*, vol. 10, f. 216 (26.12.1825).

married sons – with their fathers in terms of their willingness to aid in violent dispute, their substitutability as objects of vengeance, and their coordination of strategies of gossip and abuse.

## Parents and marriage strategy

To get at an exact balance between individual decision and family control with respect to marriage is impossible. A child who had internalized all the rules of his or her family could perhaps be given more or less free rein in deciding whom to marry. Nonetheless, there were family traditions and family strategies which could influence or be made to influence directly a child's choice of a spouse. The law was clear that a son or daughter was not free to marry without parental consent before the age of 25.[22] Thus parents had an instrument for making their choices felt. They could offer independence to their sons or daughters well before the legal age of adulthood (which came either with age 25 or with marriage) in return for a choice suitable to the family. Parents often had another weapon in their arsenal – their ability to decide the timing and size of a dowry or marriage portion – and since marriage was closely tied to property and property considerations, children had to take parental wishes into consideration. On the other hand, once there were forces pulling sons out of the village, then parents could seek to keep a hold on them by tying them to land, offering them a part of the family holding, and encouraging them to marry young. In fact, it might also have been in the interest of the family economy seen as a whole to set up one or two children relatively young, since they would have access to all the communal resources of the village, adding considerably to the wealth of a family. If the children's labor was needed all the way through anyway, endowing a new family might have seemed a wise move to make. It is quite possible that the larger endowments offered to daughters were part of a policy of tying sons-in-law to the interests of the family, or, given the fact that female agricultural labor was increasingly necessary in the nineteenth century, such endowments might have been necessary to anchor the young couple in the village and make a satellite work force available.[23] A thorough analysis of such questions can best be undertaken when we turn our attention to the demographic evidence at a later time.

*The need for parental consent for marriage is illustrated by the case of Jacob Gimmel, who became engaged to a woman from the village of Grafenberg, who was then a servant in Neckarhausen.[24] The engagement took place in his father's house with his father's consent. However, she had not informed her guardian and became afraid that he would not give his consent, so she sued to break the engagement. In another case, Andreas Grauer, 29, promised to marry Regina Pfingstag from Altenriet.[25] She came*

[22] "1. Eheordnung," (1534) in Reyscher, vol. 4, p. 66; "2. Eheordnung," (1.1.1553), pp. 86–7.
[23] See Chapter 10.
[24] *Kirchenkonvent*, vol. 2, p. 24 (7.2.1749).
[25] *Kirchenkonvent*, vol. 2, p. 82 (26.5.1752).

*to the pastor in Neckarhausen to declare her intentions and to meet and take an oath to his parents. The pastor learned that the engagement was undertaken without their permission and that they withheld their consent. Grauer's stepfather, Dorfschmid, said that the woman had misled his stepson into thinking her marriage portion would be greater than it actually was. Dorfschmid had checked and found that her father was laden with debts, so he informed Andreas that there would be no marriage portion* (Heiratsgut) *from him. Consequently, Andreas decided to give the girl up. In fact, he related that she told him she would get a strip in each field, a meadowland, a vineyard and part of a house – a classic marriage portion. He then went to Altenriet to ask the Schultheiss about getting Bürgerrecht and was informed that the girl's father would only leave 50 fl. at his death. With such poverty, he could neither become a Bürger there nor set himself up in Neckarhausen, and he therefore declared that he wanted to break off with her. In the meantime, she continued to demand that he fulfill his pledge. The disposition of the case is not known, but young Grauer ended up marrying the daughter of the Nürtingen cowherd in 1755. About the same time as this case, Johannes Keller from Nürtingen engaged himself to Barbara Stauch without witnesses and without permission of his parents.*[26] *Because they would not give their permission and his aunt who was going to leave him her property had cut him off, he wanted to be fre[illegible]r. At the end of the century, Catharina Keuerleber denied she was pregnant before the consistory, although the midwife attested to the fact that she was no longer a virgin.*[27] *Finally, she said that she was afraid to admit her condition because her lover's parents had threatened to beat her up.*

The remarkable fact in dealing with the role of parents in the courtship of their daughters is that once a young woman was old enough to receive visitors, she slept alone and could receive them. There may have been times when the young woman did not want to participate in the practice of nightly visits by young men or may have wished to discourage certain visitors.

*Margaretha Christina Bosch, for example, testified before the consistory that a young man came to see her in the attic where she slept.*[28] *The next day she had complained to her parents and said she no longer wanted to sleep alone. She then moved into her parents' room, which put a stop to the unwanted visits. In Raidwangen, Johann Jacob Hentzler prevented Michael Holpp from climbing through his daughter's window after midnight.*[29] *She already had a friend and did not want any such visits. Johannes Falter complained about the way Johann Friedrich Hentzler and Johannes Schniering treated his granddaughter, Magdalena Zeug.*[30] *Hentzler had told her a few days earlier that he would come to see her on Saturday night, but she made sure that the shutters were securely locked so that he could not get in. The following Monday he smashed her window out of revenge.*[31]

[26] *Kirchenkonvent*, vol. 2 (5.16.1753).
[27] *Kirchenkonvent*, vol. 3 (21.10.1793).
[28] *Kirchenkonvent*, vol. 3 (21.9.1784).
[29] *Kirchenkonvent*, vol. 3 (7.4.1779).
[30] *Kirchenkonvent*, vol. 3 (16.12.1781).
[31] *Gericht*, vol. 2, f. 220 (11.11.1779).

In all of these cases, the fathers (or grandfather) were supporting the expressed will of their daughters. The situation itself demonstrates that the young women slept alone in the first place and were used to receiving visitors. That does not mean parents were excluded from an interest in their marriages, however. A constantly repeated theme in the depositions for extramarital pregnancy is that a woman became pregnant in her room in her parent's house.[32] Despite the fact that this kind of freedom was accorded – sometimes openly, sometimes tacitly – the father and mother were forced into action when a daughter became pregnant. The father then had to attempt to negotiate a marriage or express his dissatisfaction by reducing the marriage portion.

*A good example of the context in which premarital sex took place in the eighteenth century is provided by the case of Elisabetha Hess, 28.*[33] *She thought she was pregnant, although she had no other proof than the fact that she had lost her virginity, and gave as the father, Jacob Baur, son of a Bauer from Oberlenningen. Young Baur had come to Neckarhausen over Christmas to help Christoph Rieth with his threshing. While he was there, he visited the Hess family with his cousin, David Baur, from Neckarhausen, and made an arrangement with Elisabetha to visit her at night, which he did three times. According to her testimony, he promised to marry her but offered no ring or any other form of pledge. He also told her he was free, even though in fact he was involved in a paternity suit at home.*[34] *In January, he returned to visit his cousin and at that time Elisabetha's father sent him a message that he should consider himself bound to his daughter. Since Jacob did not make a visit, however, the father, Georg Hess, requested a letter of intent in order to rescue his paternal honor* (ehrlichen Namen). *Hess, in his testimony, said that his brother-in-law, David Baur, cousin to Jacob, had urged him to let his daughter go to the young man, which he agreed to do. He wished, in fact, that the matter had turned out that way, when he considered his honor and that of his daughter, but he did not expect anything from the fellow, since he had treated at least three other women in a shabby manner. He would no longer trust him with his daughter.*

In this case, the web of kinship is the context in which acquaintance, visiting, and pregnancy took place. The father tied his honor, his good name, his reputation, not to his daughter's behavior but to that of her lover. He made it clear that everything had run according to form: his brother-in-law had introduced the cousin to his household. There seems to have been nothing unusual about effecting an arrangement between two young people in such a short space of time. No blame was accorded to the daughter, for she had not mistakenly expected marriage with a man of the wrong station, who had left her in the

[32] *Kirchenkonvent*, vol. 1, p. 85 (28.12.1740); p. 134 (3.5.1744); vol. 2 (25.5.1753); (29.8.1756); (21.12.1761); (7.9.1765); *Gericht*, vol. 7, f. 190 (–.–.1811).

[33] *Kirchenkonvent*, vol. 1, p. 134 (3.5.1744).

[34] See David Sabean, "Unehelichkeit: Ein Aspekt sozialer Reproduktion kleinbäuerlicher Produzenten. Zu einer Analyse dörflicher Quellen um 1800," in *Klassen und Kultur. Sozialanthropologische Perspektiven in der Geschichtsschreibung*, ed. Robert Berdahl, et al. (Frankfurt, 1982), pp. 54–76.

lurch. In this case, all the kinship information and the key role of the brother-in-law are designed to show that Elisabetha had conformed to what was expected of her. In any event, there is no hint that her loss of virginity had anything to do with the reputation of the "house." Two reputations were mentioned – that of the father and that of the daughter, and they were to some degree detachable from each other. That the father's honor could be mentioned at all suggests that the nightly visits to daughters (this one was 28) did not occur outside the framework of family interest and knowledge.

*In one rather obscure case, there is a suggestion of a young couple making an arrangement which involved mismatched families. The father of the young woman was not about to let that reflect on himself. Antonius Häfner had agreed to marry Agnes Feldmaier, daughter of Johann, and he had spoken about his intent to his mother, suggesting that he wanted to wait until after the harvest.*[35] *Feldmaier said he never encouraged his daughter. He obviously did not expect things to work out and protected his own reputation by expressing hesitancy. Nonetheless, when the young couple went ahead, the pastor spoke darkly of marriage fraud.*

Most of the cases in which parents were involved in the marriage negotiations of their children occur in the records for the period 1730–90. The declarations of pregnancy after the 1780s contain less and less information and by the 1820s registered only the barest facts. Nonetheless, taking the evidence as a whole, fathers in the earlier period were only concerned publicly with the honor of their daughters in relationship to marriage and premarital pregnancy. After 1820, they were increasingly concerned with the general reputation of their daughters and appeared before the court in their defense against rumor, gossip, and verbal abuse. Perhaps the social control mechanisms ceased to be as effective once class conflict began to develop, which necessitated the new kinds of interventions.

In the earlier period, a typical case was that of Ursula Schwarz who was made pregnant by Melchior Butzer.[36] Her stepfather cut down the marriage portion because she had acted so immorally. We do not, of course, have to take his allegations at face value. After all, the stepdaughter was negotiating to have her paternal inheritance, which would have been in the usufruct of her mother and therefore in the control of her stepfather, passed down. Getting pregnant could have been a move on her part to force the issue and an excuse on his part to cut her short. In another incident of the period, Maria Agnes Baur, daughter of Balthasar, from Raidwangen, was made pregnant by Johannes Horz, a soldier in Stuttgart, in the house where she was a servant.[37] He promised to marry her and gave her a ring. Although on his two visits to Raidwangen her parents would not allow him to visit the house, they were not willing to hinder the marriage. Four decades later, Maria Dorothea Falter

[35] *Kirchenkonvent*, vol. 2, (1.3.1754).
[36] *Kirchenkonvent*, vol. 2, p. 43 (10.7.1750).
[37] *Kirchenkonvent*, vol. 1, p. 62 (2.12.1739).

announced that she had been pregnant for 18 weeks.[38] She had promised to marry the father of the child, Johannes Heinser, with the foreknowledge and will of both sets of parents. Each of them would bring 400 fl. to the marriage. There are many other examples in the eighteenth-century court records with similar information.

According to the nineteenth-century evidence, fathers seem to have been more concerned with the overall reputations of their daughters. For example, Jacob Feldmaier complained that Mathes Sterr had slandered his daughter.[39] Sterr had come into the Lichtstube (spinning bee) and called her a "bad person" (*schlechte Mensch*) and threatened to punch her. Feldmaier referred to this as "dishonourable slander" against his daughter. Jacob Bauknecht complained that Friedrich Bauknecht called his daughter Louisa "trash" (*Lumpenmensch*) and "whore," and that she was struck by Johannes Dammel.[40] He wanted proof that she was a whore. The two men were fined for their actions. The Gemeindepfleger, Falter, complained in the name of his daughter that the wife of the schoolmaster called her a "bad person" (*schlechte Mensch*).[41] Apparently she had been scolding her son for coming home late and was referring to the company he kept.

An important aspect of mother and daughter relations revolved around courtship and marriage. As in other matters, the standing of the families involved and property considerations were central issues. But the logic of property was specific to class and time. Before 1760, for example, pregnancy before marriage was not a common occurrence. By 1800, there were examples of wealthy peasant daughters, daughters of council members, of the Bürgermeister, and even of the pastor who bore illegitimate children. Early in the eighteenth century, it was probably scandalous to have a pregnant daughter, and parents brought great pressure to see that they were properly married, preferably to the parent of the child. After 1800, even though pregnancy before marriage became increasingly common among poorer families, it also became part of more complex family strategies even for more well-to-do villagers. The labor potential of a daughter might well have outweighed any consideration of family "honor." Certainly the shame of a mésalliance would have been worse than the shame of lost virtue. Thus although over time a mother's chief concern might have been to see her daughters married well, the nature of calculations changed.

It is clear from the earliest cases of illegitimacy in the records – from the 1730s and 1740s – that women of marriageable age had their own sleeping quarters and that they received male visitors. This practice suggests that at least some degree of freedom was accorded to peasant daughters. In this early period,

[38] *Kirchenkonvent*, vol. 3, (22.1.1784).
[39] *Gericht*, vol. 9, f. 178 (17.3.1821).
[40] *Schultheißenamt*, vol. 2, f. 246 (11.5.1853).
[41] *Schultheißenamt*, vol. 2, f. 279 (5.4.1858).

marriage usually entailed mismatched couples as far as marriage portions and inheritance was concerned.[42] By the end of the century, fortune was much more closely matched with fortune, and propertied families would simply reject an unsuitable suitor even if their daughter was pregnant. A case from the 1750s demonstrates the logic of the transition and reveals the considerations present in such a case.

*Anna Maria Schober announced that she was pregnant, and her mother was not pleased.*[43] *Salomon Grauer, the father of the child, had no marriage portion – he was a "poor fellow" with 50 fl. inherited from an aunt* (Base). *He testified that he had not promised marriage but had often told his mother in Oberensingen that he wanted to marry Anna Maria. Apparently it was not at all certain that she was pregnant, and the mother suspected collusion. She tried to get evidence that the young people had in fact not had intercourse and put pressure on the maid to testify – in this unusual instance the daughter and the maid apparently shared a room. In fact, the illegitimate child was born in February, 1759, and Anna Maria and Salomon were married over a year and a half later in November 1760. Although the mother apparently delayed the marriage as long as she could, there was no real chance of preventing a mésalliance during that period.*

Even a widow could be dependent on parental consent for contracting a marriage. Margaretha, the widow of Johann Georg Zeug, agreed to marry Johann Feldmeyer if her mother would give her consent, and accepted a Taler as pledge.[44] Unfortunately for Feldmeyer, her mother objected and said he was too young.

*In another instance about the same time, Johann Michael Schütz, Dragoner, wrote to the pastor that he had slept with Rebecca Bauknecht several times and given her 18 Batzen as a pledge.*[45] *Since she would not marry, he required 40 fl. as satisfaction. She testified that she would never promise marriage without parental consent and that she had sent him away from her bed, telling him not to seek her out like a "whore." This is further evidence that the visiting of young women in their rooms was done in the context of parental knowledge and consent and without that, the relationship had something illicit about it.*

## Abusive language in parent–child relations

The cases of conflict between fathers and sons demonstrate that this relation had a very small repertory when it came to abusive language. This was also true for stepfather–stepson relationships, in marked contrast to that of stepmother–stepchildren. Violence, rudeness, and bad treatment could often take place, but the symbolic load reduced itself to a few reproaches about work habits. The

[42] Chapter 9.
[43] *Kirchenkonvent*, vol. 2 (21.6.1758); (22.6.1785).
[44] *Kirchenkonvent*, vol. 2 (21.12.1758).
[45] *Kirchenkonvent*, vol. 2 (25.7.1759).

only epithet to be found is *liederlich*, once used by a father and once by a son.[46] Johann Georg Sterr complained about his married son's rudeness (*Grobheit*) and requested that he be put in jail in order to learn to treat him better.[47] Another father reported that his son treated him immorally (*unsittlich*) and wanted him corrected *auf einer suptille Weise*.[48] Johannes Kühfuss was being restrained by the village policeman and his father, Johannes, while he was drunkenly cursing. Kühfuss turned on his father, but the text never implies that he turned from general cursing to swearing at his father. The general impression throughout the record is that even in the extremity of conflict, imprecations between fathers and sons remained restricted.[49]

*A typical altercation between father and son is provided by Gottlieb and Michael Hentzler. Gottlieb came home to get some animals to take to the market in Grötzingen.[50] His son Michael wanted to take different ones and Gottlieb called him a "violent disorderly fellow"* (liederlicher Geselle), *whereupon Michael punched him in the mouth. Gottlieb went to the Schultheiss who noted that he was bleeding and had a wound on his mouth. Gottlieb told the court that this kind of thing happened frequently and that he would no longer tolerate it. He returned a while later to say that when he got home, his wife claimed that she had hit him, which was not true. Back for a third time with his son, he withdrew his complaint. Another case involved Johannes Brodbeck, Gemeinderat, who was called to his son's house.[51] Wilhelm had spent the morning in the pub, which prompted his wife to complain that he was not tending to his business. He began to treat his wife rudely* (gröblich) *so she called her father-in-law. Wilhelm said that his father was as "disorderly"* (liederlich) *as his wife, which prompted Johannes to report to the Schultheissamt that he would not allow such an expression from a son and demanded that his son prove in what way he was disorderly. Wilhelm got 12 hours in the village jail.*

There are no cases of a daughter using abusive language against a father and only one of a father doing so against a daughter. A man in general conflict with his wife called his daughter a "witch" (*Hexe*).[52] In this case, it could have been one of his two daughters who never married, one living to the age of 49, the other to 72. He said to the court that he did not actually believe it but was irritated because she was a "fool" (*Narr*). In any event, he first called his wife a "witch" and probably let loose at the whole lot. The context of the case puts this term in a special light. The wife was in fact locally considered to be a witch, and people sent their sick children to her to be cured. Probably the daughter was a bit strange (never married and referred to by her father as a "fool") and was considered to have inherited her mother's powers. In his testimony, the

[46] *Gericht*, vol. 12, f. 89 (23.3.1883); *Schultheißenamt*, vol. 1, f. 62 (25.10.1841).
[47] *Gericht*, vol. 4, f. 21 (12.5.1785).
[48] *Gericht*, vol. 11, f. 50 (27.2.1827).
[49] *Gericht*, vol. 4, f. 166 (28.4.1791); vol. 11, f. 51 (29.3.1827); vol. 13, f. 73 (2.3.1840).
[50] *Gericht*, vol. 12, f. 89 (23.3.1833).
[51] *Schultheißenamt*, vol. 1, f. 62 (25.10.1841).
[52] *Kirchenkonvent*, vol. 1, p. 138 (24.8.1744).

husband said that his wife had not purchased her character but inherited it, which I take to mean that her powers were not the product of learned witchcraft – selling herself to the devil – but something in the blood.[53] This then would connect mother and daughter. The accusation of being a witch in this case was not associated with aggressive or evil intent but with superstitious practice. The abusive term *Hexe* could have three meanings: (1) the person practiced black magic (against the accuser); (2) the person acted agressively or evilly or witch-like (against the accuser); (3) the person accused was known to have inherited special powers, not necessarily of an evil, although perhaps of an ambiguous, nature. In this case, the father accused the wife and daughter of the third, although the ambiguity implied by the other meanings could also have been there. In any event, the father was in no way suggesting that the daughter used any special powers against him. She was just irritating.

A striking instance of abusive language occurred between a stepfather and stepdaughter. Georg Lötterle, 47, complained that his stepdaughter, Anna Maria Vogler, 29, called him a "pighead" (*Saukopf*).[54] She denied saying that but alleged in turn that he called her a "whore," to which she answered, "like you" (*per Du*). He claimed she then said, "you would have been the longest part there." The Oberamt sentenced her to be punished for her immoral conduct. The term *Saukopf*, which is derived from "pig," carried the general meaning of "rude, mean fellow" (*roher, gemeiner Kerl*), and was thus used for men. The term *Hur* used by the stepfather was turned by Anna Maria in the crudest way possible to imply sexual impropriety on his part of the gravest kind. The original exchange between them counterposed meanness to dissoluteness, which suggests issues having to do with property and propriety. The symbolic load of an incest accusation seems often to imply homologies between illicit sexuality and scrambled lines of inheritance. Perhaps they were involved in negotiations over her marriage portion.

There are no examples of sons using abusive language against mothers. One mother called her son "rascal" (*Spitzbube*) and a "poor booby" (*elender Tropf*).[55] In contrast to such paucity of abuse, step-relations often provoked strong words. In 1740, a stepson called his stepmother a "dog" (*Hund*) and "thunder" (*Donner*).[56] She called him a "lazy dog" (*fauler Hund*), *Grobenkoll* (*grob* = uncivilized), and a *Welschen* (foreigner, Frenchman). Another man called his stepmother a *Raffel* (chatterbox).[57] In 1840, two sons called their stepmother "witch" and "whore."[58]

There are no examples of mother–daughter abuse of a scurrilous kind, but the step-relationship was full of such terms. Christoph Rieth's married daugh-

[53] See the discussion in David Warren Sabean, *Power in the Blood: Popular Culture and Village Discourse in Early Modern Germany* (Cambridge, 1984), pp. 107–10.

[54] *Gericht*, vol. 11, f. 65 (7.6.1827).

[55] *Gericht*, vol. 11, f. 203 (28.12.1830).

[56] *Kirchenkonvent*, vol. 1, p. 76 (24.2.1740).

[57] *Kirchenkonvent*, vol. 2 (17.5.1768).

[58] *Gericht*, vol. 13, f. 73 (2.3.1840).

ter Eva called her stepmother, Margaretha, *tausendsakraments Bestie* and *Schlutte* (slut). Rieth's other daughter, Anna Maria Häussler, said that no dog would accept a piece of bread from her stepmother.[59] A month later the stepmother, Margaretha Rieth, called Anna Maria *Schwätzerin, Läuferin, Mussiggängerin.*[60] In general, such abuse is in the direction of bad work habits, idleness, and refusal to pay attention to work. A *Schwätzer* is a babbler or gossip. A *Läuferin* is a woman who does not like to stay at home, who runs around. A *Mussiggängerin* is an idler, a loafer. The daughter called her stepmother in turn *Brüller* and *Bräuger*. She said she was responsible for her husband's death (made him *selig*). She then called her *Canallie, Bestie,* and *Dreck*. She told her to kiss her ass (*leck mich*) and then raised her dress and said, *Du Scheckwahr* (*Scheckware*). The terms *Brüller* and *Bräuger* refer to someone who makes a lot of noise – that in answer to the stepmother's blame. The daughter-in-law then progressed to stronger terms, *Kanallie*, "beast" and "shit." Kanallie is a malicious person, full of craft, which might be brought into connection with the accusation of killing the husband/father. The final expression of contempt was to raise her dress and to use the stepmother's maiden name (Scheck) coupled with the suffix *-ware* (baggage, pack). A few days later, Margaretha Rieth called her stepdaughter a *faule Schlauffe*, a *Mistmacherin*, *Lahmmagen*, *tausendsacraments Vetterl.*[61] She needed two or three men to bugger her (*die du den Hinterst verhuren*). Schlauffe is a term for a thoughtless or wanton woman. A Mistmacher is literally a maker of shit. I am not sure about the term Lahmmagen. It probably has to do with the adjective *lamm*, slow, sluggish. Vetter (literally, "cousin") is a general name used in mockery, usually with some kind of adjective, in this case *tausendsakraments*, a play on the holy sacrament, a move into the region of cursing or *sacramentieren* usually reserved for men. Before the village court, Margaretha alleged that her stepdaughter was upset about the inheritance and had been continually calling her *Bestie, Cannalie*, and *Glunt* (whore). Anna Maria said she was called in turn *Faullentzerin* (idler), *Laman* (sluggard), *Mistmacherin*, and told her husband was not man enough for her. One stepmother called her daughter a "black pig asshole" (*schwarzes Sauloch*), and wished she would drop dead (*verrecken*).[62] Then she called her a *faules Luder* and *Schentmerr* (*Schindmäre*). "If only the devil would take you away, you *Hurenloch*." The stepmother claimed the daughter had called her a *Sauloch* and wished her to drop dead. She had only answered, "drop dead yourself." She also denied calling the daughter a *roziger Hund* (snotty dog). The terms Sauloch and Hurenloch are partly ambiguous. *Loch* literally means "hole," and could imply "asshole" or "cunt." In the case of Hurenloch (whore's hole), the metonymy suggests both wantonness and buggery. Sauloch is a term used exclusively for women. A Luder is a crafty or cunning person, and Schindmäre

59 *Kirchenkonvent*, vol. 2, p. 48 (25.7.1750).
60 *Kirchenkonvent*, vol. 2, p. 49 (24.8.1750).
61 *Kirchenkonvent*, vol. 2, p. 54 (28.8.1750).
62 *Gericht*, vol. 10, f. 226 (28.12.1825).

is a term of abuse used for women – an old mare. Rozig (from *Roz*, snot) is a typical term of abuse used by women, in this case directed against a stepdaughter.

Perhaps we can look at the terms of abuse more systematically.

| *Stepdaughter to stepmother* | *Stepmother to stepdaughter* |
| --- | --- |
| bawler (*Brüller*) | gossip (*Schwätzerin*) |
| squawker (*Bräuger*) | idler (*Mussiggängerin*) |
| malicious person (*Cannalie*) | loafer (*Faullentzerin*) |
| | sluggard (*Laman, Lahmmagen*) |
| | gadabout (*Läufer*) |
| | rotten sneak (*faules Luder*) |
| whore (*Glunt*) | wanton (*Schlauffe*) |
| beast (*Bestie*) | insatiable bugger (*Hinterst verhuren*) |
| baggage (*-ware*) | old mare (*Schindmäre*) |
| slut (*Schlutte*) | |
| shit (*Dreck*) | shit-maker (*Mistmacherin*) |
| pig's asshole (*Sauloch*) | black pig's asshole (*schwarzes Sauloch*) |
| "lick my ass" (*leck mich*) | |
| snotty dog (*roziger Hund*) | whorehole (*Hurenloch*) |
| "drop dead" (*verrecken*) | "drop dead" (*verrecken*) |
| husband killer (*Seligmacher*) | "devil take you" (*Teufel dich nehmen*) |
| thousand sacrament beast (*tausendsakraments Bestie*) | thousand sacrament "coz" (*tausendsakraments Vetterl*) |
| *Stepson to stepmother* | *Stepmother to stepson* |
| chatter box (*Raffel*) | |
| dog (*Hund*) | lazy dog (*fauler Hund*) |
| whore (*Hur*) | foreigner (*Welschen*) |
| witch (*Hexe*) | uncivilized (*Grobenkoll*) |
| thunder (*Donner*) | |

The agressiveness of much of this terminology is striking – "drop dead", "devil take you," cursing. Yet we must not draw the conclusion from these few cases that step-relations were particularly prone to conflict. What is more interesting is the symbolic content of the sometimes latent, sometimes overt tension in the relationship. We have suggested earlier that animal terms – breast, dog, mare – tend to model relations in terms of boundaries. People who are dogs or beasts are either outside normal human social categories or have illegitimately crossed boundaries. Similarly, the association with "shit" and "dirt" suggests social impurities, the lack of proper order.[63] Terms such

[63] See the suggestive remarks by Mary Douglas, *Purity and Danger: An Analysis of Concepts of Pollution and Taboo* (London, 1966), pp. 120–8.

as "wanton," "whore," "bagage" and "bugger" all vividly picture sexual and social irregularities, people who are a threat to familial organization, proper distribution of rights and property devolution. Furthermore, "asshole," "cunt," "snot," and words suggesting noisy communication model social relations by use of bodily entrances and exists. Taken altogether, the metaphorical content of abusive terms used between stepmothers and stepdaughters suggests issues of boundaries, order, and legitimacy, the problems consonant with replacing the mother/wife, adjusting lines of authority in the household and between households, confusions of generation and role (stepparents were often the same age as the children, and sometimes even younger), redistribution of resources, and readjustment of lines of inheritance.

Generational turnover is difficult business in any society. It involves great complexity despite the fact that the outcome ultimately is inexorable. By describing the processes in a partible inheritance, small peasant, and handicraft society, I have perhaps too readily implied that the situation is much more straightforward for areas marked by single-son inheritance. But the transitions there are marked by a complexity of their own. Large farms have to have competent managers of both sexes, which creates the significant problem of stepfathers and stepmothers and generational asynchronism. All of the cadets have to be provided for or dispersed in some manner nonthreatening to the home farm. In some societies, parents systematically sought to form different kinds of personalities among their children. In the Basque country, for example, noninheriting, younger sons were adventurous and entrepreneurial, while the heir became placid and rooted.[64] In Upper Austria, older sons developed an authoritarian, self-confident style, while younger children became obsequious, resentful, and furtive.[65] Observers have noticed the divergent traits being systematically constructed while children are very young.[66] In all societies of Europe, notarial records full of disputes, compromises, and settlements give us quite a different picture from the folkloristic one. A careful study of such records would also show that forging a marital union and making a transition between generations both have many steps and call for complicated strategies.

In Neckarhausen society, the shiftover was marked by the fact that the village accommodated in one way or another a large population. The resources available were of widely divergent kinds, ranging from communal plots, to family land, commercial products, pubs, and skilled and unskilled marketable labor.

[64] Leonard Kasdan, "Family Structure, Migration and the Entrepreneur," in *Comparative Studies in Society and History*, 7 (1965): 345–57.

[65] Sigrid Khera, "An Austrian Peasant Village under Rural Industrialization," in *Behavior Science Notes*, 7 (1972): 29–36.

[66] Bernard Vernier, "Putting Kin and Kinship to Good Use: The Circulation of Goods, Labour, and Names on Karpathos (Greece)," in *Interest and Emotion*, ed. Medick and Sabean, pp. 28–76; idem, "Emigration et dérèglement du marché matrimonial," in *Actes de la recherche en sciences sociales*, 15 (1977).

14

# Family charges on the transfer of property

> Since the [reserved portion] is not sufficient for her necessary support and she cannot be expected in her old age and helpless circumstances to suffer hunger and need, and because it is only just that her children supply the necessary victuals in return for the transferred property . . . .
>
> – Voluntary maternal devolution of Anna Bauknecht[1]

In our analysis of nuclear family relations, we have looked at the many ways property provided an idiom in which social and emotional life was expressed. In this chapter, I want to extend the analysis to the reciprocities, expressed or unexpressed, involved in immovable property changing hands. As we have seen, a great deal of land and many buildings shifted ownership in the process of inheritance, but many parcels were also sold or exchanged among fellow villagers, some related to each other by marriage or blood and some not. Of particular interest here are the conditions put on property devolution and sales, especially the setting up a lifetime *rente* or annuity.

## Annuities

When an aged parent retired, he or she could pass on property in return for specified agricultural labor, produce, care, room, or board. Sometime this was done in the course of an inventory for a deceased spouse and sometimes with a specific inventory for the occasion, a *Güterübergabe*, *Vermögenstradition*, or *traditio bonorum*. In all but one instance of the sample we will examine, this act involved a single parent, which shows that it was unusual in Neckarhausen for an elderly couple to retire at the same time. As long as they were both alive, they normally maintained ownership in a house and continued to farm their parcels of land together, hiring labor if necessary. But the formal documents may well hide a far more flexible practice. There are many indications that parents sloughed off property in fits and starts throughout their lives. The

[1] See n. 4.

process of devolution began when each child married. Depending on the strength of the elderly couple and the availability of their children's labor, various strategies could be used to regulate intergenerational needs. We have already noticed that parents and children frequently depended on each other for labor; the basic agricultural tools seldom fell together with the transmission of land. When a son or son-in-law got a horse, plow, and harrow, he could work the parent's land in return for part of the crop or for a wage. Each year, family members could make informal agreements exchanging the use of some parcels for help in cultivating others. We have seen how dependent families were on each other for agricultural equipment, and we can imagine that a complex set of reciprocities were worked out to ensure the proper cultivation of the land. There is far less to go on in terms of female labor, but given the fact that women became so crucial in the more intensive agriculture at the end of the eighteenth century, daughters may well have become a more important connecting link between parents and sons-in-law – which might explain the larger marriage portions given to daughters – or sisters, between brothers-in-law. Taken altogether, there seems to have been a far more flexible practice in the use of land than an analysis of mere ownership would suggest. The formal documents we possess may have been drawn up against a background of informal renting, leasing, sharecropping, and various forms of usufruct.

The language of the documents of transfer (*Übergaben*) suggests that the problem for the aged parent was not so much being unable to work as it was being unable to *manage* the enterprise, which implies not being able to carry out farming without hiring labor or renting out part of the land.

*Alt Hans Mayer transferred his property to his children in 1707 because "over the long run he was not inclined to manage his fields, not only because of age and decrepitude but also because of daily increasing bodily ailments" (seine Feldguth nicht nur allein alters und bawfälligkeit halber, sondern auch wegen täglich anwachsender grossen Anlaagen und Beschwerden in die länge nimmer vorzustehen vermag).*[2] *Wolfgang Waldner's widow could not administer the property alone any more (da sie dem Gut nimmer mehr alleinig vorzustehen können).*[3] *Anna Bauknecht, 67, recently widowed at the death of her husband, Johannes, a carpenter, passed the property on to the children because she could not run her own enterprise (daß sie zu Führung einer aigenen Oeconomie ausser Stand ist).*[4] *Agnesa Bauknecht, widow of Johann Georg, Richter, in 1798 transferred some of her land* (Feldgütern) *to the children because she could not run it with the necessary diligence* (erforderlichen Fleiß).[5] *Barbara Häfner, the widow of Michael, was unable to manage* (administrieren) *her property.*[6] *Jacob Zeug, 89, in 1827 was unable to cultivate* (unfähig zu bauen) *his fields.*[7] *Friedrich*

[2] *Inventuren und Teilungen*, 328 (–.–.1707).
[3] *Inventuren und Teilungen*, 305 (3.4.1704).
[4] *Inventuren und Teilungen*, 710 (21.3.1749).
[5] *Inventuren und Teilungen*, 1112 (28.1.1788).
[6] *Inventuren und Teilungen*, 1062 (26.11.1781).
[7] *Inventuren und Teilungen*, 1540 (24.11.1827).

Table 14.1 *Life annuities, five selected decades*

| Annuity characteristics | 1700–1709 | 1740–9 | 1780–9 | 1820–9 | 1860–9 |
|---|---|---|---|---|---|
| Number of inventories[a] | 14 | 53 | 54 | 58 | 120 |
| Number of transfers (*Übergaben*) | 2 | 4 | 14[b] | 8 | 11 |
| Mean age | 77.5 | 64.3 | 66.0 | 68.0 | 70.7 |
| Age range | 72–83 | 53–70 | 54–80 | 56–89 | 63–80 |
| Male | 1 | 0 | 6 | 3 | 7[c] |
| Female | 1 | 4 | 8 | 5 | 5[c] |
| Reserved portion | 2 | 3 | 14 | 5[d] | 10 |
| Expected produce | 2 | 2 | 9[e] | 7[e] | 3 |
| Right to room | 1 | 2 | 10 | 5 | 2[f] |
| Repossession rights | 2 | 2 | 7 | 2 | 0 |

[a] Includes all nonmarriage inventories.
[b] Includes one single woman, aged 54.
[c] Includes one couple, aged 72 and 74.
[d] Two inventories only property transferred, the inference being that some property was reserved.
[e] One received board.
[f] Room implied in one case.

*Hentzler was no longer capable of profitable administration* (nicht mehr mit Vorteil zu verwalten imstande).[8]

Through the 1820s an explanation for passing on property was always provided, and the reasons overwhelmingly involved managing and administrating (*führen*, *vorstehen*, *verwalten*, *administrieren*).[9] Later on in the century, no explanation was offered for a Vermögenstradition. Perhaps the eighteenth-century ideology of the house prompted a public statement of incapacity, a formal confirmation that an aged adult was giving up the role of Hausvater or Hausmutter. As the nineteenth century progressed, property transfer at a full or partial retirement became a matter of private contract in which explanations were superfluous.

The annuities (*Leibgedinge*, *Ausdinge*) from five selected decades between 1700 and 1869 are summarized in Table 14.1.

[8] *Inventuren und Teilungen*, 1522 (23.6.1826).
[9] I read through all of the inventories for five selected decades: 1700–1709, 1740–9, 1780–9, 1820–9, 1860–9.

In some instances, the retiring parent expressly required an annuity (*Leibrente, Leibgedinge*) consisting of foodstores and maintained the right to the lifetime occupation of a room or place in the house. Sometimes, he or she also kept a reserved portion of the property (*Reservat*), which could comprise a portion of the vegetable garden or a considerable number of arable fields, which the children might be required to farm. Just in case things did not work out, the parents could maintain the right to take back whatever was needed to support themselves.

Most often, the required produce involved a certain amount of spelt each year (usually 1 Scheffel from each child) and whatever summer grain was most often being grown – oats in the eighteenth century and barley in the nineteenth (1 or 2 Simri per child) – some lard (1 Pfund from each child), and a small amount of money (1 Gulden). Alt Hans Mayer in 1707 expected 6 Scheffel spelt and 2 Scheffel oats from his four heirs collectively.[10] Clearly, the specific nature of the support of the elderly person was tied to the fact that property was given up. The contracts made it clear that this was an exchange relation, and even the law recognized the responsibility of a child for a parent to be commensurate with the amount of property passed on. The preamble to the Güterübergabe of the 70-year-old Barbara Falter, stated that she was giving up all of her land to her five children in return for various provisions.[11] The document also noted that since she was giving up everything, it was only fair (*billig*) that the children take care of her needs in her old age. Each was to provide her annually with 1 Scheffel spelt and 2 Pfund lard. When a parent kept back a significant portion, the annuity could be dispensed with. In 1740, Margaretha, the widow of the recently deceased Schultheiss, Johann Georg Rieth, kept a considerable Reservat amounting to 1,347 fl. while transferring 1,064 fl. to each of two children.[12] They were expected in return to cultivate her land, plant the crops, and harvest, transport, and thresh the grain, and deliver it to her storage room. They also had to deliver her communal wood portion, take her grain to the mill, mow her meadows and bring the hay to the barn. In such an instance, no specific amounts of produce were necessary. By contrast, the 67-year-old Anna Bauknecht reserved only a few movables, which "for her necessary support were not sufficient."[13] And it was not reasonable (*zuzumuten*) for her in her old age and helpless (*ratlos*) condition to suffer hunger and need and was only fair that her children provide her sufficient foodstuffs because of the transferred property (*wegen des ihnen übergebenden Vermögens*). Each of them was responsible each year for 1 Scheffel spelt, 1 Simri barley, 1 Imi wine, a quarter Wannen hay, and 2 fl. When Andreas Feldmaier, a field guard, gave up his land because he could no longer manage it, he specified

[10] *Inventuren und Teilungen*, 328 (–.–.1707). This was far more than he would have needed for his personal use and would have allowed him to sell a portion.
[11] *Inventuren und Teilungen*, 691 (13.5.1747).
[12] *Inventuren und Teilungen*, 609 (10.8.1740).
[13] *Inventuren und Teilungen*, 710 (21.3.1749).

an annuity, but said that he would not expect it to be paid as long as he could work and earn his bread working for the village.[14] In the 1780s, many villagers kept a small reserved portion, a garden, a vineyard, a meadow, or a flaxland, and some movables, not enough to live on without a regular supply of provisions. In many cases, this was just enough to keep the elderly person busy, although even then he or she might need help. Johanna Speidel, 70, kept a garden and, of course, maintained her rights in a communal plot.[15] Besides the annual supply of provisions, she expected to have her garden and flaxland plowed, harrowed, and manured. Margaretha Heinser kept a considerable reserved portion and expected her two sons to provide all of her labor needs free of charge.[16] Johannes Bauknecht kept a small Reservat but required no further Leibgeding than an annual 1.5 fl. from each child, since he wanted to cultivate his own parcels. By the 1860s, it was unusual for a parent to demand a specific annuity. Most of them kept sufficient land to support themselves. Barbara, the widow of Salomon Brodbeck, 66, did not require a Leibrente because she possessed the necessary means of subsistence.[17] Margaretha Waldner, 63, the widow of Christoph Zeug, kept enough property to live on, but maintained the right to require an Ausgeding if necessary.[18] Ludwig Friedrich Federschmid, carpenter, 67, demanded an Ausding of 5 fl. each from three of his children but for the rest had enough property not to require more.[19] Jacob Bauknecht, Bauer, 74, did not request an annuity, since he reserved so much property that he could live from it free from care (*sorgenlos*).[20] Friedrich Petermann, 74, and his wife Christina Catharina Schach, 72, kept the house and barn and vegetable garden, a meadow, all of the movables with livestock and agricultural implements, and the communal plots for their support (*Sustentation*).[21] Maria Catharina Deuschle, 66, widow of Salomon Hentzler, kept more than enough for her support (*Unterhalt*).[22] The 80-year-old Friedrich Baur, carpenter, allowed some land to go to his grandchildren because his property situation (*Vermögensverhältnisse*) allowed it.[23]

Besides having the necessary victuals, aged parents also needed a place to live. Many of the property transfers spelled out their rights to specific living quarters, most often a place to sleep in the main living room (*Wohnstube*) together with the small unheated room (*Kammer*) next to it. They also frequently set aside space in the attic, in the stall, and in the shed or barn.

*Wolfgang Waldner's widow, 72, in 1704 kept the use rights to the whole house.*[24]

[14] *Inventuren und Teilungen*, 1041 (15.3.1780).
[15] *Inventuren und Teilungen*, 1079 (13.1.1783).
[16] *Inventuren und Teilungen*, 1082 (16.2.1785).
[17] *Inventuren und Teilungen*, 3136 (27.1.1860).
[18] *Inventuren und Teilungen*, 3170 (12.11.1862).
[19] *Inventuren und Teilungen*, 3177 (3.3.1863).
[20] *Inventuren und Teilungen*, 3179 (7.4.1863).
[21] *Inventuren und Teilungen*, 3211 (10.12.1864).
[22] *Inventuren und Teilungen*, 3284 (25.2.1868).
[23] *Inventuren und Teilungen*, 3290 (19.5.1868).
[24] *Inventuren und Teilungen*, 305 (3.4.1704).

*Margaretha Rieth, who kept a great deal of land, expected lifelong possession of the front room* (Wohnstube) *and chamber* (Stubenkammer).[25] *Barbara Falter sold her remaining quarter house to her son Adam in return for lifelong domicile* (Sitz).[26] *The 67-year-old Anna Bauknecht, who could not manage her own* Oeconomie *because she lived in such miserable circumstances* (lebt in solch betrübten Umständen), *kept not only the right to the* Wohnstube *and* Stubenkammer *but also enough stall space to maintain her livestock.*[27] *Barbara Häfner, 71, had a 47-year-old daughter incapable of taking care of herself* (simpel und krüppelhaft).[28] *Both were to have lifelong domicile in the house. Juliana Speidel sold a quarter house to her son to add to the one he already had.*[29] *She kept the use of the front room and chamber, while he got the right to purchase the remaining half house at the current price after her death. Johann Georg Sterr, whose sister had lived with him for a long time, specified life-long domicile in the house for her.*[30] *His 10-year-old daughter was to remain with him in the front part of the house until she married. As for himself, if he could not get along with his son, Matheus, the latter was required to pay his rent* (Hauszins) *wherever he moved to. Margaretha Heinser was to get the* Stubenkammer *and enough wood for fireplace and oven* (Herd and Ofen).[31] *Agnesa Bauknecht, 62, kept the front room, the portion of the attic above it, and place in the shed, celler, courtyard, and stall.*[32] *The 75-year-old Johannes Bauknecht also kept storage space for his grain and a place in the shed and requested enough wood for his fireplace and heating oven.*[33] *In 1826, Anna Maria Baur, 72, was concerned with room, wood, and light, and was especially anxious to have space for washing and cooking, a typical set of demands in the 1820s.*[34]

*By the 1860s, parents seldom specified the right to domicile. Instead they almost always kept back a portion of the house for themselves. Margaretha, the widow of Christoph Zeug, allowed one son to purchase three-quarters of the house and provided that he could purchase her remaining quarter at the same price rate after her death.*[35] *Jacob Bauknecht, Michael Murr, Michael Ebinger, and Friedrich Petermann made similar arrangements.*[36] *Through the 1820s, most parents inserted a clause to the effect that if they could not get along with the new householder, the latter would have to pick up their rent somewhere else. There were no such clauses in the 1860s, which reflects the fact that the parents either kept at least part of the buildings in their ownership or had enough resources to support themselves. It goes without saying that a child could not*

25 *Inventuren und Teilungen*, 609 (10.8.1740).
26 *Inventuren und Teilungen*, 691 (13.5.1747).
27 *Inventuren und Teilungen*, 710 (21.3.1749).
28 *Inventuren und Teilungen*, 1062 (26.11.1781).
29 *Inventuren und Teilungen*, 1079 (13.1.1783).
30 *Inventuren und Teilungen*, 1081 (15.2.1785).
31 *Inventuren und Teilungen*, 1082 (16.2.1785).
32 *Inventuren und Teilungen*, 1112 (28.1.1788).
33 *Inventuren und Teilungen*, 1126 (9.3.1789).
34 *Inventuren und Teilungen*, 1494 (25.3.1826).
35 *Inventuren und Teilungen*, 3170 (12.11.1862).
36 *Inventuren und Teilungen*, 3179 (7.4.1863); 3190 (20.6.1864); 3204 (3.9.1864); 3211 (10.12.1864).

*alienate a parent's right to domicile by selling the house, and any purchaser had to assume whatever conditions the seller was obligated to.*[37]

In most cases, parents made provisions for the eventuality that children might not fulfill the contract.

*Alt Hans Mayer in 1707 specified that if the children were negligent* (saumselig), *he could take back whatever property was necessary to pay for what was in arrears.*[38] *Wolfgang Waldner's widow said that if she were to be left in need, she could reclaim usufruct of the transferred property.*[39] *Barbara Falter maintained the right not just to take back the transferred property to use to support herself but the children's marriage endowments as well.*[40] *In 1780, Rebecca Brodbeck, the widow of Johannes Georg, Bauer, 80, specified that if the children proved themselves to be hard-hearted* (lieblos), *she could take the land and sell it.*[41] *Barbara Häfner, 71, maintained ownership of everything she transferred.*[42] *Juliana Speidel wanted her children to take care of her additional needs should she fall sick.*[43] *She could sell portions of the property if the children did not fulfill the contract or were hard-hearted. Johann Georg Sterr warned his children not to act* moros.[44] *And Margaretha Heinser kept ownership rights just in case her children would prove* moros *or wasteful.*[45] *Johannes Bauknecht wanted to take care of his own necessities from the reserved parcels.*[46] *If that did not prove to be enough, the children were to supply his needs or allow him to take back parts of the transferred property. In 1825, Margaretha Burckhardt said that if the children did not act as they should, she could take back the property.*[47] *Friedrich Hentzler specified that if one of his five children did not act in a proper filial fashion* (kindlich), *the others were responsible for him or her.*[48] *By the 1860s, parents no longer maintained the right to attach the transferred property or revoke it in any way. Typically, old Salomon Häfner specified that the property rights of his children were to be unlimited.*[49] *Once Barbara Brodbeck transferred property to her children, all competing claims of ownership could be expunged from the property registers.*[50] *Jacob Bauknecht divided all his property on slips to be apportioned to the children by lot.*[51] *They had eight days*

[37] See, for example, the case of Alt Hans Mayer who sold his house to his DDH, Salomon Falter, with the condition that he would have lifetime domicile. Falter in turn sold it to Hans Michael Haye with the condition that Mayer would continue to have lifelong domicile; *Kaufbuch*, vol. 2, f. 62 (14.12.1707); f. 71 (26.8.1709).

[38] *Inventuren und Teilungen*, 328 (–.–.1707).

[39] *Inventuren und Teilungen*, 305 (3.4.1704).

[40] *Inventuren und Teilungen*, 691 (13.5.1747).

[41] *Inventuren und Teilungen*, 1042 (31.10.1780).

[42] *Inventuren und Teilungen*, 1062 (26.11.1781).

[43] *Inventuren und Teilungen*, 1079 (13.1.1783).

[44] *Inventuren und Teilungen*, 1081 (15.2.1785).

[45] *Inventuren und Teilungen*, 1082 (16.2.1785).

[46] *Inventuren und Teilungen*, 1126 (9.3.1789).

[47] *Inventuren und Teilungen*, 1504 (17.3.1825).

[48] *Inventuren und Teilungen*, 1522 (23.6.1826).

[49] *Inventuren und Teilungen*, 3138 (13.12.1859).

[50] *Inventuren und Teilungen*, 3136 (27.1.1860).

[51] *Inventuren und Teilungen*, 3179 (7.4.1863).

*to sell or exchange parcels to each other, after which the property would be in their unlimited ownership. By the mid-nineteenth century, parents kept enough property for themselves to ensure their survival and apartments in their houses to maintain their independence. What they passed on to their children was property they no longer needed to support themselves or their minor children.*

One of the things which emerges from this material is the fact that retiring parents ensured their own independence. They had their own cooking place, their own wood supply, and enough flour and lard to maintain themselves, and in many instances enough to sell.[52] Quite often, they also kept livestock in the barns, and they had garden plots, arable fields, meadows, vineyards, and flaxlands. Since they were still Bürger, they had the right to village gardens, cabbage plots, and kindling. In very few cases is there any evidence that parents and married children made up a commensal group. In the occasional instance where a parent expected cooked food, the circumstances of health suggest that he or she was bedridden. Quite frequently, as parents transferred property to their children, they were concerned with the eventuality of their final illness and specified that they would receive nursing, care, and support during that time. But at the moment of the transfer itself, they were still independent. By passing on property, they were ensuring themselves a labor supply and farm produce. What these documents capture is a tension between family care and independence. The entire transaction makes the terms of reciprocity explicit – the children got land in return for specified actions, which if not fulfilled would lead to a revocation of the agreement. We must not imagine, however, that such clauses reflect the experience of filial neglect. In the annual list of poor, there were seldom old people to be found with close relatives living in the village. In fact, the most likely candidates for public support were orphans without any property, middle-aged widows, work-shy men, or people with physical disabilities who had no immediate relatives to care for them. Elderly people either held onto property until they died or made a deal with their children which was designed not so much to ensure their support as to provide a foundation for their independence.

When we survey the documentation as a whole, what is impressive is how infrequent the practice of setting up an annuity was. In the first and fifth decades of the eighteenth century, we only find two and four instances, respectively (Table 14.1). The peak of the practice occurred late in the eighteenth century, but declined again already by the early nineteenth century. Measured in terms of available documents of transfer – pre- and postmortem inventories – the

[52] Compare the treatment in George C. Homans, *English Villagers of the Thirteenth Century* (Cambridge, Mass., 1941), pp. 144–9; also Alan Macfarlane's critique, *The Origins of English Individualism: The Family, Property and Scoial Transition* (Cambridge, 1978), pp. 140–4. I am arguing here that ownership and contracts are not adequate criteria for sorting out "individualism" and "familism." See also David Gaunt, "Formen der Altersversorgung in Bauernfamilien Nord- und Mitteleuropas," in *Historische Familienforschung*, ed. Michael Mitterauer and Reinhard Sieder (Frankfurt, 1982), pp. 156–91.

rates of premortem property devolution during the first half of the eighteenth century and the early decades of the nineteenth were about the same (about 14 percent). By the mid-nineteenth century, the rate had declined to well under 10 percent. Apart from the 1780s, all of our figures suggest that premortem property transfers of a surviving parent fluctuated between 8 and 14 percent of all instances of inheritance. But only a subset of these involved annuities at all – in the first two and last decade, only two, two, and three, respectively. In every instance we have studied, the children were in fact capable of supplying the parents' labor needs. Usually they were married, and in most instances there were several of them living in the village. Most likely, the children had disputes among themselves about equality of effort. Therefore, what the parent could no longer administer were the labor inputs of the children. Or perhaps the latter refused to work for the parents unless they finally gave up a part of the land. In any event, a complex set of pressures and demands probably lay behind premortem property transfers. Annuities were there in order to ensure as much independence as a parent could muster and the threats operated to secure equality among the children. Each child had his own portion of the contract to fulfill – so many Scheffel to spelt and so forth – and the parent could attach specific portions belonging to individual children to insure compliance. Even those contracts which required labor set up an annual system of rotation so that responsibility was individualized, and children were not collectively responsible for providing goods from tilling the soil.[53]

Despite the possibility of setting up an annuity, the documents show that over the entire period, the most common practice was for the parent to hold onto property until he or she died. Children received a property settlement at marriage and may well have gotten some more at the death of their first parent. At that moment, instead of the estate being apportioned among the heirs by a *Realteilung*, an inventory was taken, laying out the shares accruing to the widow or widower and the other heirs, but leaving all the property in the usufruct of the surviving spouse (*Eventualteilung*). The survivor could allow all or part of the estate of the deceased partner to be portioned out, but such a practice was, in fact, infrequent, especially if there were still dependent children at home or the widow or widower still had hopes of marrying. The evidence suggests that most parents were able to utilize their children's labor in some manner or other until they died without bowing to pressure to give over.

Finally, we might ask in what way the practices after the mid-nineteenth century differed from earlier. To begin with, the average age of retirees rose progressively from the 1740s onwards. By the 1860s, almost all of them were between the ages of 66 and 75. By this time as well, men were just as prominent as women in making premortem property transfers. Although the reasons for retiring were no longer specified, the situation here may reflect greater longevity and a culturally established norm for retirement. In any event, almost all

[53] *Inventuren und Teilungen*, 3441 (28.1.1788).

of these cases involve people who retained enough land to ensure their economic independence, and none of them maintained the right to attach any of the transferred property. Apparently they did not have any minor children or dependents at home and could manage on reduced agricultural land. Still, most landholders during the period retained the bulk of their estates until they died. All of the documentation testifies to the nineteenth-century trend of increased dependence of the younger, married population on their elders.

## Conditional sales

Another possible form of premortem transmission was, of course, through the sale of real estate. The land market is discussed in Chapter 15; however, we need to note here the possibility that, just like Übergaben, sales could take place with conditions. Table 14.2 summarizes conditional sales for the same decades examined earlier.

In almost every case of conditional sale, the property being conveyed was a house. In one curious incident, Conrad Geiger's widow sold a large number of parcels to her sons, son-in-law, and grandchildren in return for an annuity and labor on her reserved strips.[54] Subsequently, the sale was canceled because she had not been provided with a Kriegsvogt and the minor children involved had not had a guardian (Pfleger) present. An official from Nürtingen wrote that the transaction had taken place because those involved had corrupted the local officials (*zusammengeschmiert*). For the rest, conditional sales most often involved selling a house for a specified amount of money in exchange for lifelong domicile and eventual care. Such conditional sales were not frequent; one occurred about every five years or so in the nineteenth century. In more than half of the instances here, the sale was to other than a lineal heir, in contrast to the Vermögenstraditionen studied above. It appears that selling a house, perhaps at a favorable price, outside the lines of inheritance was a residual method for ensuring independence at retirement. Along with the secured room usually went a place to cook and firewood and lighting. In a few instances, a house encumbered with the provision of lifetime tenure of an aged parent had gone to a lineal heir, who in turn sold the house to a nonrelative, inserting the necessary clause of conditional ownership.

## Redemption

We have dealt in the course of the book with many of the ways property structured family relations in Neckarhausen. The process of transition from one generation to another involved a complicated discourse about dependence, self-sufficiency, equality, right and obligation. The expectations generated in

[54] *Kaufbuch*, vol. 2, f. 41–3 (9.12.1703).

Table 14.2 *Conditional sales of real property, selected decades*

| Sales | 1700–1709 | 1740–9 | 1780–9 | 1820–9 | 1860–9 |
|---|---|---|---|---|---|
| Number of buildings sold | 19 | 48 | 46 | 116 | 81 |
| Number of conditional sales | 5 | 2 | 0 | 10 | 3 |
| Buildings with conditions | 5 | 2 | — | 9 | 3 |
| To son | 1 | 0 | — | 3 | 1 |
| To son-in-law | 0 | 0 | — | 1 | 1 |
| To other relation | 2[a] | 1[b] | — | 2[c] | 0 |
| To no relation | 2[d] | 1 | — | 4 | 1 |

[a] Brother-in-law, DDH.
[b] One BS.
[c] MH, B.
[d] Buyer four years later married seller's M-in-L.
*Source*: *Kaufbücher*.

the process of inheritance may have continually shifted as the character of various family members developed, or the economic situation, governmental interference, or the fortunes of war altered the situation. In one way or another, parents and children were concerned with land as a fundamental means of livelihood and social existence. Perhaps no villager ever looked at others without placing them consciously or unconsciously in a hierarchy of esteem derived from how much land they held, where it came from, and what they did with it. The rules of access to property were therefore fundamental to family and village dynamics. So far we have been looking at the various issues that have to do with property devolution. Land and buildings, plows and sacks of grain could be disbursed with or without a will after the death of a parent, portioned out with the marriage of children, or passed on in the complex negotiations between senior and junior adults. The distribution of real property was also subject to the village land market. In Chapter 15, we examine the nature and size of that market (in Chapter 16 we look at the way family interest and village interest in immovable property interconnected). The particular institution of concern here is the *Losungsrecht*, or the right to redemption – or what sometimes, too globally, is referred to as *retrait lignager*.

The right of redemption was handled in the Third Württemberg Law Code of 1610 under the title "Von Losungen" or "De jure retractus."[55] Only one of three types of redemption was directly based on family principles. The first was

[55] "3. Landrecht," (1610), in Reyscher, vol. 5, pp. 203–9.

called *Zinslosung* (later also *Gültlosung*) and had to do with land which was held in inheritable tenure (*Zins* and *Gült* were forms of rent). In general, there was a good deal of tension in Württemberg state practice about allowing tenancies to fractionalize either through sale or inheritance, and ordinances were continually promulgated to forbid it unless there were pressing reasons (*bewegende Ursachen*). In the course of time this latter clause led to the rise of the smallholding peasantry which characterized most of the territory by the eighteenth century. Whenever a fractionalized tenancy was sold, one of the holders of the property could redeem that portion, the greater right going to the person with the largest holding. *Marklosung* specified that a village Bürger had the right within a year and a day to redeem any parcel sold to an outsider. Finally, the heirs to an estate could make the portioning out of an inheritance or the sale of any real estate conditional (*anbedingen*). That is, the participants would have the right to redeem (*Erblosung*) any parcel subsequently sold, choosing among themselves by lot in the case of several interested parties. In the 1610 version of the law, lineal descendants participated in the right even if they were not specifically mentioned in the original agreement, and conflicting interests were sorted out by stem. Whenever a plot was sold outside the group of heirs and not redeemed according to law, it was no longer subject to redemption.

Only the Erblosung was a true retrait lignager, the recovery of family property by a line. It was possible only when an original agreement among a set of heirs established the right of redemption, as the law code put it, "by understandable words." And the exercise of the right was limited to a year and a day after a contract of sale was concluded. An *Auslöser* could only redeem a property for his own use. Somewhat earlier, an ordinance had sorted out precedence among the various forms of redemption.[56] Zinslosung took precedence over the other two forms, with the larger holder having first right unless he or she was an outsider to the village. Marklosung went before a conditional Erblosung. All of these forms of redemption were meant to combat the fractionalization of land and the dispersal of rights outside the village. In many instances, they offered family members different ways of exercising their rights against each other. Because more land, as I shall show, passed to individuals through inheritance than through sale, and since tenancies were broken up for the heirs in the process of devolution, people redeeming parcels through Zinslosung were likely to be related to each other. By exercising the right of Marklosung, a villager might well be excluding a close relative who had moved out of the village from maintaining rights there. Still, the balance of the system favored recomposing the larger farm units over the maintenance of a family estate. It therefore frequently gave more extended kin or unrelated people greater rights over closer kin. However, redemption was not inimical to a market. A person could only redeem after a sale had taken place and at the contracted price.

[56] "Verordnung, den Vorzug unter verschiedenen Losungsberechtigten betreffend" (24 April 1588), in Reyscher, vol. 4, pp. 451–2.

Despite its various forms, redemption had little effect on fractionalization over the long run.

Various ordinances defined the law of redemption more closely from time to time. In 1739, houses which were sold to relatives with lifelong rights to domicile, board, and care were excluded from redemption.[57] Also parents were permitted to redeem property in favor of their children. In 1815, all forms of redemption, except for conditional Erblosung and the recovery of property officially sold for debt, were abolished.[58] Even the right of heirs to redeem real property was limited to 30 days and could not be exercised against someone who him- or herself also had Losungsrecht or was a lineal descendent of the seller. Above all, lineal descendents of the parties of the original conditional contract no longer participated in it – the right disappeared with the person. In the case of several interested parties, the one who first fulfilled the condition of the contract – paid up – had the redemption right. In this fashion, after 1815, state ideology shifted its focus as far as land was concerned from maintaining viable farms to encouraging efficient production through a free market in real estate. In the process, fellow villagers were placed on an equal footing as far as the access to land was concerned and not distinguished from outsiders. Any legal limitations to the land market rooted in family considerations were severely restricted.

Apparently the actual exercise of the right of redemption only became important in the course of the eighteenth century. It would be very difficult to sort out which form of Losung was being exercised at any time, since the nature of the right was only occasionally specified in the registers of sales (Kaufbücher). For example, during the decade of the 1780s, there were 81 redemptions but only in 15 instances was the particular right under which they were exercised mentioned. During this period, 9 were expressly Erblosungen; 5, Zins- or Gültlosungen; and 1, a Marklosung. As far as I can see, this would overestimate the conditional heirship redemption, which probably (judging from the relative frequency of similar surnames) occurred rather less often than that based on ownership of part of a tenancy. Redemption of land sold to outsiders could, in any event, not have been considerable, since comparatively little real estate was sold to them. Table 14.3 compares the number of redemptions and the total number of sales in the five decades under consideration.

One of the characteristics of peasants is said to be an interest in keeping property in the family. There is absolutely no evidence that in Neckarhausen any particular properties were regarded as belonging to a lineage, kindred, or house. But that did not mean that kin were not interested parties in real estate transactions. Good land and suitable buildings were scarce goods, and people might well have given relatives first shot at a parcel without being willing to

[57] "Generalreskript, des Losungsrecht betreffend" (29.5.1739), in Reyscher, vol. 6, pp. 439–40.

[58] "Königliche General-Verordnung, die Aufhebung der Losungen betr." (2.3.1815), in Reyscher, vol. 7, pp. 446–9.

Table 14.3 *Frequency of redemptions, selected decades*

| Transactions | 1700–1709 | 1740–9 | 1780–9 | 1820–9 | 1860–9 |
|---|---|---|---|---|---|
| Sales of real estate | 183 | 351 | 585 | 818 | 494 |
| Redemptions | 7 | 25 | 81 | 0 | 0 |
| Percentage | 3.83 | 7.12 | 13.85 | 0 | 0 |

lower the price. Or kin might well have been able to get land from each other on favorable terms – at a *Freundschaftspreis* (kinship price), as the Kaufbuch occasionally put it, or with payments over a long term with low or no interest. Furthermore, kinship could cut two ways. A person might wish to sell to a friend or relative as part of a move to develop or maintain certain relations. A closer relative who redeemed the land would be violating the political strategy of near kin. Each move had its own meaning as part of an intricate web of transactions, and a purchase in the name of kinship might be the most selfish and interested one. Indeed, some sellers put in a reversion clause in the case of redemption.

In Neckarhausen, redemptions were always a residual factor in the market, and formally, at least, those on the basis of lineal rights made up only a fraction – probably at the height only 6 or 7 percent – of all sales. The rise of redemption correlated with the rise of the market. But by the 1820s, even when lineal redemption was formally possible, no one was interested in it any more.

Württemberg law specified various ways in which real estate could be subject to legal encumbrances, divided use, and reversionary rights. Some of the institutions appear to have been inimical to a free market in land and buildings, but we must not put too much weight on that interpretation. As a practical matter, annuities, retirement contracts, and conditional sales were all relatively infrequent. Even then, they occurred with declining frequency by the end of the eighteenth century. There is nothing "peasant" about most such practices, and modern, capitalist societies employ many such encumbrances. Indeed, the modern legal systems provide for far more complicated possibilities. As for redemption, the only inhibition with regard to the market is that the buyer might conclude it would be useless to bid on a parcel if a relative was sure to redeem it. Still, formally at least, the market set the price. By the early nineteenth century, whatever brake the practice put on prices and transactions was done away with.

# 15

# The real estate market

The number of inhabitants here has increased all too much so that the [already] high price of property has gone up.

– Gerichtsprotocoll (1751)[1]

It might be argued that a truly kin-controlled land system would be one in which land never comes onto the market. Commercialization of property might then be considered one indicator of a move away from ascribed relationships to ones of convenience and mutual advantage. Simply to measure an increasing commercialization of land – the amount coming onto the market, its price, and its rate of turnover – would be a first step in showing the rate at which it lost its capacity to integrate family interests. An increase in the amount of land bought and sold and in the volume of transactions, a decline in barter, a decrease in the average-size plot, a rise in the average price, an increase in the formality of transaction, and a decline in encumbrances on property – each of these things would seem to describe separately sufficiently but together overwhelmingly the rate at which property holding was divorced from family considerations. They might even be taken as a measure of the trajectory of individualism.[2] A further step in the analysis would be to trace the relationships between buyers and sellers to see if kin sold to one another and to what kind of kin. Whatever results might be found would not, however, be lacking in ambiguity. Suppose that in a period of low market turnover of land people did not sell to kin, but under opposite conditions did. Would we be witnessing the strengthening of kin ties in the face of the assault of money? In the first instance, we might conclude that most land remained in the family and was transmitted through inheritance. For whatever reasons, occasional parcels were sold outside the sphere of family interest now and then and in any event would only have been "released" when family members had no interest in holding them. In the second instance, inheritance plays less of a role and family relations get caught up in the general monetization of all relationships. If relatives want land, they have to bid for it on the open market like everyone else.

[1] *Gericht*, vol. 1, f. 37 (3.3.1751).
[2] See the discussion in Chapter 16.

That means that the market mediates the extent to which land is sold to kin and correspondingly the nature of relations within the family. Furthermore, in a situation where inheritance institutions sort out access to land, the rhythms of generational turnover are respected, and rights are bestowed according to ascriptive rules – age, sex, and position in the sequence of siblings. The market ought to break up such rhythms in favor of the young because it reinforces the calculation of interest and profitability and undercuts customary authority relations inside the family founded on the ability to command resources.

Another important consideration is the degree to which land and houses were sold to family and nonfamily members. First, however, we need to assess the size and nature of the real estate market. Although the exact weight of retrait lignager cannot be assessed, family claims of this nature could not have affected more than 6 or 7 percent of sales even at the peak in the 1780s. Although heirship redemption remained a possibility after 1815, no one – at least in the 1820s or 1860s – bothered to use it. Few if any families placed a redemption clause in an inventory or sales contract, and even well before the restrictions in the code of 1815, the practice was in decline. In contrast to sales of houses, sellers rarely put conditions on the sales of land. As far as dwellings were concerned, conditions were more frequently placed on premortem transfers than on sales. By the mid-nineteenth century, in terms of the volume of cases, neither form of transaction was very likely to involve anything but the transfer of full ownership. Even earlier, encumbrances on real estate were rare.

If these data suggest that property was subject to ever fewer restrictions of ownership in the course of the eighteenth and nineteenth centuries, there are also indications of an increasing formality in market transactions themselves. By the 1740s we frequently, and by the 1780s usually, find that real estate was sold in the village by public auction. Every such sale was announced "at the church door" before it was to take place and then was publicly offered for bidding "by burning light" on three separate occasions. The highest bidder won, and it was only subsequently that a redemption right could be exercised. Whatever price the Löser paid was ostensibly set by a public, open, and formal market.

Trends in property transactions over the period can be demonstrated in the sales recorded in the Kaufbücher for five selected decades between 1700 and 1870 which are about 40 years apart. In the decade 1700–1709, there were a total of 229 transactions, about a fifth of which were exchanges – one piece of arable for another, a vineyard for a flaxland (Table 15.1). Most transactions involved Neckarhausen inhabitants, although there were some sales in which one party lived in another village or town, usually because an outsider had sloughed off a bit of inheritance too far away to be of use. In the 1740s, a significant proportion of transactions were still made up of exchanges, in contrast to the 1780s and thereafter, when no transactions went around the market. Yet even in the mid-eighteenth century the significance of exchanges had declined to half the proportion they had had earlier. Whereas the absolute number of

Table 15.1 *Frequency of sales and exchanges of real estate among villagers and with outsiders, selected decades*

| Transfer | 1700–1709 | 1740–9 | 1780–9 | 1820–9 | 1860–9 |
|---|---|---|---|---|---|
| *Sales* | | | | | |
| Both NH[a] | 137 | 285 | 471 | 721 | 408 |
| 1 NH | 43 | 50 | 99 | 79 | 69 |
| Neither NH | 5 | 16 | 15 | 18 | 17 |
| *Exchanges* | | | | | |
| Both NH | 41 | 40 | 2 | 0 | 0 |
| 1 NH | 3 | 6 | 0 | 0 | 0 |
| Neither NH | 0 | 1 | 0 | 0 | 0 |
| Total | 229 | 398 | 587 | 818 | 494 |

[a] Neckarhausen.

exchanges remained stationary, sales rose 89.7 percent. Even though the market for land had heated up, it was just as much an internal one: 81.2 percent compared with 81.5 percent. It would never fall below 80 percent, peaking in the 1820s at 88.1 percent.

By the ninth decade of the eighteenth century, direct trading of land or houses had ceased. All transactions were simple sales of one kind or another, some contracted for privately, but a majority sold at public auction. Between the 1740s and 80s, sales rose another 66.7 percent. The extraordinary market of the 1820s was in part due to bankruptcy and general disarray in the period following the Napoleonic Wars, when extreme famine was followed by the collapse of grain prices. There were almost four-and-a-half times more sales in the 1820s than in the first decade of the eighteenth century. By the 1860s,

Table 15.2 *Frequency of sales of real estate by type, selected decades*

| Type of sale | 1700–1709 | 1740–9 | 1780–9 | 1820–9 | 1860–9 |
|---|---|---|---|---|---|
| Single strips (total) | 130 | 282 | 507 | 635 | 372 |
| Arable | 68 | 183 | 353 | 455 | 245 |
| Meadow | 5 | 24 | 28 | 38 | 87 |
| Garden | 7 | 17 | 26 | 26 | 18 |
| Flaxland | 18 | 18 | 49 | 46 | 21 |
| Vineyard | 32 | 40 | 51 | 70 | 1 |
| Buildings | 19 | 48 | 46 | 116 | 81 |
| Mixed/more than one | 33 | 16 | 24 | 46 | 19 |
| Other | 3 | 5 | 8 | 21 | 22 |
| Total sales | 185 | 351 | 585 | 818 | 494 |

transactions had fallen to close to what they had been in the mid- to late 1700s. The drop after 1820 was equal to the rise after 1780 (about 40 percent).

Table 15.2 lists the sales by kind of property being transferred. At the beginning of the eighteenth century, two-fifths of the sales involved one parcel of arable land. In all the other periods single arable strips made up over 50 percent of the property market, peaking in the 1780s at three-fifths. Early in the eighteenth century, the category "mixed/more than one" made up a substantial proportion of the sales (17.8 percent), but that category declined (to about 5 percent) as sales came to consist largely of specific plots or buildings sold one item at a time. In the 1820s, the principal change in the market was the rise in the sale of buildings. There was an acute shortage of houses, as well as stalls, barns, and sheds to take care of the needs of an agriculture newly committed to stall feeding. Not until the 1830s would a new wave of house building take place, but the demand was clearly reflected in the sharp turnover of buildings and parts of buildings in the 1820s. By the 1860s, the absolute sale of houses and buildings was twice that of the eighteenth century, and as a percentage of the market (16.4 percent) it was even higher than in the 1820s (14.2 percent versus 7.9 percent in the 1780s). Capital equipment for stall feeding – barns, sheds, stalls – and homes for a larger population more heavily committed to artisanal trades kept that market lively. And the new group of factory workers had most of their assets in portions of buildings. Viniculture disappeared in the 1820s, and with it land classified as vineyard.[3] Much arable land had been converted to meadow in the 1830s and 1840s as intensive stall feeding and cattle raising developed, which accounts for the fact that meadowland transactions increased from 4.6 to 17.6 percent (a fourfold increase in sales matched a fourfold rise in the area devoted to meadowland).

Structurally, one of the main changes in the land market of the nineteenth century was the entry of women (Table 15.3). They were no longer restricted to marginal pieces but were prominent in the arable and building markets. Earlier, just the occasional widow purchased land, but now many unmarried women became involved. Altogether women accounted for 10 percent of the purchases in the 1820s, and even later in the century their part remained comparatively significant. This is another difference between the nineteenth and the eighteenth centuries. We have already pointed to the fact that the percentage of adult women in the population rose in the nineteenth century and that many of them spent fewer years married, either never marrying or remaining widowed when the opportunity arose.

We need to be able to assess the development of the real estate market in more exact terms before we ask questions about its overall function in the system of village social exchange. The market, after all, is frequently treated as an abstraction rather than as a social formation, which can be rather different

[3] Technically, viniculture was given up in 1817, but it took more than a decade for those plots to be labeled "meadow."

Table 15.3 *Frequency of real estate sales to women*

| Status | Arable | Meadow | Garden[a] | Buildings | Mixed/more than one | Not given/ other | Total | Percentage of sales |
|---|---|---|---|---|---|---|---|---|
| 1700–1709 | | | | | | | | |
| Widowed | 0 | 0 | 0 | 0 | 0 | 0 | 0 | |
| Married | 0 | 0 | 0 | 0 | 0 | 0 | 0 | |
| Single | 0 | 0 | 0 | 0 | 0 | 0 | 0 | |
| NG | 0 | 0 | 0 | 0 | 0 | 0 | 0 | |
| Total | 0 | 0 | 0 | 0 | 0 | 0 | 0 | 0 |
| 1740–9 | | | | | | | | |
| Widowed | 0 | 0 | 0 | 3 | 0 | 0 | 3 | |
| Married | 0 | 0 | 0 | 0 | 0 | 0 | 0 | |
| Single | 0 | 0 | 3 | 1 | 0 | 0 | 4 | |
| NG | 0 | 0 | 0 | 0 | 0 | 0 | 0 | |
| Total | 0 | 0 | 3 | 4 | 0 | 0 | 7 | 2.0 |
| 1780–9 | | | | | | | | |
| Widowed | 8 | 3 | 1 | 2 | 0 | 0 | 14 | |

Table 15.3 *(cont.)*

| Status | Arable | Meadow | Garden[a] | Buildings | Mixed/more than one | Not given/ other | Total | Percentage of sales |
|---|---|---|---|---|---|---|---|---|
| Married | 0 | 0 | 0 | 1 | 0 | 0 | 1 | |
| Single | 3 | 1 | 1 | 3 | 0 | 0 | 8 | |
| NG | 0 | 0 | 0 | 0 | 0 | 0 | 0 | |
| Total | 11 | 4 | 2 | 6 | 0 | 0 | 23 | 3.9 |
| 1820–9 | | | | | | | | |
| Widowed | 7 | 0 | 1 | 2 | 0 | 0 | 10 | |
| Married | 4 | 0 | 0 | 1 | 1 | 0 | 6 | |
| Single | 33 | 2 | 11 | 9 | 1 | 0 | 56 | |
| NG | 7 | 0 | 2 | 0 | 0 | 0 | 9 | |
| Total | 51 | 2 | 14 | 12 | 2 | 0 | 81 | 9.9 |
| 1860–9 | | | | | | | | |
| Widowed | 6 | 1 | 0 | 5 | 1 | 0 | 13 | |
| Married | 2 | 3 | 0 | 2 | 0 | 1 | 8 | |
| Single | 6 | 6 | 1 | 3 | 1 | 0 | 17 | |
| NG | 0 | 0 | 1 | 0 | 1 | 0 | 2 | |
| Total | 14 | 10 | 2 | 10 | 3 | 1 | 40 | 8.1 |

[a] Includes gardens, flaxlands, and vineyards.

Table 15.4 *Arable land market from selected decades*

| | 1700–1709 | 1740–9 | 1780–9 | 1820–9 | 1860–9 |
|---|---|---|---|---|---|
| Total arable (Morgen) | 1028.9 (1728)[a] | 1028.9 (1728) | 1028.8 (1769) | 1028.8 (1769) | 927.3 (1846) |
| Number of arable plots sold | 132 | 199 | 392 | 522 | 275 |
| Number of arable plots transacted[b] | 193 | 264 | 392 | 522 | 275 |
| Total arable sold (M)[c] | 121.61 | 146.20 | 269.31 | 309.57 | 148.93 |
| Total arable transacted | 183.25 | 192.33 | 269.31 | 309.57 | 148.93 |
| Price/Morgen (fl.)[d] | 30.77 | 53.60 | 109.16 | 126.74 | 564.25 |
| Percentage arable sold | 11.82 | 14.21 | 26.18 | 30.09 | 16.06 |
| Percentage arable transacted[b] | 17.82 | 18.69 | 26.18 | 30.09 | 16.06 |
| Mean population/decade | 340 | 455 | 516 | 738 | 924 |
| Amt arable sold/head (M)[c] | 0.358 | 0.321 | 0.522 | 0.419 | 0.161 |
| Amt arable trans./head[b] | 0.539 | 0.423 | 0.522 | 0.419 | 0.161 |
| Number of Buyers[e] | 41 | 102 | 135 | 232 | 198 |
| Number of buyers/ percentage of mean population | 12.1 | 22.4 | 26.2 | 31.4 | 21.4 |
| Mean size arable plot (M)[c] | 0.95 | 0.73 | 0.69 | 0.59 | 0.54 |
| Largest accum. purchase[f] | 11.63 | 13.49 | 8.78 | 11.21 | 4.46 |
| Mean accum. purchase[f] | 3.13 | 1.60 | 2.06 | 1.41 | 0.94 |
| Median accum. purchase[f] | 2.63 | 1.03 | 1.19 | 1.05 | 0.69 |
| Percentage arable and meadow purchased by top 10% | 26.0 | 32.9 | 34.4 | 34.0 | 26.9 |
| Percentage arable and meadow purchased by bottom 50% | 22.5 | 21.0 | 17.3 | 20.5 | 24.0 |
| Mean age sellers | 49.4 | 41.6 | 43.1 | 50.3 | 52.6 |
| Mean age buyers | 42.2 | 36.6 | 33.4 | 37.0 | 41.8 |
| Percentage arable sold of expected inheritance | 35.5 | 42.6 | 78.5 | 90.3 | 48.2 |

[a] The sources for land use in Neckarhausen are 1728, WHAS, A 261, Bü 1345; 1769, A 8, Kabinettsakten III, Bü 88; 1848, Königliches statistisch-topographisches Bureau, *Beschreibung des Oberamts Nürtingen* (Stuttgart and Tübingen, 1848), Tabelle II.

[b] Sold or traded.

[c] Morgen.

[d] Florin, Gulden.

[e] The number of individual buyers active in the land market during the decade.

[f] Arable and meadow, in Morgen.

depending on what is traded, what social values are involved, what kinds of people take part, and so forth. The results can be misleading if the market is treated in simple quantitative terms and no effort is made to consider its components and the context in which it operated. Table 15.4 summarizes a number of variables having to do with real estate sales in Neckarhausen. Since arable land made up a large portion of all transactions, I have used them as a convenient measure.

At the beginning of our period, the players in the land market were relatively old, although the disparity in age between buyers and sellers would not be as great as in the nineteenth century. The age group 40–54, as we found in Chapter 10, held about 60 percent of the village wealth in real property. Here we see they tended to trade among themselves. Nevertheless there is a clear sign of property devolution in the land market as by and large older people sold to younger people. As the population increased during the eighteenth century, the average age of buyers dropped, so that by the 1780s they were just about nine years younger than at the beginning of the century. It appears that the generations in the last several decades of the century were the youngest buyers during the whole period we are studying, that they got their hands on significant amounts of property, and that they began to sell in the second and third decades of the nineteenth century, when they were relatively old. They held onto land longer over their lifetime than any other generation. By the time they sold off much of their land, the age of buyers was already significantly on the rise. During the period of agricultural intensification and population growth, the span between generations grew, and each successive generation entered the market older than the one before. This fits nicely into our earlier findings about the ever greater accumulation of land by older age groups. The profile of each cohort shows us that generational dynamics were radically altered over time.

There are several ways to measure the market itself and a good deal of confusion about what it means to speak about a market in quantitative terms. From the point of view of a population tripled in size, a market that merely doubled would appear to be a decline. For example, between decades I and II, the population increased by 33.8 percent while the *number* of arable plots sold increased by 50.8 percent. Measured, however, in terms of the *amount* of arable sold per head, there was actually a decline. At the end of the period, there was far less arable sold per head of population than at the beginning, which suggests that the simple equation of market and modernity is ambiguous. We can measure the market in terms of the absolute number of transactions, the volume of trade, the size of the average transaction, and the price per unit of land. All of these must be set against the size of the population, the number of active participants, and the tendency to accumulate.

Between the first and second cohorts, the number of arable plots transacted (sold, exchanged, or sold in complex transactions) rose from 193 to 264, or 36.8 percent, but the average size parcel fell 23.2 percent, from 0.95 Morgen to 0.73 Morgen. In turn, the average price per Morgen rose from 30.77 to

53.60 fl. (74.2 percent). Although the increase in the number of sales and the price per unit of land would be much greater later on, there was already more competition for village resources. The population of the village climbed 33.8 percent between the two decades, from 340 to 455. The question is, did the market affect the distribution of resources, and did its function in that capacity increase? If we assume that about a third of the entire land of the village would turn over every decade by the natural process of inheritance, then during cohort I about 35.5 percent of that amount of arable was sold during the decade.[4] The corresponding figure for the second cohort is 42.6 percent. In both situations the market was greatly overshadowed by inheritance as a method for obtaining landed resources, and even though the market's influence increased slightly, such a calculation helps put the change in perspective. In terms of population growth, the average amount of land sold or transacted per head actually declined: from 0.358 M. to 0.321 M. sold or 0.539 M. to 0.423 M. sold and exchanged.

Altogether, it appears that a modest population increase was part of the mechanism leading to a quickened market – more transactions, more land, smaller plots, higher prices. It was also a young market – from the sellers' point of view the youngest over the whole period under study. The buyers were younger than early in the century, but they would be younger still later in the century. The average difference in age between both parties was only 5 years, compared with 10 or more in the later three cohorts, which suggests that the market mediated intergenerational transfers far less than it would later on. The contrast becomes clear when we consider that inheritance was largely a matter for people between 20 and 30 years apart in age. The market also worked as a mechanism to increase inequality during the period. A Lorenz curve describing the average land accumulation per purchaser in the two decades shifts to the right toward inequality. The top 10 percent of the buyers in 1700–1790 bought 26.04 percent of the land purchased in the decade, whereas in 1740–1749, they bought 32.9 percent and yet the average purchaser bought much less land: 1.6 M. compared with 3.13 M. in the earlier cohort. The total number of individuals who bought any land was 41 in the first decade

[4] It is very difficult to use the documentation at our disposal to arrive at a figure for the amount of property which was transmitted at any period by inheritance. Because of the numerous gaps in the *Inventuren und Teilungen*, a trustworthy estimate cannot be arrived at by adding up figures from these documents. Moreover, collating so many documents is a daunting task. I have decided to make do with a rough-and-ready measure for the moment and just assume that all land would turn over in a generation if there was no market at all. Setting the length of a generation is arbitrary, given the fact of changes in fertility, multiple marriages, and changing life expectancies. For the moment, let us assume for each cohort a generational length of 30 years, which means that a third of the land would be transferred by inheritance every decade. The degree to which land was bought and sold would affect the amount inheritable, but not in any easy way to figure, since a plot sold, say, by A to B might be inherited by B's heirs instead of A's during the same generation. The purpose of this procedure is to have some measure against which to set the market. If we reduce the length of a generation, then the relative importance of the market declines.

and 102 in the second. Expressed as a percentage of the average population of the respective decades, the corresponding figures are 12.1 percent and 22.4 percent. Not only were just more people in competition for land but also a greater percentage of the population. Many people were entering the market for smaller amounts of land, while a few people were able to accumulate what was for Neckarhausen a significant collection of holdings, the largest accumulation in the decade being 13.49 M. We are left with a number of ambiguities, but a general sense of greater competition for land. The idea that a market tends to break down hierarchies of age and the like seems to be borne out but is contradicted by the fact that when the peak of land transactions occurred in the 1820s, the trend to older buyers was already well under way. Another question of interest is whether under conditions of increased trade the family grip on property was loosened. This will be the central question of Chapter 16.

By the 1780s, the disparity between the ages of buyers and sellers had almost doubled from midcentury and was even greater than at the beginning by several years. This was due in large part to a continuing decline in the age of purchasers and a slight trend back to older sellers, which continued throughout the nineteenth century. The rise of the market throughout the eighteenth century brought increased overall activity and coincided with a rapid lowering of the age of those buying real estate. No generation in the future would be able to get their hands on land at such an early age and hold onto it for so long.

Between the second and third cohorts, the number of arable plots sold, exchanged, or sold in complex transactions rose 48.5 percent, from 264 to 392. Meanwhile, the average size plot fell from 0.73 to 0.69 Morgen, a modest erosion of 5.5 percent. This time the mean price jumped a considerable 103.5 percent, from 53.6 to 109.16 fl. Part of the explanation for the increase in prices lies in the rise of the village population exercising greater demand (from an average per decade of 340 (I), to 455 (II), to 516 (III)), 33.8 percent to midcentury and 13.3 percent between the next two cohorts.

If our estimate is based on a third of the land turning over every decade by the process of inheritance, then during cohort III about 78.5 percent of that amount was sold (35.5 percent in I, 42.6 percent in II), which means that the market played a considerably larger share in the distribution of resources than it had early in the century. In fact, much more land was now sold per head of population during this decade than in the previous ones (0.358 M. in I, 0.423 M. in II, and 0.522 M. in III).

Overall, the rise in market activity apparently outstripped the modest population rise, which suggests an institutional transformation such that transactions inter vivos competed substantially with inheritance. Although the size of parcels had not been whittled away at the earlier rate, far more property per head moved over the market at greatly inflated prices. Increasingly, younger men and even a few women were entering the market. During the first decade, no women purchased lands or buildings. At midcentury women bought 7 properties (comprising 2 percent of all sales). Now they purchased 23 properties

(3.9 percent of sales). The market allowed even more accumulation in this decade than in the previous two, and the Lorenz curve of average land accumulated by purchasers shifts farthest to the right, toward inequality. The top 10 percent of the buyers purchased 34.4 percent of the arable land (26.04 in I, 32.9 in II). On the other hand, the average purchaser bought more land than in the previous cohort (3.13 M. in I, 1.6 M. in II, and 2.06 M. in III), even though a larger percentage of the population entered the market altogether (12.1 percent in I, 22.4 percent in II, and 26.2 percent in III). Part of the pressure on land and prices is the result not so much of the rise in population as the rise in the number of people who were willing and able to buy land (in absolute numbers, 41 in I, 102 in II, and 135 in III). In other words, the market for land was being driven by something more than population pressure. The fact that some people could accumulate more was part of the process of social differentiation during this period. Bauern profited from the erosion of the economic and political position of individual handicraftsmen. By this time, the Bauern dominated the village magistracy and a small committee sat as a special court for dispensing the right to purchase credit. Anyone attempting to borrow from a *rentier* in Stuttgart, for example, had to have the application approved by the local *Unterpfandsrichter*. One of the most political activities in the village had to do with the judgment of creditworthiness and reputation. Also during this period, Bauern began to create a tightly knit marriage alliance system, which helped them dominate the land market.

Many more people were competing for small bits of land, while a few were accumulating somewhat more. Although the Lorenz curve pushes towards inequality in this decade, it is by no means a description of drastic inequality. The largest single accumulation of land was 8.8 M. over the decade, which is relatively modest compared with most other periods. In any event, more people entered the market (135) than the average number of household heads in the village for the decade (116), which suggests that most of them bought at least some land. By comparison, at the beginning of the century, the number of purchasers was half of the average number of householders in the village.

The number of arable plots on the market rose by 33.1 percent between cohorts III and IV (from 392 to 522). Meanwhile, the average size of arable plot sold fell from 0.69 Morgen to 0.59 Morgen, or 14.5 percent. At the same time, the mean price per Morgen arable went from 109.16 to 126.74 fl. (up 16.1 percent), although the figure for the 1820s hides enormous fluctuations and a continuing downward trend after the inflationary Napoleonic War period (see Table 15.5). By the 1820s the average population of the village was 738, a rise of 43.1 percent between the respective cohorts, the sharpest rise since the beginning of the eighteenth century.

In this period, almost as much land was sold as could have been inherited under normal conditions of generational turnover, a sharp departure from the eighteenth century but also from later in the nineteenth. During the 1820s, the figure is 90.3 percent, which suggests that the market was a key element in

Table 15.5 *Price per Morgen arable, 1821–30*

| Year | Price/Morgen[b] | Percentage change |
|---|---|---|
| 1821[a] | 153.82 | 0.0 |
| 1822 | 144.11 | −6.3 |
| 1823 | 133.58 | −7.3 |
| 1824 | 142.51 | +6.7 |
| 1825 | 113.30 | −20.5 |
| 1826 | 109.72 | −3.1 |
| 1827 | 102.37 | −6.7 |
| 1828 | 104.52 | +2.1 |
| 1829 | 71.25 | −31.8 |
| 1830 | 146.49 | +105.6 |

[a] I used the decade 1821–30 instead of 1820–9 in order to highlight the drop and fall between 1828 and 1830.
[b] In gulden.

distributing resources, almost equaling what we have estimated would have been transmitted by the process of inheritance (compared with 35.5 percent in I; 42.6 percent in 2; 78.5 in III). But we cannot view this as a linear development for a number of reasons. For one thing, four decades later under an expanded economy, the amount of land bought and sold was much less. Many of the transactions during the 1820s were the result of economic disarray, bankruptcy, and forced sales. Despite a peak in the number of sales, measured in terms of the population, less land was sold per head than in the 1780s (0.419 M. compared with 0.358 in I, 0.321 in II, and 0.522 in III). The comparative figures for total transactions (sales and exchanges) are 0.539, 0.423, 0.522, and 0.419, respectively.

Altogether, we find a more active market in terms of volume and in terms of other means of redistribution (inheritance, gift, trading). We also see the effects of population pressure and more intensive production methods on the size of plots and the cost of land. Yet as far as the individual purchaser was concerned, there was less available and at an older age. Whatever expansion there was seems to have been due not to a change in the institutions of exchange but to the sheer increase in numbers of people buying and selling. Landowners held onto landed resources until they were much older, with the result that a larger proportion of young people were dependent on them at any given age and the average age of dependence rose. Taking the buyers as a whole, the Lorenz curve shifts slowly back to the left, toward equality. The top 10 percent of the buyers purchased 34.0 percent of the arable land, about the same as the peak in the 1780s, but the mean accumulated purchase fell to a new low (3.13 M.,

1.60 M., 2.06 M., and 1.41 M., respectively). The crisis in farming permitted more people to purchase smaller amounts and to deepen the trend to fractionalized holdings. The number of buyers expressed as a percentage of the average population for the decade rose to a new high during this period (12.1, 22.4, 26.2, and 31.4 percent, respectively). The trend to many more people entering the market (41, 102, 135, 232 respectively) for ever smaller bits of land continued on into the early decades of the nineteenth century.

As we have already noted, the average age of sellers hit a new high in the 1860s: 52.6. The age of buyers had been rising since its low in the 1780s and reached 41.8, about what it was at the beginning of the eighteenth century. The average difference in age between buyers and sellers remained high at 10.8, but not as high as earlier in the century, owing to the sharp rise in the age of buyers, those constituting a generation of extended dependence. It may well have been the case that those who controlled the Unterpfandsgericht (mortgage court) increasingly enforced their notion of who was creditworthy. Certainly younger villagers involved in migratory labor received their blessing only with great difficulty, unless they had exceptional backing from wealthier families.

The number of arable plots sold on the market declined by 46.2 percent between the 1820s and 1860s. Meanwhile, the average plot continued to decline somewhat (8.5 percent), from 0.59 M. to 0.54 M. (the figures per cohort were 0.95 M., 0.73 M., 0.69 M., 0.59 M., and 0.54 M., respectively). The dramatic story is in the changing price. Between the 1820s and the 1860s, the average cost per Morgen went from 126.74 to 564.25 fl., a rise of 345 percent. Nothing like that had happened in the previous period; indeed, the "steep" rise between the 1780s and 1820s amounted to 16.1 percent. The rise in value was due to a mixture of forces, including population pressure, intensified production, and the redemption of tithes. The increase in land values outstripped the prices of other goods considerably. Between the 1820s and 1860s, for example, the price of spelt rose by 46 percent. Comparative figures for wages exist only for a shorter period (1830 to 1860s), but they, too, indicate a rate of inflation far below the value of land.[5] At the top of the scale, wages for masons rose 91 percent, while those for cobblers went up a far more modest 67 percent. Access to land became centered on a combination of credit, family connections, guarantees, and inheritance.

By the 1860s, the average population of the village was 924.3, 25.3 percent more than 40 years earlier. The rise was less steep than that between the 1780s and 1820s (43.1 percent) but each period added about 200 more people to the village. The market had fallen to about half of what would theoretically have

[5] The price and wage series have been calculated by Wolfgang von Hippel, "Bevölkerungsentwicklung und Wirtschaftsstruktur im Königreich Württemberg 1815/65. Überlegungen zum Pauperismusproblem in Südwestdeutschland," in *Soziale Bewegung and politische Verfassung, Beiträge zur Geschichte der modernen Welt*, ed. Ulrich Engelhardt, Volker Selin, Horst Stuke (Stuttgart, 1976), pp. 270–371.

been transmitted by inheritance (48.2 percent), which was way down from its peak in the 1820s (by cohort: 35.5 percent, 43.6 percent, 78.5 percent, 90.3 percent, and 48.2 percent, respectively). If we can speak of a structural transformation in the late eighteenth century, then we certainly find that the market mechanism had failed to transform the situation. By the second half of the nineteenth century, the market seems to have played about the same overall role in the distribution of resources as it did early in the eighteenth century. Measured in terms of the amount of land transacted by head, a new low was reached: 0.161 M. (compared with 0.358, 0.321, 0.522, and 0.419), half the lowest point reached in the eighteenth century.

As far as the volume sold and its ability to act as a means of property redistribution are concerned, we have a less active market. Population pressure drove prices up but did not help to increase the volume of sales. Along with more intensive agriculture, it did help erode the size of plots even more. As far as the individual purchaser was concerned, there was far less available and at a much greater age. Most people entering the market as buyers were well into their 40s. They were not prospective brides and grooms or neogami. The subjection of the young to resources held by the old increased considerably as the age of dependence and the population as a whole increased. As far as buyers are concerned, the Lorenz curve shifts again, back to the left toward equality. The top 10 percent of the buyers purchased 26.9 percent of the arable land, about the same as at the beginning of the eighteenth century. The mean accumulated purchase fell to an absolute low of 0.94 M. (compared with 3.13, 1.60, 2.06, and 1.41). Despite the fact that the average purchaser bought less and the top did not accumulate excessively, the number of buyers expressed as a percentage of the population was back to what it had been in the mid-eighteenth century (12.1, 22.4, 26.2, 31.4, and 21.4 percent). Furthermore, the total number of buyers, while greater than at any time during the eighteenth century, was down 14.7 percent from the high of the 1820s (41, 102, 135, 232, 198, respectively).

It is difficult to follow trends because each element of the relationships went in an independent direction. There was certainly no simple linear development of market relationships. Our description leads to an analysis of economic change and changes in stratification. But our focus is still on property and family. Thus, the market must be understood in the context of socially structured exchanges. At any point that we care to look, age was clearly an important factor in the terms of exchange, and the market was not an unchanging neutral mechanism, nor one which transformed the situation in any specific direction. The accumulation and exercise of power also played a key role at various periods in gaining access to the market. The main question for our purposes is whether people preferred to buy and sell to kin and whether the increase in the number of transactions and the volume of trade reduced the family's influence in obtaining access to real estate or, whether the nature of family and kin interaction changed over time. It *is* true that the market can operate within the family and larger kin group in ways that inheritance rules and direct devolution cannot. In fact, the market can be a more adaptable instrument for developing and maintaining kin relations. At the level of the closest relatives, selling a property to a child could work more flexibly than an annuity. A parent most often sold real estate to be paid off over time. Each year for an extended period, the son or son-in-law would pay off a percentage, sometimes with interest. As long as the debt remained, this particular transaction played a role in their relationships. From another perspective, the market can extend the number of choices available and allow property to play a more flexible role in the creation and maintenance of alliances. Although a first cousin might only have residual interest in a strip of land, and would be excluded by lineal heirs, he could assert his interests through a favored transaction. What has already been said about continued relations built on time payments is also true in this instance.

Relations between generations involve a complex interlinking of households. Only for a brief period would parents and married children make up a commensal unit, even though they might share a kitchen and fireplace for a considerable time. Each maintained a separate food and wood supply and carefully demarcated space and utensils. The households in a particular building constantly reformed and regrouped. When parents retired they continued to maintain their independence and contracted for victuals or labor, depending on their circumstances. The visible sign of shifting responsibilities and obligations was the shifting of property ownership.

Family interest and practices and state policies could run along on different courses but would interlink from time to time. State planners thought that land should be freed from all encumbrances so that an industrious, capable peasantry would be able to unleash all of its energies. Thus older rules about family redemption were curtailed, but they had not been utilized to any extent except under the pressure of a growing population and a livelier land market. Before bureaucrats got a chance to change the law, villagers were already using redemption rules less often. Families were sorting out their interests in new ways through the marketplace itself, as we shall see in Chapter 16. There were fewer and fewer encumbrances on property in the nineteenth century. It became even less usual to sell real estate with conditions such as residency, although the effect might have been the same. The retired parent maintained ownership of an apartment rather than passing on the whole property with rights reserved to use a room or two.

Thus, the number of overlapping rights to use declined, but these had never been great in the first place. Parents and married children had always had separate economies, and one party kept the tools, renting them out or hiring out labor to the other. For a time, shared rights in tools existed, but usually between young farmers – brothers and brothers-in-law. By the time they reached maturity and maximum holdings, they usually had a complete set of equipment through which they managed some of the relations with their children.

Paralleling the general move to reducing encumbrances and residual rights was an increasing formality in market transactions. Soon after the mid-eighteenth century, people stopped trading property directly and sold only for cash. More and more transactions were sold at auction, and even a redemption took place only after a competitive price was established. But the market worked as a redistributing agent in complex ways. At certain times anyone with enough labor could outbid large landholders simply because he or she could exploit him or herself. Population pressure could give a push to fractionalization in this way. On the other hand, greater social differentiation could lead to social distinctions about who was creditworthy, and this in turn could be operationalized through the village power apparatus to give differential access to credit. Around the mid-nineteenth century, the high price of land was at least in part an expression of population pressure and self-exploitation, but the reduction in the number of people who could get access to land through purchase probably came out of differential access to village power.

Whatever the market did do, it did not act as some kind of a grand abstracting apparatus breaking down age hierarchies through the calculation of interest and profit or by destroying relations based on other principles such as kinship. It might have been that the older villagers were breaking an implicit contract with the young by holding ever more resources in their hands, but they can hardly be blamed for living longer. Their credit and resources, however, did give them greater chances for real estate accumulation. The striking thing is that during the period of increasing social differentiation, agricultural intensification, mobilization of land, capitalization of production (whether of cattle, flax, shoes, or cloth), and regional mobility, a system of family alliances was constructed which channeled the flow of marriage partners, godparents, guardians, pledges, labor, and land. The complicated analysis of the kinship system awaits separate treatment, but we can take the first steps by looking at the real estate market and family.

16

# Kinship and the sale of property

Johann Georg Riempp complains that his brother-in-law Mühleisen in Altdorf sold a meadow in Schimmel to David Henzler in Raidwangen and drove up the price of the meadow so high that Riempp as brother-in-law would not be able to get any of it.

– Ruggerichtsprotocoll (1803)[1]

This chapter investigates the degree to which the kinship network in Neckarhausen was mobilized for various purposes. In any society, kin are found interacting in some situations and not in others. And there are many times when kin can transact business with each other but when kinship as a principle of their dealings is not the pertinent point. In Neckarhausen, for example, the group of young men out on the streets together at night constituted first and foremost an age cohort. That some of them might have been cousins had little to do with the fact of their being together. In order to approach the problems of the structure, meaning, and perception of kinship, we will have to map out systematically certain regularities of behavior. Much of the available documentation involves complicated manipulations and clumsy, roundabout methods for getting at rather simple issues. Even then the practices we want to expose often remain frustratingly elusive. Only when we trace enough paths through the material will we be able to survey the network of interconnections. Given our sources, we can, for example, look at the names people gave their children as an indicator of the relative weight they gave to those kin selected as namesakes. But the tabular descriptions of frequency distributions suffer from "thinness" and abstraction. By looking systematically at a number of social transactions besides naming children, however, such as choosing godparents or selling land, we can construct an ever clearer and more detailed map of interconnection for any period, and by superimposing a series of such maps on each other, we can delineate the shifts in the morphology of kinship, the development of fault lines and rifts, the erosion of visible formations, and the appearance of new routes. Our charts will provide necessary guides for further exploration and travel, some of which we will undertake in later analysis. Unfor-

[1] *Gericht*, vol. 5, f. 207 (28.12.1803).

tunately, we will not be able to travel comfortably and with much pleasure until the tedious and exacting mapwork has first been accomplished.

Details on the role of kinship in the real estate market in Neckarhausen will help us to put the family holding of land and the household's access to resources in their proper perspective. To ask questions systematically, it is necessary to take a series of transactions and find out if and in what way the two parties in each instance were related to each other. For this study, I have taken the same five cohorts discussed earlier. Since the tracing of genealogical relationships is tedious and presents problems even when assisted by a computer, it was necessary to keep the number of individuals small while at the same time ensuring that the sample was large enough to represent the material adequately. For each cohort, I randomly chose 20 individuals who were involved in at least one sale in the decade and then expanded the sample to include all of their transactions. The size of each sample described in Table 16.1 varies according to the population of the village, the number of active participants in the market, and the average amount of land individuals bought and sold. In no instance did it fall below 15 percent, which appears to be adequate, given the size of the universe under observation. In constructing the statistics, I used the connection between the original seller and buyer. To add in redemptions would only have increased the number of kin links, giving added weight to the most immediate family members. In those instances where an estate was being sold because of death or insolvency, I took the seller to be the original owner, not the court-appointed executor.

At the outset, it seems wise not to define what constitutes a kinship connection narrowly. In the discussion of godparents in another volume, the exact universe considered will be described in detail. Suffice it to say here that the search for consanguineal kin went back two generations through lineal ascendants (to a person's father's father, father's mother, mother's father, or mother's mother), to their siblings, and downward three generations to include all second cousins once removed (e.g., FFBSSS, MMZDDD). For affinal relations, the search went as far as the BWBWBWB or ZHZHZHZH (taking all the permutations of in-laws such as BWZHBWB or FBSZH) and their parents

Table 16.1 *Sales of real estate from selected decades, sample size*

| Transactions | 1700–1709 | 1740–9 | 1780–9 | 1820–9 | 1860–9 |
|---|---|---|---|---|---|
| Number of sales | 185 | 351 | 585 | 818 | 494 |
| Number of sample | 90 | 102 | 234 | 148 | 83 |
| Percentage of sample | 48.6 | 29.1 | 40.0 | 18.1 | 16.8 |
| Number of exchanges | 44 | 47 | 2 | 0 | 0 |
| Number of sample | 28 | 17 | 0 | 0 | 0 |
| Percentage of sample | 63.6 | 36.2 | 0 | 0 | 0 |

and children – people who were connected in a chain up to four "households" away from each other. Tracing out genealogical connections was strictly cognatic, through males and females equally, and was carried out for both spouses (e.g., FMZSD and WFMZSD).

## Cohort I, 1700–1709

The land market in Neckarhausen during the early part of the eighteenth century was largely an internal one. Not much land was yet sold at auction and the market was not as lively as later in the century. Buyers and sellers tended to be in their 40s, active heads of household, and often of the same generation, even though buyers tended to be younger than sellers. In contrast to the later years, land was sold in fairly large parcels, almost a Morgen (1 M. = 0.78 acres) for each arable plot. The market probably accounted for not much more than a quarter of all property transfers, the rest being taken care of by inheritance in the form of both premortem (Übergabe) and postmortem devolution. There were proportionally fewer buyers in the population, who accumulated on average more land and had more equal chances to do so than later on.

We now turn to the question of how much the players in the land market were linked to each other (Tables 16.2 to 16.4). It is not yet clear whether 35 percent of the transactions between completely unrelated people constitutes a substantial proportion or not. One note of caution must be sounded: The category "no established relation" means, mutatis mutandis, that there is always the possibility that a link has been missed. There are several gaps in the documentation in this earlier period which make genealogical investigation of some families difficult. But overall this weakness does not affect the structural aspects very much. Through hand linkage, I have been able to establish more extended connections between some people, although it stretches the imagination to think that a sale to a wife's brother-in-law's sister-in-law's brother-in-law's brother-in-law (WZHBWZHZH) has anything but random meaning in itself. Of course, if one of the men in the middle of the series was putting together a complex transaction, he might be able to use the two sides of his network. What appears to be a very extended connection when we examine the two termini might well have been mediated through a figure much closer to both sides. We are left, in any event, with a substantial proportion of transactions where the movement of property stayed within a fairly restricted familial range (Table 16.4).

Certain facts stand out immediately in the structure of kin-related transactions (nuclear family, cousins, close in-laws). First, a substantial majority (62.1 percent) of such sales went to members of the nuclear family of "origin": to the son, daughter (son-in-law), brother, or sister (brother-in-law). Second, while sales to miscellaneous relatives outside this group were substantial, the collateral *blood* relatives (cousins, uncles, nephews, etc.) were not very important. Third, within the nuclear family, there seems to have been a clear prefer-

Table 16.2 *Kinship relations between buyers and sellers, 1700–1709*

| Buyer's relation to seller | Number | Percent |
|---|---|---|
| Nuclear family | 36 | 40.0 |
| S, DH (14,2)[a] | 16 | 17.8 |
| B, xB, ZH (10,3)[b] | 12 | 13.3 |
| WB, WZH (4,3) | 7 | 7.8 |
| WF | 1 | 1.1 |
| First cousins, nephew[c] | 5 | 5.6 |
| xBS[a] | 1 | |
| WFZS | 3 | |
| WFBDH | 1 | |
| FBSDH | 1 | |
| Affines | 17 | 18.9 |
| DHB | 1 | |
| WZHB | 1 | |
| FBWxZH | 1 | |
| MBDDHB | 2 | |
| WBWZHB | 1 | |
| BWZHB | 1 | |
| BWZHBWB | 1 | |
| BWBWZHB | 1 | |
| BWZHZHB | 3 | |
| BWHBWZH | 1 | |
| MBWZHB | 1 | |
| FZHFZD | 1 | |
| WZHBWZHZH | 1 | |
| WBWBWZHB | 1 | |
| No established relation | 32 | 35.6 |
| Total | 90 | 100.1 |

[a] One purchased by a xBS and DH together.
[b] One purchased by a B and ZH together.
[c] Including first cousins, once removed. No second-cousin or second-cousin once–removed links were discovered.

ence for the son and brother against the daughter and sister (son-in-law and brother-in-law).

Selling land can be part of the process of inheritance and can involve a progressive divestment over time. The turnover from one generation to another does not have to be abrupt. In a partible inheritance region, as we have stressed several times, it can take place over a very long period. Several factors are at play, among which are the need for the older generation to provide for retire-

Table 16.3 *Kinship relations between exchange partners, 1700–1709*

| Exchange partners | Number | Percent |
|---|---|---|
| Nuclear family | 3 | 10.7 |
| B/B | 2 | |
| B/Z | 1 | |
| First cousins | 5 | 17.9 |
| WFBDH/WFBDH | 1 | |
| MBDH/WFZS | 1 | |
| MBDS/MFZS | 1 | |
| MBDDH/WMFZS | 2 | |
| Second cousins | 1 | 3.6 |
| WMMZSS/FMZDDH | 1 | |
| Affines | 8 | 28.6 |
| ZHB/BWB | 1 | |
| WZH/WZH | 1 | |
| ZHZH/WBWB | 2 | |
| MZHB/BWZS | 1 | |
| BWZHZHB/BWBWZHB | 1 | |
| BWHBWBWB/ZHZHBWHB | 1 | |
| BWHWFBSWH/WHFDHWHB | 1 | |
| No established relation | 11 | 39.3 |
| Total | 28 | 100.1 |

Table 16.4 *Sales and exchanges: kinship relations, 1700–1709*

| Kinship relations | Number | Percent |
|---|---|---|
| Nuclear family | 39 | 33.1 |
| Cousins | 11 | 9.3 |
| Close in-laws | 25 | 21.2 |
| No established relation | 43 | 36.4 |

*Note*: In addition there were two gifts. No relation can be established between the parties.

ment and the desire of the younger generation to get their hands on the means of production. Donations inter vivos, gifts, and sales can all come under the heading of premortem inheritance. The father or mother could slough off pieces of land, while keeping enough for declining needs and energies – this would be a form of partition. Or they could bestow gifts, expecting in return some kind of support – for example, two sacks of flour in return for a portion of the house. Just as functional is the step of selling a piece of land to an heir, providing the father or mother with a kind of annuity. If a son or daughter paid in a lump sum, the parent could invest in loans to other villagers, earning 5 percent according to the legal rate of interest. But the child could also pay off the outstanding amount progressively over time, paying interest on the balance. Put in this perspective, selling a plot to a child, or giving it to him or her with the stipulation of support could amount to the same thing. We would be turning things around to argue that selling property to a child implies that market considerations have intruded themselves into family relations or that the latter were dominated by a "cash nexus."

There appears to be a bias in nuclear family sales to sons and to brothers, which runs against the argument in Chapter 10 that children were treated more or less equally. Closer inspection of the data suggests that the sample itself led to a distortion of the evidence. A good case in point has to do with the Geiger family; three Geiger brothers were in the group from which statistics were drawn. They accounted for six purchases from their father, Conrad (d. 1703), and eventually widowed mother, Catherine (d. 1712). One brother had died in the 1690s and a daughter and her husband, Johannes Sturtz, were not in the sample. In 1703, Conrad Geiger sold three arable fields to his son-in-law. In that same year, when the widow sold property to the three living sons, she sold an equal amount to Sturtz and to her grandchild, the son of the deceased Conrad II. In this case, children were treated with strict equality, and even the rights of a deceased child were passed along to his children. In all the other instances, there is no evidence of special treatment, although one child or other might have gotten an extra parcel of land. Since the temporal bounds of the study do not go beyond the decade, we cannot see if things were evened out in the long run. But it is clear that there was no general policy of favoring sons or particular children through land sales or gifts to get around the rules of inheritance, even though a small advantage might have been traded for service.

The various sibling relationships (B, ZH, WB, WZH) were far more important in this period for providing claims to land through purchase than those of cousinhood. A few first cousins (or first cousins once removed) are to be found, but no second cousins at all. As a whole, the relatively close in-law connections played a substantial role, but there was no particular bias in any direction. Especially noticeable is the absence of a bunching up around "once-removed in-laws," say, ZHB, WZHB, BWB, WBWB. Once outside the close circle of nuclear family relations, there does not seem to have been a system of diminishing claim based on distance. Rather, a variety of coordinated interests may have played some role – a relationship claimed by blood or some in-law connection. Apart from the sales from father or mother to children, most transactions do not have the flavor of intergenerational transmission: They tended to be among people of the same generation, at least as far as in-laws and cousins are concerned.

The data for exchanges reinforce our findings for sales, although there nuclear family relations did not play much of a role. While cousinship was of rather more importance for trading, taken as a proportion of all transactions, it did not loom large. Whatever residual rights cousins had in land by virtue of the fact that they inherited from the same pool, they did not seem in that generation to extend very much claim to special consideration on the land market. Exchanging was a different matter, since holdings of cousins were often in part the result of partitioning in earlier generations. They would end up with contiguous parcels, which could lead to exchanges of mutual advantage. By contrast, the rather increased importance of exchanges among cousins emphasizes the relatively few sales.

Affinal links have statistical prominence in this generation, although there is no evidence to suggest that buying and selling property through such a chain was governed by anything more than chance. For example, in 1706 Michael Schober bought a meadow from Salomon Hentzler in Raidwangen, his ZHBWZHB (see Figure 16.1).[2] The plot he purchased happened to be contiguous to one he already owned. It is possible that the two plots were split in an earlier inheritance and fell to two people related through a different path than the one discovered here and that they were simply sorting out the tangle. It is also possible that Schober utilized his relation to a third party, A, to pry the parcel loose from Hentzler. Or it could have simply been a business transaction in which kinship played no role at all.

Another example points to some of the possibilities. On one day, Michael Rentzler participated in three separate transactions (Figure 16.2).[3] In the two exchanges, he traded away one arable field contiguous to another he held and got another piece next to another. These may well have fallen to him and his two cousins through the normal course of inheritance. Perhaps the sale to his MBDDHB was part of a complex deal in which affinal demands as well as consanguineal claims played a role.

Real estate transactions were not, of course, isolated and may well have been part of a wider structure of exchange relations. We will see in Volume 2 that affinity played a very important role in marriage exchange in this period. Al-

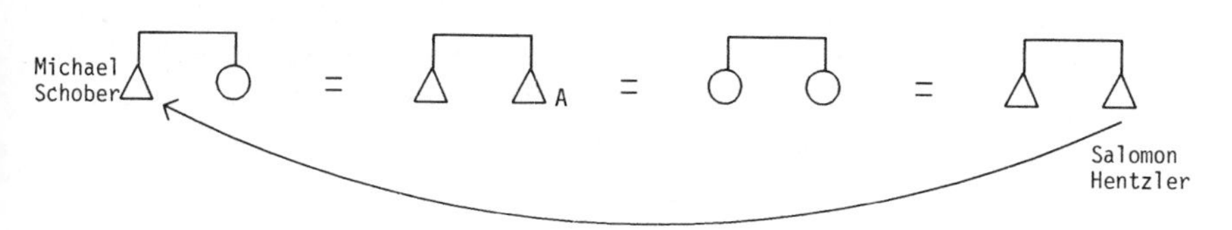


Figure 16.1

[2] *Kaufbuch*, vol. 2, f. 59, 13.12.1706.
[3] *Kaufbuch*, vol. 2, f. 53, 4.12.1705.

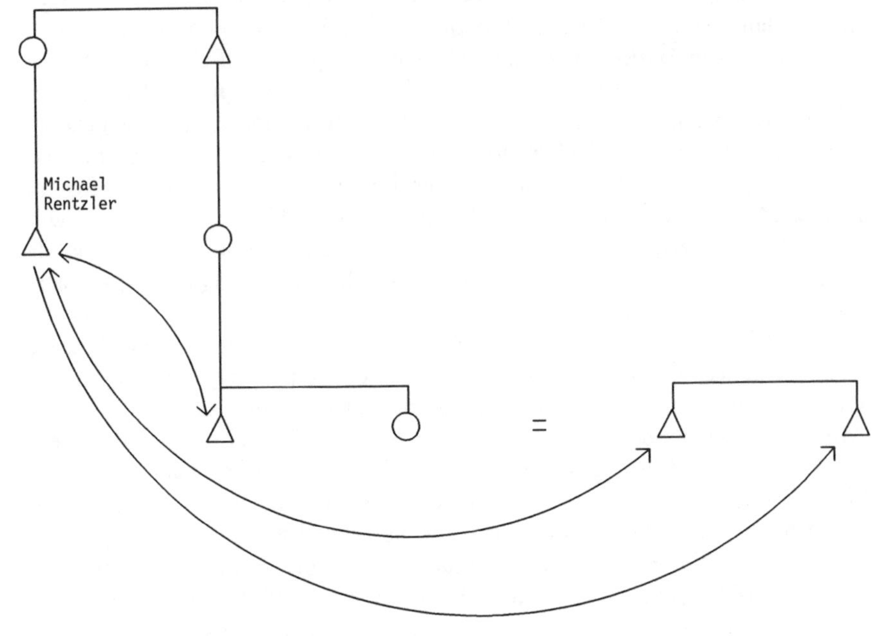


Figure 16.2

though the argument cannot be developed here, we can point to one recurrent form of kin-related marriage – the interlocking set of siblings (Figure 16.3).

Some of the in-law land sales seem to be variations on this – for example, BWZHB or WBWZHB. They point to the possibility that selling land was part of a wider set of exchanges of which marriage formed a part (Figure 16.4).

The degree to which affinal principles were at work in mediating relationships between people is difficult to assess from the networks we have reconstructed. Without direct testimony, we can only follow a chain of reasoning based on whatever material is available. Some evidence is provided by the fact that quite frequently several transactions took place on the same day. On the assumption that a person might be willing to enter into particular negotiations if a friend or relative arranged a *quid pro quo*, we can examine such groups of transactions to see if they were interconnected in some way. Altogether there were 23 occasions when more than one transaction took place. Careful tracing out of genealogical networks has not produced any clear results. Either a few

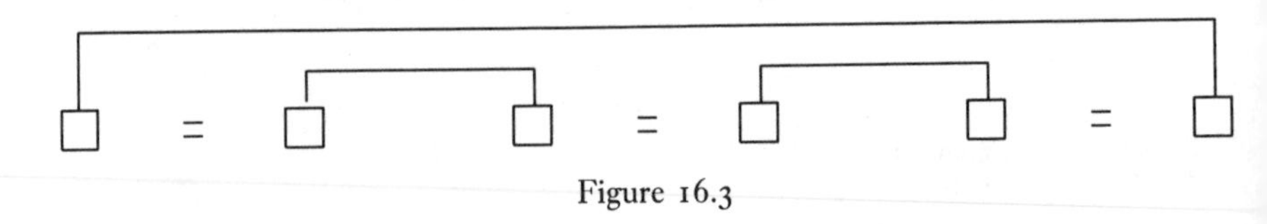

Figure 16.3

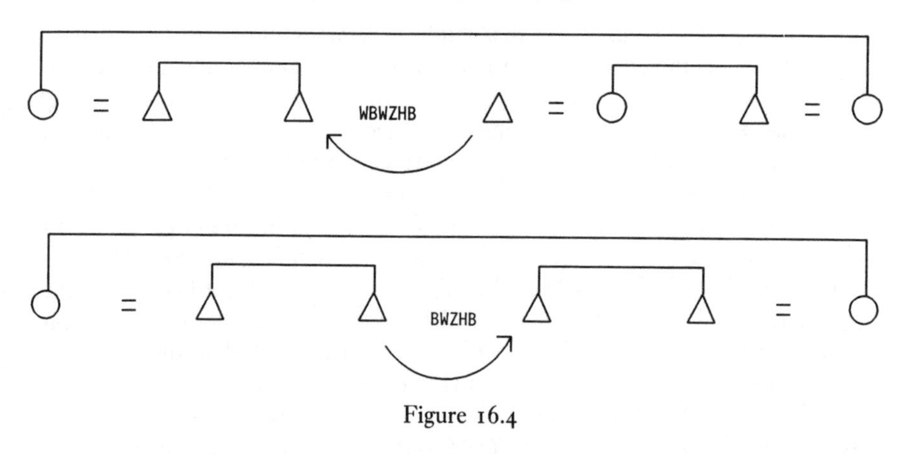


Figure 16.4

crucial links are missing or such affinal connections were not very important for sorting out resources among villagers. We must remember, however, that the strength and importance of a tie cannot be measured by its all-purpose inclusivity. Kinship is always marked by territorialization by which some relationships are utilized for some concerns and others for others. In any event, I was only able to find examples such as those shown in Figure 16.5.[4]

*Rudolph Schober's sale to Salomon Falter involved a flaxland contiguous with his own property and that of Hans Jerg Beck, a brother to their respective wives. This was almost certainly a sorting out of property descended to them through inheritance. Nicolaus Hess and Hans Jerg Schober exchanged parcels in the same field, not contiguous to any plots either one possessed. Given their own relation, they did not require any mediation of the others. Friedrich Häussler sold a noncontiguous flaxland to his WZHB, Michael Schober. Perhaps Rudolph Schober was instrumental in effecting the sale, but perhaps not.*

There may have been other ways in which help, influence, and favor were offered to people. Godparentage during this period connected older villagers with younger and richer with poorer (see the Conclusion). Everything points to a system of patronage and clientage. Perhaps once one moved outside the

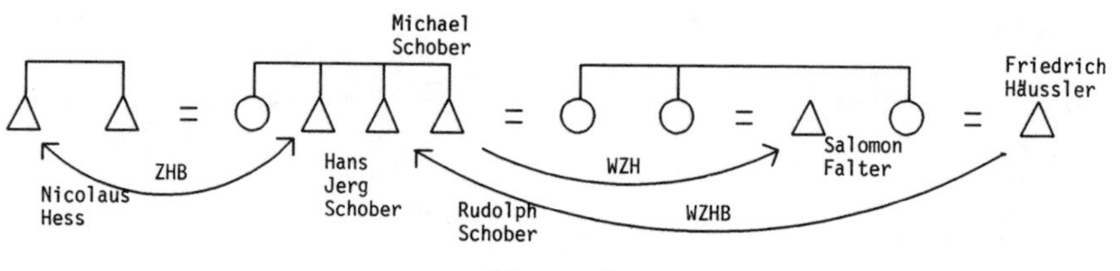


Figure 16.5

[4] *Kaufbuch*, vol. 2, f. 72, 3.12.1709.

circle of the closest kin – parents/children, siblings, direct in-laws – there were no expectations of claims on real estate of any kind at all. Either people bought or sold for direct advantage, or bits of land were pried loose through influential connections, neighborliness, or friendship. Since godparentage was one institution available for the purpose, we can examine some of the connections we find tying buyers and sellers together through it.

Let us take one person who "exchanged" land with two other people: Hans Michael Dalm. Dalm bought land from Joseph Hentzler, his WxZHBS (i.e., Hentzler sold to his FBWxZH).[5] We might want to argue that Dalm got some preference on the market or persuaded his partner to sell because of a relationship to his stepsister-in-law's nephew. But when we look at the godparent connections, we see that they overlap (Figure 16.6).

*Michael Hess, Schultheiss, was* Döte *for Joseph Hentzler, and both* Döte *and* Gevatter *for Hans Michael Dalm. (Döte, masc., and Dote, fem., express the relation between the godparent and child,* Dötle, *while* Gevatter[in] *stands for the relation between the godparent and the parent of the child.) His wife was* Dote *for Joseph Hentzler's wife. Michael Hess's son succeeded him as* Gevatter *for Dalm. In many ways, the Hess family functioned as godparents for the two men who transacted land. Furthermore, the father-in-law and brother-in-law of Dalm were both* Gevatter *for the seller, Hentzler.*

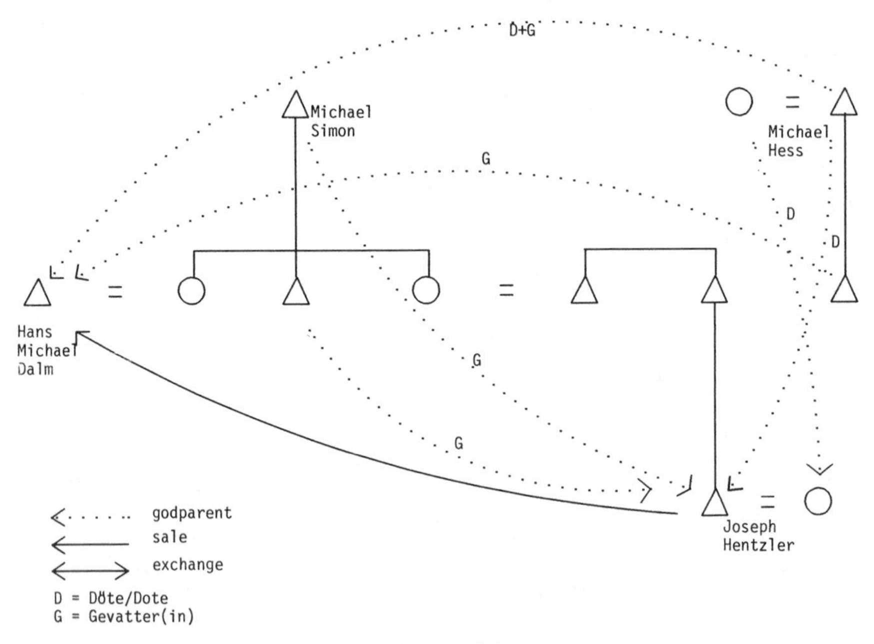


Figure 16.6

[5] *Kaufbuch*, vol. 2, f. 52, 7.6.1705.

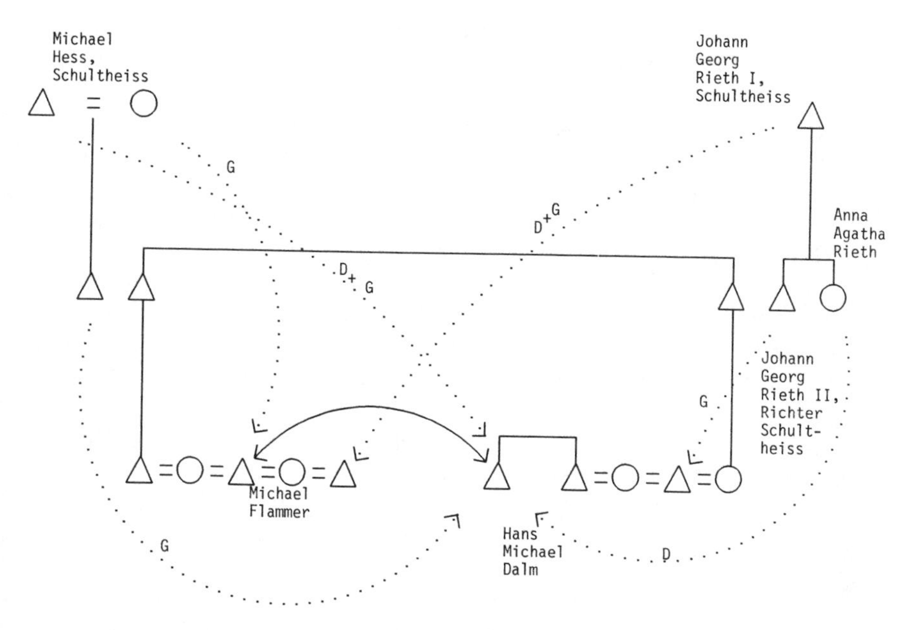


Figure 16.7

Let us look at the other transaction, interesting because the kinship connections there were extremely remote – an exchange between BWHWFBSWH and WHFBDHWHB (Figure 16.7).[6]

*Here the mediating connection of godparents is not as tidy. Johann Georg Rieth I and his son were both Schultheissen in Neckarhausen. The former dominated the period after the Thirty Years War through the 1680s. His son was a Richter already in the 1690s and eventually, during the second decade of the 1700s, became Schultheiss himself. The son often succeeded the father as godparent, either finishing out a string of siblings when Johann Georg I died, or becoming godparent for the children of people for whom the father had earlier been godparent. Anna Agatha, Johann Georg I's daughter, also was clearly part of the family patronage system. Whatever role she played on her own, she also functioned in the power sphere of her father and brother. In this instance, Johann Georg Rieth I was* Döte *for the immigrant Flammer's* Ehepredecessor *(wife's first husband) and Gevatter as well, that is,* Döte *for the child of Flammer's wife. Johann Georg Rieth II was* Gevatter *for Dalm's brother's* Ehepredecessor. *As we shall see, the* Gevatter(in) *for a couple held the position for all of the children and usually continued where a remarriage was concerned.*[7] *Anna Agatha was Dalm's* Dote. *Together the Rieth's were able to stand as intermediaries*

[6] *Kaufbuch*, vol. 2, f. 65, 6.12.1708. In this case, we have a series of remarriages, the second spouse being the Ehesuccessor of the first. If we disregard multiple marriages, the relationship here can be conflated to BWFBS/FBDHB.

[7] See vol. 2.

*between the two men. More direct was the connection to the Schultheiss Michael Hess family. Hess himself was both* Döte *and* Gevatter *for Dalm, while his wife was* Gevatterin *for Flammer.*

These two examples are repeated many times in the data. It is hard to give a summary, and multiplying cases would just be tedious. I have noted every instance where the contracting parties were "unrelated" or where the affinal relation was so stretched as to be tenuous. From a genealogical tree, for example, I have been able to find rather remote affinal connections between some individuals (e.g., BWFMBSWZHB), six of which are in the "no established relation" category of the table on sales and five in the exchanges. I have tried to determine whether the two parties are connected through a third party as godparent. A link was established where members of a nuclear family stood as godparents for two contracting parties (or their spouses, including Ehesuccessor and Predecessor), or were parents of one party and godparents for the other (Figure 16.8). The results are given in Table 16.5.

Exactly how the "mediation" of a Gevatter/Dote played a role in land and building transactions can only be surmised. For us, the startling fact is how often seemingly unrelated people transacting business were linked together in a more or less direct way through a godparent. The fact that land was so frequently traded and the market itself played so little role in distributing resources suggests that a good deal of persuasion might have been involved. Only a relatively small group of villagers were able to purchase any land at all –

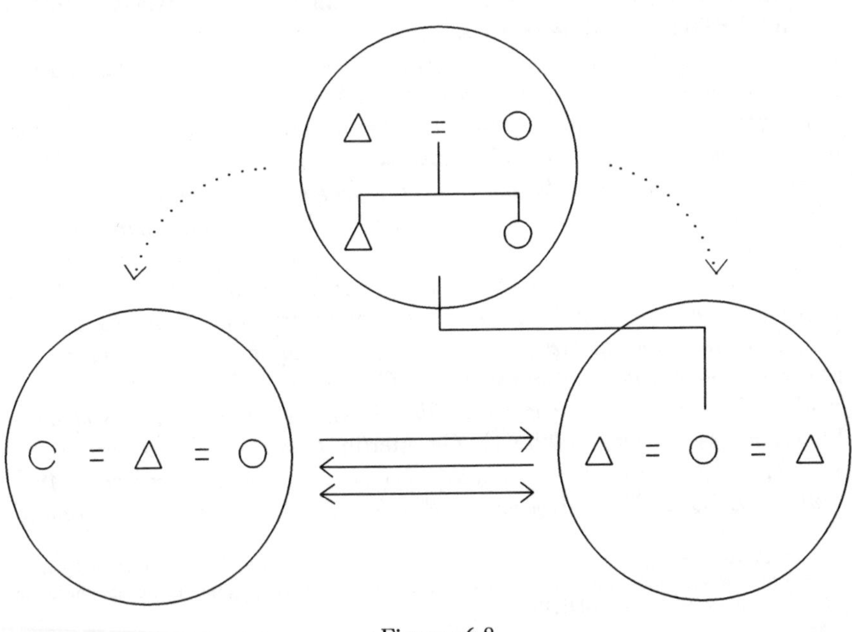

Figure 16.8

Table 16.5 *Sales and exchanges between parties linked through godparents, 1700–1709*

| | Sales | Exchanges |
|---|---|---|
| Total | 32 | 13[a] |
| Number linked | 18 | 10 |
| Percentage linked | 56.3 | 76.9 |

[a] Includes the two most extended affines from the table.

perhaps those with the most effective political connections. We are left in the end with inferences based on paths recurring in an abstract network.

This exercise, however, has added some understanding to the role of godparent. In only two cases here were godparents or their kin directly involved in a transaction. That is, the position did not give the godparent a direct advantage in the process of accumulation. He did not utilize his position or the position of his wife or children to get access to land or other immovable property. The godfather seems to have brought people together and exercised his position and prestige by acting as a kind of real estate agent. It may well have been a problem here of setting the price in a situation of noncompetitive bidding or guaranteeing payments, the mutual godparents acting as trusted go-betweens. Or perhaps it simply went against the grain to sell land outside the family – here the "ritual kin" position of the godparent would have established the moral conditions for such a transaction. In a similar fashion, village magistrates were also supposed to be intermediaries, and it is precisely the Richter, Räte, Bürgermeister, and Schultheissen, as we shall see, who so often acted as Gevatter for the villagers.[8] In any event, our data here suggest that godparents played an important role in patron/client social relations in the first part of the eighteenth century.

In the early part of the eighteenth century, as we have seen, a substantial proportion of property sales were between members of the immediate nuclear family, or what might better be described as the "nuclear family of origin," since the parents and children and siblings involved were usually living in separate households. We estimated earlier that the sale of property during the decade transferred rather more than a third as much land as the normal process of inheritance would have. Most property, therefore, moved between members of the nuclear family, or failing them, to the direct collateral heirs. In this period, there is no evidence that collateral heirs were the beneficiaries of the restricted market – at least, first cousins and nephews and nieces did not take a very large share. As a rough estimate, sales of property to people outside

[8] Discussed in vol. 2.

the immediate family accounted for about 10 percent of all property transfers (sales and inheritance) during the decade.

Property rights thus were generally sorted out within the nuclear family – between husbands and wives and parents and children. We will discuss later the importance of close kin (for example, as Kriegsvögte and guardians) in administering and watching over those rights, but relatives with residual claims to heirship did not frequently assert claims to the occasional crumb dropped out of an estate for sale. Even the right to redeem a property was seldom used during this period. Marriage and heirship determined to a large extent how resources were distributed, and however much collateral relatives were important in the larger set of social relations, they were not, by and large, interested parties in the landed estates of households other than their own.

The small bits of land that did make their way into "free" circulation seem largely to have done so through political connection – either through the affinal network of 40-year olds or with the help of the village elite in their dual roles as officials and godparents. A great deal of communal social life around the year 1700 seems to have been regulated less by a wider kinship network – certainly not by the circle of consanguineal kin – than by a system of clientage. Since at this time husbands and wives were seldom equals as far as wealth was concerned, affinal relations linked together people from different strata and themselves offered the possibilities of clientage. Patrons could build up their networks through position in the magistracy, godparentage, and affinal ties, an amalgam which did not make for tight groupings so much as overlapping, open-ended spheres of influence.

The next question to ask is how property came onto the market or was traded. We have already seen that a frequent motive had to do with farming contiguous plots. Equal inheritance could lead to the fissioning of various parcels, which trade or sale could reunify. Perhaps the fact that so many strips that did trade hands went to the directly interested party made redemption unnecessary, the buyer himself having the strongest claim. On several occasions, villagers with no relatives in the community left estates which were subject to piecemeal partition through auction. Or the estate of an occasional bankrupt could not be absorbed by the family. The most active participants in the property market in the first decade of the eighteenth century by far were the three Waldner brothers – Johannes, Hans Jerg, and Michael. Michael was described as a "very volatile person, who for many years not only started all kinds of disorderly disputes [*Händel* = business deals, lawsuits], but also led a wretched and destructive household" (ein sehr unruhiges Kopf, schon geraume Jahr her so wohl allerhand liederliche Händel angefangen, als auch sonsten eine heilose und verderbliche Haushaltung geführt).[9] Much of his estate was auctioned off in 1727 for debts. While the other two brothers seem to have had a good deal

[9] *Inventuren und Teilungen*, 441 (16.4.1724); also 473 (19.12.1726), where reference was made to *beständigen Processieren* – continual lawsuits.

of success managing their affairs, the example of Michael suggests that considerable activity in the property market might not always have been the result of business acumen or evidence for the commercialization of land.

## Cohort II, 1740–9

Market activity had risen considerably by the mid-eighteenth century. And very much younger villagers were buying and selling property. Most of the transactions where we can study the relations between people point overwhelmingly to the same generational plane (siblings, cousins, affines), the average player being in his late 30s or very early 40s. Even though the intergenerational aspects of market activity early in the century were not strong, they were even less significant 40 years later. The proportion of householders who bought some property almost doubled, but the average person purchased much less. Contrary to what might be expected in such a heated market, the percentage of kin-related sales rose considerably (see Tables 16.6 to 16.8). The category "no established relation" was halved, from 35.6 percent to 17.6 percent. At the same time, there was an important restructuring of the nature of the kinship connections between buyers and sellers. Whereas in the earlier decade sales between nuclear family members accounted for more than 60 percent of the kin-related sales (to nuclear family, cousins, and affines), in this decade they accounted for just over 40 percent. Affines had been the second most important category early in the century, making up almost 30 percent of the kin-

Table 16.6 *Kinship relations between buyers and sellers, 1740–9*

| Buyer's relation to seller | Number | Percent |
|---|---|---|
| Nuclear family | 33 | 32.4 |
| S, DH (3,7) | 10 | 9.8 |
| B, ZH, xZH [FWHDH] (3, 5, 1) | 9 | 8.8 |
| WB, WZH (10,1) | 11 | 10.8 |
| F, WF (1,1) | 2 | 2.0 |
| DS | 1 | 1.0 |
| First cousins, nephews, nieces | 21 | 20.6 |
| xZDH [FWHDDH] | 1 | |
| WZS | 1 | |
| FZS | 1 | |
| MBDS | 2 | |
| WMBS | 3 | |
| WMZS | 1 | |
| WFBS | 3 | |
| WxFBS | 1 | |
| WFBDH, WHWHFBDH | 2 | |
| FFBDH | 1 | |

Table 16.6 *(cont.)*

| Buyer's relation to seller | Number | Percent |
|---|---|---|
| First cousins, nephews, nieces cont. | | |
| MHWBDS | 1 | |
| WMMBS | 3 | |
| WxFBSDH | 1 | |
| Second cousins | 11 | 10.8 |
| FFZSS | 1 | |
| FFBDDH | 2 | |
| FMBSDH | 1 | |
| WFFZSDH | 3 | |
| WFFZSWBS | 1 | |
| WFMZSS | 1 | |
| WFFZSDH | 1 | |
| WMFZSDH | 1 | |
| Affines | 16 | 15.7 |
| BWH | 1 | |
| BWZS | 1 | |
| BWBDH | 1 | |
| ZHB | 1 | |
| ZHZH | 1 | |
| ZHFBS | 1 | |
| DHZH | 1 | |
| HWHBWH | 1 | |
| WFZHB | 2 | |
| MZHZHB | 1 | |
| MFZHBD | 1 | |
| WFBSWZH | 1 | |
| WBWBWFBS | 1 | |
| xDHBWxB | 1 | |
| FBSWMZH | 1 | |
| No established relation | 18 | 17.6 |
| No information | 3 | 2.9 |
| Total | 102 | 100.0 |

related sales, but by midcentury, they were reduced to about 20 percent of such sales. The fundamental structural change was the increased importance of first and second cousins, who together accounted for about 40 percent of all kin-related sales (compared with less than 10 percent early in the century). This fits in tidily with our information about marriage and godparentage. The major structural change in marriage was the increase in marriages to cousins (especially second cousins in this period). And godparents were also more frequently

Table 16.7 *Kinship relations between exchange partners, 1740–9*

| Exchange partners | Number | Percent |
|---|---|---|
| Nuclear family | 4 | 23.5 |
| B/B | 3 | |
| xDH/WxF | 1 | |
| First cousins | 2 | 11.8 |
| MFZS/MBDS | 1 | |
| WHFBS/FBSWH | 1 | |
| Second cousins | 1 | 5.9 |
| FMZSDH/WFMZSS | 1 | |
| No established relation | 6 | 35.3 |
| No information | 4 | 23.5 |
| Total | 17 | 100.0 |

Table 16.8 *Sales and exchanges: kinship relations, 1740–9*

| Kinship relations | Number | Percent |
|---|---|---|
| Nuclear family | 37 | 31.1 |
| Cousins | 35 | 29.4 |
| Affines | 16 | 13.4 |
| No relation established | 24 | 20.2 |
| No information | 7 | 5.9 |
| Total | 119 | 100.0 |

chosen from among consanguineal relations. The same relationship became fundamental for gaining access to land during the same period. There seems to have been some moral commitment in a more active market to selling property to people related by blood. And it is clear that the reckoning extended to second cousins. There also seems to have been a line of diminishing claim as one moved out from the nuclear family (33 sales) to first cousins (21 sales) to second cousins (11 sales). The declining line of sales ought to be superimposed on a rising curve of potential customers.[10]

Nuclear family transactions remained strong in this cohort but lost their intergenerational character. While land transfers (inheritance and sales) still took place by and large inside the nuclear family (estimated 80 percent), a few small steps were taken to develop horizontal movement through the market. In addition, that generation showed more interest in redeeming family land from

[10] For example, if there were three children for each couple, a person would have 12 first cousins and 36 second cousins.

Table 16.9 *Cousin connections between buyers and sellers, 1740–9*

| Buyer to seller | Frequency | Seller to buyer |
|---|---|---|
| FBS | 4 | FBS |
| FBD | 2 | FBS |
| FZS | 1 | MBS |
| MBS | 3 | FZS |
| MZS | 1 | MZS |
| FBSD | 1 | FFBS |
| FFBD | 1 | FBSS |
| MBDS | 3 | MFZS |
| MMBS | 3 | FZDS |
| FFBDD | 2 | MFBSS |
| FFZSS | 1 | FMBSS |
| FFZSD | 4 | FMBSS |
| FMBSD | 1 | FFZSS |
| FMZSS | 1 | FMZSS |
| MFZSD | 1 | FMBDS |

collateral heirs – at least all kinds of redemptions doubled to account for 7 percent of all sales.

To examine some of the cousin relations more closely, I have listed all of the first and second cousin relationships, conflating those traced through husbands and wives and disregarding the fact of a sale to a spouse rather than to the actual relative (WFBDDH becomes FBDD) and disregarding step-relations (Table 16.9). As noted earlier, there is a cognatic reckoning here. People traced freely through men and women over agnatic and uterine relations. Still, there is an agnatic bias in terms of the first link in the chain of reckoning from either buyer or seller. Relatives traced through the father outweigh those through the mother 20:9. We therefore need to develop an explanation not just for the new importance of sales to cousins but also for the agnatic bias to the networks. Given the population increase, it could be that the process of fissioning through inheritance had created an interest in sorting out strips that had fallen to various blood relations. But then we would expect more "exchanges" between cousins than we find. In addition, it is not wise to try to explain the increase in sales to cousins by looking outside the larger context of developing cousin relations. If devolution had reduced farming strips into smaller parcels, it was incumbent upon first cousins, first cousins once removed, and second cousins with contiguous parcels to deal with each other in a whole new set of ways. They either had to farm the land in such a manner as not to encroach on each other's territory, arrange for efficient plowing and harrowing, and cooperate closely at harvest time, or sell out to one another.

It serves little purpose to argue that cousinship had a latent value that could be put into play in the new situation. The values of cousinship were more likely forged in practice – in specific material conditions. Since the process of fissioning would continue through the 1860s at least, the instances of cousins working plots that had been held in earlier generations in one hand or living together in houses that had fallen to them through inheritance would only increase. Over the period we are studying, the erosion of the size of plots due to the process of fissioning took its greatest jump between 1700 and 1740 (23 percent). Another important period of erosion would take place between 1780 and 1820 (14 percent).[11] In Chapter 12, we studied two examples from the late 1730s and early 1740s in which villagers plowed for each other or carried on agricultural work for pay. Central to those networks were cousin relations. Land tenure and production appear to have been two factors in developing social networks in which cousins were important. Throughout the eighteenth century, there was a general decline in the patron-client structuring of relations. At midcentury, a transition took place whereby new networks based on horizontal connections between consanguineal kin, whose agnatic bias suggests a principle of male centeredness, were operating alongside old ones which utilized office, affinity, and ritual kinship.

The procedure for studying the role of godparents in market transactions is the same as before. I examined all the cases in which there was "no established relation" between parties, insufficient kinship information, or the kinship relationship was sufficiently extended to warrant further exploration. As before, I tried to determine whether two contracting parties (H or W) were linked to a third family (H,W,S,D) as Gevatter(in) or Döte/Dote. The results are presented in Table 16.10.

We see here that the relationship of godparentage in land sales where close consanguineal or affinal relations cannot be established was even clearer than at the beginning of the century. And it continued to be a *mediating* role; that is, in only two cases out of those studied did a godparent or a member of his

Table 16.10 *Sales and exchanges between parties linked through godparents, 1740–9*

| | Sales | Exchanges |
|---|---|---|
| Total | 24 | 11 |
| Number linked | 19 | 8 |
| Percentage linked | 79.2 | 72.7 |

[11] See Table 15.4.

or her family sell or buy to the family he was linked to, and even then they were in turn connected through third parties as godparents. This evidence suggests once again that godparentage was a crucial institution in the first half of the eighteenth century in village social life and that although it had undergone a transformation by midcentury, it was still significant for mobilizing resources. Even though people were more likely to go to kin for the selection of godparents than their parents and grandparents had been, the institution was still part of a clientage and favor system. More transactions took place within the web of kinship relations, however, and we can see that the tendency toward increased market activity and the tendency toward greater stratification both implied a new reliance on consanguineal kin. For a generation or so, fictive kinship played a kind of swing role – still central in its mediation function, while becoming less and less independent of previously formed kinship ties with every generation. The midcentury is perhaps a turning point. As classes deepened their divisions and as endogamy came to play an ever more central role in class formation, godparentage remained for a time one of the crucial mechanisms for tying the interests of individuals together. Several examples of land sales and fictive kinship are presented in Figures 16.9 and 16.10.

*In this case Johann Georg Rieth I was the* Döte *of both Hans Jerg Thumm and his wife. Johann Georg Rieth II and the Ehesuccessor or Johann Georg Rieth I's daughter were both* Gevatter *for Thumm. Barbara Beck and Johann Georg Rieth III were the* Gevattern *for Johann Georg Bauknecht (Figure 16.9).*

*Joseph Häfner and young Jacob Geiger traded properties. Young Jacob Geiger's wife's brother was Häfner's Gevatter. Michael Maichinger and his wife were* Gevattern *for the two contracting parties (note also that Maichinger had taken over the role from his father-in-law, Heinrich Pfeiffer). Finally Geiger's mother-in-law had been a*

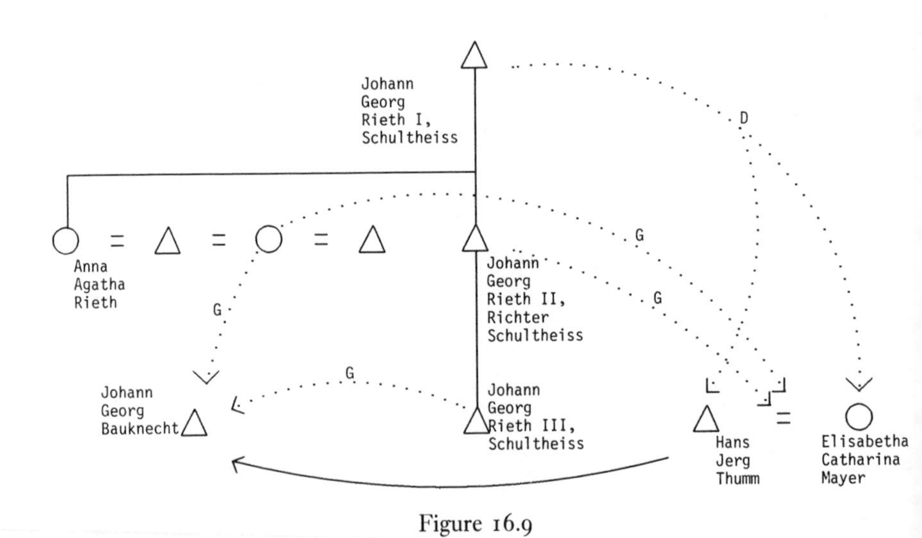


Figure 16.9

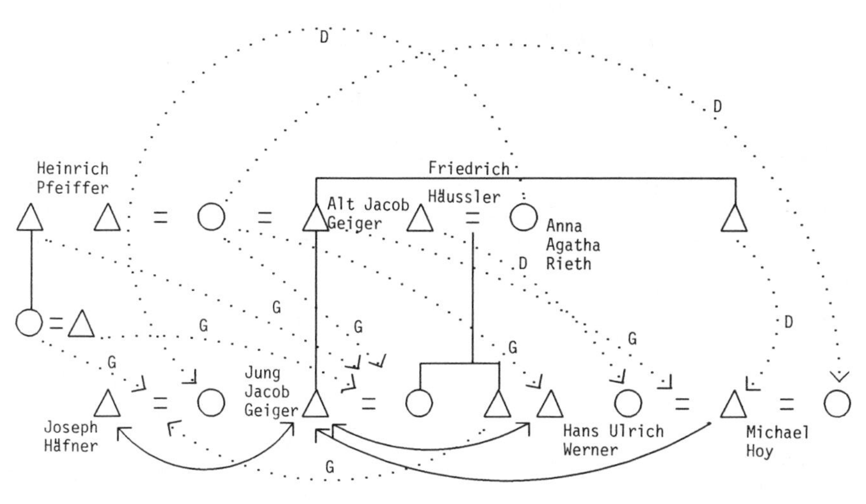


Figure 16.10

Dote *for Hafner. Geiger also traded properties with Hans Ulrich Werner. Anna Elisabetha Burkhart, first married to David Böbel and later to young Geiger's father was* Gevatterin *for both parties. Michael Hoy sold a strip of arable to young Geiger, whose father-in-law had been Hoy's first wife's* Döte. *Geiger's uncle was Hoy's* Döte *and his father Hoy's* Gevatter. *Anna Elisabetha Burkhart, Geiger's* Gevatterin, *had been Hoy's second wife's* Dote.

## Cohort III, 1780–9

By the 1780s, most household heads entered the market to buy real estate. The age of purchasers had fallen to its lowest level and is reflected in the fact that so many collateral descendants such as nephews and husbands of nieces purchased property (17, or 7.3 percent). Almost half of the purchases by affines were extended downward by a generation, and the first cousins once removed and second cousins once removed each offset the relation between sellers and buyers by one generation. In this manner, the market played a strong role in devolution for the first time in the eighteenth century, but not so much between parents and children as between collateral relatives. In other words, the market became a mechanism for integrating a larger group of kin than the rules of inheritance would have allowed. During this period, redemptions reached a peak of almost 14 percent of sales, half or more of which were probably carried out by collateral heirs. Earlier we estimated that at the beginning of the eighteenth century about 90 percent of transfers of land (through sales and inheritance) were contained within the nuclear family. By midcentury, this had been eroded somewhat to about 80 percent. But by the 1780s, the market had clearly become an important force for the redistribution of property in the village,

Table 16.11 *Kinship relations between buyers and sellers, 1780–9*

| | Number | Percent |
|---|---|---|
| Nuclear family | 37 | 15.8 |
| S, xS (11), xDH (4) | 15 | 6.4 |
| B, xB (10), ZH (7), xBWH (1) | 18 | 7.7 |
| WB, WZH (2,2) | 4 | 1.7 |
| First cousins, nephews, uncles[a] | 48 | 20.5 |
| BS | 5 | |
| xBDH | 3 | |
| WBS | 1 | |
| ZS | 1 | |
| ZHDH | 1 | |
| WZSS | 2 | |
| WZSDH | 1 | |
| WZSSS | 1 | |
| WHDS | 1 | |
| WHDDH | 1 | |
| MB | 1 | |
| MZH | 3 | |
| FBS, FxBS | 2 | |
| FZS | 5 | |
| WFZS | 1 | |
| WFBDH | 1 | |
| MBS | 4 | |
| FWHS | 1 | |
| FBWHBS | 2 | |
| FFBS | 1 | |
| FBSDH | 1 | |
| HFBSS | 2 | |
| WFZSS | 1 | |
| WFxZDH | 2 | |
| MBSS | 1 | |
| WMBSS | 1 | |
| MZDS | 2 | |
| Second cousins[b] | 23 | 9.8 |
| FFBSS, FFxBSS | 2 | |
| WFFxBSS | 2 | |
| FMBSS | 6 | |
| FMHSDS | 2 | |
| MFZDS | 1 | |
| HMMBSS | 1 | |
| FFZSSS | 1 | |
| WFFBSDS | 1 | |
| FFBSSDH | 1 | |

Table 16.11 *(cont.)*

| | Number | Percent |
|---|---|---|
| Second cousins cont. | | |
| WFFZSDSW | 1 | |
| MFFWHSS | 2 | |
| MMFBSDH | 1 | |
| WHFMBSS | 1 | |
| WHWFBSS | 1 | 14.5 |
| Affines | 34 | |
| xBWZH | 1 | |
| BWxZH | 1 | |
| xBWHF | 1 | |
| BWBS | 2 | |
| xZHB | 1 | |
| MZDHB | 1 | |
| MZSWF | 2 | |
| WZHB | 4 | |
| WZHBS | 1 | |
| ZHF | 2 | |
| HZH | 1 | |
| WZDH | 1 | |
| BDHZH | 1 | |
| BDHMZS | 1 | |
| WZHBSS | 1 | |
| WZHZSS | 3 | |
| WZSDH | 1 | |
| WZHBS | 1 | |
| MZDHBS | 1 | |
| HFBWFBS | 2 | |
| HxZHSDH | 1 | |
| WHFZHZHZ | 1 | |
| WHZDDHM | 2 | |
| WZHBWH | 1 | |
| No relation established | 78 | 33.3 |
| No information | 14 | 6.0 |
| Total | 234 | 99.9 |

[a] Includes first cousins once removed and grandnephews.
[b] Includes second cousins once removed.

reducing nuclear family property transfers to rather more than 60 percent (63.0). If we assume that when more properties are bought and sold, fewer are inherited, then transactions within the confines of direct lineal kinship would have accounted for a somewhat lower percentage.

In comparison with the two previous cohorts, a very large rise took place in the absolute numbers of transactions which were kin-related, from 58 to 81 to 142 (see Table 16.11). Yet the market outpaced the capacities of families to absorb property, and the percentage taking place between nonrelatives became a substantial third of all sales, back to where it had been at the beginning of the century.

The structural shifts which we encountered between the first two decades continued and deepened. At the beginning of the century, the nuclear family accounted for slightly more than 60 percent of kin-related sales (nuclear family, cousins, affines), whereas by midcentury, their purchases had dropped to just over 40 percent. Toward the end of the century, they had fallen to a little more than 25 percent. Affines went from 30 percent to 20 percent to somewhere in between (24 percent). The importance of "cousins" (first and second) continued to increase: It was less than 10 percent early in the century, about 40 percent at midcentury, and 50 percent by the 1780s, although this last figure includes a substantial number of nephews. Even within the affinal networks, "cousin elements" were structurally important, as the examples in Figure 16.11 show.

It is difficult to draw any firm conclusions about the effect of kinship on such sales without further evidence. However, the cousin constellation appears to have been quite significant. And even affinal relations can frequently not be traced out on a horizontal line. Such figures as a cousin's cousin or a niece's

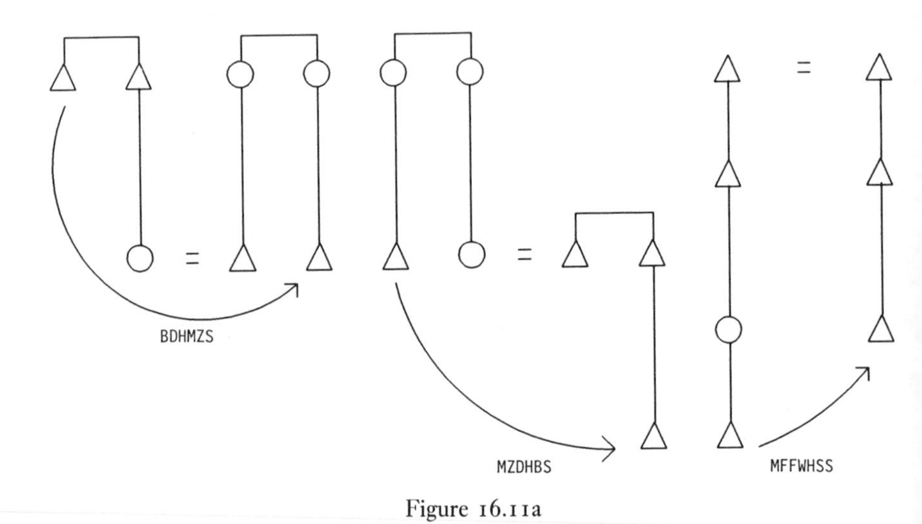


Figure 16.11a

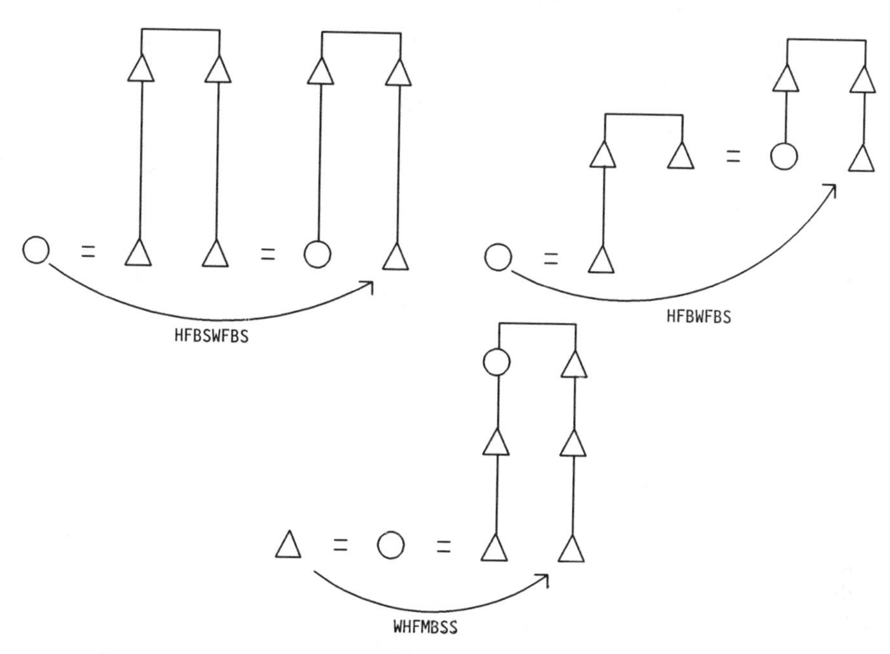


Figure 16.11b

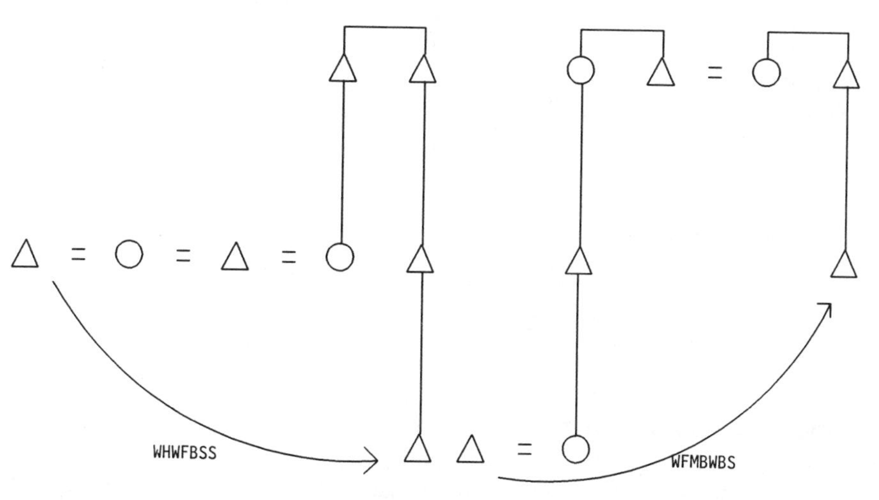


Figure 16.11c

husband's cousin or the second cousin of an Ehepredecessor all point to the greater role consanguineal relations played in social relations.

Let us carry out the same exercise regarding first and second cousins as we did for the previous cohort. We will conflate relations of husband and wife and

Table 16.12 *Cousin connections between buyers and sellers, 1780–9*

| Buyer to seller | Frequency | Seller to buyer |
|---|---|---|
| FBS | 4 | FBS |
| FBD | 1 | FBS |
| FZS | 6 | MBS |
| MBS | 4 | FZS |
| MBD | 1 | FZS |
| FFBS | 1 | FBSS |
| FBSD | 1 | FBSS |
| FBSS | 2 | FFBS |
| FBDS | 2 | MFBS |
| FZSS | 1 | FMBS |
| FZSD | 2 | FMBS |
| MBSS | 2 | FFZS |
| MZDS | 2 | MMZS |
| FFBSS | 4 | FFBSS |
| FMBSS | 6 | FFZSS |
| MFZDS | 1 | MMBDS |
| MMBSS | 1 | FFZDS |
| FFZSSS | 1 | FFMBSS |
| FFBSDS | 1 | MFFBSS |
| FFBSSD | 1 | FFFBSS |
| FFZSD | 1 | FMBSS |
| MMFBSD | 1 | FFBDDS |

disregard step-relations. Also we will disregard the spouse rather than the actual relative – FBDDH becomes FBDD.

There is a clear agnatic bias here (Table 16.12). Relations in the list traced through the father outweigh those traced through the mother 17:6 – almost 3:1 compared with 2:1 at midcentury. A constellation such as FBDH or FZSS or FZDS shows that the links in a chain between two people could go over women just as well as men, however. These are not male networks as such and it would be a great mistake to dismiss women in the eighteenth century as insignificant social actors. Nonetheless, it does appear that children more frequently utilized family networks that had been built up and maintained by their fathers. Perhaps this reflects the main issue in agriculture up to that point, which was to ensure adequate cultivation and to amortize investments in livestock and heavy agricultural equipment by offering them for hire. We would expect the structure of such networks to lose their strong agnatic character when agriculture became more closely connected with the availability of female labor.

Table 16.13 *Sales between parties linked through godparents*

| Cohort | Total | Number linked | Percentage linked |
|---|---|---|---|
| I | 32 | 18 | 56.3 |
| II | 24 | 19 | 79.2 |
| III | 86 | 52 | 60.5 |

Godparentage narrowed its focus a great deal by the 1780s, as parents increasingly chose close relatives and cousins – especially second cousins – for the position. Just as cousins became more important for *ritual* kin relations – and also for marriage partners – they played an ever more prominent role in land transactions. Yet godparentage as such still seems to have played an important mediating role while these shifts were going on. Carrying out the earlier exercise with sales between unrelated or distantly related people gives us the results shown in Table 16.13.

The connection through godparents still appears to be very important and in absolute terms accounts for many more sales than in previous periods. Even

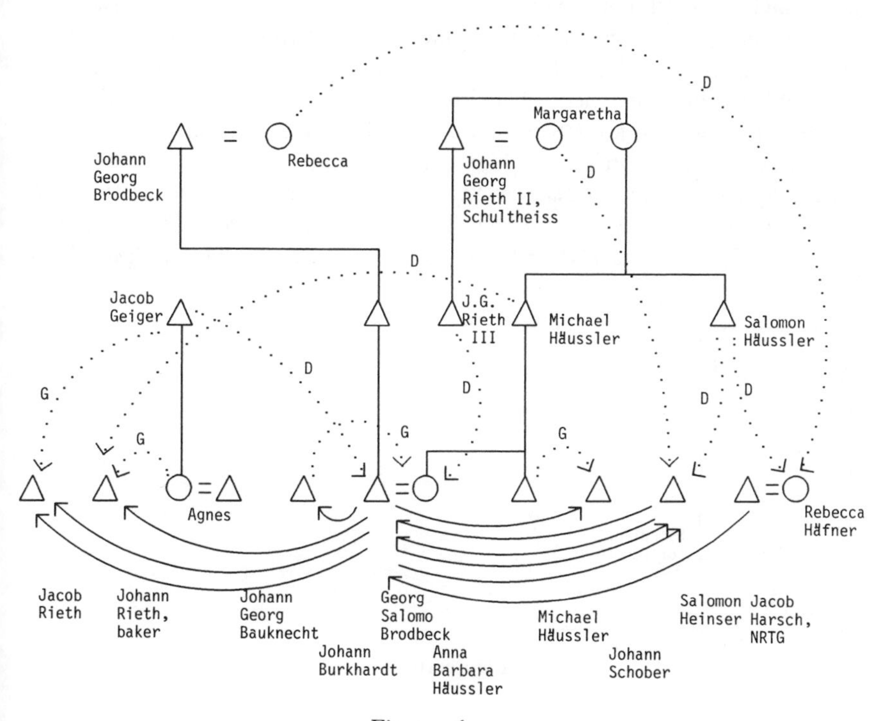


Figure 16.12

though godparentage had altered a great deal in structure, it continued to play a political role in the village in sorting out access to land. Several examples are presented in Figure 16.12.

*In this case, there is one direct instance of godparentage and land sales. Johann Burkhardt was* Gevatter *for Georg Salomon Brodbeck and sold property to him. Brodbeck's brother-in-law Michael Häussler was* Gevatter *for Johann Schober, to whom Brodbeck also sold land. In the case of Jacob Rieth, Jacob Geiger was his* Gevatter *and Brodbeck's* Döte. *Brodbeck sold to him twice. Salomon Heinser presents a more complex case. Brodbeck bought twice from him and sold twice to him. Brodbeck's wife's uncle was* Döte *for Heinser. Johann Georg Rieth, Schultheiss, was* Döte *for Brodbeck's wife, and Rieth's mother was* Dote *for Heinser. In the case of Johann Rieth, baker, who purchased land from Brodbeck, Jacob Geiger was Brodbeck's* Döte *and Geiger's daughter was Rieth's* Gevatterin. *Michael Häussler, Brodbeck's wife's father, was also* Döte *for Rieth. Finally, there is the case of Jacob Harsch from Nürtingen, husband of Rebecca Häfner who left the village upon marriage. Her Dote was Brodbeck's grandmother. Her other* Döte *was Brodbeck's wife's uncle. Harsch sold property probably inherited by Rebecca to Brodbeck.*

On many occasions, several transactions were made on the same day. Someone could unload the bulk of his or her property all at once when in shaky economic circumstances or at retirement, but our concern here is the transactions which involved more than one person selling property. Such transactions occurred on 14 occasions. We can assume for argument's sake that all the sales on one day were coordinated in one fashion or another. A person might have been willing to give up a piece of land in return for a parcel which would satisfy an obligation owed to a relative. As a result, the sale of several pieces of land would have involved intricate political arrangements.

*The simplest example took place on 24.3.1784.*[12] *Friedrich Häfner sold to Heinrich Dorfschmid who sold to young Salomon Hentzler. Dorfschmid and Häfner were first cousins and Hentzler and Häfner had a mutual* Gevatterin/Dote *in Agnes Bauer*

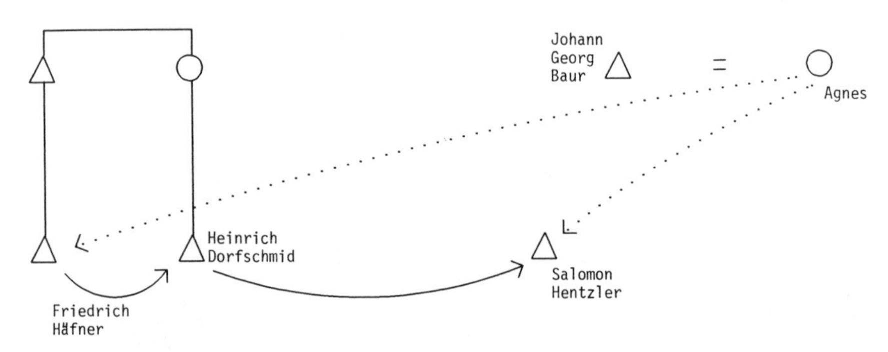


Figure 16.13

[12] *Kaufbuch*, vol. 5, f. 282, 24.3.1784.

*(Figure 16.13). This instance combines the two principles we have discovered for this period: godparentage and cousinship.*

*A second example combined principles of kinship and godparentage as well, but this time affinal connections seem to have been operative.*[13] *Johann Feldmaier and Nicolaus Vogler were linked by a common* Gevatter, *the schoolmaster, Johann Jacob Gantter (Figure 16.14). Vogler sold Feldmaier an arable strip at the same time as Feldmaier's brother-in-law's brother sold Vogler's son-in-law a vineyard.*

*The third example is more complicated and contains cousin, affinal, and fictive kin connections.*[14] *Jacob Geiger and his wife were godparents for the three contracting parties, two of which (Brodbeck and Bosch) had married sisters (Figure 16.15). The third, Nicolaus Vogler's daughter and their wives' brother, were married to first cousins.*

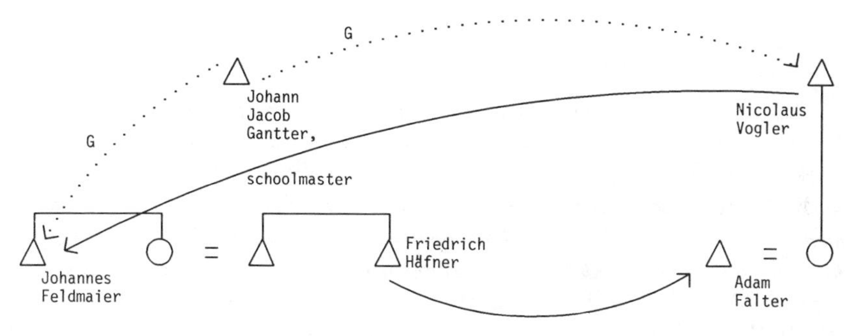


Figure 16.14

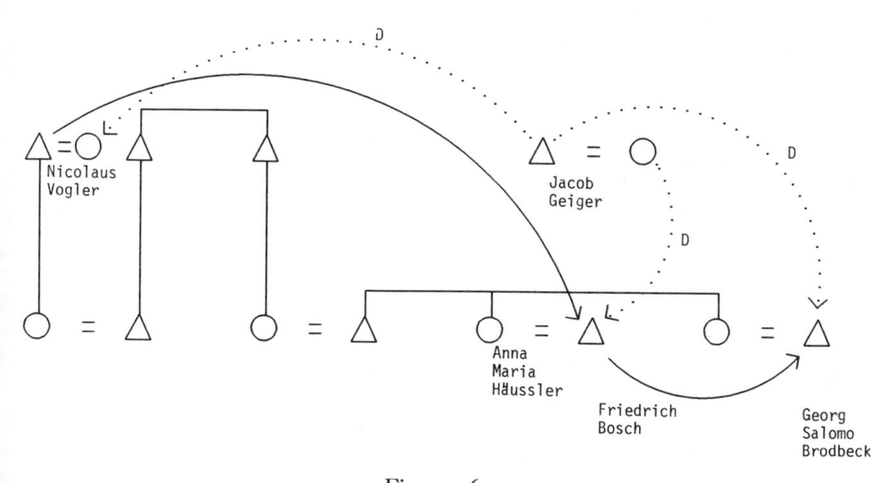


Figure 16.15

[13] *Kaufbuch*, vol. 6, f. 32, 29.3.1787.
[14] *Kaufbuch*, vol. 5, f. 239, 29.1.1782.

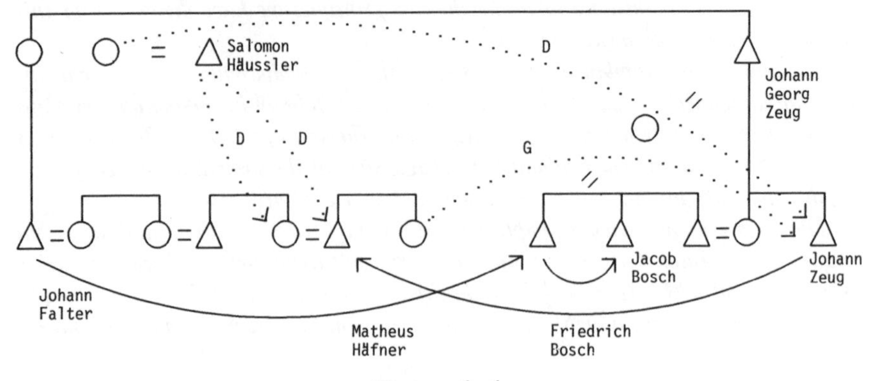


Figure 16.16

*This example is even more complicated.*[15] *Johann Falter sold a meadow to Friedrich Bosch, and Johann Zeug sold an arable strip to Matheus Häfner. This is not a case where one party gave up something to get something else in direct return. Häfner was probably anxious to get the parcel he purchased because it lay next to one he already owned. He and the seller, Zeug, had common godparents in Salomon Häussler and his wife, but they had both long been dead (Figure 16.16). Häfner's sister was* Gevatterin *for Zeug. Häfner was connected to Falter as brother-in-law's brother-in-law (WBWZH), and his dead godfather was Falter's father-in-law. Jacob Bosch actually*

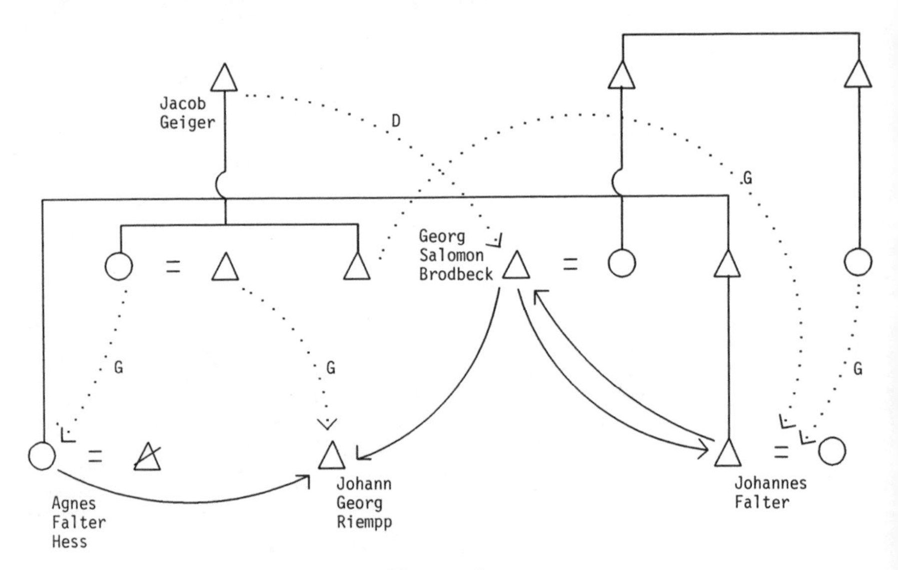


Figure 16.17

[15] *Kaufbuch*, vol. 5, f. 240, 15.2.1782.

*purchased two parcels that day but the one from his brother was redeemed and the sale was therefore called off. Both parcels were contiguous and would have combined very nicely. Jacob Bosch was married to Zeug's stepmother and was also his BWB. He was the* Ehesuccessor *to Johann Georg Zeug, Falter's uncle. Zeug and Falter, of course, were first cousins. Whether the two (or three) sales were coordinated in any way is hard to tell, but the interrelationships of the various actors nonetheless demonstrate combined principles of consanguinity, affinity, and godparentage.*

*In the final instance, Georg Salomo Brodbeck sold two parcels and received one in return.*[16] *One of those he sold was actually contiguous to one he had. The widow Agnes Hess sold Johann Georg Riempp a parcel next to one he already had. Agnes Hess was Johann Falter's aunt (Figure 16.17). Georg Salomon Brodbeck's wife's cousin was Falter's* Gevatter. *A key connection seems to have been the Geiger family. Jacob Geiger had been Brodbeck's* Döte. *His daughter was* Gevatterin *for Agnes Hess and her husband* Gevatter *for Johann Georg Riempp. Geiger's son, Jacob Friedrich, was* Gevatter *for Johann Falter.*

## Cohort IV, 1820–9

During the second decade of the nineteenth century, the market for land was greater than it had been at any time during the eighteenth. In part, this was due to the economic dislocation following the Napoleonic Wars, when many villagers went bankrupt and a significant amount of property was sold at forced, public auction. For several decades before this time, villagers had been using their land more intensively, which might well have helped erode the size of parcels. Even then, far more land was sold than ever before and to a larger percentage of a sharply increased population. There seems to have been a land hunger during the period to match the newly available supply, which not only drove prices upward but also led to wild fluctuations in price. Apparently the older generation had held onto land longer than any previous one, and those entering the market were themselves older than their counterparts in the late eighteenth century. Despite the expanded size, velocity, and formalism of the market, the nuclear family played twice as large a role as it had 40 years earlier (Table 16.14). At the same time, redemption was no longer utilized to recover family property. In this generation, a larger percentage of all kinds of land transfers were retained within the nuclear family (through inheritance and sales) – more than 67 percent. While this did not attain the levels of the first half of the eighteenth century (between 80 and 90 percent), it did reverse the trend from the later decades (63 percent). During the early nineteenth century, the interest in retaining family property was very strong. One man even went to court to complain about the fact that he had been outbid by a nonrelative for a parcel of land sold by his brother-in-law (WZH).[17] Property had gotten so

[16] *Kaufbuch*, vol. 5, f. 254, 23.12.1782.
[17] *Gericht*, vol. 5, f. 205 (28.12.1803).

Table 16.14 *Kinship relations between buyers and sellers, 1820–9*

| Buyer's relation to seller | Number | Percent |
|---|---|---|
| Nuclear family | 47 | 30.9 |
| M | 1 | .7 |
| S, DH (19,7) | 26 | 17.1 |
| B, ZH | 9 | 5.9 |
| WB, WZ, WZH (8,1,2) | 11 | 7.2 |
| First cousins, uncles[a] | 13 | 8.6 |
| FZS | 1 | |
| HFBDH | 1 | |
| MBD | 1 | |
| MZS | 1 | |
| WMZS | 2 | |
| FFBS | 1 | |
| WMFZDH | 1 | |
| WFBSS | 2 | |
| WFBDS | 1 | |
| MBSDH | 1 | |
| MBDDH | 1 | |
| Second cousins[b] | 19 | 12.5 |
| WFFZSS | 1 | |
| WFMBSDH | 1 | |
| WFMZSS | 1 | |
| WFMZSDH | 3 | |
| WFMZDDH | 1 | |
| WMFZSS | 2 | |
| MFZSS | 1 | |
| MMZSS | 1 | |
| FFFBSDH | 2 | |
| WMFBDSS | 1 | |
| WMMZSDDH | 1 | |
| FFBSSS | 1 | |
| WFFBSDS | 1 | |
| FMBSDS | 1 | |
| FMBDDDH | 1 | |
| Affines | 10 | 6.6 |
| SWZ | 1 | |
| DHB | 1 | |
| ZHBS | 1 | |
| FFWBS | 1 | |
| WBWB | 1 | |
| WBDH | 1 | |
| WSWZH | 2 | |

Table 16.14 *(cont.)*

| | Number | Percent |
|---|---|---|
| Affines cont. | | |
| WHSWBS | 1 | |
| WZHZSDH | 1 | |
| No established relation | 52 | 34.2 |
| No information | 11 | 7.2 |
| Total | 152 | 100.0 |

[a] Including first cousins once removed.
[b] Including second cousins once removed.

expensive that it was difficult to build up large holdings through purchase. On the other hand, there is considerable evidence from the earlier period when redemptions were possible that people often sold land more cheaply to brothers and sisters and children (at a "price for relatives," Freundschaftspreis).[18] There are also cases of heirs arranging matters among themselves so as to avoid public auction of a father's or father-in-law's estate.[19]

Given the age differential between buyers and sellers during the decade, the market clearly functioned as a means of turning property over to a younger generation, but one comparatively long in the tooth (average age 37). Altogether, nonrelatives made no deeper inroads into the market than they had during the eighteenth century, the proportion fluctuating between 33 and 36 percent (except during the 1740s when strangers got their hands on little family property at all). As for the structure of kin-related purchases (nuclear kin, cousins, and affines), there was a remarkable change. The nuclear family came to account for more than half of the purchases (53 percent), although not as much as at the beginning of the eighteenth century (over 60 percent), clearly a reversal of the subsequent trend (40 percent, 25 percent). Cousins retained their structural position – more than 35 percent, while affines accounted for well under half of their earlier position (11 percent). Altogether, nuclear family members and cousins bought over half of all parcels of land and parts of buildings offered for sale during the decade. Some of the sales where "no relation" was established were between third cousins. That such an extended relation may have played some role can be inferred from the structural importance of

[18] E.g., *Kaufbuch*, vol. 5, f. 279 (30.12.1783): "Zu Wohlfeil und ein Freundschaftskauf zwischen Geschwistern." Perhaps this was noted so that the price could be renegotiated in case of a redemption.

[19] E.g., *Inventuren und Teilungen*, 1340 (9.2.1808); see the discussion in my "Young Bees in an Empty Hive: Relations between Brothers-in-Law in a South German Village around 1800," in *Interest and Emotion: Essays on the Study of Family and Kinship*, ed. Hans Medick and David Warren Sabean (Cambridge, 1984), pp. 171–86, here 179.

marriages between first and second and third cousins during the period. The fall in affine connections is related to the fact that by marriage cousins became in-laws, and it only introduces unnecessary complications to trace all possible kinship links between partners. Similarly, godparents became restricted to siblings and cousins and by this generation were the same age as the parents. They no longer mediated between classes and age groups in the village. Carrying out the same exercise with regard to godparents as before shows a radical drop in the percentage of unrelated buyers and sellers who had a common godparent (from 60 transactions studied, 16, or 26.7 percent). By contrast, during the 1780s, over 60 percent of such transactions were found to have had such a link. It seems that the family maintained a firm grasp on land but that consanguineal principles became far more important by the early decades of the nineteenth century than either affinal or patronage ones. Transactions were at once narrowed down to the nuclear family and widened to blood relatives to and beyond second cousins.

When we examine cousin relations as we did for the last two cohorts (conflating relations of husband and wife and disregarding step relations – WFBDDH = FBDD), we obtain the results shown in Table 16.15. In general in this period, the agnatic bias was 5:3, compared with 3:1 in the 1780s and 2:1 in the 1740s. As before, we are looking at the first step in the chain above an actor, say, in the relation MFBS, where the mother is the first step for "A" and the father for "B" (Figure 16.18). We suggested earlier that children might be utilizing networks established by their parents – in the case below, those between the uncle and the niece, D/C. The agnatic bias suggests that we are examining networks maintained more by men than by women and that for the purchase of land, at least, such agnatic networks were important. The links, however, went over women as well as over men, and a significant number of networks may well have been maintained by women. The ratio by the 1820s certainly had moved more in their favor (6:3, 9:3, 5:3). Another point of interest in the networks is at the apex, where lines descend from two siblings. Counting

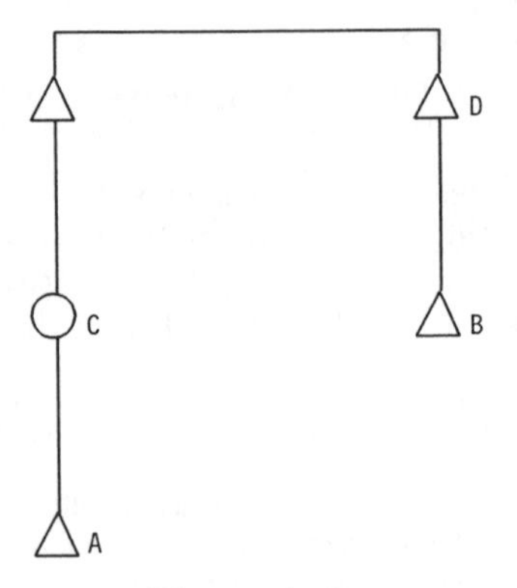


Figure 16.18

Table 16.15 *Cousin connections between buyers and sellers, 1820–9*

| Buyer to seller | Frequency | Seller to buyer |
|---|---|---|
| FBD | 1 | FBS |
| MBD | 1 | FZS |
| MZS | 3 | MZS |
| FFBS | 1 | FBSS |
| MFZD | 1 | MBDS |
| FBSS | 2 | FFBS |
| FBDS | 1 | MFBS |
| MBSD | 1 | FFZS |
| MBDD | 1 | MFZS |
| FFZSS | 1 | FMBSS |
| FMBSD | 1 | FFZSS |
| FMZSS | 1 | FMZSS |
| FMZSD | 3 | FMZSS |
| FMZDD | 1 | MMZSS |
| MFZSS | 2 | FMZSS |
| MFZSS | 1 | FMBDS |
| MMZSS | 1 | FMZDS |
| FFFBSD | 2 | FFBSSS |
| MFBDSS | 1 | FMFBDS |
| MMZSDD | 1 | MFMZDS |
| FFBSSS | 1 | FFFBSS |
| FFBSDS | 1 | MFFBSS |
| FMBSDS | 1 | MFFZSS |
| FMBDDD | 1 | MMFZSS |

them from both sides, we get FB-20, FZ-11, MB-9, MZ-22. All combinations of siblings are to be found, but siblings of parallel sex (FB and MZ) outweigh the cross gender by 2:1. It may be that networks were maintained through a sense of having descended from a sibling group but that parallel sex relationships were important for developing and maintaining such networks over generations.

## Cohort V, 1860–9

By the 1860s, the market was no longer overheated. With the long-term population rise, prices had skyrocketed and the size of plots had been whittled away to a level just over half of what levels had been around 1700 (56.8 percent). The mean purchaser bought far less land than ever before, and the percentage of the population entering the market had fallen to that of the

Table 16.16 *Kinship relations between buyers and sellers, 1760–9*

| Buyer's relation to seller | Number | Percent |
|---|---|---|
| Nuclear family[a] | 26 | 30.9 |
| S, D, DH WDH[b] (1,1,7,2) | 11 | 13.1 |
| B, Z, ZH, xZH (3,1,2,1) | 7 | 8.3 |
| WB, WZH, WBW, HZH (2,2,1,1) | 6 | 7.1 |
| SS, DS (1,1) | 2 | 2.4 |
| First cousins, nephews,[c] | 15 | 17.9 |
| MB | 2 | |
| BS | 1 | |
| ZS | 4 | |
| WZD | 1 | |
| FBS | 1 | |
| FZS | 1 | |
| MBDH | 1 | |
| WFZS | 1 | |
| WMZDH | 2 | |
| WMZDS[d] | 1 | |
| Second cousins[e] | 4 | 4.8 |
| MFZDS | 1 | |
| MMBDDH | 1 | |
| MZDSDH | 1 | |
| MFZDSDH | 1 | |
| Affines | 10 | 11.9 |
| BWB | 1 | |
| HBWB | 1 | |
| WBWB | 1 | |
| WZHB | 1 | |
| BWZH | 2 | |
| DHFZD | 1 | |
| WMBWWZH | 1 | |
| WZHZDH | 1 | |
| WMHWHW | 1 | |
| No established relation | 27 | 32.1 |
| No information | 2 | 2.4 |
| Total | 84 | 100.0 |

[a] Including linear descendants.
[b] Also BDH.
[c] Including first cousins once removed.
[d] Also WBWDH.
[e] Including second cousins once removed.

Table 16.17 *Kin-related sales for five cohorts*

| Percentage | 1700–1709 | 1740–9 | 1780–9 | 1820–9 | 1860–9 |
|---|---|---|---|---|---|
| Kin | 64.4 | 81.8 | 64.5 | 63.1 | 67.1 |
| Nuclear family | 62.1 | 40.7 | 26.1 | 52.8 | 47.3 |
| Cousins | 8.6 | 39.5 | 50.0 | 36.0 | 34.5 |
| Affines | 29.3 | 19.7 | 23.9 | 11.2 | 18.2 |

1740s. Sellers were on the average well into their 50s and buyers in their early 40s. In this period, the nuclear family probably accounted for well over three-quarters (78 percent) of all property transfers (inheritance and sales), a continuation of the trend we saw in the 1820s, almost back to the situation of the 1740s (80 percent) (see Table 16.16).

On the whole, the percentage of property sold to family members did not change very much over the whole period studied, despite fluctuations in every aspect of the market: number of participants, size of plots, tendency to accumulate, formal auction. In fact, 16 out of 20 sellers of property in the 1860s sold more than 50 percent of the time to kin. There is one phenomenon more difficult to assess, which also shows a kinship configuration. Several sellers sold properties at different times to various buyers who were only distantly related to themselves but who were closely related to each other. If anything, more property appears to have been sold to kin by the mid-nineteenth century than earlier, as Table 16.17 demonstrates. This table presents only kin and nonkin sales and disregards those for which there is no genealogical information.

By the 1860s, the nuclear family seems to have maintained its strong position, which had first been eroded in the eighteenth century but recovered early in the nineteenth. At the same time, consanguineal kin – first and second cousins – remained important. Throughout this period, people continued to marry cousins, which means that consanguineal and affinal relations were often really or potentially the same. During the nineteenth century, there were also frequent marriages with affinal kin – the deceased wife's sister or sister-in-law – which also reinforced previous kin ties. As we have seen, an important shift had taken place between 1700 and 1740 with the cousins' rise to a prominent position. At the beginning of the century, affinal and godparent relations suggested a system of patron/clientage which was slowly eroded during the eighteenth century, to be replaced by a structure based on consanguineal kin, who also provided a large part of the pool of marriage partners. By the 1820s, godparents no longer seemed to have played a mediating role connecting unrelated buyers and sellers, and inspection of the data for the 1860s proved it unnecessary to construct further statistics in that regard.

We have seen that the age structure of the market varied considerably throughout the study period. Sometimes buying and selling seems to have been

Table 16.18 *Generational plane of buyers and sellers having kinship to each other, five cohorts*

| Plane | 1700–1709 | 1740–9 | 1780–9 | 1820–9 | 1860–9 |
|---|---|---|---|---|---|
| Percentage horizontal | 57.6 | 61.3 | 50.0 | 41.6 | 50.9 |
| Percentage vertical | 42.4 | 38.8 | 50.0 | 58.4 | 49.1 |

largely a matter of adult males of the same generation, connected or unconnected by kinship. At other times, much of the market was supplemental to the inheritance process, devolving property onto the next generation in a more flexible way than intestate rules provided for. We can draw up a rough balance by calculating the generational position of participants in each kin transaction, for example, a sale to a B or FBS being on a horizontal plane, to an S or ZS on a vertical (Table 16.18).

In the early part of the eighteenth century, horizontal relations were stressed. This was a period when the market did not play as great a role in determining the allocation of property rights in the society as it did later on. The difference in age between buyers and sellers was lower than it would ever be again. Some parcels came onto the market as a kinless person died, and a few plots or houses were sold to children. For the rest, there was a relatively inactive system of exchange among adults of the same generation. By the 1780s and into the first decades of the nineteenth century, the age difference between buyers and sellers grew and vertical relations came to be increasingly stressed. Older adults sold to their children, nephews, and children of cousins. After midcentury, at least, the balance achieved in the 1780s and distorted by the heated-up market of the 1820s was reestablished. This time the buyers and sellers were 10 years older than in the 1780s but not as far apart in age as in the 1820s. About half the sales involved property devolution and another half involved transactions between brothers, brothers-in-law, and cousins. The principle of diminishing claim seems very clear here: 13 sales among brothers and sisters (brothers-in-law), 7 sales to first cousins and first cousins once removed, and 4 sales to second cousins and second cousins once removed, in reverse order to their supply.

When we consider the cousin networks, we find that buyers and sellers traced through their mothers more often than through their fathers (M:F = 13:9), tipping the bias away from an agnatic to a uterine one (Table 16.19). The approximate ratios of agnatic to uterine relations from the 1740s are 6:3, 9:3, 5:3, and 2:3, respectively. When we look at the apex of each consanguineal network, we get the following results: FB-2, FZ-6, MB-6, and MZ-8. The parallel brother relation (FB) has become insignificant in favor of cross sibling (FZ, MB) and parallel sister (MZ) connections. These data suggest that the

Table 16.19 *Cousin connections between buyers and sellers, 1860–9*

| Buyer to sellers | Frequency | Seller to buyers |
|---|---|---|
| FBS | 1 | FBS |
| FZS | 2 | MBS |
| MBD | 1 | FZS |
| MZD | 2 | MZS |
| MZDS | 1 | MMZS |
| MFZDS | 1 | MMBDS |
| MMBDD | 1 | MFZDS |
| MZDSD | 1 | FMMZS |
| MFZDSD | 1 | FMMBDS |

Table 16.20 *Sales to sons, sons-in-law, brothers, and brothers-in-law*

| | 1700–1709 | 1740–9 | 1780–9 | 1820–9 | 1860–9 |
|---|---|---|---|---|---|
| S | 14 | 3 | 11 | 19 | 1 |
| B | 10 | 3 | 11 | 3 | 3 |
| D, DH | 2 | 7 | 4 | 7 | 10 |
| Z, ZH, WB, WZH | 10 | 17 | 11 | 17 | 9 |
| Percentage S/B | 66.7 | 20.0 | 62.9 | 47.8 | 17.4 |
| Percentage B-in-law | 27.8 | 56.7 | 31.4 | 37.0 | 39.1 |
| Percentage S-in-law | 5.3 | 23.3 | 10.8 | 15.2 | 43.5 |

nineteenth century witnessed a growth in networks established and maintained by women. On the one hand, this may have been due in part to the fact that they had a greater role in the new intensive agriculture. On the other hand, it may have been due to the "feminization" of the village population – which also was rooted in the nature of production. Another way to look at the situation is to ask what percentage of sales went to sons and brothers in comparison with daughters (sons-in-law) and sisters (brothers-in-law). Table 16.20 shows that the trend over the entire period was ever in favor of daughters and sisters. We pointed out earlier that this was not a result of parents favoring one sex over the other. It does reflect patterns of outmigration and the structure of networks. As for the aberrant decade of the 1740s, I cannot explain the extra importance of sons- and brothers-in-law, but we should note that they are structurally important throughout the study period.

In this chapter, we have been considering one aspect of market transactions: the interrelationship with family and kin. A number of other important issues suggested by the data have to do with economic change and social stratification, but our concern has been whether the expanding market for land in the eighteenth and nineteenth centuries had a transforming effect on the family. This question has been hotly debated by English historians concerned with the late Middle Ages. Many of them believe that the land market was so active then that abstract considerations of profit dominated even small producers and the family did not provide the basic framework for mobilizing and distributing resources. Part of the problem seems to be the radical fluctuations in population and agricultural production from the thirteenth to the sixteenth centuries, which led to rather contradictory results.

Recent analyses of local judicial records from medieval England (called court rolls) have given rise to an interesting controversy concerning the economy and family of peasants attached to manorial estates in the period after 1250.[20] The debate first revolved around the processes of social differentiation and redistribution of resources. The evidence for a lively market in real estate from the thirteenth to the sixteenth century led Alan Macfarlane to conclude that there was no link between the family group and land. Property was continually sold to people outside the direct lines of inheritance. According to Ian Blanchard, things had gone so far in the postplague period that "the cohesive family unit had disappeared, shattered, fragmented into atomistic elements" – this all on the basis of a lively land market and the fact that few buyers and sellers had a common surname.

However, statistics about the size of the market – number of transactions, rate of turnover, size of individual sales – can be confusing if one does not have a clear understanding of the size of the population or the amount of the land at risk. I have tried to compare the Neckarhausen statistical material with several of the estate series for late Medieval England and found that in terms

[20] The following discussion is based on Bruce M. S. Campbell, "Population Pressure, Inheritance and the Land Market in a Fourteenth-Century Peasant Community," in *Land, Kinship and Life-Cycle*, ed. Richard M. Smith (Cambridge, 1984), pp. 87–134; Richard M. Smith, "Families and Their Land in an area of Partible Inheritance: Redgrave, Suffolk 1260–1320," in ibid., pp. 135–96; Bruce M. S. Campbell, "Population Change and the Genesis of Common Fields on a Norfolk Manor," in *Economic History Review*, 2 ser., 33 (1980): 174–92; P. D. A. Harvey, "Chronology of the Peasant Land Market," in *Peasant Land Market in Medieval England* (Oxford, 1984), pp. 19–28; Paul Hyams, "The Origins of a Peasant Land Market in England," in *Economic History Review*, 2 ser., 23 (1970), pp. 18–31; Ian Blanchard, review of Rodney Hilton, *English Peasantry in the Later Middle Ages*, *Social History* 5 (1977), pp. 661–4; M. M. Postan, "The Charters of the Villeins," in *Essays on Medieval Agriculture and General Problems of the Medieval Economy* (Cambridge, 1973), pp. 107–49; Andrew Jones, "Land and People at Leighton Buzzard in the Later Fifteenth Century," in *Economic History Review*, 2 ser., 25 (1972), pp. 18–27; Christopher Dyer, *Lords and Peasants in a Changing Society: The Estates of the Bishopric of Worcester, 680–1540* (Cambridge, 1980), chap. 4, pp. 301–15; Zvi Razi, *Marriage and Death in a Medieval Parish, Economy, Society and Demography in Halesowen 1270–1400* (Cambridge, 1980); idem, "Family, Land and the Village Community in Later Medieval England," in *Past and Present*, 92 (November 1981): 3–36; idem, "The Erosion of the Family–Land Bond in the Late Fourteenth and Fifteenth Centuries: A Methodological Note," in *Land, Kinship, Life-Cycle*, ed. Smith, pp. 295–304; Alan Macfarlane, *The Origins of English Individualism. The Family, Property and Social Transition* (Cambridge, 1979).

of turnover, the two situations are quite similar. Remember that the land market has to have some real limits. After all, land was being used for agricultural purposes and had to be plowed, harrowed, and harvested, and its owners had to undertake long-term and short-term investments, with buildings, tools, fences, and livestock maintained in proper order.

In my reckoning of the land market in Neckarhausen, I found that at the beginning of the eighteenth century about 12 percent of the entire arable was sold in a decade. If one took direct trading into account, another 5 percent changed hands. This figure rose steadily to a peak in the 1820s of 30 percent and dropped by the 1860s to a more modest 16 percent. By re-reckoning Zvi Razi's figures for preplague Halesowen, we find a turnover of about 11 percent per decade. The statistical series for Leighton Buzzard compiled by Andrew Jones is difficult to use for our purposes, since he does not give the size of the principal manor, which accounted for the bulk but not all of the parish of 8,900 acres. During the period 1464–1508, an average of 759 acres were sold in a decade, or 8.43 percent of the land of the parish. If we assume that the principal manor held about 80 percent of the land, then the rate of turnover in a decade was close to 11 percent. Bruce Campbell has studied the East Norfolk manor of Martham, particularly the pre- and postplague markets. Between the 1290s and 1340s, 15 to 19 percent of the land was sold in a decade. Subsequent to the 1390s, 30 to 42 percent turned over in a 10-year period. In Richard Smith's study of Redgrave in Suffolk between 1260 and 1320, about 17 percent of the land turned over in a decade. He warns that one drawback of the documentation for all of these studies is that sales, gifts, and premortem transmission are all recorded in the same form. Most of these statistics of land market activities should be therefore viewed as open to considerable inflation. Campbell has also studied a manor in Coltishall in East Norfolk. His figures appear to offer the largest land market studied so far, but he may have underestimated the size of the manor, which he sets at 200 acres. Thus in the early decades of his study, 1280–1309, about 15 percent turned over every 10 years. The famine period 1310–19 saw the rate jump to almost 40 percent. The next two decades had a land market around 30 percent, with a leap to 50 percent during the decade of the Black Death. The following three decades fell to a rate just above 30 percent. For 1380–9, we find another leap to 47 percent, followed by a fall to 20 percent for 1390–9. I think that his market is inflated by a considerable underestimation of the size of the manor, since until 1380, the size of transactions was relatively small (between 0.34 acres and 0.87 acres on average per decade, compared with 0.42 to 0.74 for Neckarhausen) and the number of buyers both in absolute terms and as a percentage of the population (45 to 95 buyers per decade, compared with 41 to 232 in Neckarhausen, and 9–34 percent of the population compared with 12–32 percent in Neckarhausen) was not too much different from the number calculated in this study.

Our results suggest that the market in early eighteenth-century Neckarhausen was about the same size as that found in many manors and villages in preplague

England. The market in the postplague situation in terms of the amount sold was frequently two to three times greater and was not unlike the situation for the late eighteenth and early nineteenth centuries in Neckarhausen. In terms of population trends, the lower English market appeared in a context of population pressure, whereas the opposite was the case in Neckarhausen. The market reached new heights in the period of depopulation in England but was driven by population pressure in the South German period of comparison. Perhaps the situation in Germany is best compared to the preplague English one, in that both were marked by population growth and pressure. In that case, the German market was two to three times *greater* than the comparable English one.

The question is whether the market in land could be a mechanism for dissolving family relations. One thing to remember is that the study of Neckarhausen begins in the eighteenth century. What the market there was like at the end of the Middle Ages or in the sixteenth century is not and cannot be known. Nonetheless, we can surmise from solid studies of other regimes, such as those by Razi, that family possibilities and strategies alter considerably from situation to situation. How resources are distributed and redistributed has everything to do with family dynamics, and the market is not an independent mechanism but can be an instrument of family strategies in competition with each other.[21]

Razi does not make the mistake of measuring all families by one type. He looks for different forms and relations according to the economic situation and demographic regime. In preplague Halesowen, for example, he finds that the richer families continually purchased land from the poorer ones, using that land to set up younger sons and daughters. This prevented the accumulation of property over generations, but meant that different groups in the population would have different family structures, and that only the well-off were organized around the dynamics of inheritance. Furthermore, he points out that wealthy families passed on their resources in a variety of ways, including leasing, credit, and pledging. No smallholder who was not the son of a substantial landholder succeeded in climbing to the top of the propertied class. In the postplague situation, with fewer direct heirs available, property and the land market created ties among a larger group of kin and made daughters and sons-in-law crucial for family continuity. The wealthy profited most from the situation, and with fewer heirs to provide for accumulated wealth from generation to generation.

We have seen in this chapter that the size of the market gives little indication of whether it is an abstracting force or has the potential to coordinate or conflict

[21] Razi found that other researchers had underestimated considerably the number of properties sold to kin in both periods, but especially after 1348. They relied on surname matches, but he had carried out a careful family reconstitution. Had he done the same, he would have missed 80 percent of the links. He gives one example where land over a 21-year period went from a father-in-law to a son-in-law and then to another son-in-law. Another example involved property between 1357 and 1402 going from a woman to her husband to her brother, then to her second husband to her brother's son-in-law and finally to her cousin. All of these family transactions would have been missed by a method matching only surnames.

with family interest. The tendency in European family analysis has been to treat kinship as a residual issue. If actions can be explained in terms both of class and kinship, the latter category becomes disvalued. Or if the market distributes resources, then the family is only interesting if it can be demonstrated that it acts against the forces of the market by controlling prices, redeeming sales, or mitigating its effects in some way. To understand kinship as a matrix for class or the market as an instrument for kinship interaction seems to go against fundamental categories.

However, the market exists inside a kin-structured universe. Without understanding how rights and obligations are territorialized in a particular society, we cannot ask how buying and selling land interacts with existing relationships, reproducing or transforming them. Kinship in Europe can be structured along an affinal axis or a consanguineal one, and the history of Neckarhausen provides an example of a society which underwent a transformation from one to the other. Ritual kinship is another factor, which may alternatively supplement or reinforce existing relations. In the affinally structured situation at the beginning of the eighteenth century, it seems to have acted as a supplement, and in the consanguineal one which followed, it offered reinforcement. We have found that the market was able to work as a distribution mechanism to integrate a developing set of relations among consanguineal kin. Given the intestate rules, which narrowed claims, as in most European societies, to lineal claimants, inheritance was a poor means for integrating kin in a situation of extreme fragmentation of land and growing social stratification. The shift from an inheritance-driven system to one balanced more by looser exchanges of marriage partners and land among allied kin gave a familial function to the market. At the beginning of the eighteenth century, property rights were sorted out largely within the nuclear family. Marriage and heirship determined most of the distribution of resources. The exchange system that emerged in the remainder of the eighteenth century was organized around male networks rooted in production routines and political negotiations. Alliances between consanguineal kin developed with the exchange of godparents, marriage partners, and land as alternative forms of mediation. As land became more monopolized by older cohorts in the nineteenth century, nuclear family dynamics came to capture more of the forces of distribution. Even in the heated situation of the 1820s, there is a trend back to nuclear family transfers. After midcentury, once the overheated market had collapsed, we are back into a world dominated by nuclear family transactions. Women now played a crucial role, in part because of their intensive involvement in agricultural production, in part because they were beginning to hold more land (as widows, for example), and in part because the demographic restructuring of the village was in their favor. Uterine networks can be discerned in sales to cousins, but the fact that 80 percent of nuclear family sales were to sons- and brothers-in-law attests to the importance of links through daughters and sisters.

In the relations between husbands and wives and between parents and adult children, we see again that the household was the locus for a changing set of alliances. A wife gave her husband access to a set of potential political and productive partners and a set of claimants or clients when it came to trading around productive resources. It appears that women played a far more crucial role in this regard and therefore exercised greater power in the nineteenth century. In addition, the relations between generations reflected a tendency for parents to hold onto land longer and longer, which created a more drawn-out period of dependence. Still, selling property to children was always an option, and it introduced flexibility into the system. In the 1820s, most sales of this kind were to sons. This was a time when many of them were still largely rooted in the village, or at least were at an age when they were giving up their handicrafts to take over agricultural tasks. By the 1860s, sons were emigrating and daughters were playing a key role in the reproduction of agricultural enterprises. In absolute terms, they purchased twice as many items of real estate in the 1860s than they did in the 1820s, despite the fact that the overall number of transactions had fallen by 40 percent.

The dynamics of the nuclear family cannot be assessed without taking into account the larger system of alliances in which it is found. In Neckarhausen, the system evolved in three stages, each dominated by a peculiar kind of kinship structure, which may give a particular form to the whole but does not exclude other kinds of interactions and connections. Early in the eighteenth century, households were linked asymmetrically through godparents and affinal kin. Married children tended to be linked more closely to the set of parents who provided the largest portion of land, had the largest set of resources, provided work opportunities, or had the best political connections. Relations between spouses themselves were shaped by the fact that one or the other brought more property to the marriage or offered the most important links to other households. Soon after midcentury, productive and political linkages came to be driven by agnatic consanguineal principles. Husbands and wives contributed to the marital estate on equal terms. At first, children got their hands on property quite young, but by the end of the century, the new generation was forced into an ever-longer period of dependence. The practical effect of marriage alliance was to reinforce divisions inside the system of stratification, and godparentage no longer mediated between age groups and classes. Links between households frequently consisted of continuing alliances between patrilines, which exchanged marriage partners and godparents, as well as land. In the third stage of the alliance system, networks were more and more frequently constructed by women. One can almost speak of a "matrifocal" structure. When two people married, the common relative was frequently a woman. People also chose godparents through a uterine network. Land was frequently exchanged in networks with a woman at the center, and local officials frequently allied with the wife/mother. Women were more ready on the basis of their productive position to construct multiple alliances or to demand a greater voice in decisions about the commercial aspects of the household and the division of its resources. On no account did this mean that a wife/mother was less subject to back-breaking work. Enormous discipline and self-exploitation lay behind the reconstruction of the village economy and brought it back from catastrophic pauperization to what the pastor in the 1860s described as a "prosperous peasantry." The peasantry remained rooted in an agriculture of small and smallest enterprises supplemented by nonagricultural sources of income, where each spouse "husbanded" his or her own resources and forced the other into sober behavior and orderly work.

# Conclusion

An egalitarian system is profoundly disturbing by virtue of the fact that it tends to undermine family and village holdings.

– Martine Segalen[1]

## Realty and reciprocity

We have pointed out many ways in which obligation was tied up with the exchange of land and other forms of wealth. In Neckarhausen, in the nineteenth century, the authority exercised by parents over adult children and the respect the latter were supposed to demonstrate were both derived expressly from the fact that parents were the source of wealth. Having to make explicit what had always been implicit suggests a weakness in the argument, but parents also wove a web of obligation through a calculated strategy of property devolution.

The paradoxes and ambiguities of family obligation are best illustrated by the readiness of family members to care for each other. Whenever an aged parent or uncle or a long-ill brother or sister was nursed for any length of time, the relatives responsible for the care kept careful book. They expected to be able to utilize any common rights such as a garden or portion of firewood, and they always put in a bill at the final division of the estate.[2] Siblings some-

[1] "'Avoir sa part': Sibling Relations in Partible Inheritance Brittany," in *Interest and Emotion: Essays on the Study of Family and Kinship*, ed. Hans Medick and David Warren Sabean (Cambridge, 1984), pp. 129–44, here p. 129.

[2] One man left his wealth to a child of his stepmother. One of the heirs challenged the will on the grounds she had taken care of him for 20 years. They came to a compromise; *Inventuren und Teilungen*, 1274 (30.10.1816). A brother, Jacob Schmid, 28, returned sick from the *Wanderschaft* and was taken care of by his brother, who billed the estate 20 fl. Barbara Walker kept house for her mother and stepfather and had especially cared for them (*gewartet und gepflegt*) in their last days, billing the estate 10 fl.; *Inventuren und Teilungen*, 1249 (2.7.1801). Michael Zeug left his stepmother's daughter, Maria Catharina Murr, most of his property, but the will had not been done with proper form (*wegen Mangels an Solemnitation*) and was challenged by his sister's daughter. Maria Catharina Murr protested that she had provided room, board, and care for 20 years, and a bill for 19 fl. was recognized; *Inventuren und Teilungen*, 1274 (19.3.1803). Johann Georg Ebinger gave up all rights to his father's inheritance – his widowered father was arranging his retirement – and so his two siblings had to take over all care of the parents; *Inventuren und*

times agreed among themselves how the matter should be taken care of and paid a specified amount to the one who offered care.[3] But more frequently, a parent or uncle contracted for the care, passing on various properties and making specific agreements with one child or niece or nephew for cooking, washing, and nursing, explicitly setting the price.[4] The evidence suggests that some family member or other took on the obligation – and that others shirked their "responsibilities" – but everyone treated the situation quite soberly and

*Teilungen*, 1343 (23.1.1809). Barbara Walker excluded her brother from inheritance because he never helped her; *Inventuren und Teilungen*, 1348 (17.2.1809). Johann Georg Falter, 59 and single, excluded his mentally ill sister from expectation to his property and set up a retirement contract (*Leibgeding*) with his nephews and nieces in which his sister was to receive lifelong room, board, and care; *Inventuren und Teilungen*, 1375 (6.2.1813); 1378 (10.2.1813).

3 Salomon Waldner came to such circumstances that he could not eat and was incontinent. During the previous several years, no one wanted to take him into their care. The siblings agreed with one brother to take over the duties at the rate of 150 fl. per year. At his death, the bill was 525 fl., which was reckoned against the estate; *Inventuren und Teilungen*, 1330 (16.3.1808). After Johannes and Margaretha Häfner died, they left a married daughter and a deaf and dumb imbecile daughter, whose brother-in-law was given permission to take her property into possession, caring for her from the annual proceeds. He and his children were then given the right to her inheritance; *Inventuren und Teilungen*, 1332 (16.3.1808).

4 A typical retirement contract was made by Anna Maria Grauer. When she passed on the property to her children, she specified an *Ausding*. She sold the house to her son and expected lifelong room even though she would take care of her own board (*Unterhalt*). If there was a lack of accord, the son would have to pay for her room elsewhere; *Inventuren und Teilungen*, 1258 (4.2.1802). Jacob Kraut bought the house inherited by him and his three sisters. His unmarried sister and her child had the right to live there, but if the sister died, the child had no claim to stay; *Inventuren und Teilungen*, 1287 (31.8.1804). Johann Adam Falter's daughter married Friedrich Bauknecht in Wolfschlugen but she never moved there. She remained sick in her father's house and died there after six months. The father deducted 101 fl. for her care and burial from her estate; *Inventuren und Teilungen*, 1295 (23.2.1805). The sibling of Johannes Schober demanded that he pay rent for having lived so long with their father. One of the daughters produced a testament which described what she had done for her mother; *Inventuren und Teilungen*, 1320 (26.11.1806). Margaretha Baur was excluded from an inheritance because she had not shared the costs of supporting her father with her brother and sister; *Inventuren und Teilungen*, 1432 (26.2.1818). Johannes Holpp before his death set aside an extra 200 fl. for his wife because of her extra costs and care in his illness; *Inventuren und Teilungen*, 1447 (21.10.1818). Johannes Bauknecht was allowed to keep the extra he had received because it had to be considered more as wages (*Verdienst*) for taking care (*Wart und Pfleg*) of his mother than as a bequest; *Inventuren und Teilungen*, 1496 (12.1.1822). Maria Agnes Falter cared for her mother for seven and a half years, for which she was accorded 18 fl. wages per year. Since there was not much left, her brother gave up all claim, but she then promised to offer him lodging with no board whenever he was around and to take care of him when sick; *Inventuren und Teilungen*, 1488 (17.2.1824). Friedrich Arnold left an extra 210 fl. to his wife for her services to him; *Inventuren und Teilungen*, 1493 (26.8.1824). Rosina Barbara Hentzler was mentally weak. Her father at his retirement concluded a three-year contract with his son, Jacob Friedrich, to provide her with food and clothing and in return have the use of her fields. At her marriage, it was noted that Magdalena Hentzler had property to use in return for maintaining her mother; *Inventuren und Teilungen*, 1545 (28.11.1827). Johannes Brodbeck demanded 12 fl. per year for having cared for his mother; *Inventuren und Teilungen*, 1561 (2.11.1829). Agatha Maria Thumm received bedding and linen from her mother as well-deserved wages (*wohverdiente Belohnung*); *Inventuren und Teilungen*, 1016 (22.11.1775). Wilhelm Rentzler received 21 fl. for lodging and taking care of his stepsister for two years; *Inventuren und Teilungen*, 1024 (18.3.1777). The two daughters of Martin Bosch agreed to share the costs of taking care of him in order to share in future inheritances; *Inventuren und Teilungen*, 1026 (13.5.1778). The widow of schoolmaster Gantter made a deal with her daughter Margaretha Heinser, wife of a member of the Gericht. Besides other things, each of their six children was to

arranged property devolution as a counterpayment.[5] The documents speak of earnings (*Verdienst*), rewards (*Belohnung*), and wages (*Liedlohn*).

Village officials made sure that an heir offered as much care for the person who was the source of their property as they had received. If a son or daughter wished to avoid all participation, he or she would refuse to share in the devolution. Parents and siblings provided for their sickly or mentally deficient offspring or siblings by making contractual deals with the other heirs. Yet responsibility did not run very far. A sister might be taken care of, but after her death, her child would have no claim to support. Altogether we get a sense from the documents of a group of people who exchanged resources and property for care, attention, and respect. The group which was most clearly bound to each other was composed of parents and children and siblings, but obligation and trust could also extend to step-relations and to uncles, aunts, nieces, and nephews. Whenever we find an extension to collateral relatives, we also find a property settlement. Yet we also have to see the exchange system as a generalized one that was not simply based on cold calculation and devoid of sentiment. Not a few siblings left a legacy to support a long lost brother or sister in case he or she should return some day to the village. And parents who could no longer support their children put in the lowest bid when the latter were auctioned off for room and board.

We have spoken of property as an idiom – in Esther Goody's phrase – a "relational idiom."[6] In Neckarhausen, family discussions and disputes were never very far away from issues having to do with sorting out claims and obligations to real estate or support. A husband or wife might well reward the other partner for extra effort by seeing to it that he or she received a few extra Gulden from the estate. And bitter quarrels frequently came down to the issue of wasting the wife's contribution to the estate or offering insufficient support to the husband's Oekonomie. Behind charges of drunkenness, idleness, and slovenliness were problems which had to do with defending and increasing the property a couple brought together in a marriage.[7]

People expected that a marriage alliance would create a set of social relationships which would structure and make possible a lifetime of fruitful exchanges.

pay her the handsome sum of 54 fl. per year. The daughter agreed to take her into her house and cook. The mother allowed her the use of all of her communal rights and privileges and paid her 18 fl. per year; *Inventuren und Teilungen*, 1028 (23.4.1778). At her death, the other children were excluded from the inheritance until they paid their share of the contract; *Inventuren und Teilungen*, 1040 (3.3.1780). Johann Georg Falter received a wage (*Liedlohn*) from his elderly parents for supporting them with labor and energy; *Inventuren und Teilungen*, 1044 (4.4.1780).

[5] The Oberamt ordered that Johann Friedrich Hentzler be given out to board. He wanted to be taken care of by the wife of Matheus Sterr, his dead brother's daughter. His Pfleger agreed and was to arrange to have her paid from the estate; *Gericht*, vol. 8, f. 15 (11.3.1812).

[6] Esther Goody, *Contexts of Kinship* (Cambridge, 1973), pp. 2–3, 41–50, 121–18.

[7] Maria Bidlingmaier argued from her study of women in two Württemberg villages that the ultimate goal of a couple was "durchzukommen" (to get through), which meant to succeed by increasing property to the extent that all the children could be properly established; *Die Bäuerin in zwei Gemeinden Württembergs*. Tübinger staatswissenschaftliche Dissertation (Stuttgart, 1918), pp. 166–7.

It was not that anyone had a *particular* claim on an in-law, but one expected a good deal of consideration and cooperation. When a man and his brother-in-law faced each other in court to transact business affecting the wife/sister's interests, they were caught in a field of cooperation and tension. People frequently expected to be able to get their hands on an arable strip or two at a price for relatives. Young Johann Georg Riempp actually stood up in the annual village assembly (Ruggericht) and denounced his brother-in-law Johann Georg Mühleisen for selling a piece of land the latter's wife had inherited for so much money that Riempp could not bid on it.[8]

There is one involved family dispute which can illustrate the interplay of "emotion and material interest."[9] Old Johann Georg Riempp married Anna Maria Falter in 1773, and her sister, Margaretha, married Johann Wilhelm Hentzler a year later. Riempp and his wife were well off, and he – like many an immigrant – apparently expected to be voted onto the Gericht. In any event, his brother-in-law Hentzler did become a Richter, and the two seemed destined to forge an ever tighter alliance. Over the next several years, they exchanged strips of land, and stood as godparents for each other's children. However, during the early 1780s, Riempp and Hentzler came to loggerheads over the inheritance of their two wives. Riempp had to appear before the Gericht for slandering Hentzler, and Hentzler stopped calling on Riempp to act as godparent for his children. Other problems arose at home for Riempp, and he began a life of drunkenness and erratic behavior, which forced him into debt and into selling off some of his property. He always attached a rider to his transactions to the effect that if anyone redeemed a piece it was to fall back to him. In this manner, he specifically excluded Hentzler from getting his hands on any of his wife's land. During the 1780s, he was in trouble several times for slandering Hentzler and was roundly denounced by the court for all of his behavior. Any reading of the documentation makes it clear that Riempp was an incompetent wastrel and that he and Hentzler had broken off relations in a decade of vituperation and recrimination, yet surprisingly, after Hentzler died, the court appointed Riempp to be the guardian of his children and administrator of his estate. Over the next two decades, he frequently sold land to his nephews.

This kind of story illustrates the complexity of involvement between kin and to what extent property was part of a larger set of exchanges and responsibilities. All the texts point toward a permanent split between the two families beginning with the problems of inheritance between the sisters, and continuing on with the breaking off of godparentage and Riempp's ranting and raving against his brother-in-law. Yet within the wider set of concerns, he was clearly considered to be an aggressive defender of family rights, just the kind of person who would

[8] *Gericht*, vol. 5, f. 205 (28.12.1803).

[9] See my much longer discussion of this case in "Young Bees in an Empty Hive: Relations between Brothers-in-Law in a South German Village around 1800," in *Interest and Emotion: Essays on the Study of Family and Kinship*, ed. Hans Medick and David Warren Sabean (Cambridge, 1984), pp. 177–86, here 173–80.

protect the interests of his nephews. The conflict in interest between the two sisters did not preclude a "devolution" in the form of sale from uncle and aunt to nephew. Real estate acted as a permanent mediation between the two families, splitting them up and drawing them together at the same time.

Over the course of the history of the village, there were two (or three) over-arching systems of exchange connecting the various families with each other and setting up channels through which goods and services flowed. At the beginning of the eighteenth century, marriage was one of the institutions which connected families of differential wealth and station. From one point of view, the village formed a conubium; it provided a space in which wealthy and poor people created lines of connection between themselves through marriage. We do not yet know, however, if there were other forms of cleavage by which the village was segmented vertically, so to speak, with groups of people defined by marriage alliances. Certainly the policy of forming marital estates, with marriage partners bringing different amounts of wealth, made brothers-in-law of people, some of whom had power and wealth and some of whom acted as a group of "clients." This was paralleled by a similar asymmetricality linking families through godparentage. For example, a Richter or Schultheiss and his son and grandson would maintain godparent relations with another family over several generations. In this affinal/ritual kin/patron–client system, families from different strata were systematically linked together over generations. Access to property was almost completely a matter of descent, and most of it was either inherited, given, or sold to nuclear kin.

This system gave way to one in which stratification was clearly horizontal. A key institution for cementing the new structure was endogamous marriage. Husbands and wives came to bring the same amount of wealth to their marriages. It could be argued that marriage within a particular stratum reduced the possibilities of finding mates who were not related to each other by blood. Yet close examination of the system (as we will see in the next volume) shows that the move to create a tighter, consanguineally driven system of relationships was the causal factor. Systematic alliances between families defined along patrilineal principles came to dominate the politics and dynamics of distribution within the village. As the land market opened up, more resources were channeled to a wider set of consanguineal kin, the same kind of people who also became ritual kin, guardians, Kriegsvögte and guarantors.

After this system of alliance was well established, the village was shaken up by a crisis in credit, leading to the bankruptcy of a significant number of families, and a redistribution of labor stemming from agricultural intensification and the development of wage labor in construction. The effects of bankruptcy in the village are not at all easy to measure, since land was simply sold to other villagers and no radical reordering of the hierarchy of wealth took place. Over the long term, recovery brought the solidification of the Bauern class economically and politically. Women came to play a key role in the negotiation of marriage alliances, agricultural production, and land ownership and distribution. All of this merits more detailed investigation, but its outline provides a schematic overview of some of the fundamental ways the flow of property was altered and channeled.

We have repeated the notion many times that property, or better, land and buildings, mediated between people. In this sense, Bourdieu's argument that the land inherits the heir is very useful. According to the nature of particular forms of property and the productive ends to which it is put, it disciplines individuals and forms a central focus for socialization, the development of character, and the formation of emotional and sentimental bonds. The many different strategies and tactics which governed the distribution of rights to land, buildings, and productive equipment provide some insight into the particular exigencies of family property in Neckarhausen.

The patrimony was never understood in terms of a fundamental unity of house, courtyard, and land. Nor was it some transcendental objectification for which all family members labored, with each generation holding it in trust for the next. Property in Neckarhausen was always considered to be something possessed by individuals. They were not guardians of a lineal substance. Any pieces could be sold off, and there was little familial continuity of ownership of any particular field, meadow, or house. Nonetheless, access to land, to the "patrimony," was always a combination of devolution and credit. The family provided starting capital, and children remained tied to their parents' economies and discipline over a long period of adult life. Property disciplined the individual to sobriety, thrift, and diligence, and in the nineteenth century at least, access to credit, without which most purchases were impossible, was accorded only to those who displayed those character traits. The fact that by 1860 the average purchaser of land was well over 40 is testimony to the period of apprenticeship necessary to convince the village authorities that one was creditworthy.

The early years in the marital life of a young couple demonstrated a tension between independence and integration into the economies of their parents. Their small farms were dependent on the traction and heavy equipment provided by the older generation, and they in turn provided labor in exchange. In the early eighteenth century, they were more frequently attached to the parents who had provided the larger endowment, but in the nineteenth in a more balanced way to both sets of parents. As a couple produced children and took on more and more adult responsibilities, they formed a node in an ever more complex alliance system. Ritual kin from both sides of the family interacted with them. As long as the institution of Kriegsvogtschaft lasted, the husband and a representative of the wife discussed family business together, and even after 1828, wives frequently brought along their fathers or brothers. With the high mortality rates of the time, minor children were frequently without one parent alive. In every such instance, they were provided with a Pfleger (guardian) from the side of the family represented by the deceased parent, another opportunity for brothers-in-law to cooperate or conflict. Marriage, therefore, was continually, in many practical ways, at the center of an alliance. So strong was the sense of exchange, no one ever thought of alienating lineal property permanently in favor of a spouse.

But obligation did not come without discipline. Husbands and wives attempted to "educate" each other to a common responsibility and used violence, threat, tongue lashings, and parental and official interference. The fulcrum for maneuver was always the diligent contribution to an economic endeavor. The father-in-law could be called in to correct a husband's behavior, or the pastor could be asked to exclude a husband from communion. Inadequate food preparation or a lack of housewifely efficiency could prompt a husband to self-help. Parents had a long period between the marriage of their offspring and their own retirement to teach them the terms of obligation. And property came from them at the rate that they were prepared to give it up. The fact that children and children-in-law worked with and for them over such a long period gave ample opportunity for creating reciprocal ties. Through the death of a child, many a parent found a son-in-law or daughter-in-law, the marital successor to the son or daughter, or eventually a grandchild tied through production routines to him- or herself. All the indications are that space and tools were subject to a careful delineation of rights. Ownership, use rights, tools, and labor were elements of complex reciprocities which structured relationships between parents and children. The concept of patrimony is a useful one in this situation as long as it is understood as a flexible instrument for disciplining one generation into assuming responsibility and another into dying off.

## Property and class

One of the objections to analyzing the social dynamics in Neckarhausen in terms of class has to do with scale. Class simply does not have the same meaning when we compare the British working class or the Chinese peasantry or the American middle class with forms of social differentiation inside a small south German village. In any event, the usefulness of the category for analyzing national political processes has been systematically whittled away during the past few decades.[10] It is not our intent to bring it back for small-scale political and social dynamics. Nonetheless, we have had a good deal to say about the social hierarchy and the distribution of power, and some remarks about social stratification are in order.

To begin with, the shape of property distribution did not change substantially over the study period. If we were to classify villagers by wealth, with the cut-off at some arbitrary point, each class would have substantially more people by the end of the period but would not look much different from before. Clearly, however, some changes were taking place, as local observers spoke of the

[10] See the summary of the literature in William M. Reddy, *Money and Liberty in Modern Europe: A Critique of Historical Understanding* (Cambridge, 1987), pp. 1–33.

destruction of village prosperity by the early decades of the nineteenth century and by midcentury of the growth of a "proletariat." But by the 1860s, a "prosperous" peasantry had been reestablished. We can never be sure whether observers were looking at similar phenomena and changing the signs or whether some real alterations had taken place and under which categories. Most of the reports we have access to were written by local pastors whose main concerns were drunkenness, marital conflict, illegitimacy, church attendance, and the like. A hard-drinking, disputatious, aggressive peasantry might look quite different to them from a sober, thrifty group where husbands and wives kept their disagreements to themselves and controlled the sexuality of their daughters, even though in many other essential ways the two groups might be indistinguishable. In one generation, the vocabulary of "house" would serve to encode social differences, while in another, terms such as "pauperism" and "proletariat" would provide lenses through which villagers were perceived. That is not just a change in vocabulary, however. In the eighteenth century, the pastor and local officials divided the village up into good and bad householders. As I have shown in another context, this could jibe fairly closely with our own socioeconomic categories – rich aggressive landholders being the good householders and poor, dependent artisans and laborers the bad ones.[11] Yet the very vocabulary sets up a dynamic situation and allows for various kinds of discriminations across the hierarchy of wealth. Once one speaks in terms of a proletariat, a vocabulary of strata has appeared and individual properties and characteristics have been erased.

But behind the vocabulary change there might well have been significant parallel changes in the social and political processes. Size, for example, may have had a great deal to do with the situation. Under population expansion, groups may have reached a critical mass, which changed the tenor of politics and village culture. It is obvious, for example, that recourse to a stable Lorenz curve for a hamlet of 50 that became a town of 3,000 would say very little in itself. In Neckarhausen, where the village tripled in size, independent agriculturalists became more exclusive, and dependent farm laborers, half-time craftsmen, and village workers more visible in the pubs and at the village assembly. We have also found that a discourse about property and prosperity developed in the village around the turn of the century, and both husbands and wives against each other and villagers among themselves were apt to carry out their conflicts by labeling each other poor or corrupt. Yet such charges were usually embedded in another discourse about family – a father and son thrown together, a family labeled as trash. There was no language of class to be found in the village which was not mediated or filtered through one of family and kinship.

Yet there were clear hierarchical distinctions which sorted out villagers even

[11] David Warren Sabean, *Power in the Blood: Popular Culture and Village Discourse in Early Modern Germany* (Cambridge, 1984), pp. 161–73.

in death. In Neckarhausen, there were two cemeteries, one by the church in the middle of the village and one at the edge of the living area in the direction of Nürtingen. The former was reserved for the village patriciate (*Honorationen*) and their families.[12] Every so often, if one paid enough, someone else could be buried there.[13] In other words, members of the village magistrates together with the richest families were buried prominently at the center of the village, next to the church, while everyone else was shunted to its margins. This dualism of magistrate and Gemeinde was central to village dynamics and its social reproduction.

One central tendency we have found is the exclusion of artisans and eventually all wage-dependent workers from positions in the Gericht or Rat. Certainly by 1800, only those with considerable amounts of land were able to obtain a seat on the ruling body. As we shall see in the next book, an endogamous marriage practice first arose among the magistrates in the 1740s, and not until a whole generation later do we find most of the Bauern following suit by marrying second cousins. Only around 1800 were artisans, building workers, and farm laborers marrying second cousins, and by that time magistrates and Bauern were making even closer consanguineal matches. Explaining changes in the structure of kinship alliances would take us too far afield now, but it is useful to remark that the development of horizontal ties among villagers and tightening up of stratification was driven by kinship and family considerations. And the opening was begun by a group of people defined by their political position in the village, not by their prior "class" position – understood either in terms of wealth as such or in terms of ownership of land.

The point of these remarks is to demonstrate that family dynamics took place in a changing field of alliance. And stratification is itself a problematic notion. It presumes some way of sorting out individual men or individual families into categories of similar characteristics. And it is assumed that there will be correlations between such categories and attitudes and behavior – cultural, social, and political. But we have found that the best way to capture the social processes in Neckarhausen is to examine the different relations, exchanges, and alliances which ordered the interplay among social "strata" in many ways. For example, at the beginning of the eighteenth century, there were clearly wealthy and poor members of the community and access to power was, of course, differentiated. Yet rich and poor were continually weaving webs of connection by marrying each other. And they created long-term relationships through ritual kinship. At the end of the century, this kind of interweaving no longer took place at all. Nor were godparents chosen from nonrelated, wealthier patrons anymore but were brothers and sisters and first and second cousins. Prospective marriage partners weighed each other's wealth very care-

[12] *Pfarrbericht*, LKA, A39, 3060 (1828).

[13] *Kirchenkonvent*, vol. 3 (10.9.1781): The gravedigger was expressly told not to bury anyone in the central graveyard without the pastor's permission.

fully and if they made a mistake chided each other for the rest of their lives. Affinal relations early in the eighteenth century connected people vertically but in the nineteenth, horizontally. The networks of family became the mechanism through which "class" relations were managed and reproduced.

What we are describing is not a simple relationship between class position and class interest. There were several reasons why cousins became useful for each other. We have already noted, for example, that the process of inheritance split up plots which were designed to be plowed as a unit. After a generation, this threw cousins together to cooperate in plowing and gave them an interest in selling out to one another or trading. In fact, in the 1740s, cousins suddenly played a prominent role in the newly expanded market. More important for the development of cousin networks, however, appears to have been the sale of tithe collection, which offered considerable pickings for those who could best coordinate their interests. The first hints of collusion and tithe auction corruption come precisely from this period.[14] Probably the attempts on the part of the "patricians" to create a close network of affinal and consanguineal relations through marriage and ritual kinship was rooted in this kind of strategical consideration. By the later part of the century, population pressure and harsher state exactions brought greater competition for land, higher prices, and a livelier real estate market – fed eventually by a rising tide of bankruptcy. Getting some control of the trade in productive resources was only possible when the landed class as such followed the practice of endogamy. Especially during the crisis of the 1820s, cousins played a prominent role in the village land market. During the following decades, the nuclear family reestablished itself as the central distributor of resources, both through inheritance and through sales. But the tight network of allied families continued to exchange land and, what is more important, controlled access to credit. A small committee of the Gemeinderat considered every application for mortgage money from whatever source, whether one of the regional foundations or a merchant in Esslingen or an official's widow in Stuttgart. Control of the land and credit markets played a considerable role in riding out the crises of the 1840s and reestablishing a solvent peasantry.

Whenever we consider the distribution of wealth in the village we run up against family. The older married villagers always had more resources in their hands than the younger married ones did. This disjunction was exacerbated with time as people lived longer and retired less frequently and at greater ages. As a result, senior and junior generations coordinated their production through ever more complex and intricate ways. Young people were rooted in the village through ownership in some land, but they were dependent on their elders for equipment to cultivate it, or had to pay for plowing and carting services. They also depended on parents and older kin for agricultural jobs. In the nineteenth century, the village could not contain all the young people, especially the young

[14] *Vogtruggericht*, vol. 1, f. 29 (14.12.1751).

men. There was a long period in which many of them had to find outside work for their support. Some of these men accumulated savings which they sank into land, leaving it in the hands of their elders until such time as they could piece together a holding by combining marriage portion, purchases, and inheritance. In these circumstances, women were crucial in a number of ways. In the new agricultural situation, their labor was fundamental. Not only did they anchor down the family holding and communal rights, creating a seasonal skewing of the sex ratio of the population, but by the 1850s they also made up a larger percentage of the permanent population. In many ways the "class" distribution of goods, work, and services in the village was also a gender distribution. The permanent men in the village tended to be the older men who had accumulated their holding over time, and they were assisted by a population of women whose labor was plentiful and cheap. Families even developed a strategy of giving daughters much larger marriage portions than sons in order to root them in the village and make their labor available. Consequently, many women remained single for most of their lives, and a large percentage of them bore illegitimate children. And widows tended less frequently to remarry in the nineteenth century, holding on to land until well into old age. By the 1840s and 1850s a good deal of social weight was accrued by these women.

Any consideration of hierarchy, class, social stratification and the like for Neckarhausen has to pay close attention to the practices of families and households. In many ways, the key to understanding the social dynamics of the village is the discipline of property. Families were put together after careful consideration of mutual wealth and reciprocal exchanges of resources. Husbands and wives and surrounding kin carried on a continual discussion about diligence and thrift, and kin both capitalized on the failure of other kin and shored up each other's credit. A brother underwriting another would castigate him publicly if he did not behave, and a father would strike a long-married son who had had too much to drink. Wives allied with the pastor or Schultheiss to control their husband's habits. And neighbors reminded each other if they lost credit, went broke, or failed to pay their taxes.

There were, of course, losers and winners. Not everyone could accept the discipline. Whatever divisions there were in wealth, occupation, piety, and sobriety cut through families vertically and horizontally, differentiating fathers and mothers from sons and daughters and siblings from each other. The last son of three successive Schultheissen blew one of the largest village fortunes ever in a decade-long drinking bout. More specifically, we can compare the fate of siblings and find in many families a successful son or daughter and a failure. There is nothing surprising in this, and Neckarhausen has no lessons to teach us here. For those who are only satisfied with a historical narrative when it rests securely on issues of exploitation, such stories do not get at the heart of the issue. The political history of the village demonstrates a running conflict between the magistrates and other villagers over corruption and favoritism, and certainly there were periods, especially from the 1780s to the 1820s when the closely coordinated interests of an oligarchy were important for deciding how accumulation would take place and who would profit from the spoils. There were various ways in which the wealthy could profit from control of village institutions – through bribes, corrupt use of the sheep herd, manipulation of grain reserves, collusion in the auction of tithe collection, and so forth. But just as people at the bottom of the pyramid were gouged, many at the top also went broke. And the profit went to their close relatives.

One of the effects of partible inheritance was always to break up accumulated wealth according to the demographic fortunes of a family. Certainly a wealthy family could accumulate over its lifetime through the use of cheap dependent labor – some from its own sons and daughters – through purchase of bits and pieces of land, and through the perquisites of office and family connection. But all the accumulated wealth was partitioned to a generation slimmed down whenever more than two children succeeded to their parents. Passed down in addition, however, was a set of real and potential alliances which were just as much a part of a young person's capital as the bits of landed endowment. Few people made it to the top who did not have these resources, but many failed to capitalize on them. At one level, we find a static distribution of resources, at another a continual reproduction of family lines, and at yet another a constant fall into a permanent class of dependent wage-earners busy in construction, agriculture, and the new factories.

## Lord and peasant

Families have to be understood within a field of power. State and church institutions continually shaped their existence, and the dynamics of particular families and the strategies of family members cannot be understood without taking the logic of Herrschaft into consideration. Once officials provided the institution of inventory making, for example, no family could escape its defining power. Parents were forced to commit themselves at a certain time, and the period of negotiation between the senior and junior generation was marked by rhythms unique to the institution. The family is not something which has existence outside of Herrschaft and can be counterposed to church and state in a simple manner. In all of its aspects, it emerges from the dialectics of a particular context of power. In those situations where it is considered a refuge, a counterpoise to involvement with exploiting and dominating institutions, its very forms of resistance arise from multiple points of the exercise of power.

Because we have been concerned with property and production in this volume, the ways the state affected the family have been much more visible than those of the church. One of the silences in the Neckarhausen texts is the religious values of the villagers. We know that there was a lively religious discourse and that pietism had a considerable impact, but such matters have a shadowy existence in the records. When the Bauknecht and Geiger boys got into a bloody street brawl, Agnes Bauknecht criticized her brother Friedrich Geiger, a Richter, for mishandling the incident. She said that although he read the Bible assiduously, he treated her orphaned children wretchedly, to which he responded by threatening to shove the Bible into her mouth.[15] This is the only directly Christian discourse recorded in the entire history of the village. We also know from the periodic pastoral reports that a pietist group, which met for Bible study and singing each week, had formed in the village early in the nineteenth century. In 1819, they met on Sunday, Thursday, and Saturday rather late in the evening.[16] The temporary Schultheiss, Salomon Brodbeck, was critical of the wasted time and the lack of order, especially the mixing of the sexes and frequent visiting by strangers. According to the various reports between 1821 and 1842, the group varied in size from 25 to 60.[17] Although the pietist community was in tension with the pastor and with the rest of the village, there simply is no conflict of value in all the court protocols to allow us to assess the effects of the movement on family life. In a study of peasant women at the turn of the twentieth century, Maria Bidlingmaier suggested that pietism was the religion of self-exploited farm women.[18] It organized their energies and provided an escape from what was otherwise an intolerable work situation. It could well be the rise of pietism in Neckarhausen and the changed working conditions had a good deal to do with each other and that over the long run the religious movement worked to still conflicts between husbands and wives. Certainly, conversion and regular religious exercise were understood in this century to go closely together with the self-discipline necessary to master the life of a small peasant producer.[19]

Discipline was surely the issue for the establishment of the church consistory. The churchman/administrator who was most responsible for founding the institution in 1644, Johann Valentin Andreae, was on the cutting edge of the first pietist movement.[20] Early in the seventeenth century, he argued that new behavior should be institutionalized to match the correct doctrine established by the Reformation. His attitude was made clear in the report he helped write against the peasant prophet Hans Keil in 1648.[21] An emphasis on sudden conversion was far less important than a long-term program of discipline, and the church consistory was meant to be a chief instrument for this. Andreae read all the various judgments of God as punishment for the trespasses of the broad strata of the population, and he wanted to find ways of controlling popular culture and creating a set of hard-working, well-ordered family groups. We can view the actions of the church consistory in Neckarhausen from this point of view. It was part of a broad church–state program to propagate the ideology of

15 *Gericht*, vol. 3, f. 173 (10.7.1784).
16 HSAL, F190II, Bü 1123/19 (24.6.1819).
17 Dekanat Nürtingen, I, 3, reports from 1825, 32, 42, 45.
18 Maria Bidlingmaier, *Bäuerin*, p. 139ff.
19 This was made clear to me in an interview with a pietist farm woman, whose family had one of the large properties (6 hectares) in Neckarhausen.
20 See my discussion in *Power in the Blood*, pp. 73, 79, 207–9.
21 Ibid., pp. 70–3.

the well-ordered house and to establish an everyday practice of sober living and hard work.

The history of the consistory in Neckarhausen indicates that insofar as family quarrels were concerned, this institution was primarily used by women, and their alliance with the pastor calls for some comment. The reigning ideology viewed the house as ordered and maintained by the Hausvater, the pater familias, although the hidden agenda had to do with the Hausvater's subjection to civil and religious authority. The pastor heard many a complaint from the wives of the village and during confession and registration for communion received detailed knowledge about the inner life of many of the families of the village. He had the power to summon offenders to the parsonage to offer spiritual advice and issue relevant warnings about behavior. In those instances where his authority was challenged, the consistory was the vehicle for reestablishing it or getting even. Looked at quantitatively, the number of marital cases which came before the consistory was very small – less than one a year. They appear to be a selection culled by the pastor from a larger set.

On formal grounds then, most cases appear to have been a collusion between the pastor and wife against the husband. But in the eighteenth century, their alliance was always in tension with the hierarchical schema in which the Hausvater had a necessary place and role. If we look at the matter in purely power terms, we can balance the independent husband with his legal power of chastisement against the wife–pastor alliance with the powerful backup institution of the consistory. In this setup, the woman's room for maneuvering was more round about than her husband's. She had to establish the fact that he violated the principles of proper house government. Even though she herself might choose a language of reciprocity, she had to ally herself with men who saw matters according to hierarchical principles.

The ideology of the house was also originally given definition by the fiscal interests of the state. In the sixteenth and seventeenth centuries, it was concerned with the rules of property holding and management and with developing instruments for locating tax, tithe, and rent responsibilities. One of its major and continuing concerns lay in the area of inheritance law. But the inheritance practices were not simply forced onto the population. The redaction of the law code proceeded by first surveying all of the practices of each village in the entire territory. The codification, however, brought uniformity and surveillance. By the eighteenth century, there were clear mechanisms for sorting out rights between siblings, parents and children, and husbands and wives. When women felt threatened by wastrel husbands, they could bring suit in court to have the entire estate inventoried. The potential embarrassment of such a threat must have been a powerful weapon in and of itself. Should an inventory offer sufficient grounds, the husband could be put under a guardian and the wife's property safeguarded, which did not offer her any more freedom to act, however.

We have pointed out that state interest shifted grounds in the eighteenth century away from the issues of property surveillance, measurement, listing, and appropriation to those of production, disencumbering, mobilization, and development. Officials became concerned with freeing land of everything which hindered its efficient use. Agricultural experimentation, agronomical science, and populationist policies were all possible precisely because of several centuries of bureaucratic control and taxation policies. Advice as to how to use different kinds of land more efficiently came on the heels of measurement and classification. Over the long run, the mobilization of resources and the stress on productivity had serious consequences for the way village institutions interacted with families. A threat to property became grounds for the dissolution of a marriage, and whatever the real nature of familial conflict, women became adept at framing their attacks within its terms of reference.

One of the many steps taken to mobilize property was to support the credit market by making a wife's wealth available to her husband's creditors. The older institution of Kriegsvogtschaft had always inserted the values and interests of a wider kin group into the transactions of the family by the very fact that the husband had to convince one of the wife's relations to go along with whatever property deal he wanted to make. The end to gender tutelage in 1828 left the husband and wife alone to make their own decisions. This took place in the context of increasing demands that the wife place her property at risk to guarantee her husband's performance. At the beginning of the nineteenth century, the state also insisted on a complete revision of all the village records of mortgages and liens, which had become antiquated and so full of errors that an overview of solvency was difficult. With the state's ability to oversee encumbrances and the registration of the liability of wives for their husbands' debts, the amount of property available for underwriting debt and performance increased considerably. Now wives frequently offered surety (Bürgschaft, Caution) for their husbands' dealings.

In this new situation, the threat to property was more acute. In the eighteenth century, a woman could, at least in theory, keep her own property out of her husband's commercial transactions. She could, of course, still do so. But then her husband could not become Bürgermeister, and he could not take on a carpentry contract down the road. He would also have difficulty explaining to the mortgage (Unterpfand) committee why he should be given a loan if there was to be no lien on the rest of the familial estate. These conditions made the issue of a hard-drinking, idle husband a threat to the property substance of the wife. If she could demonstrate to the satisfaction of the court that she was the more effective commodity producer, then she had a powerful case. And we also find a great deal more criticism put into the framework of alienated labor. Furthermore, as the ideological focus changed, the center of court responsibility changed. Familial quarrels were shifted away first from the consistory to the Gericht and then to the office of the Schultheiss.

The way the state and church interacted with the village has been central to our consideration of the family – from the rules of inheritance to the political constitution of the village. The same local officials who were responsible for channeling substantial amounts of grain and wine to the central storehouses of the duke and ducal institutions were charged with inculcating sober living and encouraging practical piety. The state created formal grounds for penetrating and regulating families precisely at the points at which it considered that the family reflected its interests. It encouraged the production of a vast amount of paper which listed, categorized, and matched taxable property and people and which described the lines of devolution and transfer of rights. State officials took a reading of every family at its inception and conclusion and made that activity a central part of the strategies of husbands and wives and parents and children. The state developed practices for discriminating between families, for defining activities, and perceiving moral characteristics. But its own institutions became instruments for villagers in pursuit of their own ends. Officials participated in the alliance system by being present at every inventory. But each inventory was also a moment for enforcing the local values of equality. If obligation was the reverse side of fairness, then the continual public staging of familial dramas was a means of ensuring reciprocity between allied partners and generations.

During the 1970s, German social historians liked to use Ernst Bloch's phrase "gleichzeitige Ungleichzeitigkeit" (simultaneous asynchronism) to describe the uneven effects of modernization on different groups, neighborhoods, and territories. The concept is useful for capturing ironies and for marking redrawn relationships between different social sectors subject to innovations in power. But it suggests that society is a curious mixture of dynamic and static elements, with some people on the cutting edge of an inexorable modernizing process and others hopelessly engaged in rearguard actions shoring up practices already consigned to the dustbin of history. We find now that traditions are continuously created and recreated and that they are often part of vanguard practices.[22] We should be wary of historical accounts which ascribe custom and immemorial usage as explanations for the existence of institutions and social practices. In any case, too often a particular institution is itself either new or changed beyond recognition by the very fact of alterations in its context. And the images of modern and traditional are the idioms of political contention, not value-free descriptions of historical processes.

The history of Neckarhausen during the period 1700 to 1870 offers an example of a locality undergoing continual change. If we had taken any other period of its history, we would not have found a more static picture, however. For example, during the 1580s, when the population of the village had reached a peak equal to that of the 1750s, villagers married over a geographical distance not found again until after 1870. The practice of remarriage coupled

[22] See, for example, Eric Hobsbawn and Terence Ranger, eds., *The Invention of Tradition* (Cambridge, 1983).

with the fact that farms were not yet subject to the fissioning processes characteristic of the seventeenth century and later meant that property continually moved sideward from marriage partner to marriage partner rather than downward from parents to children. Relatives were dispersed over a large geographical area. The old notion that "traditional" rural society was characterized by an age-old web of kinship and that urbanization and geographical mobility reoriented people away from ascriptive relationships to ones of mutual strategic advantage is increasingly unhelpful. In the history of Neckarhausen, the nature of alliance, the forms of reciprocity, the structure of social divisions, and the systemic character of conflict all changed continuously. Reference to a "web of kinship" is just an admission that there were social processes which we do not yet know how to think about. Furthermore, the contrast between kinship and contract was developed by observers precisely at a time when rural kinship was being reordered toward a complex, flexible – modern – system of alliance and exchange. Kinship and contract were not sequentially ordered but were simultaneously synchronized within the context of men and women contending about management, work, and expenditure, neighbors competing in land, labor, and commodity markets, and families exploited and disciplined by officials, creditors, and village oligarchs.

# Appendix

## A. Intensification of commonland use

A series of village financial records (*Gemeindepflegerechnungen*) from 1710 to 1870 allow us to trace various parcels of land over the entire period, and to show not only ever more intensive use, but also qualitative changes in the nature of production. There are some gaps in the series of records, which we shall have to take into consideration, but in general we can adequately show the trends by selecting volumes every 20 years over the period.[1]

One of the best indicators of change is the use to which a set of grasslands making up part of the commonland (*Allmende*) was put. Many of them were designated *Wasen*, which means turf or grassy area, or a well-watered meadow. At various times, they were in use as year-round pasture, part-time grazing meadow, orchards or gardens. Most of them lay in the vicinity of the Neckar River south of the housing area of the village and were subject to periodic or occasional flooding. The best way to study them is to follow the fortunes of several of the larger parcels over the period.

The first piece, Insele, is at the west end of the village territory (*Markung*) bordering on the neighboring village of Neckartailfingen. South of the highway and north of the river, it is, according to the 1930 survey map, about 275 meters long and 350 deep. In the financial records of 1710 and 1730, this grassland, like all the others, was not mentioned. By 1750, there was a rubric "pasture-land" in the account book, which already suggests a more careful and system-

[1] A complete set of documents for one year contained five items: (1) a volume, called the *Steuerempfangs- und Abrechnungsbuch*, listing all taxpayers from the village, detailing their tax assessments, various taxes due, and their records of payment; (2) a similar volume for holders of property in Neckarhausen who lived in other places; (3) a notebook or journal containing daily transactions (*Rapiatbuch*); (4) the annual village accounts, more particularly the *Gemeindepflegerechnungen*; (5) a sheaf, sometimes bound, of supporting documents – bills, receipts, memoranda, accounts, and lists of various kinds. For Neckarhausen, the earliest surviving financial records – all kept in the Rathaus – are for the years 1710, 1720, and 1730. For each of these years, the whole set of records still exist, but thereafter until 1790, only the account books themselves remain for selected years. Beginning in 1790 and through the end of the period under study (1870), except for an occasional gap, the complete set of records is again available, but this time for every year. For the information we need in this appendix, we will use the account books and supporting documents for the years 1710, 1730, 1790, 1810, 1830, 1850, and 1870. For the intervening period between 1730 and 1790, the account books for 1750 and 1770 will have to suffice.

atic accounting for all the parts of village commonland. Even when no income could be obtained from a plot, it came to be regularly listed. In the exceptional case of Insele, however, it was first mentioned in 1790 as a small patch of grass (*gering gras Plätzle*). A note said that it formerly had been leased as a single piece of land, but now served as a stock pasture and was totally covered with gravel. In 1810, Insele alternated for the most part between stock pasture (*Viehweide*) and sheep pasture (*Schafweide*), which was an important distinction. A small part of Insele was divided into portions (*Allmendeteile*) for the younger villagers. By 1830 it was leased out to 33 villagers for a total of 185.3 fl. In 1850, its dimensions were given as 22.03 M., and it was leased to 37 villagers for 226.9 fl. In 1870, it had attained 26.07 M., and yielded a hay and *Öhmd* (second cutting of hay) harvest sold to 43 villagers for 680.4 fl. In tracing the history of this grassland, we find that at the beginning it was small, subject to continual flooding, and covered mainly in gravel; also, it yielded an insignificant amount of grass. By the end of the eighteenth century, the village began to clear the gravel from the parcel, plow it up, and create a much-needed pasture. In subsequent years, it was partitioned into individual plots for intensive hay production and pasture, with the value of its production rising continually. At our last view, it was again farmed in one block by the village, with the substantial production sold to a considerable number of villagers. What had been a small gravelly pasture became a fairly substantial intensified meadow of just over 17 acres or about 7 hectares. Much land was reclaimed from the Neckar when it was straightened during the 1830s and flooding controlled and it became possible to clear land of gravel permanently. But the village began the clearing up job and more intensive use much earlier. Most of the other parcels we examined had similar histories.

The Biegelwiesen lies east of Insele in a thin strip under the road north of the Neckar. It is about 500 meters long and about 75 wide. Starting under the Biegelwiesen and running eastward almost to the bridge over the river to Raidwangen is another strip today called the Biegelwasen. It is about 400 meters along and 25 to 60 meters wide. These two strips made up what were eventually called the Obere- and Unterebiegelwasen. Neither were mentioned in the financial records of 1710 and 1730. In 1750, the 22.13 M. Oberebiegelwasen was "completely useless," and the little grass which grew on it was used to pasture stock. In 1770 and 1790, its dimensions were given as 22 M., two of which had been given to the bullkeeper for pasture, while the rest was grazed collectively by the village herd. In 1810, the 22 M. were used the same way, with the bullkeeper getting the use of 0.75 M.. The Unterebiegelwasen was first mentioned in 1750 as a 19.38 M. stock pasture, with 0.13 M. reserved for the bullkeeper. In the next three accounts studied, the conditions were just about the same. In 1830, 4 M. were carved out from the Oberebiegelwasen for flax cultivation and parceled out to villagers. How the rest of the land was used is not clear from the text, but it was implied that it was leased out to individual villagers for pasture. In 1850, most of the pieces of both parcels had been given out to individual villagers on a permanent basis. By 1870, 0.75 M. meadowland belonged to the bullkeeper, who leased another 2.5 M. Most of the rest was given out to villagers on a permanent basis, except for 9.13 M. which had been plowed and leased to 6 villagers annually for 66.6 fl. for the hay and Öhmd harvest.

The present-day Beutwang and Im Beutwang lie south of the river between the village territory of Neckartailfingen and the bridge leading to Raidwangen. They are both bounded on the south by the Autmutbach. Before "correction," the course of the river ran through this land, flooding it periodically. Afterward, the parcels were left on the other side of the river, and there was less danger from flooding. As with Insele and the Biegelwasen, it was now possible to remove gravel permanently. Together the two areas are about 1,125 meters long and vary in width between 150 and 290 meters. In 1710 and 1730, they were not mentioned. In 1750 and 1770, "Grosser" Beutwang had 9.38 M. and was mostly covered in gravel but had a little grass for stock grazing. In 1790 and 1810, Groß Beutwang was more than twice as large, 19.38 M, and was at the earlier date "mostly" and at the later two-thirds covered with gravel. By then the one-third that was cleared was available for leasing for 3.57 fl. Like the other parcels, the Klein Beutwang was first mentioned in 1750 and was 10.25 M. It, too, was covered by gravel and when anything grew was grazed by stock. In 1770, 1790, and 1810, it was listed as "only" (*bloß*) stock pasture. In 1830 the dimensions of the two pieces had not changed. By then only half of the Groß Beutwang was covered in gravel. From both parcels, the usable land was leased for a return of 276.7 fl. By 1870 the Beutwang was divided into the Untere Beutwang and Im Beutwang, the former with 44.13 M. as pasture and meadow and the latter with 46.38 M. as pasture and willow bushes. The whole complex was then divided into eight fields, seven of which were leased for three years to 55 villagers as pasture for 957.4 fl. The eighth portion produced 320.1 fl. worth of hay and Öhmd purchased by 54 villagers.

There is a small grassland about 115 meters square south of the railroad called Löhleswasen. It was not mentioned until 1790. Then and in 1810, its dimensions were given as 1.75 M. Before 1771, it has been a path, but at that time it was divided among villagers in 20 parcels. In 1830, it was described as a path partly used as a pasture. In 1870, the account book states that the piece had been brought under the plow in order to grow clover. Under the present rotation, it produced an oat crop sold for 50.1 fl.

To the east, just outside the Neckarhausen territory south of the Neckar in the territory of the city of Nürtingen lies a piece of land called Millot. Neckarhausen had jurisdiction over this area, which is about 625 meters long and 200 meters wide. Among other things, it contained two stone quarries, the largest about 25 by 25 meters. Again, it is not mentioned in the 1710 or 1730 accounts. In 1750 its dimensions were just over 24 M., and it was "only" a stock pasture. In 1770 and 1790, 1.5 M. was set aside for the bullkeeper. The rest of the "waste" (*Egart* = formally arable now *Öde*) was grazed by stock. By 1810, Millot was mixed orchard and pasture, and produced 46.9 fl. worth of apples. Twenty years later, the Millot was largely planted with apple trees and willows. Except for 1.3 M. for the bullkeeper and the stone quarry, and an unspecified portion leased to 16 people for 13.4 fl., the remainder was used as sheep pasture. Millot was not listed under pastureland in 1850, and the poor apple crop was sold for 5.6 fl. In 1870, 18.13 M. were listed as pasture. The Millot had been plowed and leased by the year to villagers. Fourteen people paid 59.4 fl. for the hay and Öhmd harvest. The parcel also produced over 1,400 fl. (about 6,000 liters) worth of apples, a substantial portion of the communal harvest. The stone quarry was leased for 35 fl.

A thin grassland lies east of the bridge along the north bank of the Neckar under the road to Nürtingen, the Untere Wasen or Gänswasen or Untere Böstel Wasen. In 1810, it was 7.5 M. and was a stock pasture. By 1830, it was planted with willows and served as a place for bleaching cloth (*Tuchbleiche*) and as a sheep pasture. Seventeen people leased the bleaching spots for a combined total of 12.6 fl. In 1850, only 4.3 M. were mentioned as pasture and cloth bleachery, the latter leased out to 22 people for 14.4 fl. In 1870, 3.13 M. were reserved for the bullkeeper. Half a M. had been plowed up and was leased out to villagers by the year. The rest was pasture, yielding a hay and Öhmd harvest of 86.3 fl., and bleachery leased for 6.9 fl.

Another important piece of commonland was called the Auchtert. It lies east of the village and north of the highway up against Nürtingen territory. It is about 375 meters long and about 390 wide. Again, no mention is made in the financial records in 1710 and 1730. In 1750 it measured 13.5 M. and was grazed by stock. Apparently, portions were given out to villagers before 1770 as lifetime tenures (Allmendeteile) without any obligations except for a small entry fee. This involved the upper, larger part of the area described in the 1790 accounts. The lower portion served as a sheep pasture, but for part of the year was leased to 19 people for 49.1 fl. By 1830, many fruit trees had been planted on the Auchtert as a whole and willows on the lower part. In 1870, the dimension of the common pastureland was 8 M. This area was planted with fruit trees, and part was plowed up for greater production. At that time the three-year leases were bringing in 94.7 fl. annually. The area also produced the largest crop of apples in the village (15,000 liters), and a considerable amount of hay and Öhmd was sold to villagers.

There were two smaller grasslands on the hill above the village. Kapf today is an area about 250 meters long and 175 meters wide and consists of arable in the center and orchards and pastureland on the south and west edges. In 1830, its 2 M. already produced an important apple crop (from Kapf and the Obere Wasen, 122 fl.). It also was one of the two bleacheries being leased to one person for 0.2 fl. In 1850, the poor apple crop yielded only 5 fl., but in 1870 it was up to 241 fl. In the accounts for 1870, five leaseholders had bleaching places for a total of 0.8 fl. For part of the year, Kapf was used as sheep pasture. The other small grassland was Katzenohr, which lies north of the west end of the village. Today its dimensions are 175 meters wide and 200 long. The small area of about 0.38 M. was plowed up and developed as intensive sheep pasture.

The last parcel to be studied lies on the other side of the arable fields up against the village forest, the Herdhau. It is about 325 meters long and 100 wide. In 1750, its 13.13 M. were used solely as a stock pasture and waste. In 1770, it was a horse and cattle pasture, and again in 1790, and 1810. Before 1830, half of the area was divided up for commonland portions for the younger villagers to grow flax. The remaining 8.88 M. was leased in 1850 to 18 people for 14.5 fl. In the 1870 account book, flaxland portions in the Herdhau covered 20 M. Since "before anyone could remember," the area had had commonland portions, and since 1838 they were reserved for younger Bürger in plots of about 1 Are in exchange for an entry fee of 0.3 fl. A smaller portion of 5.25 M. remained pasture.

## B. Agricultural tables

Information on agriculture was obtained from the *Gemeindepflegrechnungen* and is presented in Tables A.1 to A.4.

Table A.1 *Total income from the commonland fruit harvest (in Gulden)*

| 1710 | 1730 | 1750 | 1770 | 1810 | 1830 | 1850 | 1870 |
|---|---|---|---|---|---|---|---|
| 2.06 | 1.10[a] | 4.27[b] | 5.90[c] | 55.53 | 388.95 | 16.50[d] | 1441.80 |

[a] No division among villagers because fruit harvest unsuccessful (*nicht geraten*).
[b] Not a large crop, but enough to divide among 104 people.
[c] Fruit trees frozen.
[d] Poor harvest.

## C. Stock and sheep raising in Neckarhausen

There were two different animal populations in the village as far as pastureland was concerned – stock (horses and cows) and sheep (see also Appendix D). In 1710, the financial records contained information about income from pastureland or about its use, but in a form different from wheat appears later. The sheep ran in a common herd, and there were two separate herds for horses and cows. Each Bürger or widow had the right to have an animal or two in the common herds and paid pasture money (*Pfründegeld*). That year the herd averaged 147 cows belonging to 63 individuals (altogether there were 59 Bürger and 6 widows in the village). Most household heads, therefore, had at least one cow, and no one had more than four. On average, there were 72 horses, with 40 owners; on one had more than 4. For each animal, an individual paid 6 kr. 3 h.,

Table A.2 *Pay of agricultural specialists (in fl.)*

| Specialists | 1710 | 1730[a] | 1750 | 1770 | 1790 | 1810 | 1830 | 1850 | 1870 |
|---|---|---|---|---|---|---|---|---|---|
| Cowherd | 29. | —[b] | —[b] | —[b] | —[b] | 45.0 | | | |
| Horse herder | 38. | —[b] | —[b] | —[b] | —[b] | 45.0 | | | |
| Gooseherd | 18. | | | | 12.0 | 14.0 | | | |
| Bullkeeper | 0.[c] | —[d] | —[d] | —[d] | 7.0 | 2.0 | 10.0[e] | —[d] | 167.0 |
| Boarkeeper | | | | | | | | | 15.0[f] |
| Tree surgeon | | 3.0 | | 10.0 | 8.0 | 18.0 | 18.0 | 16.8 | 17.9 |
| Stock inspector | | | | | | 4.0 | 4.0 | 16.0 | |
| Mole catcher | | 2.8 | | 22.4 | 19.9 | 34.0 | 25.0 | 24.9 | 60.0 |
| Shepherd: | | | | | | | | | |
| Pförch | | 65.1 | 40.3 | 115.7 | 154.7 | 340.3 | 642.2 | | |
| Lease | | | | | | 720.0 | 855.0[g] | 310.0[h] | 640.0 |

[a] Account book incomplete.
[b] Directly paid from Bürger.
[c] Two bullkeepers mentioned, but "0" was set in the income side of the ledger.
[d] Mentioned but no details.
[e] Two bullkeepers.
[f] Plus fees.
[g] 1832 contract.
[h] 1851 contract.

Table A.3 *Wages of village protection officers (in fl.)*

| Protection Officers | 1710 | 1730[b] | 1750 | 1770 | 1790 | 1810 | 1830 | 1850 | 1870 |
|---|---|---|---|---|---|---|---|---|---|
| Polizeidiener | | | | | | | | 28.0 | |
| Dorfschütz | 9.0 | — | 16.0 | 20.0 | 30.0 | 50.0 | 65.0 | 72.0 | 70.0 |
| Feldschütz | | 2.0 | 18.0 | 20.0 | 16.5 | 26.0 | 35.0 | 26.9 | 55.0 |
| 1. Nachtwächter | 9.0 | | 13.0 | 14.0 | 14.0 | 9.0 | 20.0 | 25.0 | 45.0 |
| 2. Nachtwächter | | 13.0 | 14.0 | 14.0 | 9.0 | 20.0 | 25.0 | 45.0 | |
| Nachthut | | | | | | 3.0 | | | 2.3 |
| Weinberghut | —[a] | | | | 12.0 | 14.6 | | | |
| Wasserbauschütz | | | | | | | | 26.4 | |
| 1. Obsthut | | | | | | | 9.8 | | 18.6 |
| 2. Obsthut | | | | | | | 9.8 | | 4.0 |
| Flugschütz | | | | | | | 16.0 | | |
| 1. Waldschütz | | | 40.0 | 42.0 | 43.5 | 56.0 | 53.0 | 77.0 | 275.0 |
| 2. Waldschutz | | | | | | 28.7 | 53.0 | 77.0 | 19.5 |
| Bettelvogt | | | 12.0 | 5.0 | 9.0 | 16.0 | 14.0 | | |
| Maulwurffänger | | 2.8 | | 22.4 | 19.9 | 34.0 | 25.0 | 24.9 | 60.0 |
| Total | 18.0 | 17.8[b] | 113.0 | 137.4 | 153.9 | 257.3 | 325.6 | 402.2 | 549.4 |

*Note*: *Polizeidiener* = policeman; *Dorfschütz* = policeman, beadle, bailiff; *Feldschütz* = field policeman; *Nachtwächter* = nightwatchman; *Nachthut* = harvest night guard; *Weinberghut* = vineyard guard; *Wasserbauschütz* = river bank policeman; *Obsthut* = fruit harvest guard; *Flugschütz* = guard of harvest against birds; *Waldschütz* = forest policeman; *Bettelvogt* = beggar administrator and rouster; *Maulwurffänger* = mole and mouse catcher.

[a] No entry in the ledger, but two put on oath.

[b] Account book incomplete.

Table A.4 *Sale of wood in Neckarhausen (in fl.).*

| Wood type | 1710 | 1730[a] | 1750 | 1770 | 1790 |
|---|---|---|---|---|---|
| Number of Bürger and widows | 65 | | | 112 | |
| Oak | (5)13.3 | (4)14.4 | 23.3 | 1.8 | 13.3 |
| White willow | | | | | |
| Beech | | (2)8.0 | 0.0 | 35.0 | 0.8 |
| Hornbeam | | | | | |
| Linden | | | 6.0 | 164.3 | 44.7 |
| Ash | | | 0.0 | 0.0 | |
| Birch | | | 0.0 | 1.0 | 0.0 |
| Aspen | | | 0.0 | 1.3 | 0.0 |
| Stumps | | | | | 15.9 |
| Timber waste | (18)10.5 | (14)5.1 | 16.7 | 151.2 | 55.1 |
| Oak bark | | | | 2.5 | 3.5 |
| Kindling | | | | | .5 |
| Miscellaneous | | | (1)3.3 | 20.9 | 7.2 |
| Kindling portions | | | | 5.6 | |
| Willow portions | | | | 0.0 | |
| Total | 23.8 | 27.5 | 49.3 | 383.6 | 141.0 |

| | 1810 | 1830 | 1850 | 1870 |
|---|---|---|---|---|
| Number of Bürger and widows | 154 | 175 | 245 | 228 |
| Oak | (22)568.4 | (23)125.6 | 168.3 | (41) 1637.7 |
| White Willow | (13) 9.9 | | 12.3 | (102) 92.1 |
| Beech | (8) 101.5 | | 130.8 | |
| Hornbeam | (6) 13.7 | | | |
| Linden | (20)101.2 | (23)132.3 | | (11) 111.0 |
| Ash | (2) 4.8 | (10) 29.1 | | |
| Birch | | (17) 55.1 | | |
| Aspen | | | 2.7 | |
| Stumps | (20) 51.6 | (40)123.1 | | |
| Timber waste | (24) 64.3 | (41) 16.6 | 116.3 | (15) 247.6 |
| Oak bark | (1) 117.0 | (1) 150.0 | 97.0 | (1) 366.5 |
| Kindling | (27) 28.6 | | | (166) 717.5 |
| Miscellaneous | (91)112.3 | (59) 42.8 | 181.1 | (65) 233.7 |
| Kindling portions | (172) 4.8 | | | (469) 261.6 |
| Willow portions | | | | (235) 109.7 |
| Total | 1178.1 | 674.6 | 708.5 | 3777.4 |

*Note*: Number of buyers in parentheses.
[a] Ledger incomplete.

making a total collected that year of 71.3 fl. for the use of the pastureland. Since the two herders received 67 fl. together, the excess income to the village from all of the stock pastureland amounted to just over 4 fl. In 1810, the herds still existed, and the two herders received 45 fl. each, but they took fees directly from the villagers, so that there is no information on the number of animals in the accounts. In any event, the number of Bürger and widows totaled 154, more than double the population since 1710, and the income from the pasture money rose only 34 percent. This is probably an indication that already a substantial proportion of the villagers had switched to stall feeding and did not run their animals with the herd. Already some of the old pastures – part of Insele, a portion of the Beutwang, and the greater part of the Auchtert – had been apportioned to individual villagers. Still, there was a substantial portion of land designated as stock pasture for the common herd.

The evidence exists that as far back as 1710 the village had a communal bull. In 1790 two bulls were taken care of for 7 fl. wages. By 1810, a bullkeeper had to pay 2 fl. for the privilege of keeping an animal, collecting a fee from the people who made use of it. In 1830 there were two bullkeepers receiving 5 fl. each. By 1870, there was only one bull, leased to a man for the period 1868 to 1875, who received 167 fl. in that year. Whether, in addition, he could charge a fee is not clear from the text. In 1870, as well, for the first time a communal boar was introduced; its keeper received 15 fl. Early in the eighteenth century, there was also a gooseherd, whose salary in 1710 of 18 fl. can be compared to the 9 fl. for the village policeman. There were 91 geese and 36 individual owners in that year, paying a total of 9.8 fl., which meant that the village made a net loss on its pasture. By 1810 the gooseherd received 14 fl. less than a century earlier. By 1830, with the trend to individual keeping of animals and the daily collection of fodder, no gooseherd was hired by the village any more.

The shepherd is not as easy to follow in the financial records. In 1710, the herd consisted of 185 sheep belonging to the villagers plus 65 belonging to the shepherd and Bürgermeister. Altogether, 39 individuals had animals in the flock, paying a sum of 24.7 fl. Villagers paid for the privilege of having the sheep folded on their land (*Pförch*), which in that year began on March 28 and lasted to September 30. The total collected was 65.1 fl. In 1750, the Pförch brought in 115.7 fl.; in 1770, 154.7 fl.; and in 1790, 340.3 fl. In the last year, there were 193 sheep owned by 26 people. Because there were not enough animals for the Pförch, the village allowed 63 sheep from outside, setting the total for that year at 275. A few villagers had as many as 30 sheep, the shepherd, 41. On December 9, sheep were given to their owners to spend the winter in stalls. In that year, the shepherd received a wage of 61 fl. By 1810, the amount collected for folding the sheep on private land had risen considerably. The shepherd paid 720 fl. for the privilege of leasing the flock, collecting in return 642.2 fl. from the Pförch alone. In that year, the period for the Pförch was just about the same as in 1710, from March 31 to November 26, extended rather later into the fall.

From these data, we can see that villagers were ready to invest a much greater amount into the fertility of their fields. At the same time, the commonland available for the flock had been whittled away. By 1870, the lease brought in 640 fl., which shows a stability over the course of the nineteenth century. The dates of the Pförch, however, had changed, now running from July 25 to April 4, instead of over the long summer. In the earlier Pförch, the sheep had been folded on the fallow field, moving from strip to strip as villagers paid for the privilege. In the meantime, however, the fallow had been planted with clover, alfalfa, and various root crops, and the sheep were brought onto the stubble following the summer crop. What made it possible to maintain the herd was the development of intensively cultivated meadows in the Herdhau, Millot, Gänswasen, Beutwang, and Insele. One can trace the policy of a more rational rotation whereby sheep were brought onto land with pasture and orchards for a few years and then moved to another area, while the former was plowed under for a hay or clover crop. The size of the flock was limited by the stubble and the few commonland pastures. Meanwhile, stall feeding of stock had added enormously to the output of manure for the fields. Most villagers had never kept sheep in the herd and indeed at times there was difficulty finding enough sheep for the flock at all. A few people, however, sometimes kept a large number. There was a trend to individualized agriculture, so that from time to time sheep pasture was leased to individuals who folded their own animals, and with more concentrated folding the land was periodically released for rotating other crops.

## D. Agricultural intensification

There is no simple way to find out exactly what was grown in the village nor in what amounts. But there are some clues. At the end of the period under study, a report from the Oberamt Nürtingen detailed all the field crops from the district as a whole, giving the total land under cultivation together with the average total output over the previous 10 years.[2] Although any one village in the district might deviate somewhat from the overall pattern – for example, as far as I can tell, hops were not grown in Neckarhausen – the report gives a good picture of the general distribution of crops for the village.

From the information in Table A.5, which covers the period after the commutation of tithes, we can still see the outline of the three-field system. No garden produce as such or wine was listed. The total produce of the meadows was not figured, just an average yield. It is not clear whether the products of the flax and hemplands were included or whether the table essentially chronicled the yields of the arable land. For example, the carrots on the list were clearly not from vegetable gardens but must have been part of the field rotation. The problem is whether flax and hemp and cabbages in the list were those grown only in the arable fields or included those grown in the Länder as well.

[2] STAL, E258V, Bodensbenutzungsberichte, Kreis Nürtingen, Übersichtstabelle, 1860.

Table A.5 *Average crop production in the Oberamt Nürtingen, 1850–9*

| Crop | Land cultivated (M.) | Mean output (Scheffel) | Weight per Scheffel (Pfund) |
|---|---|---|---|
| Winter wheat | 25 | 100 | 280 |
| Winter rye | 107 | 402 | 265 |
| Winter barley | 2 | 8 | 240 |
| Winter spelt | 7,136 | 57,088 | 160[a] |
| Summer wheat | 383 | 1,341 | 280 |
| Summer rye | 0 | 0 | 0 |
| Summer barley | 3,731 | 14,924 | 240 |
| Oats | 2,692 | 13,460 | 165 |
| Peas | 148 | 296 | 240 |
| Lentils | 99 | 198 | 280 |
| Vetch | 234 | 351 | 240 |
| Field beans | 296 | 592 | 280 |
| Maize | 88 | 264 | 224 |
| Potatoes | 2,878 | 359,750 Simri | 28[b] |
| Cabbage | 192 | 384,000 Simri | |
| Carrots | 3 | 300 Zentner | |
| Rape and rapeseed | 501 | 1,503 | |
| Poppies | 63 | 126 | |
| Flax | 357 | 35,700 (Pfund)[c] | |
| Hemp | 487 | 97,400 (Pfund) | |
| Hops | 10 | 30 | |
| Tobacco | 0 | 0 | |

| | *Zentner per M. in 1860* |
|---|---|
| *Red clover* | 60 |
| *Alfalfa and sainfoin* | 44 |
| *Fodder beets, mangolds* | 80 |
| *Hay and second cutting (Öhmd)* | 40 |

[a] 3.5 Simri *Kernen* (dehusked spelt) per Scheffel (34 Pfund per Simri).
[b] Per Simri.
[c] Combed (*gehechelt*).

The list appears to deal only with the production of the arable fields.

The entire winter field rotation seems to have been given over to spelt production, altogether 7,270 M. for all of the winter grains, except on a small percentage of land. In Neckarhausen, the winter field was seldom planted with anything else but spelt. I have examined all of the postmortem inventories for eight selected decades beginning in 1650.[3] After the 1740s, the value of the crop was often given separately from the value of the field, which allows us to see what was planted on the winter and summer fields. In the 1740s, there were 23 examples of winter field crops, all of which were spelt. In the 1770s, out of 26 inventories with winter field information, only one had anything but spelt, one single strip of einkorn wheat, usually a summer grain. In the decade of 1800–1809, there were 33 inventories with winter field information. In two cases, some clover was introduced on some strips, and in one case a strip was being cultivated as a meadow. The number of instances with separate information on the produce of a field was sharply reduced in the 1830s, 19 cases. Out of these, three strips had been put to grass, and one strip, which for several years had been cultivated as a meadow, was sown with a mixture of spelt and barley. The 4 cases from the 1860s show only spelt grown on the winter field. In general, the winter field remained almost exclusively planted to spelt throughout the period, although some portions of the field were nibbled away for meadowland. Since the winter field seems relatively inviolate, the 7,270 M. in the above list probably encompass one of the fields in the rotation.

By the early eighteenth century, the summer field was already far more complex. Since inventories tended to be written far less frequently when the summer crops were on the field, their description occurs far less often. In the 1740s, the eleven cases show that the "oat field" (*Haberfeld*) grew barley, einkorn wheat, vetch, oats, with strips frequently carrying a mixture of oats and einkorn wheat, oats and vetch, or einkorn wheat and barley. One field was planted with hemp. In the 1770s, the einkorn wheat, oats, and barley combination were found together in the 13 examples. In the first decade of the nineteenth century, einkorn wheat was not encountered in the 10 examples, which detailed barley, oats, vetch, some clover or grass, and on one strip, spelt. In the 1830s, barley and oats still predominated (12 instances), with one strip of summer wheat and some grass. In the four examples from the 1860s, barley and oats were mentioned. From information about mixed fodder stores, we also know that peas, field beans, and maize were sometimes cultivated in the summer field. If we assume that this field was about the same size as the winter field, then the following products in the list probably made up that field: summer wheat, summer barley, oats, peas, lentils, and vetch. We might also add the field beans and maize – altogether accounting for 7,671 M., only a little over 10 percent of which was planted to nongrains.

Following the fortunes of the fallow field is more difficult. For one thing, the term "fallow" (*Brache*) is ambiguous. Even today, nongrain produce (beets and turnips and the like), are referred to as "fallow fruits" (*Brachfrüchte*). So a reference to the fallow does not imply that nothing was being grown on the plots. Certain crops seem not to have been evaluated very often, such as clover,

[3] From the series of *Inventuren und Teilungen* in the Rathaus.

alfalfa, and mangold, as in the list above, since they were generally mowed continually or harvested progressively for green fodder. Following the logic of the list, the fallow crops seem to have been potatoes, cabbage, carrots, rape and rapeseed, poppies, and most likely flax, hemp and hops, accounting for 4,491 M., or about 60 percent of the field, the rest being planted to the fodder grasses or lying truly fallow. The information from the inventories in Neckarhausen only hint at some of the uses of the fallow, since crops on that field were seldom mentioned. In the 1740s, the records mention two cases of hemp and flax being grown there; in the 1770s one case of linseed. In the first decade of the nineteenth century, clover, meadow, grass, and spelt were mentioned on four occasions. By the 1830s we find spelt, meadow, flax, and potatoes. The 1860s simply mention "fallow cultivation" (*Brachanbau*), without giving a closer description or valuating the crop.

We can see how the overall structure of the three-field system could be maintained, with its monocultural winter field, while considerable changes could take place in the summer field and the fallow. Any one strip could be subject to a complex rotation. One observer in the 1850s described a typical nine-year rotation for the region as potatoes, spelt, barley, rape (or poppies, flax, or one of the brassicae), spelt, barley, clover, spelt, oats.[4]

Potatoes, clover, and other fallow crops were introduced progressively in the eighteenth century. But some crops were apparently introduced on some fields for several years at a time. For example, three petitioners and their "Consorten" applied in 1778 to the central government to be allowed to plant "artificial grass" (*Kunstgrass*) on 26.6 M. of poor arable for nine years.[5] Apparently they had already planted sainfoin and other fodder crops there previously and wanted to be able to continue the practice, and refer to the shortage of meadowland in the village. This was the first of many petitions preserved in the state archives for the period 1778 to 1804. Apparently the desire to plant fodder crops increased substantially then, but in this document it is possible to see that the practice had begun somewhat before. The logic of the change was spelled out earlier by the Schultheiss, who argued that the meadow in Neckarhausen was only about 100 M. compared with the 1,000 M. arable.[6] There was never enough fodder and it was impossible to manure the farms properly. For some time, other villages had introduced clover and alfalfa and an experiment had been tried in Neckarhausen itself. In this instance, it seemed wise to change the cultivation of such poor land from arable to clover. A later document mentions the field planted to spelt and then alfalfa, which means that a regular rotation had been established. Similar petitions during the period

[4] Karl Göriz, *Die landwirtschaftliche Betriebslehre als Leitfaden für Vorlesungen und zum Selbststudium für Landwirte*, Teil 1–3 (Stuttgart, 1853–4), Teil 2, p. 101. Göriz was a professor at the university of Tübingen and taught farm economics (*Betriebslehre*) at the agricultural college in Hohenheim.

[5] HSAS, A249, Bü 2066, "Kulturveränderungen zu Neckarhausen 1778–1804" (26.2.1778).

[6] HSAS, A249, Bü 2066, "Kulturveränderungen zu Neckarhausen 1778–1804" (15.2.1769).

Table A.6 *Percentage of field crops found in inventories*

| Crop | 1650s | 1680s | 1710s | 1740s | 1770s | 1800s | 1830s | 1860s |
|---|---|---|---|---|---|---|---|---|
| Spelt | 70.0 | 69.6 | 67.6 | 65.0 | 50.6 | 53.6 | 57.4 | 65.8 |
| Oats | 20.7 | 25.9 | 28.5 | 19.1 | 16.7 | 21.1 | 18.6 | 4.0 |
| Barley | 4.1 | — | — | 7.5 | 13.2 | 18.6 | 15.6 | 24.0 |
| Einkorn wheat | 2.9 | — | 2.0 | 3.7 | 7.4 | 0.2 | 2.6 | 3.3 |
| Peas | 1.5 | 1.9 | 0.3 | 1.4 | 1.1 | 1.6 | 0.5 | 0.4 |
| Beans | — | — | — | 0.3 | 2.2 | — | 0.7 | 0.1 |
| Vetch | — | — | — | 0.4 | 1.4 | 0.7 | 0.5[a] | — |
| Rye | 0.3 | 1.6 | 0.2 | 0.4 | — | — | — | — |
| Hempseed | 0.4 | 0.9 | 1.3 | 2.0 | 2.1 | 2.0 | 2.1 | 0.7 |
| Linseed | — | — | — | 0.2 | 0.7 | 0.7 | 1.2 | 0.2 |
| Mixed grain[b] | — | — | — | — | 3.4 | — | — | — |
| Maize | — | — | — | — | 0.7 | 1.3 | 0.5 | 1.5 |
| Lentils | — | — | — | — | 0.4 | 0.1 | 0.1 | 0.1 |
| Wheat | — | — | — | — | — | — | 0.1 | — |

[a] And oats.
[b] "Mischling."

were approved for planting sainfoin, alfalfa, perennial grass, "artificial" fodder, clover, and hemp. In most of these cases, the parcels of land were on the edge of one of the three arable fields in difficult areas which were heavy, wet, ill-drained or stony, with poor returns. Planting the new crops meant additional heavy labor inputs for improved drainage. Reports were continually made about the shortage of fodder crops and meadow and occasionally about the lack of land for the cultivation of hemp, which suggest two directions for the intensification of agricultural production.

We need further clues to be able to assess the rhythm of agricultural innovation in Neckarhausen. Some documents which shed some light on the issues are the postmortem inventories, but they are difficult to work with. The sections devoted to movables listed cattle, grain stores, dried fruits, sauerkraut, and the like. I have taken selected decades, and in Table A.6 given the relative percentage of each arable product (except for potatoes) according to the sum total of Scheffel. In Table A.7, the relative value of grain, hay, and straw is given, and in Tables A.8 and A.9 the number of cattle and horses.

From time to time, inventories were taken of the livestock in Neckarhausen. After 1830, the data are based on triennial censuses.[7] This discontinuous series can be compared with the data presented in Tables A.8 and A.9.

[7] For the period 1831–73, STAL, E258V/40, "Ergebnisse der Viehzählungen," Oberamt Nürtingen, 1831–1907; 1816, E141, Bü 260, "Viehtabelle"; 1769, HSAS, A8, Kabinettsakten III, Bü 88; 1710, Neckarhausen *Gemeindepflegerechnungen*.

## D. *Agricultural intensification*

Table A.7 *Percentage value of grain, hay, and straw found in inventories*

| Crop | 1650s | 1680s | 1710s | 1740s | 1770s | 1800s | 1830s | 1860s |
|---|---|---|---|---|---|---|---|---|
| Grains | 91.4 | 60.2 | 89.0 | 68.1 | 61.7 | 70.0 | 65.0 | 57.1 |
| Hay | 8.6 | 30.2 | 9.8 | 24.2 | 26.4 | 16.1 | 17.7 | 29.3 |
| Straw | 0. | 9.6 | 1.1 | 7.7 | 11.9 | 13.8 | 17.3 | 13.1 |

Table A.8 *Number of animals listed in the inventories*

| Number | 1650s | 1680s | 1710s | 1740s | 1770s | 1800s | 1830s | 1860s |
|---|---|---|---|---|---|---|---|---|
| Inventories | 6 | 14 | 14 | 33 | 29 | 39 | 47 | 42 |
| Horses | 2 | 22 | 14 | 15 | 15 | 11 | 5 | 0 |
| Foals | 2 | 3 | 1 | 1 | 5 | 3 | 0 | 0 |
| Oxen | 1 | 0 | 1 | 0 | 11 | 4 | 21 | 31 |
| Young oxen | 0 | 0 | 2 | 0 | 2 | 0 | 2 | 9 |
| Cows | 6 | 17.5[a] | 18 | 18 | 25 | 34 | 33 | 31 |
| Calves | 1 | 27.5[a] | 10 | 14.5[a] | 16.5[a] | 18 | 19 | 15 |
| Pigs | 3 | 11 | 1 | 3 | 4 | 5 | 5 | 12 |
| Goats | 0 | 5 | 1 | 1 | 2 | 0 | 0 | 3 |

[a] Occasionally a person had half rights to an animal.

Table A.9 *Percentage of animals in inventories*

| Animals | 1650s | 1680s | 1710s | 1740s | 1770s | 1800s | 1830s | 1860s |
|---|---|---|---|---|---|---|---|---|
| Total number horses and cattle | 12.0 | 70.0 | 46.0 | 48.5 | 74.5 | 70.0 | 80.0 | 86.0 |
| Percentage horses | 33.3 | 35.7 | 32.6 | 33.0 | 26.8 | 20.0 | 6.3 | 0.0 |
| Percentage cattle | 66.7 | 64.3 | 67.4 | 67.0 | 73.2 | 80.0 | 93.8 | 100.0 |
| Percentage Oxen | 8.3 | 0.0 | 6.5 | 0.0 | 17.4 | 5.7 | 28.8 | 46.5 |

Before we draw any conclusions from Tables A.10 and A.11, there is another statistic that will help us understand the agricultural changes in Neckarhausen. At various dates, reports were sent to the central government regarding the distribution of different forms of land use in the village (Table A.12).[8] The

[8] HSAS, A261, Bü 1345 (1828); A8 Kabinettsakten III, Bü 88, (1769); *Oberamtsbeschreibung Nürtingen* (Stuttgart, 1848), with tables from 1846.

Table A.10 *Animal population in Neckarhausen from periodic censuses*

| Census period | Horses | Cattle | Donkeys | Sheep | Pigs | Goats |
|---|---|---|---|---|---|---|
| 1710[a] | 72.0 | 147.0 | | | | |
| 1769 | 53.0 | 208.0 | 0.0 | 272.0 | 12.0 | 0.0 |
| 1816 | 44.0 | 235.0 | 0.0 | 80.0 | 5.0 | 2.0 |
| 1830–9 | 20.3 | 446.7 | 0.0 | 474.0 | 35.3 | 4.3 |
| 1840–9 | 11.0 | 266.5 | 0.5 | 532.3 | 26.0 | 6.8 |
| 1850–9 | 7.5 | 388.3 | 0.0 | 452.8 | 29.0 | 11.3 |
| 1860–9 | 8.3 | 499.0 | 0.0 | 528.3 | 87.0 | 9.3 |
| 1873 | 8.0 | 566.0 | 0.0 | 424.0 | 127.0 | 18.0 |

[a] Not a census, but size of communal herds listed in the *Gemeindepflegerechnungen*.

Table A.11 *Percentage of animals in censuses*

| Census period | Total number horses and cattle | Percentage horses | Percentage cattle |
|---|---|---|---|
| 1769 | 261.0 | 20.3 | 79.7 |
| 1816 | 279.0 | 15.8 | 84.2 |
| 1830–9 | 467.0 | 4.5 | 95.9 |
| 1840–9 | 277.5 | 4.0 | 96.0 |
| 1850–9 | 395.8 | 1.9 | 98.1 |
| 1860–9 | 507.3 | 1.6 | 98.4 |
| 1873 | 574.0 | 1.4 | 98.6 |

cropping patterns indicate that a number of changes were under way during or just before the 1740s. While peas seem to have been part of the normal rotation early in the seventeenth century, we now find beans and vetch commonly grown. For the first time there are also several inventories with cabbages and *Rüben* mentioned in the stores. It is not clear what is to be understood by the latter term, since the family of *brassicae* (Rüben) included different kinds of plants, such as turnip, kale, and cabbage, some grown for their leaves and some for their roots. In any event, they were measured by the wagon load, and may well have been introduced into the field rotation, but could have been confined to the *Länder*. Later, in the nineteenth century, most of the brassicae – mangolds and the like – introduced into the arable were meant for green fodder. What we encounter in the 1740s seem to be the first experiments in this kind of field cropping. In all of the inventories in the samples up to that point, besides the field produce in Tables A.5–A.7 we find only wine, dried pears

Table A.12 *Land use in Neckarhausen (Morgen)*

| Year | Arable | Meadow | Vineyard | Garden | Land | Pasture | Forest | Total |
|---|---|---|---|---|---|---|---|---|
| 1728 | 1028.85 | 70.03 | 40.22 | 48.11 | 20.02 | 119.50 | 447.5 | 1774.23 |
| 1769 | 1028.75 | 69.25 | 40.00 | 69.50 | | 119.50[a] | 447.5 | 1774.50 |
| 1846 | 927.26 | 264.75 | 15.13 | 47.75 | | 119.13[b] | 422.38 | 1796.40 |

[a] *Allmende* (commons) and *Egarten* (waste)
[b] *Waiden* (pasture) and *Oeden* (waste)

and apples, some lard and flour, and an occasional side of bacon. In the inventories from the 1740s, those staples, except for bacon, continue to be found, together with cider, schnaps, sauerkraut, fresh apples, and zwetschgen (a plum variety). In the 1770s we encounter several new products: most significantly potatoes, introduced probably in the 1760s, maize, dried beans, and lentils.[9] Again, it is difficult to say what precisely was introduced into the field rotation, and what remained in gardens and Länder, but from this period onward, more and more of these products found their way into the arable. The first firm reference in court protocols to potatoes in the arable field rotation comes from 1769, but not until the 1790s were they mentioned frequently.[10] We also find examples of the industrial crops, flax and hemp, being planted outside the Länder in the fields.

As we have seen, significant interest in new fodder crops was evident in the mid- to late 1770s. In part this was due to the growing population pressure on

[9] Karl Göriz, *Beiträge zur Kenntnis der württembergischen Landwirtschaft* (Stuttgart and Tübingen, 1841), p. 3, says the potato was introduced to Württemberg in 1710 and spread as a result of bad harvests during the period 1770–1.

[10] The earliest reference in the protocols to potatoes comes from 1769; *Vogtruggericht*, vol. 1, f. 96 (11.2.1769). In order to create more communal portions for the increased number of households, the village decided to plow up a part of the Auchtert and plant it with potatoes. For the following three years, the area was to be sown with clover and then portioned out for fodder production. In the 1790s, there are many references to sacks of potatoes stored in cellars (*Gericht*, vol. 4, f. 174 [19.9.1791], *Vogtruggericht*, vol. 2, f. 7 [12.12.1791], *Gericht*, vol. 4, f. 220 [14.1.1793]) or grown on the arable (*Gericht*, vol. 4, f. 172 [5.9.1791], f. 240 [10.10.1793]), or in a garden (*Gericht*, vol. 5, f. 1 [13.12.1794]). There are references after the turn of the century to potatoes grown in communal portions in the Auchtert (*Gericht*, vol. 5, f. 192 [3.9.1803]) and in the arable (*Gericht*, vol. 7, f. 85 [14.8.1813], *Oberamtsgericht*, HSAL, F190, vol. 11 f. 174 [23.6.1815]). When the Gericht spelled out what a man was to receive daily as part of his board in 1805, potatoes were included on the menu (*Gericht*, vol. 6, f. 105 [9.8.1805]). In 1817, potatoes were provided in the soup kitchen (*Gericht*, vol. 9, f. 3 [3.5.1817]). In 1818, 76 Bürger were given seed potatoes to plant in their garden portions or fields (*zur Anpflanzung ihrer Güther und Theile*) (*Gemeindepflegerechnungen 1818*). References in the 1820s are to potatoes planted in the arable (*Gericht*, vol. 10, f. 159 [28.12.1824]), f. 139 [15.5.1824], f. 138 [13.5.1824]), or to preparation for meals (*Gericht*, vol. 10, f. 174 [18.4.1825]), or storage (*Gericht*, vol. 11, f. 161 [11.12.1829]). By the 1830s, potatoes were clearly established in the arable crop rotation and further references to the protocols are not necessary. The following are explicit references in the protocols to other crops in the arable fields. Clover: *Vogtruggericht*, vol. 1, f. 55 (20.4.1763), f. 94 (11.2.1769), f. 96 (11.2.1769), f. 99 (20.3.1770), f. 100 (20.3.1770), f. 103 (11.3.1772), f. 120 (11.12.1778), *Gericht*, vol. 2, f. 196 (29.12.1778), f. 158 (9.4.1777), vol. 3, f. 226 (28.12.1779), vol. 4, f. 33 (27.12.1785), f. 33 (27.12.1785), vol. 5, f. 29 (5.10.1795), f. 52 (9.7.1796), f. 53 (9.7.1796), f. 128 (28.12.1798), f. 202 (28.12.1803), vol. 6, f. 7 (26.6.1804), f. 100 (23.7.1805), vol. 7, f. 133 (15.6.1810), f. 200 (6.8.1811), vol. 9, f. 9 (15.6.1817), vol. 10, f. 144 (21.6.1824), vol. 11, f. 87 (28.12.1827), f. 153 (10.10.1829); *Vogtruggericht*, vol. 2, f. 29 (17.2.1808); f. 48 (28.9.1813). Lucerne: *Gericht*, vol. 10, f. 70 (12.10.1822), f. 183 (13.6.1825). Beans: *Gericht*, vol. 6, f. 100 (23.7.1805), vol. 10, f. 138 (13.5.1824), vol. 11, f. 83 (28.12.1827). Peas: *Gericht*, vol. 2, f. 225 (28.12.1779), *Nürtingen Stadtgericht*, vol. 28, f. 128 (13.2.1786), *Gericht*, vol. 6, f. 100 (23.7.1805), vol. 10, f. 138 (13.5.1824), vol. 11, f. 83 (28.12.1827). Vetch: *Nürtingen Stadtgericht*, vol. 4 (5.3.1659); *Gericht*, vol. 6, f. 100 (23.7.1805), vol. 9, f. 25 (11.11.1817). Rüben (leafy brassica): *Vogtruggericht*, vol. 1, f. 26 (15.2.1751), f. 106 (11.3.1772), *Gericht*, vol. 9, f. 17 (2.8.1817). Maize: *Gericht*, vol. 4, f. 172 (5.9.1791). The garden vegetable that was most frequently mentioned was kohlrabi: *Gericht*, vol. 1, f. 133 (26.8.1761), f. 218 (13.10.1770), vol. 4, f. 212 (26.11.1792), vol. 5, f. 13 (18.2.1795), vol. 9, f. 18 (13.8.1817).

village resources, and more efficient ways of using the land were sought. Even in the 1750s, villagers were complaining that, because the population was too large, land prices were soaring and yields in the forest and on communal land were declining.[11] In 1764, the Nürtingen Vogt complained that villagers for a long time had been planting peas and vetch in the fallow and cutting down the size of the flock.[12] At the end of the decade, the Auchtert was portioned out to villagers in an effort to manage the crisis in fodder crops.[13] It was to be planted for one year with potatoes to clean up the weeds and then for six years with alfalfa. Conflicts developed over alternative uses of communal pastureland. In 1773, various people had planted clover, grain, and vegetable crops in the Sandacker, all of which were supposed to be cleared by St. Gall's Day (October 16).[14] In that year, there were more cattle and horses in the village herds than anyone could remember, and so the pasture was necessary. During the 1780s and 1790s, significant amounts of land were planted with the new grasses and fodder crops, and there is evidence that part of the fallow had already been planted to the new fodder grasses. The summer field apparently was being planted with clover as well either after the harvest or in some of the strips. In 1777, the pastor demanded the second cutting of clover and alfalfa from the "Haberfeld und Brache".[15] In 1778, there was to be no clover in the fallow field, but it would be planted in the summer field.[16] By 1779, the shepherd was forbidden to feed the flock on the clover in the fallow in the spring, an ordinance that was repeated every year from then on.[17] The flocks were not allowed onto the cultivated fallow until St. Michael's (September 29). However, it appears that not everyone cultivated their fallow strips, and the flock was only gradually restricted. So much planting and sowing of the fallow had taken place by the late 1780s that the flock had to be cut down by about 15 percent, and a few years later by another 10 percent (see also Appendix C).[18] By the end of the century, it declined by still another 10 percent, to 250, and in 1803 was down to 170 head.[19] According to the census of 1816, there were only 80 sheep in the village. The flock was only slowly built back up after that by setting aside newly intensively cultivated pastures and was expanded by the 1840s to over 500 head.

The changes in agriculture were oriented in part toward ever more intensive cattle raising. In the 1770s, the number of horses in the village began to decline, replaced by oxen. The cattle plague at the turn of the century cut back the number of oxen available for a while, but Table A.9 shows their steady rise to

[11] *Gericht*, vol. 1, f. 37 (3.3.1751).
[12] *Vogtruggericht*, vol. 1, f. 70 (11.12.1764).
[13] *Vogtruggericht*, vol. 1, f. 96 (11.2.1769).
[14] *Gericht*, vol. 2, f. 53 (23.10.1773).
[15] *Gericht*, vol. 2, f. 158 (4.9.1777).
[16] *Gericht*, vol. 2, f. 196 (29.12.1778).
[17] *Gericht*, vol. 2, f. 226 (28.12.1779).
[18] *Gericht*, vol. 4, f. 36 (9.1.1786); f. 95 (9.1.1789).
[19] *Gericht*, vol. 5, f. 158 (7.1.1801); f. 187 (28.3.1803).

Table A.13 *Amount of potatoes per inventory (in simri)*

| | 1770s | 1800s | 1830s | 1860s |
|---|---|---|---|---|
| Number of inventories | 29.0 | 39.0 | 47.0 | 57.0 |
| Simri potatoes | 10.5 | 9.5 | 76.4 | 57.0 |
| Simri/inventory | 0.36 | 0.24 | 1.63 | 1.36 |

almost half the herd by the 1860s. It was characteristic of small producers to raise oxen, use them for a few years, and sell them to large farmers. But cows were also commonly used for traction. In 1873, rather more than one-fifth of the cows were used for plowing and harrowing.[20] The plague at the turn of the century also masks the trend in the size of the cattle herd as a whole. Between 1769 and 1816, there must have been a large increase in the number of cattle, followed by a precipitous decline, which had only been made good by the middle of the second decade. We have already seen that a significant shift took place as more and more cattle were fed in stalls. This development must have taken place in tandem with the production of green fodder crops. At the same time, straw became more important for the production of manure, and it tripled as a proportion of value of products stored in the barn from the first half to the second half of the eighteenth century.

The evidence suggests that the main lines of development were established by the turn of the century. Green fodder plants such as clover and alfalfa came to be increasingly rotated with the brassicae, sainfoin, vetch, peas, beans, and potatoes. Especially after the famine of 1815–16, potatoes became a staple crop for human consumption. The sample of inventories indicates a sixfold jump in potato stores between 1810 and 1830, which reflects a sharp rise in cultivation (Table A.13). In the Gemeindepflegerechnungen for 1818, there is a list of Bürger who obtained planting potatoes from Rothenburg – altogether, 13 Scheffel at 117 fl. 52 kr.

## E. Stealing in Neckarhausen

During the 1820s, pilfering among villagers seems to have peaked, but it remained high until midcentury. Table A.14 lists all cases before the local courts of people stealing from each other. Notice that no examples are found in the court records before the 1770s. That cannot mean that there was no thievery in the village before that time, but at least formal organs for accusation were in play after that time. For the most part, the stolen articles consisted of small amounts of food, fodder, flax, yarn, and kindling for immediate use, although some things, such as tools, were apparently stolen to sell in another

[20] STAL, E258V.

village for small amounts of cash. Very little money and only a few consumption items such as watches, smoking pipes, ribbons, pins, and the like were taken. Apparently large items worth considerable amounts of money – such as sacks of grain, farm animals, furniture, carts, and wagons – were not taken. It may be that until the 1810s, most things that were stolen were for direct consumption, such as food and fodder items. After that more things were stolen that could be turned into cash, such as bedding, watches, jewels, and agricultural implements. And only from that time on was money itself stolen.

Table A.14 *Incidence of stealing*

| Item | 1770s | 80s | 90s | 1800s | 10s | 20s | 30s | 40s | 50s | 60s | Total |
|---|---|---|---|---|---|---|---|---|---|---|---|
| Cider | | | | | | | | | | 1 | 1 |
| Grain | | | | | 6 | 1 | | 1 | 1 | | 9 |
| Root crops | | | 3 | | 1 | | | 5 | 2 | | 11 |
| Grass | 6 | 4 | 3 | 4 | 1 | 2 | | 1 | | | 21 |
| Hay | | | | 1 | 3 | | | 1 | 1 | 2 | 8 |
| Straw | | | | | 2 | | 1 | 1 | | 1 | 5 |
| Vegetables | 5 | | 2 | | 1 | | | 1 | 1 | | 10 |
| Nuts | 1 | | | | | | | | | | 1 |
| Fruit | | | 1 | 1 | 4 | 2 | | 2 | 7 | | 17 |
| Food | | | | 3 | | 2 | | | 1 | | 6 |
| Manure | | | | | | | | 1 | | | 1 |
| Poultry | | | | | | | | 1 | | | 1 |
| Flax/hemp | | 1 | 2 | | | | | 3 | | | 6 |
| Yarn | | 1 | 2 | | | 2 | | | | | 5 |
| Cloth | | | | 1 | 1 | | 2 | 2 | 1 | | 7 |
| Sacks | | | 1 | | | | | | | | 1 |
| Clothes | | | 2 | 1 | 4 | 3 | | 3 | | | 13 |
| Bedding | | | | | 1 | 1 | | | | | 2 |
| Wool | | | | | | | | 1 | | | 1 |
| Agricultural wood | | | 1 | 1 | 2 | 1 | 1 | | 1 | 1 | 8 |
| Materials | | | 1 | 1 | 1 | 1 | 1 | 2 | | | 7 |
| Willow wands | | | | 1 | | 1 | 2 | | | | 4 |
| Firewood | | 1 | | 2 | | | 2 | | | | 5 |
| Agricultural tools | | | | 2 | 13 | 5 | | 2 | | 1 | 23 |
| Personal effects | | | | | 3 | 2 | 2 | 1 | | | 8 |
| Household goods | | | | | 2 | | | 1 | | 1 | 4 |
| Money | | | | | 6 | 1 | | 2 | | 1 | 10 |
| Total | 12 | 7 | 18 | 18 | 41 | 24 | 11 | 31 | 15 | 8 | |

## F. Distribution of property

It has been possible to analyze the distribution of wealth and its changes through the tax records from Neckarhausen.[21] The series begins in 1710 with three selected years (1710, 1720, 1730) and then for every year afterward, beginning in 1790. The simplest technique for measuring the distribution of taxable wealth in these registers is the Lorenz curve, which tells us what percentage of the population paid a particular percentage of the tax. I have analyzed the first three years of records and every fifth between 1790 and 1870. I found that over the whole period, there was practically no change in the distribution of wealth despite a population increase of about 350 percent (65 Bürger and widows in 1710, 228 in 1870). Producing all of the curves would make the graph unreadable, since they all cross each other. Therefore, I have given the two from the beginning and end of the series and the one in the middle. Those from 1710 and 1790 (236 percent increase in population) describe practically the same curve. Thereafter there is a slight tendency in the direction of inequality, but even by 1870, the change is not very great. One can see the difference best by looking at two points on the curves: the percentage of total tax paid by the lowest 50 percent of the taxpayers and that paid by the upper 10 percent (Table A.15).

Table A.15 *Distribution of wealth*

| Category | 1710 | 1790 | 1870 |
|---|---|---|---|
| Lower 50% | 16.5 | 18.2 | 13.8 |
| Upper 10% | 28.6 | 28.0 | 32.5 |

The first question to ask here is how representative are the tax figures for the holding of property and which people were excluded from the registers? In general, all household heads were represented, that is, all Bürger and widows. They had to pay a variety of taxes, one of which was the *Bürgersteuer*, which required each Bürger to pay 1 fl. and each widow to pay half as much. Therefore, every household head came into the register even if he or she had no property. Over the whole period, there was seldom anyone living in the village who was not a Bürger or part of a Bürger's family. Occasionally, someone lived in the village who was accorded "associate" (*Beisitzer*) status, and such people were duly listed in the tax registers. From the 1710 and 1790 registers, I have chosen to use the *ordinarii*, taxes based on a percentage of a taxpayer's wealth. In the eighteenth century, they were based on land and buildings but

[21] The tax records make up one volume of the *Gemeindepflegerechnungen: Steuerempfangs- und Abrechnungsbuch*.

after 1820 included an assessment of the value of crafts and trades.[22] After that the exact assessment of the value of land, buildings, and trades were given, and each item was taxed separately and at a different rate. I therefore took the total tax bill from these registers, which combined all the elements. Because of the nature of the tax, the curves given here measure not only the distribution of taxes but also that of immovable property, modified after 1820 by including a value placed on handicrafts.[23]

The number of taxpayers with no taxable property was negligible in the first two tax years – 1710, 4 cases; 1790, 3. In 1870, there were 32, although 11 of them did not live in Neckarhausen at the time, 3 were outsiders (pastor and two schoolteachers), 5 were widowed, 3 were old men, and 3 were unmarried men. The distribution of wealth in 1870 was affected by two extraordinarily wealthy villagers, one a miller, the other an innkeeper. Both were assessed at least twice as much as the third wealthiest man in the village.

The first conclusion from the curves is that the *structure* of wealth distribution had not changed a great deal over the course of the eighteenth and the first three-quarters of the nineteenth centuries. Nonetheless, the population as a whole had increased substantially and the number of people in any one category had increased proportionally. This is not the place to offer a detailed analysis of the formation of socioeconomic strata in the village, yet some knowledge of the processes at work would be useful. It would be particularly helpful to know (1) whether the kind of people represented in the class of "poor" changed (2) and what role a handicraft played in the position one held. (In Chapter 10, we dealt with the question of the distribution of landholding by age.)

**1.** To assess changes in the poor of the village, I have ranked each taxpayer according to the amount of tax paid. Along with information from the family reconstitution, this allows us to examine the marital status, sex, and age of the property-owning population according to the rank order of wealth – in this case divided into deciles.

In 1710, the tax list can by and large be used as a direct measurement of the wealth of villagers. The tax was based on the value of land and buildings and therefore failed to take into account profession, movable wealth, and other assets such as *rentes*. The rank of at least two individuals (the pastor and the schoolmaster) was radically distorted in this way. From several postmortem inventories, it is clear that the pastor was often the richest man in the village, but his wealth was contained in debt obligations, movables, and coins. In 1710, he was not included in the tax list at all. In 1790, the two pastors both appeared in the fifth decile. The schoolmaster received a wage from the village, had the use of some strips of land, received free wood, and could build up a position as landholder, and one even became Schultheiss. In any event, the tax register would not reflect his true standing, since it did not reflect his income. It was

[22] The first tax list I used with such an assessment was for 1825.

[23] But not profession as such. Bauern, pastors, schoolmasters, day-laborers, for example, were not taxed for their professions.

also possible for individual villagers to have a strip of land in a neighboring village, where they would be taxed on that land. There were severe limitations, however, which meant that land held elsewhere could not affect the pattern of wealth distribution found in the Neckarhausen tax registers substantially. People living in neighboring villages could in turn have a piece of land in the village territory, but no one individual ever had very much, and most of the incursions were on the edges of the village area. Few people would have found it useful to cross the whole village to work a strip of land. Furthermore, the right of village members to "redeem" a piece of land held by foreigners led to a constant reversal of strips into the hands of Neckarhausen inhabitants. In any event, the taxes studied here are those based on property holding by Neckarhausen inhabitants in the village. With the few reservations mentioned, the distribution of taxes, which are directly proportional to the assessed property, is the same as the distribution of immovable property.[24]

The majority of taxpayers were Bürger, that is, in principle, married male household heads. Out of 85 taxpayers in 1710, there were 67 Bürger, 11 widows, 1 Beisitzer, and 6 unmarried men and women. In the lowest decile, out of 8 people in the category, 4 were widows, 1 was an 86-year-old man, 1 was a Beisitzer, and another was a man whose age could not be determined. In the second decile, from 8, there were two sets of unmarried siblings and one widow. Thus the very poorest of the propertied were heavily weighted toward the old and widowed and people not yet arrived at Bürger status. The break is already apparent between the first and second decile. That widows in general came off relatively poorer can be seen by the fact that there is only 1 in the upper 50 percent and 10 in the lower 50 percent. The unmarried also cluster in the lower categories, with 1 sibling set in the top 50 percent and 2 unmarried women, 1 unmarried man, and 2 sibling sets in the bottom 50 percent.

The picture for 1790 is not much different from that of 1710. The basis for the tax assessment was the same. In all, there were 140 taxpayers: 113 married Bürger, 11 widows, 1 Beisitzer, 2 pastors, 1 schoolmaster, and 12 unmarried men and women. In the lowest decile, out of 14 taxpayers, 4 were widows, 2 were single males, 1 single female, 1 Beisitzer, and 2 old men. Here we find the same weighting of the hierarchy of wealth at the bottom by the elderly, widowed, and the not-yet-Bürger or married. As before, there is a break between decile 1 and 2. We find the same overall structure for widows as in 1710: Two were in the top while 9 were in the bottom half. In the top 50 percent there was 1 single male and no single females, while in the bottom 50 percent, there were 4 single males, 5 single females, and 1 sibling group.

Although the tax list from 1870 presents a few problems, it shows some significant structural changes. First, the tax was based on an assessment of land, buildings, and profession (handicraft or trade, not including the pastor and schoolmaster), and the register gives both the assessment and the tax.

[24] I used the one tax – the *ordinarius*.

There was no "summary" tax such as the ordinarius which we used to study the two earlier tax lists. Each kind of wealth was taxed separately and at a differential rate. Therefore, I have taken as a basis of my calculations the total tax paid by each taxpayer, a procedure which would have introduced considerable distortions for the earlier lists because various "nontax" items were included in the final tax bill, such as fees for sheepfold (Pförch) rights. The drawback for the 1870 calculations is that the total bill contained two different kinds of taxes – a small fixed Bürger or widow tax and proportional taxes based on the valuation of real property and handicrafts. Because the fixed tax was not very large – 1 fl. per resident Bürger and 30 kr. per widow and nonresident Bürger – it introduces little distortion in the series. However, taxes of more than 1 fl. enter only in the third decile. Since no one in the first two deciles paid the full Bürgersteuer and practically everyone in the remainder did, this helped swing the entire curve to the right, in the direction of inequality. If the Bürger and widow taxes had been deducted, the curve would have overlapped with the other two more closely, which means that as far as the distribution of wealth – the relative inequality and equality – is concerned, there was even less change over the whole period than the graph suggests.

In 1870, there were 284 taxpayers: 203 Bürger, 42 widows, 1 pastor, 3 schoolmasters, and 35 single men and women. The percentage of Bürger in the list had eroded somewhat – from about 80 percent to about 70 percent. In the lowest decile, from 27 people, there were 6 widows, 2 old men, 7 single women, and 6 single men. In the second decile, from 30, there were 2 widows, 3 old men, 8 single women, 5 single men, 1 sibling set, 2 schoolmasters, and 1 pastor. In the third decile, from 28, there were 9 widows, 9 old men, 3 unmarried women, 1 unmarried man, and 2 sets of unmarried siblings. In the fourth decile, there were 6 widows, 7 old men (over 70), and 2 unmarried men. The poorest of the tax-paying class was again weighted toward the widowed, the old, and the young unmarried. In this instance, a larger group of unmarried men and women with a little land or part of a house and barn appeared. In 1710, single women made up 2.4 percent of the taxpayers, in 1790, 3.6 percent, and in 1870, 6.7 percent. The same rates for single men are 1.2, 3.6, and 5.6 percent. The question is whether the increase is part of a structural change or simply one in the registration of land. After the revision of the Pfandgesetz in the 1820s, land which fell to children with a surviving parent was entered into the Unterpfandbuch as their property. However, that land still remained in the tax registers under the parent, who held the land in usufruct. Thus the increase in the parcels of land and portions of houses and barns in the hands of unmarried men and women is a reflection of bits of property that they purchased, that fell to them because both parents were dead, or that were passed on by a surviving parent. Again, however, few of the unmarried accumulated much property. In the upper 50 percent of taxpayers, there was 1 unmarried woman, while in the lower 50 percent there were 18 unmarried women, 15 unmarried men, and three sets of unmarried siblings. By contrast, the structure of property holding for widows had changed. In the upper half of taxpayers, there were now 17 widows compared to 25 in the lower half. The nineteenth century not only saw a relative and absolute rise in the number of widows in the population (1710, 12.9 percent of the taxpayers; 1790, 7.9 percent; 1870, 14.8 percent), it also witnessed a significant rise in the proportion holding substantial amounts of real estate. Since they were never assessed for a handicraft, their actual property holding was higher than the table shows. Nonetheless, even with these changes in the way widows held land and the fact that unmarried men and women appeared more prominently in the tax lists, the hold of married men on the total percentage of wealth did not change very much over time. The total amount of tax paid by all those who were not married Bürger was 1710, 17.19 percent; 1790, 15.55 percent; 1870, 14.69 percent. Even if we exclude the new mill owner and the rich pubkeeper from the calculations in 1870, the part of those not making up the class of married Bürger was not substantially different: 15.59 percent.

2. Villages such as Neckarhausen were not just "peasant" in the sense that all or most of their inhabitants depended for their livelihood on small farms. A considerable number of people had handicrafts which they sometimes exercised as full-time occupations, sometimes part-time, and often only for particular phases in the life cycle. Many handicrafts were seasonal or necessitated migration for parts of the year. In Württemberg, as in the cities, skilled crafts in the villages were based on apprenticeship and guild organization. For example, the masons in all of the villages in the Oberamt Nürtingen belonged to the central guild which controlled their promotion to the status of master. For most village artisans, the *Wanderjahr* was part of the process of becoming a master, which was completed at marriage.

The problem before us is to assess the place artisans had in the distribution of wealth in the village.[25] One cannot rely only on the occupational information provided in the tax lists, because of the problem of teknonymy. "Johannes Falter, carpenter" might simply be called this to distinguish him from some other Johannes Falter. The former most certainly had been trained as a carpenter but by the time of the tax list may have long since been engaged in agriculture full time. In order to examine this problem, I have combined family reconstitution information on occupation with the three tax registers and matched the professions in the village with the distribution of tax wealth.

In the 1710 tax list, occupation was only given four times: a cooper, a baker, a shoemaker, and a tailor. Not even the schoolmaster, for example, was noted as such. By combining family reconstitution information, I was able to assign an occupation to 41 of 63 males. Out of those, only 5 were found with two occupations: weaver and Bauer (twice), shepherd and Bauer, forest guard (*Waldschütz*)

[25] On the analysis of social class, see Wolfgang Kashuba and Carola Lipp, *Dörfliches Überleben. Zur Geschichte materieller und sozialer Reproduktion ländlicher Gesellschaft im 19. und frühen 20. Jahrhundert*, Untersuchungen des Ludwig-Uhland-Instituts der Universität Tübingen, vol. 56 (Tübingen, 1982), pp. 76 ff., 87–122.

Table A.16 *Occupations from all sources for men on the 1710 tax list*

| Not given | Agriculture | | Handicrafts | | Other | |
|---|---|---|---|---|---|---|
| 22 | Bauer | (14) | Cooper | (2) | Baker | (2) |
| | Shepherd[a] | ( 2) | Cleatmaker | (1) | Innkeeper | (1) |
| | | | Smith | (4) | Schoolmaster | (1) |
| | | | Cobbler | (1) | Soldier[b] | (2) |
| | | | Tailor | (2) | Forest guard[c] | (1) |
| | | | Weaver[d] | (7) | Gravedigger[e] | (3) |
| | | | Carpenter | (2) | | |
| Total 22 | | 16 | | 19 | | 10 |

[a] One was also Bauer.
[b] Trompeter, Reuter.
[c] Was also a day-laborer.
[d] Two were also Bauern.
[e] One was a soldier.

and day laborer, soldier and gravedigger. The breakdown of occupations is shown in Table A.16.

Most of the handicrafts were such that one had to learn them and exercise them as a master. Whether this was the case with weavers is not clear, but the frequency with which Bauern took up or dropped the profession suggests that it was a casual occupation for many people. Occasionally individuals were called *Leineweber* (linen weavers), which may have designated someone subject to guild supervision, entry fees, and full-fledged apprenticeship. It is conceivable that most of the occupations were exercised to some degree by the people on the tax list in 1710, although it is clear from later evidence that many people failed to follow their learned handicraft throughout their lives. In the case of the three gravediggers, they held the job at different times, and the information is recovered from later sources. Most of the people who were never labeled in any records with some kind of occupation were probably primarily engaged in agriculture, either as peasant producers or as farm laborers. Included in that group were two Schultheissen, who were usually among the wealthiest Bauern in the village. Many individuals served at one time or another on the village court or council or held the post of Bürgermeister or Schultheiss. Election to any of these posts carried lifetime tenure. Their position in the occupational and economic hierarchies is shown in Table A.17. Of the officeholders, 1 came from the Bauer group, 5 from "Not given," and 7 from the artisans. The artisans accounted for about one-third of the male tax payers (32.8 percent), and about half of the offices.

We can further divide the taxpayers into quartile groups to see where the occupations are located (Table A.18). There are several things to note here.

Table A.17 *Tax by occupation, 1710*

| | Bauern | Not given | Artisans | Officeholders |
|---|---|---|---|---|
| Total number | 14 | 22 | 22[a] | 13 |
| Total tax[b] | 5,349 | 7,595 | 5,850 | 6,149 |
| Mean tax/head | 382 | 345 | 266 | 573 |

[a] Includes the innkeeper and two bakers.
[b] In heller.

Table A.18 *Distribution of occupations by tax bracket, 1710 (quartiles)*

| Occupation | Total | I | II | III | IV |
|---|---|---|---|---|---|
| Bauern | 14 | 0 | 4 | 5 | 5 |
| Artisans | 22 | 5 | 4 | 9 | 4 |
| Not given | 22 | 3 | 6 | 4 | 9 |
| Total | 58 | 8 | 14 | 18 | 18 |
| Officeholders | 13 | 1 | 0 | 4 | 8 |

The artisans are distributed over the whole range, with 64 percent in the two top quartiles (compared with 71 percent for Bauern). Their heaviest representation, however, is in the third quartile, while the Bauern are more evenly distributed over the top three. Other agriculturalists from the "Not given" category, however, would shift the leadership to the fourth quartile for the independent landed proprietors. Exactly how to interpret the picture is not clear. One cannot judge from the information what part of the tax was based on land and what on buildings. The property structure of the innkeeper, who figures in the uppermost quartile, may well have been tipped toward buildings. For the rest, the higher an artisan appears in the list, the more likely it is that he had considerable land and carried on some agriculture. The supplemental income from a craft may well have allowed an artisan with less land to compete in living standard with full-time agriculturalists. In any event, they were able to play a significant role in officeholding in the village. While the Schultheiss came from the more well-to-do class of landed proprietors, at least 2 of the 4 men who held the office of Bürgermeister during the period were artisans. An overall view of the Bürger would look something like this: a small group at the bottom of artisans and farm laborers. Four of the five artisans in this class were weavers (although the two Leineweber were in quartiles III and IV). Above these were a group of small landholders, some of whom were called "Bauer" in

Table A.19 *Occupations from all sources for men on the 1790 tax list*

| Not given | Agriculture | Handicraft | Village servants | Food services | Handicraft/ Agriculture | Other |
|---|---|---|---|---|---|---|
| 2 | Bauer (41) | Cooper (2) | 10[a] | Baker[b] (3) | Weaver/Bauer (10) | Pastor (2) |
| | Day-laborer (3) | Mason (2) | | Butcher (1) | Tailor/Bauer (1) | Schoolmaster (1) |
| | Shepherd (1) | Smith[c] (3) | | Butcher/ innkeeper (1) | Weaver/labor (1) | Bauer[d] (1) |
| | Bauer/day laborer (5) | Tailor (6) | | Butcher/ Bauer[e] (1) | | |
| | | Cobbler (2) | | Innkeeper/Bauer/ labor/trader (1) | | |
| | | Weaver (10) | | Innkeeper/ soldier (1) | | |
| | | Wheelwright (2) | | | | |
| | | Carpenter (4) | | | | |
| | | Brickmaker (1) | | | | |
| Total 2 | 50 | 32 | 10 | 9 | 12 | 4 |

[a] The village servants held a variety of positions, often going from one to the other: field guard (*Feldschütz*), baliff (*Flecken-(Dorf-)schütz*), horse herder, harvest guard (*Güterschütz*), forest guard (*Waldschütz*), gravedigger. These were combined with some of the other occupations: Bauer, day-laborer, weaver, tailor.

[b] One was also Bauer.

[c] One was also soldier.

[d] Was also a local tax collector (*Zoller*).

[e] Was also a soldier.

Table A.20 *Tax by occupation, 1790*

| | Bauer | Food service | Bauer/weaver | Handicraft | Village servant | Day-laborer | | Officeholders |
|---|---|---|---|---|---|---|---|---|
| Number | 41 | 9 | 10 | 32 | 10 | 11 | . | 23 |
| Total tax | 23,820 | 5,082 | 4,507 | 7,318 | 1,931 | 1,831 | . | 16,278 |
| Mean tax/head | 581 | 565 | 451 | 229 | 193 | 166 | . | 708 |

various sources. With the third quartile, we encounter the middle range of property holders in the village, equally represented by agriculturalists and artisans. At the top were small group of artisans (including the innkeeper) and a much larger group of agriculturalists.

In the 1790 tax list, occupation was given for 53 out of 119 males, for the most part only for artisans and the pastor, schoolmaster, shepherd, and some of the innkeepers (Table A.19). The occupations of day-laborers and Bauern were not noted. By combining family reconstitution information with the tax lists, however, we can assign occupations to all but two of the taxpayers (who were unmarried in 1790 and subsequently emigrated). Taking all of the sources together, 41 persons were assigned only the occupation "Bauer." Another 40 were given single occupations, mostly artisans of various kinds. Thirty-seven others in the course of their lifetimes were assigned more than one occupational category (Table A.20).

Artisans with a single occupation and not including the innkeepers and bakers accounted for less than one-third of the population (26.9 percent). They held only 2 of the 23 offices. If one adds all of the innkeepers and bakers, they account for about one-third (34.5 percent) of the taxpayers and 3 more of the offices. The Bauern who have no other occupation accounted for 13 of the offices and 34.5 percent of the population. Adding the weaver/Bauern accounts for an additional office and 43 percent of the population.

The distribution of occupations obtained after dividing the taxpayers into quartile groups is given in Table A.21. In contrast to 1710, artisans fall most heavily in the second quartile and had only 32.4 percent of their numbers in the top two quartiles. Bauern have been able to increase their position from 71 to 85.4 percent in the two top quartiles. The innkeepers and the weaver/Bauern also throw their weight toward the top. In 1710, on average, artisans held 69.6 percent as much taxable wealth as Bauern, while in 1790, they had fallen to 39.4 percent – a decline of well over 50 percent. In general, in comparison with 1710, there was a stronger expression of strata. At the bottom were a few

Table A.21 *Distribution of occupations by tax bracket, 1790 (quartiles)*

| Occupation | Total | I | II | III | IV |
|---|---|---|---|---|---|
| Bauer | 41 | 3 | 3 | 12 | 23 |
| Handicraft | 34 | 8 | 15 | 8 | 3 |
| Weaver/Bauer | 10 | 0 | 2 | 3 | 5 |
| Food service | 9 | 1 | 2 | 2 | 4 |
| Day-laborer | 16 | 8 | 6 | 1 | 1 |
| Village servant | 10 | 4 | 2 | 4 | 0 |
| Total | 120 | 24 | 30 | 30 | 36 |
| Officeholders | 23 | 0 | 0 | 4 | 19 |

artisans, some farm laborers, and some of the village servants. Just above them were a large group of artisans together with some of the day-laborers. The next group also contained a strong component of artisans who were outnumbered by Bauern. At the top, the landed agriculturalists clearly dominated the village, with a few innkeepers adding strength to their numbers. In 1790, the Bauern held most of the offices, with the officeholders more frequently from the highest quartile of taxpayers and the artisans practically excluded. In 1710, the artisans (including the innkeeper) held 29 percent of the entire wealth of the village (25.5 excluding the innkeepers). In 1790, they (not including the innkeepers) had only 14.8 percent of the entire immovable wealth (including 4 innkeepers, 20.3 percent). The *Bauern* and "Not given" in 1710 had 54.5 percent of the wealth, while in 1790, they had 48.3 percent. Together with the weaver/Bauern, they had 57.4 percent.

In the 1870 tax list, occupation was given for 170 of the 206 male taxpayers, and this time, 36 of the 49 Bauern were labeled as such. Again, by combining family reconstitution data with the tax lists, occupations could be assigned to almost all of the men (193 of the 206). Most of the 13 taxpayers with no assignable occupation in 1870 were not yet married (11). Since the family reconstitution stops with the year 1869, the information gathered from the entire lifespan of most individuals could not be collated with the tax list. Thus we only have information about who was a factory worker, farm laborer, or council

Table A.22 *Occupations from all sources for men on the 1870 tax list*

| Not given | Agriculture | Single handicraft | Food services |
|---|---|---|---|
| 13 | Bauern (49) | Bleacher (2) | Innkeeper/Bauer (1) |
| | Ackerbürger[a] (1) | Cooper (2) | Innkeeper/baker (2) |
| | Day-laborer (2) | Tinker (1) | Baker/Bauer (2) |
| | Shepherd (6) | Plasterer (1) | Innkeeper/cooper (1) |
| | Shepherd/ Bauer (1) | Mason (9) | Innkeeper/ butcher (1) |
| | Bauer/laborer (1) | Ropemaker (1) | Butcher (1) |
| | | Tailor (6) | Miller (1) |
| | | Cobbler (12) | |
| | | Smith (3) | |
| | | Pursemaker (1) | |
| | | Joiner (2) | |
| | | Stonemason (7) | |
| | | Dyer (2) | |
| | | Paver (3) | |
| | | Wheelwright (5) | |
| | | Weaver (8) | |
| | | Carpenter (6) | |
| Total 13 | 60 | 71 | 9 |

Table A.22 *(cont.)*

| Handicraft/ handicraft | Handicraft/ agriculture | Workers | Other |
|---|---|---|---|
| Weaver/ bleacher (2) | Weaver/ Bauer (16) | Factory (9) | Administrator (1) |
| Weaver/smith (1) | Dyer/ Bauer (1) | Factory/ tailor (1) | Pastor (1) |
| Weaver/ mason (1) | Dyer/ laborer (1) | Factory/ laborer (1) | District officer (1) |
| Mason/ stonemason (1) | Bleacher/ Bauer (3) | Factory/Bauer/ bailiff (1) | Bailiff/weaver (1) |
| | Stonemason/ Bauer (1) | Railway/ cobbler (1) | Bailiff/Bauer/ weaver (1) |
| | Mason/ Bauer (1) | Railway/ laborer (1) | |
| | Smith/ Bauer (1) | Factory/weaver/ laborer/ bailiff (1) | |
| | Tailor/ Bauer (1) | Factory/Bauer/ weaver (1) | |
| | Weaver/ Bauer/ laborer (1) | Factory/ dyer (2) | |
| Total 5 | 26 | 18 | 5 |

[a] In this case, a relatively poor Bauer.

Table A.23 *Tax by occupation, 1870*

| | Bauer | Food service | Weaver/ Bauer | Handicraft | Worker[a] | Officeholder |
|---|---|---|---|---|---|---|
| Number | 49 | 9 (10)[b] | 16 | 71 | 20 | 22 |
| Total tax | 138,309 | 32,709 (44,817) | 47,862 | 80,706 | 12,923 | 12,923 |
| Mean tax/ head | 2,823 | 3,634 (4,482) | 2,991 | 1,137 | 646 | 3,684 |

[a] Excludes two railway workers and includes two dyers.
[b] Including the second wealthiest man in the village.

member up to 1870. With this information, we find 49 men given the single occupation "Bauer" and 94 others single occupations, mostly artisans. Over the course of their lives up to 1870, 60 men were given more than one occupation. The category of village servant is not included in Table A.22, not because there were fewer of them – there were in fact more (the street cleaner, fountain cleaner, highway repairman, etc.) – but because it became unusual to list such occupations in the baptism, marriage, burial, and tax records.

Artisans with single occupations, not including innkeepers and bakers, comprised 34.5 percent of the male tax paying population in 1870 (an increase of 28.3 percent). They held only 2 of the 22 offices. The Bauern with no other occupations made up 23.8 percent of the population (a decline of 34.5 percent) and accounted for 11 offices. Adding the weaver/Bauern brings their share in the total to 31.8 percent (a decline of 26.0 percent) and accounts for 16 of the offices (an increase of 14.3 percent). Altogether, 19 of the 22 offices were held by Bauern or Bauern with other occupations (5 weavers, 1 bleacher, 1 baker, and 1 shepherd).

Wealth distribution by occupation is shown in Table A.24. The artisans are relatively evenly distributed among the first three quartiles, with a good representation in the third. Just about half of that group (49.3 percent) is in the top two quartiles, a substantial increase from 1790. With 85.7 percent of the Bauern in the top two quartiles, that occupation retained its structural position over the century. Similarly, the innkeepers and weaver/Bauern are close to the top. The strata are again fairly clear, with some shifts from 1790. At the bottom are a large group of artisans. Above them are factory workers, a few small agriculturalists, and another large group of artisans. The next stratum is dominated by solid artisans and has a small group of Bauern. At the top of the pyramid, we find Bauern, who also have most of the offices in their hands. There are also a few well-to-do artisans and innkeepers. Altogether, the artisans held 18.8 percent of the wealth, a few percentage points more than in

Table A.24 *Distribution of occupations by tax bracket, 1870 (quartiles)*

| Occupation | Total | I | II | III | IV |
|---|---|---|---|---|---|
| Bauern | 49 | 1 | 6 | 13 | 29 |
| Weaver/Bauer | 16 | 0 | 0 | 3 | 13 |
| Single handicraft | 71 | 16 | 20 | 26 | 9 |
| Handicraft + other occupations | 26 | 5 | 8 | 10 | 3 |
| Food service | 8 | 1 | 0 | 1 | 6 |
| Factory worker | 9 | 2 | 7 | 0 | 0 |
| Worker/agriculture | 4 | 0 | 3 | 1 | 0 |
| Miller | 1 | 0 | 0 | 0 | 1 |
| Officeholders | 22 | 0 | 1 | 4 | 16 |

1790, but distributed among 71 instead of 32 individuals (Table A.23).[26] Moreover, since part of their taxable wealth in 1870 was based on the handicrafts as such, their total share in the immovable wealth probably declined somewhat. The Bauern had 32.3 percent, or with the weaver/Bauern, 43.5 percent of the total tax-producing wealth of the village, a relative decline which reflects the rise of innkeepers and the establishment of a mill. In the course of the nineteenth century, the class structure of the village was increasingly pronounced. A smaller percentage of villagers was able to maintain itself by agriculture alone and there were proportionally and absolutely more artisans in the village, with unskilled and factory workers beginning to play a small but increasing role. With all of the changes, the landed members of the community solidified their grasp on power.

The tax list of 1870 allows a new kind of analysis not available for the earlier two. Since land, buildings, and profession were evaluated and taxed separately, we can ask if nonagriculturalists had any land and what the balance between land and buildings was for each group. Because the valuations of land and buildings were on completely different scales, the difference between groups can best be estimated by constructing ratios (Table A.25). The average artisan had 33.4 percent as much land as the average Bauer, while the average villager in food services had 22.8 percent more. The average factory hand had 12.0 percent as much land as the average peasant. None of this says anything about the economy of the peasant, laborer, or artisan. It is clear that the laborers had little land, and that to a degree much greater than in other groups, their wealth

Table A.25 *Relation between holdings in land and buildings by occupation, 1870*

| Occupation | Number | Total land valuation | Mean | Total building valuation | Mean | Ratio of land to buildings |
|---|---|---|---|---|---|---|
| Bauern | 49 | 2,537 | 51.8 | 23,349 | 476.5 | 1:9 |
| Weaver/ Bauern | 16 | 875 | 54.7 | 7,066 | 441.6 | 1:8 |
| Single craft | 71 | 1,230 | 17.3 | 16,858 | 237.4 | 1:14 |
| 1+ craft | 29 | 414 | 14.3 | 6,340 | 218.6 | 1:15 |
| Food service | 8 | 509 | 63.6 | 6,274 | 784.3 | 1:12 |
| Factory worker | 9 | 56 | 6.2 | 1,393 | 154.8 | 1:25 |
| Not given | 13 | 64 | 4.9 | 738 | 56.8 | 1:12 |

[26] If we add multiple occupations to the list (except for weaver/Bauern), the relative figures are 38 and 85, in either case an increase of more than 120 percent between 1790 and 1870.

was in buildings, probably lodgings, a few rooms and shed space inherited from the family. We have seen that exercise of a handicraft was frequently carried on by individuals in the early phase of the life cycle, and that wealth accumulated with age. It appears from Table A.25 that immovable wealth in the early years of marriage was probably disproportionately in buildings and that accumulation was largely a matter of adding strips of land.

Some of the artisans were absent from the village and only paid a half Bürger tax. And many of the artisans listed in the tax register were in fact not taxed for their craft, which indicates that they were not carrying it on in that year. In this table, we see a substantial proportion of artisans (37.1 percent) living in the village who were not practicing their crafts. Many sons of landed proprietors went through a life cycle phase as artisans. Others remained in a craft and reproduced themselves. Most children of craft producers also became craftsmen – although not frequently in the same branch of industry. Some were able to accumulate enough land to become peasant producers, or at least to balance their craft with agricultural production. A certain proportion of artisans, especially those relatively young, were more or less permanently work-

Table A.26 *Occupations listed and valuated in the tax register, 1870*

| Occupation | Single craft | Multiple craft | Total | Valued | Not valued | Not valued and not in village |
|---|---|---|---|---|---|---|
| Bleacher | 1 | 2 | 3 | 0 | 2 | 1 |
| Cooper | 2 | | 2 | 1 | 1 | |
| Tinker | 1 | | 1 | 1 | | |
| Plasterer[a] | 1 | | 1 | 1 | | |
| Mason | 8 | 4 | 12 | 10 | 2 | |
| Ropemaker | 1 | | 1 | | 1 | |
| Tailor | 6 | 2 | 8 | 5 | 1 | 2 |
| Cobbler | 12 | | 12 | 8 | 3 | 1 |
| Smith | 3 | 1 | 4 | 2 | 1 | 1 |
| Pursemaker | 1 | | 1 | | 1 | |
| Joiner | 2 | | 2 | 2 | | |
| Stonemason | 7 | 1 | 8 | 2 | 4 | 2 |
| Dyer | 1 | 1 | 2 | 0 | 2 | |
| Paver[b] | 3 | | 3 | 3 | | |
| Wheelwright | 5 | | 5 | 4 | 1 | |
| Weaver | 7 | 18 | 25 | 8 | 16 | 1 |
| Carpenter | 6 | | 6 | 5 | 1 | |
| Weaver/smith | 1 | 1 | 1 | | | |
| Total | 68[c] | 30 | 97 | 52 | 36 | 8 |

[a] *Ipser.*
[b] *Pflästerer.*
[c] This table gives only occupations which are expressly noted in the register.

ing in other towns and villages, taking their families with them if they were married. Since they had hopes of returning, they maintained their citizenship rights in the village, paying half the Bürger tax and holding little if any property there.

## G. Marriage contracts

This appendix presents a summary of all of the marriage contracts (*Pacten*) found in the postmortem inventories. In 1679, Georg Klein, widower, and his wife Agnesa, the widow of Zachar Hai from Kohlberg, made a pact two years after they were married.[27] According to its terms, the property he brought into the marriage would fall to his children. If his two stepchildren proved obedient and diligently helped work his land until they married, then they would each get a strip of arable and meadowland. In turn, her children were to pay the interest on 50 fl. capital to him after her decease for the rest of his life. The pact in 1729 between the widower Jacob Geiger, Bürgermeister, and Anna Elisabetha, widow of David Böbel, and earlier widow of Michael Hess, Schultheiss, was meant to protect the rights of their five married children.[28] While remaining in full ownership, she had given her children some property in usufruct, none of which was to come under the administration of her new husband.[29] Before the widower Rudolph Schober married the widow Veronica Häfner in 1732, they made a pact in the presence of their relatives.[30] Everything was gotten from "their mouths" onto paper. Both were to love each other, display faithfulness, and to do everything with love and unity. The husband was to support the wife in food and clothing even in sickness and to pay for her burial should she predecease him. She was not to suffer any loss of her marriage portion nor was he to inherit anything from her estate. If she survived him, she was to receive her Beibringen, half the acquisitions, and 50 fl. cash. In 1746, the widower Johann Martin Zeug and his third wife made a similar contract.[31] In 1759, old Johann Georg Waldner, Bauer and widower, married Anna, the widow of Johann Georg Vogel From Oberboihingen.[32] She was to bring her clothes and 200 fl. into the marriage and both would share any acquisitions or losses. Each would inherit only 50 fl. from the other, and she would have lifetime rights to live in his house. For the rest, their closest relations would inherit by the rules of intestate law. The same year the widower Jacob Geiger, pubkeeper, married Catherina, the widow of Jacob Walcker, Schultheiss in Degerschlacht.[33] Before the wedding, they assembled with their

[27] *Inventuren und Teilungen*, 220 (21.11.1679).
[28] *Inventuren und Teilungen*, 509 (29.11.1729).
[29] See Chapter 9.
[30] *Inventuren und Teilungen*, 542 (9.1.1733).
[31] See Chapter 9.
[32] *Inventuren und Teilungen*, 815 (16.1.1759).
[33] *Inventuren und Teilungen*, 840 (15.1.1759).

"closest relations" and children to make a Pactum which would regulate the inheritance were they to have no children. She was obligated to bring her movables and 200 fl. in cash and 15 fl. annual rent from property held by her son-in-law. They would share gains and losses, she inheriting 100 fl. from him and he, 50 fl. from her. Johann Georg and Barbara Bosch in 1768 agreed that the inheritance would take place by the rules of intestacy (*nach Landrecht*).[34] Should her husband die first, Barbara would inherit 100 fl. from his property and maintain the right to live in the house unless she remarried. He had an expectation of 50 fl. In addition, he would suffer all gains and losses to the collective property. In 1782, reference was made to a Heiratspactum from 1767 whereby Johannes Kittelberger was to receive 50 fl. in the event of his wife's death.[35] They were to share acquisitions and losses. Johannes Häfner, widowered Richter, married Anna Maria Pfau, a widow from Tischardt (1784).[36] From the *communio bonorum*, each was to share half the gains or losses but had no claim to the other's allatum. She could live in the house if she did not remarry. He married again a year after her death and agreed that his new wife, Barbara, was not to share in any gains or losses.[37] She would take 100 fl. from his property, and he, 50 fl. from hers. In 1795, however, he made a testament leaving small legacies to various relatives but made her the universal heir of his property because of her love and daily goodness (*Wohltaten*) to him. For the final example in the eighteenth century, Johannes Häfner, Richter and Waldmeister, had made a Pactum with his wife, Anna Barbara, whereby she would not share in any gains or losses.[38] In the only case I have found for the nineteenth century, the 64-year-old widowered Michael Falter made a marriage contract (*Ehevertrag*) with the unmarried daughter of Johann Ebinger, Anna Maria, 56.[39] Should he die first, she was to inherit everything without any inventory being undertaken. Should she predecease him, he would only keep her property in usufruct for his lifetime and would have to put up security. After his death, everything would go to the collateral heirs (*Seitenverwandten*). All losses would be deducted from his property alone.

## H. Testaments

In this appendix, I summarize all of the wills in the postmortem inventories by 50-year periods. Johann Trautwein and his wife made a mutual will in 1615.[40] He had three legal heirs, the children of his deceased brother, and she was a childless widow. They themselves did not expect to produce heirs. Since her

[34] *Inventuren und Teilungen*, 943 (22.12.1768).
[35] *Inventuren und Teilungen*, 1067 (2.12.1782); *Pactum* dated 14.1.1767.
[36] *Inventuren und Teilungen*, 1094 (22.3.1784).
[37] *Inventuren und Teilungen*, 1099 (30.7.1785).
[38] *Inventuren und Teilungen*, 1141 (25.10.1790).
[39] *Inventuren und Teilungen*, 2024 (5.9.1849).
[40] *Inventuren und Teilungen*, 76 (23.10.1657); testament dated 1615.

parents-in-law had left everything to her and he had no living ascendants, they were able to determine their own property completely. They each specified that upon the decease of one of them, the other was to have half of the whole property to use, or sell, or give away as he or she wished, and half in usufruct for life. After the latter's death, the property in use was to fall back to the legal heirs. Jacob Hoess in 1635 noted that he and his wife had no children and that he had no heirs in the ascending *Linea*, and that therefore he had the sole authority over his property (*aigentumliches Vermögen*).[41] He left all his movables and certain specific fields to his wife, with some land going to his "lieben" sister. Johann Sterr in 1635 was living with his niece's (*Schwestertochter*) husband in the nearby village of Grötzingen.[42] He specified that she was to get 300 fl., and that his brother's son (*Bruderskind*) was to get 100 fl. off the top. They were also to get a regular intestate share. Michel Hermann in 1637 wanted to create an extra share (*Voraus*) for his wife.[43] She would have the choice of the horse or the cow. Some grain was also to go to the poor. Friederich Clewer noted that his dead brother's son was also deceased, having left a small daughter.[44] The brother and son had owed Friederich 200 fl. for a house, and he wanted to erase the orphan's debt. He left her the top blanket from his bed and three under blankets to another niece. At the time, he was being cared for by his stepdaughter, to whom he then gave 100 fl. in return for a rent of 10 fl. until his death, as long as she continued to support him. Earlier (1628), he had made a will leaving his aged father a *Pflichteil* and stating that in three marriages he had had no children.[45] His present wife was to have all his property for her lifetime, after which it was to fall to his siblings or their children. She also made a will then, stressing that her husband helped her with her house and fieldwork because she had trouble walking, while her siblings and kin had not helped or cared for her or offered her any solace. Therefore she left everything to her husband. In 1648, Maria, the widow of Georg Laubengeyer, left a few strips of land to Georg Klein because of his daily favors and good deeds.[46] Klein's daughter was to get a coat and under blanket. The rest of the small property was to go to the widow's intestate heirs.

In 1662, Georg Rieth, the Schultheiss, and his wife, both childless, made a mutual testament allowing each other lifelong use of the survivor's property.[47] Judith, the wife of Adam Schmohl, left her entire estate after deduction of her husband's inheritance portion to a cousin (*Vetter*) and the three children of Laux Wurm because of the good deeds and faithfulness of their mother to her.[48] Jacob Beckh after an illness in 1673 in which he had been tended by his

41 *Inventuren und Teilungen*, 116 (16.7.1650).
42 *Inventuren und Teilungen*, 15 (15.12.1635).
43 *Inventuren und Teilungen*, 24 (11.5.1636); *legatum* dated 18.4.1637.
44 *Inventuren und Teilungen*, 63 (6.12.1652).
45 *Inventuren und Teilungen*, 63 (6.12.1652).
46 *Inventuren und Teilungen*, 83 (25.7.1658).
47 *Inventuren und Teilungen*, 94 (10.11.1662).
48 *Inventuren und Teilungen*, 224 (27.6.1685).

wife, left her an extra portion of land.[49] The rest was to go by intestate inheritance rules to his grandson. Hans Barthlome had no children of his own.[50] In 1676, he left a Voraus for his stepdaughter and her five children, one of which he himself had raised. He also left 10 fl. for his "lieben" sister who lived across the Rhine, but if she was not heard from, the sum was to fall to his stepdaughter's husband. The rest of his property was to go to his "freundlich lieben Stiefftochtermann," (friendly dear stepson-in-law) who was to care for Barthlome's wife as his closest in-law (*nächsten Schwieger*). The widow Margaretha Zeug in 1679 wanted a few extra pieces of furniture to go to her son Melchior and his wife Catharina for their unstinting diligence in caring for her in her long illness.[51] Everything else was to go by intestate law. In 1683, Elisabetha Beck left a small advantage to her son over her daughter because he would have to take care of her fieldwork.[52] The widow Barbara Speidel in 1684 was concerned to make sure that her two unmarried children, because of their obedience and good deeds, did not get less than the other children.[53] They were to have a few movables, but the rest of the estate was to pass by intestate law. Anna Elisabetha, the wife of the Schultheiss Michael Hess, in 1687 specified that certain properties were to go to her deceased brother's children and the rest of her goods to her "lieben" husband.[54] In 1693, the widow Anna Maria Rentzler wanted two of her children, who had demonstrated many filial good deeds, to share above the normal inheritance portion half the house and barn, three strips of land, a horse and cow, and all the bedding, linen, and furniture.[55] When she died, the officials said that the testament had given away much too much for the present state of the property and ordered that it be divided in eight equal portions for all the children.

The widow Agatha Rieth died in 1709, leaving a son, Hans Georg Grauer, and four children of another son, Andreas, as heirs.[56] Hans Georg explained that his mother had left everything to him and produced a document written by the schoolmaster in Grossbettlingen where he lived, describing her having taken refuge with him. The officials noted that everyone knew that the widow had helped her son Andreas build his house with the promise that she could live there for the rest of her life. When she tried to move in, everything turned out otherwise. They kicked her out (*mit Füssen von sich gestossen*), and she had to earn her living among strangers and pay rent for 20 years into her weak old age. When she could no longer support herself, she took refuge with her other son where she was cared for until her death. But because the document lacked the proper "solemnities," it was ignored. In 1715, Hans Conrad Hess and his

[49] *Inventuren und Teilungen*, 194 (21.1.1681).
[50] *Inventuren und Teilungen*, 177 (6.5.1676).
[51] *Inventuren und Teilungen*, 225 (–.–.1679).
[52] *Inventuren und Teilungen*, 210 (10.4.1685).
[53] *Inventuren und Teilungen*, 218 (–.–.1684).
[54] *Inventuren und Teilungen*, 263 (11.1.1695).
[55] *Inventuren und Teilungen*, 213 (–.–.1693).
[56] *Inventuren und Teilungen*, 343 (21.10.1709).

wife Anna made a mutual will after 19 years of marriage with no issue.[57] They made each other "universal" heirs, which meant that the survivor would have usufruct for life, after which the estate would revert to the heirs, namely the siblings by stem. The survivor was not allowed to be wasteful. In 1731, Michael Hauer, who was very sick, and his wife, neither of whom had had children, made a mutual will.[58] "They both describe how their marital affection towards each other has lasted for a long time, and how they cannot avoid taking it to their hearts and have taken thought about how they can reward each other." The survivor was to have the estate for lifetime enjoyment and could use it up if necessary, as long as there was no swindling or wasteful living. Besides his wife, his heirs were two brothers and a sister, who was living somewhere outside Württemberg, but no one knew where. After his wife's death, her inheritance was to be held until such time as the sister must be dead, and then to fall to the other siblings.

Johannes Sterr, who had been married four times, wrote a document by hand leaving the daughter who had cared for him in his illness an extra 30 fl.[59] Before Salomon Falter, mousquetier, went off with the army – to die at the battle of Lüthen – he and his wife made each other "universal" heirs of the whole property, expressly excluding everyone else.[60] Mathes Hermann, Bauer, made a testament in 1761, leaving legacies to his sister in Grötzingen (50 fl.), to his dead brother's two daughters (10 fl. together), and to the orphanage in Stuttgart (1 fl.). Since he had no ascendants or descendants, he left his entire property to his wife to use as she wished. Should she die intestate, then half of what he left was to revert to his collateral line.[61] The 72-year-old Rebecca Bauknecht made a will in 1781, leaving various amounts to close relatives, including her godchild, but also making a small bequest of 5 fl. to the woman who took care of her.[62] Two years later, she changed her will, since she now was being cared for by a "blood relative" (*Blutsfreund*), her cousin (*Base*), Johann Falter's wife. The Falters were left a meadow. Anna Maria Häfner (née Pfau) made her husband her universal heir, leaving bequests to various collateral heirs, all of them cousins, children or children-in-law of her mother's brother.[63] Jacob Häfner, Bauer, had lived with his wife in 40 years of "peaceful" (*friedliche*) marriage and had no direct heirs (*Leibeserben*).[64] He excluded his long-lost brother and sister who had gone to the New World and left half of his estate to his sibling's children and grandchildren – five of them by head – although his wife was to have use-rights until her death. A year later, when his widow died,

[57] *Inventuren und Teilungen*, 380 (–.–.1717).
[58] *Inventuren und Teilungen*, 539 (21.1.1731).
[59] *Inventuren und Teilungen*, 766 (17.11.1755).
[60] *Inventuren und Teilungen*, 813 (20.5.1758). The actual testament is not there.
[61] *Inventuren und Teilungen*, 940 (3.2.1768); testament dated 27.1.1761.
[62] *Inventuren und Teilungen*, 1089 (18.10.1783); the first testament was dated 6.3.1781, and the second, 20.6.1783.
[63] *Inventuren und Teilungen*, 1099 (5.7.1786); testament dated 30.6.1783.
[64] *Inventuren und Teilungen*, 1100 (6.7.1786); testament dated 15.6.1786.

she left all of the bedding and her clothing to her brother's daughter who had cared for her during her illness.[65] Barbara Bosch (née Arnold) had no direct heirs.[66] She left 5 fl. to the village poor relief fund and specific sums to her sister and sister's son. Her husband (Johann Georg Bosch) had demonstrated faithfulness and love in 19 years of marriage, so she added 50 fl. to what he would receive according to the marriage contract. All the rest was to go to her three brothers or their direct heirs. Somewhat later, Barbara changed her will, noting that her sister's son had disappeared. His designated portion was to go to her brother's daughter who at present was taking care of her. Margaretha Häfner, the widow of Johannes, Richter, noted that her sister's son, Jacob Schober, disappeared in 1772, leaving a daughter in Nürtingen.[67] Her estate was to be held for Schober to provide for him in case he returned home. In the event of his death, the property was to fall to his daughter.

In 1801, Maria, the widow of Nicolaus Vogler, specified that all of her property was to be divided among her children in five equal portions, but the inheritance of her deceased daughter in Nürtingen was to be held in guardianship by the authorities in Neckarhausen, with their father receiving the interest until the children reached adulthood.[68] The 78-year-old retired soldier, Michael Zeug, left everything to the children of his stepmother, Maria Catharina Murr.[69] Because of an incorrectness of form, a niece (sister's daughter) challenged the will, whereupon Maria Catherina put in a bill for 20 years of care. After arbitration, the niece took away 19 fl., about 15 percent of the estate. Rebecca Bauknecht (née Falter) had been married for only half a year and during that time had taken sick and returned from Wolfschlugen to her father.[70] She left the poor relief fund 3 fl., reduced her husband's legacy to the obligatory portion, and made over the rest to her other heirs, her father, and two sisters. Christina, the widow of Matheus Schober, butcher and Bauer, privileged the daughter who cared for her during her illness 40 fl.[71] Juliana, widow of Jacob Eberwein, upon the marriage to her new husband Michael Walker, brickmaker (*Ziegler*), made a testament leaving 25 fl. each to a brother and sister, but disinherited another brother because of his constant abuse in favor of the latter's son, who got 10 fl.[72] Small bequests were made to the village poor (2 fl.) and the orphanage in Stuttgart (2 fl.). The rest was to go to her husband in full ownership. Catharina, widow of the Schultheiss, left 5 fl. each to the orphanage in Stuttgart and the

[65] *Inventuren und Teilungen*, 1102 (21.2.1787). Her brother, as her closet heir, inherited her entire estate, but he had already passed his property on to his children. They then took the inheritance in return for a rent (*Leibgeding*) paid to the father.

[66] *Inventuren und Teilungen*, 1136 (18.1.1790); testament dated 28.12.1787.

[67] *Inventuren und Teilungen*, 1162 (10.4.1792); testament dated 9.3.1792.

[68] *Inventuren und Teilungen*, 1270 (2.3.1803); testament dated 27.2.1801.

[69] *Inventuren und Teilungen*, 1274 (18.3.1803); testament dated 13.9.1761.

[70] *Inventuren und Teilungen*, 1295 (23.2.1805); testament dated 24.7.1804.

[71] *Inventuren und Teilungen*, 1320 (26.11.1806); testament dated 15.10.1806.

[72] *Inventuren und Teilungen*, 1348 (17.2.1809); testament dated 22.1.1808.

village poor relief fund.[73] A cousin was to get 100 fl., with the rest of the estate to go to two siblings' children, all other heirs excluded. Maria Agnes, the widow of Johannes Waldner, specified that the two grandchildren of her sister were each to get as much as the four children of her brother, and each of these was to get as much as her four living siblings.[74] Barbara Kraut, single, illegitimate daughter of Agnes Kraut, left everything to her mother's sister, specifically excluding a cousin (Base).[75] Elisabetha Margaretha, widow of Georg Friedrich Heiler in Nürtingen, came to live with her daughter, Maria Catharina, wife of Anton Falter, in Neckarhausen.[76] She added 150 fl. to her daughter's portion for "special love and faithfulness." A year later she renounced her testament on the grounds that she had not received the expected care from her daughter and no longer wanted to prejudice any child. Friedrich Arnold, weaver, disinherited his brother's son who emigrated to Russia.[77] His widow was to get two fields for services rendered (*geleistete Dienste*), with the rest of the estate divided equally between her and his relatives, the four children of his sister, a brother, and the two children of another brother. The Stuttgart orphanage was to get 30 kr. Jacob Brodbeck, unmarried soldier, left 25 fl. to the woman who bore his illegitimate child, and the rest to his three siblings, although his brother was reduced to a fifth of the estate.[78] Mathias Ebinger disinherited his estranged wife and left everything to his three-year-old daughter. Should she challenge the will, she was to be reduced to an obligatory portion.[79] Until the daughter reached her majority, the wife would have usufruct of the property. He left 105 fl. to his mother for taking care of him and 100 fl. to his half brother for the love he had shown. The school fund was to get 5 fl. Anna Maria Beck reduced her husband to an obligatory portion because of his wastrel life.[80] The rest was to go to the children, with her eldest son receiving an extra 100 fl. for his services. The pastor Immanuel Gottlob Denk had had to pay large debts for his son Friedrich, a surgeon in a neighboring village.[81] He therefore disinherited him in favor of his children, mandating that the property be put under a guardian, with the interest falling to Friedrich. When the children reached adulthood, half was to be given to them, with the other half remaining under a guardian who would pay the interest to Friedrich until he died. In any event, the debts pastor Denk had had to pay were to be deducted from the inheritance portion. Another son, who suffered from mental illness and could not earn a living, was to have an extra 500 fl. to hold until such time as he was

[73] *Inventuren und Teilungen*, 1390 (9.5.1814); testament dated 22.3.1812.
[74] *Inventuren und Teilungen*, 1406 (20.4.1816); testament dated 24.3.1810.
[75] *Inventuren und Teilungen*, 1479 (12.11.1822); testament dated 14.2.1822.
[76] *Inventuren und Teilungen*, 1489 (2.3.1824); testament dated 21.2.1820; second testament dated 8.1.1821.
[77] *Inventuren und Teilungen*, 1493 (26.8.1824); testament dated 29.2.1824.
[78] *Inventuren und Teilungen*, 1514 (26.3.1826).
[79] *Inventuren und Teilungen*, 1685 (1.8.1835); testament dated 13.6.1835.
[80] *Inventuren und Teilungen*, 1710 (10.6.1836); testament dated 22.3.1836.
[81] *Inventuren und Teilungen*, 3017 (3.4.1841); testament dated 8.9.1840.

capable of working. Katharina, widow of Christoph Schmid, weaver, wanted to see that the children of her two deceased sisters received as much as the living siblings.[82] Catharina Bauknecht (née Rieth) had lived a "happy and satisfactory marriage" with her husband Friedrich, whom she designated as her universal heir.[83] She left 5 fl. to the poor relief fund, the interest of which was to be used for school books. Andreas Falter left everything in four equal parts to a brother and the three children of another brother.[84] Johannes Kühfuss reduced one son who had emigrated to an obligatory portion, apparently because he had helped him with his travel money.[85] Another son in America was probably dead, and his portion was to fall in turn to the grandson.

During the 20 years at the end of our period of study, making wills became rather more frequent, and the practice changed somewhat. In 1850, Anna Maria (née Hentzler), the 31-year-old widow of Johann Friedrich Bauknecht, dying in childbirth, left everything to her baby as her only heir.[86] If the latter failed to survive, her estate was to fall to her mother and siblings. When the 67-year-old widow of Friedrich Brodbeck, Catharina (née Petermann), made out her will, she reduced one daughter – whose husband had emigrated to America – to an obligatory portion and made a third of another daughter's portion over to the latter's child.[87] Maria Rosina Elisabetha (née Mathes), widow of Gottlieb Federschmid, 74, disinherited one of her daughters, living in Gegensberg, in favor of the latter's six children,[88] The children of another daughter were to get an extra 100 fl. Johann Christian Feierabend and his wife Maria Agnes (née Feldmaier) both made wills at the same time.[89] The survivor was to have full enjoyment of the estate of the other, with the remainder at his or her death falling to the collateral heirs – for the wife, her four siblings or their children. Friedrich Rieth suffered a stroke and could barely talk.[90] The officials who were summoned posed questions, to which he gave positive or negative responses. His only legal heir was his half brother, Conrad Raichle, who was to be excluded in favor of the latter's children. An illegitimate child he had fathered was not to inherit anything. Margaretha (née Brodbeck), the widow of Johannes Kraushaar, listed as heirs the 30 children of her five siblings.[91] They were to inherit in five equal portions by stem, with some individual children singled out for extra bequests of around 20 fl. each. Christoph Baur and his wife Maria Magdalena (née Beck) made out wills at the same time.[92] Both

[82] *Inventuren und Teilungen*, 1851 (21.10.1842); testament dated 3.10.1842.
[83] *Inventuren und Teilungen*, 1949 (22.10.1846); testament dated 10.5.1841.
[84] *Inventuren und Teilungen*, 1980 (3.2.1848); testament dated 21.1.1848.
[85] *Inventuren und Teilungen*, 2012 (23.3.1849); testament dated 21.12.1848. This case is discussed in greater detail in Chapter 7.
[86] *Inventuren und Teilungen*, 2045 (21.5.1850); testament dated 7.5.1850.
[87] *Inventuren und Teilungen*, 2099 (17.3.1853); testament dated 12.7.1852.
[88] *Inventuren und Teilungen*, 3012 (19.5.1853); testament dated 11.1.1853.
[89] *Inventuren und Teilungen*, 3013 (16.1.1854); testament dated 30.4.1844.
[90] *Inventuren und Teilungen*, 3015 (21.11.1853); testament dated 27.12.1851.
[91] *Inventuren und Teilungen*, 3024 (14.2.1854); testament dated 9.1.1854.
[92] *Inventuren und Teilungen*, 3032 (11.2.1854); testament dated 19.5.1854.

specified that three nephews and nieces of the husband were to get 500 fl. each. The survivor, however, was to enjoy the property for the length of his or her life, with complete administrative powers and the right to alienate it if necessary. Any legal heir who complained would be reduced to an obligatory portion. Margaretha (née Hentzler), widow of Johann Georg Ebinger, 78, reduced her grandchild to an obligatory portion and left the rest to her brother in Raidwangen, with a small bequest of 3 fl. to the poor.[93] Jacob Schnitzler, miller in Neckarhausen, 70, had had to pay substantial debts at the death of one of his sons.[94] The other son was to get the same amount before the estate was divided. A 67-year-old spinster (*Eigenbrödlerin*), Maria Catharina Weiler, left her estate to her nieces and nephews instead of to her siblings, who in any event kept lifelong use-rights and administration.[95] The one sister who did not live in the village had to post security. Maria Catharina also left 50 fl. and bedding to the illegitimate daughter of Magdalena Falter and 20 fl. to the stepdaughter of Matheus Rieth, who was married to her sister. The poor relief fund was to get 1 fl. Johann Georg Rieth, 83, former police officer, disinherited a son who had gone to America because he was a wastrel and still had considerable debts in Neckarhausen.[96] Rieth's grandchildren were to inherit in his place, but the portion of one of them, Jacob, was to be held by his sister Catharina until he returned to live in Württemberg. In order to provide for the minor children of his second wife, Jacob Friedrich Falter, carpenter, left them the house, barn, garden, and a meadow worth 600 fl.[97] The rest of the estate was to be divided equally among all the children, with lifelong usufruct reserved to the widow. Any child who challenged the will would be reduced to an obligatory portion with the difference between that and the expected inheritance going to the children of the second marriage. Johann Adam Ebinger, baker, 50, and his wife Anna Maria (née Rieger), 57, both made wills at the same time, leaving full ownership in the estate to the survivor.[98] There was to be no inventory, security, pledge, or caution money of any kind, and the holder was free to alienate the property as he or she wished. At the death of the survivor, the remainder of the estate was to be divided into two equal parts, one part going to the collateral heirs of each side. The husband's heirs were an uncle (*Oheim*) and an aunt (*Tante*), and the wife's, children of Johann Georg Falter and the illegitimate children of Magdalena Falter, whose relationship to her was not specified in the document. Other relatives of like degree were disinherited (*enterbt*). Michael Hentzler, former Gemeinderat, regulated the complicated inheritance of children from three marriages in two testaments.[99] In the first,

[93] *Inventuren und Teilungen*, 3040 (12.1.1855); testament dated 8.8.1836.
[94] *Inventuren und Teilungen*, 3053 (11.4.1855); testament dated 24.1.1853.
[95] *Inventuren und Teilungen*, 3113 (15.2.1859); testament dated 16.10.1857.
[96] *Inventuren und Teilungen*, 3152 (10.9.1861); testament dated 10.6.1861.
[97] *Inventuren und Teilungen*, 3171 (17.1.1863); testament dated 8.10.1862.
[98] *Inventuren und Teilungen*, 3204 (16.2.1863); testament dated 11.9.1861.
[99] *Inventuren und Teilungen*, 3193 (12.2.1864); testament dated 30.5.1850, second testament dated 2.7.1856; this case is discussed in more detail in Chapter 7.

he reduced the portion of his daughter Anna Maria by 50 fl. because she had received 200 fl. from him earlier and because she did not always behave properly towards him. Since the children of the third marriage were minors and therefore at a disadvantage, they were to get extra support in the form of half of the house, barn and garden. There was obviously ill-will between his son-in-law and his third wife, which prompted Hentzler to deny her use-rights in the extra share falling to her children. In the testament six years late, Hentzler specified that his estate should be divided up according to intestate law, except for some exceptions. In the first place, his grandchildren from his daughter of the first marriage did not treat him with respect even though they had received considerable property through him. Also his daughter from his second marriage did not treat him as he expected. Therefore, all the children of the first and second marriages were to be reduced to obligatory portions, with the difference going to the children of the third marriage. His present wife was not to have the use-rights in her children's inheritance because she had not displayed enough loyalty and had not been at all hardworking and thrifty. Johannes Rieth, unmarried Bauer, left his property to his brother's two children with the proviso that they pay out 400 fl. to his sister's daughter within a quarter year.[100] He apparently lived with his brother's family. Small bequests of 5 fl. were to go to the poor relief fund in the village and the orphanage in Stuttgart. Michael Ebinger, 75, and his wife, Anna Maria (née Hess), 65, both made wills leaving the survivor complete possession of the estate.[101] At the latter's death, the property would fall according to intestate law to the children and grandchildren, but the portion of a half-year-old grandchild, Friederika Bauknecht, was to be put under a guardian with the interest compounded so that her father could have no use of the property at all. Anna Maria (née Kühfuss), widow of Joahnn Georg Falter, Schultheiss, left her property to a daughter and son in equal portions.[102] The portion falling to Anna Maria, wife of a schoolmaster in Leinberg/Liebenzell, was to be put under a guardian, with the interest paid to her. Should she die without heirs, the property was to fall back to her brother, who would in any event be its administrator. Any challenge to the will would reduce her to an obligatory portion. Michael Schach and his wife Christiana (née Falter) both made testaments leaving all property in the complete possession of the survivor.[103] When the latter died, the remainder, divided into two equal parts, would fall to the husband's siblings and the wife's mother and siblings. Salomon Hentzler, weaver and Bauer, with the agreement of his children from his first two marriages, left an extra portion of 200 fl. to his wife because she had been a careful and diligent (*häusliche*) mother to them.[104] After her death the advance would revert to his children. The unmarried Johann

[100] *Inventuren und Teilungen*, 3199 (28.5.1864).
[101] *Inventuren und Teilungen*, 3205 (3.9.1864); testament dated 16.9.1863.
[102] *Inventuren und Teilungen*, 3209 (22.10.1864).
[103] *Inventuren und Teilungen*, 3215 (15.2.1864); testament dated 7.9.1863.
[104] *Inventuren und Teilungen*, 3231 (9.9.1865); testament dated 30.1.1860.

Georg Reyer, 62-year-old shepherd, left all his property to his sister and her illegitimate daughter because they had taken him in and promised to care for him until his death.[105] He disinherited his brother and two half-siblings. Friedrich Köpple, mason, and his wife, Anna Maria (née Baur) made over to the survivor complete ownership in the estate, which would fall after the latter's death to the heirs of the wife.[106] The heirs of the husband were completely excluded. Johannes Bauknecht, weaver, left all of his property equally according to laws of intestacy to his six children, two of whom were in America, but made a separate bequest of 100 fl. to his illegitimate daughter.[107] Wilhelm Deuschle, cooper and Gemeinderat, and his wife Maria Magdalena (née Beck), widow of Christoph Baur, made wills at the same time.[108] Instead of the statutory portion they had agreed to before the wedding, they each now left the other 1000 fl. in lifelong usufruct without the necessity of posting any security but with reversion rights to their respective heirs. If the survivor should challenge the will (to which they both agreed), he or she would be reduced to an obligatory portion. Johann Georg Federschmid, tailor, left a field to his son in America and the rest of the estate to his daughter in Neckarhausen.[109] The property of the son was to remain in the usufruct of his sister until such time as he or his children returned to Württemberg.

## I. Distribution of taxes by age

Table A.27 *Male Bürger tax distribution by age, 1710*

| Age | Number | Total tax paid by age group[a] | Percentage paid by age group of total tax[b] | Mean tax paid per head |
|---|---|---|---|---|
| 15–19 | 0 | — | — | — |
| 20–24 | 1 | 0 | 0 | 0 |
| 25–29 | 4 | 1,122 | 4.7 | 281 |
| 30–34 | 15 | 3,228 | 13.6 | 215 |
| 35–39 | 9 | 2,864 | 12.1 | 318 |
| 40–44 | 6 | 1,666 | 7.0 | 278 |
| 45–49 | 9 | 4,768 | 20.1 | 530 |
| 50–54 | 10 | 3,757 | 15.8 | 378 |
| 55–59 | 1 | 514 | 2.2 | 514 |
| 60–64 | 3 | 1,081 | 4.6 | 360 |
| 65–69 | 1 | 656 | 2.8 | 656 |
| 70+ | 2 | 113 | 0.5 | 57 |

[a] In heller.
[b] 17.9 percent of the total tax of 23,736 heller was paid by other than male Bürger.

[105] *Inventuren und Teilungen*, 3250 (17.10.1866); testament dated 15.5.1866.
[106] *Inventuren und Teilungen*, 3260 (22.3.1867); testament dated 21.1.1867.
[107] *Inventuren und Teilungen*, 3263 (5.4.1867); testament dated 22.3.1867.
[108] *Inventuren und Teilungen*, 3276 (6.7.1867); testament dated 6.1.1858.
[109] *Inventuren und Teilungen*, 3294 (3.7.1868); testament dated 9.5.1866.

Table A.28 *Male Bürger tax distribution by age, 1790*

| Age | Number | Total tax paid by age group[a] | Percentage paid by age group of total tax[b] | Mean tax paid per head |
|---|---|---|---|---|
| 15–19 | 0 | — | — | — |
| 20–24 | 6 | 1,950 | 4.0 | 325 |
| 25–29 | 13 | 3,248 | 6.6 | 250 |
| 30–34 | 10 | 3,348 | 6.8 | 335 |
| 35–39 | 13 | 4,956 | 10.1 | 381 |
| 40–44 | 18 | 4,647 | 9.4 | 258 |
| 45–49 | 15 | 6,932 | 14.1 | 462 |
| 50–54 | 20 | 11,053 | 22.4 | 553 |
| 55–59 | 6 | 2,122 | 4.3 | 354 |
| 60–64 | 3 | 1,767 | 3.6 | 589 |
| 65–69 | 4 | 970 | 2.0 | 243 |
| 70+ | 9 | 1,691 | 3.4 | 188 |

[a] In heller.
[b] 13.3 percent of the total tax of 49,321 was paid by other than male Bürger.

Table A.29 *Male Bürger tax distribution by age, 1870*

| Age | Number | Total tax paid by age group[a] | Percentage paid by age group of total tax[b] | Mean tax paid per head |
|---|---|---|---|---|
| 15–19 | 2 | 147 | 0.03 | 74 |
| 20–24 | 3 | 502 | 0.1 | 167 |
| 25–29 | 13 | 22,444 (10,336)[c] | 5.2 (2.4) | 1,726 (861) |
| 30–34 | 28 | 36,145 | 8.4 | 1,291 |
| 35–39 | 21 | 34,037 | 7.9 | 1,621 |
| 40–44 | 18 | 32,250 | 7.5 | 1,792 |
| 45–49 | 28 | 60,350 | 14.1 | 2,155 |
| 50–54 | 26 | 51,134 | 11.9 | 1,967 |
| 55–59 | 19 | 47,815 (35,056)[d] | 11.2 (8.2) | 2,517 (1948) |
| 60–64 | 17 | 30,518 | 7.1 | 1,795 |
| 65–69 | 3 | 7,111 | 1.6 | 2,370 |
| 70–74 | 12 | 29,111 | 6.8 | 2,426 |
| 75–79 | 7 | 12,961 | 3.0 | 1,852 |
| 80+ | 3 | 843 | 0.2 | 281 |

[a] In heller.
[b] 10.1 percent of total tax of 428,275 was paid by other than male Bürger.
[c] Excluding the immigrant new miller, the second richest man in the village.
[d] Excluding the wealthiest man in the village, an innkeeper.

# Bibliography

## Manuscript Sources

*Gemeindearchiv Neckarhausen*


*Feld- und Waldrugungsprotocolle* (1789–1870).
*Gemeindepflegerechnungen* (1710, 1720, 1730, 1795–1870).
*Gerichts- und Gemeinderatsprotocolle*, 18 vols. (1746–1870) (*Gericht*).
*Inventuren und Teilungen*, 1–3356 (1727–1871).
*Kaufbücher*, 19 vols. (1653–1870).
*Schultheißenamtsprotocolle*, 3 vols. (1839–70) (*Schultheißenamt*).
*Skortationsprotocolle*, 1 vol. (1822–69) (*Skortationsbuch*).
*Unterpfandsbücher*, 20 vols. (1717ff.).
*Vogtruggerichtsprotocolle* (*Bescheid- und Recessbuch*), 2 vols. (1747–1906) (*Vogtruggericht*).


*Pfarramt Neckarhausen*


*Taufregister* (Microfilm from LKA: S2403-5/KB429–431).
*Eheregister* (Microfilm from LKA: S2403-5/KB429-431).
*Todtenregister* (Microfilm from LKA: S2403-5/KB429-31).
*Familienregister* (1828–73).
*Kirchenkonventsprotocolle*, 4 vols. (1727–1848) (*Kirchenkonvent*).


*Stadtarchiv Nürtingen*


*Gerichtsprotocolle*, 52 vols. (1586–1841) (*Nürtingen Stadtgericht*).


*Dekanatsamt Nürtingen*


*Pfarr- und Übersichtsberichte* (1821, 32, 40). Akten I/3, 4.


*Hauptstaatsarchiv Stuttgart* (HSAS)


A8 Bü88.
A249 Bü2066.
A261 Bü1344, 1345.
A214 Bü714.

# Bibliography


*Staatsarchiv Ludwigsburg* (STAL)

*Oberamtsgerichtsprotocolle Nürtingen*, 21 vols. (1802–1891). F190 Band 9–1; F190II Band 257–74.
E10 *Bevölkerungstabelle.*
E141 Bü260.
E258V Bü40.

*Landeskirchlichesarchiv Stuttgart* (LKA)

*Syndodus Protocolle.*
A39 Bü3060.
C2 Bü6/14.

**Secondary sources**

Abel, Wilhelm. *Massenarmut und Hungerkrisen im vorindustriellen Europa.* Hamburg and Berlin: 1974.
Alverson, Hoyt. "Arable Agriculture in Botswana: Some Considerations of the Traditional Social Formation." *Rural Africana* 4–5 (1979): 33–47.
Bakhtin, Mikhail. See V. N. Vološinov.
Berkner, Lutz K. "The Stem Family and Developmental Cycle of the Household: An Eighteenth-Century Austrian Example." *American Historical Review* 76 (1972): 398–418.
Bidlingmaier, Maria. *Die Bäuerin in zwei Gemeinden Württembergs.* Tübinger staatswissenschaftliche Dissertation. Stuttgart: 1918.
Blanchard, Ian. Review of Rodney Hilton, *English Peasantry in the Later Middle Ages. Social History* 5 (1977): 661–4.
Bonnassie, P. "Une famille de la campagne barcelonaise et ses activités économiques aux alentours de l'an mil." *Annales de midi* 76 (1964): 261–303.
Boserup, Ester. *The Condition of Agricultural Growth: Economics of Agrarian Change under Population Pressure.* Chicago. 1965.
Bourdieu, Pierre. "Marriage Strategies as Strategies of Social Reproduction." Translated by Elborg Forster. In *Family and Society. Selections from the Annales*, edited by Robert Forster and Orest Ranum, pp. 117–44. Baltimore: 1976.
Bourdieu, Pierre, and Passeron, Jean-Claude. *Reproduction in Education, Society and Culture.* Translated by Richard Nice. London: 1977.
Brown, Peter. *The Body and Society: Men, Women and Sexual Renunciation in Early Christianity.* New York: 1988.
Brunner, Otto. "Das 'ganze Haus' und alteuropäische 'Oekonomik.'" In *Neue Wege der Verfassungs- und Sozialgeschichte.* 2d ed., pp. 103–27. Göttingen: 1968.
Bücher, Karl. *Industrial Evolution.* 3d ed. Translated by S. Morley Wickett. New York: 1912.
*Die Entstehung der Volkswirtschaft.* 13th ed. Tübingen: 1919.
Campbell, Bruce M. S. "Population Change and the Genesis of Common Fields on a Norfolk Manor." *Economic History Review*, 2d ser. 33 (1980): 174–92.
"Population Pressure, Inheritance and the Land Market in a Fourteenth-Century Peasant Community." In *Land, Kinship and Life-Cycle*, edited by Richard M. Smith,

pp. 87–134. Cambridge: 1984.
Certeau, Michel de. *The Practice of Everyday Life*. Translated by Steven Rendall. Berkeley: 1984.
Chambers, J. D. "Enclosure and the Labor Supply in the Industrial Revolution." *Economic History Review*, 2d ser. 5 (1953): 319–43.
Chayanov, A. V. *The Theory of Peasant Economy*. Edited by Daniel Thorner, Basile Kerblay, and R. E. F. Smith, with a foreword by Theodor Shanin. Madison, Wisc.: 1986.
Chaytor, Miranda. "Household and Kinship: Ryton in the Late 16th and Early 17th Centuries." *History Workshop Journal* 10 (1980): 25–60.
Clark, Katerina, and Holquist, Michael. *Mikhail Bakhtin*. Cambridge, Mass.: 1984.
Clifford, James. "Introduction: Partial Truths." In *Writing Cultures: The Poetics and Politics of Ethnography*. Edited by James Clifford and George E. Marcus, pp. 1–26. Berkeley: 1986.
Cole, John W. and Wolf, Eric R. *The Hidden Frontier. Ecology and Ethnicity in an Alpine Valley*. New York: 1974.
Collomp, Alain. "Famille nucléaire et famille élargie en Provence au xviii^e siècle." *Annales ESC* 27 (1972): 969–75.
"Tensions, Dissensions, and Ruptures inside the Family in Seventeenth- and Eighteenth-Century Haute Provence." In *Interest and Emotion. Essays on the Study of Family and Kinship*, edited by Hans Medick and David Warren Sabean, pp. 145–70. Cambridge: 1984.
Davis, John. *Land and Family in Pisticci*. New York: 1973.
Deleuze, Gilles and Guattari, Félix. *Anti-Oedipus: Capitalism and Schizophrenia*. Minneapolis: 1983.
Douglas, Mary. *Purity and Danger: An Analysis of Concepts of Pollution and Taboo*. London: 1966.
Dumont, Louis. *Homo Hierarchicus: The Caste System and Its Implications*. Translated by Mark Sainsbury. Chicago: 1970.
*From Mandeville to Marx: The Genesis and Triumph of Economic Ideology*. Chicago: 1977.
Dundes, Alan. *Life Is Like a Chicken Coop Ladder: A Portrait of German Culture through Folklore*. New York: 1984.
Dyer, Christopher. *Lords and Peasants in a Changing Society: The Estates of the Bishopric of Worcester, 680–1540*. Cambridge: 1980.
Elias, Norbert. *The Court Society*. New York: 1983.
*Erster Rechenschaftsbericht für das Jahr vom 1 October 1845 bis 1846 an die Gesellschaft für Hebung der Linnengewerbe in Württemberg*. Ersttattet von dem engeren Ausschuße derselben. Nürtingen: n.d. (Copy in HSAS, E70, Bü 1077.)
Finley, Moses. *The Ancient Economy*. Berkeley: 1973.
Fischer, Hermann. *Schwäbisches Lexikon*. 6 vols. Tübingen: 1904–36.
Flandrin, Jean-Louis. *Families in Former Times: Kinship, Household and Sexuality*. Translated by Richard Southern. Cambridge: 1979.
Fortes, Meyer. "Pietas in Ancestor Worship." In *Time and Social Structure and Other Essays*, pp. 164–200. LSE Monographs on Social Anthropology, vol. 40. New York: 1970.
Foucault, Michel. *The History of Sexuality*, vol. 1: *Introduction*. Translated by Robert Hurley. Harmondsworth: 1981.
Gaunt, David. "Formen der Altersversorgung in Bauernfamilien Nord- und Mitteleu-

ropas." In *Historische Familienforschung*, edited by Michael Mitterauer and Reinhard Sieder, pp. 156–91. Frankfurt: 1982.

Geertz, Clifford. "'From the Native's Point of View': On the Nature of Anthropological Understanding." In *Local Knowledge: Further Essays in Interpretive Anthropology*. New York, 1983.

Goldschmidt, Walter, and Kunkel, Evelyn Jacobsen. "The Structure of the Peasant Family." *American Anthropologist* 73 (1971): 1058–76.

Goody, Esther. *Contexts of Kinship*. Cambridge: 1973.

Goody, Jack. *Death, Property and the Ancestors: A Study of the Mortuary Customs of the Lodagaa of West Africa*. London: 1962.

"Marriage Prestations, Inheritance and Descent in Pre-Industrial Societies." *Journal of Comparative Family Studies* 1 (1970): 37–54.

"The Evolution of the Family." In *Household and Family in Past Time*, edited by Peter Laslett with the assistance of Richard Wall, pp. 103–24. Cambridge: 1972.

"Bride Wealth and Dowry in Africa and Eurasia." In *Bridewealth and Dowry*, edited by Jack Goody and S. J. Tambiah, pp. 1–58. Cambridge: 1973.

*Production and Reproduction: A Comparative Study of the Domestic Domain*. Cambridge Studies in Social Anthropology 17. Cambridge: 1976.

Göriz, Karl. *Beiträge zur Kenntnis der württembergischen Landwirtschaft*. Stuttgart and Tübingen: 1841.

*Die landwirtschaftliche Betriebslehre als Leitfaden für Vorlesungen und zum Selbststudium für Landwirte*. 3 Teile. Stuttgart: 1853–4.

Gouesse, Jean-Marie. "Parenté, famille et mariage en Normandie aux xviie et xviiie siècles." *Annales ESC* 27 (1972): 1139–54.

Grube, Walter. *Geschichtliche Grundlage*. Vol. 1 of *Vogteien, Ämter, Landkreise in Baden-Württemberg*, edited by Landkreistag Baden-Württemberg. 2 vols. Stuttgart: 1975.

Guyer, Jane. "Household and Community in African Studies." *African Studies Review* 24 (1981): 87–137.

*Handwörterbuch des deutschen Aberglaubens*. Edited by Hanns Bächtold-Stäubli. 10 vols. Berlin and Leipzig: 1927–42.

Harvey, P. D. A. "Chronology of the Peasant Land Market." In *Peasant Land Market in Medieval England*, pp. 19–28. Oxford: 1984.

Hasselhorn, Martin. *Der altwürttembergische Pfarrstand im 18. Jahrhundert*. Veröffentlichungen der Kommission für geschichtliche Landeskunde in Baden-Württemberg. Series B: Forschungen, vol. 6. Stuttgart: 1958.

Hausen, Karin. "Große Wäsche. Technischer Fortschritt und sozialer Wandel in Deutschland vom 18. bis ins 20. Jahrhundert." *Geschichte und Gesellschaft* 13 (1987): 273–303.

Henning, Friedrich Wilhelm. "Die Betriebsgrößenstruktur der mitteleuropäischen Landwirtschaft im 18. Jahrhundert und ihr Einfluß auf die ländlichen Einkommensverhältnisse." *Zeitschrift für Agrargeschichte und Agrarsoziologie* 17 (1969): 171–93.

Hess, Rolf-Dieter. *Familien- und Erbrecht im württembergischen Landrecht von 1555 unter besonderer Berücksichtigung des älteren württembergischen Rechts*. Veröffentlichungen der Kommission für geschichtliche Landeskunde in Baden-Württemberg. Series B: Forschungen, vol. 44. Stuttgart: 1968.

Hippel, Wolfgang von. "Bevölkerungsentwicklung und Wirtschaftsstruktur im Königreich Württemberg 1815/65. Uberlegungen zum Pauperismusproblem in Südwestdeutschland." In *Soziale Bewegungen und politische Verfassung. Beiträge zur Geschichte der modernen Welt*, edited by Ulrich Engelhardt, Volker Sellin, and Horst Stuke, pp. 270–371. Stuttgart: 1976.

*Die Bauernbefreiung im Königreich Württemberg.* 2 vols. Forschungen zur deutschen Sozialgeschichte, vols. 1, I and II. Boppard am Rhein: 1977.

Hobsbawm, Eric and Ranger, Terence, eds. *The Invention of Tradition.* Cambridge: 1983.

Homans, George C. *English Villagers of the Thirteenth Century.* Cambridge, Mass.: 1941.

Houston, Rob, and Smith Richard M. "A New Approach to the Family?" *History Workshop Journal* 14 (1982): 120–31.

Hradil, Paul. *Untersuchungen zur spätmittelalterlichen Ehegüterrechtsbildung nach bayrisch-österreichischen Rechtsquellen*, Teil 1: *Das Heiratsgut.* Vienna: 1908.

Hufton, Olwen. *The Poor of Eighteenth-Century France, 1750–1789.* Oxford: 1974.

Huppertz, Barthel. *Räume und Schichten bäuerlicher Kulturformen in Deutschland: Ein Beitrag zur deutschen Bauerngeschichte.* Bonn: 1939.

Huttenlocher, Friedrich. *Baden-Württemberg, kleine geographische Landeskunde.* 3d ed. Schriftenreihe der Kommission für geschichtliche Landeskunde Baden-Württemberg, vol. 2. Karlsruhe: 1968.

Hyams, Paul. "The Origins of a Peasant Land Market in England." *Economic History Review*, 2d ser. 23 (1970): 18–31.

Iggers, Georg C. "Historicism." In *Dictionary of the History of Ideas: Studies of Selected Pivotal Ideas*, edited by Philip P. Wiener, vol. 2, pp. 456–64. 4 vols, New York: 1973.

Illich, Ivan. *Gender.* New York: 1982.

Jeffreys, Sheila. *The Spinster and Her Enemies: Feminism and Sexuality 1880–1930.* London: 1985.

Jones, Andrew. "Land and People at Leighton Buzzard in the Later Fifteenth Century." *Economic History Review*, 2d ser. 25 (1972): 18–27.

Kaerger, Karl. "Die Sachsengängerei." *Landwirtschaftliche Jahrbücher* 19 (1890): 239–522.

Karnoouh, Claude. "L'oncle et le cousin." *Etudes rurales* 42 (1971): 2–53.

"Penser 'maison,' penser 'famille': Résidence domestique et parenté dans les societés rurales de l'est de la France." *Etudes rurales* 75 (1979): 35–75.

"Le Pouvoir et la parenté." In *Paysans, femmes et citoyens*, edited by Hugues Lamarche, Susan Carol Rogers, and Claude Karnoouh, pp. 143–210. Leparadou: 1980.

Kaschuba, Wolfgang, and Lipp, Carola. *1848 – Provinz und Revolution.* Tübingen: 1979.

*Dörfliches Uberleben. Zur Geschichte materieller und sozialer Reproduction ländlicher Gesellschaft im 19. und frühen 20. Jahrhundert.* Untersuchungen des Ludwig-Uhland-Instituts der Universität Tübingen, vol. 56. Tübingen: 1982.

Kasdan, Leonard. "Family Structure, Migration and the Entrepreneur." *Comparative Studies in Society and History* 7 (1965): 345–57.

Khera, Sigrid. "An Austrian Peasant Village under Rural Industrialization." *Behavior Science Notes* 7 (1972): 29–36.

Kocka, Jürgen. "Antwort an David Sabean." In *"Geschichte von Unten – Geschichte von Innen." Kontroverse um die Alltagsgeschichte.* Publication of the Fernuniversität Hagen. Hagen: 1985.

Königlicher statistisch-topographischer Bureau. *Beschreibung des Oberamts Nürtingen.* Stuttgart and Tübingen: 1848.

Koppe, J. G. *Unterricht im Ackerbau und in der Viehzucht.* 5th ed. 3 vols. Berlin: 1841–2.

Kriedte, Peter, Medick, Hans, and Schlumbohm, Jürgen. *Industrialisierung vor der Industrialisierung. Gewerbliche Warenproduktion auf dem Lande in der Formationsperiode des Kapitalismus.* Veröffentlichungen des Max-Planck-Institut für Geschichte. Göttingen: 1977.

*Industrialization before Industrialization.* Translated by Beate Schemp. Cambridge: 1981.

Laslett, Peter. "Introduction: The History of the Family." In *Household and Family in Past Time*, edited by Peter Laslett with the assistance of Richard Wall, pp. 1–89. Cambridge: 1972.

Leach, Edmund R. "Rethinking Anthropology." In *Rethinking Anthropology*, pp. 1–27. London: 1961.

*Social Anthropology*. New York: 1982.

Le Play, M. Frédéric. *L'Organisation de la famille selon le vrai modèle signalé par l'histoire de toutes les races et de tous les temps.* Paris: 1871.

Levine, David. *Family Formation in an Age of Nascent Capitalism.* New York: 1977.

Lipp, Carola, Kaschuba, Wolfgang, and Frahm, Eckart, eds. *Nehren. Eine Dorfchronik der Spätaufklärung*, by F. A. Köhler. Untersuchungen des Ludwig-Uhland-Instituts der Universität Tübingen, vol. 52. Tübingen: 1981.

Macfarlane, Alan. *The Origins of English Individualism: The Family, Property and Social Transition.* Cambridge: 1978.

Martin, Jochen. "Zur Stellung des Vaters in antiken Gesellschaften." In *Historische Anthropologie*, edited by H. Süssmuth, pp. 84–109. Göttingen: 1984.

Mayer-Edenhauser, Theodor. *Untersuchungen über Anerbenrecht und Güterschluss in Kurhessen*. Prague: 1942.

Medick, Hans. "The Proto-industrial Family Economy: The Structural Function of Household and Family during the Transition from Peasant Society to Industrial Capitalism." *Social History* 1 (1976): 291–315.

"Plebejische Kultur, plebejische Offentlichkeit, plebejische Oekonomie. Uber Erfahrungen und Verhaltensweisen Besitzarmer und Besitzloser in der Übergangsphase zum Kapitalismus." In *Klassen und Kultur: Sozialanthropologische Perspektiven in der Geschichtsschreibung*, edited by Robert Berdahl, et al., pp. 157–204. Frankfurt: 1982.

"Priviligiertes Handelskapital und 'kleine Industrie.' Produktion und Produktionsverhältnisse im Leinengewerbe des altwürttembergischen Oberamts Urach im 18. Jahrhundert." *Archiv für Sozialgeschichte* 23 (1983): 267–310.

"Village Spinning Bees: Sexual Culture and Free Time among Rural Youth in Early Modern Germany." In *Interest and Emotion: Essays on the Study of Family and Kinship*, edited by Hans Medick and David Warren Sabean, pp. 317–39. Cambridge: 1984.

"Teuerung, Hunger und 'moralische Oekonomie von Oben: Die Hungerkrise der Jahre 1816–17 in Württemberg." *Beiträge zur historischen Sozialkunde* 2 (1985): 39–44.

Medick, Hans, and Sabean, David Warren. "Interest and Emotion in Family and Kinship Studies: A Critique of Social History and Anthropology." In *Interest and Emotion: Essays on the Study of Family and Kinship*, edited by Hans Medick and David Warren Sabean, pp. 9–27. Cambridge: 1984.

Meillassoux, Claude. "From Reproduction to Production: A Marxist Approach to

Economic Anthropology." *Economy and Society* 1 (1972): 93–105.
Mendels, Franklin F. "Industrialization and Population Pressure in Eighteenth-Century Flanders." Ph.D. dissertation. University of Wisconsin-Madison: 1970.
"Agriculture and Peasant Industry in Eighteenth-Century Flanders." In *Industrialization before Industrialization*, by Peter Kriedte, Hans Medick, and Jürgen Schlumbohm. Cambridge: 1981.
Meyerhoff, Hans. "Introduction." In *The Philosophy of History in Our Time*. New York: 1959.
Mitterauer, Michael. "Zur Familienstruktur in ländlichen Gebieten Österreichs im 17. Jahrhundert." In *Beiträge zur Bevölkerungs- und Sozialgeschichte*, edited by Heimo Helczmanovski, pp. 167–222. Vienna: 1973.
"Familiengröße – Familientypen – Familienzyklus." *Geschichte und Gesellschaft* 1 (1975): 235–55.
"Vorindustrielle Familienformen." *Wiener Beiträge zur Geschichte der Neuzeit* 2 (1975): 123–85.
"Vorindustrielle Familienformen. Zur Funktionsentlastung des 'ganzen Hauses' im 17. und 18. Jahrhundert." In *Fürst, Bürger, Mensch: Untersuchungen zu politischen und soziokulturellen Wandlungsprozessen im vorrevolutionären Europa*, edited by Friedrich Engel-Janosi, Grete Klingenstein, and Heinrich Lutz, pp. 123–85. Vienna: 1975.
"Familienformen und Illegitimität in ländlichen Gebieten Österreichs." *Archiv für Sozialgeschichte* 19 (1979): 123–88.
Mitterauer, Michael, and Sieder, Reinhard. *Vom Patriarchat zur Partnerschaft*. Munich: 1977.
Moltmann, Günter, ed. *Aufbruch nach Amerika: Friedrich List und die Auswanderung aus Baden und Württemberg 1816–17. Dokumentation einer sozialen Bewegung*. Tübingen: 1979.
Murdock, George Peter. *Social Structure*. New York: 1949.
Pflaumer-Resenberger. *Die Anerbensitte in Altbayern: Eine rechts-und wirtschaftsgeschichtliche Untersuchung*. Munich: 1939.
Phillips, Roderick. *Putting Asunder: A History of Divorce in Western Society*. Cambridge: 1988.
Plakans, Andrejs. *Kinship in the Past: An Anthropology of European Family Life 1500–1900*. Oxford and New York, 1984.
Polanyi, Karl, Arensberg, Conrad M., and Pearson, Harry W. *Trade and Markets in Early Empires: Economy in History and Theory*. Chicago: 1971.
Postan, M. M. *The Medieval Economy and Society: An Economic History of Britain 1100–1500*. Berkeley and Los Angeles: 1972.
"The Charters of the Villeins." In *Essays on Medieval Agriculture and the General Problems of the Medieval Economy*, pp. 107–49. Cambridge: 1973.
Razi, Zvi. *Marriage and Death in a Medieval Parish Economy, Society and Demography in Halesowen 1270–1400*. Cambridge: 1980.
"Family, Land and the Village Community in Later Medieval England." *Past and Present* 92 (November, 1981): 3–36.
"The Erosion of the Family-Land Bond in the Late Fourteenth and Fifteenth Centuries: A Methodological Note." In *Land, Kinship and Life-Cycle*, edited by Richard M. Smith, pp. 295–304. Cambridge: 1984.
Rebel, Hermann. *Peasant Classes: The Bureaucratization of Property and Family Relations under Early Habsburg Absolutism 1511–1636*. Princeton: 1983.

Reddy, William P. *Money and Liberty in Modern Europe: A Critique of Historical Understanding*. Cambridge: 1987.

*Regierungsblatt für das Königreich Württemberg*. Stuttgart: 1811ff.

Reif, Heinz. "Vagierende Unterschichten, Vagabunden und Bandenkriminalität im Ancien Régime." *Beiträge zur historischen Sozialkunde* 1 (1981): 27–37.

Reyscher, August Ludwig, ed. *Vollständige, historisch und kritisch bearbeitete Sammlung der württembergischen Geseze*. 19 vols. Stuttgart and Tübingen: 1828–51.

Richter, Gregor. *Lagerbücher- oder Urbarlehre: hilfswissenschaftliche Grundzüge nach württembergischen Quellen*. Veröffentlichungen der staatlichen Archivverwaltung Baden-Württemberg, vol. 36. Stuttgart: 1979.

Riehl, Wilhelm. *Die Naturgeschichte des Volks als Grundlage einer deutschen Social-Politik*. 3d ed. Vol. 2: *Die bürgerliche Gesellschaft*. Vol. 3: *Die Familie*. Stuttgart and Augsburg: 1855.

Robisheaux, Thomas. *Rural Society and the Search for Order in Early Modern Germany*. Cambridge: 1989.

Roeber, A. G. "Erbberechtliche Probleme deutscher Auswanderer in Nordamerika während des 18. Jahrhunderts." *Zeitschrift für neuere Rechtsgeschichte* 2 (1986): 143–56.

"The Origins and Transfer of German-American Concepts of Property and Inheritance." *Perspectives in American History*, n.s. 3 (1987): 115–71.

Rousseau, Jean-Jacques. *Discourse on the Origin and Foundation of Inequality among Mankind*, edited by Lester G. Crocker. New York, 1967.

Sabean, David Warren. "Aspects of Kinship Behavior and Property in Rural Western Europe before 1800." In *Family and Inheritance in Rural Society in Western Europe, 1200–1800*, edited by Jack Goody, et al., pp. 96–111. Cambridge: 1976.

"Verwandtschaft und Familie in einem württembergischen Dorf 1500 bis 1870: Einige methodische Uberlegungen." In *Sozialgeschichte der Familie in der Neuzeit Europas: Neue Forschungen*, edited by Werner Conze, pp. 231–46. Stuttgart: 1976.

"Intensivierung der Arbeit und Alltagserfahrung auf dem Lande – Ein Beispiel aus Württemberg." In *Sozialwissenschaftliche Informationen für Unterricht und Studium* 6 (1977): 148–52.

"Unehelichkeit: Ein Aspekt sozialer Reproduktion kleinbäuerlicher Produzenten: Zu einer Analyse dörflicher Quellen um 1800." In *Klassen und Kultur: Sozialanthropologische Perspektiven in der Geschichtsschreibung*, edited by Robert Berdahl, et al., pp. 54–76. Frankfurt: 1982.

"The History of the Family in Africa and Europe: Some Comparative Perspectives." *Journal of African History* 24 (1983): 163–71.

*Power in the Blood: Popular Culture and Village Discourse in Early Modern Germany*. Cambridge: 1984.

"Young Bees in an Empty Hive: Relations between Brothers-in-Law in a South German Village around 1800." In *Interest and Emotion: Essays on the Study of Family and Kinship*, edited by Hans Medick and David Warren Sabean, pp. 171–86. Cambridge: 1984.

"Zur Bedeutung von Kontext sozialer Logik und Erfahrung." In *"Geschichte von Unten – Geschichte von Innen": Kontroverse um die Alltagsgeschichte*, edited by Jürgen Kocka and F. J. Brüggemeier. Publication of the Fernuniversität Hagen. Hagen: 1985.

Schlumbohm, Jürgen. "Agrarische Besitzklassen und gewerbliche Produktionsverhältnisse: Großbauern, Kleinbesitzer und Landlose als Leinenproduzenten im Umland von Osnabrück und Bielefeld während des frühen 19. Jahrhunderts." In *Mentalitäten und Lebensverhältnisse: Beispiele aus der Sozialgeschichte der Neuzeit. Rudolf Vierhaus zum 60. Geburtstag*, edited by Mitarbeitern and Schülern, pp. 315–34. Göttingen 1982.

"Bauern – Kötter – Heuerlinge. Bevölkerungsentwicklung und soziale Schichtung in einem Gebiet ländlichen Gewerbes das Kirchspiel Belm bei Osnabrück 1650–1860." *Niedersächsisches Jahrbuch für Landesgeschichte* 58 (1986): 77–88.

Schulte, Regina. "Infanticide in Rural Bavaria in the Nineteenth Century." In *Interest and Emotion: Essays on the Study of Family and Kinship*, edited by Hans Medick and David Warren Sabean, pp. 77–102. Cambridge: 1984.

Schulz, Helga. "Landhandwerk und ländliche Sozialstruktur um 1800." *Jahrbuch für Wirtschaftsgeschichte*, part 2 (1980): 11–50.

Schwab, Dieter. "Familie." In *Geschichtliche Grundbegriffe.* Historisches Lexikon zur politisch-sozialen Sprache in Deutschland, edited by Otto Brunner, Werner Conze, and Reinhard Kosellek, vol. 2: 253–301. Stuttgart: 1975.

Schwenkel, Hans, ed. *Heimatbuch des Kreises Nürtingen.* 2 vols. Published by Konrad Trilsch for the Kreisverband Nürtingen. Würzburg: 1950–3.

Schwerz, J. N. *Beschreibung der Landwirtschaft in Nieder-Elsaß.* Berlin: 1816.

Segalen, Martine. Mari et femme dans la société paysanne. Paris, 1980.

"'Avoir sa part': Sibling Relations in Partible Inheritance Brittany." In *Interest and Emotion: Essays on the Study of Family and Kinship*, edited by Hans Medick and David Warren Sabean, pp. 129–44. Cambridge: 1984.

*Ouinze générations de Bas-Bretons: parenté et société dans le pays bigouden sud, 1720–1980.* Paris: 1985.

Simmel, Georg. *Philosophy of Money.* Translated by Tom Bottomore and David Frisby. Boston and London: 1978.

Smith, Richard M. "Families and Their Land in an Area of Partible Inheritance: Redgrave, Suffolk 1260–1320." In *Land, Kinship and Life-Cycle*, edited by Richard M. Smith, pp. 135–96. Cambridge: 1984.

"Some Issues Concerning Families and Their Property in Rural England 1250–1800." In *Land, Kinship and Life-Cycle*, edited by Richard M. Smith, pp. 1–86. Cambridge: 1984.

Strathern, Andrew. "Work Processes and Social Change in Highlands New Guinea." Paper prepared for Anthropology and History Round Table I. Göttingen: 1978.

Thompson, E. P. "The Grid of Inheritance: A Comment." In *Family and Inheritance: Rural Society in Western Europe 1200–1800*, edited by Jack Goody, et al., pp. 328–60. Cambridge: 1976.

Tyler, Stephen A. "Post-Modern Ethnography: From Document of the Occult to Occult Document." In *Writing Culture*, edited by James Clifford and George E. Marcus. Berkeley: 1986.

Vernier, Bernard. "Émigration et déréglement du marché matrimonial." *Actes de la recherche en sciences sociales* 15 (1977).

"Putting Kin and Kinship to Good Use: The Circulation of Goods, Labour, and Names on Karpathos (Greece)." In *Interest and Emotion: Essays on the Study of Family and Kinship*, edited by Hans Medick and David Warren Sabean, pp. 28–76. Cambridge: 1984.

Vološinov, V. N. *Marxism and the Philosophy of Language.* (Mikhail Bakhtin). Translated by Ladislav Matejka and I. R. Titunik. Cambridge, Mass.: 1986.

Wall, Richard. "Introduction." In *Family Forms in Historic Europe*, edited by Richard Wall in collaboration with Jean Robin and Peter Laslett, pp. 1–63. Cambridge: 1983.

Wilk, Richard R., and Netting, Robert McC. "Households: Changing Forms and Functions." In *Households. Comparative and Historical Studies of the Domestic Group*, edited by Robert McC. Netting, Richard R. Wilk, and Erik J. Arnould, pp. 1–28. Berkeley: 1984.

Yver, Jean. *Egalité entre héritiers et exclusion des enfants dotés: Essai de géographie coutumière.* Paris: 1966.

# Index of villagers

Key: e = emigrated to; i = immigrated from; b = born (date and/or place); h = husband(s). Dates in parentheses indicate that a baptismal or burial record is not available but that a date is given in another record. Orthographic problems make such dates less reliable.

Baur, Agnes, 1773–1854, h. Waldner, Anton, 292

# General index

# Cambridge studies in social and cultural anthropology



1 The Political Organisation of Unyamwezi*
R. G. ABRAHAMS
2 Buddhism and the Spirit Cults in North-East Thailand*
S. J. TAMBIAH
3 Kalahari Village Politics: An African Democracy*
ADAM KUPER
4 The Rope of Moka: Big-Men and Ceremonial Exchange in Mount Hagen, New Guinea*
ANDREW STRATHERN
5 The Majangir: Ecology and Society of a Southwest Ethiopian People*
JACK STAUDER
6 Buddhist Monk, Buddhist Layman: A Study of Urban Monastic Organisation in Central Thailand*
JANE BUNNAG
7 Contexts of Kinship: An Essay in the Family Sociology of the Gonja of Northern Ghana*
ESTHER N. GOODY
8 Marriage among a Matrilineal Elite: A Family Study of Ghanaian Civil Servants*
CHRISTINE OPPONG
9 Elite Politics in Rural India: Political Stratification and Political Alliances in Western Maharashtra*
ANTHONY T. CARTER
10 Women and Property in Morocco: Their Changing Relation to the Process of Social Stratification in the Middle Atlas*
VANESSA MAHER
11 Rethinking Symbolism*
DAN SPERBER. Translated by Alice L. Morton
12 Resources and Population: A Study of the Gurungs of Nepal*
ALAN MACFARLANE
13 Mediterranean Family Structures*
EDITED BY J. G. PERISTIANY
14 Spirits of Protest: Spirit-Mediums and the Articulation of Consensus among the Zezuru of Southern Rhodesia (Zimbabwe)*
PETER FRY
15 World Conqueror and World Renouncer: A Study of Buddhism and Polity in Thailand against a Historical Background*
S. J. TAMBIAH
16 Outline of a Theory of Practice*
PIERRE BOURDIEU. Translated by Richard Nice
17 Production and Reproduction: A Comparative Study of the Domestic Domain*
JACK GOODY
18 Perspectives in Marxist Anthropology*
MAURICE GODELIER. Translated By Robert Brain

19 The Fate Shechem, or the Politics of Sex: Essays in the Anthropology of the Mediterranean*
JULIAN PITT-RIVERS

20 People of the Zongo: The Transformation of Ethnic Identities in Ghana*
ENID SCHILDKROUT

21 Casting out Anger: Religion among the Taita of Kenya*
GRACE HARRIS

22 Rituals of the Kandyan State*
H. L. SENEVIRATNE

23 Australian Kin Classification*
HAROLD W. SCHEFFLER

24 The Palm and the Pleiades: Initiation and Cosmology in Northwest Amazonia*
STEPHEN HUGH-JONES

25 Nomads of Southern Siberia: The Pastoral Economies of Tuva*
S. I. VAINSHTEIN. Translated by Michael Colenso

26 From the Milk River: Spatial and Temporal Processes in Northwest Amazonia*
CHRISTINE HUGH-JONES

27 Day of Shining Red: An Essay on Understanding Ritual*
GILBERT LEWIS

28 Hunters, Pastoralists and Ranchers: Reindeer Economies and their Transformations*
TIM INGOLD

29 The Wood-Carvers of Hong Kong: Craft Production in the World Capitalist Periphery*
EUGENE COOPER

30 Minangkabau Social Formations: Indonesian Peasants and the World Economy*
JOEL S. KAHN

31 Patrons and Partisans: A Study of Two Southern Italian Communes*
CAROLINE WHITE

32 Muslim Society*
ERNEST GELLNER

33 Why Marry Her? Society and Symbolic Structures*
LUC DE HEUSCH. Translated by Janet Lloyd

34 Chinese Ritual and Politics*
EMILY MARTIN AHERN

35 Parenthood and Social Reproduction: Fostering and Occupational Roles in West Africa*
ESTHER N. GOODY

36 Dravidian Kinship*
THOMAS R. TRAUTMANN

37 The Anthropological Circle: Symbol, Function, History*
MARC AUGÉ. Translated by Martin Thom

38 Rural Society in Southeast Asia*
KATHLEEN GOUGH

39 The Fish-People: Linguistic Exogamy and Tukanoan Identity in Northwest Amazonia
JEAN E. JACKSON

40 Karl Marx Collective: Economy, Society and Religion in a Siberian Collective Farm*
CAROLINE HUMPHREY

41 Ecology and Exchange in the Andes*
Edited by DAVID LEHMANN

42 Traders without Trade: Responses to Trade in two Dyula Communities*
ROBERT LAUNAY

43 The Political Economy of West African Agriculture*
KEITH HART

44 Nomads and the Outside World*
A. M. KHAZANOV. Translated by Julia Crookenden

45 Actions, Norms and Representations: Foundations of Anthropological Inquiry*
LADISLAV HOLY AND MILAN STUCKLIK

46 Structural Models in Anthropology*
PER HAGE AND FRANK HARARY

47 Servants of the Goddess: The Priests of a South Indian Temple*
C. J. FULLER

48 Oedipus and Job in West African Religion*
MEYER FORTES

49 The Buddhist Saints of the Forest and the Cult of Amulets: A Study in Charisma, Hagiography, Sectarianism, and Millennial Buddhism*
S. J. TAMBIAH

50 Kinship and Marriage: An Anthropological Perspective (available in paperback/ in the USA only)*
ROBIN FOX

51 Individual and Society in Guiana: A Comparative Study of Amerindian Social Organization*
PETER RIVIERE

52 People and the State: An Anthropology of Planned Development*
A. F. ROBERTSON

53 Inequality among Brothers: Class and Kinship in South China*
RUBIE S. WATSON

54 On Anthropological Knowledge*
DAN SPERBER

55 Tales of the Yanomami: Daily Life in the Venezuelan Forest*
JACQUES LIZOT. Translated by Ernest Simon

56 The Making of Great Men: Male Domination and Power among the New Guinea Baruya*
MAURICE GODELIER. Translated by Rupert Swyer

57 Age Class Systems: Social Institutions and Politics Based on Age*
BERNARDO BERNARDI. Translated by David I. Kertzer

58 Strategies and Norms in a Changing Matrilineal Society: Descent, Succession and Inheritance among the Toka of Zambia*
LADISLAV HOLY

59 Native Lords of Quito in the Age of the Incas: The Political Economy of North Andean Chiefdoms*
FRANK SALOMON

60 Culture and Class in Anthropology and History: A Newfoundland Illustration*
GERALD SIDER

61 From Blessing to Violence: History and Ideology in the Circumcision Ritual of the Merina of Madagascar*
MAURICE BLOCH

62 The Huli Response to Illness*
STEPHEN FRANKEL

63 Social Inequality in a Northern Portuguese Hamlet: Land, Late Marriage, and Bastardy, 1870–1978*
BRIAN JUAN O'NEILL

64 Cosmologies in the Making: A Generative Approach to Cultural Variation in Inner New Guinea*
FREDRIK BARTH

65 Kinship and Class in the West Indies: A Genealogical Study of Jamaica and Guyana*
RAYMOND T. SMITH

66 The Making of the Basque Nation*
MARIANNE HEIBERG

67 Cut of Time: History and Evolution in Anthropological Discourse*
NICHOLAS THOMAS

68 Tradition as Truth and Communication*
PASCAL BOYER

69 The Abardoned Narcotic: Kava and Cultural Instability in Malanesia*
RON BRUNTON

70 The Anthropology of Numbers*
THOMAS CRUMP

71 Stealing People's Names: History of Politics in a Sepik River Cosmology*
SIMON J. HARRISON

72 The Bedouin of Cyrenaica: Studies in Personal and Corporate Power*
EMRYS L. PETERS. Edited by Jack Goody and Emanuel Marx

* published in paperback